Pensions Law Handbook

by the Pensions Department of Nabarro Nathanson
Head of Department: Geoffrey Preston LLB

Joint Editors

Jennifer Bell BA (Hons)
Partner

and

Douglas Sleziak BA (Hons)
Senior Legal Manager

Members of the LexisNexis Group worldwide

United Kingdom	LexisNexis UK, a Division of Reed Elsevier (UK) Ltd, 2 Addiscombe Road, CROYDON CR9 5AF
Argentina	LexisNexis Argentina, BUENOS AIRES
Australia	LexisNexis Butterworths, CHATSWOOD, New South Wales
Austria	LexisNexis Verlag ARD Orac GmbH & Co KG, VIENNA
Canada	LexisNexis Butterworths, MARKHAM, Ontario
Chile	LexisNexis Chile Ltda, SANTIAGO DE CHILE
Czech Republic	Nakladatelství Orac sro, PRAGUE
France	Editions du Juris-Classeur SA, PARIS
Germany	LexisNexis Deutschland GmbH, FRANKFURT AND MUNSTER
Hong Kong	LexisNexis Butterworths, HONG KONG
Hungary	HVG-Orac, BUDAPEST
India	LexisNexis Butterworths, NEW DELHI
Ireland	Butterworths (Ireland) Ltd, DUBLIN
Italy	Giuffrè Editore, MILAN
Malaysia	Malayan Law Journal Sdn Bhd, KUALA LUMPUR
New Zealand	LexisNexis Butterworths, WELLINGTON
Poland	Wydawnictwo Prawnicze LexisNexis, WARSAW
Singapore	LexisNexis Butterworths, SINGAPORE
South Africa	LexisNexis Butterworths, Durban
Switzerland	Stämpfli Verlag AG, BERNE
USA	LexisNexis, DAYTON, Ohio

© Reed Elsevier (UK) Ltd 2004

All rights reserved. No part of this publication may be reproduced in any material form (including photocopying or storing it in any medium by electronic means and whether or not transiently or incidentally to some other use of this publication) without the written permission of the copyright owner except in accordance with the provisions of the Copyright, Designs and Patents Act 1988 or under the terms of a licence issued by the Copyright Licensing Agency Ltd, 90 Tottenham Court Road, London, England W1T 4LP. Applications for the copyright owner's written permission to reproduce any part of this publication should be addressed to the publisher.

Warning: The doing of an unauthorised act in relation to a copyright work may result in both a civil claim for damages and criminal prosecution.

Crown copyright material is reproduced with the permission of the Controller of HMSO and the Queen's Printer for Scotland. Any European material in this work which has been reproduced from EUR-lex, the official European Communities legislation website, is European Communities copyright.

A CIP Catalogue record for this book is available from the British Library.

ISBN 0 7545 2609 7

Typeset by Kerrypress Ltd, Luton, Beds
Printed and bound in Great Britain by Antony Rowe Ltd, Chippenham, Wiltshire

Visit LexisNexis UK at www.lexisnexis.co.uk

Preface

I am delighted to introduce this sixth edition of the highly regarded Tolley's Pensions Law Handbook. The book has been written and revised entirely by practising pension lawyers who are members of the Pensions Department at Nabarro Nathanson. The detailed work of editing it has been undertaken by Jennifer Bell and Douglas Sleziak, and we are grateful to them for that.

Nabarro Nathanson is one of the largest independent law practices in the UK. Its Pensions Department has for many years been one of its strengths. Our pension lawyers, both in London and in Sheffield, have a deep technical knowledge of their subject and advise an impressive range of clients on the areas that the book covers.

I am sure that readers will find the new edition valuable. The fact that is now in its sixth edition reflects its popularity. It also reflects the constantly changing statutory environment within which trustees of pension schemes and sponsoring employers operate. The Pensions Bill, on its passage through the House of Lords at the time of print, is just part of the current changes. Tax simplification too, which is also on the horizon, poses fresh challenges to employers, trustees and administrators of pension schemes who will all no doubt be trying to ensure that revised procedures are in place before 'A Day'. The anticipated impact of the Pensions Bill and tax simplification are reflected throughout this sixth edition where appropriate.

All of us in the Pensions Department have contributed to the book. My thanks to them all. The contributors are (in alphabetical order): Margaret Allison, Jennifer Bell, Alison Birkitt, Marika Chalkiadis, Mario Conti, Tom Dane, Amanda Day, Jemma Dean, Joan Desmond, Mike Draper, Neal Gibson, Alastair Govier, Kate Grayling, Dominic Harris, Louise Howard, Melissa Jones, Sue Jones, Victoria Lee, Josephine Manfredi, John Murray, Graham Ness, Geoffrey Preston, Kate Richards, Gowri Siva, Douglas Sleziak, Damian Smith, Michal Stein, Elizabeth Turner and Dominic Winfield.

Our aim has been to state the law as at end May 2004, and I am confident that this new edition will be as useful to those working in the field of pensions law as the previous editions have been.

Geoffrey Preston
Head of Pensions Department
Nabarro Nathanson

Contents

Table of Statutes **xi**
Table of Statutory Instruments **xxi**
Table of Cases **xxxiii**
Table of European Legislation **xxxix**
Abbreviations and References **xli**

1. **Pension provision in the UK – an introduction 1**
    Introduction **1**
    A brief history of pension provision in the UK **1**
    Retirement provision by the state **5**
    Occupational pension schemes **9**
    Membership of occupational pension schemes **18**
    Making contributions to occupational pension schemes **21**
    Benefits payable from occupational pension schemes **26**
    Increasing pensions in payment **35**
    Forfeiture and suspension of benefits **36**
    Stakeholder pension schemes **42**

2. **People involved with pensions 45**
    Introduction **45**
    Trustees **45**
    Actuaries **48**
    Auditors **52**
    Investment managers **53**
    IR Savings, Pensions, Share Schemes Office of the Board of Inland Revenue (IR SPSS) **54**
    Occupational Pensions Board (OPB) **55**
    Registrar of Occupational and Personal Pension Schemes (Registrar) **56**
    Occupational Pensions Regulatory Authority (Opra) **56**
    Pensions Compensation Board (PCB) **60**
    National Insurance Services to Pensions Industry **63**
    Pensions Advisory Service **64**
    Pensions Ombudsman **65**
    Pensions Reform **70**
    Professional Bodies **72**

3. Trustees 75
Introduction 75
Who can be a trustee? 75
Type of trustee 76
Employment protection for trustees under the Employment Rights Act 1996 80
Trustees' duties 82
Trustees' meetings 89
Member-nominated trustees 90
Internal dispute resolution 98
Protection from liability 103
Data Protection Act 1998 106
Trustees' duties to the employer 109

4. Contracting-out 111
Introduction 111
A brief history of contracting-out 112
The contracting-out certificate 113
Final salary schemes 114
Money purchase schemes 122
Mixed benefit schemes 128
Transfers between contracted-out arrangements 129
Electing for the issue, variation or surrender of a contracting-out certificate 135
Termination of contracted-out employment 140
Simplification of contracting out 145
Contracted-out rights on divorce 145
Stakeholder schemes 145
Replacement for SERPS 145

5. Inland Revenue limits and taxation 148
Introduction 148
Remuneration and final remuneration 149
Normal retirement date 152
Maximum benefits 153
Taxation 163
The April 2006 regime 172

6. Protection for early leavers 176
Introduction 176
Scope of early leaver legislation 177
Preservation 178
Revaluation 186
Transfer values – introduction 189

Contents

　　The right to a cash equivalent **190**
　　Calculating the cash equivalent **192**
　　Exercising the right to a cash equivalent **195**
　　Trustees' duties after member exercises his right **196**
　　Disclosure requirements **200**
　　Hybrid schemes **201**
　　Transitional arrangements and the implications of PA 1995 **201**
　　Summary of guaranteed cash equivalent procedure **202**

7. Employment issues 205
　　Introduction **205**
　　What is the employee promised? **206**
　　What are the employer's obligations? **209**
　　How do the trustees fit in? **216**
　　Entitlements in cases of dismissal or redundancy **217**
　　Business reorganisations **223**
　　Employer's lien **227**
　　Discrimination **227**
　　Additional changes **235**
　　Conclusion **236**

8. Pensions and divorce 237
　　Introduction **237**
　　Position prior to PA 1995 **238**
　　Earmarking – impact of PA 1995 **239**
　　Pension sharing **245**
　　Family proceedings rules **259**
　　Scheme documentation **260**
　　Overlap between earmarking and pension sharing **261**
　　Taxation **261**
　　The future **262**

9. Sex equality 263
　　Introduction **263**
　　Access/eligibility **265**
　　Benefits **274**
　　Conclusions and practical issues **280**
　　Maternity provisions **290**
　　Tables of relevant legislation and case law **293**

10. Investment 306
　　Introduction **306**
　　The meaning of investment **306**
　　Trading or investing? **307**

Power of investment **310**
Duties of trustees when exercising their investment power **311**
Statutory obligations **315**
The Financial Services and Markets Act 2000 **318**
The selection and supervision of investment advisers **322**
The liability of investment advisers **324**
Voting rights as a consequence of share ownership – is it a trust asset? **330**
Trustee liability and protection **331**
Myners' report: voluntary code of practice **332**

11. Funding, deficits and surpluses 336
Introduction **336**
Pre-PA 1995 requirements relating to funding **336**
Funding practice **337**
Actuarial valuations **338**
The minimum funding requirement **341**
What is a surplus? **355**
Why surpluses are an issue **355**
Who owns a surplus? **356**
Inland Revenue requirements relating to the reduction of surpluses **359**
Trust law requirements relating to the reduction of surpluses **362**
Legislative requirements relating to the reduction of surpluses and PA 1995 **363**
Pensions Bill **367**

12. Reconstruction and winding-up 368
Introduction **368**
Key considerations **369**
Amendments **372**
Bulk transfers – general **384**
Bulk transfers – specific issues where winding-up has not commenced **392**
Triggering a winding-up **393**
Deferral of winding-up by trustees **395**
The winding-up process **397**
Employer's debt **413**
Bulk transfers – specific issues where winding-up has commenced **418**
Bulk transfers – overview **420**
Sanctions against trustees under PA 1995 **424**
Pensions Bill **424**

Contents

13. Small self-administered schemes 430
   Introduction **430**
   Development of the regulatory framework **431**
   Funding SSASs and payment of benefits **435**
   Borrowing by SSASs **438**
   Investments by SSASs – general **439**
   Loans by SSASs **443**
   Investment in shares **444**
   Self-investment **445**
   Investment in real property **446**
   Tax avoidance and the bona fides of the scheme **447**
   Withdrawal of approval **449**
   Trading **449**
   VAT **450**
   The Pensions Act 1995 **450**
   Application of PA 1995 To SSASs **451**
   Transfers and conversions **452**
   The future **453**

14. Unapproved arrangements 454
   Introduction **454**
   Types of unapproved arrangements **454**
   Establishing unapproved arrangements **458**
   Application of pensions legislation **460**
   Taxation aspects of a FURBS **464**
   Taxation aspects of an UURBS **470**
   Insuring death benefits **472**
   Offshore arrangements **473**
   Final salary FURBS **474**
   Investment and implications of the Financial Services and Markets Act 2000 **475**
   National Insurance contributions **476**
   Company law implications **477**
   Simplification of the tax treatment of pensions **477**

15. Personal pension and stakeholder schemes 480
   Introduction **480**
   Revenue approval of the scheme **482**
   Membership of a personal pension scheme and stakeholder scheme **487**
   Benefits payable from a personal pension scheme **490**
   Income withdrawal **496**
   Contributions **501**

Tax treatment **505**
Contracting-out of the state earnings related pension scheme **507**
Transfer values **510**
Disclosure of information **512**
Investment **513**
SIPP investment requirements **516**
Stamp Duty **516**
Stamp Duty Land Tax (SDLT) **518**
Withdrawal of revenue approval **520**
Pensions Bill **520**

16. Commercial transactions 522
Introduction **522**
The sale documents **524**
Shares or assets **527**
Whether the sale will give rise to a transfer payment **531**
Transactions where the purchaser takes over the whole scheme **532**
Transactions involving a transfer payment **536**
Employer's debt **551**
Member-nominated trustees **555**
Public sector transfers **555**
Other types of scheme **557**
Conclusion **558**

17. Pensions dispute resolution and litigation 559
Introduction **559**
Non-court forums for dispute resolution **559**
Court proceedings **562**
Alternative Dispute Resolution (ADR) **584**

18. Insolvency 589
Introduction **589**
Consequences of corporate insolvency under English law – the regimes **589**
Administration **598**
Notifying trustees of a pension scheme of the appointment of insolvency practitioner **601**
Possible claims against the pension scheme by the insolvency practitioner **601**
Independent trustee requirements **602**
Insolvency of the employer and the winding-up of a pension scheme **602**
Deficit or surplus of pension scheme on insolvency **604**
Pensions Bill **610**

Appendix I Penalties under the Pensions Act 1995 and other legislation **612**
  Types of penalty **612**
  Summary of penalties **613**

Appendix II Summary of the Application of the Occupational Pension Schemes (Disclosure of Information) Regulations 1996 (SI 1996 No 1655) (The 'Disclosure Regulations') to Approved Schemes, and other Requirements to Disclose Information **628**

Index 663

Table of Statutes

1834 Civil Service
    Superannuation Act 1.2
1891 Stamp Act
    s 55 .... 15.54
1906 Public Trustee Act 3.4
1908 Old Age Pension Act 1.2
1911 National Insurance Act 1.2
1921 Finance Act 1.2
1925 Law of Property Act 18.7
    ss 99–109 .... 18.7
1925 Trustee Act 10.15
    s 14 .... 3.4, 3.11
    s 15(f) 12.84
    s 23 .... 10.32
    s 25 .... 10.32, 10.33
    s 27 .... 12.77
    s 36 .... 3.11
    s 39 .... 3.11, 18.9
    s 40 .... 3.11
    s 57 .... 12.9
    s 61 .... 1.49, 3.52
    ss 23 and 25 .... 3.19
1958 Variation of Trusts Act 12.9
1961 Trustee Investments Act 1.18, 10.15
    s 6 .... 10.20
1963 Finance Act
    s 55 .... 15.54
1965 Industrial and Provident
    Societies Act 15.2
1970 Equal Pay Act 7.26, 9.5, 9.40
    s 1(b)(a) 9.5
1970 Finance Act 1.2
1973 Finance Act 13.1
1973 Matrimonial Causes Act
    ss 21–25 .... 8.2
    s 21A 8.9
    s 23 .... 8.5, Appendix 11
    s 24B(1) 8.9
        (2) 8.10
        (3) and (4) 8.9
        (5) 8.30
    s 24C 8.10
    s 24D 8.25
    s 25 .... 8.3
        (2) 8.2
        (a) 8.2, 8.3

1973 Matrimonial Causes Act – *contd*
    s 25(h) 8.2
    s 25A(1) 8.2
    s 25B or 25C .... Appendix 11
    s 25B-25D 8.3
    s 25B(1) 8.3
        (4) 8.3
        (5) 8.3
        (6)(a) and 25C(3) 8.3
    ss 25B(6)(a) and 25C(3) 8.3
    s 25B(6)(b) 8.3
        (7) 8.3, 8.6
        (7B) 8.30
    s 25C 8.3
        (3) 8.3
        (4) 8.30
    s 25D(1)(a) 8.5
        (3) 8.3
    s 31 .... 8.3
1973 Social Security Act 1.2, 6.2, 9.2, 9.40
    Sch 16 para 7 .... 6.28
1975 Sex Discrimination Act 9.40
1975 Social Security Act 6.12
1975 Social Security (Pensions)
    Act 1.2, 9.40
1977 Unfair Contract Terms Act
    s 2(2) 3.50
1978 Employment Protection
    (Consolidation) Act 9.40
1980 Solicitors (Scotland) Act
    s 41 .... Appendix I
1981 Supreme Court Act
    s 51 .... 17.30
1984 Data Protection Act 3.55
1984 Health and Social Security
    Act 6.5
1984 Inheritance Tax Act 8.3
    s 5 .... 14.22, 14.26, 14.30
    s 58 .... 14.19
    s 151 .... 5.37
1985 Companies Act
    s 247 .... 18.2
    s 303 .... 3.27
    s 310 .... 12.47
    s 310(1) 3.51
    s 311 .... 14.16, 14.37

Table of Statutes

1985 Companies Act – *contd*
s 378 .... 18.5, 18.6
s 736 .... 4.37, 4.52, 15.2
1985 Family Law (Scotland) Act
ss 12A(2) or (3) .... Appendix II
1985 Social Security Act 1.2, 6.4,
6.6, 6.43, 15.1
1986 Building Societies Act 15.2
1986 Company Directors
Disqualification Act 18.3
1986 Finance Act 11.36
1986 Financial Services Act 10.30,
10.32
s 191 .... 8.17, 13.14
1986 Insolvency Act 18.1, 18.6
ss 1–7 .... 18.2
s 1A 18.2
ss 8–27 .... 18.8
s 23 .... 18.8
ss 28–49 .... 18.7
s 37 .... 18.7
s 44 .... 18.7
s 72 .... 18.7
s 72A 18.7
ss 72A–72H 18.7
s 89 .... 12.93
s 129 .... 12.80
s 130 .... 18.6
s 132 .... 18.6
s 136 .... 18.6
s 247 .... 18.12
(2) 12.80, 18.12, 18.13
s 249 .... 18.3, 18.8
s 278 .... 12.80
s 279 .... 1.56
(3),(4) 1.56
s 281(A) 1.56
s 283 .... 1.51
s 306 .... 1.51
s 310 .... 1.53
(6) 1.56
(A) 1.56
s 386 .... 18.3
ss 388–389 .... 18.3
s 389A(1) 18.3
s 390 .... 18.3
(4) 18.3
s 423 .... 18.20
s 435 .... 2.6, 18.3, 18.8
ss 249–435 .... 3.6
Sch 1 .... 18.8

1986 Insolvency Act – *contd*
Sch 4 .... 18.6
Sch 4A 1.56
s 2(2)(e) 1.56
Sch 6 .... 18.3, 18.16
Sch A1 .... 18.2
Sch B1 .... 18.8
para 5 .... 18.8
para 99 .... 18.8
1986 Sex Discrimination Act 9.40
1986 Social Security Act 1.2, 1.20,
7.1
s 7 .... 4.24
s 10 .... 6.28
1986 Wages Act 7.3
1987 Banking Act 3.21
1987 Finance (No 2) Act 1.31, 15.1
1988 Income and Corporation
Taxes Act 1.2, 5.1, 8.31, 13.4
Pt XIV 13.1
Chap I 5.1, 6.52, 13.35, 15.21,
15.47, 15.49
Chap IV 5.1, 6.52, 6.56, 13.35,
15.1, 15.4
s 19(1) 5.34
s 56(3) 5.31
s 74 .... 5.39, 14.15
s 129B 5.31
s 189 .... 5.35
s 226 .... 15.1
s 256 .... 14.21
s 396 .... 14.26
s 417(5)(b) 5.4
s 431(B)(2)(d),(e) 6.56
s 438 .... 5.40
(1) 15.38
s 529 .... 15.8
ss 540–547 .... 14.31
s 590(2)(a) 13.30
(3) 5.1
s 590A(3)–(4) 4.37
s 590(A)(3)–(4) 4.52
s 590C 5.3, 15.28
(5) 5.3
s 591 .... 5.1
s 591B(1) 13.31
s 592 .... 1.18, 1.32, 5.26, 10.12
(2) 5.31, 13.32
(3) 5.31
(4) 5.26, 5.30
(7) 5.28, 5.30

xii

Table of Statutes

1988 Income and Corporation Taxes Act – *contd*

s 592(8)	5.28
s 594(1)	5.30
s 595	14.6
(1)	14.29
s 598(4)	5.36
s 599	5.35
s 601	11.43
ss 601–603	11.39
ss 605, and 651	Appendix I
s 605(3)(a)	14.9
(b) and (4)	14.9
(4)	14.20
ss 605A, 619, 653 and 658	Appendix I
s 611	5.24, 12.79, 15.47, 15.49
s 611A	4.19, 15.21
s 612	1.18, 5.3, 14.17
(1)	5.24
s 615	1.27
s 615(6)	2.4, 10.23
s 619,	Appendix I
s 620	15.1
(5)	15.2
s 630	15.18
ss 630–655	15.1
s 630(1)	15.6
s 632	15.2
(1)	6.56
s 632B(4)	15.7
s 633	15.4, 15.51
s 634	15.11, 15.12
s 634A	15.18
(4)	15.18
s 635	15.13
s 636	15.14
s 637	15.15
s 638	15.25
s 639	15.33
(2)(a)	15.33
s 640(4)	15.28
s 640A	15.28
s 641	15.36
s 642	15.34
s 643(1)	15.37
(2)	15.38
s 644	15.7
s 646(1)	15.28
s 648A	15.39
s 650	15.58

1988 Income and Corporation Taxes Act – *contd*

s 651	Appendix I
(1)	15.58
s 653	Appendix I, 15.4
s 656	14.21
s 658	Appendix I
s 659A	5.31
s 659B(1)	15.2
(5), (6) and (7)	15.2
s 660A	14.16, 14.17
(4)	14.17
s 660D	14.17
s 686(2)	5.31
(c)(i)	14.17
s 703	13.29
s 707	13.23, 13.29
s 727(1)	5.31
s 840A(1)(b)	15.2
Sch 4, s 22	11.41
Sch 22	11.39, 11.43, 11.47, 12.41
para 3(3)	11.42
para 6(1)	11.47
Sch 23, para 5(5)	5.4
para 6(2)	5.3

1989 Companies Act

137(1)	3.51

1989 Finance Act ... 14.1

s 76	14.15, 14.24
Sch 7	15.13

1989 Social Security Act 4.18, 7.29, 9.36, 9.37, 9.40

Sch 5	7.29, 9.34

1990 Social Security Act 1.2, 1.45, 2.11, 3.6, 9.40

1992 Friendly Societies Act 15.2

1992 Social Security Administration Act 1.4

s 148	4.61

1992 Social Security Contributions and Benefits Act 1.4

s 2(i)(a)	14.36
s 3(i)(a)	14.36

1992 Taxation of Capital Gains Act

s 27(1)(g)	5.31

1992 Taxation of Chargeable Gains Act

s 5	14.18
s 69	14.18

Table of Statutes

1992 Taxation of Chargeable Gains Act – *contd*
- s 271(1)(g) 5.31
- Sch 1 .... 14.18
- Sch A1 .... 14.18

1993 Criminal Justice Act 10.46

1993 Finance Act
- s 78 .... 5.31

1993 Pension Schemes Act .... 1.2, 1.4, 1.11, 1.41, 2.2, 2.5, 2.13, 4.6, 4.19, 6.7, 6.10, 7.3, 9.40, 9.39, Appendix I
- Pt III 4.1
- Pt IV,
  - Chap I 6.2, 6.8
  - Chap II 6.3, 6.8, 6.31
  - Chap III 6.5, 6.8, 6.31
  - Chap IV 6.6, 6.8
- s 1 .... 1.11, 8.9, 14.12
- s 6 .... 2.11
- ss 7–13 .... Appendix I
- s 9(3) 4.19
- (5) 15.40
- s 10 .... 4.18, 4.20, 4.21, 15.42
- s 12A 7.22
- s 12B 4.6
- s 13 .... 4.11
- ss 13–24 .... 4.5, 4.11
- s 15 .... 4.11
- s 16 .... 4.61
- s 17 .... 4.13
- s 19(4) 12.74
- ss 26–33 .... 4.18
- s 27 .... 4.21
- s 28 .... 4.25
- ss 28–29 .... 4.25
- s 28(4) 4.29
- (4A) 4.30
- s 32 .... 4.28
- s 32A 12.41, 12.74
- s 38 .... Appendix I
- s 41 .... Appendix I
- s 43 .... 15.4
- ss 52–53 .... 4.65
- s 53(1) 4.65
- s 67 .... Appendix I
- s 68A–68D 8.27
- s 69 .... 6.7
- ss 69–82 .... 6.2
- s 70 .... 6.21

1993 Pension Schemes Act – *contd*
- s 70(1) 6.15
- (2) 6.12
- s 71 .... 6.16
- (1) 6.17
- (3) 6.23
- (7) 6.11
- (9) 6.11
- s 72(1) 6.22
- (3) 6.22
- s 72A .... Appendix I
- s 72C .... Appendix I
- s 73(2) 6.24
  - (a) 6.25
- (4) 6.25
- (5) 6.29
- s 74(1) 6.19
- (3) 6.20
- (4) 6.20
- (6) 6.20
- (7) 6.19
- s 75(5) 6.20
- ss 83–86 .... 6.4
- s 83(1)(a) 6.31
- s 84 .... 6.33
- (1) 6.37
- (2) 6.34, 6.35
- (3) 6.36
- s 85 .... 6.32
- ss 87–92 .... 4.64, 6.5
- ss 93–101 .... 6.6, 6.43, 15.46
- s 93A 6.60
- ss 93A, 99 and 101 .... Appendix I
- s 93A(1) 6.45
- (4) 6.45
- s 94(1)(a) 6.44
  - (aa) 6.44, 6.52
- s 95(2) 12.73
  - (a) 12.74
  - (b) 12.74
  - (c) 12.74
- (9) 6.52
- s 96 .... 6.53
- (1) 6.53
  - (b) and (2) 6.53
- s 97 .... 4.40, 4.41, 6.48
- s 98 .... 6.46, 6.47
- s 99(2) 6.55
- (4) 6.57
- (7) 6.58
- s 100 .... 6.52

Table of Statutes

1993 Pension Schemes Act – *contd*
- s 101A-101Q 8.18
- s 101C 8.18
- s 101F 8.18
- s 101G(1) 8.18
- s 101H 8.18
- s 101J 8.18
- s 102 .... 14.12
- s 108 .... 12.64, 12.72
- s 111 .... 1.31
- s 111A .... Appendix I
- s 118 .... 9.2, 14.12
- ss 119–122 .... 14.12
- ss 123–125 .... 18.17
- s 123 .... 18.17
- s 124(1) 18.17
  - (2) 18.17
  - (3) 18.17
  - (3A) 18.17
- s 129 .... 6.8
- s 131 .... 6.8
- s 132 .... 6.8
- s 144 .... 12.78, 14.12
- s 145 .... 2.26
- s 146 .... 2.27, 14.12
- ss 146 and 148 .... 17.8
- s 146(6) 9.5
- s 150(1) 2.28
- s 151 .... 17.9, 17.12
  - (2) 2.28
  - (4) 17.9
- s 152 .... 6.44
- s 153 .... Appendix I
- s 160 .... 7.1, 12.33
- s 175 .... 2.17
  - (4) 2.20, 2.21
- s 179 .... 6.13
- s 180 .... 6.14, 6.23
  - (2) 6.14, 6.23
- Sch 3 .... 6.33
  - para 1 .... 6.39
    - (1)(a) 6.42
    - (b) 6.42
  - para 2 .... 6.39, 6.40, 11.47
    - (7) 6.41
  - para 3 .... 6.34
  - para 4 .... 6.35
  - para 5 .... 6.38

1994 Finance Act 14.33

1994 Matrimonial and Family Proceedings Act 8.2

1995 Bankrupcy (Scotland) Act
- s 12(4) 12.80

1995 Disability Discrimination Act 7.28
- s 1 .... 1.24
- s 17 .... 1.23, 7.28
- s 48 .... 2.5

1995 Finance Act 13.31
- s 58 .... 15.17
- s 61 .... 13.31
- Sch 11 .... 15.17

1995 Pensions Act 1.2, 1.4, 1.11, 1.18, 1.25, 1.58, 2.2, 2.3, 2.5, 2.10, 2.13, 2.24, 2.27, 3.1, 3.7, 3.8, 3.11, 3.15, 3.16, 3.18, 3.39, 3.46, 3.49, 3.50, 3.53, 4.1, 4.4, 4.5, 4.18, 4.19, 4.23, 4.48, 4.49, 6.62, 7.1, 7.11, 7.12, 8.1, 9.5, 9.40, 10.2, 10.19, 10.29, 10.49, 11.1–3, 11.13, 11.50, 12.91, 13.1, 13.15, 13.33, 14.12, 14.7, 15.5, 16.23, 17.5, 18.8, 18.18
- s 1 .... 2.12
- s 2 .... Appendix I
- s 3 .... 2.13, 2.14, Appendix I
- ss 3, 10, 17, 19 and 21 .... 3.33
- s 3(2)(c) 3.3
  - (3) 2.13
- s 4 .... 2.13, Appendix I
- ss 6, 9 and 10 .... 13.34
- s 7 .... 2.13, 3.11
- s 7–13 .... Appendix I
- s 7(3) and (4) 3.11
  - (5) 3.11
  - (b) 3.13
- s 10 ...... 2.13, 2.14, 8.13, 8.18, 18.9, Appendix I
  - (5) 3.3
- s 11 .... 2.13, 12.51
- s 13 .... 2.13
- s 14 .... 2.13
- s 15 .... 2.13
- s 16 .... 3.24
  - (1) 3.25
  - (3)–(8) 3.27

Table of Statutes

1995 Pensions Act – *contd*
ss 17 and 19 .... Appendix I
s 17(1)(a) 3.30
  (2) 3.34
  (4) 3.26
s 18(3)–(7) 3.27
  (8) and (9) 3.37
s 19 .... Appendix I
  (1)(a) 3.30
  (2) 3.34
  (4) 3.26
s 20(1)(b) 3.29
  (2)–(5) 3.28
s 21 .... Appendix I
  (7) 3.27
  (8)(a)(i)–(ii) 3.31
s 22 .... 2.27, 3.6, 18.11
ss 22–26 .... 14.12
s 23 .... 3.6, 18.11
  (1) 3.6
    (a) 3.6
  (3) 3.6
s 25(1) 3.6
  (2) 3.6
  (4) 3.6
  (6) 3.6, 3.13, 18.11
s 26(1) and (2) 3.6
  (A) .... Appendix I
s 27 .... 2.6, 2.7, 3.2
  (2) 2.6
s 28 .... 2.6, Appendix I
s 29 .... 2.13, 3.2
s 30 .... 2.13, 3.2, 3.3, Appendix I
  (5) 2.13
s 30(A) 2.13
s 31 .... 12.77, Appendix I
  (1) 3.51
  (2) 3.53
s 32 .... 3.23, Appendix I
  (4) 3.24
s 33 .... 10.50
  (1) 3.50
s 34 ...... 2.8, 3.16, 3.19, 3.50, 10.15,
                  10.16, 10.33, 10.50
ss 34 and 35 .... 13.34
s 34(1) 3.16, 10.15
  (2)(b) 10.30, 10.37, 10.50
  (4) 3.50, 10.50
  (5) 10.30, 10.50
s 35 .... 10.23, 10.27, 11.19,
                  Appendices I & II

1995 Pensions Act – *contd*
s 35(5)(b) 3.60, 10.23
  (6) 10.23
s 36 .... 3.50, 10.19, 10.22, 10.23,
                  10.30, 10.37, 10.50
  (2) 10.20
  (5) 10.23, 10.33
s 37 .... 1.17, 1.18, 1.45, 11.47,
                           Appendix I
s 38 .... 12.57
  (1) 12.55
  (2) 12.55
  (3)(a) 12.55
s 39 .... 3.13
s 40 ...... 4.5, 4.19, 10.24, Appendix I
s 41 .... 3.22, Appendix II5
  (1) and (2) (c) .... Appendix II
s 42 .... 7.34
s 46 .... 7.35
s 47 ...... 2.4, 2.7, 10.30, 10.38, 13.34
  (1)(b) ... 1.26, 6.48, 11.15, 11.41,
                                12.21
  (2) 10.41
s 47(9)(a) 18.9
s 48 .... 1.27, 2.5, 2.7, 2.13, 13.34,
                           Appendix I
s 48(1) 2.2, 2.6
s 48(7)–(13) 2.5
s 49 .... 3.21, 10.35, Appendix I
s 49(8) 1.30
  (11) and (12) 1.26, 1.27
s 50 ..... 1.17, 3.40, 3.48, 12.14, 17.2,
                           Appendix I
  (2) 3.45
s 50A 3.48
s 50B 3.48
s 51 .... 1.3, 1.17, 1.45, 4.6, 8.19,
                           13.34, 14.12
  (6) 1.45
s 52 .... 1.45
s 53 .... 1.45
ss 56–61 .... 1.17, 11.14
s 56 .... 1.26
  (1) 13.34
  (2) 11.14
    (a) 13.34
s 57 .... 11.15, Appendix I
  (1)(a) .... Appendix II
s 58 ..... 1.18, 3.20, 11.20, Appendix I
ss 58 or 87 .... Appendix II
s 58(3)(b) 11.23

Table of Statutes

1995 Pensions Act – contd
s 58(3)(c) 11.23
    (4) 11.20, 11.21
    (6) 11.21
ss 59 and 60 .... Appendix I
s 59, 60 and 75 .... 16.24
s 59(2) 11.26
s 60(4) and (5) 11.28
s 62 .... 1.22, 7.25, 9.24, 9.29, 9.40
ss 62–66 ..... 1.17, 9.1, 9.2, 9.6, 9.17,
                 9.40, 13.34, 14.12
s 62(3) 9.1
s 63 .... 9.5
    (4)(c) 9.5
s 64(3)(b) 9.15
s 65 .... 9.1, 9.19, 9.21, 12.11
s 67 .... 1.3, 7.10, 7.12, 7.13, 8.21,
              9.21, 12.5, 12.15,
              12.18, 12.23, 12.24,
              12.26, 12.31, 12.96,
                      17.15
    (3) 8.21
    (4)(a) 12.21
       (b) 12.22
    (6) 12.24
s 68 .... 11.28, 12.11
s 69 .... 2.13, 11.45
ss 69–71 .... 12.10
s 70 .... 12.10
s 71 .... 12.10
    (2) 11.45
s 72(A) .... 12.75, Appendix II
s 73 .... 8.22, 12.89, Appendix I
ss 73 and 74 .... 1.17, 12.67
ss 73, 74, 76 and 77 .... 13.34
ss 73–77 .... 12.66
s 73(3) .... 6.51, Appendix II
    (a)-(e) 4.49
    (4) 12.67
    (5) 12.5, 12.71, 12.87, 12.89
s 74 .... 1.18, 12.67, 12.74, 12.87,
                      13.34
    (3) 12.69, 12.70
       (a) 12.74
       (b) 12.74
       (c) 12.74

1995 Pensions Act – contd
s 75 .... 11.18, 12.55, 12.65, 12.68,
           12.78, 12.79, 12.84,
           12.95, 13.34, 14.12,
           16.25, 16.62, 16.64,
           16.65, 18.12, 18.13,
               18.14, 18.20
    (1) 12.81
    (1A) 12.81, 16.63
    (1B) 12.81
    (1A)–(1E) 15.63
    (3) 12.81, 18.13, 18.14
    (4) 12.80
       (a) 18.13
    (8) 12.84
S 75A 16.64
s 76 .... 12.71, 13.34, 18.19
ss 76 and 77 .... 1.17, 1.45, 11.48,
                    Appendix I
s 77 .... 11.48, 12.72, 13.34
ss 78–80 .... 2.18
s 78(5) 2.20, 2.21
s 81 .... 2.19, Appendix I
    (1) 13.34
       (b) 2.19
s 82(5) 2.19
s 83 .... 2.19
s 87 .... 1.27, 3.20, Appendix I
    (2) 13.34
s 87–90 .... 1.17
s 88 .... 1.27, Appendix I
s 91 .... 1.46, 8.3, 13.9
ss 91–94 .... 7.24
s 91(5)(a) and (b) 1.48
       (c) 1.47
ss 91(5)(d) and 93(3) 7.24
s 91(5)(d) and (e) 1.49
ss 91(6) 7.24
s 92 .... 1.46, 1.50
    (3) 1.50
s 93(5) 1.50
s 93A 8.25
s 94 .... 8.25
s 96 .... 2.15
    (2) .... Appendix I
s 97 .... Appendix I
s 98 .... 2.16
s 99 .... 2.16
s 100 .... 2.16
s 101 .... 2.16
s 104 .... 2.16, Appendix I

xvii

Table of Statutes

1995 Pensions Act – *contd*
s 106 .... 2.16
s 107 .... 2.16
s 108(1)7 .... 2.16
    (2)7 .... 2.16
    (3)7 .... 2.16
s 109 .... 2.16
s 111 .... Appendix I
s 113 .... 3.22
s 123 .... 2.6, 3.6
s 124 .... 3.26
    (1) 12.82
    (2) 12.20
s 126 .... 9.29
s 150 .... 2.10
ss 152–154 .... 13.34
ss 156–160 .... 13.34
s 160 .... 1.20
s 165 .... 2.17, 2.20, 2.21
s 166 .... 8.2, 8.3
ss 166(4) and (5) 8.3
Sch 4, para 1 .... 1.7
1996 Employment Rights Act 3.10,
                7.15, 7.16, 9.32,
                    9.37, 9.40
s 1 .... 7.2
    (4)(d)(iii) 7.2
s 13 .... 1.30, 7.3
s 18 .... 7.19
s 46 .... 7.35
s 58 .... 3.10, 7.34
s 59 .... 3.10, 7.34
s 60 .... 3.10, 7.34
s 62(2) 3.10
s 71 .... 9.34
    (4) 9.34
s 102 .... 3.10, 7.15, 7.35
ss 123 and 124 .... 7.16
s 158 .... 7.15
s 203 .... 7.19
    (1) 7.35
1996 Family Law Act 8.9
s 28(1)(b) 8.10
1997 Finance (No 2) Act
s 19(2) 5.31
Sch 6(3) 5.40
1998 Data Protection Act ... 2.34, 3.54,
                3.55, 3.56, 3.58
1998 Finance Act 14.18
1998 Human Rights Act 9.30, 17.10

1999 Employment Relations
    Act 9.34
1999 Finance Act
s 79 .... 8.31
Sch 10 .... 8.31
1999 Social Security
    Contributions (Transfer of
    Functions etc.) Act 4.1, 4.4
1999 Welfare Reform and
    Pensions Act 1.2, 1.51, 1.52,
                1.57, 2.19, 5.1, 8.1,
                        8.9, 15.1
s 1 .... 2.14, 7.1
s 2 .... 2.4, 2.8, 2.14, 2.19, Appendix I
s 3 .... Appendix I
s 9(2B) 8.22
s 12 .... 1.54
    (2) 1.57
s 15 .... 1.55
s 23(1)(a) .... Appendix II , 8.24
s 27(1)(3) 8.9
    (2) 8.9
s 29 .... 8.23
    (1) 8.10
        (a) 8.10
    (2) 8.23
    (4) 8.23
    (7) 8.23
s 30 .... 8.23
s 31(1) 8.11
    (2) 8.11
    (3) 8.11
s 33 .... Appendix I
    (4) 8.13
s 34(1) 8.13
s 34(a) and (b) .... Appendix II
s 35 .... 8.13
s 36 .... 8.27
s 37 .... 8.17
s 38 .... 8.22
    (2) 8.22
s 41 .... 8.25
    (3)(b) 8.25
s 46(1) 8.3, 8.9
    (2) 8.3
Sch 3, para 5 .... 14.12
Sch 5
    paras 1, 2, 3 and 4 .... 8.14
    para 1(2) 8.14
    para 1(3) 8.14
    para 1(4) 8.14

1999 Welfare Reform and Pensions Act –
contd
Sch 5 – *contd*
  para 6 .... 8.14
Sch 12
  paras 45–49 .... 8.20
  para 53 .... 8.20
2000 Child Support, Pensions
  and Social Security Act 1.2,
            1.10, 2.27, 3.25,
                          4.64
2000 Finance Act
  s 17 .... 15.36
  s 94 .... 13.21
2000 Financial Services and
  Markets Act 1.58, 10.1, 10.19,
          10.25–27, 10.28,
          10.30, 10.35, 10.38,
          10.41, 10.50, 12.23,
          13.14, 14.35, 15.52
  Pt 4 .... 15.2
  s 1 .... 10.27
  ss 19 and 22 .... 10.33, 13.14
  s 22 .... 2.8, 10.24
  s 23 .... Appendix I
  s 25 .... Appendix I
  s 56 .... Appendix I
  s 66 .... Appendix I
  s 118 .... Appendix I
  s 123 .... Appendix I
  s 178 .... Appendix I
  s 190 .... Appendix I
  s 191 .... Appendix I
  s 205 .... Appendix I
  s 206 .... Appendix I
  s 241 .... Appendix I
  s 243 .... 15.2
  s 352 .... Appendix I
  s 380 .... Appendix I
  s 382 .... Appendix I
  s 397 .... Appendix I
  s 398 .... Appendix I
  Sch 1, Pt II 15.2
  Sch 2 .... 10.24
  Sch 3
    para 5(a), (b) and (c) 15.2
    para 5(d) 15.2
    para 12 .... 15.2
    para 12(1) and (2) 15.2
      (a) 15.2
      (a)-(e) 15.2

2000 Financial Services and Markets Act
  – *contd*
Sch 3 – *contd*
      (cc) 15.2
  para 15 .... 15.2
Sch 4
  para 2 .... 15.2
  para 4 .... 15.2
Sch 5 .... 15.2
Sch 8
  para 83 .... 5.3, 5.4
2000 Freedom of Information
  Act 2.34
2000 Trustee Act 3.14, 3.19
  s 11 .... 10.32
  s 23 .... 10.50
2002 Employment Act 9.34, 9.35,
                            9.40
2002 Enterprise Act ... 1.53, 1.56, 18.7,
                          18.8
  s 256 .... 1.56
  s 257 .... 1.56
  s 259 .... 1.56
  s 260 .... 1.56
2000 Insolvency Act 18.2, 18.3
2002 State Pension Credit Act 1.5
2003 Finance Act
  s 42 .... 15.56
  s 56 .... 15.56
  Sch 4, para 8 .... 15.56
  Sch 5 .... 15.56
2003 Income Tax (Earnings and
  Pensions) Act
  s 15 .... 5.3, 5.4, 5.34
  s 21 .... 5.3, 5.4, 5.34
  s 386 .... 14.6, 14.15, 14.16, 14.21,
                          14.34
    (1) 14.16
    (6) 14.16
  s 388 .... 14.16
  s 394 .... 14.25
    (1) 14.21, 14.25
    (2) 14.21
  s 395(2) and (4) 14.21, 14.22,
                          14.30
  s 396 .... 14.21, 14.22, 14.26
  s 397(1) 14.33
  s 398 .... 14.25
  Pt 6, Chap 2 .... 14.21

Table of Statutes

2003 Income Tax (Earnings and
  Pensions) Act – *contd*
  Pt 6, Chap 3 .... 5.3
2003 Local Government Act
  ss 101 and 102 .... 16.68

Table of Statutory Instruments

1965/1189 Redundancy Payments Pensions Regulations 1965 ...... 7.15
1975/1189 Public Trustee (Custodian Trustee) Rules 1975 .... 3.4
1976/142 Occupational Pension Schemes (Equal Access to Membership)
    Regulations 1976 .... 9.2
1978/1045 Matrimonial Causes (Northern Ireland) Order
    Art 25 .... Appendix II
    Art 27B .... Appendix II
    Art 27C .... Appendix II
1979/591 Social Security (Contributions) Regulations 1979 ...... 14.36
1981/1794 Transfer of Undertakings (Protection of Employment)
    Regulations 1981 .... 1.3, 7.22, 7.23
    reg 7 .... 7.22, 16.15
        (1),(2) 7.22
1985/1205 Credit Unions (Northern Ireland) Order 1985 1522
1985/1931 Occupational Pension Schemes (Transfer Values)
    Regulations 1985 .... 6.62
1986/1032 Companies (Northern Ireland) Order 1986 .... 15.2
1986/1046 Occupational Pension Schemes (Disclosure of Information)
    Regulations 1986 .... 11.5, 11.16, 14.12
1986/1925 Insolvency Rules 1986 .... 18.1
    Part 1 .... 18.2
    rule 1.19 .... 18.3
    rule 1.54 .... 18.3
    rule 4.67 .... 18.6
    rule 4, Chapter 9 .... 18.6
1986/1996 Insolvency Proceedings (Monetary Limits) Order 1986 (SI 1986
    No 1996) 18.16
1987/352 Pension Scheme Surpluses (Administration) Regulations 1987
    reg 3 .... 11.43
1987/412 Pension Scheme Surpluses (Valuation) Regulations 1987 .... 11.39, 11.41
    reg 3 .... 11.40
    reg 10 .... 11.42
    reg 11 .... 11.42
1987/516 Stamp Duty (Exempt Instruments) Regulations 1987 .... 15.54
1987/1108 Pension Scheme (Voluntary Contributions Requirements and
    Voluntary and Compulsory Membership) Regulations 1987
        reg 2(3) 14.12
            (4) 1.31
            (6) 1.31
            (8) 1.31
        reg 3 .... 1.20
1987/1110 Personal Pension Schemes (Disclosure of Information)
    Regulations 1987 .... 15.50, Appendix II
1988/1014 Personal Pension Schemes (Transfer Payments)
    Regulations 1988 .... 15.13
1988/1436 Occupational Pension Schemes (Transitional Provisions)
    Regulations 1988 .... 5.6, 16.42

Table of Statutory Instruments

1990/2075 Occupational Pension Schemes (Independent Trustee)
Regulations 1990 .... 14.12
1990/2101 Retirement Benefits Schemes (Continuation of Rights of Members
of Approved Schemes) Regulations 1990 .... 5.6, 16.42
1991/167 Occupational Pension Schemes (Preservation of Benefit)
Regulations 1991 .... 4.38, 4.42, 6.2, 7.14
    regs 5(2), (3) and (4), 8(2) 6.26
    reg 7(2) 6.26, 6.27, 6.28, 6.29
    regs 7(2) and 8(3) 6.26, 6.27
    reg 8 .... 6.26
        (1) 6.26, 6.27
        (3) 6.26, 6.27
    regs 8(4) and 11 .... 6.26, 6.27
    regs 9 and 11 .... 6.28
    reg 9(4)(a) 6.28
    regs 9(4)(b) and 9(5) 6.28
    reg 9(6) 6.28
    regs 10 and 11 .... 6.29
    reg 11 .... 6.26, 6.27, 6.28
    reg 11A 6.25
    reg 12(2) 12.33
        (3) 4.37
        (3) 12.33
        (4B) .... 12.33, Appendix II
    reg 14 .... 6.19
    reg 21 .... 6.12
    regs 27A .... Appendix II
    reg 27B .... Appendix I
1991/168 Occupational Pension Schemes (Revaluation) Regulations 1991
    reg 3 .... 6.32
1991/588 Personal and Occupational Pension Schemes (Pensions
Ombudsman) Regulations 1991 .... 7.7, 13.34
1991/1247 Family (Proceedings) Rules 1991
    rule 2.70 .... 8.5, 8.28
        (4) 8.28
        (6) 8.28
        (7) 8.28
    rules 2.70(8) and (9) 8.28
        (11) and (12) 8.28
        (13), 14 and 15 .... 8.28
1991/1614 Retirement Benefits Schemes (Restriction on Discretion to
Approve) (Small Self-Administered Schemes) Regulations 1991 ...... 13.2, 13.5,
                                                                                                                          13.24
    reg 2 .... 13.3
    reg 4 .... 13.13
    reg 5 .... 13.16, 13.18
    reg 6 .... 13.20, 13.22, 13.23
    reg 7 .... 13.24
    reg 8 .... 13.20, 13.23, 13.25, 13.26
    reg 9 .... 13.4, 13.27
    reg 11 .... 13.20

Table of Statutory Instruments

1992/246 Occupational Pension Schemes (Investment of Scheme's Resources) Regulations 1992 .... 14.12
1992/3218 Banking Coordination (Second Council Directive) Regulations 1992 .... 15.2
1994/3013 VAT (Buildings and Land) Order 1994 .... 13.33
1995/1019 Local Government Pension Scheme Regulations 1995 .... 6.58
1995/1053 Personal and Occupational Pension Schemes (Pensions Ombudsman) (Procedure) Rules 1995 .... 2.28
    reg 3 .... 2.28
    reg 5(2) 2.28
    reg 6(2) 2.28
        (3) 2.28
    reg 7 .... 2.28
    reg 16(1) 2.28
1995/1215 Occupational Pension Schemes (Equal Access to Membership) Amendment Regulations 1995 .... 13.34
1995/3103 Retirement Benefits Schemes (Information Powers) Regulations 1995 .... 5.26, 13.2
1995/3183 Occupational Pension Schemes (Equal Treatment) Regulations 1995 .... 9.2, 9.5, 9.29, 9.40, 13.34
1996/805 Personal Pension Scheme (Deferred Annuity Purchase) (Acceptance of Contributions) Regulations 1996 .... 15.25
1996/1172 Occupational Pension Schemes (Contracting-Out) Regulations 1996 .... 4.1, 4.5, 4.17, 4.18, 4.48
    reg 18 .... 11.22
    regs 2–12 .... 4.4
    reg 3 .... 4.44, 4.45
    reg 5 .... 4.47
    reg 6 .... 4.48
    reg 7 .... 4.44
    reg 9 .... 4.50, 4.51
    reg 10 .... 4.44, 4.46
    reg 12 .... 4.52
    reg 16 .... 4.17
    reg 22 .... 4.8
    regs 25–26 .... 4.6
    regs 29(a) and 40(h) 14.12
    reg 30 .... 4.19, 4.22, 4.34
    reg 31 .... 4.22
    reg 32 .... 4.22
    regs 41–69 .... 4.5
    regs 55–56 .... 4.11
    reg 72 .... 4.49
1996/1216 Occupational Pension Schemes (Member-nominated Trustees and Directors) Regulations 1996 .... 3.25, 13.34
    regs 2, 7 and 13 .... 3.34
    reg 4 .... 3.26
    reg 6 .... 3.26
    reg 7 .... 3.33
    regs 7 and 13 .... 3.35
    reg 7(2) 3.34

Table of Statutory Instruments

1996/1216 Occupational Pension Schemes (Member-nominated Trustees and Directors) Regulations 1996 – *contd*
- reg 9 .... 3.30, 3.34
- regs 9 and 15 .... 3.36
- regs 9(2) and 15(2) 3.36
- regs 9(2)(c), 15(2)(c), 20(1)(d)(ii) and 20(1)(f)(ii) 3.38
- reg 9(2)(d) 3.30, 3.38
- reg 10 .... 3.34
- reg 13 .... 3.34
  - (2) 3.34
- reg 15 .... 3.30, 3.34
- reg 16 .... 3.34
- reg 20(1) 3.36
- regs 20(1)(g) and 20(1)(h) 3.36
- reg 20(2) 3.36
- regs 8 and 14 .... 3.38
- Sch 1 .... 3.31, 3.32
- Sch 2 .... 3.29
- Sch 3 .... 3.37
  - para 7 .... 3.27

1996/1270 Occupational Pension Schemes (Internal Dispute Resolution Procedures) Regulations 1996 .... 3.48, 13.34, 17.2
- reg 2 .... 3.41
- reg 3 .... 3.41
- reg 4 .... 3.43
- reg 5(2) 3.44
  - (3) 3.44
- reg 6 .... 3.45
- reg 7 .... 3.46
- reg 8 .... 3.40
- reg 9 .... 3.47

1996/1456 Disability Discrimination (Employment) Regulations 1996
- reg 4 .... 1.23

1996/1536 Occupational Pension Schemes (Minimum Funding Requirement and Actuarial Valuations) Regulations 1996 .... 1.26, 11.14, 11.16, 12.83, 13.34
- reg 10 .... 11.17
- reg 11 .... 11.18
- reg 12 .... 11.18, 11.19
- reg 13 .... 11.18, 16.65
- reg 15 .... 11.20
  - (3) 11.20
- regs 16(1) and (2) 11.20
- reg 17 .... 11.21
  - (1) 11.20
- reg 18 .... 11.27
- reg 19 .... 11.24
- reg 21 .... 11.28
- reg 23 .... 11.26
- reg 24 .... 11.31
- regs 25–27 .... 11.25
- reg 30 .... 11.8, 11.10

Table of Statutory Instruments

1996/1536 Occupational Pension Schemes (Minimum Funding Requirement and Actuarial Valuations) Regulations 1996 – *contd*
    Sch 3 .... 11.27
    Sch 4 .... 11.28
    Sch 5, paras 1 and 2 .... 11.29
        para 3 .... 11.30
    Sch 6 .... 11.10
1996/1537 Personal and Occupational Pension Schemes (Protected Rights) Regulations 1996 .... 4.1, 4.18
    reg 4 .... 4.25
    reg 5 .... 4.26
    reg 8 .... 4.29
    reg 9 .... 4.28
    reg 12 .... 4.27
1996/1655 Occupational Pension Schemes (Disclosure of Information) Regulations 1996 .... 1.17, 7.14, 13.34, 16.31, Appendix II
    reg 2(1) 14.12
        (2) 14.12
    reg 3 .... Appendix I
    reg 4 and Sch 1 .... 3.40, Appendix I
    reg 5(10) 12.75
        (d) 12.75
        (12) 12.75
        and Sch 2 .... Appendix II
            (10) 12.74
            (d) 12.74
            (12) 12.74
    reg 6 .... 10.23, Appendix II
        (2) .... Appendix II
    reg 7 .... 11.15, Appendix II
    reg 8 .... Appendix II
    reg 10 .... 8.7
1996/1676 Divorce Regulations 1996 .... 8.4
1996/1679 Occupational Pension Schemes (Indexation) Regulations 1996
    reg 2 .... 1.45
1996/1715 Occupational Pension Schemes (Scheme Administration) Regulations 1996 .... 13.34, Appendix I
    reg 1(2) 1.27
    reg 3 .... 1.17, 6.51
        (1) 2.7
        (2) 2.4
        (3) 2.8
    regs 4 and 5 .... 10.38
    reg 4(1) 2.4
    reg 5 .... 2.4, 10.30, 10.38
        (1) 2.4
        (2)(a) 2.4
        (2)(b)(ii) 2.4
        (4) 2.4
        (8) 2.4
    reg 6(1)(b) 18.9

Table of Statutory Instruments

1996/1715 Occupational Pension Schemes (Scheme Administration) Regulations 1996 – contd
- reg 7 .... 2.6, 3.2
  - (3)(b)(iv) 6.51
- reg 8(4) 6.51
- reg 9 .... 3.24
- reg 10 .... 3.24
- reg 11 .... 3.21, 10.35
- reg 12 .... 3.21
- reg 13 .... 3.21
- reg 16 .... 1.30
- reg 17 .... 1.27
- regs 18 and 19 .... 1.27

1996/1847 Occupational Pension Schemes (Transfer Values) Regulations 1996 .... 6.43, 6.48, 6.61, 13.34
- reg 2(b) 6.44
- regs 3 and 4 .... 6.46
- reg 6(1) 6.45
  - (2) 6.45
  - (3) 6.45
  - (4) 6.52
- reg 7(1) 6.48
  - (3) 6.48
  - (5) 6.49
- reg 8 .... 6.50, 6.60
  - (1) 6.51
  - (3) 6.50
  - (4) 6.51
  - (12) 6.51
- reg 10 .... 6.58
- reg 11 .... 6.60
- reg 11 and Sch 1 .... Appendix II
- reg 12 .... 6.52
- reg 13 .... 6.57
- reg 19 .... 6.61
- reg 20 .... 6.45, 6.60
- Sch 1 .... 6.60, Appendix II

1996/1975 Occupational Pension Schemes (Requirement to Obtain Audited Accounts and a Statement from the Auditor) Regulations 1996 .... 2.7

1996/1976 Occupational Pension Schemes (Pensions Compensation Board Limit on Borrowing) Regulations 1996
- reg 2 .... 2.20, 2.21

1996/2156 Occupational Pension Schemes (Payments to Employers) Regulations 1996
- regs 4–6 .... 11.47
- regs 7–9 .... 12.72
- regs 7–10 .... 11.48
- reg 7 .... 18.19
- reg 12 .... 11.49

Table of Statutory Instruments

1996/2475 Personal and Occupational Pension Schemes (Pensions
Ombudsman) Regulations 1996 .... 2.27, 7.7
   reg 2 .... 2.27
   reg 3 .... 2.27, 3.47, 14.12
      (2) 2.27
   reg 5 .... 2.27
      (3) 2.27
1996/2517 Occupational Pension Schemes (Modification of Schemes)
Regulations 1996 .... 12.10
   reg 3 .... 12.21
   reg 4 .... 12.22
   reg 5 .... 12.24
   reg 6 .... 12.18
      (a) 8.21
   reg 7 .... 12.11
1996/3126 Occupational Pension Schemes (Winding Up) Regulations 1996 ....
                                                                                                                                 Appendix I
   reg 2 .... 12.48, 12.90
   reg 3 .... 11.19, 12.67
      (2) 12.67
   reg 4(5) 12.67
   reg 5 .... 12.56
   reg 6(2)(a) 12.74
   regs 6–8 .... 12.74
   reg 7 .... 12.74
   reg 8(4) 12.74
      (5) 12.74
   reg 9 .... 12.74
   reg 10(1) 12.55
   reg 11 .... 12.57, Appendix II
1996/3127 Occupational Pension Schemes (Investment) Regulations 1996 .... 4.5,
                                                                                                  4.17, 4.19, 4.48, 10.21, 13.34
   reg 4 .... 10.24
   reg 5 .... 10.24
   reg 6 .... 10.24
   reg 7 .... 10.24
   reg 10 .... 10.23
      (3)(a) 14.12
   reg 11 .... 10.23
1996/3128 Occupational Pension Schemes (Deficiency on Winding Up etc.)
Regulations 1996 .... 7.3, 12.78, 18.14
   reg 3 .... 12.83, 16.63
      (A) 16.63
   reg 4(3) 12.81, 16.62
   reg 5(1) 12.82
      (2) and (3) 12.82
   reg 6(2) 12.82
   reg 7 .... 1.17
   regs 7, 8 and 9 .... 12.79
   reg 10 .... 12.79
      (c) 14.12

Table of Statutory Instruments

1997/252 Occupational Pension Schemes (Independent Trustee)
Regulations 1997 .... 3.6, 13.34
    reg 2 .... 3.6
    reg 3 .... 3.6
    reg 5 .... 1.17
        (1)(f) 14.12
    reg 7 .... 3.6, Appendix I

1997/371 Register of Occupational and personal Pension Schemes
Regulations 1997 .... 14.12, Appendix I
    reg 3(2) 2.11
    reg 4 .... 14.12
    reg 5 .... 2.11, 3.10
    reg 6 .... 2.11
    reg 7 .... 2.11

1997/665 Occupational Pension Schemes (Pensions Compensation Provisions)
Regulations 1997 .... 13.34
    reg 2 .... 2.18
    reg 3 .... 2.18
    reg 5 .... 2.18
    reg 6 .... 2.18

1997/666 Occupational and Personal Pension Schemes (Levy)
Regulations 1997
    reg 2 .... 14.12
    reg 2–8 .... 2.12
    reg 13 .... Appendix I

1997/724 Pensions Compensation Board (Determinations and Review
Procedures) Regulations 1997 .... 2.18

1997/785 Occupational Pension Schemes (Assignment, Forfeiture, Bankruptcy
etc.) Regulations 1997
    reg 2 .... 1.38
    reg 3 .... 1.49, 7.24
    reg 4 .... 1.48

1997/786 Personal and Occupational Pension Schemes (Miscellaneous
Amendments) Regulations 1997 .... 4.1, 6.43
    reg 2 .... 11.14
    reg 10 .... 11.15
    reg 14 .... 11.15
    reg 28 .... 11.14
    Sch 1 .... 11.15

1998/728 Retirement Benefits Schemes (Restriction on Discretion to Approve)
(Small Self-Administered Schemes) (Amendment) Regulations 1998 .... 13.2

1997/1612 Local Government Pension Scheme Regulations 1997 .... 16.68

1998/1315 Retirement Benefits Schemes (Restriction on Discretion to
Approve) (Small Self-Administered Schemes) (Amendment/2)
Regulations 1998 .... 13.2

1998/1494 Occupational Pension Schemes (Scheme Administration)
Regulations 1998 .... 10.38

1998/3132 Civil Procedure Rules 17.11

1999/1849 Occupational Pension Schemes (Investment and Assignment,
Forfeiture, Bankruptcy etc.) Amendment Regulations 1999 .... 10.21

Table of Statutory Instruments

1999/3438 Local Government Pension Scheme (Amendment etc.)
  Regulations 1999 .... 16.68
2000/1048 Pensions on Divorce or Annulment (Provision of Information)
  Regulations 2000 .... 8.13, 8.24
  reg 2 .... 8.8, 8.24, 8.25
  regs 2(2) and 2(3)(b)-(f) 8.28
  reg 3 .... 8.4
    (7) 8.4
  reg 4 .... 8.24, 8.25
  reg 5 .... 8.24, Appendix II
  reg 6 .... 8.24
    (1) .... Appendix II
  reg 7 .... 8.24
  reg 8 .... 8.4, 8.24
  reg 9 .... 8.4, Appendix I
  reg 10 .... 8.8
2000/1049 Pensions on Divorce or Annulment (Charging) Regulations 2000
  reg 3 .... 8.7, 8.8
  reg 5 .... 8.25
  reg 7 .... 8.25
  reg 9 .... 8.25
  reg 10 .... 8.7
2000/1052 Pension Sharing (Valuation) Regulations 2000
  regs 4 and 4(1) 8.23
  reg 5 .... 8.23
2000/1053 Pension Sharing (Implementation and Discharge of Liability)
  Regulations 2000
  reg 3 .... 8.13
  reg 4 .... 8.13
  reg 6 .... 8.15, Appendix II
  regs 7, and 7(2) 8.14
  reg 11 .... 8.15
  Sch 5, paras 1, 1(2), 1(4), 2, 3,, 4 and 6 .... 8.14
2000/1054 Pension Sharing (Pension Credit Benefit) Regulations 2000 .... 8.18
  reg 25 .... 8.18
  reg 26 .... 8.18
  regs 32–35 .... 8.19
2000/1055 Pension Sharing (Safeguarded Rights) Regulations 2000 .... 8.27
2000/1085 Retirement Benefits Schemes (Sharing of Pensions on Divorce or
  Annulment) Regulations 2000
  reg 5(5) 5.8
  reg 6(1) .... Appendix II
2000/1086 Retirement Benefits Schemes (Restriction on Discretion to
  Approve Small Self Administered Schemes) Regulations (Amendment)
  Regulations 2000 .... 13.2
  reg 2 .... 8.16
2000/1116 Welfare Reform and Pensions Act 1999 (Commencement No 5)
  Order 2000 .... 8.9
2000/1123 Divorce or Annulment (Pensions) Regulations 2000
  reg 3 .... 8.4
  reg 4 .... 8.5

Table of Statutory Instruments

2000/1123 Divorce or Annulment (Pensions) Regulations 2000 – *contd*
   reg 4(5) 8.5
   reg 5 .... 8.5
      (1) 8.5
      (3) 8.5
   reg 6 .... 8.5
      (4) 8.5
   reg 9 .... 8.10
2000/1403 Stakeholder Pension Schemes Regulations 2000 .... 1.57
   reg 32 .... 2.7
2000/1551 Part-Time Workers (Prevention of Less Favourable Treatment)
   Regulations 2000 .... 1.22, 7.26, 9.5, 9.7, 9.40
2000/2975 Pension Sharing (Contracting-out) (Consequential Amendments)
   Regulations 2000 .... 4.67
2001/117 Personal Pension Schemes (Restriction on Discretion to Approve)
   (Permitted Investments) Regulations 2001 .... 15.1, 15.4, 15.51, 15.52
2001/119 Personal Pension Schemes (Transfer Payments) Regulations 2001 ..... 5.18,
                                                                   15.13, 15.18, 15.19, 15.46
   reg 8(3) 15.47
2001/358 Pension Sharing (Excepted Schemes) Order 2001 .... 8.9
2001/544 Financial Services and Markets Act 2000 (Regulated Activities)
   Order 2001 (SI 2001 No 1544) 10.29
   Art 37 .... 8.17
2001/1004 Social Security (Contributions) Regulations 2001 .... 14.36
   Sch 3, Part VI, para 1 .... 14.36
2001/1177 Financial Services and Markets Act 2000 (Carrying on Regulated
   Activities by Way of Business) Order 2001
   Art 4(6) 10.30
   reg 4 .... 2.8, 13.14
2001/1218 Occupational Pension Scheme (Pensions Compensation Provisions)
   Amendment Regulations 2001 .... 2.19
2002/380 Occupational Pension Schemes (Minimum Funding Requirement
   and Miscellaneous Amendments) Regulations 2002 .... 11.8, 11.34
2002/459 Occupational Pension Schemes (Winding up Notices and Reports
   etc) Regulations 2002 .... 12.10,, Appendix II
   reg 10 .... 12.75
      (2) 12.75
2002/681 Occupational and Personal Pension Schemes (Contracting-Out)
   (Miscellaneous Amendments) Regulations 2002 .... 4.1, 4.4
2002/836 Occupational and Personal Pension Schemes (Bankruptcy) (No. 2)
   Regulations 2002 .... 1.54
2002/2034 Fixed-Term Employees (Prevention of Less Favourable Treatment)
   Regulations 2002 .... 1.22, 1.24, 7.27, 9.8, 9.40
2002/2035 Part-time Workers (Prevention of Less Favourable Treatment)
   Regulations 2000 (Amendment) Regulations 2002 .... 7.26, 9.5, 9.7, 9.40
2002/2327 Occupational Pension Schemes (Member-nominated Trustees and
   Directors) Amendment Regulations 2002 .... 2.2, 3.25, 3.35, 3.37
2002/2675 The Control of Asbestos at Work Regulations 2002 .... 13.26
2002/3006 Retirement Benefits Schemes (Information Powers) (Amendment)
   Regulations 2002 .... 13.2

Table of Statutory Instruments

2003/1476 Financial Services and Markets Act 2000 (Regulated Activities) (Amendment) (No 2) Order 2003 .... 13.14
2003/1660 Employment Equality (Religion or Belief) Regulations 2003 .... 7.31
2003/1661 Employment Equality (Sexual Orientation) Regulations 2003 .... 7.30, 7.31, 9.30, 9.40
   reg 3 .... 9.30
   reg 4 .... 9.30
   reg 5 .... 9.30
   reg 25 .... 7.30, 7.31, 9.30
2003/1673 Disability Discrimination Act 1995 (Amendment) Regulations 2003 .... 7.28
2003/1727 Occupational Pension Schemes (Transfer Values and Miscellaneous Amendments) Regulations 2003 .... 2.3, 6.43
2003/2770 Disability Discrimination Act 1995 (Pensions) Regulations 2003 ..... 7.28
2003/2827 Employment Equality (Sexual Orientation) (Amendment) Regulations 2003 .... 7.30, 9.30, 9.40
2003/3004 Local Government Pension Scheme (Amendment) (No 2) Regulations 2003 .... 16.68
2004/403 Occupational Pension Schemes (Winding Up and Deficiency on Winding Up etc) (Amendment) Regulations 2004 .... 12.68
   reg 2 .... 12.81
2004/537 Guaranteed Minimum Pensions Increase Order 2004 .... 4.61
2004/1140 Occupational Pension Schemes (Winding up)(Amendment) Regulations 2004 .... 11.26

Table of Cases

A'Abo v Paget [2000] WTLR 863 .... 17.34
AGCO v Massey Ferguson Works Pension Trust [2003] 57 PBLR 1.36
Adams v Lancashire County Council [1996] All ER 473; [1997] IRLR 436
    (CA) 7.22
Algemeen Burgerlijk PF v Beaune Case-7/93 [1994] ECR I-4471 .... 9.12, 9.40
Allam & Co Ltd v Europa Poster Services Ltd [1968] 1 All ER 826 .... 10.43
Allen v TKM Group Pension Trust Ltd (L00370 – 25 April 2002) 3.22
Allonby v Accrington and Rossendale College [2001] IRLR 364; Case
    C-256/01 [2004] IRLR 224 (ECJ) 9.5, 9.40
Andrews v Ramsey & Co [1903] 2 KB 635 .... 10.42
Atherton v British Insulated & Helsby Cables Ltd (1925) 10 TC 155 .... 14.15
AXA Equity & Law Life Assurance Society Plc (No. 1) [2001] 2 BCLC
    447 .... 17.35

Barber v Guardian Royal Exchange Case 262/88 [1990] ECR I-1889;
    [1990] 2 CMLR 513 ...... 1.34, 7.1, 7.12, 9.1, 9.9, 9.17, 9.19, 9.40, 12.13, 12.54
Bartlett v Barclays Bank Trust Company Limited [1980] Ch 515 .... 3.14
BEC Pension Trustee Ltd v Sheppeck [2002] EWHC 101 (Ch) 12.72
Beckmann v Dynamco Whicheloe Macfarlane Ltd, Case C-164/00, [2002] 64
    PBLR; [2002] All ER (D) 05 (Jun) 7.22, 9.11, 9.40, 16.15, 16.50
Beddoe, Downes v Cottam, Re [1893] CA 17.33, 17.36
Bellinger v Bellinger [2003] UKHL 21; [2003] 2 All ER 593 .... 9.32, 9.40
Bestrustees v Stuart [2001] PLR 283 .... 12.13
Bestuur van het Algemeen Burgerlijk Pensioenfonds v Beune [1995] All ER
    (EC) 97 .... 9.12, 9.29
Bilka-Kaufhaus GmbH v Weber von Hartz Case C-170/84 [1986] ECR 1607,
    132/92 [1993] PLR 203 .... 9.2, 9.4, 9.12, 9.40
Bingham v Hoboun Engineering Ltd [1992] IRLR 298 .... 7.16
Birds Eye Walls v Friedl M Roberts Case C [1993] PLR 281 .... 9.12, 9.29
Bishop of Oxford v Church Commissioners (1991) PLR 185 .... 10.21
Boyle v Equal Opportunities Commission [1998] All ER 879 (EC) 9.34
Bradstock Group Pension Scheme Trustees Ltd v Bradstock Group plc and
    others [2002] All ER (D) 109 (Jun) 12.84
Brigden v American Express Bank Ltd [2001] IRLR 94 .... 7.19
Brook Street Bureau (UK) Ltd v Dacas [2004] EWCA Civ 217 .... 9.5, 9.40
Brooks v Brooks [1995] All ER 257 .... 8.1
Brooks v National Westminster Bank Plc, decision of 8 November 1993,
    Court of Appeal, unreported 1.36
BT Pension Schemes v Clarke [2000] PLR 157 .... 5.31
Buckton, Buckton v Buckton [1907] 2 Ch 406 .... 17.34, 17.32
Bullfield v Fournier [1895] 11 TLR 282 .... 10.42
Bullock v The Alice Ottley School [1992] IRLR 564 (CA) 9.16, 9.40

Century Life v The Pensions Ombudsman (1995) PLR 135 .... 2.27
Chapman, Re (1896) 2 Ch 763 .... 10.50
Chessels & ors v BT plc & ors [2002] PLR 141 .... 17.35
Clancy v Cannock Chase Technical College [2001] IRLR 331 .... 7.16

Table of Cases

Clark v British Telecom Pension Scheme [1999] 06 PBLR 21; [1999] PLR
51 .... 5.31, 10.12
Clark v Hicks [1992] PLR 213 .... 3.6
Coloroll Pension Trustees Ltd v Russell Case C-200/91 [1994] ECR I-4389;
[1995] All ER (EC) 23 .... 7.1, 7.13, 9.9, 9.10, 9.11, 9.13, 9.17, 9.19, 9.25, 9.26,
9.40
Cooper v C&J Clarke Ltd (1982) 54 TC 670 .... 10.12
Copnall, Mrs D, determination of Ombudsman (2000) Case no F00828,
28 September 2000 .... 9.5
Courage Group Pension Schemes, Re [1987] 1 All ER 528; 1 WLR 495 .... 7.13,
11.37, 11.46, 12.13, 16.17, 16.21
Cowan v Scargill [1984] 2 All ER 750 .... 3.12, 10.18, 10.19, 10.21
Crossley v Faithful & Gould Holdings Limited [2004] EWCA Civ 293, [2004]
All ER (D) (Mar) 295 .... 7.7

Davis v Richards Wallington Industries Ltd [1991] 2 All ER 563 .... 11.38
Defrenne v SABENA (No 2) [1976] ECR 455 .... 9.1, 9.2, 9.40
Defrenne v The Belgium State Case 80/70 [1971] ECR 445 .... 9.40
Deutsche Telekom v Schroder [2000] ECR 1-743 .... 9.5, 9.40
Duffield v Pensions Ombudsman (1996) PLR 285 .... 2.28

Eames v Stepnell Properties Ltd (1966) 43 TC 678 .... 10.6
Edge v Pensions Ombudman [1998] Ch 512; (1999) 49 PBLR 37; (1999) PLR
215 (CA) 1.36, 2.28, 3.17, 3.60
Engineering Training Authority v Pensions Ombudsman (1996) PLR 409 .... 7.7

Fisher v Harrison [2003] 49 PBLR, [2003] All ER (D) 484 (Jul) 1.46
Fisscher v Voorhuis Hengelo BV Case C-128/93 [1994] ECR I-4583 .... 9.2, 9.40
Frankling v BPS Public Sector Ltd [1999] IRLR 212, [1999] ICR 347, EAT ... 16.15
Fray v Voules [1859] 1 E&E 839 .... 10.32
French v Mitie Management Services Ltd [2002] IRLR 513; [2002] All ER
(D) 150 (Sep) 16.15

Gillespie v Northern Health & Social Services Board Case 342/93 [1996]
AER (EC) 284 .... 9.36, 9.40
Glossop v Copnall [2001] PLR 263 .... 9.5, 9.40
Goodwin v UK [2002] IRLR 664 .... 7.33, 9.32, 9.40
Grant v South West Trains Ltd [1998] All ER (EC) 193 .... 9.30, 9.40
Gray's Inn Construction Co. Lt, Re [1980] 1 WLR 711, [1980] 1 All ER
814 .... 18.6

Hagen v ICI Chemicals and Polymers Ltd [2001] 64 PBLR, [2001] All ER
(D) 273 (Oct) 7.22, 16.46
Harris v Shuttleworth (1994) PLR 47 .... 1.36, 7.7
Harwood-Smart v Caws [2000] PLR 101 .... 12.13
Halsey v Milton Keynes General NHS Trust [2004] EWCA Civ 576, [2004]
ALL ER (D) 125 (May), ... 17.36
Hazell v Hammersmith and Fulham Borough Council [1990] 2 WLR 17 .... 10.47
Hillsdown Holdings plc v Pensions Ombudsman (1996) PLR 427; (1997) PLR
161 (HC); (1999) PLR 37 (CA) 7.7, 12.6
Hoover Ltd v Hetherington and another [2002] All ER (D) 418 (May) 5.15

Table of Cases

Hopkins v Norcross (1994) 18 .... 7.17
HR v JAPT [1997] PLR 99 .... 3.49

Icarus (Hertford) v Driscoll (1990) PLR 1 .... 7.5
Imperial Foods Ltd Pension Scheme, Re [1986] 2 All ER 802 ..... 3.50, 12.12, 16.32
Imperial Group Pension Trust v Imperial Tobacco [1991] 2 All ER 597; 1
    WLR 589 .... 7.6, 7.7, 7.9, 7.10.11.37 11.46, 12.6
IRC v Fraser (1942) 24 TC 498 .... 10.5
ITN v Ward [1997] PLR 131 .... 7.2

Jeffs v Ringtons Ltd (1985) 58 TC 680 .... 14.15

KB v National Health Service Pensions Agency and anr [2001] All ER (D)
    2279; [2004] All ER (D) 03 (Jan) 7.25, 7.30, 7.33, 9.32, 9.40
Kemble v Hicks [1998] 3 All ER 154 .... 1.51, 12.60, 12.77
Kerry v British Leyland [1986] CA transcript 286 .... 7.5
Kutz-Bauer v Freie und Hansestadt Hamburg [2003] All ER (D) 327 (Mar) 9.16,
    9.40

Landau, Re [1997] 3 All ER 322 .... 1.51
Laws v National Grid [1998] PLR 295 .... 17.35
Learoyd v Whiteley (1887) 12 AC 727 .... 10.19
Leadenhall Independent Trustees v Welham [2004] All ER (D) 423 (Mar) 9.29,
    9.40
Lee v Showman's Guild (1952) 2 QB 329 .... 1.36
Legal & General Assurance Society Ltd v CCA Stationery Ltd [2003] EWHC
    2989 (Ch); [2003] ALL ER (D) 233 (Dec) 17.12
Lennon v Metropolitan Police Commissioner [2004] EWCA Civ 130,
    [2004] 2 All ER 266 .... 7.7
Lloyds Bank Pension Trust Corporation v Lloyds Bank Plc [1996] PLR 263 .... 7.12,
    9.9, 9.40
Londonderry's Settlement re Peat v Walsh [1964] 3 All ER 855 .... 3.22, 17.16
LRT Pension Fund Trustee Co Ltd v Hatt [1993] PLR 227 .... 11.37

MacDonald v Horn [1995] 1 All ER 961 .... 17.35
Marsh Mercer Pension Scheme v Pensions Ombudsman [2001] 16 PBLR (28)
    (the Williamson Case) 2.28, 9.28, 9.40
Mark Niebhur Todd v Judith Cobb Lady Barton & ors [2002] Ch.
    (Unreported) 17.31
Marshall v Southampton & SW Hampshire Area Health Authority Case
    152/84 [1986] ECR 723 .... 9.16, 9.40
Marson v Morton [1986] 1 WLR 1343 .... 10.2, 10.5
Martin v The City of Edinburgh District Council (1989) PLR 9 .... 10.21
Martin v South Bank University (OJ 2001/C61/13); C 4/01; [2003] All ER (D)
    85 (Nov); [2004] 1 CMLR 472; [2004] IRLR 74 (ECJ) ... 7.22, 9.11, 16.15, 9.40
Matthews and others v Kent and Medway Towns Fire Authority and others
    [2003] IRLR 732; [2003] All ER (D) 90 (Aug) 7.26, 9.7, 9.40
McCann Interiors Limited v Allied Dunbar Assurance plc [L00552] 2.27
Mettoy Pensions Trustees Ltd v Evans [1990] 1 WLR 1587 .... 7.5, 7.7
Mihlenstedt v Barclays Bank International [1989] IRLR 522 .... 7.5
Moore's (Wallisdown) Ltd v Pension Ombudsman [2002] 1 All ER 737 .... 17.12

Table of Cases

Municipal Mutual v Harrop [1998] PLR 149 .... 12.14, 12.15

NT Gallagher & Son Ltd, Shierson v Thompson, Re [2002] 1 WLR 2380;
  [2002] 3 All ER 374 .... 18.3
National Bus Company – Determination of the Pensions Ombudsman, 6
  September 1996 (1997) PLR 1 .... 7.9, 7.12
National Grid Company plc [1997] PLR 157 and 161 (1999) PLR 37 ...... 7.7, 11.37
Neath v Hugh Steeper Ltd Case C-152/91 [1993] ECR I-6935 .... 9.13, 9.15, 9.17,
                                                                                      9.40
Niebhur Todd, Mark v Judith Cobb Lady Barton & Others [2002] Ch.
  (Unreported) 17.28
Nolte v Landesversicherungsanstalt Hannover Case C-317/93 [1996] AER
  (EC) 212 .... 9.3, 9.40

O'Rourke v Darbishire [1920] AC 581; [1920] All ER Rep 1 .... 17.16
Outram v Academy Plastics [2000] IRLR 499 .... 7.7
Owens Corning Fibreglass (UK) Pensions Plan Ltd ,Re (The Times, 8 July
  2002); [2002] All ER (D) 191 .... 17.20

Paramount Airways Ltd (No 3), Re [1994] BCC 172 .... 18.7
Perry v Intec Colleges Ltd (1993) PLR 56 .... 7.22
Peter Pan Manufacturing Corporation v Corsets Silhouette Ltd
  [1963] 3 All ER 402 .... 10.46
Pickford v Quirke (1927) 13 TC 251 .... 10.7
Pitmans Trustees v the Telecommunications Group plc [2004] PBLR 32;
  [2004],All ER (D) 143 .... 10.23
Polly Peck International plc (in administration) v Henry [1998] All ER (D)
  647 .... 18.12
Poole v Trustees of the Cytec Industries (UK) Limited 7.8
Preston & Others v Wolverhampton Healthcare Trust Case Co C78/98 (The
  Times 19 May 2000) [2001] 2 WLR 448, HL (The Times 9 February
  2001) 5.30, 7.26, 9.40
Preston v Wolverhampton Healthcare NHS Trust [2000] All ER (EC) 714 .... 9.5
Preston (No 2) [2001] 3 All ER 947 .... 9.5
Preston & Others v Wolverhampton Healthcare NHS Trust (No.3) [2002] PLR
  389; [2004] IRLR 96; [2004] All ER (D)175 (Feb) 7.26, 9.5, 9.40

Quirk v Burton Hospital [2002] 24 PBLR 9.9, 9.40

R v Secretary of State for Employment, ex parte Seymour-SmithCase
  C-167/97 [1999] ICR 447 .... 9.3, 9.40
Re: Owens Corning Fibreglass (UK) Pensions Plan Ltd (The Times, 8 July
  2002) 17.17, 17.23
Richards v Merchant Navy Pension Scheme (unreported) 7.20
Royal Brunei Airlines v Tan [1995] 2 AC 378 .... 3.49
Royal Masonic Hospital v Pensions Ombudsman [2001] 3 AllER 408; 01
  PBLR (9) 6.7, 14.10
Rutherford v Secretary of State for Trade and Industry [2003] IRLR 858;
  [2003] All ER (D) 67 (Oct) 7.32
Rutter v Charles Sharpe & Co Ltd (1979) 53 TC 163 .... 14.15
Rye v Rye [2002] EWHC 956 (Fam) 8.9

Table of Cases

S v S [2002] All ER (D) 58 (Mar) 8.9
Salt v Chamberlain (1979) 53 TC 143 .... 10.11
Scally and others v Southern Health and Social Services Board,
   [1991] 4 All ER 563 .... 7.26
Schmidt v Rosewood Trust [2003] 2 WLR 1442, [2003] 3 All ER 76;
   [2003] UKPC 26 .... 3.22, 17.16
Secretary of State for Trade and Industry v Rutherford, Bentley and Harvest
   TownCircle Limited [2003] 78 PBLR, (EAT) 9.16, 9.40
Shillcock v Trustees of Uppingham School (1997), determination of Pensions
   Ombudsman, Case No F00317, 30 October 1997 .... 9.6
Simpson Curtis Pension Trustees Ltd v Readson Limited and others [1994]
   PLR 289, [1994] OPLR 231 .... 18.12
Smith v Avdel Systems Ltd Case C-408/92 [1994]; ECR I-4435 .... 9.9, 9.17, 9.38
Speight v Gaunt (1883) 22 Ch D 727 .... 10.50
Standard Chartered Bank v Walker [1982] 1 WLR 1410; [1982] 3 All ER
   938 .... 18.7
Stannard v Fison Pension Trust Ltd [1992] 1 PLR 27 .... 11.37, 16.7
Steel v Wellcome Trustees Ltd [1988] 1 WLR 167 .... 10.50
Stevens v Bell (British Airways) [2002] PLR 247 .... 11.37

Tellerup v Daddy's Dance Hall [1988] ECR 739 .... 16.15
Ten Oever v Stichting Case C-109/91 [1993] ECR I-4879 .... 9.10, 9.40
Thrells v Lomas (1992) PLR 233; [1993] 1 WLR 456 .... 3.60, 12.14
Turner v Last (1965) 42 TC 517 .... 10.6

UNIFI v Union Bank of Nigeria Plc (2001) IRLR 712 .... 7.1
University of Nottingham v Eyett [1999] IRLR 87 .... 7.7
Uppingham School v Shillcock [2002] EWHC 641 (Ch), [2002] 2CMLR 39 ..... 9.6,
   9.29, 9.40

Van den Akker v Stiching Shell PF Case -28/93 [1994] ECR I-4527 .... 9.21, 9.40
Venables and others v Hornby (Inspector of Taxes) [2004] 1 All ER 627 .... 5.15
Vickery, Re [1931] 1 Ch 572 .... 10.50
Vroege v NCIV Instituut Case C-57/93 [1994] ECR I-4541 .... 9.2, 9.40

Wallersteiner v Moir (No. 2) [1975] QB 373 .... 17.35
Warrener v Walden Engineering Co Ltd (1992) PLR 1; (1993) PLR 295
   (EAT) 7.22
Westminster City Council v Haywood and the Pensions Ombudsman (1996)
   PLR 161 .... 2.28
Whiteley, Re (1886) 33 Ch D 347 .... 10.19
Wild v Smith (1996) PLR 275 .... 1.39
Williamson – Determination of the Pensions Ombudsman, 7 January 2000 ...... 9.29
Williamson, Ian v Sedgwick Group Trustees (2001) HC 0000424 .... 4.16
Wilson v Law Debenture Trust Corporation Plc [1995] 2 All ER 337 ..... 3.22, 17.14
Wirral Metropolitan Borough Council v Evans and another [2001] OPLR 53 ...... 7.7
Wragg, Re [1919] 2 Ch 58 .... 10.2, 10.15

Table of European Legislation

Directives
Acquired Rights Directive (Council Directive 77/187 EEC) 7.22, 7.25, 9.11, 9.40
   Art 3 .... 16.15
   (3) 9.11, 9.40
Acquired Rights Directive (Council Directive 98/49 EC) 7.22, 7.25
Acquired Rights Directive (Council Directive 98/50 EC) 9.40

Equal Pay Directive (Council Directive 75/117/EEC) 7.29, 9.30, 9.40
   Art 6 .... 9.15
Equal Treatment Directive (76/207) 7.29, 9.16, 9.40
Equal Treatment Directive (79/7) 9.40
Equal Treatment Directive (86/378) 7.29, 9.34, 9.40
Equal Treatment 'Framework' Directive (2000/78) ... 7.28, 7.30, 7.31, 7.32, 9.16, 9.23,
                                                                                                                                                                                   9.30, 9.40
   Art 6(2) 9.16

First Life Insurance Directive (79/267/EEC)
   Art 6 .... 15.52
Fixed Term Work (Council Directive 1990/70/EC) 7.27

Insurance Mediation Directive (2002/92/EC) 13.14

Part-time Workers Directive (Council Directive 97/81/EC) 9.7, 9.40
Part-time Workers Directive (Council Directive 98/23/EC) 9.7
Pensions Directive (2003/41/EC) 10.19
Pregnant Workers Directive (ex EU Directive 92/85) 9.34
   Art 12 .... 9.32

Treaties
European Convention on Human Rights
   Art 6 .... 17.23
   Art 6(1) 17.10
   Art 8 .... 7.30, 9.32, 9.40
   Art 12 .... 9.32, 9.40
   Art 14 .... 7.30

Treaty of Amsterdam 9.1
Treaty of Rome
   Art 141 (ex 119) 7.25, 7.26, 7.30, 7.33, 9.1, 9.2, 9.3, 9.4, 9.5, 9.11, 9.12, 9.13,
                                                       9.14, 9.15, 9.19, 9.27, 9.29, 9.30, 9.40

Maastricht Protocol 9.1

Abbreviations and References

Abbreviations

APPS	=	Appropriate Personal Pension Scheme
APT	=	Association of Pensioneer Trustees
AVC	=	Additional voluntary contribution
Business Order	=	Financial Services and Markets Act 2000 (Carrying on Regulated Activities by Way of Business) Order 2001 (SI 2001 No 1177)
CETV	=	Cash Equivalent Transfer Value
COMBS	=	Contracted-out mixed benefit scheme
COMPS	=	Contracted-out money purchase scheme
Compensation Regulations	=	Pensions Compensation Board (Determinations and Review Procedure) Regulations 1997 (SI 1997 No 724)
Contracting-Out Regulations	=	Occupational Pension Schemes (Contracting-out) Regulations 1996 (SI 1996 No 1172)
CPR	=	Civil Procedure Rules
DSS	=	Department of Social Security
Deficiency Regulations	=	Occupational Pension Schemes (Deficiency on Winding Up etc.) Regulations 1996 (SI 1996 No 3128)
Disclosure Regulations	=	Occupational Pension Schemes (Disclosure of Information) Regulations 1996 (SI 1996 No 1655)
Dispute Regulations	=	Occupational Pension Schemes (Internal Dispute Regulations Procedures) Regulations 1996 (SI 1966 No 1270)
Divorce Regulations	=	Divorce etc. (Pensions) Regulations 1996 (SI 1996 No 1676)
DWP	=	Department for Work and Pensions
EC	=	European Community
ECJ	=	Court of Justice of the European Communities
ECON	=	Employer's contracting-out number
Equal Treatment Regulations	=	Occupational Pension Schemes (Equal Treatment) Regulations 1995 (SI 1995 No 3183)
ERA 1996	=	Employment Rights Act 1996
Forfeiture Regulations	=	Occupational Pension Schemes (Assignment, Forfeiture, Bankruptcy etc.) Regulations 1997 (SI 1997 No 785)
FSA	=	Financial Services Authority

Abbreviations and References

FSAVC	=	Free standing additional voluntary contributions scheme
FSMA 2000	=	Financial Services and Markets Act 2000
FURBS	=	Funded unapproved retirement benefits scheme
GMP	=	Guaranteed minimum pension
Goode Committee	=	The Pension Law Review Committee, chaired by Professor Goode, whose report was issued in September 1993 (CM 2342)
ICTA 1988	=	Income and Corporation Taxes Act 1988
IDRP	=	Internal dispute resolution procedure
IFMA	=	Institutional Fund Managers Association
IMRO	=	Investment Management Regulatory Organisation
Independent Trustee Regulations	=	Occupational Pension Schemes (Independent Trustee) Regulations 1997 (SI 1997 No 252)
Investment Regulations	=	Occupational Pension Schemes (Investment Regulations 1996 SI 1996 No 3127)
IR SPSS	=	Inland Revenue Savings, Pension, Share Schemes Office
LEL	=	Lower earnings limit
LET	=	Low earnings threshold
LIBA	=	London Investment Bank Association
LPI	=	Limited price indexation
MCA	=	Matrimonial Causes Act 1973
MFR	=	Minimum funding requirement
MFR Regulations	=	Occupational Pension Schemes (Minimum Funding Requirement and Actuarial Valuations) Regulations 1996 (SI 1996 No 1536)
MNDs	=	Member-nominated director
MNT Regulations	=	Occupational Pension Schemes (Member- nominated Trustees and Directors) Regulations 1996 (SI 1996 No 1216)
MNTs	=	Member-nominated trustees
Modification Regulations	=	Occupational Pension Schemes (Modification of Schemes) Regulations 1996 (SI 1996 No 2517)
NAPF	=	National Association of Pension Funds
NICO	=	National Insurance Contributions Office
NISPI	=	National Insurance Services to Pensions Industry
OEIC	=	Open-ended investment company
Ombudsman Regulations	=	Personal and Occupational Pension Schemes (Pension Ombudsman) Regulations 1996 (SI 1996 No 2475)

Abbreviations and References

OPAS	= Occupational Pensions Advisory Service
OPB	= Occupational Pensions Board
Opra	= Occupational Pensions Regulatory Authority
PA 1995	= The Pensions Act 1995
PCB	= Pensions Compensation Board
PMI	= Pensions Management Institute
PPRP	= Personal Pension Protected Rights Premium
PPSGN	= Personal Pension Schemes Guidance Notes
Preservation Regulations	= Occupational Pension Schemes (Preservation of Benefit) Regulations 1991 (SI 1991 No 167)
Protected Rights Regulations	= Personal and Occupational Pension Schemes (Protected Rights) Regulations 1996 (SI 1996 No 1537)
PSA 1993	= The Pensions Schemes Act 1993
PSO	= Pension Schemes Office of the Inland Revenue
QEF	= Qualifying earnings factor
Registrar	= Registrar of Occupational and Personal Pension Schemes
Regulated Activities Order	= Financial Services and Markets Act 2000 (Regulated Activties) Order 2001 (SI 2001 No 544)
S2P	= State Second Pension
Scheme Administration Regulations	= Occupational Pension Schemes (Scheme Administration) Regulations (SI 1996 No 1715)
SCON	= Scheme contracting-out number
SERPS	= State Earnings-Related Pension Schemes
SIPP	= Self-invested personal pension scheme
SMP	= Statutory maternity pay
SSAS Regulations	= Retirement Benefits Schemes (Restriction on Discretion to Approve) (Small Self Administered Schemes) Regulations 1991 (SI 1991 No 1614)
SSASs	= Small self-administered scheme
Surplus Regulations	= Pension Scheme Surpluses (Valuation) Regulations 1987 (SI 1987 No 412)
TA 1925	= Trustee Act 1925
TCGA 1992	= Taxation of Chargeable Gains Act 1992
TEP	= Traded endowment policy
Transfer Regulations	= Occupational Pension Schemes (Transfer Values) Regulations 1996 (SI 1996 No 1847)
TUPE	= Transfer of Undertakings Protection of Employment Regulations 1981 (SI 1981 No 1794)

Abbreviations and References

UCTA	= Unfair Contract and Terms Act 1977
UURBS	= Unfunded unapproved retirement benefits scheme
Voluntary Contributions Regulations	= Pension Schemes (Voluntary Contributions Requirements and Voluntary and Compulsory Membership) Regulations 1987 (SI 1987 No 1108)
Winding-up Regulations	= Occupational Pension Schemes (Winding Up) Regulations 1996 (SI 1996 No 3126)
WRPA 1999	= Welfare Reform and Pensions Act 1999

Case References

AC	= Appeal Cases (Law Reports)
All ER	= All England Law Reports
Ch	= Chancery (Law Reports)
E & E	= Ellis & Ellis Queen's Bench Report
ECR	= European Court Reports
IRLR	= Industrial Relations Law Reports
KB	= King's Bench (Law Reports)
OPLR	= Occupational Pension Law Reports
PBLR	= Pension Benefits Law Reports
PLR	= Pensions Law Reports
TC	= Tax Cases
TLR	= Times Law Reports
WLR	= Weekly Law Reports

Chapter 1

Pension provision in the UK – an introduction

INTRODUCTION

1.1 The word 'pension' is defined in the Oxford English Dictionary as 'an annuity or other periodical payment made, especially by a government, a company or an employer of labour in consideration of past services or of relinquishment of rights, claims or emoluments'.

A pension scheme is therefore a systematic arrangement for meeting these regular payments. As the definition suggests, pension schemes may be either state schemes or private arrangements. Where a scheme is established by the Government, it will often be a 'pay as you go' arrangement with no advance provision being made for funding of benefits. Private pension arrangements, whether established by an employer or by an individual, will usually be funded; contributions will be made by the individual and/or his employer during his working life to ensure that, when the individual retires, sufficient money is available to provide his pension and any other benefits which are payable.

Private pension arrangements are governed by a mixture of trust, employment, fiscal, social security and family law, which together provide the framework within which such schemes must operate. Pension provision for the public sector tends to be governed more rigidly by legislation. Many public sector schemes, including the Local Government Pension Scheme and the National Health Service scheme, are governed and administered almost exclusively by statutory instruments and are, to a degree, unaffected by other legislation. Such schemes are generally outside the scope of this book. The law relating to personal pension schemes and stakeholder pensions schemes is discussed in chapter 15.

A BRIEF HISTORY OF PENSION PROVISION IN THE UK

1.2 The first arrangement to contain features which are recognisable in modern pension schemes was established in 1671 by HM Customs and Excise. Originally the arrangement provided for a retiring employee to be paid a pension by his successor, but by 1686 employees were required to make advance provision for their own retirement by paying contributions towards a retirement fund.

1.2 *Pension provision in the UK – an introduction*

Pension protection was gradually extended to a broader range of civil servants but it was not until the *Civil Service Superannuation Act 1834* (the first enactment devoted solely to pensions) that any formal legislative framework was established. During the early nineteenth century the concept of pension provision was extended so that other employees, both in the public and private sectors, became eligible for membership of pension schemes. Insurance and life assurance schemes became available and actuarial methods for assessing risk gradually developed.

The beginning of the twentieth century saw the introduction of the first State scheme. In 1908 the *Old Age Pension Act* was passed which gave those over 70 a non-contributory, but means tested, pension. General taxation paid for this early State scheme although that was changed following the passing of the *National Insurance Act 1911*. At the same time, there was a continuing increase in the establishment of pension funds by large private sector employers.

The growth in pension provision prompted pressure for change in the tax treatment of pension funds and in 1920 the Royal Commission on Income Tax recommended that investment income earned by pension funds should be tax-free. The *Finance Act 1921* provided a statutory right to tax relief on contributions made to pension funds by employers and employees and on the investment income of Inland Revenue 'approved' pension funds. To gain Inland Revenue approval, assets constituting pension funds had to be kept separate from an employer's other assets and consequently trust funds emerged as a natural vehicle for obtaining tax approved status.

The *Finance Act 1970* established a new system of approval for occupational pension schemes. Although the legislation has been consolidated and amended in the *Income and Corporation Taxes Act 1988*, the basic underlying taxation principles for UK occupational schemes remain the same today (although see 1.3 in relation to forthcoming changes).

In addition to tax legislation, various pieces of social security legislation affecting pension schemes were passed during the 1970s which impacted on pension schemes, including the *Social Security Act 1973* which introduced provisions to protect early leavers and the *Social Security Pensions Act 1975*. The 1980s saw the introduction of further legislation; the *Social Security Acts 1985* and *1986* extended the protection offered to early leavers and, in particular, gave them the right to transfer their benefits to another pension scheme. The various Acts passed in the 1970s and 1980s, together with the relevant provisions of the *Social Security Act 1990*, are now consolidated in the *Pension Schemes Act 1993* (*PSA 1993*).

A major review of pensions provision in the UK was undertaken by the Pension Law Review Committee chaired by Professor Roy Goode following what has become known as 'the Maxwell scandal'. In their report, 'Pension Law Reform' (CM 2342-1, September 1993), the Committee made many recommendations as to how the legislative framework for pension provision could be amended to provide greater protection for employees. Many of their recommendations were adopted in the *Pensions Act 1995 (PA 1995)* which came into force on 6 April 1997. Two further significant Acts were passed by 2000, namely the *Welfare Reform and Pensions Act 1999 (WRPA 1999)* and the *Child Support, Pensions and Social Security Act 2000*. The most notable changes introduced by these Acts were the introduction of new pension sharing on divorce provisions, the stakeholder pension requirements and the State Second Pension.

Pensions Bill, Finance Bill and other recent changes

1.3 More recently, a number of consultations and reviews have been undertaken which have led to two new Bills – the Finance Bill and the Pensions Bill (which will become the *Finance Act 2004* and the *Pensions Act 2004*). In summary, the main provisions are as follows:

(*a*) simplification of the tax treatment of pensions – all pension saving after implementation (planned to be 6 April 2006) to follow a single set of rules, including:

- single lifetime limit on the amount of pension saving that attracts favourable tax treatment – currently proposed at an initial level of £1,500,000 per individual and increased thereafter as determined by the Treasury;

- an annual limit on all inflows of value to an individual's pension fund (both in the form of contributions and growth) – currently proposed at £215,000 and increased thereafter as determined by the Treasury;

- subject to scheme rules, allowing members to draw pension benefits whilst continuing to work;

- minimum age for taking early retirement benefits to be raised from 50 to 55 by 2010;

- removal of the tax advantages for unapproved schemes.

Transitional provisions are proposed to give a level of protection to those who currently have rights which are inconsistent with the new regime.

(*b*) replacing the minimum funding requirement with a scheme specific standard;

(*c*) reducing the level of prescription on selection processes for member nominated trustees, but having a strict requirement for one third of the trustees to be member nominated;

(*d*) changes to the internal disputes resolution procedure requirement (in particular to provide the option of a single stage procedure);

(*e*) a new pensions regulator whose main objectives will be to protect the benefits of members of occupational and personal pension schemes, reduce the risk of situations arising which may lead to compensation being payable by Pension Protection Fund (PPF) (see below) and promote and improve understanding of the good administration of occupa-

1.3 *Pension provision in the UK – an introduction*

tional schemes. New powers to assist the Regulator in achieving those objectives include the power to issue contribution notices and financial support directions against employers and persons associated and connected with the employer; extended information gathering powers and extended whistleblowing requirements;

(f) increasing protection of pensions rights on business transfers. Where before the transfer, an employee is a member of an occupational pension scheme to which the employer contributes, or is entitled to be a member, or would be entitled to be a member if he or she had been employed for longer, the purchaser must ensure that after the transfer the employee becomes eligible to be a member of an occupational or stakeholder pension scheme. Where the previous scheme was money purchase, then the purchaser will have to match the employees' contributions up to six per cent of pensionable salary and where the previous scheme was final salary the new scheme must at least satisfy the current reference scheme test (or such other requirements as may be included in Regulations). Alternatively the employer may offer membership of a stakeholder scheme to which it must match employee contributions up to six per cent.

(g) easement of the application of *s 67, PA 1995*;

(h) protection for early leavers with between three months and two years' pensionable service who in will in future have the right to a cash transfer sum (cash equivalent) or a contribution refund;

(i) introduction of the Pension Protection Fund (PPF) to give members of defined benefit schemes a measure of protection where their employers are in financial difficulty. The PPF will assume responsibility for eligible schemes where a relevant insolvency event has occurred in relation to the employer (or where the employer is unlikely to be able to continue as a going concern), the scheme is unable to secure its 'protected liabilities' and there is no possibility of a scheme rescue. Defined contribution schemes are not eligible to participate. Relevant insolvency events will include entering administration and passing a resolution for voluntary winding-up without a declaration of solvency.

When the PPF assumes responsibility the scheme assets will be transferred to the PPF and the trustees discharged from further responsibility. The PPF Board will then be responsible for paying benefits at the protected liability level. 'Protected liabilities' include 100 per cent of benefits for those already retired or over the scheme's normal pension age, 90 per cent of accrued benefits for other members and 50 per cent pensions for widows and widowers. Up to 25 per cent of the benefit may be taken as a lump sum. Pensions relating to service after 5 April 1997 will be increased at limited price indexation (LPI) capped at 2.5 per cent and pensions in deferment will be revalued at RPI capped at 5 per cent. Pension payments will be capped at a maximum annual rate which will be laid down in regulations, and the initial cap is likely to be £25,000.

For the first year of operation defined benefit schemes will be required to contribute a scheme-based levy. This will be calculated on the basis of the scheme membership and will not be affected by the funding position of the scheme in question. In future years the PPF Board may introduce a risk-based levy whereby schemes with poor funding positions could be required to pay more.

(j) requirement for all trustees to have an increased knowledge of the legal, financial and other aspects of pensions;

(k) the LPI requirement contained in *section 51* of *PA 1995* for statutory increases to pensions in payment will be reduced from RPI capped at 5 per cent to RPI capped at 2.5 per cent. This will apply to benefits accrued after the provisions come into force (expected to be 6 April 2005). At the time of writing, these provisions are not yet in force and so are liable to change are likely to expanded by regulations. Regulations have also recently come into force which change the calculation of the debt on employer and change the priority order on winding up. These changes are further discussed in chapter 12.

RETIREMENT PROVISION BY THE STATE

Types of State pension

1.4 The provision of retirement pensions by the State is governed by the *Social Security Contributions and Benefits Act 1992* and the *Social Security Administration Act 1992*, as amended by *PSA 1993* and *PA 1995*. There are four categories of State retirement pensions, Category A, Category B, Category C and Category D.

Category A and Category B pensions are contributory and are made up of the basic State pension and any additional element payable from the State earnings-related pension scheme (SERPS) or the State Second Pension ((SERPS/S2P) (see 1.9 and 1.10 below). The Category A pension payable to an individual is derived from his or her National Insurance contribution record. A Category B pension is payable by virtue of the contribution record of an individual's spouse and is only available to married women, widows and widowers.

Category C and Category D pensions are non-contributory and are payable only in very restricted circumstances. Category C pensions are payable to men and women who were over State pension age on 5 July 1948 and to the spouses of those men who qualified. Certain individuals who are over age 80 may receive a Category D pension if they are not entitled to any other category of State pension or if the pension they are entitled to is less than the Category D pension.

Basic State pension

1.5 The basic State pension is payable to all individuals who have:

(a) reached State pension age;

1.6 *Pension provision in the UK – an introduction*

(*b*) made sufficient National Insurance contributions; and

(*c*) made a claim for a State retirement pension.

The rate of the basic State pension is increased each year. From 12 April 2004, the full rate of the basic State pension is £79.60 per week for an individual (this is the full Category A pension payable and the amount of Category B pension payable to a widow or widower). For a married couple, the full rate of the basic State pension is £127.25 per week which comprises a Category A pension of £79.60 plus a Category B pension payable to a spouse of £47.65.

In October 2003 the *State Pension Credit Act 2002* came into force. This introduced a new State Pension Credit for persons aged 60 and over. It provides for a minimum income guarantee (subsuming the minimum level of income support payable to such persons). It consists of two main elements:

- a guarantee credit, to ensure a minimum level of income;
- a savings credit which from age 65 will provide an additional income for pensioners who have low or modest incomes in addition to the basic rate pension.

State pension age

1.6 A man reaches State pension age on his 65th birthday. A woman born before 6 April 1950 reaches State pension age on her 60th birthday. The State pension age for a woman born after 6 April 1950 will be equalised to age 65 progressively over the ten years between 2010 and 2020. The effect of this equalisation is that a woman born on or after 6 April 1955 will have a State pension age of 65. The date on which a woman born between 6 April 1950 and 6 April 1955 attains State pension age is determined in accordance with *paragraph 1* of *Schedule 4* to *PA 1995*.

National Insurance contribution record

1.7 Generally, in order to qualify for a full Category A basic State pension, sufficient Class 1, Class 2 or Class 3 National Insurance contributions must have been paid or credited to the individual for approximately 90 per cent of his working life. An individual's working life starts on 16 April immediately preceding his 16th birthday and ends on 5 April immediately preceding his attaining State pension age. An individual's working life will therefore usually be 49 years in the case of a man and 44 years in the case of a woman (although this will increase to 49 years with the equalisation of State pension age). So, to be eligible for the full basic State pension, National Insurance contributions must be paid by, or credited to, an individual for 44 years in the case of a man or 39 to 44 years (depending on her State pension age) in the case of a woman.

Where the individual's National Insurance contribution record falls short of these requirements, a reduced basic State pension may still be payable. To qualify the individual must have paid or been credited with National Insurance contributions for sufficient years to qualify for at least 25 per cent of the full rate of basic State pension.

Primary Class 1 National Insurance contributions at the rate of 11% are payable by all employees whose earnings are in excess of the earnings threshold. They are paid on earnings up to the upper earnings limit. Those earning between the lower earnings limit and earnings threshold do not pay Class 1 contributions but are treated as having done so for contributory benefit purposes. The earnings threshold and upper and lower earnings limits are statutory limits which are prescribed each year. For the tax year 2004/2005, the lower earnings limit is £4,108 per annum, the earnings threshold is £4,732 and the upper earnings limit is £31,720. In addition those earning more than £31,720 will pay 1% on earnings in excess of this amount. Secondary Class 1 contributions are payable by employers in respect of those employees whose earnings are in excess of the earnings threshold. There is no upper limit on secondary Class 1 contributions. Class 1 National Insurance contributions are collected through the PAYE system.

Class 2 National Insurance contributions are flat rate contributions payable by the self-employed. Class 3 contributions are voluntary contributions. They can be made by an individual to boost his contribution record so as to ensure that he has sufficient contributions to entitle him to a particular benefit. Class 4 contributions are paid by the self-employed on profits in excess of the lower profit limit. For the tax year 2004/2005 Class 4 contributions are payable at 8% on profit between the lower profit limit (£4,745) and upper profit limit (£31,720) and at 1% on profits in excess of the upper profit limit.

Application for a State retirement pension

1.8 An individual must apply for the State retirement pension. The Department of Social Security sends the appropriate forms to those who are eligible shortly before they reach State pension age.

State earnings-related pension scheme

1.9 The second element of a Category A or Category B pension is the additional earnings-related pension component previously known as SERPS (see 1.10 below). An individual will be entitled to this additional component if he has paid Class 1 National Insurance contributions on earnings between the lower earnings limit and upper earnings limit in any tax year since 1978/79. As a consequence, those earning less than the lower earnings limit will not build up any entitlement to a pension under this earnings related component. In order to receive an additional earnings-related pension the claimant must have reached State pension age.

An individual's additional pension is determined according to his 'surplus earnings' for each year which counts for additional pension (ie each year after

1.10   *Pension provision in the UK – an introduction*

6 April 1978 in which he has paid Class 1 National Insurance contributions). To calculate 'surplus earnings' it is first necessary to determine an individual's earnings up to the upper earnings limit, for each relevant tax year. Then the earnings in any particular tax year are increased in line with the rise in national average earnings (as set out in the most recent Revaluation of Earnings Factors Order) to take account of inflation. Finally, an amount equal to the lower earnings limit in the last complete tax year before the one in which the individual attains State pension age is deducted. The resulting amount is the individual's surplus earnings for that tax year. The way in which an individual's additional pension is calculated then depends on whether he reached State pension age before or after 6 April 1999.

The annual rate of additional pension of an individual who reached State pension age before 6 April 1999 is calculated by multiplying the aggregate of his surplus earnings for all the years which count for additional pension by 1.25 per cent.

The annual rate of additional pension of an individual who reached State pension age on or after 6 April 1999 is:

(*a*)   the aggregate of his surplus earnings in the tax years from 6 April 1978 to 5 April 1988, multiplied by 25 per cent and then divided by the total number of years between 6 April 1978 (or 6 April immediately preceding his 16th birthday, if later) and the 5 April immediately preceding his 65th birthday; plus

(*b*)   the aggregate of his surplus earnings in the tax years from 6 April 1988 to the 5 April immediately preceding his attaining State pension age is multiplied by the relevant percentage (which varies between 20 and 25 per cent depending on the year in which the individual attains State pension age) and then divided by the total number of years between 6 April 1978 (or 6 April immediately preceding his 16th birthday, if later) and 5 April immediately preceding his 65th birthday.

If an individual is contracted-out of this earnings related pension component (see chapter 4), he will not be entitled to additional pension from the State for the period during which he is contracted-out.

State second pension

1.10   From April 2002, SERPS has been replaced with a second tier state pension known as the State Second Pension, or 'S2P'. This was introduced by the *Child Support, Pensions and Social Security Act 2000* and is intended to provide a bigger pension than SERPS did by boosting the second tier pension of low and moderate earners, carers who are looking after young children or a disabled person and the long-term disabled with broken work records.

The S2P regime provides for a new low earnings threshold ('LET'), £11,600 for the tax year 2004/2005 (originally set at £9,500, and uprated in line with increases in national average earnings). In the case of low earners, individuals earning less than the LET, but in excess of the lower earnings limit ('LEL') (also called the qualifying earnings factor ('QEF')), (see 1.6 above) will be treated for S2P calculation purposes as if they had earnings equal to LET. Carers who have no earnings or earnings below the LEL will be treated for S2P purposes as if their earnings are at the LET if:

(a) they receive Child Benefit for a child under six;

(b) they are entitled to receive Invalid Care Allowance; or

(c) they are given Home Responsibilities Protection because they are caring for a sick or disabled person.

Those entitled to long-term Incapacity Benefit or Severe Disablement Allowance throughout a tax year will also be treated as if they had an earnings factor of the LET in that year, provided that by the time they reach State pension age they have either worked and paid or are treated as having paid Class 1 National Insurance contributions for at least one tenth of their working life (see 1.6 above).

S2P will operate in two phases. During Phase 1 (to last for five years), S2P accrual will be earnings-related, on the basis of three accrual bands:

Band	Earnings band	Accrual rate
1	earnings between LEL and LET	40%
2	earnings between LET and UET	10%
3	earnings between UET and UEL	20%

(The Upper Earnings Threshold (UET) is equal to three times the LET, less two times the QEF, amounting to £26,600 for the tax year 2004/2005.)

During Phase 2, S2P will be calculated at a flat rate for individuals who are under 45 at the point of change, but will continue to be earnings related for individuals who are over age 45 at the point of change. During Phase 2 the scheme will be aimed mainly at individuals earning less than the LET. It is intended that those who are aged under 45 but earning over the LET will not accrue benefits.

OCCUPATIONAL PENSION SCHEMES

What is an occupational pension scheme?

1.11 An occupational pension scheme is defined in *section 1* of the *PSA 1993* as:

'any scheme or arrangement which is comprised in one or more instruments or agreements and which has, or is capable of having, effect in

1.12 *Pension provision in the UK – an introduction*

relation to one or more descriptions or categories of employments so as to provide benefits, in the form of pensions or otherwise, payable on termination of service, or on death or retirement, to or in respect of earners with qualifying service in an employment of any such description or category'.

As can be seen, the definition of an occupational pension scheme is very wide; it can be funded or unfunded; it can relate to an entire workforce, a specified group of employees or a single individual; it can be established and governed by a single clause in a contract of employment or by a complex trust deed.

Most occupational pension schemes can benefit from tax privileges if they are correctly structured. For tax purposes, schemes can be either approved by the Inland Revenue or unapproved (see chapter 14 for further details of unapproved arrangements). Those schemes approved by the Inland Revenue receive considerably more tax privileges than unapproved schemes but are, as would be expected, more heavily regulated (see chapter 5).

Most occupational pension schemes, whatever their nature, are required to comply with the provisions of the *PSA 1993* and the regulations made under that Act. In particular, all schemes are required to comply with the provisions of the *PSA 1993* dealing with protection for early leavers (see chapter 6). Schemes which are contracted-out of the State earnings related pension component are also required to comply with the relevant provisions of the *PSA 1993* relating to contracting-out (see chapter 4).

Occupational pension schemes are also regulated by *PA 1995* which aimed to improve the administration of pension schemes and increase security for members. The effect of the *PA 1995* is discussed throughout this book where relevant. Certain types of occupational schemes have been exempted from many of the provisions of the *PA 1995* by regulations. Most notably, unapproved schemes are exempt from many, but not all, of the requirements (see chapter 14) as are most small self-administered schemes (see chapter 13).

Why establish a pension scheme?

1.12 No occupational pension scheme (unless the benefits are particularly poor) is cheap to run. Understandably employers have to think carefully about the costs involved before establishing an occupational pension scheme. A scheme can often cost an employer as much as 15 per cent of payroll in contributions alone (and sometimes more, particularly where there is a past service deficit). On top of this there are often costs such as life assurance premiums and the general day to day expenses of running the scheme.

The most common reason for an employer to establish an occupational pension scheme is that he wishes to attract the right calibre of staff. Pension benefits often form a significant part of an employee's remuneration package and so having an appropriate scheme to offer can be important in attracting the right type of recruit. This is particularly so for employers in industries where pension provision is common, in which case the type of arrangement offered may sometimes be dependent upon the 'industry norm'. If an employer in a particular industry is thinking of establishing an occupational pension scheme, it is likely to undertake a survey of other schemes operated by employers in the same sector. If it discovers the vast majority of those employers operate a 'defined contribution arrangement' rather than a 'defined benefit arrangement' it is unlikely to establish a defined benefit scheme as defined benefit schemes are generally perceived to be more expensive (and can be particularly so in times of poor stock market performance).

A good pension scheme may also encourage an employee to remain with an employer, particularly if the scheme offers benefits which are more generous than those offered by similar employers. An employer may be able to encourage long and faithful service by providing employees with a good pension on their eventual retirement.

An Inland Revenue 'exempt approved' scheme benefits from several tax advantages (see chapter 5) and so, although costly, is a relatively tax efficient way of providing employee benefits.

From the employees' point of view membership of an occupational scheme can be very attractive. The pension provided by the State is unlikely to be adequate for many employees to maintain their standard of living during retirement; and although employees often have to contribute to an occupational pension scheme they will also obtain benefit from the contributions made by their employer in respect of them.

Types of benefits provided by occupational pension schemes

1.13 Occupational pension schemes are commonly described as either defined benefit schemes or defined contribution schemes, depending on the type of benefits they provide. Defined benefit schemes are also often referred to as final salary and defined contribution schemes as money purchase schemes. In the former, the amount of pension which a member ultimately receives will be directly related to his remuneration, usually, at or around the date of his retirement (although schemes where benefits accrue on a 'career average' basis are becoming more popular). In the latter, the amount of pension a member receives will be related to the contributions made to the scheme by and in respect of him and the investment return on those contributions. The most important difference between the two types of schemes, other than the benefits they provide (see 1.32 to 1.44 below), is the way in which they are funded and the resulting implications, particularly in terms of burden of risk, for the employer and the member.

Defined benefit schemes

1.14 A member of a defined benefit scheme will generally be required to

1.15 *Pension provision in the UK – an introduction*

pay a specific proportion of his remuneration by way of contributions (although in some schemes this can fluctuate and in others the member may not be required to contribute) with the balance of the cost of providing the benefits under the scheme being met by the employer (hence these schemes are often also known as balance of cost schemes). The exact cost of providing the benefits will not be known until the last beneficiary under the scheme dies, so a defined benefit scheme represents a very open ended risk to the employer. The way in which the contributions of the employer are calculated for the funding of such a scheme is considered further in chapter 11.

Defined contribution schemes

1.15 The rules of a defined contribution scheme will likewise usually specify the contributions a member is required to pay to the scheme and will also generally specify the contributions the member's employer is required to make to the scheme in respect of him. Usually the rules will provide for the member to have a notional 'individual account' which is credited with his contributions, the contributions his employer makes in respect of him and the investment growth attributable to those contributions. When the member retires, assets equal to the value of his account will be realised and the proceeds will often be used to purchase an annuity to provide him with an income.

The amount of pension the member receives from a defined contribution scheme will be wholly dependent on the contributions made and the investment growth achieved; it will not in any way be related to the member's earnings before retirement. For many employers a defined contribution scheme represents an attractive proposition as the cost of financing the scheme can be predicted with certainty. For an employee such schemes are often less attractive because if the investments perform poorly, it is the employee upon whom this will ultimately impact, rather than the employer.

Hybrid schemes

1.16 It is possible to have a hybrid scheme which provides pensions accrued on both a defined contribution basis and a defined benefit basis. A hybrid scheme can have a defined contribution section and a defined benefit section where a member will accrue benefits under one or other section, or possibly be able to switch between the two in certain circumstances eg on attaining a certain age or on having completed a specified number of years of service. Alternatively, a hybrid scheme can provide defined contribution benefits but with a defined benefit underpin (or vice versa) so that the member will receive the greater of the benefits that can be provided by his individual account and a pension calculated by reference to his salary before retirement. As employers become more cost sensitive and wish to minimise scope for fluctuations in contribution rates for the future other variations are also becoming more prevalent.

Application of legislation to different types of occupational pension schemes

1.17 The legislation relating to occupational pension schemes generally applies equally to schemes which provide defined contribution benefits as to those which provide defined benefits. However, there are exemptions for defined contribution schemes from some of the requirements of the legislation, as referred to in the table below.

Legislation relating to:	Applicability to:	
	Defined benefit schemes	Defined contribution schemes
Protection for early leavers, ie preservation, transfers and revaluation (see chapter 6)	All occupational pension schemes are required to comply with the legislation relating to the protection of early leavers although the time limits for the payment of transfer values and ways in which benefits are calculated will vary as between defined benefit and defined contribution schemes.	
Equal treatment (see chapter 9)	The equal treatment requirements set out in *sections 62* to *66* of *PA 1995* apply to both defined benefit and defined contribution schemes.	
Independent trustees (see chapter 3)	The requirement for an independent trustee in certain circumstances involving the employer's insolvency applies to all defined benefit schemes established under trust.	Defined contribution schemes are exempt from the legislation relating to independent trustees (*Occupational Pension Schemes (Independent Trustee) Regulations 1997, reg 5 (SI 1997 No 252)*).
Debt on the employer (see chapter 12)	Where a defined benefit scheme is being wound up, a 'relevant insolvency event' occurs or an employer ceases to participate (whilst at least one other continues) and the value of the assets of the scheme is less than the value of its liabilities, a debt (calculated on different bases depending on the circumstances) may become due to the trustees of the scheme from the employer.	The legislation applies to defined contribution schemes only in limited circumstances where the assets of the scheme have been reduced due to criminal action (*Occupational Pension Schemes (Deficiency on Winding-up etc.) Regulations 1996, reg 7 (SI 1996 No 3128)*).
Disclosure (see chapter 3 and appendix ii)	Trustees of all occupational pension schemes are required to comply with the requirements of the *Occupational Pension Schemes (Disclosure of Information) Regulations 1996 (SI 1996 No 1655)* in so far as they relate to their scheme.	
Limited price indexation (see chapter 1)	Limited price indexation applies to all approved schemes and all schemes in respect of which approval has been applied for and has not been refused (*section 51* of *PA 1995*).	

1.17 *Pension provision in the UK – an introduction*

Legislation relating to:	Applicability to:	
	Defined benefit schemes	Defined contribution schemes
Investments (see chapter 10)	All trustees must comply with the statutory requirements relating to investment, including the choice of investments, the appointment of fund managers, self-investment and the maintenance of a statement of investment principles (unless their scheme has an appropriate exemption under the relevant regulations).	
	The Myners principles (non-statutory) also apply to both defined benefit and defined contribution schemes, modified appropriately in each case.	
Contracting-out (see chapter 4)	Contracting-out is permissible on a reference scheme test basis or on a protected rights basis (but if a scheme, which before 6 April 1997 was contracted-out on a guaranteed minimum pension (GMP) basis, wishes to contract-out on a protected rights basis but does not wish to secure GMP liabilities outside of the scheme, it must have elected to do so by 31 January 1998).	Contracting-out is permissible on a reference scheme test basis (if the scheme provides adequate benefits) or on a protected rights basis.
Voluntary membership (see 1.19 below)	Membership of any occupational pension scheme cannot be compulsory.	
Voluntary contributions (see 1.30 below)	Members of occupational pension schemes must be permitted to pay voluntary contributions. The Pensions Bill proposes to remove this requirement.	
Registration and levy (see chapter 2)	Trustees are required to register their scheme with the Pension Schemes Registry and are required to pay a levy.	
Dispute resolution (see chapter 3)	Trustees must put in place a dispute resolution procedure in accordance with *section 50* of *PA 1995*.	
Pensions Ombudsman (see chapter 2)	The Pensions Ombudsman has jurisdiction to investigate a wide range of complaints but cannot investigate a complaint that has not gone through the internal dispute resolution procedure unless he believes there is no prospect of a decision being made within a reasonable time.	

Legislation relating to:	Applicability to:	
	Defined benefit schemes	Defined contribution schemes
Appointment of professional advisers (see chapter 2)	Trustees of defined benefit schemes must appoint an individual as scheme actuary and an individual or firm as scheme auditor. An individual or firm must be appointed by or on behalf of the trustees as fund manager. Trustees should not rely on the advice of any professional adviser they did not appoint.	Trustees of defined contribution schemes must appoint an individual or firm as scheme auditor but do not need to appoint a scheme actuary (*Occupational Pension Schemes (Scheme Administration) Regulations 1996, reg 3 (SI 1996 No 1715)*). An individual or firm must be appointed by or on behalf of the trustees as fund manager. Trustees should not rely on the advice of any professional adviser they did not appoint.
Member-nominated trustees (see chapter 3)	Trustees must arrange for the appointment of member-nominated trustees (or directors in the case of a trustee company) unless the employer has successfully opted out of the requirements or the scheme is exempt. The Pensions Bill proposes to remove the opt-out route.	
Minimum funding requirement (See chapter 11)	Tax approved defined benefit schemes must comply with the minimum funding requirement (which includes maintaining a schedule of contributions) as set out in *sections 56 to 61 of PA 1995*. The Pensions Bill proposes to replace the minimum funding requirement with a scheme specific funding requirement (this will still include a requirement for a schedule of contributions).	The minimum funding requirement does not apply to defined contribution schemes, but trustees are required to maintain a schedule of payments in accordance with *sections 87 to 90 of PA 1995* (see 1.26 below).
Winding-up (see chapter 12)	The order in which the liabilities of a tax approved defined benefit scheme must be secured in the event of a winding-up is, to an extent, governed by *sections 73 and 74 of PA 1995*.	The order in which the liabilities of a defined contribution scheme must be secured on a winding-up is determined solely in accordance with the scheme's governing documentation.

1.18 *Pension provision in the UK – an introduction*

Legislation relating to:	Applicability to:	
	Defined benefit schemes	Defined contribution schemes
Payment of surplus (see Chapter 11)	Before a payment can be made to an employer in order to reduce a surplus, certain notice requirements must be complied with and all benefits payable under the scheme (other than GMPs and defined contribution benefits, including benefits deriving from voluntary contributions if appropriate) must be granted limited price indexation increases (*section 37* of *PA 1995* in the case of ongoing schemes and *sections 76* and *77* in the case of schemes which are in winding-up)..	Defined contribution benefits do not have to be granted increases but the notice requirements still apply (*section 37* of *PA 1995* in the case of ongoing schemes and *sections 76* and *77* in the case of schemes which are winding-up).

How are occupational pension schemes established?

1.18 As Inland Revenue approval is only available to occupational pension schemes established under irrevocable trusts (*Income and Corporation Taxes Act 1988, s 592*), the vast majority of such schemes are established by trust deed or a declaration of trust. Over the years, many schemes have been established by an interim trust deed which sets out the bare bones of the scheme but does not usually contain detailed provisions relating to the benefits to be provided. However, the Inland Revenue have now stated that any approval applications received by them after 5 April 2002 should be submitted using definitive documentation, except in limited circumstances, eg where a scheme is set up as a result of a corporate transaction. Where a scheme is approved on the basis of an interim trust deed, it will usually be a condition of approval that a full definitive deed and rules will be submitted within 12 months of the execution of the interim deed. The Inland Revenue will also now require certain provisions to be included in the interim trust deed. (See IR12 (2001) PN 2.12–2.15).

The documentation governing a scheme will usually consist of a definitive trust deed and one or more sets of rules. There is no particular agreed format as to what should be contained in the trust deed and what should be in the rules. It is quite common for the trust deed to contain the administrative provisions of the trust and for the rules to detail the benefits payable under the scheme, but there are many variations on this theme.

The first trust deed, whether interim or definitive, will generally appoint the first trustees of the scheme and set out the terms of the trust. In particular it will be necessary for the trust deed to include or make provision for a power of amendment so that the scheme can be amended for future changes in legislation and/or practice. The trustees will also need to be given sufficient powers in the trust deed to be able to administer the trust. For example, prior to the changes introduced by *PA 1995*, unless a trust deed contained a sufficiently wide investment power the trustees were restricted in the types of investments they could make to those set out in the *Trustee Investments Act 1961*.

When a scheme's documentation is first drafted, consideration needs to be given to the 'balance of power' between the trustees and the employer, ie it is necessary to decide which powers should be vested in the trustees, which powers should be vested in the employer and which powers should be vested jointly. As a general rule, if the exercise of the power could have a financial implication for the scheme, an employer will usually wish to be involved in exercising that power; the power could be vested in the employer or it could be vested in the trustees, subject to the consent of the employer. *PA 1995* has, in some instances, shifted the 'balance of power' from the employer to the trustees. For example, under *section 37* of *PA 1995*, the power to make a payment to an employer from a scheme to reduce a surplus vests with effect from 6 April 1997 in the trustees, irrespective of the rules of the scheme (see chapter 11 for further details). The trustees also have some power over the level of contributions required when preparing a schedule of contributions pursuant to *section 58* of *PA 1995*.

The rules of a scheme will generally detail the benefits which are payable under the scheme. They will usually also set out conditions for membership and specify the contributions (if any) which the members are required to pay. The exact details of the rules will, of course, depend on the benefit structure of the scheme. However, the rules should ensure that the scheme (whether approved or unapproved) provides only 'relevant benefits' if it is to benefit from the tax advantages available. 'Relevant benefits' are defined in *section 612* of *ICTA 1988* as 'any pension, lump sum or like benefit given on retirement or on death or in anticipation of retirement or in connection with past service after retirement or death'. An occupational pension scheme which provides, for example, permanent health insurance for long term illness in addition to retirement benefits, does not provide only relevant benefits. Benefits provided by the scheme must be payable only to the member, his spouse, children, dependants or (on his death) his personal representatives if they are to qualify as relevant benefits.

Centralised schemes

1.19 It may be possible for an employer to participate in a 'centralised' or 'multi-employer' occupational pension scheme, rather than establish its own scheme, thus benefiting from lower administration costs. Such schemes generally have a principal employer, which exercises those powers usually vested in the principal sponsoring employer, and a number of associated or participating employers, on whose behalf the principal employer will generally act.

In the case of an approved occupational pension scheme the Inland Revenue must be satisfied that the employers participating in the scheme are sufficiently closely associated, unless the scheme is an industry wide scheme specifically established for non-associated employers. (See Part 21 of the Inland Revenue's Practice Notes, IR12 (2001), for details of the requirements relating to centralised schemes.) Employers are associated if one directly or indirectly controls the other or both are controlled by a third person. Alternatively, employers may be associated through a permanent community of interest, such as common management or shareholders or interchangeable or jointly employed staff.

If an employer wishes to participate in a centralised scheme, it must agree to observe the rules of the scheme. This is usually achieved by the trustees, the principal employer and the associated employer executing a deed of adherence or participation. The Inland Revenue must be informed (by way of the appropriate form) if an employer commences participation in an approved scheme. If a participating employer ceases to be sufficiently closely associated with the principal employer to satisfy the Inland Revenue's requirements (for example, if the participating employer is sold out of the group), it must withdraw from the scheme (although see Chapter 16 in relation to temporary participation periods).

MEMBERSHIP OF OCCUPATIONAL PENSION SCHEMES

Non-compulsory membership

1.20 Membership of an occupational pension scheme cannot currently be made compulsory and any term in a contract of employment or any rule in an occupational pension scheme to the effect that an employee must be a member of a particular pension scheme is void. Legislation relating to non-compulsory membership was first introduced by the *Social Security Act 1986* and first became effective on 6 April 1988; it is now contained in *section 160* of *PA 1995*. The only exception to this is that membership may be compulsory for a death in service only benefit if that benefit is provided on a non-contributory basis. [*Pension Schemes* (*Voluntary Contributions Requirements and Voluntary and Compulsory Membership*) *Regulations 1987* (*SI 1987 No 1108*), *reg 3*]. In practice, it is, however, permissible (so long as the matter is correctly handled) for employees to be included automatically as members of their employer's scheme unless they specifically request to opt-out. Moreover, the Department for Work and Pensions' (DWP) consultation paper of February 2004 stated that the DWP is looking at ways to deliver increased pension saving in the UK, including the possibility of requiring automatic membership of an employer's scheme, but retaining an ability for members to opt-out if they wish.

For the time being, however, the effect of current legislation is not only that a new employee has the option to choose whether or not to become a member of his employer's scheme, but also that an existing member may choose to opt-out of membership whilst remaining employed by a participating employer.

Inland Revenue requirements

1.21 Membership of an approved occupational pension scheme must be confined to employees of the employers participating in the scheme but need not be open to all employees or to any particular category of them (IR12 (2001) PN 3.1). However, discriminatory entry conditions which cannot be objectively justified should be avoided (see Chapter 9).

The word 'employee' generally includes any director or officer of a company. However, a director of an investment company (ie a company which derives its income from investments) cannot be a member of an approved scheme in relation to that employment if he owns more than 20 per cent of the shares in the company. Even if he does not own 20 per cent of the shares, a director of an investment company cannot be admitted to membership of an approved scheme in relation to that employment if he is a member of a family which together owns more than 50 per cent of the shares (IR12 (2001) PN 3.9).

An individual who is assessed to income tax on his earnings under Schedule D cannot be provided with benefit under an approved occupational pension scheme in respect of those earnings. So proprietors and partners under Schedule D may not be permitted to become or remain active members of an approved scheme (IR12 (2001) PN 3.4 to 3.5).

An employee who is temporarily absent from work may, for Inland Revenue purposes, be considered to remain a member if there is a definite expectation that he will return to service and he does not become a member of another approved occupational pension scheme or personal pension scheme during the period of absence. It is not necessary to seek the approval of the Inland Revenue if such a period of temporary absence is of less than ten years. If an employee is temporarily absent because of incapacity he may remain a member indefinitely, regardless of whether there is a clear expectation that he will return to work. Any other period of temporary absence should be agreed with the Inland Revenue if the employee is to remain a member (IR12 (2001) PN 3.11 to 3.15).

In the past an employee could not be a member of an occupational pension scheme if he was also contributing to a personal pension scheme. The only situation where a person could be a member of both a personal pension scheme and an occupational pension scheme at the same time, and in respect of the same source of income, was where the occupational pension scheme provided only death benefits or where an 'appropriate' personal pension scheme was used for the purposes of contracting-out of the State earnings-related pension scheme. However, the changes introduced by the stakeholder legislation have provided employees with further flexibility and options. Employees with P60 earnings in 2004/2005 of less than £30,000 may also pay up to £3,600 to a personal pension or stakeholder pension, whilst at the same time continuing to be eligible for concurrent membership of their occupational pension scheme.

Equal access

1.22 The terms on which employees may become members of an occupational pension scheme must be the same for both men and women (*section 62* of *PA 1995*).

1.23 *Pension provision in the UK – an introduction*

A claim of discrimination in respect of the terms on which employees may become members of a scheme may be brought before a court or employment tribunal. Where discrimination is proven, the court or tribunal may declare that the employee has the right to be admitted on such a date on or after 8 April 1976 as it may specify and may also declare that the employer shall provide the resources necessary to provide the appropriate level of benefits for the employee (subject, in most cases, to the employee also making appropriate contributions).

The *Part Time Workers (Prevention of Less Favourable Treatment) Regulations 2000 (SI 2000 No 1551)* and the *Fixed Term Employees (Prevention of Less Favourable Treatment) Regulations 2002 (SI 2002 No 2034)* introduced measures to protect part time and fixed term workers from unjustified exclusion from pension schemes (alongside more general employment protection). The issue of sex discrimination in relation to occupational pension schemes generally, and in particular the exclusion from membership of part-time and fixed term employees, is discussed further in chapter 9.

Disability discrimination

1.23 It is unlawful for an employer with 15 or more employees to discriminate, without justification, against disabled employees in terms of the benefits provided to those employees, including access to and benefits provided from, an occupational pension scheme. *Section 1* of the *Disability Discrimination Act 1995* provides that 'a person has a disability if he has a physical or mental impairment which has a substantial and long term adverse effect on his ability to carry out normal day-to-day activities'. An employer discriminates against a disabled person if he treats that person less favourably than he treats, or would treat, a person who is not disabled and he cannot show that the treatment was justified.

Section 17 of the *Disability Discrimination Act 1995* implies an overriding 'non-discrimination rule' into the rules of an occupational pension scheme. Consequently, any discriminatory decision taken by the trustees (whether in relation to access to membership or otherwise) will be a breach of the scheme's rules unless it can be justified.

Less favourable treatment can only be justified if the reason is material to the circumstances of a particular case and substantial. In terms of pension provision, less favourable treatment for a disabled person is permissible where the cost to the scheme of benefits on termination, retirement or death would, by reason of the person's disability, be likely to be substantially greater than it would be for a comparable person without a disability. [*Regulation 4* of the *Disability Discrimination (Employment) Regulations 1996 (SI 1996 No 1456)*] For example, an employer could not exclude an employee from a pension scheme simply because she suffered from a visual impairment but could justifiably refuse admission to an employee with multiple sclerosis if the cost of an early retirement pension would be substantially greater than for an employee without that illness.

Discrimination on the grounds of disability is discussed further in chapter 7.

Procedure for becoming a member

1.24 The rules of the scheme will often set out the procedure which an employee must follow if he wishes to become a member of the scheme. Often the rules will provide for a minimum and maximum entry age, thus allowing an employer to exclude the very young (who are likely to change jobs more frequently) and the very old (for whom the costs of benefits are particularly high).

It is not uncommon for the rules of a scheme to impose a 'waiting period' where an employee has to be employed for a certain period of time before being eligible to become a member (although this is becoming less common). A waiting period may correspond to an employee's 'probationary period' under his contract of employment some rules will provide that an employee is only eligible once he is a 'permanent' employee. However, the *Fixed-Term Employees (Prevention of Less Favourable Treatment) Regulations 2002 (SI 2002 No 2034)* now provide that fixed term employees should be provided with benefits on a pro-rata basis equivalent to those provided to their permanent counterparts, unless their exclusion can be objectively justified (see chapter 7)

An employee may be required to complete an application form for membership of an occupational pension scheme; in the case of a contributory scheme, this form will normally authorise the employer to deduct contributions from the employee's salary (see also 1.28 below). It is common for employers to ask employees who do not wish to join the scheme or who choose to opt-out of the scheme to sign a waiver form confirming that they understand that they are giving up benefits.

MAKING CONTRIBUTIONS TO OCCUPATIONAL PENSION SCHEMES

Employer's contributions

1.25 Before the *1995 Act* came into force there was little in the way of statutory control over funding and the making of contributions (see chapter 11). *PA 1995* introduced provisions requiring trustees to maintain, in the case of defined benefit schemes, schedules of contributions and, in the case of defined contribution schemes, schedules of payment.

Defined benefit schemes

1.26 The trustees of a defined benefit scheme which is subject to the minimum funding requirement (see 11.14 below for details of those schemes which are exempt) must maintain a schedule of contributions which shows separately the rates and due dates of:

(*a*) all contributions, other than voluntary contributions, payable by or on behalf of active members of the scheme;

1.26 *Pension provision in the UK – an introduction*

(b)   contributions payable by or on behalf of each employer;

(c)   if made separately, the contributions payable to cover the total expenses which are likely to be incurred by the trustees in the period covered by the schedule;

(d)   in the case of schedules of contributions certified on or after 19 March 2002, any due dates and amounts of contributions required to correct serious under-provision (see Chapter 11).

(e)   such other information as the employer and the trustees may decide.

The rates of contributions shown in the schedule must be certified by the scheme actuary, ie the actuary appointed under *section 47(1)(b)* of *PA 1995*, as sufficient to secure that the minimum funding requirement will continue to be met during, or will have been met by the end of, the schedule period.

Trustees are required to keep records of the contributions made to the scheme and any action which they take to recover contributions which are not paid by the date on which they are due.

If there has been 'fraudulent evasion' in failing to pass employee contributions to the trustees or managers, criminal penalties may apply (*section 49(11)* and *(12)* of *PA 1995*)). *PA 1995* provides that non-payment is an automatic 'whistle-blowing' offence under *section 48* of *PA 1995* and must immediately be reported to the Occupational Pensions Regulatory Authority (Opra) by the scheme actuary or the scheme auditor. The trustees must also give notice of that fact to Opra within 30 days (unless it is a first or second default and payment is made within 10 days of the due date). Notice of failure to pay contributions must be given to members within 90 days of the due date (unless payment has been made within 60 days of the due date). Any contributions which remain unpaid become a debt due from the employer to the trustees.

It should be noted, however, that in its Update 5 of 2004 Opra announced that in future it will only expect reports from trustees of late payments of employer contributions (or payment over of employee contributions) where there is:

- a significant risk to the security of scheme assets; or

- a significant detrimental impact on members.

In most cases Opra now expects a report only where contributions are overdue for 90 days. Trustees must still report unpaid contributions to members after 60 days. *Section 56* of *PA 1995* and the *Occupational Pension Schemes (Minimum Funding Requirement and Actuarial Valuations) Regulations 1996 (SI 1996 No 1536)* (*MFR Regulations*) require a report to be made to Opra where any contribution is late (with one annual payment of up to 10 days later allowed to go unreported). However, trustees reporting within 90 days will not be penalised by Opra for failing to report strictly in accordance with the Regulations. Trustees complying with Opra's new standards should carefully record any late contribution and keep a note that they are relying on Update 5 when not reporting to Opra. Although they will not be penalised by Opra, trustees

Pension provision in the UK – an introduction **1.27**

applying Opra's relaxation should be aware that they will not be complying strictly with the legislation and may leave themselves open to the risk of censure from the Pensions Ombudsman or the Court.

The statutory requirements relating to schedules of contributions are discussed further in chapter 11.

Defined contribution schemes

1.27 The trustees of a defined contribution scheme must (unless the scheme is exempt, see below) ensure that a 'schedule of payments' is periodically prepared, maintained and revised in relation to the scheme. *Section 87* of *PA 1995* and *regulations 18* and *19* of the *Scheme Administration Regulations (SI 1996 No 1715)* provide that the schedule must show, for the year to which it relates:

(*a*) the rates of contributions payable towards the scheme by or on behalf of the employer (or in the case of multi-employer schemes, each employer) and the active members of the scheme;

(*b*) the amounts payable towards the scheme by the (or each) employer in respect of expenses likely to be incurred during the year in question;

(*c*) the dates on or before which payments are to be made.

Where any amounts payable in accordance with a schedule of payments by or on behalf of the employer have not been paid on or before the due date, then a civil offence has been committed under *PA 1995*, punishable by fine (unless there has been 'fraudulent evasion' in failing to pass employee contributions to the trustees or managers, in which case criminal penalties may apply (*section 49(11)* and *(12)* of *PA 1995*)). Non-payment is an automatic 'whistle-blowing' offence under *section 48* of *PA 1995* and must immediately be reported to Opra by the scheme actuary or the scheme auditor. The trustees must notify Opra if any contributions are not paid by the due date, within 30 days after the due date (again, unless it is the first or second default and payment is made within 10 days) and notice must be given to members within 90 days (unless payment has been made within 60 days of the due date). However, see 1.26 above in relation to Opra's Update 5. [*PA 1995, s 88* and the *Scheme Administration Regulations, reg 20*].

Regulation 17 of the *Scheme Administration Regulations* provides that trustees of the following schemes do not have to maintain a schedule of payments:

- unapproved occupational pension schemes;
- certain public service pension schemes;
- occupational pension schemes with less than two members;

1.28 *Pension provision in the UK – an introduction*

- schemes which provide only death benefits;
- small self-administered schemes where all the members of the scheme are trustees and all decisions are made by the unanimous agreement of those trustees who are members;
- *section 615* schemes;
- certain earmarked insured schemes (see *regulation 1(2)* of the *Scheme Administration Regulations*).

Any trustee who fails to comply with the requirement to maintain a schedule of payments may be fined and/or removed as a trustee (see also appendix I).

Inland Revenue requirements

1.28 An occupational pension scheme will not be approved by the Inland Revenue unless the employers participating in it are required to make contributions to it. Furthermore, the Revenue will not approve a scheme if the employers' contributions appear to be mere token contributions of insignificant amounts. The Revenue considers employer contributions of less than ten per cent of total contributions to be insignificant (see IR12 (2001) PN 5.1).

Employers can take 'contribution holidays', without having to report them to the Inland Revenue, provided that the duration of the holiday does not exceed two years (IR12 (2001) PN 5.4). Contribution holidays in excess of this duration must be sanctioned by the Inland Revenue. The tax treatment of contributions made by employers to approved occupational pension schemes is discussed in chapter 5.

Members' contributions

1.29 Most, but by no means all, occupational pension schemes require members to make contributions. These are discussed below.

Ordinary contributions

1.30 The level of the contributions which members are required to make is a matter of scheme design. Contributory schemes typically require a contribution of between four and seven per cent of salary. Contributions will generally be deducted from a member's salary by his employer through the payroll. The employee must specifically consent to contributions being deducted for this purpose (*Employment Rights Act 1996, s 13*) and consequently membership application forms will generally include provision for the necessary consent to be given.

Contributions deducted by a member's employer must be passed to the trustees of the scheme within 19 days (or 14 days in the case of minimum payments made by virtue of the member being contracted out of SERPS/S2P) of the end of

Pension provision in the UK – an introduction **1.31**

the month within which the contribution is deducted. [*PA 1995, s 49(8)* and the *Scheme Administration Regulations (SI 1996 No 1715), reg 16*]. Failure to do so is an offence for which the employer can be fined, imprisoned or both, depending on the circumstances (see 1.25 and 1.26 above).

Voluntary contributions

1.31 A member may wish to enhance his pension benefits by making voluntary contributions in addition to any contributions he is required to make under the rules of the scheme. The rules of an occupational pension scheme currently must not prohibit the payment of voluntary contributions, except to the extent necessary to comply with Inland Revenue requirements. [*PSA 1993, s 111*]. However, the rules may provide that a member who has reached, or is within one year of reaching, normal pension age cannot make voluntary contributions. [*Voluntary Contribution Regulations, reg 2(6)*]. The Pensions Bill proposes to remove the requirement to provide an additional voluntary contribution ('AVC') facility.

The rules of a scheme may require that members who wish to make voluntary contributions have to make a certain minimum level, but any lower limit imposed cannot be higher than 0.5 per cent of the member's earnings in any tax year or, if greater, three times the weekly lower earnings limit. [*Voluntary Contribution Regulations, reg 2(8)*]. In practice, it is not common for schemes to restrict the payment of voluntary contributions in terms of the minimum amount that must be paid.

The rules of a scheme may also require a member to give notice of his intention to pay, or vary the rate at which he is paying, voluntary contributions. The maximum notice period that the rules can require is twelve months. [*Voluntary Contribution Regulations, reg 2(4)*]. It is not uncommon for a scheme to impose a notice period of one or two months so as to allow the employer sufficient time to make adjustments to the payroll.

The benefits deriving from voluntary contributions will generally be defined contribution benefits, irrespective of whether the scheme is defined contribution or defined benefit. Voluntary contributions may sometimes be used to purchase added years of service which count toward the member's defined benefits, but this is unusual. Any voluntary contributions paid by the member must be used to provide additional benefits for, or in respect of, that member. The amount of the additional benefits must be reasonable, having regard to the amount of the contributions paid and (if the benefits provided by the voluntary contributions are not defined contribution benefits) the value of the other benefits under the scheme.

Instead of making voluntary contributions 'in-house' through the employer's scheme, a member may choose to make contributions to a 'free standing additional voluntary contributions' ('FSAVC') arrangement. Legislation to provide for these arrangements was introduced in the *Finance (No 2) Act 1987*.

1.32   *Pension provision in the UK – an introduction*

An FSAVC arrangement has much in common with a personal pension scheme (see chapter 15), although regulations relating to the payment of voluntary contributions generally also apply. An FSAVC arrangement is established by a provider in exactly the same way as a personal pension scheme. Usually the provider is an insurance company, friendly society, bank or building society. The main disadvantage with an FSAVC arrangement is that the member is obliged to meet the fees associated with the administration and management of the arrangement whereas, if voluntary contributions are paid 'in-house', the employer will usually bear these costs.

Inland Revenue restrictions

1.32   The total contributions (ordinary and voluntary) which can be made to a scheme by a member in any tax year is restricted by the Inland Revenue to 15 per cent of the member's remuneration in that year. [*ICTA 1988, s 592*].

If the payment of voluntary contributions causes benefits to be excessive, any surplus can be refunded to the member (net of tax), or in the event of his death, paid to his estate. Generally, a check only needs to be made when the member retires or requests a transfer if he has left pensionable service before retirement. However, where a member is contributing to an FSAVC, a check must be made if the member leaves pensionable service, irrespective of whether or not he requests a transfer (see IR12 (2001) PN 4.4).

If a member commences paying voluntary contributions after 8 April 1987, those voluntary contributions must be used to provide benefits in the form of pension. They cannot be commuted for a tax free lump sum although they can be taken into account when calculating the maximum lump sum that can be paid from a scheme (see IR12 (2001) PN 8.3).

The drawing of a member's AVC benefits has now become more flexible and the Scheme may now permit the member to defer drawing his AVC benefits until after his main scheme benefits have come into payment, draw them before that time or use an income drawdown facility. These options are set out in and are subject to the restrictions in appendix XII of IR12.

BENEFITS PAYABLE FROM OCCUPATIONAL PENSION SCHEMES

Inland Revenue requirements

1.33   The benefits payable from an approved occupational pension scheme, whether defined contribution or defined benefit, are limited by the Inland Revenue. To obtain Inland Revenue approval, the rules of the scheme must reflect these limits, which are discussed in chapter 5.

When are benefits payable?

1.34 Benefits will become payable under a scheme either on the death of a member or on the member's retirement, whichever is the earliest. Benefits are usually calculated on the basis of the member's 'normal retirement date' which will generally be between age 60 and 65. It is a condition of Inland Revenue approval that the rules of the scheme specify the age at which members will normally retire; the specified age must generally be between 60 and 75 (IR12 (2001) PN 6.5 and 6.6); see also chapter 5. Normal retirement date need not necessarily be the birthday at which the specified age is reached; it may be a convenient day such as the last day of the preceding or following month or the nearest scheme anniversary date.

Normal retirement date may differ for different categories of members, for example directors may have a normal retirement date of age 60 while all other members have a normal retirement date of age 65. In the past it was common to find schemes with a different retirement age for men and women (usually reflecting the State pension age) but following the decision in *Barber v GRE Insurance Group [1990] 1 ECR 1889*, this is no longer the case (see chapter 9 for a full discussion on the equalisation of normal retirement dates).

The rules of a scheme may permit benefits to be paid either before or after normal retirement date. A pension may not, however, come into payment before a member is age 50 unless that member is retiring due to incapacity. This is both an Inland Revenue requirement (see chapter 5) and a statutory requirement (see chapter 6). The Finance Bill 2004 proposes to increase this minimum age to 55 from 6 April 2010. Benefits payable on early retirement are discussed further in 1.35 below. The Inland Revenue will not permit benefits to come into payment after age 75; benefits payable on late retirement are discussed in 1.36 below.

Final salary defined benefit schemes

Pension benefits at normal retirement

1.35 In the case of a final salary defined benefit scheme a member's pension is calculated by reference to the remuneration he is receiving at or shortly before he retires or leaves service. The level of remuneration by which benefits are calculated is often referred to as 'final pensionable salary' or some similar expression. The definition of final pensionable salary is a matter of scheme design; the wider the definition, the higher a member's final pensionable salary is likely to be and consequently, the greater his resulting pension will be. A member's final pensionable salary may be his earnings at the date on which he retires, his total earnings during the previous year or his earnings averaged over a certain period, such as the previous three years; it may include fluctuating emoluments such as commissions or bonuses or it may simply be basic salary. There may be offsets against final pensionable salary, for example, it is not uncommon for a deduction equal to the lower earnings limit to be made.

1.36 *Pension provision in the UK – an introduction*

Typically, a scheme's rules will contain a formula for calculating the pension payable. This will generally be expressed as a fraction or percentage of final pensionable salary for each year of pensionable service (ie service whilst an active member and any service deemed, under the rules of the scheme, to be pensionable service); 1/60th or 1/80th are the most common annual accrual rates. A formula such as this gives the member some reassurance that, assuming that he has been a member of a scheme for much of his working life, his pension will be a reasonable proportion of the salary he was earning at the time he retired. For example, a person who has been a member of a scheme offering a 1/60th accrual rate for 30 years will receive a pension of 30/60ths, or one half of his final pensionable salary.

Pension benefits on early retirement

1.36 The rules of the scheme may allow members to retire on pension at any time if retirement is due to incapacity or at any time after age 50 for any other reason. Generally the rules will specify that either employer or trustee consent is required for early retirement and, in the case of incapacity retirement, that satisfactory medical evidence is produced.

The level of benefits payable on early retirement will often depend on whether or not the member is retiring due to incapacity. A non-incapacity related early retirement pension will generally be calculated using the same formula as for normal retirement but taking account of actual pensionable service and final pensionable salary at the date of retirement. The resulting pension will often then be reduced to take account of early receipt. This is usually done by applying a percentage reduction, for example, a member's pension may be reduced by 3 per cent for each year that actual retirement precedes normal retirement date.

Sometimes rules may provide for a different level of benefit, depending on the circumstances of the retirement. In *AGCO v Massey Ferguson Works Pension Trust [2003] 57 PBLR*, the scheme rules provided more generous benefits on early retirement when it was at the request of the employer. The court was asked to consider the meaning of the words 'retires from Service at the request of the Employer' in the context of the terms of the particular scheme and, in particular whether this included voluntary and/or compulsory redundancy?

The court held that 'retire' is intransitive (ie the employee elects to give up work rather than being required to leave) and that 'retire' covers situations different from dismissal and is distinct from 'leaving Service' which covers broader circumstances. The words 'retires from Service at the request of the Employer' did not include a case where the employer requests and subsequently enforces retirement – the natural meaning of 'request' is that the employee has a choice in the matter. There is a broad range of voluntary redundancy – from truly voluntary to a position where the employee has little choice in the matter. True 'voluntary' redundancy does fit within the wording as being 'retirement at the request of the employer'. Compulsory redundancy does not as it is a dismissal rather than a retirement.

Pension provision in the UK – an introduction **1.36**

Where the retirement is due to incapacity the benefits provided will often be more generous. They may, for example, be calculated without reduction for early receipt or possibly on the basis of the pensionable service the member would have completed had he remained a member until his normal retirement date. Such pensions are obviously more expensive than non-incapacity early retirement pensions and so are generally paid less frequently.

The definition of incapacity contained in the glossary to the Inland Revenue's Practice Notes is any 'physical or mental deterioration which is sufficiently serious to prevent the individual from following his or her normal employment, or which seriously impairs his or her earning capacity. It does not mean simply a decline in energy or ability'. The Inland Revenue will not permit an incapacity retirement pension to be paid unless the member concerned falls within this definition of incapacity. However, the rules of many schemes go further than the Inland Revenue definition of incapacity; self-induced incapacity (for example, self-inflicted injuries or drug addiction) may be excluded; employer and/or trustee consent will often be required, and the member may have to be incapacitated to the extent that he is incapable of any full-time employment, not just of working for his current employer.

The fact that there are often many conditions relating to the payment of an incapacity pension has given rise to a number of disputes between members and trustees as to whether such a pension should be paid. The decisions, to an extent, turn on the particular wording of the incapacity rule in question but generally an employer must act in good faith when considering any medical evidence provided in relation to an application for an incapacity pension. Trustees may be required to exercise a discretion in relation to the payment of benefits such as an incapacity pension. When exercising such a discretion, trustees should ensure that they ask themselves the proper questions, adopt a correct construction of the rules of the scheme and do not arrive at a perverse decision which no reasonable body of trustees could arrive at (taking into account all relevant, but no irrelevant, factors (*Lee v Showman's Guild (1952) 2 QB 329; Harris v Lord Shuttleworth and others (Trustees of the National Provincial Building Society Pension Fund) (1994) PLR 47 and Edge v Pensions Ombudsman (1999) 49 PBLR (37)*).

A distinction is sometimes drawn between voluntary and involuntary retirement. In *Brooks v National Westminster Bank plc*, an unreported decision of the Court of Appeal on 8 November 1993, the court decided that retirement was essentially a voluntary act as distinct from dismissal. In the case of a voluntary retirement, an ill-health early retirement pension was available and in the case of a dismissal, it was not. This decision was called into question by the Court of Appeal in *Harris v Lord Shuttleworth* which decided that it was possible to regard an individual who had been compulsorily retired by her employer as having retired by reason of incapacity.

Often an incapacity rule provides that the member must be 'permanently' incapacitated. The decision in *Harris v Lord Shuttleworth* suggests that being permanently incapacitated is synonymous with there being no reasonable

1.37 *Pension provision in the UK – an introduction*

prospect that the member will be able to work before normal retirement date either for the employer concerned or a similar employer.

Where a member receives his pension early he is effectively receiving benefits as an alternative to a preserved benefit and consequently the preservation legislation must be complied with. This is discussed further in chapter 6.

Pension benefits on late retirement

1.37 The rules of a scheme may permit a member to remain in service after his normal retirement date. Generally when a member of an approved scheme postpones his retirement he cannot take his benefits until he actually retires but benefits must be taken on or before the member's 75th birthday, even if he has not retired (IR12 (2001) PN 6.1). However, if the member joined (or is deemed to have joined) the scheme before 1 June 1989 he may take his benefits at any time after he attains normal retirement date even though he is continuing in service (IR12 (2001) PN 6.14). Once a member takes any part of his benefit he cannot continue to accrue further benefits.

The benefits payable on late retirement will be greater than the benefits payable on normal retirement. A member may continue to accrue pensionable service after his normal retirement date or alternatively his benefits may be calculated as at his normal retirement date and then increased by actuarial factors to take account of late receipt.

As with early retirement benefits, the provision of late retirement benefits is considered to be an alternative to a preserved benefit and so the legislation relating to preservation of benefits must be complied with (see chapter 6).

Tax free lump sum on retirement

1.38 A member may choose to take part of his retirement benefits in the form of a tax free cash lump sum if the rules of the scheme allow for this option. The maximum lump sum that can be taken is restricted by the Inland Revenue (see chapter 5) and, to an extent, depends on the circumstances of the retirement. If a member is retiring due to serious ill-health he may be able to commute the whole of his pension for a lump sum. To qualify, the member must have a very limited life expectancy, usually of less than one year. Full commutation is also permissible where the benefits payable are trivial, ie at the time of writing, less than £260 per annum. [*Occupational Pension Schemes (Assignment, Forfeiture, Bankruptcy etc.) Regulations 1997 (SI 1997 No 785), reg 2*].

Lump sum death benefits

1.39 An occupational pension scheme will usually provide a life assurance benefit in the event of the death of an active member. This benefit is usually calculated by multiplying a member's salary (which can be pensionable salary, annual salary or final pensionable salary) by a specified figure, but occasionally it is a fixed sum. The maximum lump sum death benefit a scheme will usually provide is four times salary as this is approximately the same as the maximum amount that the Inland Revenue will permit (see chapter 5).

In the event of a member's death, the life assurance benefit will usually be payable under 'discretionary trust' in order to mitigate any potential inheritance tax liability. If a payment is made through a discretionary trust, it will not form part of the member's estate and consequently will not be taken into account when assessing liability for inheritance tax. A scheme's governing rules will therefore usually contain an appropriate discretionary trust provision. When a member joins the scheme he will be asked to complete a 'statement of wishes' form to indicate to the trustees who he would wish to receive a lump sum death benefit in the event of his death. This statement of wishes does not bind the trustees but simply acts as a guidance for them. Irrespective of whether the member has completed a statement of wishes form, the trustees should make proper inquiries to establish whether or not they are paying the benefits to the most appropriate person. This is particularly true where there has been a change in the member's personal circumstances, such as a remarriage or death in the family. The trustees should tread carefully as they will be exercising their discretion and so must ask themselves the proper questions, adopt a correct construction of the rules of the scheme and not arrive at a perverse decision which no reasonable body of trustees could arrive at (taking into account all relevant, but no irrelevant, factors). (See 1.35 above; and *Wild v Smith 1996 PLR 275.*)

Lump sum death benefits are usually insured with a life assurance company. Only the largest occupational schemes are inclined to pay death benefits directly out of the fund as such benefits can be very costly.

It is common for a refund of the member's contributions also to be paid in the event of his death, sometimes with interest, but often without.

Spouse's/dependant's pension

1.40 In addition to the lump sum life assurance benefit payable in the event of the death of a member, a pension is often payable to his surviving spouse. The amount of the benefit payable will generally vary depending on whether the member died before or after retirement.

If a member dies whilst an active member the amount payable will usually be a percentage (often 50 per cent) of the member's prospective pension. This will be calculated on the basis of either his actual pensionable service at the date of death or the pensionable service he would have completed had he remained an active member until his normal retirement date and had his pensionable salary remained static.

In the case of the death of a member following his retirement, the spouse's pension is often calculated as a percentage of the member's pension at the date

1.41 *Pension provision in the UK – an introduction*

of his death. A spouse's pension of 50 per cent of the pension the member was receiving at the date of his death is common. A lump sum death benefit may be payable if the member dies within five years of the date of his retirement (often known as a five-year guarantee). For example, if a member dies within two years of his retirement date a lump sum equal to three years' worth of pension instalments may be payable as a lump sum.

The rules of the scheme may also permit a child or dependant's pension to be paid and this may be either where the member dies leaving no spouse (or a spouse who subsequently dies) or in addition to any spouse's pension which is payable. In the case of an approved scheme, the Revenue will only allow such a pension to be paid to someone who is dependent on the member at the date of his death. A child of a member who is under 18 or is undergoing full-time educational or vocational training will always be considered by the Revenue to be dependent upon his parent. In all other cases there must be a sufficient degree of financial dependency if the pension is to be paid. In the case of co-habitees this dependency can take the form of inter-dependency, for example, if both incomes are required to maintain the standard of living enjoyed by the couple in question.

Benefits on leaving service other than on retirement

1.41 A member must be entitled to a preserved benefit within a scheme if his pensionable service under that scheme is terminated before his normal pension age and he has at least two years' qualifying service. If the member has transferred his rights under a personal pension scheme to his employer's occupational pension scheme he will be entitled to a preserved benefit from that scheme, even if he has not completed two years' qualifying service.

Broadly speaking, qualifying service is pensionable service under the scheme, service in employment which was contracted-out by reference to the scheme or service which is deemed to be qualifying service by virtue of a transfer payment received by the scheme in respect of the member. A member's normal pension age is the earliest date on which he has an unqualified right to retire on an unreduced pension, other than on special grounds, such as ill-health or redundancy. In most schemes it will be the same as his normal retirement date.

PSA 1993 sets out the minimum requirements with which schemes must comply and it is not uncommon for a scheme to grant a member a preserved benefit, even if he has not completed two years' of qualifying service. Such schemes are often described as having immediate vesting of benefits. If a member has a preserved benefit under a scheme he will generally have a statutory right to require that the 'cash equivalent' of his benefits be transferred to his new employer's scheme, a personal pension scheme or another suitable tax approved arrangement.

If a member does not qualify for a preserved benefit under the scheme, he will usually be entitled to a refund of any contributions he has made to the scheme.

The refund will be net of tax (currently charged at 20 per cent) and, if the scheme is contracted-out of the State earnings-related pension scheme, will also be net of the cost of reinstating the member into SERPS/S2P. Contributions may be refunded with interest, but this is not a statutory requirement.

The protection afforded to early leavers is discussed in detail in chapter 6.

Defined contribution schemes

Pension benefits

1.42 The benefits paid to a member of a defined contribution scheme are determined by two factors, namely:

(*a*) the amount of money held by the trustees on behalf of the member at retirement; and

(*b*) the annuity rates applicable at the time when the member's benefits become payable.

The amount of money held by the trustees under (*a*) above will be determined by the level of contributions paid by the member's employer and the member himself, and the investment income realised in respect of those contributions. The total amount is generally referred to as the member's 'individual account' or, more colloquially, his 'pot'.

It is becoming increasingly common for members to be given some discretion over the way in which their individual account is invested. Often members will be given a choice of funds and are required to indicate to the trustees of the scheme what percentage of their individual account they wish to invest in each fund. The scheme must be carefully structured to ensure that the arrangements put in place, whilst offering the member choice, do not expose the trustees to potential claims from members whose investment choices do not perform as well as expected.

A member cannot have any claim to any particular asset, even if he is given some power in relation to how his account is invested. All the assets of the scheme will be invested together so that, although the member's account will be credited with interest and investment growth, no specific scheme asset will be attributable to his account.

On the member's retirement, whether at, before or after normal retirement date, assets equal in value to his individual account will be realised and the proceeds will be used to provide the member with a pension. Some defined contribution schemes provide additional benefits on the retirement of a member due to incapacity, but this will almost certainly be at the discretion of the employer.

Defined contribution schemes will usually (and in the case of small self-administered schemes, must) secure pensions by the purchase of an annuity. Often the member will be permitted to choose the insurance company from which the annuity will be purchased and will also be able to specify what conditions will apply to the annuity. Annuities can be purchased on a single life basis but, more commonly, they will allow for a spouse's pension to be payable in the event of the member's death. Particular conditions may apply if the member's pensionable service was contracted-out of the State earnings-related pension scheme and the annuity is being used to secure a member's protected rights (see chapter 4). If annuity rates are particularly poor, or if the circumstances warrant such action, the trustees may choose to provide the pension from the scheme rather than purchase an annuity, or they may permit income drawdown or annuity purchase deferral (see Inland Revenue Pensions Updates 54 and 66 and Appendix XII of IR12 (2001)).

Before 6 April 1997, there was no requirement that a pension, whether provided by the scheme directly or secured by the purchase of an annuity, had to be increased whilst in payment. However, all pensions provided in respect of contributions made after 6 April 1997 must be increased by the lesser of 5 per cent per annum and the increase in the Retail Prices Index for the relevant period. Any annuity purchased with contributions made after 6 April 1997 must therefore provide such increases (see also 1.44 below).

Death benefits

1.43 Most defined contribution schemes provide lump sum death-in-service benefits in much the same way as defined benefit schemes do (see 1.38 above).

The benefits provided to the spouse and/or dependants of a member of a defined contribution scheme may be a proportion of the member's salary or may be such level of pension as can be secured by the proceeds of the member's account. If the scheme provides a percentage of salary, there will usually be some form of insurance as it is possible (and in the case of young or new members, likely) that the member's account will be insufficient to provide the necessary funds to secure the benefit.

Benefits on leaving service

1.44 A member of a defined contribution scheme who terminates his pensionable service before his normal retirement date is entitled to benefits in much the same way as a member of a defined benefit scheme. The same statutory criteria determine whether the member has a right to preserved benefit or not, although the method of calculating the preserved benefit will, of course, be different.

A member of a defined contribution scheme who has a preserved benefit under the scheme will also generally have a statutory right to require that the 'cash equivalent' of his benefits be transferred to his new employer's scheme, a personal pension scheme or another suitable tax approved arrangement. However, the time limits within which the trustees must action his request differ from those applicable to defined benefit schemes (see chapter 6).

INCREASING PENSIONS IN PAYMENT

1.45 Any occupational pension scheme which is approved by the Inland Revenue must increase pensions in payment attributable to:

(*a*) in the case of a defined benefit scheme, pensionable service completed on and after 6 April 1997; and

(*b*) in the case of a defined contribution scheme, contributions made in respect of employment carried on from 6 April 1997.

The minimum increase for which the rules of the scheme must provide is the lesser of five per cent per annum (the Pensions Bill proposes to change this to 2.5 per cent) and the increase in the Retail Prices Index for the relevant period. [*PA 1995, s 51*]. This type of increase is commonly referred to as limited price indexation or 'LPI'.

Legislation requiring schemes to provide LPI increases to pensions was initially incorporated into the *Social Security Act 1990* but the majority of the provisions were not brought into effect. The one exception was in relation to the making of a payment to an employer. Where a surplus was being reduced by a payment to an employer, LPI increases had to be given on all pensions and prospective pensions for both past and future service other than guaranteed minimum pensions or benefits provided on a defined contribution basis. This is still the case but the appropriate statutory provisions are now contained in *section 37* of *PA 1995* in the case of ongoing schemes (see chapter 11) and *sections 76* and *77* of *PA 1995* in the case of schemes which are in winding-up (see chapter 12).

If an increase in excess of LPI is given, the excess may be offset against the following year's increase. [*PA 1995, s 53*]. LPI increases do not, however, have to be given in respect of pensions which derive from a member's voluntary contributions. [*PA 1995, s 51(6)*]. Nor do increases have to be given in respect of a pension paid to a member who has not attained the age of 55 at the time when the increase takes effect, unless he retired on account of incapacity. [*PA 1995, s 52*].

LPI increases do have to be given in respect of benefits derived from transfer payments but only to the extent that they are attributable to pensionable service completed on or after 6 April 1997. [*Occupational Pension Schemes (Indexation) Regulations 1996 (SI 1996 No 1679), reg 2*]. This requirement does not apply to transfer payments from a scheme which itself was not subject to the indexation requirement.

LPl increases do not have to be given in respect of benefits derived from a pension credit awarded as a result of a pension sharing order on the divorce of a member. [PA 1995, s 51(6)].

1.46 *Pension provision in the UK – an introduction*

FORFEITURE AND SUSPENSION OF BENEFITS

1.46 Generally a member's entitlement or accrued right to a pension cannot be assigned, commuted, surrendered or charged. However, there are various exceptions to this general rule [*PA 1995, s 91*]. Furthermore, a court is not able to make an order (other than an attachment of earnings order, income payments order, pension sharing order or earmarking order) which would deprive a member of his/her entitlement (although unapproved schemes are excluded from this provision). An example of the extent of this principle is shown in the case of *Fisher v Harrison [2003] 49 PBLR, [2003] All ER (D) 484 (Jul)*. As part of the settlement of a dispute, Mr Harrison purported to assign all his pension benefits (past and future) to Mr Fisher by way of consent order. The scheme included a fairly standard forfeiture clause, providing that benefits purported to be assigned would be forfeited.

The court held that the forfeiture clause did not apply to the attempted assignment of the benefits to which Mr Harrison already had an absolute entitlement (ie those which had become due and payable between 1996 and the date of the consent order). It also held that *sections 91* and *92* of *PA 1995* did not prevent the assignment of the benefits already due. However, both the forfeiture clause in the scheme rules and *section 91* did apply to pension payments falling due after the date of the consent order.

In this case, the consent order could not be severed (to allow Mr Fisher to claim the payments already due) and therefore even the valid assignment of past pension payments could not be enforced. Mr Harrison was entitled to payment of the benefits due before the date of the consent order (although Mr Fisher could apply for a new order in relation to the freezing of those benefits). Those payable after that date were forfeit but Mr Harrison could ask the trustees to exercise their discretion under the forfeiture clause to make payments to him.

Exceptions to inalienability

Commutation of pension

1.47 The rules of an approved occupational pension scheme may, and generally do, allow a member to commute part or, in some circumstances, all of his pension for a lump sum at retirement (see 1.37 above). [*PA 1995, s 91(5)(c)*].

Surrender in favour of a spouse and/or dependant

1.48 The rules of a scheme may also allow a member to surrender part of his pension to provide a pension for his spouse and/or dependants in the event of his death after retirement. [*PA 1995, s 91(5)(a) and (b)*]. The total amount of all pensions payable to a spouse and/or dependants must not exceed the reduced pension payable to the member. For the purpose of this calculation, the member's reduced pension can include the pension equivalent of any lump sum benefit, whether provided separately or by commutation (see IR12 (2001) PN 12.5).

Charge, lien or set-off

1.49 Section *91(5)(d)* and *(e)* of *PA 1995*, provide that the rules of a scheme may allow for a charge or lien on, or a set-off against, a member's pension benefits to be made for the purposes of:

(*a*) enabling the member's employer to recover a monetary obligation arising out of a criminal, negligent or fraudulent act or omission by him;

(*b*) discharging a monetary obligation due to the scheme arising out of:

  (i) a criminal, negligent or fraudulent act or omission by him; or

  (ii) where the individual is a trustee, arising out of a breach of trust by him (unless the court has relieved him, wholly or partly, from personal liability under *section 61* of the *Trustee Act 1925*); [*Forfeiture Regulations, reg 4*)].

The amount or any charge, lien or set-off is restricted to the amount of the monetary obligation due or, if less, the value of the member's entitlement (calculated on a cash equivalent basis (see chapter 6)). The member must be given a certificate showing the amount of the charge, lien or set-off and its effect on his benefits under the scheme. If the member disputes the amount, the charge, lien or set-off cannot be effected unless the obligation becomes enforceable by a court order or an arbitrator's award. It is questionable whether silence on the part of the member concerned amounts to consent to the amount of the charge, lien or set-off, even if the certificate specifies that any dispute must be raised within a certain time limit. In effect, unless the member agrees to the charge, lien or set-off being exercised, the safest course of action is to obtain a court order or arbitrator's award.

A charge, lien or set-off cannot be exercised against a member's protected rights or accrued right to a guaranteed minimum pension. Neither can a charge, lien or set-off be exercised against a transfer payment received by the scheme in respect of a member unless it is attributable to another scheme of the same or a financially associated employer, and the benefits transferred could have been subject to a charge, lien or set-off under the transferring scheme. [*Forfeiture Regulations, reg 3*].

Forfeiture

1.50 Under *section 92* of *PA 1995*, an entitlement, or accrued right, to a pension cannot be forfeited other than as a consequence of:

(*a*) a purported assignment, commutation, surrender, charge, lien or set-off which is of no effect; or

- (b) the bankruptcy of a member which occurs prior to 6 April 2002; or
- (c) the member being convicted of certain offences such as treason; or
- (d) the failure of the member to make a claim within six years of the benefit becoming due; or
- (e) where a pension is payable to a person nominated by the member and that person is convicted of the murder, manslaughter or unlawful killing of the member.

Where a member's benefits are forfeited under the circumstances in (a) or (b) above in accordance with the scheme's rules, the trustees have a discretion under *section 92(3)* of *PA 1995* to pay the pension or benefit to all or any of the following:

- (i) the member of the scheme to, or in respect of, whom the pension was, or would have become, payable;
- (ii) the spouse or any dependant of the member;
- (iii) any other person to whom, under the rules of the scheme, the pension was or could have been paid.

A member's benefits may also be forfeited if a charge, lien or set-off could be exercised against them. The same conditions apply to forfeiting benefits as apply when exercising a charge, lien or set-off. If a member's benefits are forfeited in these circumstances, the trustees have power to determine that the amount forfeited is paid to the employer. [*PA 1995, s 93(5)*].

Pension rights following a member's bankruptcy

1.51 When an individual is declared bankrupt the general rule is that his estate automatically vests in the trustee in bankruptcy [*Insolvency Act 1986, s 306*]. The bankrupt's estate is defined as all property belonging to or vested in the bankrupt at the commencement of the bankruptcy, except for items for the bankrupt's personal use in his employment, and items for the basic domestic needs of the bankrupt and his family, [*Insolvency Act 1986, s 283*].

How does this affect an individual's pension rights? It was previously established that trustees in bankruptcy were entitled to claim the entire pension benefits of scheme members, not just pensions in payment (see *Re Landau [1997] 3 ALL ER 322*). In order to protect scheme members many pension schemes included forfeiture clauses – these will all be slightly different but the purpose of them was automatically to forfeit the member's entitlement to scheme benefits on his bankruptcy and for the trustees to have a discretion to distribute payments, up to the value of those benefits, to the member or his family (commonly known as 'protective trusts').

As a result of the *WRPA 1999*, forfeiture clauses have become less significant. Indeed, for persons made bankrupt on or after 6 April 2002 forfeiture clauses are no longer effective (see 1.52 below).

However, while they still maintain some relevance in relation to bankruptcies prior to 6 April 2002, it is important to note that not all forfeiture clauses are automatically valid. The validity of forfeiture clauses has been scrutinised closely by the courts most notably in *Kemble v Hicks [1998] 3 All ER 154*. This shows a difference between:

(*a*) clauses which purport to forfeit an absolute life interest, which cannot be valid;

(*b*) clauses which purport to forfeit determinable life interests (ie an interest that is valid until the happening of a certain event). These are only valid if the life interest is determinable in the same events that the forfeiture clause is expressed to operate; and

(*c*) clauses which forfeit a contingent interest, which are generally acceptable (ie an interest that will only become payable on the happening of a future specified event).

The relevance of a valid forfeiture clause to an individual, depending on the time that the bankruptcy order was made, is shown more clearly in the table in 1.52 below.

The Welfare Reform and Pensions Act 1999

1.52 The law concerning the effect of bankruptcy on an individual's pension rights has changed dramatically under the *Welfare Reform and Pensions Act 1999* ('*WRPA 1999*'). This Act contains provisions on pensions and bankruptcy which apply to occupational, personal and stakeholder pension schemes, as well as retirement annuity contracts.

The treatment of a member's scheme benefits on bankruptcy will now depend on the date the bankruptcy order was made. The position, as it applies to benefits under all approved pension schemes only, is summarised below.

Date of bankruptcy order	Is there a valid forfeiture clause?	Treatment of bankrupt's benefit
Before 29 May 2000	No	Benefits vest in trustee in bankruptcy on his appointment.
Before 29 May 2000	Yes	Benefits are forfeit and may be applied by scheme trustees under 'protective trusts'.
On or after 29 May 2000 and up to and including 5 April 2002	No	Benefits do not vest in trustee in bankruptcy on his appointment and are payable from scheme under the provisions of the trust deed and rules.
On or after 29 May 2000 and up to and including 5 April 2002	Yes	Benefits do not vest in trustee in bankruptcy on his appointment but forfeiture clause will operate provided the clause is valid and benefits may be applied by scheme trustees under 'protective trusts'.

1.53 *Pension provision in the UK – an introduction*

Date of bankruptcy order	Is there a valid forfeiture clause?	Treatment of bankrupt's benefit
On or after 6 April 2002	All forfeiture clauses are void	Benefits do not vest in trustee in bankruptcy on his appointment and are payable from scheme under the provisions of the trust deed and rules.

Pensions in payment

1.53 If a member is in receipt of a pension during the period of his bankruptcy (between the date of bankruptcy order and the date of discharge) it is open to the trustee in bankruptcy to apply to the Court for an Income Payments Order under *section 310* of the *Insolvency Act 1986* requiring the pension to be paid to the trustee in bankruptcy rather than the member. This would equally apply if a lump sum payment was made from the scheme during the period of bankruptcy.

In most cases, income payments orders will be in force from the period of the commencement of the order until the bankrupt is discharged – it is currently one year until automatic discharge of the bankrupt. In certain limited circumstances, the duration of the order can be extended beyond the date of discharge of the bankrupt. It is important to remember that the trustee in bankruptcy can only exercise those rights under the pension scheme which the bankrupt himself can. Therefore, if there is a long period of time before a member reaches retirement age pension rights will be of little use to a trustee in bankruptcy. In addition it makes no difference if the bankrupt member is discharged before the pension comes into payment – if the benefits have vested in the trustee in bankruptcy, any future payments may still be made to the trustee in bankruptcy, until the bankruptcy itself, ie not the individual, is discharged.

The effect on unapproved schemes

1.54 The benefits provided by an unapproved pension scheme will vest automatically in the trustee in bankruptcy. However, the Secretary of State is able to make regulations that define what constitutes an unapproved pension scheme and how that might, in prescribed circumstances, be excluded from his estate [*WRPA 1999, s 12*]. The member is now able to apply to the Court for an order excluding all or part of his entitlement under the scheme, or he may reach a formal agreement to that effect with the trustee in bankruptcy. [*Regulation 4* of the *Occupational and Personal Pension Schemes (Bankruptcy) (No. 2) Regulations 2002 (SI 2002 No 836)*].

Excessive contributions

1.55 Under *section 15* of the *WRPA 1999*, the trustee in bankruptcy can seek an order from the court, where excessive contributions have been made to an approved pension scheme. If made, order will restore the position to what it would have been, had the excessive contributions not been made (and the trustees will be ordered to pay an amount to the trustee in bankruptcy). The court will look at whether the contributions:

(a) have unfairly prejudiced individual creditors; and

(b) have been made in an effort to keep them beyond the reach of creditors; and

(c) were excessive when looking at the individual's personal circumstances at the time.

Enterprise Act 2002

1.56 The *Enterprise Act 2002 (EA 2002)* received royal assent on 7 November 2002 and is now fully in force.

Most notably, automatic discharge of the bankrupt now occurs after one year rather than the previous position where discharge occurred after three years. The bankrupt may be discharged prior to the expiry of one year where the official receiver files a notice at court that his investigations into the bankrupt's affairs are complete or if he believes that the period of one year until automatic discharge is unnecessary. [*Insolvency Act 1986, s 279* as inserted by *section 256 of the EA 2002*]. This means that the trustee in bankruptcy will have a shortened period of time in which to secure the bankrupt member's pension payments. This period may be extended, however, where the bankrupt member's level of income exceeds that which he reasonably requires for both his own and his family's needs. In these circumstances, the trustee in bankruptcy may secure an income payments order which will continue after the discharge of the bankrupt up to a maximum period of three years from the date of the bankruptcy order. [*Insolvency Act 1986, s 310(6)* as inserted by *EA 2002, s 259*].

However, the official receiver and the trustee in bankruptcy can apply to the court for an order extending the period of discharge of the bankrupt beyond one year or until a specified condition is fulfilled by the bankrupt. An order will only be made by the court to extend the period of the bankruptcy in these circumstances where the bankrupt has failed or is failing to comply with his obligations under the bankruptcy. [*Insolvency Act 1986, s 279(3), (4)* as inserted by *EA 2002, s 256*]. Further, in certain circumstances, the official receiver or Secretary of State may apply to the Court for a bankruptcy restriction order after the discharge of the bankrupt. This allows the duration of the bankruptcy to be extended to between 2 and 15 years, if certain types of culpable behaviour by the bankrupt are identified. (*Insolvency Act 1986, s 281A* as inserted by *EA 2002, s 257*). *Schedule 4A* has been inserted in the *Insolvency Act 1986*, which outlines the type of conduct which will be taken into account when considering the culpability of the bankrupt. For example, this will include excessive pension contributions made by the bankrupt (*Insolvency Act 1986, Sch 4A, s 2(2)(e)*).

Section 260 of the *EA 2002* also introduces an 'income payment agreement'. An income payment agreement is similar to an income payments order and is a

1.57 *Pension provision in the UK – an introduction*

written agreement between the bankrupt and his trustee in bankruptcy (or official receiver) to pay an amount equal to a specified part of the bankrupt's income to his trustee or official receiver for a specified period. The income payment agreement can impact on third parties because under the terms of the income payment agreement a third party, which can include the trustees of a scheme, can be required to pay to the trustee in bankruptcy (or official receiver) a portion of the bankrupt's pension for a specified period.

Whilst, unlike an income payments order, an income payment agreement avoids the requirement of a court hearing, the terms of the income payment agreement can be enforced as if they were provisions of an income payments order. An income payment agreement must specify the period for which it is to have effect and it can continue in force past the date of the discharge of the bankrupt for up to a maximum period of three years from the date of the agreement [*Insolvency Act 1996, s 310A* as inserted by *EA 2002, s 260*].

STAKEHOLDER PENSION SCHEMES

Background

1.57 Stakeholder pensions were introduced by the government as a new way for individuals to make provision for their retirement. The stakeholder pension scheme was designed to be a low cost, easy to understand, defined contribution pension plan targeted at individuals earning between £9,000 and £18,000 per annum who were not making pension provision at the time of introduction. The original idea was first proposed in November 1997 with the issue of '*Stakeholder Pensions – A Consultation Document*' by the (then) DSS. The ideas expressed in this document were carried forward in the December 1998 '*Partnership in Pensions*' Green Paper. Throughout 1999 several consultation papers seeking comment on the proposed workings of stakeholder pension schemes were issued until finally on 11 November 1999, with the publication of the *Welfare Reform and Pensions Act 1999*, the first statutory guidance on stakeholder pension schemes was published. The first stakeholder schemes became registerable from 1 October 2000 and were available to the public from April 2001. The primary regulations governing the operation of stakeholder schemes are the *Stakeholder Pension Schemes Regulations 2000* (*SI 2000/1403*).

The basic elements of stakeholder

1.58 The following outlines the basic aspects of a stakeholder pension scheme.

(*a*) *Legal structure*

Stakeholder schemes may be run either on the basis of a trust (ie similar to that of an occupational pension scheme) or on a contractual basis with the stakeholder scheme being run by an FSA authorised 'stakeholder scheme manager'. If the scheme is to be trust based then one third of the trustees must be independent, but there is no requirement for there to be member nominated trustees; where established on a contractual basis a contract between the manager and the scheme will set out the manager's responsibilities.

(b) Regulation

All schemes must be registered with Opra in order to qualify as stakeholder schemes and Opra regulates their operation and management. Stakeholder scheme compliance broadly follows that of *PA 1995* requirements. The Financial Services Authority (the *'FSA'*) regulates marketing and advice and supervises the firms responsible for managing the funds invested, (stakeholders being 'investments' for the purposes of the *Financial Services and Markets Act 2000*). In addition, the Inland Revenue regulates the conditions for tax approval and the Pensions Ombudsman has jurisdiction to hear complaints regarding maladministration.

(c) Charging

Stakeholder schemes are intended to have a simpler and more transparent charging structure than is sometimes seen with personal pension contracts. An annual charge of 1 per cent per annum of the fund value held by an individual is currently the maximum that a stakeholder scheme provider can levy. This covers all costs associated with initial recruitment of members and the continuing costs of running the scheme. All other additional services (and attaching costs) are optional to the scheme member. Transfers in and out of the scheme do not attract charges. Investment choice options can be given, but with a default option for those who do not wish to choose.

(d) Minimum contributions

To ensure that those of modest means are not precluded from joining stakeholder schemes, the minimum permissible level of contributions is £20, with members allowed to make contributions either on a regular or an infrequent basis, thereby catering for, amongst others, individuals who take a career break.

(e) The duty on employers

Subject to the exemptions below, all employers are required to designate a stakeholder scheme, including at least one scheme which all employees can join. They are also required to pass details of that scheme to their employees, and to provide a facility for deduction of contributions from the pay of those employees who are a member of a scheme, if the employee wishes.

1.58 *Pension provision in the UK – an introduction*

The requirement to provide access to stakeholder schemes applies to all employers, the current exemptions only applying to:

(*a*) Employers who already offer occupational schemes where the employee may join within a year of starting work and where the qualifying age is no older than 18 and no younger than 5 years before the scheme's normal retirement date;

(*b*) Employers with fewer than five employees;

(*c*) Employers whose employees all earn below the National Insurance Lower Earnings Limit;

(*d*) Employers who offer a group personal pension to which they contribute at least 3 per cent per annum of their employees' earnings, and which levies no charges when an individual leaves the scheme to move to a new employer.

Further details relating to Stakeholder Pension Schemes are set out in chapter 15.

Chapter 2

People involved with pensions

INTRODUCTION

2.1 This chapter considers the roles of the individuals and organisations involved in the administration, management and regulation of pension schemes. The people involved in pensions fall within four main categories:

(*a*)   those whose involvement is specific to the scheme in question; this group includes the trustees of the scheme and the professional advisers appointed by the trustees (ie the actuary, auditor and fund manager) to assist them in carrying out their functions;

(*b*)   those which can broadly be termed the regulatory bodies; this group includes the IR Savings, Pension, Share Schemes Office of the Inland Revenue (IR SPSS) (formerly the Pension Schemes Office), the Occupational Pensions Regulatory Authority (Opra), the National Insurance Services to Pensions Industry (formerly the Contracted-out Employments Group) of the National Insurance Contributions Office (which is an agency operated by the Inland Revenue) (previously the Contributions Agency of the DSS) and the Registrar of Occupational Pension Schemes and Personal Pension Schemes;

(*c*)   the Occupational Pensions Advisory Service (OPAS) and the Pensions Ombudsman, both of whom may have a role to play when disputes arise; and

(*d*)   the various professional bodies, the most important of which are the Pensions Management Institute and the National Association of Pension Funds.

The Pensions Bill, published in February 2004, also establishes two further bodies: a new Pension Protection Fund ('PPF') and a Pensions Regulator (see 2.29 below).

TRUSTEES

2.2   Where a pension scheme is established by an employer under trust, the role of the trustees is to hold the scheme's assets separately from the employer's assets and to apply them for the benefit of scheme members in accordance with the trust documents, general trust law and overriding legislation. If the scheme's liabilities are funded in advance over a period of time by employers' and

2.2 People involved with pensions

employees' contributions, the use of a trust creates a degree of security for scheme members by placing the scheme's assets beyond the reach of the employers' creditors. For schemes seeking the tax advantages of 'exempt approval' (see chapter 5), the existence of a trust is a Revenue requirement.

The role of a pension scheme trustee is evolving. In the past, there were few restrictions as to who could be a pension scheme trustee; a trustee could be an individual, the scheme's principal employer, a company, an elected employee or a member representative. For practical reasons, however, a scheme's trustees would usually be either at least two individuals or a company, whose board of directors would take the relevant decisions. The *Pensions Act 1995* (*PA 1995*) imposed requirements as to who may and may not be a pension scheme trustee (see 3.2 below) and in broad terms, entitled scheme members to nominate at least one third of the trustees (unless the scheme members accept alternative arrangements proposed by the employers) (see 3.24 to 3.27 below). The Government was concerned that many schemes do not have member nominated trustees as a result of alternative employer arrangements. As a consequence, the existing arrangements have been amended by the *Occupational Pension Schemes (Member-nominated Trustees and Directors) Amendment Regulations 2002 (SI 2002 No 2327)* (the *'MNT Amendment Regulations'*).

At the beginning of 2002, the Department for Work and Pensions (DWP) (explained in further detail at 2.35 below) circulated draft regulations relating to member-nominated trustee arrangements to various organisations (including the NAPF and the PMI for their consideration. Primarily this was because the first approvals for an employer's alternative arrangements under the current requirements were due to expire in 2002. Employers needed direction on what action (if any) should be taken as a consequence.

The *MNT Amendment Regulations* came into force on 6 October 2002 and their main effect was to extend the approval of existing arrangements by an additional four years. They provide that schemes with approved employer opt-outs or trustee arrangements in place need to take no further action. From the 6 October 2002, employers are able to propose new arrangements subject to the Trustees' approval but any employer opt-out arrangements approved after this date will be limited to four years. Trustee proposed arrangements are extended for an additional four years also. Further details are provided at 3.29.

Trustees must act in the best interests of their beneficiaries (generally considered to mean their best financial interests) and in accordance with statute and the scheme's trust deed and rules. Chapter 3 takes a more detailed look at trustees' duties and responsibilities in light of recent developments. In 2002, Paul Myners published his review of institutional investment in the UK setting out the 'blueprint' for change and recommendations for pensions schemes.

The Government published consultation papers back in the beginning of 2002 focusing on three of the Myners' Report recommendations on which they intended to legislate. These included whether schemes should have independent custodians, encouraging shareholder activism and the need for trustees to be

People involved with pensions   **2.2**

familiar with the issues concerned when reaching investment decisions. The Government's response to the Myners Report provided that March 2003 would see a public review to assess the effectiveness of the principles in bringing about the changes (which involved case studies using a small number of pensions schemes).

Further information on the Myners Report and its impact is provided at 3.14 below.

In January 2004 the Occupational Pensions Regulatory Authority ('Opra') published an update (Opra Note 1) to provide guidance to scheme actuaries and auditors to the legal requirements and circumstances in which Opra would expect them to make a report under *section 48(1)* of *PA 1995*. In respect of the payment of contributions, legislation sets out in detail when trustees of occupational pension schemes must receive all the pension contributions due to the scheme. If the trustees do not receive the contributions by the due dates, the trustees are under a duty to report to Opra within 30 days unless:

- the trustees receive the contributions within ten days after the due date; or

- it is the only late payment, or there has only been one other late payment in the twelve months ending on the due date.

Opra have now decided to focus their attention on the areas they believe are "critical" to the protection of members' interests. In practical terms, this means that:

- any contributions paid late but received within the 90 day period do not normally have to be reported to Opra;

- trustees must report all contributions still outstanding at the end of the 90 day period to Opra immediately; and

- when reporting to Opra, trustees should confirm that they have notified the members of the late payment of the contributions. If they receive any contributions after the 90 day period, but before they make their report to Opra, this should be noted in the report.

Opra are hoping this change in their approach will reduce the number of late payment reports that they currently experience. It should also be noted that trustees who follow the procedures laid down in Opra Note 1 will not be penalised for failing to report in accordance with legislative requirements.

PA 1995 introduced civil and criminal penalties for trustees in respect of breaches of certain sections of the *PA 1995* (and *PSA 1993*, as amended) and the disqualification or suspension of trustees in certain circumstances (see 2.14 below). Details of these appear throughout this book and are summarised in appendix 1.

2.3 *People involved with pensions*

ACTUARIES

The role of the actuary

2.3 An actuary must be a Fellow of the Institute of Actuaries (or of the Faculty of Actuaries in Scotland). For the purposes of *PA 1995*, an actuary can also be a person approved by the Secretary of State (in practice, such approval is likely to be granted only to actuaries with overseas qualifications). Actuaries assess financial problems, using mathematical and statistical methods, specialising, in particular, in problems concerning uncertain future events. In the context of pension schemes this most often involves predicting movements in the scheme (deaths, retirements and withdrawals) and estimating the costs of providing the benefits due and accruing in the future.

The actuary to a scheme will recommend the assumptions and methods to be used to value the scheme's assets and liabilities, will periodically value these (see chapter 11) and, where the scheme promises final salary benefits, will recommend the rate of contribution which is necessary to provide those benefits. He will advise on a day to day basis on benefit issues, such as the calculation of cash equivalents (an area of practice recently amended pursuant to the enactment of the *Occupational Pension Schemes (Transfer Values and Miscellaneous Amendments) Regulations 2003 (SI 2003 No 1727)*) (see chapter 6) and early retirement factors (for example, the extent to which an early retirement pension should be discounted to take account of early payment). An actuary may also advise the trustees on strategic investment decisions.

The appointment of the actuary under *PA 1995*

2.4 Under *section 47* of *PA 1995*, the trustees of most occupational pension schemes and stakeholder schemes (if registered in accordance with *section 2* of the *Welfare Reform and Pensions Act 1999* ('WRPA 1999')) must appoint an actuary. The actuary so appointed must be a named individual, even if working in a large actuarial firm (*section 47(1)(b)*). The individual actuary appointed under this provision ('the scheme actuary') has specific functions to perform under *PA 1995*. In particular, it is the scheme actuary who is responsible for producing valuations (see chapter 11).

Under *regulation 3(2)* of the *Scheme Administration Regulations (SI 1996 No 1715)*, the requirement for a scheme actuary does not apply to:

(*a*)   unfunded schemes;

(*b*)   unapproved schemes;

(*c*)   public service schemes or schemes which are backed by a government guarantee;

(*d*)   money purchase schemes;

People involved with pensions **2.5**

(e) centralised schemes for non-associated employers providing non-commuted lump sum benefits;

(f) schemes with less than two members;

(g) schemes which provide only death benefits and to which members have no accrued rights;

(h) expatriate schemes under *section 615(6)* of the *Income and Corporation Taxes Act 1988*; and

(i) certain schemes established by statute.

Regulation 4(1)(b) of the *Scheme Administration Regulations (SI 1996 No 1715)* sets out the qualifications and experience or approval required for appointment as the scheme actuary. An actuary must be a Fellow of the Institute or Faculty of Actuaries or must be approved by the Secretary of State. Additionally, an actuary cannot be a trustee of the pension scheme nor must he be connected with or an associate of a trustee of that scheme (see 2.7 below).

Any actuary can perform functions which do not have to be performed by the scheme actuary, but if the trustees rely on the skill or judgement of an actuary not appointed by them, they will risk incurring civil penalties or removal. Consequently whenever trustees of a pension scheme (even one that is exempt from having to appoint a scheme actuary) seek advice from an actuary, they should ensure that the actuary has been properly appointed in accordance with the requirements of *PA 1995*.

There are specific requirements for trustees to observe in making the necessary appointments (see *Scheme Administration Regulations (SI 1996 No 1715), reg 5* which includes stakeholder schemes and the actuarial guidance note, GN29, issued by the Institute and Faculty of Actuaries). The notice must be in writing, must specify the date of the appointment, and must set out to whom he shall report and take instructions from. (*Scheme Administration Regulations, reg 5(1)*). The actuary must acknowledge the notice in writing within one month of its receipt. (*Scheme Administration Regulations reg 5(2)(a)*) In addition, the actuary must confirm in writing that he will notify the trustees of any conflict of interest to which he is subject in relation to the scheme immediately on becoming aware of the existence of the conflict (*Scheme Administration Regulations, reg 5(2)(b)(ii)*). If the actuary resigns from the appointment or is removed by the trustees, he is required to certify whether the circumstances of the resignation or removal are likely to affect the members (*Schemes Administration Regulations, reg 5(4)*). Subject to these requirements, the trustees are free to determine the terms of the appointment and where an actuary resigns or is removed from the appointment, the trustees are required to appoint a replacement within three months (*Schemes Administration Regulations, reg 5(8)*).

Whistleblowing

2.5 The scheme actuary is required by *section 48* of *PA 1995* to be a 'whistleblower', although Opra's expectations in respect of what scenarios

2.6 *People involved with pensions*

should be reported has recently been clarified (see 2.6 below). In accordance statutory requirements, if the actuary has 'reasonable cause to believe' that:

(*a*) any duty relevant to the administration of the scheme imposed on the trustees, professional advisers, the principal employer or any 'prescribed person' has not been or is not being complied with; and

(*b*) the failure is likely to be of 'material' significance to the Occupational Pensions Regulatory Authority ('Opra') (see 2.14 below) in the exercise of any of its functions;

he must give an immediate written report to Opra. None of the words recited above in inverted commas are defined in the Act, which does not render interpretation easy. The intention is to catch all people who have statutory duties under *PSA 1993* and *PA 1995*. Other people involved with the scheme may also blow the whistle (for example, the trustees, solicitors or fund managers) but they are not under a statutory duty to do so. The confusion over the interpretation of the legislation has lead to reports being made to Opra which do not constitute a significant risk to members' benefits. In an attempt to stem the number of reports being made and to assist the scheme actuary, Opra have published a Note (to replace Opra Note 1) which sets out a 'traffic light' framework and guidance on when reports should be made (see 2.6 below).

The *PA 1995* contains a mechanism for Opra to impose penalties on actuaries who fail to comply with *section 48* (although at the time of writing the relevant *sub-sections* ((*7*) – (*13*)) *of section 48* have yet to be brought into force). This is on the understanding that, instead, Opra will make a complaint to the relevant professional body who will then employ their own disciplinary measures).

The actuary's professional obligations are set out in Guidance Note 29, Occupational Pension Schemes – Advisers to the Trustees or a Participating Employer (GN 29). The Guidance Note is updated and the latest version (5.0) is effective from March 2003. The Guidance Note is subject to further future amendment, in the event of there being conflict between it and the current or any future Opra (or subsequent appointed body) guidance notes. The Guidance Note applies principally to actuaries advising scheme trustees, but also contains guidance on advising an employer or the trustees (but not as the scheme actuary). The Guidance Note makes it clear that the scheme actuary is not expected to search for circumstances which would be reportable to Opra, but does have a duty to report circumstances which come to his or her attention (GN 29, para 6.4, version 5.0) 'immediately' (although it should be noted that immediately is not a defined term). The scheme actuary is therefore required to assess whether any information may be of material significance to Opra (GN 29, para 6.5, version 5.0) which should be read in conjunction with Opra Note 1 (see 2.6 below).

The traffic light framework

2.6 Opra published new guidelines for scheme actuaries and auditors in October 2003 (referred to as 'Opra Note 1') on the circumstances in which Opra would expect scheme actuaries or auditors to report breaches of legal requirements in accordance with *section 48(1)* of *PA 1995*.

There has been a shift of emphasis and although Opra still expects trustees (together with their advisers) to comply with the law, they no longer wish to receive reports which do not constitute a significant risk to the security of scheme assets or have any 'significant detrimental impact on members' benefits' (Opra Note 1).

Opra Note 1 explains that Opra's focus is on the areas it considers critical to protecting members' interests. Examples include:

- breaches that could result in delaying, preventing access to or reducing members' benefits;
- breaches that carry a criminal penalty; and
- breaches that indicate potential dishonesty or misuse of assets or contributions.

The emphasis of Opra Note 1 is to assist scheme actuaries and auditors in reaching a decision about whether or not to make a report. Opra have devised a 'traffic light' framework that will assist in the determination of whether a breach should be reported.

In summary, the reporting scenarios are illustrated in the table below.

Red	Red scenarios involve breaches which Opra will always regard as materially significant because of the risk it constitutes to members' interests. Examples of red scenarios can be found in Opra Note 1 and should always be reported.
Amber	Amber scenarios involve breaches where the risk to members' interests is less clear. The scheme actuary and auditor must take into account the context of the breach in relation to the scheme before deciding whether or not the breach constitutes a significant/immediate/potential risk to members' interests and is therefore reportable. Examples are provided in Opra Note 1.
Green	Green scenarios involve breaches which Opra does not regard as materially significant because their experience has shown that such breaches do not constitute any significant risk to members' interests. Again, examples of green scenarios can be found in Opra Note 1. Opra would not expect to receive a report in a green scenario but they do expect trustees to put matters right and to comply in the future.

The lists published are not definitive and further examples can be found on Opra's website regarding the new 'traffic light' reporting system. Details of how to contact Opra are found at **2.18** below.

Ineligibility to act if a trustee

2.7 Under *section 27* of *PA 1995* a trustee of a pension scheme (including

2.8 *People involved with pensions*

stakeholder schemes) (and any person 'connected' or 'associated' with such a trustee) may not be an actuary to the same scheme. (The terms 'connected' and 'associated' are defined in *section 123* of *PA 1995* by reference to *section 249* and *section 435* of the *Insolvency Act 1986*. See 13.3 and 13.23 for tables which illustrate the effect of these definitions).

However, a director, partner or employee of a firm of actuaries may act as a scheme's actuary even though another director, partner or employee of the firm is a trustee of that scheme (*PA 1995, s 27(2)*), and the firm may also provide trustee services to the scheme. [*Scheme Administration Regulations (SI 1996 No 1715), reg 7*].

Breach of *section 27* is a criminal offence (*PA 1995, s 28*) and may also lead to a prohibition order by Opra.

AUDITORS

2.8 An auditor is a person who is authorised by the Institute of Chartered Accountants of England and Wales or similarly recognised supervisory body (or, for the purposes of *PA 1995*, is approved by the Secretary of State) who receives, examines and officially verifies accounts of money in the hands of an individual or company.

Trustees of occupational pension schemes and, *with effect from 1 October 2000*, stakeholder schemes (*Stakeholder Pension Schemes Regulations 2000 (SI 2000 No 1403), reg 32*) must appoint an individual or a firm as auditor under *section 47* of *PA 1995*. However, under *regulation 3(1)* of the *Schemes Administration Regulations*, this requirement does not apply to:

(*a*) unapproved schemes;

(*b*) unfunded schemes;

(*c*) schemes which provide only death benefits and to which members have no accrued rights;

(*d*) schemes with less than two members;

(*e*) public service pension schemes, schemes backed by a Government guarantee and certain schemes established by statute;

(*f*) money purchase small self-administered schemes in which all members are trustees and all trustee decisions are made by unanimous agreement;

(*g*) expatriate schemes under *section 615(6)* of the *Income and Corporation Taxes Act 1988*; and

(*h*) schemes providing money purchase benefits where all benefits are by insurance or annuity contracts specifically allocated to members.

Rules similar to those applying to the appointment of actuaries apply to the appointment of auditors under *PA 1995* (see 2.4 above). However, the bar on a trustee (or anyone 'connected' or 'associated' with a trustee) acting as auditor (see 2.7 above) is arguably wider, in that there is no specific provision enabling a director, partner or employee of a firm of auditors to act as auditor where another director, partner or employee of that firm is a trustee of the scheme. The same sanctions as referred to in 2.7 above apply to any auditor who breaches the provisions of *section 27* of *PA 1995*. The auditor is also required to whistle blow in the circumstances set out in 2.5 above (which includes the requirements as set out in the new 'traffic light' approach as detailed under 2.6 above).

The *Occupational Pension Schemes (Requirement to obtain Audited Accounts and a Statement from the Auditor) Regulations 1996 (SI 1996 No 1975)* which apply to all schemes except insured schemes which earmark insurance policies for each member, require:

(i) the trustees in respect of scheme years ending on or after 6 April 1997 to obtain audited accounts and the auditor's statement regarding payment of contributions within seven months of the end of the scheme year;

(ii) the trustees to make provision as to the form and content of the accounts; and

(iii) the accounts to contain a statement that they have been prepared and audited in accordance with the regulations.

Further guidance for auditors can be found in the Auditing Practices Board's (APB) Practice Note 15 – 'The Audit of Occupational Pension Schemes in the United Kingdom' and the APB's bulletin 2000/2002, 'Supplementary Guidance for Auditors of Occupational Pension Schemes in the United Kingdom', both of which can be ordered through the APB's website: www.abs.org.uk/apb/ Scheme auditors are advised to familiarise themselves with these publications before undertaking work in relation to pension schemes.

INVESTMENT MANAGERS

2.9 A scheme's trust deed and rules will usually give the trustees wide investment powers to enable the trustees to deal with trust assets as if they were the beneficial owners and to maximise their investment opportunities. In addition, *section 34* of *PA 1995* confers on occupational scheme trustees (including stakeholder scheme trustees registered in accordance with *section 2* of the *WRPA 1999*) an investment power which is the same as if they were absolutely entitled to the scheme's assets themselves and which is subject only to any restrictions imposed by the scheme.

Trustees will generally delegate their investment power to a fund manager who is authorised rather than seek authorisation themselves. This is usually achieved by way of an investment management agreement ('IMA'). The IMA must contain certain information as prescribed by the *PA 1995*, which includes dealing with any conflicts of interest that may arise.

Trustees are required under *section 47(2)* of *PA 1995* to appoint a fund manager if their scheme has 'investments', which include 'any asset right or interest' as

2.10 *People involved with pensions*

defined in *section 22* of the *Financial Services and Markets Act 2000* (*'FSMA'*). The regulated activities are described more fully under *Schedule 2* of *FSMA* and separated into the following headings:

- dealing in investments;
- arranging deals in investments;
- deposit taking;
- safekeeping and administration of assets;
- managing investments;
- investment advice;
- establishing collective investment schemes; and
- using computer-based systems for giving investment instructions.

The *Scheme Administration Regulations* (*SI 1996 No 1715*) exempt (amongst others) unfunded schemes, schemes with less than two members, wholly insured schemes and small self-administered schemes in which all members are trustees and all investment decisions are made by all or a majority of the trustees (further exemptions are provided for under *reg 3(3)* of the *Scheme Administration Regulations* and *para (4)* of *reg 4* of the *Financial Services and Markets Act 2000* (*Carrying on Regulated Activities by Way of Business*) *Order 2001*) (*SI 2001 No 1177*).

IR SAVINGS, PENSIONS, SHARE SCHEMES OFFICE OF THE BOARD OF INLAND REVENUE (IR SPSS)

2.10 2001 saw a number of executive offices of the Inland Revenue replaced by 'business streams'. The four offices involved were the Capital Taxes Office, the Financial Intermediaries and Claims Office, the Stamp Office and the Pensions Scheme Office. The work of these offices has been brought together to form a new organisation – Inland Revenue Capital and Savings. The previous structure was largely historical and by organising the work in a different way, the service provided has been improved.

IR SPSS is one of the business streams of the Inland Revenue's Capital and Savings. It is responsible for work on pensions, including personal pensions, savings products, employee share schemes and equity remuneration, and any continuing MIRAS issues. Its role is to protect the valuable tax reliefs on offer, through the granting and monitoring of tax approved status for retirement benefit schemes. The tax treatment of occupational pension schemes is dealt with further in chapter 5 and of personal pension schemes in chapter 15. The organisation of IR SPSS incorporates:

- Audit and Pension Schemes Service; and
- Pension Schemes Technical Advice.

People involved with pensions **2.11**

In particular, the main functions of the Audit and Pension Schemes Service include:

(*a*) dealing with the issue, variation and cancellation of contracting out certificates;

(*b*) supervising contracted out schemes to ensure their resources meet their contracted out liabilities and continue to satisfy the conditions for contracting out;

(*c*) allocating employer contracting-out numbers (ECONS) and scheme contracted out numbers (SCONS);

(*d*) supplying contracted out employers with:

- a toolkit when the contracting out certificate is first issued to newly contracted out schemes;

- National Insurance contracted out contribution tables; and

(*e*) dealing with contracting out certificates for insolvent employers.

The Inland Revenue's guidelines are set out in its Practice Notes, IR12 (2001) (as updated from time to time) for occupational schemes and IR 76 (2000) for personal pension schemes (including stakeholder schemes) and a general enquiry service is available. The IR SPSS is located in Nottingham, and can be contacted at Audit and Pension Scheme Services, Yorke House, PO Box 62, Castle Meadow Road, Nottingham, NG2 1BG (Tel: 0115 974 1600; Fax: 0115 974 1480).Website: www.inlandrevenue.gov.uk

OCCUPATIONAL PENSIONS BOARD (OPB)

2.11 The OPB was dissolved by *section 150* of *PA 1995* with effect from 5 April 1997. Some of the OPB's overseeing functions were, following the OPB's dissolution, taken over by Opra (see 2.12 below). The OPB's responsibilities for contracting-out have now been taken over by the National Insurance Services to Pensions Industry (otherwise known as NISPI), a department of the National Insurance Contributions Office of the Inland Revenue (previously the Contracted Out Employment Group) (see 2.24 below).

To place these matters in context it is worth mentioning the OPB's main functions before its dissolution on 5 April 1997, which were:

(*a*) running the Pensions Registry (see 2.12 below, now a function of Opra);

(*b*) making grants to approved bodies, eg OPAS (see 2.25 below);

(*c*) making modification orders, now a function of Opra (see 12.10 below);

(*d*) monitoring and advising schemes on overriding legislation (eg on preservation (see chapter 6) responsibility now rests with the trustees);

(*e*) administering and dealing with the statutory disclosure requirements (see chapter 3, now a function of Opra); and

2.12 *People involved with pensions*

(*f*) supervising schemes which have ceased to be contracted-out (see chapter 4, now a function of the National Insurance Services to Pensions Industry).

REGISTRAR OF OCCUPATIONAL AND PERSONAL PENSION SCHEMES (REGISTRAR)

2.12 The office of Registrar was established by the *Social Security Act 1990* (the relevant legislation is now contained in *section 6* of *PSA 1993*). Opra took over the management of the Registry from the OPB on 6 April 1997. The provisions of the *Register of Occupational and Personal Pension Schemes Regulations 1997* (*SI 1997 No 371*), allow Opra to appoint an agent to perform any function of the Registrar [*regulation 2(3)*].

The main functions of the Registrar are:

(*a*) to obtain and record details [*regulation 3(2)*] (such as details of the trustees, the name of the scheme administrator, the number of members and the type of benefits provided) of all occupational pension schemes, personal pension schemes and their respective predecessor arrangements (trustees must provide this information within three months of the scheme becoming a registrable scheme) [*regulation 4(1)*];

(*b*) to maintain the register and to amend it to take into account changes to scheme details as and when they are reported (trustees are required to report changes within twelve months) [*regulation 5*];

(*c*) to carry out searches of the register on request by any person who is or may be entitled to a benefit under the scheme (or their representative) to trace the location of their preserved pension rights [*regulation 6*]; and

(*d*) to collect a levy from registered schemes (*Regulation 2–8* of the *Occupational and Personal Pension Schemes* (*Levy*) *Regulations 1997* (*SI 1997 No 666*)).

The Registrar is not obliged to contact relevant schemes about individual members' rights or to record details of individual transfers made. Trustees can be fined for failing to provide the Registrar with the necessary information within the required time frame [*regulation 7*].

The Registrar can be contacted at the following address: PO Box 1NN, Newcastle upon Tyne, NE99 1NN (Tel: 0191 225 6393; Fax: 0191 225 6390/1).

OCCUPATIONAL PENSIONS REGULATORY AUTHORITY (OPRA)

2.13 Opra, the statutory regulator of the pensions arrangements offered by employers, was established by *section 1* of *PA 1995*, and came into effect from 6 April 1997. As an executive non-departmental public body, it is accountable to the Secretary of State for Work and Pensions. However, all of this is set to change. In 2002 the Pickering Report recommended that a new kind of regulator should be established to be more 'proactive' in the role it undertakes. The long awaited Pensions Bill was published in February 2004 and establishes the 'Pensions Regulator', the new body to replace Opra. Further details can be found at 2.29 below. In the interim and until the Pensions Bill is enacted, Opra remains the UK's regulatory body

Principal powers of Opra

2.14 Opra has a number of powers under *PA 1995* which it can use to ensure that members' interests are protected and occupational pension schemes comply with *PA 1995*. Its responsibilities have been extended by the introduction of stakeholder pensions and it now also supervises employers who make employer or employee payments into personal pensions.

(*a*) Prohibition order. Opra can prohibit a person from being a trustee of a particular trust scheme (*section 3* of *PA 1995*), primarily if that person has been in serious or persistent breach of specified duties under *PSA 1993* and *PA 1995*. A prohibition order has the effect of removing that person as a trustee (*section 3(3)* of *PA 1995*).

(*b*) Suspension order. Opra can suspend a trustee (*section 4* of *PA 1995*), for example where a prohibition order (see (a) above) is under consideration or where proceedings have been commenced for an offence involving deception or dishonesty. A suspension order prevents the individual from acting as a trustee during the period of suspension (generally for an initial period of 12 months, but this may be extended by Opra for a further 12-month period).

(*c*) Disqualification order. Opra can disqualify a trustee 'of any trust scheme' (*section 29* of *PA 1995*), for example for involvement in an offence involving dishonesty or if, in the opinion of Opra, he is incapable of acting or, in the case of a company, it has gone into liquidation. In certain circumstances, such as disqualification as a company director, disqualification as a trustee is automatic. Under *section 30* of *PA 1995*, a person acting in breach of a disqualification order is guilty of an offence and subject to a fine or imprisonment, but the actions of a disqualified trustee are not automatically invalidated and do not affect the personal liability of the person so acting (*section 30(5)* of *PA 1995*). Opra is required to maintain a record of all disqualified persons – the 'disqualification register' – and to disclose details on request (*section 30(A)* of *PA 1995*).

(*d*) Appointing additional trustees. Opra can appoint additional trustees in certain circumstances (*section 7* of *PA 1995*), for example to replace those it has prohibited or disqualified. Opra may require that the additional trustees' expenses are met out of the scheme's assets, may specify the powers or duties of the trustee and may remove a trustee so appointed.

(*e*) Imposition of penalties. Opra can impose civil penalties (subject to a maximum of £5,000 in the case of an individual or £50,000 in any other

2.15 *People involved with pensions*

case, either of which may be increased by the Secretary of State) for breaches of the *1995 Act* (*section 10*) in a wide range of circumstances set out in *PA 1995*. (These circumstances are referred to wherever relevant throughout this book and are collected together for ease of reference in appendix I.). Most penalties apply to trustees or employers but Opra can also penalise an actuary or auditor for failing to 'whistle blow' (see 2.5, 2.6 and 2.7 above) (*section 48* of *PA 1995*).

(*f*) Winding-up of a scheme. Opra can order the winding-up of a scheme under *section 11* of *PA 1995* in limited circumstances; see 12.52 below.

(*g*) Make applications to court. Opra may apply to the court:

- for an injunction to restrain misappropriation of assets (*section 13* of *PA 1995*); or

- for an order for the repayment to a pension scheme where assets have wrongly been refunded, or a loan wrongly made, to an employer (*section 14* of *PA 1995*).

(*h*) Issue directions for trustees to pay benefits. Opra can direct trustees to arrange for the payment of benefits which should have been paid by an employer (*section 15* of *PA 1995*).

(*i*) Modification Orders. Opra has power to make modification orders to achieve the reduction of pension scheme surpluses or the distribution to employers of a surplus on a winding-up (*section 69* of *PA 1995*).

(*j*) Circulation of statements made by Opra. Opra can direct the trustees (in writing) to include a statement prepared by Opra in their annual report or to send members a copy of a statement prepared by Opra (*section 15* of *PA 1995*).

Stakeholder pensions

2.15 *Section 2* of *WRPA 1999* extended Opra's powers to maintaining a register of stakeholder pension schemes. The register enables members of the public to identify stakeholder schemes and allows employers to ensure compliance with legislation. Opra have the discretionary powers to impose a fee for registering schemes (which is currently £200.00) and may also remove schemes from the register which do not comply with section 1 of WRPA 1999. If a scheme does not comply with the conditions set out under *section 1*, Opra may prohibit named individuals from acting as a trustee (*section 3* of *PA 1995*) or impose fines (*section 10* of *PA 1995*). Criminal sanctions can also be imposed where a trustee has 'knowingly or recklessly' provided Opra with information which is false or misleading (*section 2(5)* of *WRPA 1999*).

Determination by Opra

2.16 Generally determinations by Opra are final, except that reviews can be made, under *section 96* of *PA 1995*, in the following situations:

(a) on the application of any person to review a prohibition order, a disqualification order or an order in relation to the payment of penalties;

(b) on the application of an interested person, a determination may be reviewed if Opra is satisfied that there has been a relevant change in circumstances or a determination was made in ignorance of, or was based on a mistake as to, a material fact; and

(c) Opra may review any determination within six months (or such longer period as it shall determine) on any ground.

Opra may, following such a review, vary or revoke any previous determination.

Obtaining information

2.17 Opra may require the trustees, managers, professional advisers, employers or any other person likely to hold documentation relevant to the discharge of Opra's functions to supply that information to Opra (*section 98* of *PA 1995*). 'Document' for this purpose includes information recorded in any form.

An Opra inspector may enter premises to ascertain whether certain regulatory provisions are being complied with (*section 99* of *PA 1995*), which includes power to examine orally any persons on the premises. The inspector may require the production of documents from persons at the premises. For the purposes of these provisions, 'premises' means any premises where members of the pension scheme are employed or where documents relevant to the administration of the pension scheme may be held or where the administration itself is being carried out.

Opra can apply for a warrant if it believes that there are documents on premises which have not been supplied or it suspects that documents have been tampered with or that an offence has been committed or assets will be misappropriated (*section 100* of *PA 1995*). A warrant authorises an Opra inspector to enter the premises using reasonable force, to search the premises and to take possession of documents (or copies of documents). Opra may retain documents seized for a period of six months or, if proceedings have been brought in that period, until the conclusion of the proceedings.

In the following circumstances, non-co-operation with Opra is an offence leading to a fine and/or imprisonment (*section 101* of *PA 1995*):

(a) refusal to produce documents without reasonable excuse;

(b) intentionally obstructing an Opra inspector without reasonable excuse;

(c) knowingly or recklessly providing Opra with false or misleading information; and

(d) intentionally and without reasonable excuse altering, suppressing or destroying documentation.

2.18 *People involved with pensions*

Generally, restricted information must not be disclosed by Opra except with the consent of the person to whom it relates or the person from whom Opra obtained it. Any such disclosure is an offence (*section 104* of *PA 1995*). Restricted information is information obtained by Opra relating to the business or affairs of any person (except for information already in the public domain or information which is in summary form only and which does not relate to any individuals).

Exceptions to this are:

(i) where disclosure is required to enable Opra to carry out its functions (*section 106* of *PA 1995*);

(ii) where Opra considers that disclosure would enable any of a list of named individuals and institutions (for example, the Secretary of State, Treasury, Bank of England, IR SPSS, Pensions Ombudsman, Registrar and others) to carry out their functions (*section 107* of *PA 1995*);

(iii) disclosure to the Secretary of State or the Inland Revenue if it is in the interest of members of an occupational scheme or in the public interest (*section 108(1)* of *PA 1995*);

(iv) disclosure for the purpose of instituting criminal proceedings and certain other specified proceedings, for example, in connection with proceedings arising under *PA 1995* (*section 108(2)*); and

(v) disclosure to the Director of Public Prosecutions (*section 108(3)* of *PA 1995*).

Specific provisions apply regarding the disclosure of tax information by the IR SPSS to Opra although in most instances such information would itself be treated as restricted information (*section 109* of *PA 1995*).

Cost of Opra

2.18 For the purposes of meeting the expenditure of Opra and the Pensions Compensation Board ('PCB') (see 2.19 below), regulations under *section 175* of *PSA 1993* (as amended by *section 165* of *PA 1995*) make provision for imposing a levy. The levy is payable to the Secretary of State by or on behalf of the administrator of public service schemes or the trustees or managers of occupational or personal pension schemes.

Opra can be contacted at Invicta House, Trafalgar Place, Trafalgar Street, Brighton, East Sussex BN1 4DW (Tel: 01273 627 600; Fax: 01273 627 688. E-mail: helpdesk@opra.gov.uk. Website: www.opra.gov.uk).

PENSIONS COMPENSATION BOARD (PCB)

Establishment of the PCB

2.19 The PCB was established by *sections 78* to *80* of *PA 1995* and became operational on 6 April 1997. It consists of not less than three part-time members, appointed by the Secretary of State. Its remit is restricted to occupational pension schemes established under trust and the intention is to exclude only those schemes where there is equivalent or better existing protection for scheme members, or where compensation would be inappropriate. Determinations made by the PCB are governed by the *Pensions Compensation Board (Determinations and Review Procedure) Regulations 1997 (SI 1997 No 724)*.

Making a claim

2.20 Under *section 81* of *PA 1995*, claims for compensation can only be made where:

(*a*) the scheme is a trust scheme;

(*b*) an employer is insolvent (or the employers are insolvent in the case of a multi-employer scheme);

(*c*) the value of the scheme's assets has been reduced by reason of an offence involving dishonesty, including an intent to defraud (*regulation 3 of the Occupational Pension Schemes (Pensions Compensation Provisions) Regulations 1997 (SI 1997 No 665)* the 'Compensation Regulations');

(*d*) the value of the assets in a final salary scheme immediately before the application is less than the protection level (the combined value of 100 per cent of its most urgent liabilities and 90 per cent of its other liabilities. The most urgent liabilities include pensions in payment and members within 10 years of retirement); and

(*e*) it is 'reasonable in all the circumstances' that the members of the scheme should be assisted in such a way.

Under *regulation 2* of the *Compensation Regulations*, assistance from the PCB is not available to:

(i) small self-administered schemes with less than 12 members all of whom are trustees and under the rules of which trustee decisions must be made unanimously;

(ii) public service pension schemes and schemes backed by a Government guarantee;

(iii) unapproved schemes;

(iv) schemes with less than two members and no beneficiaries; and

(v) schemes which provide only death benefits and under the provisions of which no member has accrued rights.

The impact of the *Welfare Reform and Pensions Act 1999* ('*WRPA 1999*') should also be considered in this context. With effect from 1 April 2000, but with the exception of *section 81(1)(b)* of *PA 1995*, this paragraph 2.20 will

2.21 *People involved with pensions*

also apply to a stakeholder scheme if it has been registered under *section 2* of WRPA 1999.

Under *section 82* of *PA 1995*, the period for making a claim to the PCB is within 12 months of either the insolvency date (on or after 6 April 1997) or upon which the auditor, actuary or trustees knew or ought reasonably to have known that a reduction in value had occurred. Under subsection (5) of *section 82* of *PA 1995* the PCB may extend the period for making a claim beyond 12 months. Members, beneficiaries, trustees and any person who financed, provided benefits or administered the scheme (or persons acting on those persons' behalf) are authorised to make the claim. Payments are made to the trustees. The amount of the payment is determined in accordance with *regulation 5* of the *Compensation Regulations (SI 1997 No 665)* as amended by the *Occupational Pension Scheme (Pensions Compensation Provisions) Amendment Regulations 2001 (SI 2001 No 1218)*, but the amount cannot exceed the shortfall at the application date, plus interest at the prescribed rate of 2 per cent above base rate (*section 83* of *PA 1995*). Additionally, for a salary related scheme, it cannot exceed the amount required to secure the aggregate of the protected liabilities, as at the application date calculated on the basis of the minimum funding requirement (see chapter 11). Any interim payments made in anticipation will be deducted (*regulation 6* of the *Compensation Regulations*).

Interim payments are intended to enable schemes to continue paying non-discretionary benefits (that is pensions in payment and deferred pensions and ill-health early retirement pensions which become payable between the application date and the settlement date, but excluding any lump sum liabilities) to the extent that they are unable to do so from the scheme's remaining assets. If it subsequently transpires that a scheme was not eligible to receive an interim payment (for example, if the loss was as a result of innocent maladministration), the PCB may recover the interim payment made, provided that pensions in payment will not be reduced and that recovery by the PCB would not result in the trustees acting in breach of trust (*regulation 6* of the *Compensation Regulations*).

Funding of the PCB

2.21 The PCB has imposed an annual levy on pension schemes (*section 175(4)* of *PSA 1993*, as amended by *section 165* of *PA 1995*), which is payable by the trustees for the first time since its initial levy in 1997. The levy has been set at a flat rate of 23p per member. The PCB, on the basis of past expenditure and expected future expenditure, determines the amount of the levy.

The PCB has power to borrow money required to perform their functions up to a limit of £15 million. [*PA 1995, s 78(5)* and *regulation 2* of the *Occupational Pension Schemes (Pensions Compensation Board Limit on Borrowing) Regulations 1996 (SI 1996 No 1976)*].

Obtaining information

2.22 The PCB may require the trustees, managers, professional advisers, employers or any other person likely to hold documentation relevant to the discharge of the PCB's functions, to produce that documentation to the PCB.

Neglecting or refusing, without reasonable cause, to produce documents can result in a fine. Knowingly or recklessly providing false or misleading material particulars or intentionally or without reasonable cause altering, suppressing or concealing documents can result in a fine and/or imprisonment.

The PCB can be contacted at 11 Belgrave Road, London, SW1V 1RB, Tel: 020 7828 9794, Fax: 020 7931 7239.

The future of the PCB

2.23 The Government has sealed the fate of the PCB by publishing the first draft of the Pensions Bill in February 2004. There will be a new Pension Protection Fund ('PPF') which will provide members of defined benefit schemes with security in the event of insolvency by their employers. The Board will administer the PPF and, as part of that role, will also deal with claims of fraud, thereby taking on the functions of the PCB – which in turn is to be dissolved. Further details on the Pension Bill can be found at 2.29 below.

NATIONAL INSURANCE SERVICES TO PENSIONS INDUSTRY

2.24 NI Services to Pensions Industry (formerly the Contracted-Out Employments Group (COEG)) is a Directorate within the Inland Revenue National Insurance Contributions Office and is responsible for ensuring that the pension rights of employees contracted-out of the State Second Pension (S2P) (which replaced the State Earnings Related Pension Scheme (SERPS) with effect from 6 April 2002) are maintained and safeguarded (see chapter 4). In particular, NI Services to Pensions Industry is responsible for:

(*a*) dealing with the termination of contracted out employment, and all related matters;

(*b*) approving and supervising schemes if they cease to be contracted out;

(*c*) withdrawing approval of arrangements or refusing to approve them;

(*d*) issuing certificates of non-approval and discharge of liabilities directives;

(*e*) approval of arrangements for securing pension rights when a scheme ceases to contract-out;

2.25 *People involved with pensions*

(*f*) communicating with scheme authorities about the facility for checking National Insurance numbers, dates of birth etc. for funding purposes; and

(*g*) answering general queries regarding contracted-out arrangements (including personal pension arrangements).

NI Services to Pensions Industry can be contacted at the Inland Revenue, National Insurance Contributions Office, Service Development Group, Benton Park View, Newcastle upon Tyne, NE98 1ZZ. Contracting-out pensions helpline: 08459150150 (or 0191 213 5000). Fax: 0191 225 0067.

PENSIONS ADVISORY SERVICE

2.25 The Occupational Pensions Advisory Service ('OPAS'), is an independent, grant-aided, non-profit making company limited by guarantee with a network of local volunteer advisers, who are experienced pensions professionals. The aim of OPAS is to provide free assistance to members of the public with difficulties which they have failed to resolve with the trustees, administrators or pension provider of their pension scheme. The OPAS service is available to anyone who believes he or she has pension rights. This includes active members of pension schemes (including company, personal and stakeholder arrangements), pensioners, those with deferred pensions from previous employment, and dependants. OPAS can be contacted directly or via the Citizen's Advice Bureau.

OPAS's remit is to explain pension scheme benefits to members and liaise directly with trustees or administrators to provide further information to members or to assist a member in obtaining his correct legal entitlement from a pension scheme.

If OPAS is unable to resolve the problem but believe that the complaint is valid it will assist a member in making a formal complaint to the appropriate Ombudsman (the Pensions Ombudsman or the Personal Investment Authority Ombudsman). OPAS cannot:

(*a*) initiate legal action on a member's behalf;

(*b*) give financial advice;

(*c*) deal with complaints from a group or body of pension scheme members;

(*d*) act as a lobbying force for any improvement in pension scheme benefits;

(*e*) act through intermediaries;

People involved with pensions **2.27**

(f) offer advice on State pension benefits; or

(g) assist if legal proceedings have been initiated or if the Pensions Ombudsman (see 2.26 below) has already investigated a complaint.

OPAS can be contacted at 11 Belgrave Road, London, SW1V 1RB. National telephone helpline: 0845 6012923. Fax: 020 7233 8016. Email enquiries should be sent to: enquiries@opas.org.uk. Website: www.opas.org.uk).

PENSIONS OMBUDSMAN

The role of the Pensions Ombudsman

2.26 The Pensions Ombudsman's office was established on 1 October 1990. The Ombudsman is appointed by the Secretary of State under *section 145* of *PSA 1993* which also sets out his role. Under *PA 1995* the Ombudsman has power to appoint his own staff (with the approval of the Secretary of State for Work and Pensions) and has taken advantage of this by seeking to appoint professional staff from the pensions industry and legally qualified pensions experts. The Ombudsman's budget is paid for out of the levy imposed on all occupational pension schemes.

The role of the Pensions Ombudsman is to investigate and decide complaints and disputes about the way that pension schemes are run. He is completely independent and acts as an impartial adjudicator.

The Pensions Ombudsman is dealing with more and more disputes; this is due to a number of factors including:

(a) the extent of the Ombudsman's jurisdiction; and

(b) a greater awareness of the existence of his office (particularly as all pension schemes are now required to notify their members of the existence of both OPAS and the Pensions Ombudsman).

In the light of this increased activity on the part of the Pensions Ombudsman's office it is more likely that, should a dispute not be resolved by the trustees under the internal dispute resolution procedure or by OPAS, a complaint will be made to the Pensions Ombudsman.

Jurisdiction

2.27 The complaints and disputes which the Ombudsman may investigate are described in *section 146* of *PSA 1993* (as amended by the *Child Support, Pensions and Social Security Act 2000*) and are summarised in the following table:

2.27 *People involved with pensions*

Type of scheme	Who may complain or refer a dispute to the Ombudsman	Parties against whom a complaint may be made or a dispute may be referred to the Ombudsman	Nature of complaint or dispute
'Complaints of maladministration'			
Occupational or personal	By or on behalf of any actual or potential beneficiary.	Trustees, managers, employers and/or administrators.	Complaint of injustice in consequence of maladministration of the scheme.
Occupational	By or on behalf of any trustee or, manager of a scheme.	Trustees, Employers.	Complaint of maladministration of that scheme.
Occupational	An employer in relation to a scheme.	Trustees or managers of that scheme.	Complaint of maladministration of that scheme.
Occupational	By or on behalf of any trustee or manager of a scheme.	Trustees or managers of another scheme.	Complaint of maladministration of the other scheme.
Trust scheme	By or on behalf of an independent trustee.	Trustees or former trustees who are/were not independent trustees of that scheme.	Complaint of maladministration of that scheme.
'Disputes of fact or law'			
Occupational or personal	By any actual or potential beneficiary.	Trustees, managers and/or employers	Dispute of fact or law.
Occupational	By or on behalf of any trustee or manager of a scheme.	Trustees, managers or employers of that scheme. (Note that trustees/managers cannot refer disputes with managers; and employers cannot refer disputes with other employers.)	Dispute of fact or law.
Occupational	An employer in relation to a scheme.	Trustees or managers of that scheme.	Dispute of fact or law.
Occupational	By or on behalf of any party to the dispute.	Trustees or managers of another scheme.	Dispute of fact or law in relation to the other scheme.
'Complaints or disputes'			
Occupational	By or on behalf of at least half the trustees of the scheme.	Different trustees of the same scheme.	Dispute of fact or law or maladministration of that scheme.
Occupational subject to insolvency procedures	By or on behalf of the independent trustee who is a party to the dispute.	Trustees or former trustees of the scheme who are not independent.	Any dispute (in relation to a time when *section 22* of *PA 1995* applies).
Occupational	By or on behalf of the sole trustee.		Any question relating to the carrying out of functions of that trustee.

The word 'maladministration' is not defined in the legislation, although the Pensions Ombudsman's booklet describes it as including bias, neglect, inattention, delay, incompetence and arbitrariness. The complaint must include behaviour which constitutes maladministration which in turn has lead to 'injustice'. Again, this is not defined but is described by the Pension Ombudsman as not only including a financial loss, but incorporating distress, delay or inconvenience.

The *Personal and Occupational Pension Schemes (Pensions Ombudsman) Regulations 1996 (SI 1996 No 2475)* (*'Ombudsman Regulations'*), introduced under *PA 1995*, provide that the Ombudsman may not investigate or determine a complaint unless the internal dispute resolution procedure has first been followed. [*Ombudsman Regulations, reg 3*]. (The internal dispute resolution procedure is discussed in chapter 3). The only exception to this is where a complaint has been referred to the internal dispute procedure and the Ombudsman is satisfied that there is no prospect of a decision being reached within a reasonable period (*regulation 3(2)* of the *Ombudsman Regulations*).

Regulation 5 of the *Ombudsman Regulations* cover the time limits for referring a dispute to the Ombudsman's office. The Ombudsman is not permitted to investigate a complaint if it is received by him more than three years after the date on which the act or omission complained of occurred, or three years after the date on which the complainant knew or ought to have known of its occurrence. However, this period can be extended where the Ombudsman believes it was reasonable for a complaint not to be made before the end of this period, in which case the time limit may be extended to such further period as he considers reasonable (*regulation 5(3)* of the *Ombudsman Regulations*).

Regulation 2 of the *Ombudsman Regulations* also confirms the extension of the Ombudsman's jurisdiction to administrators of pension schemes. The definition of 'administrator' includes any person 'concerned' with the administration of a scheme. It has been held that the jurisdiction of the Ombudsman extends to situations where an insurance company manages a scheme from day to day (*Century Life v The Pensions Ombudsman (1995) PLR 135*) even where there are separate trustees and that, in these circumstances, the insurance company can fall within the definition of a 'manager'. It may also extend to other advisers in some circumstances, as shown in the Pension Ombudsman's determination in the 2003 case of *McMann Interiors Limited [L00552]*, when the incorrect actuarial guidance produced by the insurance company's actuary was held to be maladministration.

Investigating a complaint

2.28 The procedure which the Ombudsman follows during his investigations is set out in the *Personal and Occupational Pension Schemes (Pensions Ombudsman) (Procedure) Rules 1995 (SI 1995 No 1053)* ('The Procedure Regulations' as amended)); it is summarised in the booklet accompanying the complaint form, which is sent out, on request, to those wishing to bring a complaint. Upon receipt of the complaint form a caseworker at the Ombudsman's office will make an initial review of the case to decide whether it should

2.28 *People involved with pensions*

be accepted for formal investigation. Then the complaint form and accompanying papers, if any, are copied to the respondent (ie the employer, trustees, managers or administrators) and any other person against whom allegations are made in order to allow them an opportunity to respond to the allegations (*regulation 5(2)* of the *Procedure Regulations*).

The Ombudsman has powers to demand papers from parties (*section 150(1)* of *Part X* of *PSA 1993*) who may hold them and can also hold oral hearings if he considers this necessary (although to date, these have been rare (*regulation 10(1)* of *Procedure Regulations*)). Both the complainant and the respondent have an opportunity, with leave of the Ombudsman, to submit a supplementary statement and/or amend details of their original complaint/response (*regulations 3* and *7* of the *Procedure Regulations*).

In conducting the investigation the Ombudsman must comply with the statutory rules to ensure fairness and must also comply with the principles of natural justice (*Duffield v Pensions Ombudsman (1996) PLR 285*). In particular, he must:

(*a*)   make clear to the respondent the specific allegation(s) to be investigated;

(*b*)   express the substance of the allegation(s) in plain and simple language; and

(*c*)   disclose to the respondent all potentially relevant information obtained by him (particularly all evidence and representations made by the complainant).

The Court of Appeal's 1999 decision in *Edge v Pensions Ombudsman (1999) PLR 215* emphasised this need for the Ombudsman to observe the principles of natural justice. In particular, it was decided that he could not consider complaints which could only be remedied by steps which would adversely affect someone who was not a party to the investigation. Turning this the other way, in the recent case of *Marsh Mercer Pension Scheme v Pensions Ombudsman [2001] 16 PBLR (28) (the Williamson Case)* heard in the High Court, the Ombudsman's decision that a pension scheme should equalise all GMP's between men and women was set aside. Principally, it was held that the Pension Ombudsman had affected all members of the scheme, not only the complainant. Accordingly, he should have either declined jurisdiction or made a decision which would only affect the complainant.

After receiving a copy of the complaint the respondent has 21 days within which to produce a written reply (*regulation 6(3)* of the *Procedure Regulations*), although time extensions can be requested (*regulation 16(1)* of *Procedure Regulations*). The reply can include a reference to any other person (such as a manager or administrator of the scheme) who, in his opinion, has a direct interest in the subject matter of the complaint (*regulation 6(2)* of *Procedure Regulations*). It is not, however, possible for the respondent to join a third party as a second respondent. The Ombudsman will then issue a written determination of his decision, which will initially be sent out to both the respondent and the complainant in draft form for their comments. At this stage, changes to the determination can still be made.

After investigating the complaint, and examining the comments of both parties, the Ombudsman will issue a final written determination. This determination will direct the trustees or managers of the scheme concerned 'to take or refrain from taking' such action as the Ombudsman considers appropriate (*section 151(2)* of *Part X* of *PSA 1993*). Following a number of conflicting authorities it is now thought that the Pensions Ombudsman can award compensation for distress and inconvenience to a complainant although this is not beyond doubt. In *Westminster City Council v Haywood and the Pensions Ombudsman (1996) PLR 161*, the council appealed against the Ombudsman's directions for damages to be paid. The award was set aside by the High Court and an appeal was made to the Court of Appeal. The Court of Appeal did not rule on the matter as it held that the Ombudsman did not have the requisite power to hear the complaint at all.

However, the courts have made clear that if the Ombudsman does have power to award compensation he should consider not only the amount of compensation but also upon whom the ultimate liability for this will fall (for example, it may not be appropriate for a liability to fall on a scheme which is in deficit). The Ombudsman's determination is binding on the parties, subject only to an appeal to the High Court on a point of law, and can be enforced through the County Court. Costs cannot be awarded against a complainant, even if the complaint is not upheld.

It is becoming increasingly common for the Ombudsman's determinations to be appealed to the High Court under the High Court's general jurisdiction to hear appeals from any court, tribunal or person. This is referred to in Part 52 of the Civil Procedure Rules.

Notice of the appeal must be served and the appeal entered within 28 days after the date of the Ombudsman's determination. The appeal may only be made on a point of law and the Ombudsman himself will be a respondent to the Appeal (although in practice he may not appear), in addition to the original complainant. A High Court judge has discretion to remit matters on appeal to the Ombudsman for further consideration. The Ombudsman has stated that the number of appeals against his determinations may threaten his role as 'a provider of a cheap and informal service in relation to pension disputes'.

David Laverick (a solicitor who was Director for the North of England with the Office of the Local Government Ombudsman and more recently, former Chief Executive of the Family Health Services Appeal Authority), took over the role of Pensions Ombudsman from Dr Julian Farrand on 1 September 2001. In the first year of David Laverick's tenure, he has already changed the structure of the office. Complaints are now handled throughout their life in the office 'within one multi-disciplinary team'. This allows the complainant to understand who their point of contact is, as well as avoiding internal delays where files were

2.29 *People involved with pensions*

previously passed between members of staff. Further information on David Laverick's first year as Pension Ombudsman can be found in his annual report, published on the Pensions Ombudsman website (details of which are provided below).

The Pensions Ombudsman website can be found at www.pensions-ombudsman.org.uk and determinations issued from 1 April 2001 (and frequently requested determinations issued before 1 April 2000) are available for review. The Pensions Ombudsman can be contacted at 11 Belgrave Road, London, SW1V 1RB (Tel: 020 7834 9144; Fax: 020 7821 0065; E-mail: enquiries@pensions-ombudsman.org.uk).

PENSIONS REFORM

The Pensions Bill

2.29 In July 2002, the Pickering Report was published. One of its recommendations was that a new kind of regulator should be established which would be in essence 'more proactive than the existing Occupational Pensions Regulatory Authority' acting as an adviser as well as a regulator. This was only one of the many reforms the Government was envisioning should take place to simplify pensions and provide better security for members of occupational pension schemes.

The Government's programme for pensions reform continued with the publication of the Green Paper on 17 December 2002 and the White Paper: 'Simplicity, Security and Choice: Working and Saving for Retirement' in 2003. In February 2004 the Government then laid the Pensions Bill before Parliament. At the time of writing the Bill is still working its way through the Standing Committee who meet three times a week to discuss its contents and review each section. With 248 clauses the projected commencement date of 6 April 2005 appears rather optimistic. At this stage, the detail is to be left to the regulations and the codes of practice and therefore it is difficult to say with any certainty exactly what will be enacted in 2005. In its current draft, the Pensions Bill establishes a new fund, the PPF, and a new regulator, the Pensions Regulator. A summary of both is set out below. The Bill also has provision for the Secretary of State to appoint one or more persons to act as a deputy to the Pensions Ombudsman (see 2.26 to 2.28 above) on such terms as may be determined from time to time.

Pension Protection Fund

2.30 The Pensions Protection Fund ('PPF') 'will allow individuals to save with confidence' said Andrew Smith, Secretary of State for Work and Pensions on 12 February 2004. Its aim is to provide compensation to members of defined benefit schemes (and hybrid pension schemes) if an employer becomes insolvent and the value of the scheme's assets is less than the protected liabilities.

Broadly, it will provide compensation in two areas:

- 100% of pensions in payment for those who have reached the scheme's normal retirement age; and
- 90% of the accrued pensions of others.

Both of which will be subject to a salary cap, which is currently stated to be £25,000 (although this figure could be subject to change when the Pensions Bill and subsequent legislation receives royal assent).

The PPF will be funded by a levy on the scheme trustees or 'or any other prescribed person', for example an employer. The levy will be based on 'scheme factors' such as the number of members and the balance between active members and deferred members. The other element of the levy will be based on the 'risk factors', linked to the level of under-funding and other risk factors. However, for the first couple of years the levy is expected to be a flat rate. There will also be an administration levy and a fraud compensation levy.

An independent Board ('Board') will run the PPF. The Board will consist of a chairman (to be appointed by the Secretary of State) and directors drawn from relevant sectors of the pension and financial markets. The Board will be responsible for:

- paying the compensation;
- paying the fraud compensation (taking over the functions of the current Pensions Compensation Board);
- managing and calculating the applications of the three levies; and
- setting and overseeing the investment strategy.

Whilst the Board is considering an application and assessing a scheme, certain restrictions will be invoked in relation to the scheme in question, including:

- winding up not commencing and if it has been triggered when the Board became involved, it will stop;
- no transfer payments being made (except in certain prescribed circumstances);
- no new members being admitted and no further contributions being paid other than those outstanding at the time of the insolvency of the employer or a notification from the trustees of a scheme or from the Regulator; and
- benefits ceasing to accrue, although increases in benefits, which have already accrued, will be allowed.

There is also provision for appeal to the PPF Ombudsman who can review decisions taken by the Board and investigate complaints of maladministration.

2.31 *People involved with pensions*

The Pensions Regulator

2.31

'The Pensions Bill sets out proposals for a new Pensions Regulator. It will focus on protecting the benefits of pension scheme members, concentrating its effort on schemes where it assesses that there is a high risk of fraud, bad governance or poor administration.'

Andrew Smith, Secretary of State for Work and Pensions, February 2004.

The format of the Pensions Regulator is said to be based on the findings of the report of the Quinquennial Review of the Occupational Pensions Regulatory Authority and the findings of the Pickering Report in July 2002.

The aim of the approach is to create a Pensions Regulator that is able to identify and focus on the areas of greatest risk and provide better protection to members of work-based pension schemes. The Pensions Regulator will adopt a pro-active approach, by concentrating on the areas that threaten members' interests. The focus will be on fraud and maladministration, as well as tough new powers on under-funding. It will encourage best practice though an increased education and guidance role.

With the birth of the Pensions Regulator, we will see the demise of Opra. The functions of Opra will be transferred to the Pensions Regulator as well as having the range of increased powers which will assist to fulfil its objectives. Its powers will include:

- the ability to freeze a scheme whilst investigations take place to protect the members' benefits or scheme assets;
- increased powers covering the suspension and removal of trustees;
- increased whistleblowing responsibilities and duties to report certain events; and
- issuing improvement notices compelling schemes to take specific action to remedy problems within a specified timescale.

The governing board of the Pensions Regulator will consist of a chairman and at least six other members. The Secretary of State for Work and Pensions will appoint the chairman and the members of the board. To ensure that the Pensions Regulator is fair, some functions, such as making a penalty order, will be exercised by a Determinations Panel, a body appointed by the Regulator.

PROFESSIONAL BODIES

Pensions Management Institute (PMI)

2.32 The PMI was established in 1976 to promote professionalism amongst those working in the field of pensions. It is an independent non-political organisation which establishes, maintains and improves professional standards in every aspect of pension scheme management and consultancy. There are four grades of membership: the first is student membership, which is the introductory level for those wishing to study the Institute's examinations. After student membership, there are a further three grades of qualified membership; Ordinary Member (someone who has passed one of the Institute's examinations), Associate Member (someone who has passed the Institute's examinations and has three years' experience in pensions management or administration) and Fellowship (an individual who was an Associate and has eight years' experience, five of which must have been spent in a position with 'substantial pensions accountability and responsibility'). The PMI is directed by a Council of 16 elected fellows, who are actively involved in pension schemes.

The PMI also offers examinations for trustees in basic pensions knowledge, a qualification in administration, a Diploma in international employee benefits and the retirement provision certificate to name a few.

The PMI can be contacted at PMI House, 4–10 Artillery Lane, London, E1 7LS (Tel: 020 7247 1452. Fax: 020 7375 0603). E-mail: enquiries@pension-pmi.org.uk. Website: www.pensions-pmi.org.uk.)

The National Association of Pension Funds (NAPF)

2.33 The NAPF describes itself as the 'principal UK body representing the interests of the employer sponsored pensions movement'. Among its members are large and small companies, local authority and public sector bodies which provide pensions for over ten million employees and five million people in retirement, accounting for more than £600 billion of pension funds. NAPF members also include corporate trustees and other organisations providing professional advice to schemes. The NAPF have also recently announced a new membership category which allows individual trustees, trustee directors and chairmen of trustee boards of NAPF member funds to join. The NAPF's principle aim is to encourage pension provision by employers by representing the interests of members to the UK Government, Europe, regulators and other professional bodies (including the media). It seeks to achieve this by:

(*a*)   influencing public opinion;

(*b*)   consulting government bodies;

(*c*)   collecting and disseminating information on best practice and trends involving schemes;

(*d*)   publishing guidelines and information; and

(*e*)   providing education in the form of seminars and conferences.

The NAPF can be contacted at NIOC House, 4 Victoria Street, London SW1H 0NX (Tel: 020 7808 1300; Fax: 020 7222 7585); E-mail: mail@napf.co.uk; Website: www.napf.co.uk.

2.34 *People involved with pensions*

Information Commissioner

2.34 Although not a pensions body as such, the Information Commissioner's Office regulates the holding, use and protection of personal information relating to living individuals by data controllers. The Information Commissioner enforces and oversees the *Data Protection Act 1998* and the *Freedom of Information Act 2000*. The Commissioner is a UK independent supervisory authority.

The Information Commissioner maintains a public register of data controllers. Each register entry contains the names and address of the data controller and a general description of the processing of personal data by a data controller. The public register is updated weekly, but new notifications, renewal and amendments may take several weeks to appear during busy periods. Under the *Data Protection Act 1998* the Information Commissioner can, in certain circumstances, serve an information notice and assess compliance with the *Act* and where there has been a breach, serve an enforcement notice ordering compliance. The impact of the data protection legislation and in particular, the *Data Protection Act 1998* is considered further in Chapter 3.

The Information Commissioner's Office can be contacted at:

Wycliffe House
Water Lane
Wilmslow
Cheshire
SK9 5AF

Information Line: 01625 545 745/545 700 Website: www.informationcommissionergov.uk/

The Department for Work and Pensions

2.35 The Department for Work and Pensions (DWP) is responsible for employment, equality, benefits, pensions and child support. It was formed in June 2001 from parts of the former Department of Social Security and the Department for Education and Employment.

The DWP's priorities include (amongst others) a new pension service to provide information and support to today's and tomorrow's pensioners. The Secretary of State for Work and Pensions is currently Andrew Smith MP and he has overall responsibility for all work and pension matters. Malcolm Wicks MP is the Minister for Pensions whose responsibilities include (but are not limited to): pensions overview, pensions legislation, the Pensions Service and regulatory reform.

To contact the DWP or any minister write to the Correspondence Unit, Room 540, The Adelphi, 1 – 11 John Adam Street, London WC2N 6HT or via their website: www.dwp.gov.uk. Tel: 020 7712 2171. Fax: 020 7712 2386.

Chapter 3

Trustees

INTRODUCTION

3.1 The role of a pension scheme trustee is to apply the scheme assets for the benefit of scheme members and other beneficiaries, in accordance with the scheme's trust documents. This has long been a considerable responsibility and, under *PA 1995*, trustees' responsibilities increased further. Now the Pensions Bill, as introduced in the House of Commons on 10 February 2004, looks set to make further changes to the role of trustees, raising the standard of care that they are expected to attain while altering the requirements and procedure for member nominated trustees and internal dispute resolution. However, this is in Bill form and subject to change, and therefore *PA 1995* currently remains the key legislation guiding pension scheme trustees.

PA 1995 introduced civil penalties (of up to £5,000 for individuals and £50,000 for companies) and criminal penalties (ie fines and/or imprisonment) for breaches of certain provisions of the *PA 1995*. It also gives Opra power to suspend or prohibit a person from acting as a trustee of a particular scheme (most particularly, where he has been in serious or persistent breach of *PA 1995*) and disqualify a person from trusteeship of any scheme. appendix I summarises the penalties which may be imposed by Opra under *PA 1995*.

WHO CAN BE A TRUSTEE?

3.2 Anyone who is legally capable of holding property can act as a trustee. In effect this means that anyone aged 18 or over can be appointed as a trustee. There are, however, circumstances where an individual may be disqualified from being a trustee. Under *section 29* of *PA 1995*, a person is disqualified from acting as a trustee if, for example:

(*a*) he has been or is convicted of an offence involving dishonesty or deception;

(*b*) he is an undischarged bankrupt;

(*c*) he has made an arrangement with his creditors and has not been discharged in respect of it;

(*d*) he is disqualified as a company director; or

3.3 *Trustees*

(e) in the case of a trustee which is a company, any director of the company is disqualified for any of the reasons set out above.

Additionally Opra has the power to disqualify a person from being a trustee if, in their opinion, it is not desirable for him to act as a trustee of a trust scheme and the person (or company) either:

(i) has been prohibited from being a trustee by Opra; or

(ii) has been removed as a trustee by the Court on grounds of misconduct or mismanagement.

Opra may also disqualify a trustee from being a trustee of any trust scheme where:

(i) in the case of an individual, he is incapable, in the opinion of Opra, of acting as a trustee by reason of mental disorder; or

(ii) in the case of a company, it has gone into liquidation.

The consequences of disqualification are set out in *section 30* of *PA 1995*; see also chapter 2.

A trustee is prohibited from acting as actuary or auditor to the scheme of which he is trustee and so, in effect, the actuary and auditor will be prevented from acting as a trustee. This will not, however, prevent another person in the same firm from acting as a trustee. [*PA 1995, s 27* and the *Scheme Administration Regulations (SI 1996 No 1715), reg 7*].

TYPE OF TRUSTEE

Individual trustees and corporate trustees

3.3 A trustee will either be an individual, acting in a personal capacity, or a corporate body. A company will often be specifically formed to act as a trustee but any company may act as a trustee if its memorandum and articles of association contain the necessary powers. Although it is the company (not the directors) which is the trustee, in practical terms, the directors will take all the relevant trustee decisions. Whilst the exposure to liability of a director of a corporate trustee may be reduced (as compared with the position of an individual trustee), the director concerned may not escape all liability to the beneficiaries. For further discussion of this topic see 3.49 below.

A director (or other officer of a trustee company) is also subject to the same civil penalties as individual trustees under the *PA 1995* where it can be shown that a breach of the provisions of the *PA 1995* took place with his consent or connivance (*section 10(5)* of *PA 1995*). In these circumstances, Opra can prohibit him from acting as a trustee, in which case the trustee company is also prohibited from acting as a trustee. [*PA 1995, s 3(2)(c)*].

Trust corporations

3.4 A trust corporation is a corporate trustee which is:

(*a*) formed under the laws of the UK and has a place of business in the UK; and

(*b*) empowered by its constitution to act as a trustee; and

(*c*) either incorporated by a special Act of Parliament or Royal Charter or is a registered company with an issued share capital of at least £250,000, of which £100,000 is paid up. [See *Public Trustee (Custodian Trustee) Rules 1975* under *SI 1975 No 1189*].

A notable example of a trust corporation is the Public Trustee which was established by the *Public Trustee Act 1906*.

The main advantage of a trust corporation over a trustee company is that a trust corporation can give a valid receipt for the proceeds of a sale of land on its own. Otherwise at least two trustees will be necessary before a valid receipt can be given. [*TA 1925, s 14*].

Pensioneer trustees

3.5 This type of trustee is required by the Inland Revenue for a small self-administered pension scheme and is considered further in chapter 13.

Independent trustees

Statutory appointments

3.6 In certain circumstances an independent trustee must be appointed. This legislation was first introduced by the *Social Security Act 1990* but, since 6 April 1997, such appointments have been governed by *sections 22* to *26* of *PA 1995* and the *Occupational Pension Schemes (Independent Trustee) Regulations 1997 (SI 1997 No 252)* (the '*Independent Trustee Regulations 1997*'). Under this legislation, if, in relation to an occupational pension scheme which is established under trust:

(*a*) an insolvency practitioner is appointed in relation to an employer participating in the scheme; or

(*b*) the official receiver becomes:

- the liquidator or provisional liquidator of a company which is an employer; or
- the receiver and the manager, or the trustee, of the estate of a bankrupt who is an employer;

then it is the duty of the insolvency practitioner or official receiver to satisfy himself that, at all times, at least one of the trustees of the scheme is an independent person. If the insolvency practitioner or official receiver is not satisfied that this is the case he must appoint or secure the appointment of an independent person as a trustee of the scheme as soon as reasonably practicable. [*PA 1995, ss 22* and *23*].

The requirements do not apply to money purchase schemes, (including schemes which would be money purchase schemes except for the fact that they provide GMPs), unapproved schemes, schemes where all the members are trustees, schemes which provide only death benefits (and under the provisions of which no member has accrued rights), schemes under which all the benefits to be provided are secured by specifically allocated insurance policies or annuity contracts and 'section 615(6) schemes' (a type of approved scheme for expatriates). [*Independent Trustee Regulations 1997, reg 5*].

A person is 'independent' under *section 23(3)* of *PA 1995* and *regulation 2* of the *Independent Trustee Regulations 1997* only if:

(i) he has no interest in the assets of the employer or of the scheme, otherwise than as trustee of the scheme;

(ii) he has not provided services to the trustees or the employer, in relation to the scheme, at any time since the day which fell three years before *section 22* of *PA 1995* started to apply in relation to the scheme;

(iii) he is neither connected with nor an associate of:

- the employer;
- any person for the time being acting as an insolvency practitioner in relation to the employer; or
- the official receiver, acting in any of the capacities mentioned above in relation to the employer; or
- a person who has an interest in the assets of the employer or of the scheme, otherwise than as a trustee of the scheme; or
- a person who has provided services to the trustees or the employer, in relation to the scheme, during the past three years.

The terms 'connected' and 'associated' are defined in *section 123* of *PA 1995* by reference to *sections 249* and *435* of the *Insolvency Act 1986*. See chapter 13 for tables which illustrate the effect of these definitions.

If the official receiver or insolvency practitioner fails to appoint an independent trustee when such appointment is required under *section 23* of *PA 1995* a member may apply to court under *section 24* for an order requiring him to discharge his statutory duty to appoint.

An independent trustee may cease to be independent whilst acting as a trustee. For example, if he or his firm provide services (other, of course, than the specific service of acting as an independent trustee) to the scheme he will cease to be independent. (*Clark v Hicks [1992] PLR 213.*). If an independent trustee ceases to be independent in relation to the scheme, he must advise the insolvency practitioner or official receiver of that fact and (unless he is the sole trustee) will automatically cease to be a trustee of the scheme. [*PA 1995, s 25(4)*].

Where an independent trustee is required under *PA 1995*, all discretionary powers of the trustees, and any discretionary powers of the employers which are of a fiduciary nature, automatically vest in the independent trustee and are exercisable only by him irrespective of whether or not the previous trustees are removed from office. [*PA 1995, s 25(2)*].

The legislation is modified in relation to a multi-employer scheme, where an insolvency practitioner has been appointed or the official receiver has become liquidator or provisional liquidator in relation to an employer. In such a case, the requirement for an independent trustee only applies if the employer concerned is a trustee of the scheme or has (or has had, within the previous three years before *section 22* of *PA 1995* applied) sole power to appoint or remove any trustee, or any director of a company which is a trustee, of the scheme and no other employer has such power or another employer has the power but an insolvency practitioner has been appointed or the official receiver has become liquidator or provisional liquidator in relation to the employer.[*Independent Trustee Regulations, reg 3*].

If, immediately before the appointment of an independent trustee, there was no trustee of the scheme other than the employer, the employer will cease to be a trustee upon the appointment of the independent trustee [*PA 1995, s 25(1)*].

Where an independent trustee has been appointed under *section 22* of *PA 1995*, it is the responsibility of the trustees of that scheme to supply in writing to every member (excluding deferred members whose address is not known to the trustees) or relevant trade union within two months of the appointment of the independent trustee the following information:

(i) the name and address of any person who has been appointed as an independent trustee of the scheme under *section 23(1)(b)* of *PA 1995*;

(ii) the scale of fees that would be chargeable by any independent trustee and payable by the scheme;

(iii) details of the amounts charged to the scheme by any independent trustee in the past 12 months; and

(iv) the name and address of any trustee who is an independent person for the purposes of *section 23(1)(a)* of *PA 1995*. [*Independent Trustee Regulations 1997, reg 7.*]

The insolvency practitioner or official receiver must provide the trustees, as soon as practicable after the receipt of a request, with any information which the trustees may reasonably require for the purposes of the scheme. Any expenses incurred by the insolvency practitioner or the official receiver in complying with this request are recoverable by him as part of the expenses incurred by him in the discharge of his duties. [*PA 1995, s 26(1) and (2)*].

3.7 *Trustees*

Regardless of the provisions of the scheme's trust deed and rules, an independent trustee is entitled to be paid out of the scheme's resources his reasonable fees for acting as an independent trustee and any expenses reasonably incurred by him in doing so, and this is to be paid in priority to all other claims falling to be met out of the scheme's resources. [PA *1995, s 25(6)*].

Non-statutory appointments

3.7 An employer may still wish to appoint a trustee who is independent of the employer, even though there is no statutory requirement to make such an appointment. The main reason for doing so would be to demonstrate to the membership that the employer is not using its position as an employer to influence the trustee's decisions. Such an appointment would be made by exercising the scheme's power of appointment, as modified by *PA 1995* requirements in relation to member-nominated trustees (See 3.25 to 3.39 below).

Member-nominated trustees

3.8 *PA 1995* provides for the appointment of member-nominated trustees. This is dealt with in 3.25 to 3.39 below.

Constructive trustees

3.9 In certain circumstances, a person (although not formally appointed as such) may find that he is treated in law as being a trustee of a scheme. This will usually happen because the person has, by his conduct, assumed trustee-like responsibilities. For example, where a person has never validly been appointed as a trustee but has nevertheless acted as one, he could at law be regarded as a constructive trustee. Another example is where a scheme has a pensions committee whose role includes exercising discretionary functions which relate directly to members' interests.

EMPLOYMENT PROTECTION FOR TRUSTEES UNDER THE *EMPLOYMENT RIGHTS ACT 1996*

3.10 The *Employment Rights Act 1996* (*ERA 1996*) offers protection for employees who are trustees of their employer's occupational pension scheme (see also chapter 7). In particular the *ERA 1996*:

(*a*)   entitles employee trustees to time off to perform their trustee duties and undergo trustee training (*ERA 1996, s 58*);

(*b*)   entitles employee trustees to payment for time taken off due to his trustee role (*ERA 1996, s 59*);

(*c*)   permits employee trustees to complain to an employment tribunal if the employer has failed to comply with (*a*) or (*b*) above (*ERA 1996, s 60*) (generally, such a complaint must be made within three months (ERA 1996 s 62(2));

(*d*) provides that employee trustees are to be regarded as unfairly dismissed if the reason, or the principal reason for the dismissal is that they performed any functions as a trustee (*ERA 1996, s 102*).

Appointment, removal and discharge of trustees

3.11 Generally a scheme's documentation will contain a specific provision vesting the power to appoint and remove trustees, such power most frequently being vested in the principal employer. There are, in addition, statutory provisions governing the appointment and removal of trustees contained in the *Trustee Act 1925* and, in relation to member-nominated trustees, in *PA 1995* (see 3.25 to 3.39 below). In the majority of schemes, the power of appointment should be sufficiently widely drawn that reliance need not be placed on the *Trustee Act 1925*.

Section 36 of the *Trustee Act 1925* deals with the power of appointing new or additional trustees where a trustee:

(*a*) is dead;

(*b*) remains out of the UK for more than twelve months;

(*c*) desires to be discharged;

(*d*) refuses or is unfit to act; or

(*e*) is incapable of acting; or

(*f*) is an infant.

In such a situation, the power of appointment is exercisable by the person as specified in the governing documentation. If there is no-one in whom such a power is vested (for example, because the employer has been liquidated) or no-one who is able and willing to act, then the surviving or continuing trustee or trustees or his or the personal representatives of the last surviving or continuing trustee may make the appointment. The court also has power to appoint trustees, either in addition to or in substitution for existing trustees, where it is otherwise difficult or impracticable to do so.

Section 39 of the *Trustee Act 1925* permits the retirement of a trustee without a new appointment being made, provided that, after the trustee's retirement, there remains either a trust corporation or at least two individuals appointed. In such circumstances, the retiring trustee is deemed to be discharged from the trust, provided a deed is executed by the retiring trustee, the remaining trustees and the person who has the power to appoint trustees. The appointment of a trustee who is also a member of the scheme does not automatically end on his leaving employment or ceasing to be a member of the scheme (but see 3.26 below regarding member-nominated trustees).

3.12 *Trustees*

The Registrar of Occupational and Personal Pension Schemes (see chapter 2) must be informed of changes of trustees (however they are appointed or removed) within twelve months of the change taking place. [*Register of Occupational and Personal Pension Schemes Regulations 1997 (SI 1997 No 371, reg 5)*].

An employer's power to remove or appoint trustees is generally regarded as a fiduciary power and so must be exercised in the interests of the scheme's beneficiaries. If an employer disregards those interests, his position will be similar to that of a trustee who has committed a breach of trust. Whenever there is a change in the trustees of a pension scheme, it is important to ensure that the ownership of the assets of the pension fund is transferred accordingly. Land and chattels (but not stocks and shares) vest automatically in a new trustee if the appointment is by way of a deed. [*TA 1925, s 40*].

In addition to the power to suspend, prohibit and disqualify trustees referred to in 3.2 above, Opra also has power to appoint a trustee or trustees to a scheme. [*section 7, PA 1995*]. Such an appointment may be made following the prohibition or disqualification of a former trustee or may be where Opra is satisfied that an appointment is necessary:

(*a*) to ensure that the trustees as a whole have the necessary knowledge and skill for the proper administration of the scheme;

(*b*) to secure that the number of trustees is sufficient for the proper administration of the scheme; or

(*c*) to secure the proper use or application of the assets of the scheme.

Opra Note 5 ('Pensions Act 1995: Appointment of Trustees by Opra') provides guidance on the circumstances when it is deemed necessary by Opra for it to exercise these powers.

When making an order Opra may also determine the appropriate number of trustees for the proper administration of the scheme; require a trustee appointed by them to be paid fees and expenses out of the scheme's resources and provide for the removal or replacement of such a trustee. [*Section 7(5), PA 1995*]. Finally, in most cases, unlike a statutory independent trustee, a trustee appointed by Opra under *section 7* shall have the same powers and duties as the other trustees of the scheme, unless the order appointing the trustee restricts those powers and duties or provides that those powers and duties are to be exercised by the trustee so appointed to the exclusion of the other trustees. [*Section 8(3) and (4), PA 1995*].

TRUSTEES' DUTIES

3.12 The following are some of the general duties with which trustees must comply. Except where those duties are stated as arising under a particular piece of legislation, they are general trust law duties and may, to some extent, overlap. Trust law duties are fiduciary; they must be exercised in the best interests of the scheme's beneficiaries.

Whilst there is argument as to what may or may not be in the best interests of the members, it is an established principle that the best interests of the beneficiaries of a scheme are usually the best financial interests of those beneficiaries. In *Cowan v Scargill [1984] 2 All ER 750* Megarry stated: '... under a trust for the provision of financial benefits, the paramount duty of the trustees is to provide the greatest financial benefits for the present and future beneficiaries.' The question as to how this duty may be modified by the duty of trustees to consider and to specify in their statement of investment principles their approach to 'socially responsible investment' remains to be seen.

Duty not to profit from position as a trustee

3.13 As a general principle, a trustee may not receive any benefit from the scheme (including benefits payable by virtue of his being a member of the scheme) or exercise his powers in a way which creates a conflict between his personal interest and his duties to the scheme's beneficiaries. However, *section 39* of *PA 1995* provides that this principle does not apply to a trustee who is also a member of the scheme, if on exercising his powers in any manner, he benefits merely because the exercise of a power in that manner benefits (or may benefit) him as a scheme member (eg granting an augmentation to members' benefits). Despite this provision of *PA 1995*, a trustee may still not profit in other ways: for example, a trustee cannot buy assets from or sell assets to the scheme.

A trustee may, if the trust documents expressly permit it, be paid for acting as a trustee from out of the trust fund. An independent trustee appointed under *PA 1995* (see 3.6 above) may be paid his reasonable fees and expenses out of the trust fund regardless of whether this is permitted by the trust instrument. [*PA 1995, s 25(6)*]. Under *section 7(5)(b)* of *PA 1995*, Opra has the power to order that the fees and expenses of a trustee appointed by it are paid out of the scheme's resources.

Duty of prudence

3.14 Each trustee has an obligation to act as a prudent person would, not only in the conduct of his own affairs, but also in looking after the affairs of third parties. In doing so, trustees must also use any skills or expertise which they possess (so a higher standard will be required of professional trustees). (*Bartlett v Barclays Bank Trust Company Limited [1980] Ch 515* illustrates this point).

The Government has adopted Paul Myner's proposal in his report entitled 'Institutional investment in the United Kingdom: A Review' (6 March 2001) that trustees' duty of care in investment decision-making must be raised. The Government has said that it will legislate to enforce the new standard, and the Pensions Bill is an example of this intention. It has stated that where trustees are

3.15 Trustees

taking a decision, they should be able to take it with the care and skill of someone familiar with the issues concerned and that they should have appropriate training. If trustees do not wish to take investment decisions, they must delegate responsibility for these decisions to someone who does have the skills and resources to take them effectively. See 3.23 below for an outline of what issues trustees will have to be conversant with if the Pensions Bill is brought into force.

The *Trustee Act 2000* also introduced a new statutory duty of care for trustees, including trustees of occupational pension schemes (but they are excluded from the ambit of the duty as concerns the performance of their investment functions). The statutory duty of care is subject to the provisions of the trust documentation.

Duty to act in accordance with the trust deed and rules

3.15 Decisions and actions of trustees must be taken in accordance with the scheme's trust documents, and will be open to challenge if they are not. Trustees must therefore familiarise themselves with the scheme's documentation and if they are unsure as to the interpretation of any trust documentation (and any announcement which has not been incorporated into the trust documentation) suitable professional advice should be sought. Trustees should bear in mind that the effect of the trust deed and rules may be qualified or even contradicted by overriding legislation (a good example of this being *PA 1995* and regulations, and should, therefore, ensure that scheme documents are kept up to date. Opra recommends that amendments to the scheme are consolidated approximately every five years.

Duties relating to investment decisions

3.16 All trustees should familiarise themselves with their investment powers. This is one of the most fundamental duties of a trustee and must be exercised within the parameters of the trust deed, legislation and case law. *Section 34(1)* of *PA 1995* gives trustees of occupational pension schemes power 'to make an investment of any kind as if they were absolutely entitled to the assets of the scheme', subject only to any restrictions imposed by their scheme documents. If trustees disregard any such restrictions, they may find themselves liable for any resulting loss to the value of the fund.

The fact that trustees have power to make a particular investment does not necessarily mean that it is an appropriate investment for them to make; for instance, a high proportion of investment in property would be inappropriate in a fund where liquidity was required to pay pensions. Similarly, trustees should generally diversify their investments so as to maintain a balance between achieving good returns and protecting the fund against unnecessary risk.

PA 1995 contains specific provisions relating to the delegation by trustees of their investment discretions. (See chapter 10.) See also 3.14 above concerning the recommendations of the Myners Report, and 3.23 in relation to the Pensions Bill.

Duty to act impartially between the different classes of beneficiaries

3.17 A trustee must act fairly between different classes of beneficiary (namely pensioners, active members, deferred pensioners, contingent beneficiaries and, in some cases, prospective members) and must also act fairly as between individuals. In some cases the employer may also be regarded as a beneficiary (see paragraph 3.60 below). This issue could arise where trustees are considering the allocation of surplus on the winding-up of a scheme. The trustees must consider the interests of all beneficiaries (including, as appropriate, the employer as residual beneficiary) when deciding how to allocate any surplus.

That is not to say that all classes of beneficiary must be treated in an identical manner. In the case of *Edge v Pensions Ombudsman [1999] 49 PBLR (37)* Chadwick LJ summarised the current legal position when he confirmed that the duty to act impartially 'is no more than the ordinary duty which the law imposes on a person who is entrusted with the exercise of a discretionary power: that he exercises the power for the purpose for which it is given, giving proper consideration to the matters which are relevant and excluding from consideration matters which are irrelevant. If pension fund trustees do that, they cannot be criticised if they reach a decision which appears to prefer the claims of one interest – whether that of employers, current employees or pensioners – over others. The preference will be the result of a proper exercise of the discretionary power.' (paragraph 50)

Duty to seek appropriate professional advice on matters which a trustee does not understand

3.18 This duty is self-explanatory and should be complied with in areas where a trustee is not an expert. A trustee's decisions will generally be harder to challenge if it can be shown to have been based on suitable professional advice. Specific requirements as to the use of professional advisers have been introduced by *PA 1995* (see chapter 2).

Delegation

3.19 Trustees must not generally delegate their powers or discretions unless they are authorised to do so by the trust deed and rules (although there are some statutory powers of delegation, most notably the limited general power to delegate under *sections 25* of the *Trustee Act 1925*, the narrow default powers contained by the *Trustee Act 2000* and the power to delegate investment discretions under *section 34* of *PA 1995* – see chapter 10).

3.20   *Trustees*

It will generally be appropriate for the trustees (provided there is power under the scheme's documentation), to appoint a person (whether one of the trustees or an external person), as pensions manager to administer the scheme on a day to day basis. The person so appointed should be fully informed of the duties and responsibilities which the trustees have delegated to him. This person will usually be in the employment of the sponsoring company. The trustees may also appoint an outside party to provide other administration services such as payment of pensions, retention of their membership records and other services. There should be a written agreement between the trustees and the administrator not least because the trustees are required to ensure that the external administrator has appropriate systems in place to ensure the security and proper processing of membership data and the trustees should receive undertakings to that effect in the agreement. Some schemes use the employer's in-house staff to provide these services. The trustees are required to act prudently in choosing any person to whom they delegate any of their duties or responsibilities.

Duty to collect contributions

3.20   *PA 1995* requires trustees to arrange for a schedule of contributions (in the case of a final salary scheme – see *s 58*) or schedule of payments (in the case of a money purchase scheme – see *s 87*) to be prepared. In either case the schedule must show the rates of contributions payable and the dates on or before which such payments are due. *PA 1995* (and regulations made under it) set out the steps to be taken by the trustees if these contributions are not paid (see also chapter 11).

Duty to keep receipts, payments and records

3.21   *Section 49* of *PA 1995* requires trustees to keep any money received by them in a separate bank account kept at an institution authorised under the *Banking Act 1987*. Trustees may arrange to keep money in a separate account operated by a third party if they have entered into a suitable arrangement or contract. Any such arrangement or contract must ensure that records (including details of the amount paid, date of payment, and from whom it was paid, the amount paid out, the date of withdrawal and to whom, and the interest earned) are kept for at least six years and that all interest is credited to the scheme. [*Scheme Administration Regulations 1996, reg 11*].

Trustees are required by *section 49* of *PA 1995* and *regulation 13* of the *Scheme Administration Regulations* (*SI 1996 No 1715*) to keep written records of their meetings (including meetings of any of their number, for example sub-committees of the trustees), for at least six years from the end of the scheme year to which they relate, stating:

(*a*)   the date, time and place of the meeting;

(*b*)   the names of all the trustees invited to the meeting;

(c) the names of the trustees who attended the meeting and those who did not attend;

(d) the names of any professional advisers or other persons who attended the meeting;

(e) any decisions made at the meeting; and

(f) whether since the previous meeting there has been any occasion when a decision has been made by the trustees and if so the time, place and date of such a decision, and the names of the trustees who participated in the decision.

In addition, trustees are required by *section 49* of *PA 1995* and *regulation 12* of the *Scheme Administration Regulations* (*SI 1996 No 1715*) to keep, for at least six years from the end of the scheme year to which they relate, books and records relating to certain transactions including records of:

(i) any amount received in respect of any contribution payable in respect of an active member of the scheme;

(ii) the date on which a member joins the scheme;

(iii) payments of pensions and benefits;

(iv) payments made by or on behalf of the trustees to any person including a professional adviser, including the name and address of the person to whom the payment was made and the reason for that payment;

(v) any movement or transfer of assets from the trustees to any person including a professional adviser, including the name and address of the person to whom the assets were moved or transferred and the reason for that transaction;

(vi) the receipt or payment of money or assets in respect of the transfer of members into or out of the scheme along with certain prescribed details;

(vii) payments made to a member who leaves the scheme including the name of that member, the date of leaving, the member's entitlement at that date, the method used for calculating any entitlement under the scheme and how that entitlement was discharged;

(viii) payments made to the employer;

(ix) other payments to, and withdrawals from, the scheme, including the name and address of the person the payment was made to or from whom it was received; and

(x) generally where a scheme is wound up, details as to how protected rights were discharged (see chapter 4).

Disclosure of information to members

3.22 Trustees are obliged to disclose certain documents and information to scheme members, prospective members, beneficiaries and recognised trade

3.22 Trustees

unions under *section 41* of *PA 1995*, *section 113* of *PSA 1993* and the *Disclosure Regulations (SI 1996 No 1655)*. The requirements do not apply to schemes with only one member nor to schemes which only provide death benefits.

There are other regulations which also require disclosure of information to members in certain situations, eg divorce. These are referred to in the context of the relevant chapter in this book and a general summary of the information which must be disclosed is given at Appendix II.

Under the legislation, trustees are obliged to disclose, amongst other things, details of the scheme's governing documentation, basic scheme information (which is usually contained in the scheme's explanatory booklet), an annual report commenting on the accounts and funding of the scheme and details of benefits payable.

Most information need only be disclosed at the request of the member, prospective member, beneficiary or trade union although some information (most notably the basic scheme information) must be provided, as a matter of course, regardless of whether or not a request is made. The legislation does not entitle a person to receive information which is not relevant to his own rights or entitlements under the scheme.

Beneficiaries of a trust also have the right to compel trustees to disclose certain information so they can be satisfied that the trustees are performing their duties.

The right of a beneficiary to have access to certain trust documents was considered in the leading case of *Londonderry's Settlement re Peat v Walsh [1964] 3 All ER 855*. The Court of Appeal held that, whilst a beneficiary is entitled to see trust documents, this rule did not extend to requiring trustees to disclose documents recording the reasons behind the exercise of a discretion. Trust documents are documents in the possession of the trustees as trustees, which contains information about the trust which the beneficiaries are entitled to know and in which the beneficiaries have a proprietary interest.

The later case of *Wilson v Law Debenture Trust Corporation plc [1995] 2 All ER 337* applied the position in *Londonderry* more directly to the pension context. It showed that it is only in exceptional circumstances that trustees should be compelled to give reasons for the exercise of a discretion, for example where there was evidence that the trustees had failed to take into account a relevant consideration when exercising that discretion. However, the general presumption was that 'in the absence of evidence to the contrary a trustee has exercised his discretion properly' (paragraph 29).

However, this long help position has come under attack recently both in the courts and in front of the Pensions Ombudsman. Firstly, in the decision in *Allen v TKM Group Pension Trust Ltd (L00370 – 25 April 2002)* the current Pensions Ombudsman took a different view from the established position at law as concerns the disclosure of trustees' reasons. He decided in this case that it was maladministration for the trustees not to provide reasons for their decisions, not to have disclosed in full the minutes of their meetings and not to provide copies of the material they considered in taking their decision. This case illustrates the importance of trustees keeping clear records of decisions and it would appear that when making decisions, trustees will be expected by the Pensions Ombudsman to give their reasons or be at risk of a finding of maladministration.

Secondly, in *Schmidt v Rosewood Trust [2003] 2 WLR 1442, [2003] 3 All ER 76* a case before the Privy Council, the belief that a beneficiary's right to view trust documents was based on the sort of proprietary interest espoused in *Londonderry* was dismissed. Instead, the right was viewed as a part of the courts inherent powers of supervision over trusts. This is a difficult concept for a trustee to consider in practice, as it would seem to be at the court's discretion what documents ought to be disclosed to a beneficiary. However, trustees should seek to consider the competing interests of all different beneficiaries, the trustees and third parties when considering what ought to be disclosed.

The Pensions Bill

3.23 Following a trend highlighted by the Myners Report, the Pensions Bill may impose added burdens on pension scheme trustees. The Pensions Bill will require trustees to be conversant with:

(*a*)   the scheme's trust deed and rules;

(*b*)   the scheme's statement of investment principles;

(*c*)   where relevant, the scheme's statement of funding principles; and

(*d*)   any document detailing the trustees' policies generally.

The trustees will also have to have knowledge and understanding of the law relating to pensions and trusts, the principles relating to the investment of assets and scheme funding, as well as any other prescribed matter. Opra's successor will be given the power to issue codes of practice to detail how these requirements might be effected.

These burdens are equally imposed on the directors of corporate trustees.

TRUSTEES' MEETINGS

3.24 Specific provisions relating to the conduct of trustees' meetings are sometimes specified in the trust documents (or, in the case of a corporate trustee, its articles of association) and will typically cover such matters as how notice of meetings is to be given, that notice must be given to all the trustees, the number of trustees that will constitute a quorum, how a chairman of the trustees is to be appointed and whether he has a casting vote. If not set out in the trust documents (or articles), there should be some written record of these details, perhaps in a minute or resolution passed at a trustees' meeting.

3.25 *Trustees*

It is important to comply with these requirements. If, for example, notice has not been given to all of the trustees of a forthcoming meeting, then the validity of any resolutions passed at that meeting may subsequently be open to challenge.

Under *section 32* of *PA 1995*, unless the scheme provides otherwise, decisions of trustees may be made on the basis of a majority vote and trustees may set their own quorum for meetings at which majority decisions may be taken. In certain situations specific requirements apply (see *section 32(4)* of *PA 1995*), for example, the removal of a member-nominated trustee will require a unanimous vote (*section 16* of *PA 1995*). Notice of occasions where decisions may be taken by majority must be given to each trustee to whom it is reasonably practicable to give such notice.

Regulation 10 of the *Scheme Administration Regulations (SI 1996 No 1715)* specifies the way in which notice for trustees' meetings has to be given. The notice must state the date, time and place of the meeting and must be sent, at least ten business days before the meeting, to the last known address of each trustee entitled to attend the meeting or take part in the decision-making process. However, notice of a meeting does not have to be given where it is necessary, as a matter of urgency, for trustees to make a decision. [*Scheme Administration Regulations (SI 1996 No 1715), reg 9*].

MEMBER-NOMINATED TRUSTEES

Introduction

3.25 This section considers the current legislation concerning member-nominated trustees and directors, however, the Government has stated that the regime will be changing. Originally the Government proposed to introduce changes which were contained in the *Child Support, Pensions and Social Security Act 2000*. However, following the publication of the Pickering Report into the simplification of pensions legislation entitled 'A Simpler Way to Better Pensions' (published in July 2002), the Government decided not to introduce the changes to the member-nominated trustee regime which were proposed in that Act.

The Government set out its long-term intention to simplify the member-nominated trustee regime in its Green Paper published in December 2003 (CM 5677 'Simplicity, Security and Choice: Working and Saving for Retirement'), much of which has been subsequently carried through into the Pensions Bill. The Government wants schemes to have greater flexibility to manage themselves in a more efficient and effective way that reflects and supports the business of the sponsoring employer. It intends to reduce the level of prescription on selection processes for member-nominated trustees so that legislation focuses upon the outcome to be achieved – at least one-third of trustees should be member-nominated – and not, as now, on the detailed processes that schemes must follow to achieve that outcome (paragraph 61).

However, in view of the fact that schemes would soon be required to take action to review approval of their existing arrangements under the current law, the Government brought into force the *Occupational Pension Schemes (Member-nominated Trustees and Directors) Amendment Regulations 2002 (SI 2002 No 2327)* (the *'MNT Regulations 2002'*) on 6 October 2002. The intention of these *Regulations* is to continue the status quo so as to allow the Government sufficient time to develop a more simplified regime as set out in the Green Paper and Pensions Bill. For an outline of the proposals contained in the Pensions Bill see 3.39 below.

The *MNT Regulations 2002*:

(a) extend the validity of current approvals for existing arrangements from six years to ten years;

(b) allow employers to propose new arrangements at any time, with the consent of the trustees, for a period of up to four years.

Employers and trustees of schemes where the existing member nominated trustee arrangements are due to expire under the statutory six year period need do nothing to extend the approval period for the existing arrangements. The *MNT Regulations 2002* automatically extend the approval period by a further four years. Express periods within existing arrangements for the appointment of trustees or directors are not affected by the MNT Regulations 2002. Nominations and elections would still have to be undertaken in accordance with the existing arrangements.

Other than for the above changes the legislation remains basically unchanged. The provisions of the existing legislation are set out below.

Under *PA 1995* and the *Occupational Pension Schemes (Member-nominated Trustees and Directors) Regulations 1996 (SI 1996 No 1216)* ('the *MNT Regulations'*) the trustees of occupational pension schemes are under a duty to secure arrangements for the selection of member-nominated trustees ('MNTs') and the implementation of the arrangements and the appropriate rules (*PA 1995, s 16(1)*) unless the employer 'opts out' of the MNT requirements (see 3.30 below) or the scheme in question is exempt (see 3.26 below).

There is a parallel duty upon the directors of a corporate trustee to appoint member-nominated directors ('MNDs') where:

(a) the employer is 'connected' to the trustee company; or

(b) the trustee company is:
 - sole trustee of the scheme; or
 - all the other trustees are also companies.

Exceptions

3.26 There are some important exceptions to the application of the member-nomination requirements. For example, schemes where the trustees of the scheme consist of all the members, schemes with less than two members, certain executive schemes, relevant small self-administered schemes, death benefit only schemes, relevant industry-wide schemes, certain insured schemes, schemes with a statutory independent trustee and unapproved schemes. Schemes in winding-up and 'closed' schemes are not automatically exempt. [For more details see *PA 1995, ss 17(4), 19(4)* and the *MNT Regulations (SI 1996 No 1216), reg 4* (for MNTs) and *reg 6* (for MNDs)].

The arrangements

3.27 The trustees are required by *sections 16(3)* to *(8)* (MNTs) and *sections 18(3)* to *(7)* (MNDs) of *PA 1995* to put in place arrangements which ensure that:

(*a*)   persons are nominated and selected by 'qualifying members' under appropriate rules to become trustees. A 'qualifying member' in relation to a trust scheme means a person who is an active, deferred or pensioner member of the scheme (*PA 1995, s 21(7)*). A 'pensioner member' means a person who in respect of pensionable service under the scheme or by reason of transfer credits, is entitled to present payment of pension or other benefits (ie excluding dependent pensioners) (*PA 1995, s 124*);

(*b*)   the removal of an MNT/MND may only occur with the agreement of all the other trustees. However, the right under *section 303* of the *Companies Act 1985* for shareholders to remove directors can be exercised in respect of an MND unless the corporate trustee is a wholly-owned subsidiary of the employer of a single-employer scheme (*MNT Regulations (SI 1996 No 1216), Sch 3 para 7*);

(*c*)   vacancies are filled where there are insufficient nominations (or alternatively the arrangements may specify that vacancies may remain until the expiry of the next nomination period);

(*d*)   the term of office is not less than three and no more than six years;

(*e*)   the minimum number of MNTs/MNDs is:

- two where the scheme has more than a hundred members (or one, where there are less than a hundred members)(members in this context including active, deferred and pensioner members); and

- one third of the total number of trustees.

If the trustees propose a greater number of MNTs/MNDs the employer must consent to the trustees' proposals;

(*f*)   the functions of an MNT are exactly the same as all the other trustees. This requirement does not apply to MNDs or to Opra-appointed trustees or to independent trustees appointed under statute;

(*g*)   where a member appointed as an MNT/MND ceases membership of the scheme, he/she must resign from his/her post as MNT/MND.

The appropriate rules

3.28 The trustees must decide whether to formulate their own rules for the selection of MNTs/MNDs which must be approved under the statutory consultation procedure, or to adopt the prescribed selection rules which are set out in the MNT Regulations.

If the trustees adopt their own selection rules they must cover the following areas (*PA 1995, s 20(2) to (5)*):

(*a*) the procedure for nomination and selection of MNT/MND vacancies;

(*b*) eligibility for reselection – an MNT/MND must be eligible for re-selection at the end of his/her period of service;

(*c*) insufficient nominations – the rules must deal with the filling of vacancies;

(*d*) the requirement that (where the employer so requires) employer approval must be obtained where a person who is not a 'qualifying member' (see 3.27 above) is proposed for appointment as MNT/MND;

(*e*) nomination conditions.

The prescribed appropriate rules

3.29 The prescribed appropriate rules can be adopted by the trustees if they do not want to formulate their own selection rules and do not require member approval. The prescribed appropriate rules will apply by default if the trustees do not put in place their own rules in the timescale provided. [*PA 1995, s 20(1)(b)*].

The prescribed appropriate rules are designed to satisfy the minimum requirements of the *PA 1995* as it is intended that they should be capable of quick implementation. The requirements are set out in *Schedule 2* of the *MNT Regulations* (SI 1996 No 1216) and require the trustees to give notice only to active members of the scheme, requesting nominations within a specified period (which cannot be less than a month). Nominations can only be made, or supported by, active members of the scheme but any person may be nominated. Where a nominee is not a scheme member his nomination must either be approved by the employer or the employer must have stated that his approval is not required. The vacancies for member-nominated trustees shall then be filled following a ballot of the active members, unless the number of nominations does not exceed the number of vacancies, in which case the nominees shall become member-nominated trustees.

Employer's alternative arrangements (opt-out)

3.30 The employer can opt-out of the member-nomination requirements by proposing 'alternative arrangements'. The employer can propose a continuation

3.31 *Trustees*

of existing arrangements, or the adoption of new arrangements, for selecting the trustees of the scheme. [*PA 1995, s 17(1)(a)* (MNTs) and *s 19(1)(a)* (MNDs)]. In formulating its proposals, the employer is not constrained by any of the statutory requirements relating to MNTs/MNDs.

The procedure for the employer is as follows. The employer:

(a) where necessary, first obtain the consent of the trustees to the employer giving notice of opt out (*MNT Regulations (SI 1996 No 1216) reg 9(2)(d)*). This will not be necessary in every circumstance but where the employer decides to change the opt out arrangements mid-way through the four year statutory approval period, the consent requirement will need to be fulfilled.

(b) gives notice to the trustees at a 'permitted notice time' (see 3.34 below) that he intends to propose alternative arrangements; and

(c) before the end of the 'approval period':

- member approval to the proposals is obtained; and
- written notice is given by the employer to the trustees of their approval. [*MNT Regulations (SI 1996 No 1216), reg 9* (MNTs) and *reg 15* (MNDs)].

If the opt-out is approved by the membership, it is the trustees' duty to ensure that those arrangements are made and implemented (although, if continuation of the existing arrangements is proposed and approved, the trustees may not need to take any action).

The statutory consultation procedure

3.31 Under the *PA 1995*, members must be consulted where:

(a) the trustees are formulating their own selection rules; or

(b) the employer is proposing to opt out.

If the trustees are formulating their own selection rules, conduct of the approval procedure is the trustees' responsibility; if the employer proposes to opt out it is the employer's responsibility.

Active and pensioner members must be consulted under this procedure. It is only necessary to include 'such deferred members of the scheme as the trustees may determine'. If the employer is opting out he must, therefore, consult the trustees in advance on this issue. [*PA 1995, s 21(8)(a)(i)* and *(ii)*].

The MNT Regulations set out details of the approval procedure which is referred to as the 'statutory consultation procedure'. [*MNT Regulations (SI 1996 No 1216), Sch 1*].

Trustees/employers can decide in operating the statutory consultation procedure to adopt:

(i) the objection procedure; or

(ii) the ballot procedure.

The objection procedure

3.32 Under this procedure members are given at least one month to object to the proposals beginning with the date on which the notice is given. If 10 per cent (or 10,000 members if less) object to the proposals, a ballot may be held, if specified in the notice. If fewer than ten per cent of the members object, then the proposals are automatically approved.

The ballot procedure

3.33 Under this procedure, trustees/employers can put their proposals straight to the ballot. A majority of those eligible members voting can approve the proposals. If members reject the trustees' or the employer's proposals, the proposals may be withdrawn and refined before putting them to the members again. The overriding timescales (see 3.34 below) for gaining member approval and implementing the proposals must be adhered to.

The notice to eligible members must contain the prescribed information set out in the *MNT Regulations (SI 1996 No 1216) (Schedule 1)*. Records must be kept of the steps taken to comply with the procedure. If Opra considers that the requirements for implementing MNT/MND proposals or alternative arrangements have not been complied with, a penalty could be imposed and trustees or (where relevant) the employer could be fined. [*PA 1995, ss 3, 10, 17, 19* and *21*].

Timescales

Schemes established before 6 April 1997

3.34 Assuming that the employer did not opt-out, MNTs/MNDs had to be in place by the end of six months beginning with the commencement date of *PA 1995* ie by 5 October 1997. [*MNT Regulations (SI 1996 No 1216), regs 7(2) (MNTs)* and *13(2) (MNDs)*].

Employers who put forward alternative arrangements had one month beginning with the commencement date of *PA 1995* to initiate the 'opt-out' process. [*MNT Regulations, reg 9* (MNTs) and *reg 15* (MNDs)]. An employer's opt-out arrangements had to be approved by the membership by the end of the six months beginning with 6 April 1997 (ie by 5 October 1997). It is the trustees' responsibility to implement the opt-out arrangements by the end of six months beginning with the date on which the employer gives notice to the trustees that

3.35 Trustees

the opt out arrangements have been approved by the membership. [*PA 1995, ss 17(2)* (MNTs) and *19(2)* (MNDs) and the *MNT Regulations, regs 10* (MNTs) and *16* (MNDs)].

If the employer's opt-out failed, the trustees had six months beginning with the end of the opt-out approval period, or the date within the approval period that the employer notified the trustees that the opt-out had failed, to put in place MNT/MND arrangements in accordance with paragraphs 3.28 or 3.29 above. [*MNT Regulations, regs 2, 7* and *13*].

Schemes established after 6 April 1997

3.35 MNTs/MNDs must be in place by the end of six months beginning with the date that the MNT/MND requirement first applies to the scheme (usually the commencement date of the scheme), unless the employer opts out within one month of that date. If the opt-out fails, the trustees must put in place MNT/MND arrangements within six months of the opt-out failure. [*MNT Regulations, regs 7* (MNTs) and *13* (MNDs)].

Cessation of approval of appropriate rules and alternative arrangements

3.36 Following the bringing into force of the *MNT Regulations 2002*, member approval of arrangements where the employer gave notice to the trustees of his intention to opt out on or after 6 October 2002, will expire after four years. For those schemes where the opt out arrangements or the trustees' rules were approved prior to that date, in normal circumstances the arrangements would expire after six years but the effect of the *MNT Regulations 2002* is to extend the period of approval by another four years, making ten years in total. At the end of the statutory approval period, the appropriate rules/alternative arrangements will have to be put to the members for approval again to ensure that approval is maintained. [*MNT Regulations (SI 1996 No 1216), reg 20(1)*].

If an employer successfully opted out first time round (or subsequently), not more than twelve nor less than six months before the date on which approval of 'opt-out' arrangements ceases, the employer must notify the trustees that it intends to opt out again. Before the end of six months beginning with the date the employer notifies the trustees that it intends to opt out again, the employer must implement the statutory consultation procedure to obtain fresh members' approval of its proposals and notify the trustees of their approval (once obtained). [*MNT Regulations, regs 9* and *15*].

If an employer's attempt to opt out is unsuccessful, it can try to opt out again, broadly speaking, at the end of the ten/four years (depending upon whether member approval was originally obtained before or after 6 October 2002) following previous attempt. [*MNT Regulations, regs 9(2)* and *15(2)*].

In certain circumstances, approval of the appropriate rules/alternative arrangements may cease before the end of the normal approval period. This may happen as a result of a 'relevant event' (*MNT Regulations, reg 20(2)*), which under the *MNT Regulations* occurs where:

(a) there is bulk transfer without consent;

(b) an employer starts or ceases to be a participating employer in the scheme; or

(c) the employer becomes a wholly owned subsidiary of a company which is not an employer participating in the scheme.

If a relevant event has occurred and the trustees consider that it would be detrimental to the members' interests for approval of the appropriate rules/alternative arrangements to continue, they can serve notice upon the employer (for alternative arrangements) and the eligible members (for the appropriate rules) to the effect that approval will cease at the end of six months beginning with the date of service of that notice. [*MNT Regulations, regs 20(1)(g) and 20(1)(h)*]. If the employer had alternative arrangements in place prior to service of the notice, it can seek to 'opt-out' once again.

Special cases

3.37   The *MNT Regulations* modify the member-nomination provisions in their application, for instance, to multi-employer schemes, schemes where the employer is sole trustee and where a sole corporate trustee is trustee of several schemes. In the latter case, aggregation of the membership may take place. [*PA 1995, s 18(8), (9)* and *MNT Regulations (SI 1996 No 1216), Sch 3*].

Changes to the arrangements

3.38   One issue that is likely to arise from time to time is the extent to which the approved trustee arrangements can be changed during the statutory approval period. If the employer has opted out, prior to 6 October 2002 it was the case that generally the arrangements could not be changed during the six year period unless the original statutory consultation procedure notice provided sufficient latitude to do so. This has been changed by the *MNT Regulations 2002* which allow an employer to opt out at any time, provided it has gained the trustees' prior consent to it opting out at any time. [*MNT Regulations (SI 1996 No 1216), reg 9(2)(d)*]

It is open to the employer to withdraw the opt-out arrangements but, in broad terms, if this is done the employer cannot opt-out again for another four years. If the withdrawal of the arrangements took place before 6 October 2002, the employer would be unable to opt out again before a 10 year period has elapsed. Detailed provisions concerning the times when new arrangements can be put in place are set out in the *MNT Regulations*. [*MNT Regulations (SI 1996 No 1216), regs 9(2)(c), 15(2)(c), 20(1)(d)(ii) and 20(1)(f)(ii)*].

3.39 *Trustees*

Trustees can withdraw the existing arrangements at any time and propose new arrangements. [*MNT Regulations, regs 8* and *14*]. However, in adopting that course of action, the trustees would need to have regard to whether the change proposed is in the best interests of the members.

The Pensions Bill

3.39 The Pensions Bill, if it comes into force, will change the MNT/MND requirements for a scheme. As was indicated in the Government's Green Paper, the emphasis is on the principle of securing member representation, rather than rigid adherence to an imposed procedure.

The most notable change is that the employers right to opt out of the MNT/MND requirements, currently allowed under *PA 1995*, will be removed. Instead, the trustees of a scheme must ensure that at least one-third of the trustees or trustee directors are MNTs or MNDs respectively. This would have to be achieved within a reasonable timeframe, such timeframe to be determined in a code of practice to be issued by Opra's successor, the Pensions Regulator. The Bill also seeks to put in place a procedure to ensure that MNT/MND vacancies do not go unfilled for any length of time.

INTERNAL DISPUTE RESOLUTION

Introduction

3.40 *Section 50* of *PA 1995* requires trustees of occupational pension schemes to secure that arrangements are made and implemented for the resolution of disagreements about matters in relation to the scheme. Schemes of which all the members are trustees or which have only one member are exempt from the requirements. [*Occupational Pensions Schemes (Internal Dispute Resolution Procedures) Regulations 1996 (The 'Dispute Regulations') (SI 1996 No 1270), reg 8*].

The Act requires trustees to establish a two stage procedure. The arrangements must provide for a specified person (which could be one of the trustees or a third party, for example the administrator) to make an initial decision and for the trustees to reconsider the matter if the aggrieved individual so requests within six months of the initial decision.

Details of the internal dispute resolution procedure, including who to contact, must be set out in writing and must be given as part of the 'basic information about the scheme' under the *Disclosure Regulations* to:

(*a*) any prospective member or, if this is not practical, within two months of a person becoming a member;

(*b*) all members who were members on 6 April 1997, by 5 April 1998 at the latest; and

(c) any member, prospective member or beneficiary, the spouse of any member or prospective member and any independent trade union, within two months of them requesting the information. [*Disclosure Regulations (SI 1996 No 1655), reg 4 and sch 1*].

Ideally the internal dispute resolution procedure should be in addition to other efforts to resolve the matter and should be operated to provide an opportunity to resolve misunderstandings before they escalate. Bearing this in mind, it is useful to provide a simple form to assist individuals who have a complaint. Failing to help individuals with a grievance may, in some situations, amount to 'maladministration' and lead to criticism of the trustees.

The Government's Green Paper, 'Simplicity, Security and Choice: Working and Saving for Retirement' published in December 2002 included proposals to improve the procedures for dealing with internal disputes, in particular by giving scheme trustees more flexibility to adopt a procedure which best suits the scheme and its members and setting a shorter timescale for the process to be completed (paragraph 61). These proposals then formed the basis for parts of the Pensions Bill, which are discussed at 3.48 below.

Who can make a complaint?

3.41 Under the current legislation, the internal dispute resolution procedure must cover disagreements between the trustees and:

(a) members (ie active members, deferred pensioners and pensioners);

(b) the spouse or dependants of a deceased member;

(c) prospective members of the scheme. A 'prospective member' means any person who, under the terms of his contract or the scheme rules is:

  (i) an individual who has satisfied the eligibility conditions of the scheme and could elect to become a member;

  (ii) an individual who will satisfy the eligibility conditions providing he or she remains in employment for long enough;

  (iii) an individual who will automatically become a member unless he or she elects otherwise;

  (iv) an individual who may become a member if his or her employer consents;

(d) any individual who was in one of the above categories within the six months prior to making a complaint;

(e) any individual claiming to be within one of the above categories.

[Dispute Regulations (SI 1996 No 1270), reg 2].

A claimant can nominate a representative to make or continue the complaint on his behalf. If the claimant is incapable of acting for himself or is a minor, a family member or other appropriate person can bring or continue a claim. In the

3.42   *Trustees*

case of a deceased member, his personal representatives can bring or continue a claim. [*Dispute Regulations (SI 1996 No 1270), reg 3*].

The first stage of the procedure

The nominated person

3.42   The first stage of the procedure must provide for a person, on the application of a complainant, to give a decision on the disagreement. [*PA 1995, s 50(2)*]. *PA 1995* does not specify who the person should be; it could be one of the trustees, a committee of the trustees, the secretary to the trustees, the pensions manager, a representative of the employer (such as the personnel manager) or possibly an independent third party. When deciding who to appoint, trustees should consider factors such as:

(*a*)   whether the person they appoint will be able to deal with the disputes within the required time frame (see 3.46 below);

(*b*)   whether he will be, and be seen to be, impartial – it is unlikely that the procedure will be of any use in practice if members simply see it as a further hurdle to cross before being able to put a claim to OPAS or the Pensions Ombudsman;

(*c*)   whether he has sufficient knowledge of the scheme, and of pensions issues generally, to deal with complaints; and

(*d*)   if an independent third party is to be appointed, whether the scheme or the employer is able and willing to meet any cost involved.

It should be remembered that the person appointed has no special powers. His decisions are not binding on the trustees and he cannot exercise the trustees' powers. It is recommended formally to appoint the person chosen in writing, setting out parameters within which that person may operate.

Making an application

3.43   An application for a decision under the first stage must include:

(*a*)   the name, address, date of birth and National Insurance number of the complainant and, where the complaint is made by a spouse or dependant of a deceased member (or a person claiming to be a spouse or dependant), the relationship to the member and the member's full name, address, date of birth and National Insurance number must be stated;

(*b*)   the name and address of any representative acting on behalf of the complainant and whether that person's address is to be used for service of documents in relation to the complaint; and

(*c*)   a summary of the facts relating to the disagreement, with sufficient detail to show why the complainant is aggrieved.

The application must be signed by or on behalf of the complainant. [*Dispute Regulations (SI 1996 No 1270), reg 4*].

Giving a decision

3.44 The first stage decision, which will have to be given, in writing, within two months after receipt of the complaint, must include:

(*a*)   a statement of the decision;

(*b*)   a reference to any part of the scheme rules, trust deed or legislation which has formed the basis for the decision and where a discretion has been exercised, a reference to the relevant part of the scheme rules conferring it; and

(*c*)   a reference to the complainant's right to ask the trustees to consider the dispute within the appropriate time limit (see 3.45 below). [*Dispute Regulations (SI 1996 No 1270), reg 5(2)*].

If a decision is not given within two months, an interim reply must be sent immediately setting out the reasons for the delay and an expected date for the decision. [*Dispute Regulations (SI 1996 No 1270), reg 5(3)*].

Although the Regulations do not require an explanation for the decision to be given, it will usually be sensible to give one. An explanation should remove any misunderstandings and hopefully prevent the complainant proceeding to stage 2 of the process.

The second stage of the procedure

Making an application

3.45 The second stage of the procedure must oblige the trustees, on the application of a complainant, to reconsider the matter and give a decision or confirm a previous decision. [*PA 1995, s 50(2(b))*]. Such an application will have to be made by the complainant within six months of the date on which the first stage decision was given. [*Dispute Regulations (SI 1996 No 1270), reg 6*]. The application must include:

(*a*)   the name, address, date of birth and National Insurance number of the complainant and, where the complaint is made by a spouse or dependant of a deceased member (or a person claiming to be a spouse or dependant) the relationship to the member and the member's full name, address, date of birth and National Insurance number must be stated;

(*b*)   the name and address of any representative acting on behalf of the complainant and whether that person's address is to be used for service of documents in relation to the complaint;

(*c*)   a copy of the stage 1 decision;

3.46 *Trustees*

(*d*) a statement of the reason why the complainant is dissatisfied with the first stage decision; and

(*e*) a statement that the complainant wishes the disagreement to be reconsidered by the trustees.

The application must be signed by or on behalf of the complainant.

Giving a decision

3.46 The trustees will then have to give a decision within two months of receipt of the complaint, or explain the reason for the delay. [*Regulation 7* of the *Dispute Regulations* (*SI 1996 No 1270*)]. In addition to the information set out above, the second stage decision will have to include:

(*a*) a statement of the decision and an explanation as to whether and, if so, to what extent it either confirms or substitutes the previous decision;

(*b*) a reference to any part of the scheme rules, trust deed or legislation which has formed the basis for the decision and, where a discretion has been exercised, a reference to the relevant part of the scheme rules conferring it; and

(*c*) information about, and the address of, OPAS and the Pensions Ombudsman.

Although the legislation only requires a statement of the decision and an explanation as to whether and, if so, to what extent it confirms or substitutes the previous decision to be given, it will usually be sensible to give an explanation of the reasons for the decision.

Exempted disagreements and the Pensions Ombudsman

3.47 Under *regulation 9* of the *Dispute Regulations* (*SI 1996 No 1270*), internal dispute resolution procedure does not have to be used where proceedings have begun in a court or tribunal or where the Pensions Ombudsman has commenced an investigation into the same complaint. In addition, the Pensions Ombudsman will not be able to accept a complaint unless the complainant has first made full use of the internal dispute resolution procedure available to him unless he is satisfied that:

(*a*) there is no real prospect of a notice of a decision under the procedure being issued within a reasonable period from the date on which he received a complaint; and

(*b*) it is reasonable, in the circumstances that he should investigate and determine the complaint. [*Personal and Occupational Pension Schemes (Pensions Ombudsman) Regulations 1996* (*SI 1996 No 2475*), *reg 3*].

The Pensions Bill

3.48 The Pensions Bill proposes to make a number of key changes to how schemes should deal with dispute resolution. Most notably *section 50* of the *PA 1995* will be replaced and new *sections 50A* and *50B* will be added to *PA 1995*. There would no longer be a requirement for a two stage dispute resolution procedure, instead just one stage would be sufficient, though the trustees of a scheme would not be prevented from having a two stage process should they so desire.

New *section 50A* will define, in line with the *Occupational Pension Schemes (Internal Dispute Resolution Procedures) Regulations 1996 (SI 1996 No 1270)*, who can make an application under a scheme's internal dispute resolution procedure. New *section 50B* shows what particular issues should be dealt with by a scheme's internal dispute resolution procedure, such as time limits, and would also compel the procedure to allow a person who is party to a dispute to be represented by another person where that party has died, or is incapable of acting (for example, because of being a minor) or because another person has been nominated to act as a representative.

PROTECTION FROM LIABILITY

General

3.49 Trustees who act outside of their powers, or who act in a way which is in breach of their trust law duties to scheme beneficiaries, may find themselves personally liable to the beneficiaries for breach of trust. Alternatively, where they are in breach of a statutory duty, they will usually be liable as stated in the relevant Act (see appendix I, for instance, in relation to breaches of *PA 1995*). In practice, directors of a trustee company may have more protection than they would if they were individual trustees, although the position is not straightforward. The extent to which directors of a trustee company can be held directly liable to scheme beneficiaries was considered in the case of *HR v JAPT [1997] PLR 99* where the court found that directors of a trustee company do not normally owe a direct fiduciary duty to beneficiaries of a trust. The exception to this principle is where a director is found guilty of 'accessory liability'. In order to be found liable as an 'accessory' to a breach of trust, the director must have acted dishonestly in the sense described in the case of *Royal Brunei Airlines v Tan [1995] 2 AC 378* and referred to in the case of *JAPT* as follows:

> 'It is Royal Brunei dishonest for a person, unless there is a very good and compelling reason, to participate in a transaction if he knows it involves a misapplication of trust assets to the detriment of the beneficiaries or if he deliberately closes his eyes and ears or chooses deliberately not to ask questions so as to avoid his learning something he would rather not know and for him then to proceed regardless' (paragraph 61).

There are, however, some protections from liability available to trustees. These are considered below.

3.50 *Trustees*

Exclusion clause in the trust deed

3.50 Most pension schemes' trust deeds will contain a provision under which the trustees (or directors of a trustee company) will not be liable except in limited circumstances. These circumstances will typically be conduct which involves some degree of bad faith or negligence on the part of the person sought to be made liable. 'Wilful neglect or default' is a phrase commonly used in exclusion clauses; 'deliberate and knowing breach of trust' is another. Clauses of this nature have been upheld by the courts in relation to trustees' liabilities to beneficiaries (eg Walton J in *Re Imperial Foods Ltd Pension Scheme [1986] 2 All ER 802*), although such wording in a trust deed would not be sufficient to exclude liabilities to third parties (ie liabilities to persons with whom the trustees deal who are not beneficiaries or parties to the trust deed; such liability will most usually arise under the terms of a contract with that third party, rather than under the terms of the trust deed), or penalties imposed by statute, most particularly, those imposed under *PA 1995* (see appendix I) which cannot be met from the assets of the scheme.

Section 2(2) of the *Unfair Contract Terms Act 1977* restricts the validity of certain clauses which seek to exclude liability for negligence. However, this restriction applies only to business liability, and so (in the context of actions brought by beneficiaries) is likely only to apply to professional trustees who charge for acting as such; it is for this reason that some exclusion clauses in trust deeds specify that liability for the negligence of a professional trustee is not excluded.

Section 33(1) of *PA 1995* prohibits the exclusion or restriction of any liability for breach of an obligation under any rule of law to take care or exercise skill in the performance of any investment functions (where that function is exercisable by a trustee of the scheme or by a person to whom that function has been delegated under *section 34* of *PA 1995*). However, where the trustees have delegated to a fund manager under *section 34, section 34(4)* relieves of them of responsibility for any act or default of that fund manager in the exercise of any discretion delegated to him, so long as they (or anybody else making the delegation on their behalf) have taken all reasonable steps to satisfy themselves as to the fund manager's knowledge and experience and that he is carrying out his work competently and complying with the requirements of *section 36* of *PA 1995* (see Chapter 10).

It should be noted that the Law Commission in January 2003 issued a Consultation Paper (CP171) on exemption clauses, entitled 'Trustee Exemption Clauses'. The Law Commission's view is that increased regulation of trustee exemption clauses is necessary because their increased use in recent years has reduced the protection afforded to beneficiaries in the event of breach of trust. The Law Commission therefore proposes to draw a distinction between the professional and the lay trustee. The Consultation Paper suggests that professional trustees should no longer be able to rely on clauses which exclude their inability for breach of trust arising from negligence nor would professional trustees be able to be indemnified from the trust fund in respect of breaches of trust arising from negligence. Professional (and lay) trustees would however have the right to use trust assets to buy indemnity cover. Lay trustees would still be able to benefit from exemption/indemnity clauses. The closing date for comments upon the proposals in the Consultation Paper was 30 April 2003, and further proposals are awaited at the time of writing.

Indemnity clause in the trust deed

3.51 A scheme's trust deed will often provide for the trustees to be indemnified against liability. The clause may entitle them to be indemnified by the employers or from the trust fund or from the trust fund in the event of default on the indemnity by the employer. In any case, any kind of liability which is not covered by the trust deed's exclusion clause will typically also not be covered by the indemnity clause.

Section 310(1) of the *Companies Act 1985* throws some doubt over the validity of an indemnity from the scheme's principal employer. This section renders void:

'(1) ... any provision, whether contained in a company's articles or any contract with the company or otherwise, for exempting any officer of the company or any person (whether an officer or not) employed by the company as auditor from, or indemnifying him against, any liability which by virtue of any rule of law would otherwise attach to him in respect of any negligence, default, breach of duty or breach of trust of which he may be guilty in relation to the company'.

However, *section 310* is amended by *section 137(1)* of the *Companies Act 1989* so that a company is not prevented 'from purchasing and maintaining for any such officer or auditor insurance against any such liability'.

Two points arise from *section 310*:

(*a*) there is the question as to whether the directors of a trust company (who may be seeking to rely on the indemnity) are also officers of (or auditors employed by) the company providing the indemnity. If not, then *section 310* does not appear to apply to the indemnity; and

(*b*) the section applies only to liability 'in relation to the company'. The question as to whether the liability does relate to the company will depend upon the facts of a given case.

Where there is a corporate trustee with directors who are also officers of the company providing the indemnity (often the principal employer), as discussed in (*a*) above, it has been possible to argue that, as is shown in (*b*) above, they are not acting 'in relation to the company' and therefore the indemnity would remain valid. This has not been tested in court, though would seem to have some merit. However, this argument would seem less likely to succeed where the principal employer (and company providing the indemnity) and trustee are one and the same entity. Here it becomes more difficult to separate the role of the

3.52 *Trustees*

directors acting as trustee directors and as officers of the indemnifying company, as in both cases they would always be acting 'in relation to the company'.

It may be hard for trustees to justify as being in the members' best interests an amendment to a scheme so as to enable them to be indemnified from the trust fund if no such indemnity previously existed. In any event, *section 31(1)* of *PA 1995* prevents trustees from being indemnified out of the fund in respect of fines or civil penalties under the Act (see appendix I).

Court's discretion

3.52 Under *section 61* of the *Trustee Act 1925*:

> 'If it appears to the court that a trustee ...is or may be personally liable for breach of trust ...but has acted honestly and reasonably, and ought fairly to be excused for the breach of trust ...the court may relieve him either wholly or partly from personal liability for the same'.

This is only a discretion of the court, and trustees should be reluctant to place too much reliance on it. In most situations the trustees are likely to rely on the indemnity in the Trust Deed and Rules and only where none exists, would the trustees need to seek an Order under the provisions of this section.

Insurance

3.53 Trustees may wish to take out insurance against liability, but should be mindful as to how far the terms of the policy restrict the circumstances in which they could make a claim. If it is intended that the premiums be paid from the trust fund, advice should be sought as to whether the circumstances and the terms of the scheme will permit this. In any event, *section 31(2)* of *PA 1995* prohibits the payment of premiums from a scheme's assets to insure against the imposition of fines or civil penalties under the *PA 1995* (see appendix I). More commonly insurance tends to be used to protect the trustees against claims by 'lost beneficiaries', rather than liabilities generally in relation to their actions.

It can therefore be seen that *PA 1995* does considerably more to introduce penalties and sanctions for trustees than it does to introduce protections for trustees from liability.

DATA PROTECTION ACT 1998

3.54 Pension fund trustees will need to comply with the *Data Protection Act 1998* (the *DPA 1998*) which, despite its title, came into force on 1 March 2000. In most cases trustees will be 'data controllers' since they determine the purpose for which and the manner in which information is held and processed. The emphasis of *DPA 1998* is on compliance with the data protection principles and the rights of individuals in respect of whom information is held.

The data protection principles have been modified from previous legislation. In summary, the data protection principles require that information relating to individuals must be:

(a) processed fairly and lawfully – in certain circumstances it will be necessary to obtain the consent of the data subject and provide certain information to him;

(b) obtained and processed only for specified and lawful purposes;

(c) adequate, relevant and not excessive;

(d) accurate and kept up to date;

(e) kept for no longer than necessary;

(f) processed in accordance with the rights of data subjects;

(g) kept secure, by ensuring appropriate technical and organisational measures are in place; and

(h) not transferred outside the European Economic Area unless adequate data protection safeguards are in place.

The new law enhances the rights of data subjects by giving them:

(i) stronger rights of access to information;

(ii) express rights to prevent direct marketing;

(iii) rights to rectify and erase inaccurate data;

(iv) rights relating to decisions taken by computer;

(v) certain rights to prevent processing of data; and

(vi) greater rights to compensation.

Manual data

3.55 Paper records as well as computerised data are covered by the *DPA 1998*. Paper records will be covered if they are part of a 'structured filing system' where specific information relating to a particular individual can be readily accessed. Manual files organised by reference to individual policy holders will, therefore, be caught.

Transitional relief

3.56 There was transitional relief from part (but not all) of *DPA 1998* for computerised records until October 2001. There is also relief from many provisions of *DPA 1998* for a further six years for manual data. These reliefs will only apply if the data is part of a collection which existed before 24 October 1998. Data added to such collections after that date will also benefit from this relief. However, data controllers will need to comply with the whole of *DPA 1998* straightaway in relation to new collections of data created after that date.

3.57   *Trustees*

Registration of pension fund trustees

3.57   The registration procedure is being simplified although precise details are still awaited. Advice on registration can be sought from the Data Protection Office. They have indicated that it may be appropriate for pension fund trustees to register for the purpose of 'investment management' in addition to 'pensions administration' which is the main (if not sole) purpose for which pension fund trustees hold data.

Data processors

3.58   Under *DPA 1998*, data processors (known as computer bureaux under *The Data Protection Act 1984*) will no longer need to register. This means that pension fund administrators (who often act as agents on behalf of pension fund trustees in terms of processing data) will not need to register in that capacity.

A data controller will, however, need to ensure that its data processors comply with data protection legislation. A data controller will need to have a contract in writing with its data processors under which they agree only to act on the instructions of the data controller and to put in place sufficient technical and organisational measures to keep data secure. This is to comply with the seventh data protection principle referred to above. Processing is defined extremely widely and includes merely holding data on behalf of another and so would encompass data held by the likes of administrators and actuaries.

Practical steps to ensure compliance

3.59   Pension fund trustees would do well to take the following steps to show that they are complying with the new legislation:

(*a*)   appoint one person to take overall responsibility for data protection;

(*b*)   carry out an audit of current personal data activity;

(*c*)   update the forms used to collect personal data;

(*d*)   ensure that suitable agreements are in place with all data processors;

(*e*)   address security issues both technical and organisational;

(*f*)   establish procedures to deal with data subjects' requests; and

(*g*)   review how necessary it is to collect data, especially 'sensitive' data as defined under the 1998 Act.

Of particular impact on pension fund trustees will be:

(i)   changes to data protection notices which need to be given to scheme members;

(ii)   the requirement to obtain express member consent for the use of 'sensitive' data;

(iii) the security obligations, particularly with regard to data held by third parties; and

(iv) restrictions on transferring data outside Europe.

TRUSTEES' DUTIES TO THE EMPLOYER

3.60 Whilst it is true that trustees must act in the best interests (and that usually means best financial interests) of their members and other beneficiaries, case law requires trustees in certain circumstances to take into consideration the interests of the sponsoring employer. This follows on from the trustees' fundamental duty to give effect to the trust deed and rules which in turn is a reflection of the employer's contractual promise made to its employees to provide pension benefits. The trust deed and rules will confer a variety of powers, duties and discretions on the trustees to enable them to give effect to the contractual promises of the employer to the employees. How the trustees exercise their powers can have a significant impact on the ultimate costs borne by the employers.

An employer's interests in the occupational pension scheme which it sponsors are varied. One particular example of a trustee power which can significantly affect the interests of the employer is the trustee's power of investment. In a balance of cost scheme, any failure by the trustees to obtain reasonable returns on the investment of the pension fund will result in the employer having to make greater contributions to the scheme to fund the promised benefits. In support of this is *section 35(5)(b)* of *PA 1995* which obliges trustees to consult the employer when preparing or revising the statement of investment principles. Whilst the consultation process does not require the consent of the employer, the employer nevertheless may have rights against the trustees, should they cause loss to the employer by exercising their powers in an imprudent manner.

Another example where the employer's interests are evident is in the case of the distribution of a surplus, especially upon the winding-up of a scheme. There is a significant body of case law on this subject, the most useful of which is the case of *Thrells Limited v Lomas [1993] 1 WLR 456*. In *Thrells* the scheme was winding up and was in surplus with an insolvent employer. The ultimate beneficiaries of any refund of surplus to the employer would be the creditors. The case set out factors that trustees should take into account in deciding how to exercise their discretion on allocation of surplus monies. The principal factors to consider are the scope of the discretion and its purpose, the source of the surplus (for example, is it due to excessive contributions from the employer), the size of the surplus, the financial position of the employer and the needs of members of the scheme. The usual duties of trustees will also apply when exercising their powers and they should, therefore, give proper consideration to all matters relevant to the exercise of the power.

This duty to the employer was noted by the Court in *Edge v Pensions Ombudsman [1998] Ch 512* where the Court stated '... the proposition that the trustees were not entitled, when deciding how to reduce the £29.9 million surplus, to

3.60 *Trustees*

take any account of the position of the employers is one with which I emphatically disagree. The Employers play a critical part in this Pension Scheme. They have to pay contributions sufficient to keep the Scheme solvent.'

It is clear from the above that it would be wrong for the trustees blindly to ignore the interests of the employer when exercising their powers, especially in the often delicate situation of distributing a surplus. On those occasions when it is appropriate for the trustees to enter into negotiations with the employer for benefit improvements, the trustees should be mindful that any extra financial burden which they succeed in placing upon the employer could ultimately jeopardise the ability of the employer to continue sponsoring the scheme. The circumstances of each exercise of the trustees' powers should be carefully examined and the rights of the employer taken into consideration.

Chapter 4

Contracting-out

INTRODUCTION

4.1 The combination of a 'pay as you go' arrangement, where the contributions of the workers pay for the pensions of the pensioners, and an ageing population has placed a heavy burden on the State. As a consequence, when the State earnings-related pension scheme ('SERPS') was introduced in 1978, the Government decided to allow employers to contract-out of it if the contributions were instead paid to a suitable private arrangement. Initially, only final salary occupational pension schemes were permitted to contract-out of SERPS but in 1988 the facility was made available to money purchase arrangements.

Employers and employees who participate in a contracted-out scheme pay a reduced rate of National Insurance contributions. The reduction is known as the contracted-out rebate. The total contracted-out rebate for final salary schemes 5.1 per cent of band earnings, ie earnings between the lower and upper earning limits; the employee benefits from a 1.6 per cent reduction, and the employer from a 3.5 per cent reduction in the contributions paid) has remained the same for the tax year 2004/2005. The lower earnings limit for the tax year 2004/2005 is £4,108 and the upper earnings limit is £31,720. These limits are increased each year.) The calculation of the contracted-out rebate for money purchase schemes depends on the age of the member (see 4.23 below).

Commentators have criticised these rebates as not fully reflecting the cost of providing pensions due to increased life expectancy and lower interest rates. In addition, some believe it will be difficult to justify the use of an occupational money purchase scheme for contracting-out under new terms, since individuals may enjoy much higher rebates (at least 1 per cent of band earnings higher) under stakeholder/personal pension plans.

However, the Government has gone some way to addressing these concerns by replacing SERPS from April 2002 with the State Second Pension ('S2P'). The aim of S2P is to provide a bigger pension than SERPS.

The new state pension is described in more detail in chapter 1 and in 4.69 and 4.73 below. It is proposed that rebates remain earnings-related.

Further changes to simplify contracting out legislation were introduced by the *Occupational and Personal Pension Schemes* (*Contracting-Out*) (*Miscellaneous Amendments*) *Regulations 2002* (*SI 2002 No 681*) which came into force from 6 April 2002.

4.2 Contracting-out

This chapter examines the way in which occupational pension schemes can contract-out. Contracting-out by way of an appropriate personal pension scheme is dealt with in chapter 15. The requirements a scheme must fulfil in order to contract-out of SERPS are set out in *Part III* of *PSA 1993* (as amended by *PA 1995* and the *Social Security Contributions (Transfer of Functions etc.) Act 1999*), the *Occupational Pension Schemes (Contracting-Out) Regulations 1996 (SI 1996 No 1172)* ('the *Contracting-Out Regulations*') (as amended by the *Personal and Occupational Pension Schemes (Miscellaneous Amendments) Regulations 1997 (SI 1997 No 786)*) and, in the case of a money purchase scheme, the *Personal and Occupational Pension Schemes (Protected Rights) Regulations 1996 (SI 1996 No 1537)* ('the *Protected Rights Regulations*') and the *Social Security Contributions (Transfer of Functions etc.) Act 1999*. In the case of both final salary and money purchase schemes these *Regulations* have been amended by the *Occupational and Personal Pension Schemes (Contracting-Out) (Miscellaneous Amendments) Regulations 2002 (SI 2002 No 681)*.

A BRIEF HISTORY OF CONTRACTING-OUT

Final salary schemes

4.2 Initially, final salary schemes could only contract-out if they satisfied two tests:

(*a*) a qualitative test, namely the requisite benefit test, which in simple terms meant providing $\frac{1}{80}$th of pensionable salary for each year of pensionable service; and

(*b*) a quantitative test, namely the provision of a guaranteed minimum pension ('GMP') broadly equivalent to the SERPS entitlement being given up.

The requisite benefit test was abolished in November 1986 and schemes only had to satisfy the GMP test in order to contract-out. As from 6 April 1997 ('the appointed date'), final salary schemes wishing to contract-out are once again required to pass a scheme quality test but for future service do not have to satisfy the GMP test. This new quality test, introduced by *PA 1995*, is based loosely on the requisite benefit test; it aims to ensure that a certain overall level of benefits will be provided for members of the scheme generally. Although members of final salary contracted-out schemes ceased accruing GMPs on 5 April 1997, GMPs are retained in respect of service completed before that date and so, in order to continue to be contracted-out, schemes must continue to comply with the requirements relating to GMPs (see 4.11 to 4.16 below).

Money purchase arrangements

4.3 In April 1988 it became possible for members of money purchase arrangements, including personal pension schemes and free standing additional voluntary contribution schemes, to contract-out of SERPS. In the case of an employer-sponsored arrangement, generally a contracted-out money purchase scheme ('COMPS'), each member has to be provided with benefits based on contributions actually made and the investment return on those contributions. The employer's contributions must be at least equal to the contracted-out rebate to the COMPS.

In order to promote contracting-out for new arrangements, the Department of Social Security (now known as the Department of Work and Pensions ('DWP')) paid an 'incentive' of two per cent of earnings between the upper and lower earnings limit. This payment ceased in April 1993 but from 6 April 1997 age-related rebates are payable in addition to the flat rate contracted-out rebate. Irrespective of how an individual is contracted-out, the same reduced S2P pension is paid to an individual by the State.

THE CONTRACTING-OUT CERTIFICATE

4.4 In order to deduct and pay National Insurance contributions at the reduced rate, an employer must have a valid contracting-out certificate.

A contracting-out certificate is issued by reference to the employments which are contracted-out. The certificate generally has to relate to all employments with an employer but may exclude:

(*a*) those employees who opt in writing not to join the part of the scheme which is contracted-out, provided that this is allowed under the rules of the scheme; and

(*b*) those employees who are within five years of normal pension age at the date of joining the scheme.

On 6 April 1997, the Secretary of State assumed responsibility (from the Occupational Pensions Board) for the issue, variation and withdrawal of contracting-out certificates. The Contributions Agency, an executive agency of the Department of Social Security (now the DWP), acted on behalf of the Secretary of State in this regard. The Contracted-Out Employment Group ('COEG') within the Contributions Agency had day to day responsibility for the monitoring of contracted-out schemes (see also 2.21 above). In accordance with the provisions of the *Social Security Contributions (Transfer of Functions, etc) Act 1999*, from 1 April 1999, the Commissioners of Inland Revenue (through agency of the National Insurance Contributions Office ('NICO')), took over responsibility for matters related to contracted-out employment. Although COEG, now National Insurance Services to Pensions Industry, ('NISPI') remains as the sub-division of that office responsible for the day to day administration. The operational aspects of determining new elections to contract out and maintaining information on current contracted-out schemes were moved to the Inland Revenue Audit and Pension Schemes Services in Nottingham from May 2003. Responsibility for policy will remain with the DWP and NISPI will continue to provide technical expertise on contracting out. NICO has updated its guidance manuals and forms to reflect the changes introduced by the

4.5 *Contracting-out*

Occupational and Personal Pensions Schemes (Contracting-Out) (Miscellaneous Amendments) Regulations 2002 (SI 2002 No 681).

As a consequence of the changes introduced by *PA 1995*, all final salary schemes which were contracted-out prior to 6 April 1997 were required to re-elect to contract-out by 31 January 1998, at the latest, if they wished to continue to be contracted-out after 6 April 1997. Failure to re-elect resulted in the cancellation of contracting-out certificates with retrospective effect to 6 April 1997.

Schemes contracting-out for the first time after 6 April 1997 are required to comply with the election procedure set out in *regulations 2* to *12* of the *Contracting-Out Regulations (SI 1996 No 1172)* (see 4.43 to 4.48 below).

A contracting-out certificate shows both an employer's contracting-out number (ECON) and a scheme contracting-out number (SCON). An ECON is specific to a particular employer so even if an employer participates in several contracted-out schemes it will generally only have one ECON. Each scheme will have its own SCON. ECONs and SCONs are used by NISPI to monitor National Insurance contributions and liability to secure contracted-out rights.

FINAL SALARY SCHEMES

Requirements for contracting-out

4.5 A final salary scheme can be contracted-out of the S2P after 6 April 1997 only if:

(*a*) in relation to service completed before 6 April 1997:

  (i) the scheme complies with the requirements of the *1993 Act* relating to the provision of GMPs (as set out in the *1993 Act, ss 13* to *23* and the *Contracting-Out Regulations (SI 1996 No 1172), regs 41* to *69*); and

  (ii) the rules of the scheme applying to GMPs are framed so as to comply with any requirements relating to the form and content of contracted-out rules as may be prescribed in regulations or specified by NICO; and

(*b*) in relation to service completed after 6 April 1997, NICO is satisfied that:

  (i) the scheme satisfies the reference scheme test (see 4.6 to 4.10 below);

  (ii) the scheme is subject to, and complies with, the provisions of *PA 1995* relating to employer-related investments (as set out in *PA 1995, s 40* and the *Occupational Pension Schemes (Investment) Regulations 1996 (SI 1996 No 3127)*, see 10.24 below);

  (iii) the scheme satisfies the minimum funding requirement or, in the

Contracting-out **4.6**

   opinion of the actuary, will do so within the schedule period (which broadly speaking is the following five years) (and see 11.20 below);

(iv) the scheme does not permit the payment of a lump sum instead of a pension, unless the amount involved is trivial or the payment is permitted in accordance with Inland Revenue limits (see 5.8 below);

(v) the scheme provides for benefits to be payable by reference to an age which is equal for men and women and is permitted by the Inland Revenue (see 5.5 below); and

(vi) the rules of the scheme are framed so as to comply with any requirements relating to the form and content of contracted-out rules as may be prescribed in regulations or specified by NICO.

[PSA 1993, s 9 and the Contracting-Out Regulations (SI 1996 No 1172)].

Schemes which are not exempt approved by the Inland Revenue (see chapter 5) are not permitted to contract-out. A small self-administered scheme cannot contract out if its rules are drafted so as to exempt it from the provisions of the *PA 1995* relating to employer-related investments.

Post 6 April 1997 – the reference scheme test

The reference scheme

4.6 The reference scheme test is a statutory scheme quality test. It aims to ensure that the pensions to be provided for members (which includes active members and deferred members) and their spouses, from a contracted-out scheme, are broadly equivalent to, or better than, the pensions which would be provided under the 'reference scheme'. Details of the reference scheme are set out in *section 12B* of the *PSA 1993* and *regulations 25* and *26* of the *Contracting-Out Regulations (SI 1996 No 1172)*. Essentially the reference scheme is an occupational pension scheme which:

(a) has a normal pension age of 65 for both men and women;

(b) provides a pension for life at normal pension age of $\frac{1}{80}$th of average qualifying earnings in the last three tax years for each year of pensionable service, subject to a maximum of 40 years (qualifying earnings for the purpose of the reference test means 90 per cent of earnings between the lower and upper earnings limits for National Insurance contributions);

(c) provides that, on the death of a member, a pension is payable to the member's spouse unless:

- the member marries his or her spouse after having received benefits under the scheme; or

- the spouse remarries or cohabits with another person after having received benefits under the scheme; or

4.7 *Contracting-out*

- the spouse is cohabiting with another person at the time of the member's death;

(*d*) provides that any spouse's pension payable on the death of a member before normal pension age is equal to 50 per cent of the pension the reference scheme would have been obliged to provide in respect of the member, based on the service he actually completed;

(*e*) provides that any spouse's pension payable on the death of a member after normal pension age is equal to 50 per cent of the pension the reference scheme was obliged to provide for the member at the date of his death;

(*f*) provides annual pension increases in accordance with *section 51* of *PA 1995* (see chapter 1);

(*g*) revalues deferred pensions between the date of leaving and normal pension age in accordance with *PSA 1993* (see chapter 6).

The test – actuarial certification

4.7 A scheme meets the reference scheme test only if the scheme actuary (or an actuary appointed for this purpose if the trustees are not required to appoint a scheme actuary) certifies that the benefits of at least 90 per cent of the members and their spouses are broadly equivalent to, or better than, those payable under the reference scheme. Money purchase benefits (such as additional voluntary contributions) and the pensions to be provided under the scheme in respect of members who are not contracted-out under the scheme are ignored. In calculating the benefits payable to and in respect of members of a scheme, the actuary must follow the professional guidance note, 'Retirement Benefits Schemes – Adequacy of Benefits for Contracting-out on or after 6 April 1997', (GN 28), issued by the Institute of Actuaries and Faculty of Actuaries and approved by the Secretary of State.

A scheme does not have to match the benefit structure of the reference scheme in order to contract-out but if it provides pensions equal to or better than the reference scheme in every respect, including spouse's pensions, the actuary can provide a certificate without further investigation (GN 28 para 4.1). If the benefit structure of a scheme does not match or better the benefit structure of the reference scheme, the actuary will have to determine whether the benefits are broadly equivalent to, or better than, the benefits payable under the reference scheme. Where benefits under a scheme are not directly comparable to the benefits provided for under the reference scheme, the actuary has to compare the actuarial value of the benefits.

For the purposes of providing the required certificate the benefits to be compared are those that members are expected to accrue during the three years following the effective date of certification, assuming that they leave service at the end of that period or on reaching normal pension age, if earlier. Spouses' pensions must be compared separately in respect of death in service, death in deferment (assuming in each case that the member in respect of whom the benefit is payable dies at the end of the three year period) and death in retirement (assuming that the member in respect of whom the benefit is paid dies on the day after the scheme's normal pension age). In the case of a scheme with a normal pension age of less than 65 the spouse's death in retirement benefit payable to a spouse will have to be compared with the reference scheme's death in service benefit.

To be able to certify that the benefits are broadly equivalent to or better than the benefits payable under the reference test, the actuary therefore has to make four separate comparisons, namely:

(*a*)   members' pensions;

(*b*)   spouses' pensions payable on death in service;

(*c*)   spouses' pensions payable on death in retirement; and

(*d*)   spouses' pensions payable on death in deferment.

For a scheme to be able to contract-out, the actuary must be able to certify that at least 90 per cent of the persons within each group are entitled to benefits at least equal to the benefits they would receive from the reference scheme.

Schemes with more than one benefit structure

4.8   If a scheme has different sections which apply to different categories of employment or which offer different benefit structures, each section which is to be contracted-out must satisfy the reference scheme test independently. [*Contracting-Out Regulations (SI 1996 No 1172), reg 22.*] If a scheme with two separate sections has one section which does not satisfy the reference scheme test that section cannot be contracted-out, even if, overall, the scheme would satisfy the reference scheme test.

Schemes with more than one employer

4.9   Where there is more than one employer participating in a scheme each employer must either have its own contracting-out certificate or be included in a holding company certificate. If an employer wishes to have its own certificate in respect of its own employees, the reference scheme test must be complied with separately in respect of those employees. Where a holding company certificate is used, separate tests are not required unless different employers operate different benefit structures.

How stringent is the reference scheme test?

4.10   There are a number of reasons why a scheme may not satisfy the reference scheme test. The most obvious example is a scheme which has an accrual rate of less than 80ths, but the relationship between pensionable earnings and band earnings is equally significant, as shown in 4.6 above.

4.11   *Contracting-out*

The reference scheme uses an average of 'qualifying earnings' in the last three tax years for calculating benefits. Qualifying earnings are defined as 90 per cent of earnings between the lower and upper earnings limits. If a scheme's benefits are based on a pensionable salary which is lower than a member's actual salary (for example because it excludes commission, bonuses, overtime and other fluctuating emoluments or because there is an offset for the lower earning limit) there is a possibility that the benefits provided will not better those provided under the reference scheme. This is best illustrated by way of an example:

> A member's actual earnings during the tax year 2004/2005 are £24,500 comprising of £12,000 basic salary, £10,000 commission and bonuses and £2,500 overtime. The scheme's definition of pensionable salary for the purpose of calculating benefits is basic salary plus overtime (but excluding commission and bonuses) during the previous tax year. The member's pensionable salary is therefore £14,500. The average of 90 per cent of his band earnings (which will take into account commission and bonuses) over the last three years (ie 2001/2002, 2002/2003 and 2003/2004) is £19,624.80. For the purposes of the reference scheme test, the member's scheme benefits, calculated on a salary of £14,500, will be tested against benefits based on a salary of £19,624.80.

If a significant proportion of a scheme's membership receive much of their earnings in fluctuating emoluments which do not form part of pensionable salary, it is possible that the scheme will not satisfy the reference scheme test even if the accrual rate is greater than 80ths.

The other area where many schemes may need to re-examine their benefit structure is in relation to spouse's pensions on death in deferment. The reference scheme provides a 50 per cent spouse's pension on death in deferment whereas, in the past, many schemes have provided only a spouse's GMP. To meet the reference scheme test a scheme has to satisfy the test for all of the four categories referred to in 4.7 above separately, so a scheme which provided only a spouse's GMP on death in deferment is unlikely to pass the reference scheme test.

The reference scheme benefits do not form any kind of an underpin, they are simply a benchmark against which a scheme's benefits are measured. Once a scheme has met the contracting-out conditions, the scheme's normal benefit formula applies. A scheme could be designed so as to provide an underpin of the reference scheme benefits, with the rules being appropriately drafted to ensure that those benefits are provided as a minimum. This will clearly be more complicated to administer, and more costly to provide, as additional records will have to be maintained and checks made whenever a benefit becomes payable. However an underpin may be attractive to employers, particularly if the scheme generally provides benefits greater than the reference scheme but has difficulty demonstrating that it meets the reference scheme test.

Pre 6 April 1997 – guaranteed minimum pensions

Conditions relating to GMPs

4.11   If a scheme was contracted-out of SERPS (now S2P) on a salary related basis prior to 6 April 1997, or if a scheme wishes to be able to accept transfers of GMPs from a contracted-out salary related scheme, it must comply with the requirements of the *1993 Act* relating to the provision of GMPs. These requirements are contained in *sections 13* to *24* of the *1993 Act* and *regulations 55* to *69* of the *Contracting-Out Regulations (SI 1996 No 1172)*.

To be contracted out of SERPS (now S2P) on a salary related basis prior to 6 April 1997, the rules of the scheme had to provide for the member and, if applicable, the member's spouse to be entitled to a pension of not less than the guaranteed minimum. This guaranteed minimum pension or 'GMP' must be payable for life and must commence generally no later than State pension age. Although State pension age is being equalised (so that by April 2020 it will be 65 for both men and women), GMPs will continue to be payable on the appropriate State pension age when they ceased to accrue ie 60 for women and 65 for men. A scheme can provide for the commencement of the GMP to be postponed for any period during which a member continues in employment after attaining State pension age. However, the consent of the member must be obtained if the period of postponement exceeds five years from State pension age or if the postponement relates to employment which is not contracted-out by reference to the scheme. [*PSA 1993, s 13*]. Where payment of a GMP is postponed until after State pension age it must be increased to take account of late receipt. [*PSA 1993, s 15*].

All GMPs in payment which are attributable to service completed since 6 April 1988, must be increased each year by the lesser of the retail prices index and three per cent per annum. [*PSA 1993, s 109*].

Calculating the GMP

4.12 The original aim of the GMP legislation was to ensure that, on retirement, a member was entitled to a pension which was at least equal to that to which he would have been entitled had he remained contracted into SERPS (now S2P). A GMP does not, however, directly equate to the S2P entitlement being given up.

The GMP payable to a member is based on the level of his earnings whilst in contracted-out employment and is calculated according to the member's 'earnings factors' during the relevant period. A member's earnings factors are derived from his earnings between the lower earnings limit and upper earnings limit each year, revalued in accordance with the increase in the earnings index over the relevant period. The basis on which earnings factors are calculated changed in April 1987 so separate calculations must be made in respect of pre- and post-April 1987 service. The method of calculation also depends on the age of the member at 6 April 1978. Essentially the calculation is:

(*a*) for a person within 20 years of State pension age on 6 April 1978 (ie a man born before 6 April 1933 and a woman born before 6 April 1938), 1.25 per cent of his revalued earnings factors for each year between

4.13 *Contracting-out*

6 April 1978 and 5 April 1988 *plus* one per cent of his revalued earnings factor for each year between 6 April 1988 and 5 April 1997;

(*b*) for any other person (ie a man born after 6 April 1933 or a woman born after 6 April 1938), 25 per cent of his revalued earnings factors for each tax year between 6 April 1978 and 5 April 1988 divided by the number of complete tax years after 5 April 1978 (or the start of working life) up to State pension age *plus* 20 per cent of his revalued earnings factors between 6 April 1988 to 5 April 1997 divided by the number of complete tax years after 5 April (or the start of working life) up to State pension age.

A member is only entitled to a GMP from a scheme if he has been paid earnings in excess of the lower earnings limit from employment which is contracted-out by reference to the scheme. The above calculations therefore only need to be made in respect of periods of contracted-out pensionable service where the member's earnings exceeded the lower earnings limit.

Spouse's GMPs

4.13 If a member of a contracted-out salary related scheme who is entitled to a GMP dies, leaving a widow or widower (whether before or after attaining State pension age), the widow or widower will be entitled to a GMP under the scheme. The GMP payable to a widow is one half of the GMP payable to the member. The GMP payable to a widower is one half of that part of the member's GMP which is attributable to her earnings factors for the period 6 April 1988 to 5 April 1997.

The scheme must provide for the widow or widower's pension to be payable to the widow or widower for the periods set out in the legislation. For example, the scheme must make provision for a widow's pension to be payable to her for any period for which a widowed mother's allowance or widow's pension is payable to her by virtue of the "earner's" contributions (*PSA 1993, s 17*).

Trivial commutation

4.14 A member's GMP can only be commuted for a lump sum if the amount of all the benefits payable from the scheme to the member is trivial, ie less than £260 per annum (or such other amount as may be prescribed by regulations).

From 6 April 2002 the law changed to allow commutation of trivial amounts of GMP for members who have not reached state pension age ('SPA'). The conditions for this are:

(*a*) the total scheme benefits do not exceed £260 per annum;

(*b*) the scheme is winding up or a member retires before SPA;

(*c*) the GMP is revalued at fixed or limited rate.

The future of GMPs

4.15 Although it is no longer possible to accrue GMPs in respect of service completed after 6 April 1997, schemes which were contracted-out on a salary related basis prior to that date, must continue to provide GMPs in accordance with the statutory requirements some of which are detailed above.

Equalisation of GMPs

4.16 Julian Farrand, the then Ombudsman, ruled in 2000 that pensions that differ for genders doing equal service violate European Union law on equal treatment of pensions as 'pay'. On 23 February 2001, in the High Court of Justice, Rimer J decided that the Ombudsman did not have jurisdiction to direct that GMPs are to be equalised. (*Ian Williamson v Sedgwick Group Trustees (HC 0000424)*). The Ombudsman only had jurisdiction to make determinations affecting those directly party to the dispute. Rimer J left open the question of whether legislation requires GMPs to be equalised and if so how. Consequently, the detailed issue remains unresolved. Members could therefore still raise discriminatory issues on this point with trustees. Trustees and companies would then be left with uncertainty as how to address the point. However, they should be thinking about reserving costs to cover the issue if it is raised in the future and also about who is to bear the risk on a transfer-in, and in the context of share acquisitions, and transfers of past service rights. Sex equality of scheme benefits is dealt with in chapter 9.

Triennial re-certification

4.17 To ensure that contracted-out schemes continue to meet the necessary standard, schemes were required to re-certify at regular intervals. [*Contracting-Out Regulations (SI 1996 No 1172), reg 16*]. To re-certify a statement had to be submitted to NISPI (on form CA7322), at intervals of no more than three years, confirming that:

(*a*) GMP requirements are met if the scheme was originally contracted-out before 6 April 1997 or if any GMP liabilities have been transferred into the scheme;

(*b*) the scheme is not one which is excluded from contracting-out under the *Contracting-Out Regulations*;

(*c*) the scheme is not exempt from and is complying with the *Occupational Pension Schemes (Investment) Regulations 1996 (SI 1996 No 3127)*;

(*d*) a certified schedule of contributions is in place confirming that, in the opinion of the actuary, the rates of contributions are adequate for the purposes of securing that the scheme meets or will meet the minimum funding requirement during the period covered by the schedule (see 11.20 below).

4.18 *Contracting-out*

When submitting the triennial statement a reference scheme test certificate was also required to be submitted. From 6 April 2002, schemes are no longer required to submit a Reference Scheme Test Certificate tri-annually and will instead rely on exception reporting. The requirement to re-certify every three years has also been dispensed with.

MONEY PURCHASE SCHEMES

4.18 Since April 1988, when the relevant provisions of the *Social Security Act 1986* first came into force, it has been possible for employers and individuals to contract out of SERPS (now S2P) by way of money purchase arrangements. Such arrangements are now governed by *sections 10* and *26* to *33* of *PSA 1993* (as amended by *PA 1995*), the *Contracting-Out Regulations* (as amended) and the *Personal and Occupational Pension Schemes (Protected Rights) Regulations 1996 (SI 1996 No 1537)* ('the *Protected Rights Regulations*').

Requirements for contracting-out

4.19 *Section 9(3)* of *PSA 1993* and *Regulation 30* of the *Contracting-Out Regulations (SI 1996 No 1172)* provide that a money purchase scheme can contract out of S2P only if:

(*a*) it complies with the requirements of *PSA 1993* regarding the provision of protected rights (see 4.20 to 4.29 below);

(*b*) it is subject to, and complies with, the provisions of *PSA 1993* relating to employer related investments (as set out in *section 40* of *PA 1995* and the *Occupational Pension Schemes (Investment) Regulations 1996 (SI 1996 No 3127)* see 10.24);

(*c*) its rules provide that contributions made by members are invested so as to provide money purchase benefits;

(*d*) its rules require 'minimum payments' to be invested on behalf of the member within one month of the end of the tax month to which they relate and age-related payments to be invested on behalf of the member within one month of the date of payment by the Secretary of State;

(*e*) its rules are framed so as to comply with any requirements relating to the form and content of contracted-out rules as may be prescribed in regulations or specified by the Secretary of State.

A scheme which is not exempt approved by the Inland Revenue (see chapter 5) is not permitted to contract-out unless it is a relevant statutory scheme as defined in *section 611A* of the *Income and Corporation Taxes Act 1988*. As with final salary schemes, a small self-administered scheme cannot contract out if its rules are drafted so as to exempt it from the provisions of *PA 1995* relating to employer-related investments.

Minimum payments and protected rights

4.20 A money purchase scheme contracts out of S2P by providing 'protected rights'. These are the rights derived from the 'minimum payments' made to the scheme in respect of a member and certain other payments, including age-related rebates and transfers to the scheme of rights accrued in another contracted-out arrangement. [*PSA 1993, s 10* and the *Protected Rights Regulations (SI 1996 No 1537), reg 3*].

Identification and valuation of protected rights

4.21 Unless the rules of a scheme specify otherwise, a member's protected rights are his rights to money purchase benefits under the scheme. However, protected rights exclude 'the appropriate percentage' of the rights which were his protected rights immediately before the day on which a 'pension debit' arose – for details on pension sharing on divorce, see Chapter 8. Under *section 10* of *PSA 1993* the rules of the scheme may limit a member's protected rights to:

(*a*)   the rights derived from the payment of minimum payments (see 4.22 below), age-related rebates (see 4.23 below) and incentive payments (see 4.24 below) made in respect of the member; and

(*b*)   protected rights which have been transferred to the scheme from another arrangement (see 4.40 below); and

(*c*)   money purchase benefits which represent a guaranteed minimum pension or post-1997 contracted-out rights deriving from a transfer made to the scheme from a contracted-out final salary scheme or an annuity contract (see 4.38 below).

If a scheme is seeking Inland Revenue approval (see chapter 5) its rules should limit the definition of protected rights (IR12 (2001) PN 7.30). If the rules of a scheme limit a member's protected rights they must also make provision for their identification. The value of protected rights must be calculated in a manner which is no less favourable than that in which the value of any other money purchase benefits are calculated. [*PSA 1993, s 27*].

Minimum payments

4.22 To contract out of S2P through a contracted-out money purchase scheme (commonly referred to as a 'COMPS') the employer must make minimum payments to the scheme for the benefit of each member who is contracted-out by reference to the scheme. Minimum payments represent the contracted-out rebate, ie the difference between the full rate of National Insurance contribution and the reduced, contracted-out rate, payable on band earnings (ie earnings between the lower earnings limit and the upper earnings limit). This rebate, which is also known as the flat rate rebate, is set at 2.8 per cent of band earnings from 6 April 2004 (being 1.6 per cent for the employee and 1.0 per cent for the employer) for money purchase schemes.

4.23 *Contracting-out*

The Government Actuary has reviewed the technical issues underlying the calculation of rebates. Rebates must take account of benefits given up, life expectancy, investment returns to be achieved before and after retirement and expenses incurred in private pension arrangements.

The employer may recover the member's share of the rebate from the employee but this is not a requirement. [*Contracting-Out Regulations (SI 1996 No 1172), reg 31*]. If the member's share of the rebate is to be recovered, the scheme effectively becomes contributory for the members, even if no other contributions are payable, and the rules of the scheme should be framed accordingly so that the members receive tax relief on the contributions.

The employer must make the required minimum payments to the trustees of the scheme within 14 days of the end of the income tax month to which the payments relate, ie on or before the 19th of the following month. [*Contracting-Out Regulations, reg 32*]. Minimum payments must be invested within one month of the end of the tax month to which they relate. [*Contracting-Out Regulations (SI 1996 No 1172), reg 30*].

Age-related rebates

4.23 The contracted-out rebate was originally intended to be equivalent to the cost of providing the S2P benefit being given up (which increases with the age of the person in respect of whom the benefit is provided). The contracted-out rebate has historically been based on the cost of providing the benefit for a person of 'average' age. As, prior to 6 April 1997, the same contracted-out rebate was available in respect of all members irrespective of age, it was financially advantageous for those younger than the average age to contract-out of, and for those older than the average age to contract-in to S2P.

PA 1995 changed the way in which the contracted-out rebate applies to money purchase schemes by introducing age-related rebates. As from 6 April 1997 an age-related top-up became payable in addition to a flat rate rebate. Age-related rates will from April 2002, range from 0 per cent to 7.9 per cent.

Age-related rebates are not payable in respect of a member for the tax year in which he reaches State pension age (or would have done but for his death) although the flat rate rebate is still available.

Once protected rights have been secured, no age-related rebate will be paid in respect of the member unless the amount due is at least ten times the weekly lower earnings limit. In such a case the payment will be made to the insurance company, if protected rights have been secured through the purchase of an annuity, or to the trustees if they are secured by the payment of a scheme pension. If effect has been given to protected rights by means of a transfer payment, the age-related rebate, up to the date on which the transfer payment was made, becomes payable to the trustees or managers of the scheme which accepted the transfer. If effect has been given to protected rights and the age-related rebate due is less than ten times the weekly lower earnings limit, the rebate may be paid to the member, the member's spouse or if the member dies unmarried, to any person at the discretion of the Secretary of State.

Age-related rebates are payable at the end of each tax year and must be invested by the trustees within one month of receipt. A member may be required to provide documentary evidence of his date of birth and that evidence may be disclosed by the authorities to the trustees or any person responsible for administering the scheme.

As the age-related rebate is effectively paid a year in arrears, the amount due will have to be taken into account on transfers and on the death or retirement of a member. The employer may choose to make arrangements to actually 'credit' the member on a month by month basis but the additional costs and cash flow implications will fall on the employer who would recover the expenditure at the end of the tax year.

Incentive payments

4.24 Prior to 6 April 1993 an 'incentive' payment of two per cent of band earnings was payable to those schemes which contracted-out for the first time between 1 January 1986 and 5 April 1993. [*SSA 1986, s 7*]. Although incentive payments are no longer payable, any made in the past still form part of a member's protected rights.

Giving effect to protected rights

Member's pension

4.25 The rules of a COMPS must provide for a member's protected rights to be used to provide a pension from the scheme or be used to purchase an annuity. [*PSA 1993, ss 28* and *29* and the *Protected Rights Regulations (SI 1996 No 1537), reg 4*]. The pension or annuity must commence on or after the member's 60th birthday but before his 65th birthday, unless he agrees to a later date, and must continue for life. The rate of the pension or annuity must be calculated on a basis which does not discriminate on the basis of sex.

If the rules of the scheme do not provide for the payment of a pension from the scheme, or if the member requires that an annuity be purchased, the member must be given the opportunity to choose the insurance company which is to provide the annuity. The member must generally notify the trustees of his choice, in writing, at least one month, and not more than six months, before his normal retirement date. If the member does not notify the trustees of his choice, the trustees can decide from whom to purchase an annuity. A lump sum may be paid instead of a pension if the annual rate of pension is trivial (see 4.29 below).

In certain circumstances, effect may also be given to protected rights, by the making of a transfer payment in the case of an occupational pension scheme, to

4.26   *Contracting-out*

another occupational pension scheme, to a personal pension scheme or to an overseas arrangement (*PSA 1993, s. 28*).

Benefits payable on death after retirement

4.26   The rules of a COMPS must provide for a member's protected rights to be used to provide a pension or annuity for the member's widow or widower on the death of the member after retirement. [*PSA 1993, s 29* and the *Protected Rights Regulations (SI 1996 No 1537), reg 5*]. The only exception to this is if the member is not married at the date of his retirement and specifically elects not to make provision for a spouse. The annuity or pension need only be paid to a qualifying spouse, ie a person who is the widow or widower of the member and who was at least age 45 when the member died, was entitled to child benefit in respect of a qualifying child under age 18 or was residing with a qualifying child under age 16. A qualifying child for this purpose is a child of the member and his widow or her widower or any child in respect of whom they were entitled to child benefit.

The rate of any qualifying spouse's pension or annuity must be one half of the amount that would have been payable to the member if he or she had survived. The rules of the scheme must provide for the pension or annuity to be payable:

(*a*)   for life, if the qualifying spouse was over 45 when the member died; or

(*b*)   until he or she ceases to be eligible for child benefit or ceases to reside with a qualifying child under the age of 16; or

(*c*)   until he or she remarries while under State pension age.

The rules of the scheme may provide for the pension or annuity to be payable for a longer period. They may, for example, provide for the benefit to be payable for life irrespective of whether or not the widow or widower remarries. Provision may also be made in the rules for benefits to be payable to a surviving spouse even if he or she does not fall within the definition of a qualifying spouse. They may, for example, provide for a pension to be payable to a spouse even though she has not reached age 45 and does not have any qualifying children.

Where a benefit is not payable, or ceases to be payable, to a surviving spouse the rules of the scheme may provide for a pension to be paid to or for the benefit of any qualifying children until they reach 18. The rate of the pension must not exceed one half of the amount of pension which would have been paid to the member had he survived.

The rules may provide for the pension or annuity attributable to protected rights to continue to be paid, at the full rate payable to the member, to any person for up to five years from the date on which the member's pension or annuity commenced.

Benefits payable on death before retirement

4.27 The rules of a COMPS must provide that if a member dies before the benefits deriving from his protected rights come into payment, his protected rights will be used to provide a pension, an annuity, or, in certain circumstances, a lump sum. [*PSA 1993, s 28* and the *Protected Rights Regulations (SI 1996 No 1537), reg 12*]. The benefit must be payable to any qualifying spouse who is at least age 45 when the member dies or who is entitled to child benefit in respect of a qualifying child under age 18 or is residing with a qualifying child under age 16.

The annuity or pension must be paid to the qualifying spouse from a date which is as soon as practicable after the member's death and is payable until the surviving spouse either dies, remarries before State pension age or ceases to be a qualifying spouse.

The pension or annuity may contain a provision for the payment of a pension to qualifying children on the death of a qualifying spouse. It may also include a five year guarantee period in the same manner as the pension payable on the death of a member after retirement.

Where the trustees of the scheme find that, after making reasonable enquiries, the member was not survived by a qualifying spouse, they must make provision for the cash equivalent of the member's protected rights to be paid to the member's estate or to or for the benefit of any person nominated, in writing, by the member.

Suspension and forfeiture

4.28 The rules of a COMPS must not permit the suspension of a member's protected rights or of payments giving effect to them. [*PSA 1993, s 32* and the *Protected Rights Regulations (SI 1996 No 1537), reg 9*]. However, the rules may permit the benefits deriving from protected rights to be suspended where the person entitled to payment is, in the opinion of the trustees, unable to act for himself, for example, because he has a mental disorder. In such a situation, the trustees may pay the benefit to another person for the maintenance of the incapacitated person and/or his dependants. The rules may also permit the suspension of the pension when the recipient is in prison, in which case the benefit can be paid to his dependants.

Generally, the rules of the scheme must not permit forfeiture of a member's protected rights. However, the rules may permit forfeiture where the trustees of the scheme do not know the address of the person to whom the payment should be made and at least six years have elapsed since payment was due.

4.29 *Contracting-out*

Lump Sum

Trivial commutation

4.29 If the pension which could be provided by a member's protected rights, and all other benefits attributable to him under the scheme, is less than £260 per annum (or such other amount as may be prescribed by regulations), the member can elect to receive his benefits, including his protected rights, in the form of a lump sum. [*PSA 1993, s 28(4)* and the *Protected Rights Regulations (SI 1996 No 1537), reg 8*].

Other circumstances

4.30 A lump sum is also permitted to be paid in certain cases of terminal illness (*PSA 1993, s 28(4A)*).

MIXED BENEFIT SCHEMES

Governing legislation

4.31 Prior to 6 April 1997 a scheme could only be contracted-out on either a salary related basis or a money purchase basis. A scheme could not contract-out by both methods simultaneously nor could it convert to a different method unless it ceases to contract-out on the original basis and discharged its liability to pay either guaranteed minimum pensions or protected rights and then subsequently elected to contract-out on the other basis.

From 6 April 1997 it became possible for schemes to contract-out via both the money purchase and salary related routes at the same time. These schemes are referred to as contracted-out mixed benefits schemes or 'COMBS'. Initially, only schemes which are contracting-out for the first time and salary related schemes which are re-electing to contract-out on or after 5 April 1997 are able to become COMBS. However this flexibility has been extended to contracted-out money purchase schemes from 6 April 1998.

COMBS are essentially treated as two different schemes so that the requirements relating to a salary related scheme apply to the salary related part and the requirements relating to a money purchase scheme apply to the money purchase part. Similarly elections for contracting-out certificates must comply with all the requirements for both salary related and money purchase schemes (see 4.43 to 4.49 below).

Electing to become a COMBS

4.32 A salary related scheme which was contracted-out prior to 6 April 1997 and continued to be contracted-out after that date can become a COMBS by opening up a money purchase section. The rules of the scheme may permit members to move between the salary related and the money purchase parts of the scheme or may restrict membership of each section depending on, for example, age or job description. Schemes contracting-out for the first time on or after 6 April 1997 can elect to be a COMBS from the outset.

From 6 April 1998, existing money purchase schemes have been able to become a COMBS by opening up a salary related part and then will be treated in much the same way as a salary related scheme which elected to become a COMBS.

All COMBS will be issued with a COMBS contracting-out certificate and two scheme contracting-out numbers or 'SCONs', one for the salary related part of the scheme and one for the money purchase part.

Ceasing to become a COMBS

4.33 A COMBS can elect to become a pure money purchase or salary related scheme by closing the salary related or money purchase part, as appropriate, without discharging its liabilities in respect of existing contracted-out rights. NICO will treat the inactive part of the scheme as if it were a scheme which has ceased to contract-out (see 4.65 below). Such a scheme will then be issued with a money purchase or salary related contracting-out certificate, as appropriate.

Transitional provisions

4.34 During the period 6 April 1997 to 31 January 1998 an existing salary related scheme could switch to being a money purchase contracted-out scheme for future service without first having to discharge its liability for GMPs. Such an election had to be made with effect from 6 April 1997. Future benefits accrue on a money purchase basis although the scheme will continue to have liability for the accrued GMPs. The GMPs in such schemes will be supervised as if they were provided by a scheme which has ceased to contract-out.

Such a scheme is technically not a COMBS as it does not have two separate active sections; it will be treated as a money purchase scheme for contracting-out purposes although it will provide salary related benefits. The rules of the scheme must state whether the member's contributions (in excess of minimum payments) will be used to provide money purchase benefits or salary related benefits. [*Contracting-Out Regulations* (*SI 1996 No 1172*), *reg 30*].

TRANSFERS BETWEEN CONTRACTED-OUT ARRANGEMENTS

4.35 Broadly speaking, a member who terminates pensionable service at least one year before his normal retirement date has a statutory right to require the trustees of the scheme to transfer the cash equivalent of his benefits to another pension arrangement and since 6 April 2002 both pre and post 1997 protected rights can be transferred to an overseas arrangement as well as an overseas occupational pension scheme (see chapter 6 for details of conditions applying to such transfers). In certain circumstances, such as the sale of a business, a group or bulk transfer of the accrued rights of a group of members may be made to another scheme. In either case, where the transfer would include the accrued rights to which a member is entitled by virtue of his contracted-out employment, additional restrictions may apply.

A tabulated summary of 4.36 to 4.41 below is included at 4.42 below.

Transfers from a contracted-out final salary scheme to a contracted-in scheme

4.36 Before 6 April 1997, it was possible for a transfer to be made from a contracted-out final salary scheme to a contracted-in final salary scheme; the member's accrued rights in excess of his GMP can be transferred to the contracted-in scheme and his GMP can be secured by some other means. It is no longer possible to make such a transfer if the member has any post-1997 contracted-out salary related rights. A member's post-1997 contracted-out salary related rights are his rights to all benefits accrued after 6 April 1997 by virtue of contracted-out employment. Unlike an entitlement to a GMP, the member's rights under the scheme which are attributable to the fact that he is contracted-out cannot be separately identified and so cannot be secured elsewhere.

Transfers from a contracted-out final salary scheme to another contracted-out final salary scheme

4.37 A transfer in respect of a member's GMP and post-1997 contracted-out salary related rights can be made from a contracted-out final salary scheme to another contracted-out final salary scheme if:

(a) the member consents in writing; and

(b) the member is either employed by an employer who contributes to the receiving scheme or has previously been a member of the receiving scheme;

(c) the part of the transfer payment representing post-1997 contracted-out rights is applied to provide benefits for the member, in accordance with the rules of the receiving scheme relating to contracted-out employment, as if they had accrued in the receiving scheme; and

(d) if the transfer includes accrued rights to a GMP, the receiving scheme's rules provide for the conditions relating to the payment of GMPs accrued under the receiving scheme to apply equally to the transferred GMPs.

If the member does not enter contracted-out employment under the receiving scheme, the transfer can be made only if the receiving scheme provides for a GMP to be payable of at least the amount which would have been payable by the transferring scheme had the transfer not taken place. The receiving scheme must revalue GMPs for such members in accordance with the rules relating to the scheme's own GMPs.

If the transfer includes liability for the payment of a GMP to or in respect of a person who has become entitled to it, the pension must commence from the date on which the receiving scheme assumes liability for the GMP. Any spouse's GMP must be calculated and paid in the same manner as under the transferring scheme.

Where the transferring scheme and the receiving scheme apply to employment with the same employer or the transfer is a bulk transfer as a consequence of a financial transaction between employers or between connected employers (ie where each of the employers is one of a group of companies consisting of a holding company and one or more subsidiaries, within the meaning of *section 736* of the *Companies Act 1985*) or associated employers (within the meaning of *section 590A(3)* and *(4)* of the *Income and Corporation Taxes Act 1988*) the first two conditions set out above do not apply. However, the transfer must be made in accordance with conditions set out in *regulation 12(3)* of the *Occupational Pension Schemes (Preservation of Benefit) Regulations 1991 (SI 1991 No 167)* ('the *Preservation Regulations*') (see chapter 12).

Transfers from a contracted-out final salary scheme to a contracted-out money purchase scheme or a contracted-out personal pension scheme

4.38   A transfer in respect of a member's GMP and post 1997 contracted-out rights can be made from a contracted-out final salary scheme to a contracted-out money purchase scheme if:

(*a*)   the member consents in writing; and

(*b*)   the member is employed by an employer who contributes to the receiving scheme or has previously been a member of the receiving scheme;

(*c*)   the transfer payment is applied so as to provide money purchase benefits under the receiving scheme; and

(*d*)   if the transfer includes a GMP, the amount of the transfer payment is at least equal to the cash equivalent of the GMP.

Again, the first two conditions do not apply where the transferring scheme and the receiving scheme apply to employment with the same employer or the transfer is a bulk transfer as a consequence of a financial transaction between employers or between connected or associated employers, provided the transfer is made in accordance with conditions set out in the *Preservation Regulations* (*SI 1991 No 167*).

4.39   *Contracting-out*

Transfers from a contracted-out money purchase scheme to a contracted-in money purchase scheme or a contracted-in personal pension scheme

4.39   It is possible for a transfer to be made from a contracted-out money purchase scheme to a contracted-in money purchase scheme or a contracted-in personal pension scheme if the member's protected rights are separately identifiable. In this situation, the member's rights in excess of his protected rights can be transferred to the contracted-in scheme and his protected rights can be secured by some other means, such as a transfer to a suitable annuity contract or a contracted-out personal pension scheme.

Transfers from a contracted-out money purchase scheme to another contracted-out money purchase scheme or a contracted-out personal pension scheme

4.40   A transfer in respect of a member's protected rights can be made from a contracted-out money purchase scheme to another contracted-out money purchase scheme or contracted-out personal pension scheme if:

(*a*)   the member consents in writing; and

(*b*)   the member is either employed by an employer who contributes to the receiving scheme or has previously been a member of the receiving scheme;

(*c*)   the part of the transfer payment representing protected rights is of an amount which is at least equal to the cash equivalent of those rights, calculated in accordance with the requirements of the *section 97* of *PSA 1993* (see 6.49 below);

(*d*)   the transfer payment is applied to provide money purchase benefits for or in respect of the member.

Transfers from a contracted-out money purchase scheme to contracted-out final salary scheme

4.41   A transfer in respect of a member's protected rights can be made from a contracted-out money purchase scheme to a contracted-out final salary scheme if:

(*a*)   the member consents in writing; and

(*b*)   the member is either employed by an employer who contributes to the receiving scheme or has previously been a member of the receiving scheme;

(*c*)   the part of the transfer payment representing protected rights is of an amount which is at least equal to the cash equivalent of those rights, calculated in accordance with the requirements of the *section 97* of *PSA 1993* (see chapter 6);

(*d*) any part of the transfer payment representing pre-1997 protected rights must be used to provide a GMP in accordance with the receiving scheme's rules;

(*e*) any part of the transfer payment representing post-1997 protected rights must be used to provide the member with contracted-out rights under the rules of the receiving scheme.

Transfers between contracted-out arrangements: tabulated summary

4.42

	Type of Transfer	Is transfer permitted?		Conditions
		Pre-1997	Post-1997	
1.	*Contracted-out* final salary to *contracted-in* final salary	Rights over GMP could be transferred, and GMP secured separately	Not if rights to benefits after 6 April 1997 by virtue of contracted-out employment	Not applicable
2.	*Contracted-out* final salary to *contracted-out* final salary	Yes – subject to conditions	Yes – subject to conditions	Except in the case of employments with the same employer and bulk transfers (where (a) and (b) below will not apply, but conditions set out in the *Preservation Regulations* will): (*a*) member consents (*b*) member employed by employer who contributes to/or has previously been member of, receiving scheme (*c*) part of transfer representing post-1997 rights applied as if accrued in receiving scheme (*d*) receiving scheme's rules apply same conditions to transferred GMP's
3.	*Contracted-out* final salary to *contracted-out* money purchase	Yes – subject to conditions	Yes – subject to conditions	Except in the case of employments with the same employer and bulk transfers (where (a) and (b) below will not apply, but conditions set out in the *Preservation Regulations* will): (*a*) member consents

4.42 *Contracting-out*

	Type of Transfer	Is transfer permitted?		Conditions
		Pre-1997	Post-1997	
				(b) member employed by employer who contributes to/or has previously been member of, receiving scheme
				(c) transfer payment applied to provide money purchase benefits under receiving scheme
				(d) if transfer includes GMP, transfer payment is at least equal to cash equivalent of GMP
4.	*Contracted-out* final salary to *contracted-out* personal pension	Yes – subject to conditions	Yes – subject to conditions	See 3 above
5.	*Contracted-out* money purchase to a *contracted-in* money purchase	If protected rights are separately identifiable, excess rights can be transferred, and protected rights secured separately		Not applicable
6.	*Contracted-out* money purchase to *contracted-in* personal pension	If protected rights are separately identifiable, excess rights can be transferred, and protected rights secured separately		Not applicable
7.	*Contracted-out* money purchase to *contracted-out* money purchase	Yes – subject to conditions		(a) member consents
				(b) member employed by employer who contributes to/or has previously been member of, receiving scheme
				(c) transfer payment representing protected rights is at least equal to cash equivalent of those rights
				(d) transfer payment is applied to provide money purchase benefits

	Type of Transfer	Is transfer permitted?		Conditions
		Pre-1997	Post-1997	
8.	Contracted-*out* money purchase to *contracted-out* personal pension	Yes – subject to conditions		See 7 above
9.	Contracted-*out* money purchase to *contracted-out* final salary	Yes – subject to conditions		(a) member consents (b) member employed by employer who contributes to/or has previously been member of, receiving scheme (c) transfer payment representing protected rights is at least equal to cash equivalent of those rights (d) transfer payment representing pre-1997 protected rights used to provide a GMP (e) transfer payment representing post-1997 protected rights used to provide contracted-out rights

ELECTING FOR THE ISSUE, VARIATION OR SURRENDER OF A CONTRACTING-OUT CERTIFICATE

4.43 Full details of the election procedures for obtaining, varying or surrendering a contracting-out certificate are given in the manuals 'Contracted-out Guidance for Salary Related Pension Schemes and Salary Related Overseas Scheme', (CA14C) 'Contracted-out Guidance for Money Purchase Pension Schemes and Money Purchase Overseas Schemes', (CA14D) and 'Contracted-out Guidance for Mixed Benefit Pension Schemes and Mixed Benefit Overseas Schemes,' (CA14E) all of which are available from NISPI.

Notices of intention and notices of explanation

4.44 Before making an election for the issue, variation or surrender of a contracting-out certificate, the employer must give either a notice of intention or a notice of explanation. [*Contracting-Out Regulations* (*SI 1996 No 1172*), *regs 3 and 10*].

4.45 *Contracting-out*

Notice of intention

4.45 A notice of intention must be issued in all cases unless the election to be made will not result in a change in contracted-out status for the employees involved (in which case a notice of explanation may be given (see 4.46 below)).

Notices of intention must be in writing and must contain the information specified in *regulation 3* of the *Contracting-Out Regulations (SI 1996 No 1172)*, which includes an explanation of the effect of making the election. Specimen notices of intention are given, for a final salary scheme, in the manual 'Contracted-out Guidance for Salary Related Pension Schemes and Salary Related Overseas Schemes', (CA14C) and, for a money purchase scheme, in the manual 'Contracted-out Guidance for Money Purchase Pension Schemes and Money Purchase Overseas Schemes', (CA14D), copies of which are available from NISPI.

A notice of intention must be given to all employees in the employments which are to be covered by the certificate whether or not they are members of the scheme or can complete the minimum period of service before normal pension age. The notice must also be given to any appropriate independent trade unions, the trustees of the scheme, the scheme administrator and, if applicable, the insurance company. Notices can be given by sending or delivering them to all relevant parties or, in the case of employees, by exhibiting them conspicuously at the place of work and drawing each employee's attention to it.

A notice of intention must specify the notice period, which generally must be at least three months from the date on which the notice is given. If there are no independent trade unions involved or if all unions involved agree, the notice period can be shortened but it cannot be less than one month. During the notice period employees can raise objections with the employer or with the Commissioners of Inland Revenue.

An employer can amend his election at any time before the issue, variation or withdrawal of the contracting-out certificate but only if the amendment would not alter the categories or descriptions of the employees to which the election relates or the date from which it is intended that the certificate is to have effect. However, if incorrect information is shown in the original notice of intention the employer must issue fresh notices and the notice period will start to run again.

Notice of explanation

4.46 Regulation 10 of the *Contracting-Out Regulations (SI 1996 No 1172)* permits a notice of explanation to be given (rather than a notice of intention) if:

(*a*) the employees covered by the election will continue to qualify for either GMPs and post-April 1997 contracted-out salary related rights or protected rights, as the case may be, under the same scheme after the election takes effect;

(b) the accrued rights of those employees to GMPs and post-April 1997 contracted-out salary related rights or protected rights, as the case may be, under the scheme will be unaffected; and

(c) the employment of those employees will continue to be contracted-out by reference to the same scheme.

A notice of explanation will generally be used where changes occur within a group of companies. For example, if all the employees of a company are transferred to another company within the same group they may remain members of the same scheme, assuming that the new employer participates in the scheme. In such a situation, it would be appropriate to use a notice of explanation as the election would not result in any change of contracted-out status for any of the employees involved.

One notice of explanation can cover more than one election. For example, in the scenario referred to above, the notice would explain both the surrender of the certificate held by the original employer (or its removal from a holding company certificate) and the election for a contracting-out certificate by the new employer (or for its inclusion on a holding company certificate). A notice of explanation will have to be tailored to the exact requirements of the elections to be made but specimen notices of explanation are given in the appropriate manual issued by NI Services to Pensions Industry as referred to in 4.43 above.

Where a notice of explanation is used no notice period need be given and employees do not have to be allowed the opportunity to object to the election. Otherwise the requirements relating to how a notice is to be given are the same as in respect of notices of intention.

Making an election to contract-out

Timing of elections

4.47 An election to contract-out must be made within three months of the expiry of the notice of intention or explanation. [*Contracting-Out Regulations (SI 1996 No 1172), reg 5*]. Elections made outside this period may be accepted if a satisfactory explanation can be given for the delay. Where possible, an election to contract-out should be submitted before the date from which the contracting-out certificate is to have effect but back-dating may be permitted, at the discretion of NISPI, in some circumstances.

The election

4.48 The election must contain the information specified in *regulation 6* of the *Contracting-Out Regulations (SI 1996 No 1172)*. In particular, in the election to contract-out the employer must confirm that:

(a) the scheme is not exempt from and is complying with the *Occupational Pension Schemes (Investment) Regulations 1996 (SI 1996 No 3127)*;

4.49 *Contracting-out*

(*b*) that a notice of intention or explanation has been given and that, if appropriate, consultation requirements have been complied with.

If a scheme is contracting-out on the money purchase basis the employer must also confirm that he will comply with obligations concerning minimum payments as set out in *PSA 1993* and the *Contracting-Out Regulations*. In particular confirmation must be given that the rules of the scheme make provision for:

(*a*) the investment of minimum payments within one month of the end of the tax month to which they relate;

(*b*) the investment of age-related rebates made to the scheme within one month after payment;

(*c*) employee's contributions to be used for money purchase benefits unless those contributions are being used for salary related benefits payable in addition to the benefits accruing from minimum payments.

The election will generally be made by completing Form CA7300 in respect of a final salary scheme, Form C7301 in respect of a money purchase scheme or Form C7302 in respect of a mixed benefit scheme (all of which are available from NISPI). The Form must be signed by both the employer and the trustees or by someone authorised to sign on behalf of either or both of these parties.

Supporting documents

4.49 When making an election in relation to a final salary scheme, until the minimum funding requirement is fully in place (ie 5 April 2007) an employer must provide a 'Certificate T' from the scheme actuary (*Contracting-Out Regulations (SI 1996 No 1172), reg 72*) confirming that:

(*a*) the scheme complies with the funding requirements for contracting-out;

(*b*) the requirements of *PA 1995* relating to the minimum funding requirement (see 11.14 to 11.31) and employer-related investments (see 10.24) are complied with; and

(*c*) if the scheme winds-up it will be able to meet the liabilities specified in section 73(3)(*a*)–(*e*) of *PA 1995* (as amended by the *Winding-Up Regulations*) (see 12.66).

In order to complete a certificate, the actuary must carry out a full minimum funding requirement valuation and certify a schedule of contributions within twelve weeks of signing of the valuation (see chapter 11 for further details). The Certificate T must then be submitted within one month of the actuary certifying the schedule of contributions. Where a minimum funding requirement valuation is not available, the election package can contain a statement from the actuary confirming that an interim schedule of contributions is in place which, in his opinion, is adequate for the scheme to be able to meet its contracted-out liabilities and any prescribed liabilities with a higher priority on a winding-up.

The employer must also submit a reference scheme test certificate signed by the scheme actuary confirming that the scheme satisfies the reference scheme test.

Variation of the contracting-out certificate

4.50 Minor variations to a contracting-out certificate may be made by notifying NISPI in writing or by submitting an appropriate form. Minor variations include the change of the name of an employer, an employer's address or the name of the scheme. Such changes must be notified within three months of the effective date of the change. Notice of such changes does not have to be given to employees or other interested parties.

Major variations require full election action including the issue of a notice of intention and consultation with independent trade unions or the issue of a notice of explanation, if appropriate. Specimen notices of intention are given in the appropriate manual issued by NISPI. Major changes include a change to the effective date of contracting-out, the addition or deletion of a subsidiary to the schedule of the holding company's certificate or changes to the categories of employment covered by the contracting-out certificate. Major changes must be notified to NISPI on the appropriate form (Form CA7306) within three months of the effective date of change. [*Contracting-Out Regulations (SI 1996 No 1172), reg 9*].

Election to surrender a certificate

4.51 Before making an election to surrender a contracting-out certificate an employer must give a notice of intention and undertake consultation with any independent trade unions. Specimen notices of intention are given in the appropriate manual issued by NISPI. The notice period is the same as for the making of an election for a certificate, ie a minimum of one or three months depending on whether there are any independent trade unions involved and whether they agree to the shorter period. In order to surrender a contracting-out certificate a Form CA7313 must be submitted to the NISPI. [*Contracting-Out Regulations (SI 1996 No 1172), reg 9*]

Holding company certificates

4.52 An employer may hold a contracting-out certificate as a holding company whether or not it is itself contracted-out by reference to the scheme. An employer can be a holding company if it is:

(*a*) one of a group of companies which consists of a holding company and subsidiaries (within the meaning of *section 736* of the *Companies Act 1985*); or

(*b*) an employer who controls associated employers (within the meaning of *section 590(A)(3)* and *(4)* of *ICTA 1988*); or

(*c*) an employer who is the principal employer in accordance with the rules of

4.53 *Contracting-out*

the scheme or who has power to act on behalf of all employers in the scheme in accordance with the rules.

A holding company may elect for a single contracting-out certificate which includes its associated or subsidiary companies on a schedule to the certificate. The requirements relating to the reference scheme test differ if a single contracting-out certificate is issued to a holding company rather than separate certificates being issued to each company (see 4.9 above). [*Contracting-Out Regulations (SI 1996 No 1172), reg 12*].

The periodic return system

4.53 In April 1993 the Occupational Pensions Board (now dissolved) introduced the periodic return system whereby notification of changes to holding company certificates were supplied on a six-monthly basis instead of as and when the changes occurred. Employers with holding company certificates participate in this system on a voluntary basis. The system has been continued by NICO but the periodic returns are now required to be made on an annual basis. The changes that may be notified on the periodic return Form CA7312 are:

(*a*) the addition or deletion of employers from the schedule to the contracting-out certificate held by the holding company;

(*b*) a change of scheme name;

(*c*) a change of name of the principal employer and/or any participating employer;

(*d*) the appointment of a new principal employer.

TERMINATION OF CONTRACTED-OUT EMPLOYMENT

4.54 Full details of the procedures which must be adopted following the cessation of contracted-out employment are given in the manuals 'Termination of Contracted-out Employment – Manual for Salary Related Pension Schemes and Salary Related Parts of Mixed Benefit Schemes', (CA14) 'Termination of Contracted-out Employment – Manual for Money Purchase Pension Schemes and Money Purchase Parts of Mixed Benefits Schemes', (CA14A) and 'Cessation of Contracted-out Pension Scheme', (CA15) all of which are available from NISPI.

When does contracted-out employment cease?

4.55 A member will be treated as having terminated contracted-out employment if:

(*a*) his contract of employment expires or is terminated; or

(b) in the absence of a contract of employment, the employment itself has ended; or

(c) he has ceased to be a member of a contracted-out scheme; or

(d) the contracting-out certificate by virtue of which his employment was contracted-out has been surrendered or cancelled; or

(e) the contracting-out certificate by virtue of which his employment was contracted-out has been varied in such a way that the certificate no longer applies to his employment; or

(f) the earner's employer dies or disposes of the whole or part of his business so that the member ceases to be employed by that employer and the contracted-out employment is not, or cannot be, treated as continuing with any new employer.

When is a member's contracted-out employment treated as not having ceased?

4.56 A member's contracted-out employment is not treated as having ceased if he resumes membership of the same scheme within six months as a result of either, employment with the same employer or employment with a new employer. However his contracted-out employment will be treated as having ceased if his protected rights or accrued GMP and post-1997 contracted-out salary related rights, as applicable, have been secured outside the scheme.

If the contracting-out certificate relating to the member's contracted-out employment has been varied, surrendered or cancelled so that it no longer applies to the member, the member's contracted-out employment will not be treated as having ceased if, within six months, he becomes a member of another contracted-out scheme of the same employer. The member's protected rights or accrued GMP and post-1997 contracted-out salary related rights, as applicable, must be transferred to the new scheme.

A member's contracted-out employment will not be treated as terminated if his employer's business is taken over by another employer provided the new employer accepts the liabilities and responsibilities of the old employer. The new employer must notify NISPI of the change within one month of the change taking place.

Securing contracted-out rights when a member leaves a scheme

4.57 Where a member's pensionable service terminates after he has completed two years of qualifying service he is entitled to a preserved benefit under the scheme (see chapter 6). In the case of a contracted-out scheme the member's protected rights or GMP and rights attributable to his post-6 April 1997 contracted-out employment, as appropriate, will form part of the preserved benefit and, as such, must be appropriately secured.

4.58 Contracting-out

A member who leaves pensionable service before completing two years of qualifying service will usually only be entitled to a refund of his contributions. In this situation he will generally be reinstated into S2P.

The three options set out in 4.58 to 4.60 below are available for securing the contracted-out rights of early leavers.

Reinstatement into S2P

4.58 It may be possible to reinstate the member rights into the State scheme by a payment of a contributions equivalent premium. The consequence of paying such a premium is that the member is treated as if he had not contracted-out for the period in respect of which the premium was paid. The member's protected rights or accrued GMP and post-1997 contracted-out salary related rights, as appropriate, are extinguished.

As from 6 April 1997 it is only possible to buy an employee back in to S2P if he had less than two years of qualifying service and took a refund of his contributions on leaving the scheme.

Retention of liability within the scheme

4.59 The second alternative is to retain the liability for the member's protected rights or accrued GMP and post-1997 contracted-out rights, as appropriate, within the scheme. Any such rights retained within the scheme must be revalued to take account of inflation (see 4.59 below).

Transfer to another arrangement

4.60 The third option is that liability for the member's protected rights or accrued GMP and post-1997 contracted-out rights, as appropriate, could be secured outside the scheme. This may be done by way of a transfer to another contracted-out scheme, such as the scheme of a new employer or a contracted-out personal pension scheme. Alternatively the liability could be bought out by the purchase of an insurance policy or an annuity contract (see 4.34 to 4.40 above for conditions relating to transfers).

Revaluation

Revaluing GMPs

4.61 To counter some of the effects of inflation and to allow for the fact that a GMP will be based on band earnings at the date of termination of pensionable service, *section 16* of *PSA 1993* provides that GMPs of early leavers must be revalued from the date of leaving up to State pension age. The two methods currently available to revalue GMPs are:

(a) revaluation of earnings factors – this involves increasing the earnings factors used for calculating the GMP by the last earnings factor order made under *section 148* of the *Social Security Administration Act 1992* in the same way as for active members; or

(b) fixed rate revaluation – in this case the rate of revaluation is fixed at a certain level depending on the date of the termination of contracted-out employment. Where contracted-out employment terminated before 6 April 1988 the rate is 8.5 per cent compound, for terminations during the period 6 April 1988 to 5 April 1993 the rate is 7.5 per cent compound, for terminations during the period 6 April 1993 to 5 April 1997 the rate is 7 per cent compound and for terminations on or after 6 April 1997 the rate is 6.25 per cent compound. The rate of revaluation for early leavers will be reduced to 4.5 per cent per year for leavers on or after 6 April 2002. The new fixed rate is reviewed every five years and this has consistently been reduced since its introductory level of 8.5 per cent per annum in 1978.

To a limited extent it is possible to revalue GMPs by what is known as limited rate revaluation. Using this method GMPs must be increased by the lesser of:

(i) five per cent compound for each complete tax year after that in which contracted-out service terminated; and

(ii) the increase which would apply using the last order made under *section 148* in the tax year before the member reaches State pension age.

From 6 April 2004, the figure for limited rated evaluation of GMPs by virtue of the *Guaranteed Minimum Pensions Increase Order 2004 (SI 2004 No 537)* is 2.8%. If limited rate revaluation is used a limited rate revaluation premium has to be paid to NICO. Limited rate revaluation can only apply in respect of members for whom limited revaluation premiums were being paid prior to 6 April 1997. Otherwise the option is no longer available and schemes which previously adopted this method must adopt one of the other two methods available. The trustees and the employer must decide which method of revaluation is to be adopted and NISPI must be notified of any changes.

Post-1997 contracted-out salary related rights

4.62 The benefits payable to members in respect of post-6 April 1997 contracted-out employment are revalued in the same way as other benefits accruing under the scheme (see chapter 6).

Protected rights

4.63 The protected rights of a member must be revalued on the same basis as other money purchase benefits (see chapter 6).

Anti-franking

4.64 The GMPs of early leavers are further protected by the principle of 'anti-franking'.

The legislation relating to anti-franking was contained in *sections 87* to *92* of *PSA 1993*.

The *Child Support, Pensions and Social Security Act 2000* introduced new rules on anti-franking, which become effective from 6 April 2002. These automatically apply to members and their beneficiaries who have an entitlement to a GMP from a scheme, provided that the earner leaves pensionable service on or after 6 April 2002. This applies equally where the member's service ended by death after 6 April 2002 and a widow/widower's pension is payable. Scheme managers/trustees will be able to make an election to choose to operate the alternative rules to calculate the pensions of members and beneficiaries where pensionable service ended before 6 April 2002. If an election is made, scheme mangers/trustees need to be careful not to discriminate between categories of earners.

The alternative anti-franking rules:

(*a*) protect increases to GMPs;

(*b*) prevent statutory increases arising in one period of pensionable service from being offset against those arising in a different period of service; and

(*c*) prohibit the offsetting of pensions derived from service prior to 6 April 1997 against those derived from service after that date.

The alternative anti-franking rules introduce a new minimum benefits test. The new rules try to ensure that a member leaving pensionable service after 5 April 2002, but before SPA, will receive at least the better of his pre-6 April 1997 accrual and his GMP, plus his post-5 April 1997 benefits.

There is guidance on anti-franking requirements, contained in Joint Office Memorandum 77.

Supervision of formerly contracted-out schemes

4.65 When a scheme ceases to be contracted-out it must secure members' protected rights or accrued GMPs and post-1997 salary related contracted-out rights, as appropriate, in one of the ways mentioned in 4.57 to 4.60 above. The Secretary of State, acting through NICO and NISPI, has a duty to continue to supervise schemes which have lost their contracted-out status for whatever reason. [*PSA 1993, ss 52* and *53*]. The trustees of such a scheme can be directed to take such action as the Secretary of State may, in writing, specify. [*PSA 1993, s 53(1)*]. This will usually take the form of monitoring the funding of the scheme, by requiring actuarial certification, so as to ensure that the scheme has sufficient assets to meet its liabilities for protected rights or accrued GMPs and post-1997 salary related contracted-out rights, as appropriate.

SIMPLIFICATION OF CONTRACTING OUT

4.66 The *Occupational Personal Pension Schemes (Contracting-out) (Miscellaneous Amendments) Regulations 2002 (SI 2002 No 681)* which came into force from 6 April 2002 introduced changes intended to simplify contracting out for both occupational and person pension schemes. A summary of these changes is contained in 4.73.

CONTRACTED-OUT RIGHTS ON DIVORCE

4.67 The *Pension Sharing (Contracting-out) (Consequential Amendments) Regulations 2000*, which came into force on 1 December 2000, amend the *Contracting-Out Regulations*. The aim is to ensure that those pension rights conferred under pension sharing arrangements, which are derived from the rights of a member protected under the contracting-out arrangements, receive similar protection to that accorded to contracted-out rights.

STAKEHOLDER SCHEMES

4.68 If an individual contracts out of S2P using a stakeholder pension plan, a rebate of National Insurance contributions is paid into their stakeholder plan.

There is a NICO manual explaining the procedures to be used from April 2001 where an individual uses a stakeholder pension to contract-out of S2P. This is manual CA84: Stakeholder Pension Scheme Manual. The manual is available from the Inland Revenue (website http://www.inlandrevenue.gov.uk/stakepension).

REPLACEMENT FOR SERPS

4.69 SERPS was based on a standard target benefit of 20% of average revalued earnings over a working lifetime restricted to earnings between the Lower and Upper Earnings Limits. This has been replaced with effect from 6 April 2002 by S2P which provides different accrual rates and target benefits depending on earnings.

Benefits under S2P

4.70 Different accrual rates apply depending on earnings:

(*a*) accrual for a target benefit of 40% for earnings between LEL (£4,108) and the new Lower Earnings Threshold (LET) (£11,600);

4.71   *Contracting-out*

(*b*)   accrual for a target benefit of 10% between LET and new Upper Earnings Threshold (UET) (£26,600);

(*c*)   accrual for a target benefit of 20% between second threshold and UEL (£32,330);

(*d*)   everyone earning at least LEL will be treated as if earning LET.

It is intended that in 2006 all contracted in employees will receive the same flat rate benefit based on LET.

Non-earners

4.71   S2P provides benefits for some non-earners, based on assumed earnings of LET. They are:

(*a*)   those receiving long-term incapacity benefits;

(*b*)   those caring for a disabled or sick person or a child under 6.

Other non-earners remain excluded from S2P (as they were from SERPS) including:

(*a*)   self employed;

(*b*)   students;

(*c*)   unemployed;

(*d*)   early retired and short term sick.

4.72   The main differences between SERPS and S2P are that the latter is intended to provide higher benefits to people on lower earnings and to provide assumed earnings equal to the LET in respect of non-earners such as those on long-term incapacity benefit.

Contracting out of S2P

4.73   Occupational schemes already contracted-out under SERPS will continue to do so on a similar basis with the state providing pension top ups to the new S2P level for low and moderate earners. The NI rebate for COSRs is 3.5% of band earnings (previously 3.0%) and the employee rebate remains at 1.6%. Age related rebates for COMPs are retained.

Personal Pension Schemes (see 15.30) will contract out at the S2P level of benefit with the state topping up to LET level for those earning between LEL and LET. Rebates will be calculated by reference both to age and to the different levels of accrual. It is intended that this will continue after the flat rate S2P is introduced.

Proposed legislative changes

4.74 In the government's White Paper issued on 11 June 2003 entitled 'Action on Occupational Pensions', the government indicated its intention to streamline the rules of contracting-out. In particular, it stated its intention to find a 'workable and affordable solution to the problems created by the complexity of the Guaranteed Minimum Pension (GMP) element of contracted-out schemes'.

In a press release dated 17 October 2003 the Secretary of State for Work and Pensions, Andrew Smith, announced measures that would enable occupational pension schemes which had contracted-out of SERPs to convert the GMP element into their own scheme benefits, as long as the value of members' previously accrued rights are maintained. If schemes take up this option they will have to convert on the basis of actuarial equivalence with the proviso that any resulting changes will not affect the value of individual accrued rights.

However, the Pensions Bill published on 12 February 2004 did not contain any of these proposed changes, and it is currently unclear when the government will be legislating to give effect to these proposals.

Chapter 5

Inland Revenue limits and taxation

INTRODUCTION

5.1 This chapter deals with the tax treatment of those occupational pension schemes which are 'exempt approved' by the Inland Revenue under *Chapter I* of *Part XIV* of the *Income and Corporation Taxes Act 1988* (*ICTA 1988*). The taxation of occupational pension schemes which are not so approved is covered in chapter 14. The tax treatment of personal pensions is summarised in chapter 15. (It is possible for *Chapter I* approved schemes to convert to become approved under *Chapter IV* of *ICTA 1988*. Guidance was given by the Inland Revenue when new Part 24 was added to IR12(2001) by Pension Update 127 issued on 4 March 2002.)

The Inland Revenue/Treasury Consultation Paper 'Simplifying the Taxation of Pensions – Increasing Choice and Flexibility for All' which was released in December 2002 proposed various changes which would have a dramatic impact on the subject matter of this Chapter. That was followed in turn by a further Consultation Paper 'Simplifying the Taxation of Pensions: the Government's proposals' which was issued in December 2003, the Chancellor's statement in the March 2004 Budget and the Finance Bill which was published 8 April 2004. The revised changes are summarised in 5.41 and 5.42 below.

Schemes which are approved by the Inland Revenue's Savings, Pensions, Share Schemes ('IR SPSS') gain certain tax advantages, namely:

(*a*) the employer obtains tax relief on his contributions;

(*b*) the employee obtains tax relief on his contributions;

(*c*) the employee is not charged on his employer's contributions as a benefit in kind;

(*d*) some relief from income tax and capital gains tax is available on the investment income and gains of the fund;

(*e*) pensions are taxed as earned rather than unearned income (although the tax rates for both types of income are the same at present); and

(*f*) part of the pension may be taken in the form of a lump sum which is (currently) tax-free.

To obtain all the available tax advantages in respect of contributions and investment income and gains, a scheme must be not only an approved scheme but an 'exempt approved scheme' under *section 592* of *ICTA 1988*. To be exempt approved, an approved scheme must:

(i) be established under irrevocable trusts (and the IR SPSS must be satisfied that this is the case); or

(ii) be a scheme which the Revenue, having regard to any special circumstances, decide to treat as an exempt approved scheme.

The Revenue is required to approve a scheme which meets the requirements set out in *section 590(3)* of *ICTA 1988*; this is known as mandatory approval. These requirements are very strict and the vast majority of schemes do not meet them. Consequently most schemes seek 'discretionary' approval in accordance with the requirements set out in *section 591* of *ICTA 1988*. This chapter, therefore, addresses the requirements for discretionary (rather than mandatory) approval.

The IR SPSS exercises its discretion to approve schemes in accordance with guidelines set out in an office manual which is summarised in the IR SPSS's practice notes. (IR12 (2001)); these Practice Notes, rather than the earlier IR12 (1997), now apply to the vast majority of approved schemes). The office manual and the Practice Notes reflect legislation and discretionary practice but they do not have the force of law. The IR SPSS do, however, work closely from them.

The requirements which a scheme must meet to obtain approval relate primarily to the maximum benefits which can be paid from the scheme, but there are also limits on the contributions which members may pay. Further details of these limits are summarised in 5.6 below.

It is important to note that the IR SPSS's practice notes set out the maximum benefits that may be paid. Pension schemes are not obliged to pay maximum benefits and, in the vast majority of final salary schemes, the rules will effectively limit the benefits payable to lesser amounts. If a scheme is of the money purchase type, the benefits will depend on the contributions paid to it and the growth of the funds invested, and these benefits will usually be insufficient to provide the Revenue maxima. If the funds available in a money purchase scheme are more than sufficient to provide the Revenue maxima then the excess (less any tax) may have to be refunded.

As from 1 December 2000, yet a further complication has been added to any consideration of Revenue maxima (as a result of the *Welfare Reform and Pensions Act 1999*), namely the ability of the courts to issue a pension sharing order. The issue of pension sharing orders is dealt with in more detail in Chapter 8.

REMUNERATION AND FINAL REMUNERATION

5.2 The maximum benefits a member may receive from an exempt approved occupational pension scheme and the maximum contributions he may

5.3 Inland Revenue limits and taxation

make to such a scheme are calculated by reference to his 'final remuneration'. As the expression suggests, final remuneration is itself calculated by reference to 'remuneration'.

Remuneration

5.3 Remuneration includes any emoluments chargeable to tax under *sections 15* or *21* of the *Income Tax (Earnings and Pensions) Act 2003* (ITEPA 2003) except:

(*a*) sums arising from the acquisition or disposal of shares or from a right to acquire shares; and

(*b*) payments on the termination of office (eg redundancy payments and golden handshakes).

[*Chapter 3* of *Part 6* if *ITEPA 2003*].

(Glossary to the Practice Notes and *ICTA 1988, s 612*).

Remuneration is limited in certain circumstances by legislation.

For members joining pension schemes on or after 17 March 1987, but before 1 June 1989, generally known as 'high earners' the amount of remuneration which can be used to determine cash lump sum benefits may not exceed £100,000. [*ICTA 1988, Sch 23 para 6(2)*].

The level of remuneration which may be taken into account for the purposes of determining the maximum benefits payable is restricted to the 'permitted maximum' or, as it is colloquially known, the 'earnings cap' imposed by *section 590C* of *ICTA 1988*.

The earnings cap was first introduced in 1989 and was set at £60,000 p.a. for the tax year 1989/1990. There is provision in the legislation for the earnings cap to be increased annually in line with the retail prices index rounded up to the nearest multiple of £600. [*ICTA 1988, s 590C(5)*]. The earnings cap for the tax year 2004/2005 is £102,000.

The earnings cap generally applies to all members of schemes established on or after 14 March 1989. It also applies to members of schemes established before 14 March 1989 who became members on or after 1 June 1989. However, it does not apply where employees are considered to have continuity of membership from before 1 June 1989. [*Retirement Benefits Schemes (Continuation of Rights of Members of Approved Schemes) Regulations 1990 (SI 1990 No 2101)*]. For example, if a member moves from one pension scheme of an employer to another scheme of the same employer he may be treated as if he had always been a member of the second scheme and so will not necessarily become subject to the earnings cap.

Pension Update 110 reported amendments to recognise participation in employee share ownership plans and restrictive undertakings.

Amounts deducted from pay to purchase 'Partnership Shares' (which are not subject to tax under *section 15* or *21* of *ITEPA 2003*) as part of a Share Incentive Plan can be included in the calculation of remuneration (and final remuneration – see 5.4 below) (*Finance Act 2000, Sch 8, para 83*). Payments made to employees on leaving in consideration for them agreeing (for example) not to work for a competitor, are not to be included in remuneration as they are not a reward for working for the employer. Schemes wishing to incorporate these changes will need amendment. Where standard documents have been agreed, extended wording may be added to Documentation Certificates PS5 or PS6

Final remuneration

5.4 The definition of final remuneration is set out in the IR SPSS's Practice Notes (IR12 (2001) Appendix I). There are two basic definitions of final remuneration depending upon the category of member involved. Broadly these definitions are:

(*a*) the highest remuneration liable to income tax under *section 15* or *21* of *ITEPA 2003* for any one of the five years preceding a member's date of retirement, leaving pensionable service or death (whichever is earlier), being the total of:

   (i) the basic pay for the year in question ('the basic pay year'); and

   (ii) the yearly average over three or more consecutive years ending with the expiry of the corresponding basic pay year of any fluctuating emoluments; or

(*b*) the yearly average of the total remuneration liable to income tax under *section 15* or *21* of *ITEPA 2003* for any three or more consecutive years ending not earlier than ten years before the date of retirement, leaving pensionable service or death (whichever is earlier).

Whichever formulae gives the best results may be used for most members but only the second formula can be used for controlling directors or other members whose remuneration after 5 April 1987 exceeds £100,000 per annum. The restriction was introduced because the directors of private companies are able to control the remuneration paid to them. Their ability to increase their remuneration just before they retire is therefore restricted by the imposition of the three year averaging. The three year averaging also applies to any member who was a controlling director at any time in the last ten years before retirement. These restrictions prevent a director who has relinquished control just before retirement from using the best year in the last five for final remuneration purposes. A controlling director is any member who, at any time after 16 March 1987 and within ten years of retirement or leaving pensionable service, has been a director and, either on his own or with one or more associates, has beneficially owned or been able to control directly, indirectly or through other companies, 20 per cent or more of the ordinary share capital of the company. ('Controlling

5.5 Inland Revenue limits and taxation

director' is defined, in *paragraph 5(5)* of *Schedule 23* to *ICTA 1988*, as a person who is a director (as defined in *section 612*) and is within *paragraph (b)* of *section 417(5)* in relation to the employer company).

Fluctuating emoluments include any remuneration other than basic salary which fluctuates from year to year, for example, bonuses and profit related pay (IR12 (2001) Appendix I). If only one year's fluctuating emoluments were used to arrive at the figure for final remuneration it could distort the final figures considerably or could be manipulated. This type of remuneration must be averaged over a period of three years. If fluctuating emoluments are only paid in a single year and are to be included when calculating final remuneration the agreement of IR SPSS should be sought beforehand.

The 'basic pay year' used for calculating final remuneration will not necessarily end at the date of retirement or leaving service or death. In some cases it may be several years before then. To allow for inflation, remuneration paid in earlier years may be increased in line with the Retail Prices Index up to the last day of the basic pay year.

The date of the particular year's end that is used for calculating final remuneration is flexible provided it falls in the relevant period prior to the date of retirement, leaving service or death (as the case may be). It may, for example, be convenient to use the company's accounting year, the tax year, or the year ending on retirement.

Pension Update 110 reported modifications to recognise absences on paid maternity leave and participation in employee share ownership plans and restrictive undertakings.

Where an employee leaves service during a year which includes paid maternity leave or within twelve months of the end of paid maternity leave then final remuneration can include a notional amount based on the greater of the remuneration the employer would have been obliged to pay under the contract in force prior to the start of the paid maternity leave and the actual remuneration received in the twelve months immediately prior to the commencement of paid maternity leave.

As mentioned in 5.3 above, amounts deducted from pay to purchase 'Partnership Shares' (which are not subject to tax under *section 15* or *21* of *ITEPA 2003*) as part of a Share Incentive Plan can be included in the calculation of final remuneration (*Finance Act 2000, Sch 8, para 83*).

NORMAL RETIREMENT DATE

5.5   The normal retirement date of any member must be specified in the rules of the scheme (IR12 (2001) PN 6.5 to 6.11). It can differ for different categories of member but must be between the ages of 60 to 75. Lower ages may be permitted in some employments, for example, for sportsmen or those with

Inland Revenue limits and taxation **5.7**

hazardous occupations. However, the IR SPSS pointed out in Pension Update 120 that lack of success as a result of waning popularity or the deterioration of a solo singer's or pop group's technique were not arguments that prove sufficient grounds for agreeing a low normal retirement date. Female members of occupational pension schemes who joined before 1 June 1989 may have a normal retirement date of 55. This Revenue distinction does not, however, override the requirements for equal treatment of men and women.

MAXIMUM BENEFITS

The three regimes

5.6 The maximum benefits in respect of a member are partly governed by his date of admission to membership of the pension scheme. There are three regimes in this respect:

(*a*) admission to membership before 17 March 1987;

(*b*) admission to membership of a scheme established before 14 March 1989, between 17 March 1987 and 31 May 1989 (inclusive); and

(*c*) admission to membership from 1 June 1989.

In some circumstances a member who would otherwise fall within categories (*b*) and (*c*) may be treated for these purposes as if he had joined the scheme on an earlier date. [*Occupational Pension Schemes (Transitional Provisions) Regulations 1988 (SI 1988 No 1436); Retirement Benefits Schemes (Continuation of Rights of Members of Approved Schemes) Regulations 1990 (SI 1990 No 2101)*]. One example of this is where a member moves between schemes following the sale of his employer. Another is where a member is re-instated to membership following a successful claim relating to mis-selling of personal pensions.

Members who fall within categories (*a*) and (*b*) are said to have 'continued rights' (IR12 (2001) Appendix III). Such a member can elect to be treated as if he was admitted to membership on or after 1 June 1989. An election can be made at any time before benefits commence, are bought out or transferred, or attainment of age 75 whichever first occurs. Following such an election the member's benefits will be based on the Inland Revenue's permitted maxima for members joining pension schemes on or after 1 June 1989, but they will become subject to the earnings cap (see 5.3 above).

Pension at normal retirement date

Maximum total benefits

5.7 The maximum total benefits that may be provided on retirement under an approved scheme are calculated by reference to an employee's length of service with the employer and his or her final remuneration. Total benefits are

5.8 *Inland Revenue limits and taxation*

measured in terms of an annual pension for the member payable for life being the aggregate of any pension payable (including, where the member does not fall within the administrative easement described in 5.8 below (IR12 (2001) PN 7.7), any pension debit) and the pension equivalent of any non-pension benefits (IR12 (2001) PN 7.2). The maximum aggregate benefit payable without taking account of 'retained benefits' (see 5.24 below) is a pension (of which part may be taken in lump sum form as described in 5.11 below) of $\frac{1}{60}$th of final remuneration for each year of service (up to 40 years) (IR 12 (2001) PN 7.3). However, this is subject to special provisions relating to controlling directors (IR 12 (2001) PN 7.10) and the aggregation of benefits with other approved schemes (IR 12 (2001) PN 7.25 and 7.26).

Pension sharing easement

5.8 Under an administrative easement, pension debits can be ignored in calculating the member's maximum permissible total benefits, both pension and lump sum, under IR 12 (2001) PN 7.2. With two important exceptions, the easement applies to members of schemes other than simplified defined contribution schemes. The first exception would be a controlling director (within the meaning in *regulation 5(5)* of the *Retirement Benefits Schemes (Sharing of Pensions on Divorce or Annulment) Regulations 2000 (SI 2000 No. 1085)*. The second exception relates to members whose earnings exceed one quarter of the permitted maximum determined at its level for the year of assessment in which the marriage was dissolved. For this purpose, earnings mean those in respect of pensionable service to which the scheme relates, and which were received during the year of assessment immediately preceding the year of assessment in which the dissolution or annulment of the marriage occurred, and from which tax was deducted under PAYE.

The test is applied as at the date of divorce and once it is satisfied, the pension debit may be permanently ignored, that is irrespective of subsequent employment changes (IR 12 (2001) PN 7.7).

Pre-17 March 1987 member

5.9 For a member who became, or is treated as having become, a member prior to 17 March 1987, the maximum permissible pension of two thirds of final remuneration can be accrued over a period of ten years' service, in accordance with the following table:

Years of service to normal retirement date	Maximum pension (before any commutation and including the annuity value of any lump sum entitlement) expressed as 60ths of Final Remuneration
1–5	1 for each year
6	8
7	16

Years of service to normal retirement date	Maximum pension (before any commutation and including the annuity value of any lump sum entitlement) expressed as 60ths of Final Remuneration
8	24
9	32
10 or more	40

Regardless of the date on which the member joined the scheme, the pension (unless it does not exceed 1/60th of final remuneration for each year of service) must not, when aggregated with any 'retained benefits' (see 5.24 below), exceed two thirds of final remuneration.

Post-17 March 1987 member

5.10 The maximum pension payable to a member on retirement at normal retirement date is, as indicated in 5.7 above, two thirds of his final remuneration (IR12 (2001) Part 7). For a person who became, or is treated as having become, a member on or after 17 March 1987 (that is a person who is within either category (b) or (c) as described in 5.6 above) this is restricted to 1/30th of final remuneration for each year of service subject to a maximum of 20 years.

Cash lump sum at normal retirement date

5.11 Members are allowed to commute some or all of their pension for a tax free cash lump sum (IR12 (2001) Part 8). Pension Update 135 issued on 20 December 2002 clarifies how the Inland Revenue expects approved schemes to administer tax free lump sum retirement benefits. The lump sum is limited to no more than 3/80ths of final remuneration for each year of service up to a maximum of 40 years. This allows a cash lump sum of one and a half times final remuneration to be paid after 40 years of service. A higher accrual rate is permitted if the member has continued rights (see 5.6 above).

The actual accrual rate depends on when the member is treated as having joined the scheme and is calculated in accordance with 5.12 to 5.14 below as appropriate.

Pre-17 March 1987 member

5.12 If the member is treated as having joined the scheme before 17 March 1987, the following table applies:

5.13 *Inland Revenue limits and taxation*

Years of service to normal retirement date	Maximum lump sum expressed as 80ths of final remuneration
1–8	3 for each year
9	30
10	36
11	42
12	48
13	54
14	63
15	72
16	81
17	90
18	99
19	108
20 or more	120

The limits described in this paragraph do not apply where a member's benefit entitlement in a scheme is permanently reduced following a pension sharing order and the member does not fall within the pension sharing administrative easement described in 5.8 above. The calculation of the maximum lump sum benefit, in these circumstances, depends on whether the lump sum is obtained by commutation of pension or whether the scheme rules provide for a pension and a separate lump sum rather than a commutable pension. In the former case the maximum lump sum benefit is the greater of:

(*a*) 2.25 times the initial annual rate of pension after reduction to take account of the pension debit; or

(*b*) an amount determined in accordance with the scheme rules as if there had been no pension share, then reduced by 2.25 times the amount of pension from the pension debit calculated at the member's normal retirement date.

Where scheme rules provide for a pension and a separate lump sum as opposed to a commutable pension, the maximum lump sum benefit is the greater of:

(*a*) three times the initial annual rate of the separate pension after reduction to take account of the pension debit; or

(*b*) an amount determined in accordance with the scheme rules as if there had been no pension share, but then reduced by three times the amount of pension from the pension debit calculated at the member's normal retirement date. (IR 12 (2001) PN 8.26.)

Post-17 March 1987 but pre-31 May 1989 member

5.13 If the member is treated as having joined the scheme during the period

Inland Revenue limits and taxation **5.15**

from 17 March 1987 to 31 May 1989 (inclusive) then (except for schemes commencing on or after 14 March 1989 (see 5.14 below)) a more complex formula applies. The member may use the higher accrual rate set out in the table in 5.12 above, but only to the same proportionate extent that his pension from the scheme (before any part of it has been exchanged for a lump sum or given up to provide further pensions for dependants) falls within the range between $\frac{1}{60}$th and $\frac{1}{80}$th of final remuneration for each year.

These limits do not apply where a member's benefit entitlement in a scheme is permanently reduced following a pension sharing order and the member does not fall within the administrative easement. In such circumstances, the maximum lump sum benefit is calculated in accordance with 5.12 above.

Post-1 June 1989 member

5.14 If the member is treated as having joined the scheme on or after 1 June 1989 (or before then if the scheme itself commenced on or after 14 March 1989), and his pension (before any part of it has been exchanged for a lump sum or given up to provide further pensions for dependants) exceeds $\frac{1}{60}$th of final remuneration for each year of service, his lump sum may be increased to 2.25 times the annual amount of that pension.

However, in any of the above cases, the lump sum plus any 'retained benefits' (see 5.24 below) must not exceed one and a half times final remuneration.

For the purpose of calculating Revenue limits, commutation factors are set by the Inland Revenue to determine the cash value provided for each £1.00 of pension given up (IR12 (2001) Part 7). A commutation factor of 12:1 must be used irrespective of age, sex or escalation rate for current members and those members with continued rights who opt for the current regime. For members with continued rights, commutation factors differ according to age. At age 60 a commutation factor of between 10.2 and 11.0 may be used; at age 65 the range is 9.0 to 9.8 (IR12 (2001) PN 7.59). It is possible to agree enhanced commutation factors with the IR SPSS outside these ranges.

Early retirement and leaving service before normal retirement date

5.15 The rules of approved occupational pension schemes may permit members to draw early retirement benefits at any age after 50 (or earlier on grounds of incapacity) provided they actually retire or cease pensionable service with the employer concerned (IR12 (2001) PN 10.8). A female member with continued rights may receive early retirement benefits from age 45 if she retires within ten years of her normal retirement date as such members were permitted to have a normal retirement date of 55.

The receipt of an early retirement pension will not preclude a member from taking up employment elsewhere although the early retirement benefits may have to be taken into account as 'retained benefits' (see 5.24 below) if the

5.16 *Inland Revenue limits and taxation*

member joins the subsequent employer's pension scheme. If a member is subsequently re-employed by the employer from whose scheme early retirement benefits have been, or are being, paid the rules of the scheme may permit the suspension of the early retirement pension (IR12 (2001) PN 7.32); if the member is to accrue further benefits under the scheme the early retirement benefits must be suspended (IR12 (2001) Appendix IV).

Two recent cases merit some attention. The case of *Venables and others v Hornby (Inspector of Taxes) [2003] UKHL 65, [2004] 1 All ER 627*, which went to the House of Lords, concerned the managing director of a company that operated a small self-administered scheme. The Court of Appeal had held that under the legislation 'retire' must mean cessation of service as an employee or director of the employer in question. It did not include merely a change in the nature of the employment. Under the terms of the Scheme there was no support for a conclusion that 'retirement' was anything other than cessation of service. The House of Lords overturned the decision of the Court of Appeal. Lord Millett gave the leading speech. He said that 'it does not follow from the fact that the word Employee is defined to include a director that an employee who is also a director must retire from both his employment and his office as director before he can be said to retire within the meaning of the Trust Deed'. The case, therefore, turned on the definition of the word 'employee'.

In *Hoover Ltd v Hetherington and another [2002] All ER (D) 418 (May)* the High Court had to consider whether the member had 'retired' at 57 when he had left one employer and started a completely different employment. The Court held there that 'retire' meant withdrawal from some office or business without necessarily saying anything about any other office. Hoover is still relevant when considering the position of an individual intending taking up employment elsewhere.

Early retirement on grounds of incapacity

5.16 If a member retires early at any age on grounds of incapacity, his benefits may be calculated in the same manner as if he had retired at normal retirement date. Both his actual service and potential service (ie the service he would have completed had he remained a member up to his normal retirement date) can count towards the calculation. Final remuneration is calculated as at his date of actual retirement.

'Incapacity' is defined in the Glossary to IR12 (2001) as 'physical or mental deterioration which is sufficiently serious to prevent the individual from following his or her normal employment, or which seriously impairs his or her earning capacity. It does not mean simply a decline in energy or ability'.

Early retirement other than on grounds of incapacity

5.17 The maximum pension payable from an approved scheme on early retirement, other than on grounds of incapacity (IR12 (2001) PN 10.9 to 10.14), for a member without continued rights is the greater of:

(a) 1/60th of final remuneration for each year of service up to a maximum of 40 years; and

(b) the lesser of:

  (i) 1/30th of final remuneration for each year of service up to a maximum of 20 years; and

  (ii) 2/3rds of final remuneration less 'retained benefits' (see 5.24 below).

Where the member has a pension debit in relation to the scheme and does not fall within the administrative easement described in 5.8 above, the maximum benefits are calculated in accordance with the requirements set out above but must be reduced by the pension debit.

The maximum cash lump sum payable in such circumstances (IR 12 (2001) PN 10.15 to 10.18) is 3/80ths of final remuneration for each year of service up to a maximum of 40 years or, if greater, an amount equal to 2.25 times the initial annual rate of pension to be paid (before any part of that pension has been commuted for the lump sum or given up to provide further pensions for dependants). However, (unless the lump sum does not exceed 3/80th of final remuneration for each year of service) the lump sum must not, when aggregated with any 'retained benefits' (see 5.24 below), exceed one and a half times final remuneration.

For members with continued rights (see 5.6 above), the maximum pension on early retirement is either 1/60th of final remuneration for each year of service up to a maximum of 40 years or, if more favourable, the amount calculated by the formula:

$$N/NS \times P;$$

where:

N is the number of actual years of service up to a maximum of 40 years;

NS is the number of actual years of service plus years of potential service to normal retirement date; and

P is the maximum pension the member could have received had he remained in service until normal retirement date calculated by reference to final remuneration as at the date of termination of pensionable service.

For members with continued rights (see 5.6 above) the maximum cash lump sum available on early retirement is either 3/80ths of final remuneration for each year of service up to a maximum of 40 years or, if more favourable, the amount calculated by the formula:

$$N/NS \times LS;$$

5.18 *Inland Revenue limits and taxation*

where:

N is the number of actual years of service with a maximum of 40 years;

NS is the number of actual years of service plus years of potential service to normal retirement date; and

LS is the maximum lump sum the member could have received had he remained in pensionable service until normal retirement date calculated by reference to final remuneration at the date of termination of pensionable service.

Leaving service benefits

5.18 If a member leaves service before reaching normal retirement date, several options are available regarding his accrued benefits (IR12 (2001) Part 10). If the member is at least age 50, retirement benefits may be paid immediately if the scheme's rules permit this. If the member has not reached age 50 benefits may be left in the scheme and paid after age 50 as early retirement benefits or at normal retirement date. The maximum benefits payable on leaving service in respect of pensions and cash lump sums are, broadly, the same as those payable on early retirement.

Alternatively a deferred annuity may be purchased or a transfer value paid to another occupational or personal pension scheme. In these circumstances, it is important to remember that the amount used to purchase the annuity or the amount of the transfer value cannot exceed the Inland Revenue maximum amount for early retirement benefits. In particular, there are limitations on making transfer payments to personal pension schemes for controlling directors and other members whose remuneration exceeds the earnings cap. [*Personal Pension Schemes (Transfer Payments) Regulations 2001 (SI 2001 No 119)*].

Retirement after normal retirement date

5.19 In certain circumstances, a member may be permitted to postpone receipt of his benefits until after normal retirement date (IR12 (2001) PN 7.43 to 7.46). The calculation of the maximum pension permissible by the Revenue on late retirement will depend on whether the member has continued rights.

If the member has continued rights (see 5.6 above), his maximum pension will be the greatest of:

(a) his maximum pension at normal retirement date, but substituting the date of actual retirement for normal retirement date;

(b) his maximum pension at normal retirement date plus $1/60$th (up to a maximum of $5/60$th) for each further year of service over 40 years after normal retirement date; and

(c) his maximum pension at normal retirement date increased by increases in the Retail Prices Index or by actuarial increases (whichever produces the greater result) since normal retirement date;

except that the first two options are not available to controlling directors other than in respect of service after age 70.

If the member does not have continued rights (see 5.6 above), the maximum pension will be the maximum pension he could receive if his date of actual retirement was substituted for his normal retirement date.

Death benefits

Lump sums payable on death in service before normal retirement date

5.20 On a member's death in service before reaching normal retirement date (IR12 (2001) Part 11), a lump sum may be paid equal to the greater of:

(a)   £5,000; and

(b)   four times final remuneration less 'retained benefits' (see 5.24 below).

In addition, a refund of the member's own contributions may be paid with or without interest. As a member's death cannot be foreseen, the definition of final remuneration is more generous than at normal retirement date. Final remuneration on death may be:

(i)   the annual basic salary immediately before death; or

(ii) the annual basic salary immediately before death plus the average of fluctuating emoluments during the three years up to the date of death; or

(iii) the total remuneration, fixed and fluctuating, paid during any period of 12 months falling within the three years prior to death.

If a scheme's rules provide for a lump sum benefit on death that does not exceed twice the member's final remuneration 'retained benefits' (see 5.24 below) need not be taken into account.

Spouses and dependants benefits

5.21 Following the death of a member in service or after retirement, a spouse's and/or dependant's pension may be provided. The maximum level of all such pensions must not exceed two thirds of the maximum pension that could have been provided for the deceased member had he retired due to incapacity immediately before death, calculated on the basis of there being no lump sum commutation at retirement and as if the deceased had no 'retained benefits' (see 5.24 below) from earlier occupations.

Death of an early leaver

5.22 If a former member dies before age 50, having deferred benefits in the

5.23 Inland Revenue limits and taxation

scheme, a cash lump sum may be paid. Spouse's and dependant's pensions may also be provided, calculated by reference to the deceased member's maximum approvable deferred pension.

Death in service after normal retirement date

5.23 Where a member dies in service after normal retirement date, maximum benefits may be provided on the basis of death in service (see 5.20 and 5.21 above). In the case of a member with continued rights, benefits may be provided on the basis that the member died in retirement having retired the day before the date of death.

Retained benefits

5.24 Retained benefits (IR12 (2001) Appendix I) generally are retained rights to relevant benefits and, where appropriate, pension debits built up in previous employments or periods of self-employment from schemes or contractual arrangements which have benefited from tax privileges. These include:

(*a*) retirement benefit schemes approved by the Inland Revenue or seeking approval;

(*b*) retirement annuity contracts and personal pension schemes; and

(*c*) certain overseas schemes.

Retained benefits may be ignored in any of the following circumstances:

(i) in the case of pensions benefits, if they do not exceed £260 in total from all sources;

(ii) in the case of lump sum retirement benefits, if they do not exceed £2,500 in total from all sources;

(iii) in the case of death benefits if they do not exceed £2,500 in total from all sources;

(iv) refund of a member's personal contributions.

Appendix 1 to IR12 (2001) describes 'relevant benefits' as follows:

'*Relevant Benefits* are defined in *section 612 (1)* of *ICTA 1988* in very wide terms, and broadly cover any type of financial benefit given by an employer on retirement or death or by virtue of a pension sharing order but excluding benefits given in connection with genuine redundancy (as opposed to retirement). The definition does not include benefits receivable only in the event of death by accident or disablement by accident during service'.

Appendix 1 to IR12 (2001) describes 'retirement benefits scheme' as follows:

'*Retirement Benefits Scheme* is defined in *section 611* as a scheme for the provision of *relevant benefits* for one or more employees but does not include any national scheme (such as the State Earnings Related Pension Scheme) providing such benefits. In this context 'scheme' needs to be interpreted widely to include any arrangement creating an enforceable right to such benefits and an arrangement to pay ex-gratia *relevant benefits* (although the latter type of arrangement is not approvable unless the benefit is in the form of a lump sum and satisfies certain conditions). Employee includes an ex-employee.' 'Employees' and 'employee' are replaced by 'scheme members' and 'scheme member' in *subsection (3)* and *(4)(b)* of *section 611* and *subsection (b)* defines 'scheme member' as including both employees and ex spouses.'

TAXATION

5.25 Occupational pension schemes which are granted exempt approved status obtain a number of advantages in the form of tax reliefs.

Employers' contributions

5.26 Contributions actually paid by an employer to an exempt approved scheme are generally allowable as deductions for income or corporation tax purposes. [*ICTA 1988, s 592*]. Deductions for ordinary annual contributions are allowable in the accounting period in which they are paid. (There are special rules applicable to fully insured money purchase schemes in the Funding Guidance Notes to be found in Appendix VIII to IR12 (2001), a revised version of which was issued on 4 March 2002 with Pensions Update 124.)

Any other contributions (generally referred to as special contributions) paid to a scheme by an employer within a chargeable period ending on or after 1 June 1996 which amount to £500,000 or over and exceed the total of other contributions made by the employer to that scheme in the same chargeable period, can, at the discretion of the Revenue, be 'spread' for tax relief purposes. [*ICTA 1988, s 592*]. Aggregate special contributions amounting to less than £500,000 will not be spread for tax relief purposes. (See Pensions Update No. 53 for details of the Inland Revenue's recent clarification of current policy regarding spreading). The period over which special contributions can be spread (IR 12 (2001) PN 5.9 is determined by reference to the amount of the contribution in accordance with the following table:

Total special contributions within a chargeable period	Maximum number of years over which the total contribution can be spread
£500,000 or over, but less than £1,000,000	2 years
£1,000,000 or over, but less than £2,000,000	3 years
£2,000,000 or over	4 years

5.27 *Inland Revenue limits and taxation*

The amount of any special contribution is apportioned equally over the relevant period for the purposes of spreading. For example, if £800,000 is paid in chargeable period ended 31 December 1996 it would be spread as £400,000 in that year and £400,000 the following year. Where a chargeable period is less than or more than twelve months, allowance is given on a pro-rata basis. For example, if the first chargeable period is eight months and a special contribution of £800,000 was paid during this period it would be spread as £320,000 over the eight months and £480,000 in the following twelve months.

If the IR SPSS believes chargeable periods are being manipulated to reduce the period of spreading, it reserves the right to determine the spread on some other basis.

Special contributions (ie any contributions other than ordinary contributions) paid by any employer since 31 December 1995 to any exempt approved occupational pension scheme must be reported to the IR SPSS within 180 days of the end of the scheme year in which they are paid. [*Retirement Benefits Schemes (Information Powers) Regulations 1995 (SI 1995 No 3103)*]. The only exceptions to this are if:

(*a*)   the total special contributions made by the employer in a chargeable period do not exceed one half of the earnings cap or the employer's ordinary annual contribution, whichever is the greater; or

(*b*)   the special contributions are made solely to finance cost of living increases.

With regard to part-time employees who are given back dated rights to membership of occupational pension schemes, the Inland Revenue confirmed the tax position in Pensions Update 131 issued on 23 April 2002. Employer contributions to fund back service will be allowable for tax purposes in the normal way under *ICTA 1988, s 592(4)*.

Pension sharing orders

5.27   Generally, when a pension credit is established for an ex-spouse within a scheme, the employer should not make any further contributions in respect of that pension credit. The prohibition will not occur, however, where contributions are required to be paid in accordance with a pensions sharing order (IR 12 (2001) PN 5.15). When, as a result of a pension sharing order, a member's benefit entitlement is permanently reduced and the member does not fall within the PN 7.7 administrative easement (see 5.8 above), the maximum approvable total benefits of that member are reduced. Further contributions by an employer for such a member should be based on no more than the reduced maximum approvable total benefits for that member. They should not be based on the maximum approvable benefits that would have applied for that member had the pension sharing order not been made (IR12 (2001) PN 5.16).

Employees' contributions

5.28 Contributions paid personally by members to an exempt approved scheme are allowable as an expense, for the purposes of calculating Schedule E income tax liability, in the tax year in which they are paid. [*ICTA 1988, s 592(7)*]. The maximum permitted contribution on which tax relief is allowed is 15 per cent of the member's remuneration from the employment to which the scheme relates. [*ICTA 1988, s 592(8)*]. The rules of the scheme should limit the amount of contributions a member can make to the scheme to the amount which qualifies for tax relief.

The Inland Revenue has a discretion to prescribe a higher limit than 15 per cent but will only do so in exceptional circumstances. One example of where the Revenue have been prepared to allow a greater contribution is where a member is reinstated into an occupational pension scheme following a successful claim relating to the mis-selling of a personal pension scheme (IR SPSS Update No. 21).

Although, for Inland Revenue purposes, members may or may not be required to make basic or contractual contributions to an approved scheme, Department for Work and Pensions' (DWP) legislation does require schemes to permit certain members to pay additional voluntary contributions to secure additional benefits subject to the requirements for approval (IR12 (2001) PN 4.1). 'Additional voluntary contributions' are described in Appendix 1 to IR12 (2001) as 'contributions by an employee other than basic or contractual contributions ie over and above contributions (if any) required as a condition of membership and include any such contribution paid under a *free-standing additional voluntary contribution scheme*'. A 'free-standing additional voluntary contribution scheme means a *retirement benefits scheme* approved by the Board by virtue of *section 591(2)(h)*, established by a pension provider or the trustees of an approved centralised scheme for non-associated employers ... to which the employer does not contribute and which provides benefits additional to those provided by a scheme to which the employer does contribute'.

Tax relief on employee contributions (other than those to a free-standing additional voluntary contributions scheme) is given through a special arrangement under the PAYE system whereby the contributions are deducted from gross pay before the member's PAYE tax deductions are calculated. The result of this is that, as the contributions are paid, the correct tax relief is given automatically (IR12 (2001) PN 4.3).

With regard to part-time employees given back dated rights to membership, guidance is given in Pensions Update 131. Paragraph 8 of the Update states that scheme rules would normally preclude the payment of contributions by members which are in excess of the limit for tax relief (IR 12 (2001) PN 4.4). However, the Inland Revenue has confirmed that there would be no objection to an employer paying contributions in excess of the 15% limit in the circumstances covered by Update 131. The Inland Revenue confirmed, therefore, that scheme rules may be amended accordingly. Nevertheless, tax relief would not

5.29 *Inland Revenue limits and taxation*

be available on any excess contributions over the 15% limit. An alternative approach, described in paragraph 9 of Update 131, would enable on-going contributions to be made. This would enable contributions to be spread over additional tax years and qualify for tax relief.

Pension sharing orders

5.29 For a member who does not fall within the administrative easement described in PN 7.7 and whose benefit entitlement is permanently reduced following a pension sharing order, the maximum approvable total benefits are reduced. Where there is scope to do so, however, contributions may be paid by such a member up to the maximum described in 5.27 above to rebuild some or all of the pension debit. Contributions cannot be paid by an ex-spouse to a scheme in respect of a pension credit held for that ex-spouse (IR 12 (2001) PN 4.6). However, where the ex-spouse is also entitled to benefits under the scheme as a result of being employed by a participating employer, contributions may be paid to the scheme up to the maximum described in 5.27 above. There may be circumstances where an ex-spouse has a pension credit held in a scheme in respect of which there is an entitlement to benefits as an employee and the scheme does not treat the pension credit rights as separate from the employee rights. In those circumstances, the pension credit rights will be taken into account in applying the tax approval limits to the total benefits that the individual receives as an employee scheme member. Again, in these circumstances, contributions must relate solely towards the provision of benefits that arise as a result of being an employee. This means that those contributions will be based on the reduced maximum approvable total employee benefits for that member, that is after taking into account the pension credit (IR 12 (2001) PN 4.6.).

Contributions and part-time employees

5.30 Pensions Update 131 was issued by IR SPSS following the House of Lords decision in *Preston & Others v Wolverhampton Healthcare Trust Case Co C78/98 (The Times 19 May 2000) [2001] 2 WLR 448, HL (The Times 9 February 2001)*. The Update was issued to confirm the tax position on pension contributions in respect of part-time employees who are to be given backdated rights to membership of occupational pension schemes. Paragraph 6 of the Update confirmed that contributions from an employer to fund back service would be allowable for tax purposes in the normal way under *section 592(4)* of *ICTA 1988*. With regard to employee contributions, paragraph 7 of the Update confirmed that contributions made by the employee to the scheme in order to catch up may be made as a single contribution or alternatively as on-going contributions. Tax relief under *section 592(7)* or *section 594(1)* of *ICTA 1988* is available. However, the limit of such relief remains at 15% of remuneration paid in the tax year in which the contribution is made.

Paragraph 8 of the Update points out that scheme rules would normally preclude the payment of contributions by members which are in excess of the 15% limit for tax relief (IR 12 (2001) PN 4.4). However, IR SPSS has no objection to an employee paying contributions in excess of the 15% limit in circumstances covered by the Update. It is possible for the scheme rules, therefore, to be amended accordingly but the tax relief would not be available on any excess contributions over the 15% limit.

Paragraph 9 of the Update describes the alternative approach of on-going contributions. Although an employee cannot opt to carry back or have payments otherwise related back to earlier years, contributions in relation to back years may, with the agreement of the scheme trustees, be made by instalments over future years. This would enable the amount of any contribution paid in a tax year to remain within the 15% limit.

Paragraph 10 of the Update deals with an employee who has left the employment concerned. Contributions may be made to the former employer's occupational pension scheme but no tax relief will be available in respect of those contributions.

Fund income

General

5.31 Investment income derived from assets held for the purposes of an exempt approved scheme is exempt from income tax at the basic rate of tax which applies to individuals (*ICTA 1988, s 592(2)*) and additional rate of tax which applies to discretionary trusts (*ICTA 1988, s 686(2)*). Thus income received gross by the trustees, eg rents and certain interest payments, is not subject to tax. Where tax was deducted before receipt by the trustees, for example, in the case of dividends, it may be reclaimed; up to the 1992/93 tax year the tax credit that can be reclaimed is 25 per cent of the dividend plus any tax credit. For the period 6 April to 1 July 1997, the value of the tax credit that can be reclaimed is only 20 per cent of the dividend plus the tax credit. [*Finance Act 1993, s 78*]. From 2 July 1997, the payment of tax credits on dividends paid by UK companies to tax approved pension schemes was abolished. [*Finance Act (No 2) 1997, s 19(2)*].

Any gains realised by the trustees on a disposal of an asset are not chargeable to capital gains tax. [*Taxation of Chargeable Gains Act 1992 (TCGA 1992), s 271(1)(g)*].

It had been considered that underwriting commission received by trustees, to the extent that it was applied for the purposes of the scheme, was exempt from income tax (*ICTA 1988, s 592(3)*). The Inland Revenue succeeded in its appeal before Lightman J. in the High Court case of *Clarke v. British Telecom Pension Trustees and Others [1999] PLR 51* to have reversed a decision made by the Special Commissioners who had earlier taken the view that the BT Trustees were not carrying on a trade. The Inland Revenue have expressed the view (IR 12 (2001) PN 17.11) that income from trading by an exempt-approved scheme

5.32 *Inland Revenue limits and taxation*

does not fall within the exemption from income tax (*ICTA 1988, s 592(2)*). It is interesting to compare PN17.10 (c) and PN17.11 and the statement in the latter that income from trading by an exempt-approved scheme does not fall within the exemption described as PN17.10 (a) – trading is not income derived from investments or deposits. PN17.10 (c) provides that underwriting commissions, to the extent that they are applied for the purposes of the scheme and would otherwise be chargeable under Case VI of Schedule D are exempt from Income Tax (*ICTA 1988, s 592 (3)*). In the *Clarke* case, the Revenue contended – initially successfully in the High Court – that the underwriting commissions did not fall within Case VI (which would have meant that they were tax-exempt under PN17.10 (c)) but rather they constituted receipts of a trade carried on by the trustees and, therefore, fell within Case I. The Court of Appeal, in *BT Pension Schemes v. Clarke [2000] PLR 157*, reversed the decision of Lightman J, holding in favour of the trustees, on the somewhat unsatisfactory ground that it was not open to the judge to make his own entirely independent evaluation of the evidence. The Court of Appeal held that this was not a test case but one very much resting on its facts. This leaves open the possibility of a successful attack by the Revenue in the future.

Profits on gains from transactions in certificates of deposit to the extent that the deposits are held for the purposes of the scheme are exempt from income tax. [*ICTA 1988, s 56(3)(b)*].

Income or capital gains derived from dealing in financial futures or traded options are exempt from capital gains tax (*TCGA 1992, s 271(1)(g)*) and income tax. [*ICTA 1988, s 659A*].

Stock lending fees received by the trustees after 1 January 1996 are exempt from income tax. [*ICTA 1988, s 129B*]. Such fees received prior to 2 January 1996 were liable to income tax. [*ICTA 1988, s 727(1)*]. Where manufactured payments are received under the terms of an approved stock lending arrangement such payments are exempt from income tax (Extra Statutory Concession C19).

Overfunding

5.32 Where the IR SPSS considers that a scheme is overfunded and proposals acceptable to the IR SPSS have not been forthcoming, the IR SPSS may withdraw approval from that part of the scheme which is overfunded. In such cases the tax reliefs described above will not be available to that part of the fund from which approval has been withdrawn (see chapter 11).

Trading

5.33 Certain activities undertaken by pension scheme trustees may be classed as trading by the Inland Revenue. This does not prejudice the exempt approval of a scheme provided the scheme's rules permit the trustees to trade. However, tax is payable on the income derived from such activities.

The question as to whether the trustees are trading or not is a matter for the inspector of taxes to decide, not the IR SPSS, although general guidance is given in the IR SPSS's Practice Notes (IR12 (2001) PN 17.10, 17.11 and 20.80). The relevant considerations in deciding whether a transaction involves trading or not are usually described as the six 'badges of trade' (1954 Royal Commission (Command 9474 paragraph 116). These are discussed in chapter 10, but broadly speaking they relate to:

(a) the subject of the transaction;

(b) the length of the period of ownership;

(c) the frequency or number of similar transactions;

(d) supplementary work carried out on or in connection with the property realised;

(e) the circumstances responsible for the transaction; and

(f) the motive for the transaction.

An indication of the types of activity that could result in the trustees paying tax as a result of trading are:

(i) bond washing and dividend stripping;

(ii) frequent purchases and sales of property particularly where the property is developed before being sold on;

(iii) commission received from underwriting new issues of stocks and securities;

(iv) purchases and sales of commodities;

(v) directly operating a commercial business; and

(vi) acquisition and leasing of plant, machinery, fixtures and fittings.

Benefits paid out

Pension benefits

5.34 Pensions paid either directly or indirectly (via an annuity) from a scheme to retired members or their spouse or dependants are liable to income tax under *section 15* or *21* of *ITEPA 2003*. The tax is collected by the trustees via the PAYE system. Where an annuity has been purchased by the trustees from a life office, the life office will be responsible for deducting tax through the PAYE system.

Where arrears of pension are paid that relate to more than one tax year tax will be deducted at the date of receipt. However, the recipient may request the inspector of taxes to assess the arrears of pension for the purposes of *section 15* or *21* of *ITEPA 2003* in the tax year in which they were earned. [*Finance*

5.35 *Inland Revenue limits and taxation*

Act 1989, s 41(2)]. This could be advantageous if rates of tax are lower in the earlier year(s) than in the year of receipt.

Lump sums

5.35 Cash lump sums payable on retirement either by way of commutation of pension or as an additional payment are generally tax-free subject to the benefit limits explained earlier (see 5.11 to 5.14 above). [*ICTA 1988, s 189*].

However, trivial pensions (ie pensions below a certain limit, currently £260 per annum) or pensions prospectively payable in circumstances of serious ill-health (ie where the recipient is not expected to live for more than 12 months) which are wholly commuted and paid to the member as a lump sum are subject to income tax under Case VI of Schedule D on the excess of the commutation payment over the greater of:

(a) $3/80$th of final remuneration for each year of service less any lump sum received other than by commutation, and

(b) the maximum lump sum payable in commutation of pension under the scheme rules otherwise than on grounds of triviality or exceptional circumstances of serious ill-health.

[*ICTA 1988, s 599*; IR (2001) PN 17.27].

Refunds of contributions

5.36 Where a member who has made contributions to the scheme leaves service without having become entitled to a deferred benefit under the preservation legislation (see chapter 6), repayment of those contributions plus interest is permissible (IR12 (2001) PN 10.53). Such a refund is liable to income tax at a rate of 20 per cent under Case VI of Schedule D and is not classed as taxable income for any other purposes of the ICTA 1988. [*ICTA 1988, s 598(4)*].

Lump sum death benefit

5.37 Any lump sum death benefit, if paid by the trustees under discretionary powers to an individual or an organisation, is not liable to inheritance tax. [*Inheritance Tax Act 1984, s 151*]. In the case of a controlling director who dies in service on or after age 75, however, any lump sum death benefit must be paid to the member's estate (IR12 (2001) PN 11.12) and so must be taken into account when considering liability for inheritance tax.

Transfer payments

5.38 Transfer payments between tax approved pension schemes representing the retirement benefits of members, provided they do not exceed Inland Revenue limits, carry no tax implications as they are a transfer of assets between tax exempt bodies.

Administration expenses

5.39 If a pension scheme bears the costs of its administration itself it will not be able to obtain tax relief on those costs as its income is not taxable (unless it is trading and the costs relate to the trading activity). Whilst a pension scheme's rules may provide for administration costs to be paid either by the employers or from the scheme's resources, it is advisable for the employer and trustees to have a clear idea of which costs will be borne by each party. The employer may obtain tax relief in respect of the costs of establishing and operating a pension scheme if the expenses concerned are wholly and exclusively incurred in running the employer's business. [*ICTA 1988, s 74*]. However, if the employer pays costs which are attributable to the trustees, for example, a valuer's fees incurred on property valuations, tax relief will not be given.

If the trustees employ someone (as opposed to appointing an agent) to carry out duties in connection with the pension scheme then they will be responsible, as the employer of that person, for deducting income tax via the PAYE system on the remuneration paid.

Value Added Tax (VAT) incurred by the trustees is an expense of the pension scheme and may be recoverable in certain circumstances. HM Customs and Excise has published useful guidance on VAT and pension schemes covering registration and VAT costs which can and cannot be recovered by the trustees. [Value Added Tax Funded Pension Schemes: VAT Notice 700/17.]

Life offices

5.40 Employers' and employees' contributions paid to (and benefits paid from) an exempt approved scheme administered by a life office will receive the same tax treatment as any other exempt approved scheme.

It is the tax treatment of the funds held by life offices for pensions purposes that differs from other exempt approved schemes. Such funds are exempt from corporation tax and capital gains tax in respect of income and gains accruing on them. However, life offices expect to make a profit from pensions business as they do on any other business they transact, so whilst income derived from funds under their control is not liable to tax apart from dividends received from 2 July 1997 from UK companies (*Finance Act (No 2) 1997, Sch 3 para 6*), profits arising out of the exercise of control of those funds are liable. [*ICTA 1988, s 438*].

5.41 *Inland Revenue limits and taxation*

Simplification of tax treatment of pensions

5.41 The December 2002 consultation paper followed a review of the current tax rules carried out by a team made up of members of the Inland Revenue and nominees from pensions industry representative bodies. The consultation paper proposed a clean break. Although there would be no change in respect of pension rights accrued before implementation of the reform, all pension saving after implementation would follow a single set of rules – and there would be a simple set of rules relating to the conversion of pension savings into benefits.

The second consultation paper issued in 2003 set out how the simplified regime would work, if introduced, and proposed a number of modifications following the consultation on the first paper.

In his March 2004 Budget statement, the Chancellor announced that the Government would be proceeding with the proposals set out in the December 2003 consultation paper. Implementation of the new regime of 'registered schemes' which will replace all current pension tax regimes, has been put back to April 2006 (the second consultation paper having indicated April 2005) and the detailed legislation would be introduced in the *Finance Act 2004*. The Finance Bill was published by the Treasury on 8 April 2004. The impact of the changes under the Finance Bill is discussed in paragraph 5.42 below.

THE APRIL 2006 REGIME

Registered schemes

5.42 The new provisions will apply to all 'registered' schemes (the equivalent of current approved schemes). This will include defined benefit and defined contribution occupational schemes, Small Self-Administered Schemes, Self-Invested Personal Pension Schemes and other personal pension schemes.

Existing approved schemes will automatically be registered under the new regime unless the scheme elects to opt out and become what will be known as an 'employer-financed retirement benefits scheme'.

Lifetime allowance

5.43 There will be a lifetime allowance of £1.5 million. The explanatory notes to the Finance Bill confirm that the allowance will increase to £1.8 million by 2010/2011. For defined benefits there will be a standard valuation factor of 20:1. This is based on the assumption that there are annual retail price index increases and dependants' pensions don't exceed the member's pension. Schemes offering more generous benefits can negotiate different factors with the Revenue.

The recovery charge for sums in excess of the lifetime allowance will be 25 per cent, or 55 per cent if the excess funds are taken as a lump sum. Schemes will be expected to deduct the recovery charge and make net payments to the member.

Lifetime allowance – transitional provisions

5.44 Individuals with rights in excess of the lifetime allowance at A-Day can register those rights as a percentage of the lifetime allowance. When they draw their benefits they will have a personal lifetime allowance of the same percentage of the indexed lifetime allowance as at the date of retirement. So, for example, a member with accrued benefits valued at £2.25 million on A-Day could register a figure of 150 per cent. If, when that member came to draw his/her benefits, the lifetime allowance had increased to £2 million, his or her personal lifetime allowance would be £3 million.

Alternatively members (even those below the lifetime limit) can stop contributing (and stop benefits accruing) at A-Day and they will not then suffer a recovery charge on any excess to the lifetime limit when they retire.

Annual allowance

5.45 Maximum annual contributions of £215,000 will be allowed. This will be increased to £255,000 by April 2010. Contributions or accrual in any year in which benefits are taken in full will be exempt. Individuals will be taxed on any pensions growth in excess of the annual allowance.

Transfers from one registered scheme to another will not count towards the annual allowance.

Tax-free lump sum

5.46 Up to 25 per cent of the capital value of benefits below the lifetime allowance can be taken as a lump sum.

Pension age

5.47 Schemes must move to a minimum pension age of 55 by 2010. It is to be left to individual schemes as to how they achieve this. Members with existing contractual rights (as at 10 December 2003) to draw an early pension at 50 may have that right honoured. Incapacity early retirement will be allowed.

People in schemes with low normal retirement dates (NRDs) at A-Day may retain that NRD but the lifetime limit will be reduced by 2.5 per cent for each year before 55 which the pension is taken. The reduction will not apply to the police, fire service and armed forces. New schemes for all three groups are proposed before 2010 and they will have minimum NRDs of 55.

5.48 *Inland Revenue limits and taxation*

Members will not be required to take all their benefits in one go at retirement. People will be able to be flexible in combining working with drawing benefits.

Benefit rules

5.48 The following rules will apply to all benefits:

- members can take a 25 per cent tax-free lump sum that is below the annual allowance;
- members must draw benefits before 75;
- no benefits payable before 55 (except incapacity benefit);
- are payable for life;
- are paid in instalments at least annually;
- are not assignable other than where permitted by Revenue;
- are not guaranteed for a minimum period of more than ten years;
- up to age 75, there will be no capital guarantee greater than 'value protection';
- there will be maximum and minimum income limits;
- are taxed as income under PAYE.

Securing benefits at 75

5.49 This must be done either by annuity, employer promise (which includes paying from scheme assets) or an Alternative Secured Income (ASI). ASIs are essentially for those who object on religious grounds to the pooling of mortality risk.

Death benefits

5.50 When death occurs before retirement, benefits can either be paid as pensions to dependants or, before the member reaches 75, as a lump sum (or as a combination of pension and lump sum). The lump sum will be tested against the lifetime allowance. There will be no test against the lifetime allowance if all benefits are taken as pension.

When death occurs after benefits are in payment, no capital payments will be allowed after age 75. On death before 75, where income has not been secured, funds that are not drawn may be repaid as a capital fund subject to 35 per cent tax.

Pension sharing

5.51 For pension sharing orders effective post A-Day, pension credits will count towards the lifetime allowance for the recipient but pension debits will not count against the donor's lifetime allowance (ie the donor will be able to rebuild to the lifetime allowance). Neither a pension debit nor credit will count towards the annual allowance.

For pension sharing orders effective pre-A-Day, in calculating pension rights as at A-Day, the value of the pension debit/credit will be ignored for both spouses.

Investment

5.52 Schemes will be allowed to engage in all types of investment, including residential property. Restrictions on investment in the sponsoring employer will remain. The non-commercial use of an asset by a member will be subject to a tax charge.

Tax relief on contributions

5.53 Employers will be able to claim a deduction in profits chargeable to UK tax for employer contributions paid to registered pension schemes.

Individuals will be able to claim tax relief on contributions up to 100 per cent of their UK earnings (subject to the annual allowance). Those earning less than £3,600 can obtain relief on contributions of up to £3,600.

Funded and Unfunded Unapproved Retirement Schemes

5.54 Unapproved schemes will no longer have any tax-favoured status. Amounts in Funded Unapproved Retirement Schemes (FURBS) at A-Day will have some transitional protection. Benefits in Unfunded Unapproved Retirement Schemes (UURBS) and FURBS will not be tested against the annual or lifetime allowances and no recovery charge will apply but payments out will be charged at the member's usual marginal tax rate.

Chapter 6

Protection for early leavers

INTRODUCTION

General

6.1 One of the main sources of dissatisfaction with occupational pension schemes historically has been the treatment of members who leave such schemes (usually because they have left employment) before normal pension age. (The meaning of 'normal pension age' is discussed in 6.23 below.)

Consequently, legislation has introduced the following protections for early leavers relating to 'preservation' (see 6.2 below), revaluation (see 6.3 to 6.5 below) and transfer values (see 6.6 below).

Preservation requirements

6.2 The preservation requirements set out the benefits which occupational pension schemes are required to provide for early leavers. These requirements are summarised in 6.10 to 6.30 below.

The preservation requirements were first introduced by the *Social Security Act 1973* with effect from 6 April 1975, but have since been amended to give increased protection to leavers. They are now consolidated in *Chapter I* of *Part IV* (ie *sections 69* to *82*) of the *Pension Schemes Act 1993* and the *Occupational Pension Schemes (Preservation of Benefit) Regulations 1991 (SI 1991 No 167)* (*'Preservation Regulations'*).

Revaluation

6.3 An early leaver's scheme entitlement under the preservation requirements (see 6.2 above) will most typically take the form of a deferred pension from the scheme, prospectively payable from his normal pension age.

Legislation requires the calculation of any such pension to be revalued in respect of the period of deferment. Two separate types of revaluation apply, depending on whether or not the benefit concerned is a 'guaranteed minimum pension' earned in relation to pre-6 April 1997 contracted-out employment (see chapter 4).

Revaluation of benefits other than guaranteed minimum pensions

6.4 This is governed by *Chapter II* of *Part IV* (ie *sections 83* to *86*) of *PSA 1993*. (These requirements were first introduced by the *Social Security Act 1985*, but have since been revised; they are discussed in 6.31 to 6.42 below).

Revaluation of guaranteed minimum pensions

6.5 This is governed by *Chapter III* of *Part IV* (ie *sections 87* to *92*) of *PSA 1993*. These requirements (which were originally introduced by the *Health and Social Security Act 1984*) are summarised in chapter 4.

Transfer values

6.6 *Chapter IV* of *Part IV* (ie *sections 93* to *101*) of *PSA 1993* sets out certain statutory entitlements for an early leaver to require that a sum representing his rights under the scheme be used in one of a number of ways (eg transferred to another scheme or used to buy him an annuity). This right (first introduced by the *Social Security Act 1985*) is covered further in 6.44 below.

SCOPE OF EARLY LEAVER LEGISLATION

Schemes affected

6.7 The legislation referred to in 6.1 to 6.6 above applies to occupational pension schemes (as now defined in *PSA 1993*). The High Court, in the case of *Royal Masonic Hospital v Pensions Ombudsman [2001] 01 PBLR (9)* overturned the decision of the Pensions Ombudsman concerning the scope of the preservation requirements. The Court held that *section 69* of *PSA 1993* did not cover unfunded private sector schemes as the pension promise was merely a contractual one that would be met in the future from the general assets of the employer rather than from an accrued fund.

Relationship of early leaver legislation to scheme rules

6.8 *Chapter I* of *Part IV* of *PSA 1993* (which relates to preservation) effectively requires that scheme rules contain provisions which comply with the preservation requirements (summarised in 6.10 to 6.30 below). However, *Chapter I* does not actually go so far as to override the scheme rules if they do not comply. [*PSA 1993, s 131*]. Nevertheless, even though *Chapter I* does not override the scheme rules, employers and trustees can still be challenged by members and beneficiaries for operating a scheme whose rules do not fulfil the preservation requirements (see 6.9 below). In particular, it should be noted that *section 132* of the *PSA 1993* requires trustees, where their scheme's rules do not meet the preservations requirement, to take such steps as are open to them for rectifying this.

6.9 *Protection for early leavers*

By contrast, *Chapters II, III* and *IV* of *Part IV* of *PSA 1993* (which relate to revaluation and transfer values) do override the scheme rules (subject to limited exceptions). [*PSA 1993, s 129*].

Enforcement of preservation legislation

6.9 Until 6 April 1997 the Occupational Pensions Board (OPB) had certain functions relating to preservation, including the power to determine whether a scheme's rules complied with the preservation requirements and powers to modify scheme rules so as to ensure compliance with those requirements.

However, the OPB was dissolved on 5 April 1997, and the functions of the OPB relating to preservation were not transferred to any other regulatory body. A member who is not satisfied that his scheme complies with preservation can instead seek recourse against the employer and/or the trustees through an application to the Pensions Ombudsman (see chapter 17) or through the courts.

PRESERVATION

Defined terms

6.10 *PSA 1993* uses a number of defined terms in relation to the preservation requirements. These are broadly summarised below.

'2 years' qualifying service'

6.11 This is defined in *section 71(7)* of *PSA 1993*. It means two years (whether a single period of that duration or two or more periods, continuous or discontinuous, totalling two years) in which the member was at all times employed either:

(*a*)　in 'pensionable service' (see 6.12 below) under the scheme; or

(*b*)　in service in employment which was contracted-out by reference to the scheme; or

(*c*)　in 'linked qualifying service' (see 6.13 below) under another scheme.

There are special provisions in relation to periods of service previously terminated. [*PSA 1993, s 71(9)* and the *Preservation Regulations (SI 1991 No 167), reg 21*].

'Pensionable service'

6.12 This is defined in *section 70(2)* of *PSA 1993*. In effect, pensionable

Protection for early leavers **6.15**

service means actual service in employment to which the scheme relates which qualifies the member (assuming it continues for long enough) for retirement benefits at normal pension age.

There are detailed regulations regarding breaks in pensionable service. [*Preservation Regulations (SI 1991 No 167), reg 21*]. In particular, the service before and after the break must be added together (in ascertaining whether there are two years' qualifying service – see 6.11 above) where one or more of the following conditions are satisfied:

(*a*) the break does not exceed one month; or

(*b*) the break corresponds to the member's absence from work wholly or partly because of pregnancy or confinement and the member returns to pensionable service no later than one month after returning to work in exercise of her statutory rights to return to work; or

(*c*) the break corresponds to the member's absence from work in furtherance of a 'trade dispute' as defined in the *Social Security Act 1975*.

(Whether or not the break counts towards pension benefits is determined not only by the rules of the scheme, but also by any relevant employment and pensions legislation – particularly where the period is a period of maternity leave (see chapter 9).)

'Linked qualifying service'

6.13   Linked qualifying service is relevant where the scheme has accepted a transfer payment from another occupational pension scheme or a buy-out policy. The qualifying service under the transferring scheme or noted in the buy-out policy, is added to qualifying service in the scheme receiving the transfer payment. The trustees will be given certified details of the qualifying service as part of the conditions for accepting the transfer payment. The detailed definition of linked qualifying service is contained in *section 179* of the *1993 Act*. This includes restrictions on what can and cannot count as linked qualifying service. For example, regard can only be had to 'actual service'.

'Normal pension age'

6.14   Normal pension age is defined in *section 180* of *PSA 1993* and is discussed in detail in 6.23 below. The term is relevant to the questions as to whether a member is an early leaver and when a preserved pension for him becomes payable.

'Long service benefit'

6.15   Long service benefit is defined in *section 70(1)* of *PSA 1993*. It can broadly be seen as those:

(*a*) retirement benefits for a member at normal pension age; and

6.16   *Protection for early leavers*

(*b*)   benefits for his spouse, dependants or others on his attaining normal pension age or, if later, death;

which would have been payable under the scheme had the member remained in pensionable service until normal pension age.

'Short service benefit'

6.16   Short service benefit is the benefit which a scheme may be required to provide in respect of an early leaver unless one of the prescribed 'alternatives to short service benefit' (see 6.24 to 6.29 below) applies instead. The definition is contained in *section 71* of *PSA 1993*.

Qualifying for short service benefit

6.17   Under *section 71(1)* of *PSA 1993*, a scheme must provide short service benefit (consisting of benefit of any description which would otherwise have been payable as long service benefit) where a member's pensionable service is terminated before normal pension age and:

(*a*)   he has at least two years' qualifying service; or

(*b*)   a transfer payment in respect of his rights under a personal pension scheme has been made to the scheme.

The short service benefit is generally payable from the member's normal pension age or age 60 if later (see 6.23 below).

Calculating the short service benefit – an overview

6.18   The method of calculation of short service benefit is set out in *section 74* of *PSA 1993*.

Same basis as long service benefit

6.19   *Section 74(1)* of *PSA 1993* requires that, except where the principle of 'uniform accrual' applies (see 6.20 below), 'a scheme must provide for short service benefit to be computed on the same basis as long service benefit'.

The application of this requirement to money purchase benefits is relatively simple. If a scheme provides long service benefit on a money purchase basis, the corresponding short service benefit should also be money purchase and computed on the same basis. Further details regarding money purchase benefits are contained in *regulation 14* of the *Preservation Regulations* (*SI 1991 No 167*).

Where long service benefits are calculated by reference to a member's salary at normal pension age, short service benefits must also be calculated in a corresponding manner by reference to the member's salary at the date of termination of pensionable service. Similarly, if the member's salary is averaged over a specified period before normal pension age when calculating his long service benefits, a period of the same duration must be used to average the member's salary for the purpose of calculating short service benefits. [*PSA 1993, s 74(7)*].

The calculation of short service benefit in relation to final salary benefits can be illustrated by the following example:

> A member's pension, calculated at normal pension age, is $\frac{1}{60}$th of final pensionable salary for each year of pensionable service. Final pensionable salary is defined as the average of the member's salary over the three years immediately preceding normal pension age. The member joins the scheme at age 30 and his normal pension age is 65. The calculation of his pension will be as follows:
>
> (*a*) if the member stays to normal pension age, and so completes 35 years of pensionable service, his long service benefit will be a pension of $\frac{35}{60}$th of final pensionable salary, calculated by averaging his salary over the three years immediately preceding normal pension age; but
>
> (*b*) if the member leaves pensionable service, say, at age 40, having completed ten years of pensionable service, his short service benefit will be a pension of $\frac{10}{60}$th of final pensionable salary, calculated by averaging his salary over the three years immediately preceding the date of leaving pensionable service. This pension will be payable from the scheme at the normal pension age of 65.

Uniform accrual

6.20 There are a number of circumstances where the legislation requires that short service benefits be computed on the basis of 'uniform accrual' rather than as set out in 6.19 above. [*PSA 1993, s 74(6)*]. In particular, uniform accrual must be applied where the following situations arise, namely:

(*a*) the long service benefit formula is not related to the length of pensionable service or the number or amount of contributions paid (*PSA 1993, s 74(4)*); or

(*b*) the long service benefit accrues at a higher rate or otherwise more favourably if the member's pensionable service is of some specified minimum length or if he remains in pensionable service up to a specified minimum age (*PSA 1993, s 74(3)*).

The common strand running through those instances where uniform accrual is required is that there is no obvious accrual rate in the scheme rules or the only accrual rate available would give an anomalous result.

The principle of uniform accrual is that benefits accrue evenly over the period of pensionable service (thus creating a notional accrual rate). This is best illustrated by way of an example:

6.21 *Protection for early leavers*

A member joins a scheme at age 30 and is promised a pension of two thirds of his salary on retirement at age 60. This formula is not related to his length of pensionable service and so, under *sections 74(4)* and *74(6)* of the *PSA 1993*, uniform accrual applies. The principle of uniform accrual treats the 'two thirds' pension, which he will receive at age 60 if he remains in pensionable service, as accruing uniformly throughout the 30 years of his pensionable service (ie from age 30 to age 60). If the member leaves at age 45, he will have completed one half of this 30 year period (ie 15 years), so his short service benefit will be one half of the 'two thirds' pension which he would have received had he stayed to age 60 (ie one third of his salary at the date of termination of pensionable service).

Uniform accrual also applies (in a slightly different way) to any part of a member's long service benefit which derives from a benefit improvement granted in relation to previous pensionable service. In these circumstances, the benefit improvement is treated as accruing uniformly over the period from the date when the improvement was granted to the attainment of normal pension age. [*PSA 1993, s 75(5)*].

Death in service benefits not preserved

6.21 It should be noted that the definition of 'long service benefit' contained in *section 70* of *PSA 1993* does not cover death in service benefits. Consequently a scheme is not required by the preservations laws to provide death benefits where an early leaver subsequently dies before normal pension age (although many schemes do provide some level of benefit in these circumstances).

Discretionary benefits

6.22 A further question which arises is how far discretionary benefits must be preserved. *Section 72(1)* of *PSA 1993* provides that a scheme must not contain any rule which could result in an early leaver being treated less favourably for any purpose relating to short service benefit than he would have been treated for the same purpose relating to long service benefit if he had stayed in service. However, this does not apply to a rule which merely confers discretion on the trustees or some other person, so long as the rule does not specifically require the discretion to be exercised in any discriminatory manner against members in respect of the short service benefit. [*PSA 1993, s 72(3)*]. It is therefore arguable that a scheme rule relating to discretionary augmentation which provides that the trustees cannot consider deferred members is discriminatory.

Date of payment of preserved benefits

6.23 Short service benefits are payable from 'normal pension age' or age 60 (whichever is the later). [*PSA 1993, s 71(3)*].

A member's 'normal pension age' is defined in *section 180* of *PSA 1993* as the earliest age at which the member is entitled to receive benefits (other than a guaranteed minimum pension), on his retirement from any employment to which the scheme applies. Where the scheme only provides a guaranteed minimum pension, the normal pension age is the earliest age at which the member is entitled to receive the guaranteed minimum pension on retirement from such employment.

For the purposes of determining a member's normal pension age, any special provision as to early retirement on grounds of ill-health or otherwise must be disregarded. [*PSA 1993, s 180(2)*]. The former OPB's interpretation of this (which is still generally followed) was that a member's normal pension age would be the earliest date on which the member had an unqualified right to retire on an unreduced pension (other than on special grounds such as ill-health or redundancy). For example, if the rules of a scheme specify a normal retirement date of age 65 but allow a member to retire, without the consent of the trustees or his employer and without any actuarial reduction, at any time after age 62, the member's normal pension age will be 62.

Alternatives to short service benefits

6.24   Section 73(2) of *PSA 1993* permits the rules of a scheme to provide one or more of a number of alternatives to short service benefits.

Transfer payments

6.25   A member's accrued rights may be transferred to another occupational pension scheme, or to a personal pension scheme, with a view to acquiring rights for the member under the receiving scheme. [*PSA 1993, s 73(2)(a)*]. Furthermore, a scheme may provide for the member's accrued rights to be transferred, if the member consents, to an overseas arrangement. 'Overseas arrangement' means a scheme or arrangement, other than an occupational pension scheme, which:

(*a*)   has effect, or is capable of having effect, so as to provide benefits on termination of employment or on death or retirement to or in respect of earners;

(*b*)   is not an appropriate scheme; and

(*c*)   is administered wholly or primarily outside the United Kingdom [*Preservation Regulations (SI 1991 No167), reg 11A*].

Except in limited circumstances (see 12.33 below), the consent of the member must be obtained if a transfer is to be made as an alternative for providing short service benefits within the scheme. [*PSA 1993, s 73(4)*].

6.26 Protection for early leavers

Early retirement

6.26 The rules of a scheme may permit payment of benefits to commence before normal pension age. In such a situation, the benefits payable may be of different amounts, and be payable to different recipients, than applies in relation to short service benefit. [*Preservation Regulations (SI 1991 No 167), reg 8(1)*].

However, where a scheme provides an early retirement pension as an alternative to short service benefits, the following requirements will apply:

(*a*) the benefits must include a benefit payable to the member (*Preservation Regulations (SI 1991 No 167), reg 8(1)*);

(*b*) it must be the case that either:

- the member's earning capacity is destroyed or seriously impaired by physical or mental infirmity; or
- the member has become incapable of following his normal employment because of physical or mental infirmity; or
- the member has attained age 50 or is within ten years of normal pension age (*Preservation Regulations (SI 1991 No 167), regs 8(2), 5(2), (3) and (4)*);

(*c*) the member's consent must be obtained unless:

- his earning capacity is destroyed or seriously impaired because of physical or mental infirmity; and
- in the opinion of the scheme's trustees, he is incapable of deciding whether it is in his interests to consent (*Preservation Regulations (SI 1991 No 167), regs 7(2) and 8(3)*); and

(*d*) the relevant scheme rule must require the trustees to be reasonably satisfied that the total value of the benefits when they become payable is at least equal to the value of the accrued benefits which they replace. [*Preservation Regulations (SI 1991 No 167), regs 8(4) and 11*].

Late retirement

6.27 The rules of a scheme may also permit payment of benefits to commence after normal pension age as an alternative to short service benefits. The benefits payable may be of different amounts, and be payable to different recipients, than applies in relation to short service benefit. [*Preservation Regulations (SI 1991 No 167), reg 8(1)*].

In this situation, the following requirements will apply:

(*a*) the benefits must include a benefit payable to the member (*Preservation Regulations (SI 1991 No 167), reg 8(1)*);

(b) the member's consent to this alternative must be obtained (*Preservation Regulations (SI 1991 No 167), reg 7(2)*); and

(c) the relevant scheme rule must require the trustees to be reasonably satisfied that the total value of the benefits when they become payable is at least equal to the value of the accrued benefits which they replace. [*Preservation Regulations (SI 1991 No 167), regs 8(4) and 11*].

Bought-out benefits

6.28 A scheme may provide for a member's benefits to be appropriately secured or 'bought out' by the purchase of an annuity contract or insurance policy from an insurance company. The benefits provided may be different from those required to constitute short service benefit. If this option is to be exercised the trustees must be reasonably satisfied that the payment made to the insurance company is at least equal to the value of the benefits that have accrued to or in respect of the member under the rules. [*Preservation Regulations (SI 1991 No 167), regs 9 and 11*].

Generally the consent of the member is required before benefits can be bought out. [*Preservation Regulations (SI 1991 No 167), reg 7(2)*]. However, consent is not required if the insurance policy or annuity contract to be purchased satisfies certain prescribed conditions (set out in the *Preservation Regulations (SI 1991 No 167), reg 9(4)(a)*) and either:

(a) the scheme is being wound up; or

(b) the member has less than '5 years qualifying service' (as defined in *paragraph 7* of *Schedule 16* to the *Social Security Act 1973* immediately before the coming into force of *section 10* of the *Social Security Act 1986* (changes to preservation requirements); or

(c) the trustees consider that, in the circumstances, it is reasonable for the benefits to be bought out without member consent. [*Preservation Regulations (SI 1991 No 167), regs 9(4)(b) and 9(5)*].

In the case of (b) and (c) above, the following further requirements must be satisfied:

(i) the member's rights under the scheme must not include protected rights (see chapter 4);

(ii) at least twelve months must have elapsed between the purchase of the insurance policy or annuity contract and the termination of the member's pensionable service;

(iii) the trustees must generally give the member at least thirty days' written notice of their intention to take out the policy or enter into the contract; and

(iv) when the trustees actually take out the policy or enter into the contract

6.29 *Protection for early leavers*

there must be no outstanding application by the member for a cash equivalent (see 6.52 below). [*Preservation Regulations (SI 1991 No 167), reg 9(6)*].

Money purchase benefits

6.29 A scheme may provide money purchase benefits as an alternative to short service benefits. The relevant scheme rule must require the trustees to be reasonably satisfied that the total value of the benefits when they become payable is at least equal to the value of the accrued benefits which they replace. [*Preservation Regulations (SI 1991 No 167), regs 10 and 11*]. The member's consent is required if this alternative is to be provided. [*Preservation Regulations (SI 1991 No 167), reg 7(2)*]. In practice this alternative is not widely used.

None of the alternatives to short service benefits discussed above may include a return of contributions except in limited circumstances relating to service completed before 6 April 1975. [*PSA 1993, s 73(5)*].

Inland Revenue limits

6.30 In some circumstances, there may be a conflict between the minimum benefits which the preservation legislation requires and the maximum benefits which the Inland Revenue will allow (see chapter 5). Where this happens, the preservation requirements will usually prevail (IR12 (2001), PN 10.4), subject to certain overall limits in respect of money purchase schemes (IR12 (2001), PN 10.13).

REVALUATION

Background

6.31 In spite of the preservation legislation described from 6.10 above, there was for many years a continuing dissatisfaction with the law's failure to protect members' preserved pensions from the impact of inflation in respect of the period from leaving pensionable service to normal pension age.

Chapters II and *III* of *Part IV* of *PSA 1993* now provide for an element of revaluation in respect of this period. Effectively, two separate systems of revaluation apply:

(*a*) guaranteed minimum pensions accrued by reference to contracted-out employment before 6 April 1997 are subject to revaluation under *Chapter III* of *Part IV* (this is summarised in chapter 4);

(*b*) revaluation of other benefits is as set out in *Chapter II* of *Part IV* of, and in *Schedule 3* to, *PSA 1993*. It is these provisions which are summarised in 6.32 to 6.42 below.

General application of the revaluation requirements

6.32 Under *section 83(1)(a)* of *PSA 1993*, the revaluation requirements of *Chapter II* apply where benefits are payable to or in respect of a member of an occupational pension scheme and:

(a) his pensionable service ends on or after 1 January 1986;

(b) when his pensionable service ends, he has accrued rights to benefits under the scheme;

(c) there is a period from his date of leaving to his normal pension age of at least a year (see 6.23 for meaning of 'normal pension age'); and

(d) in the case of benefits payable to any other person in respect of the member, the member dies after normal pension age.

However, revaluation is not required to be applied separately in respect of the 'alternatives to short service benefit' referred to in 6.24 above. [*PSA 1993, s 85*].

For the purposes of the revaluation requirements, where 'normal pension age' is before the age of 60, it is taken to mean the age at which short service benefit is made payable under the scheme rules (see 6.23) [*Occupational Pensions Schemes (Revaluation) Regulations 1991 (SI 1991 No 168)*, reg 3].

Determining which method of revaluation applies

6.33 There are four different methods of revaluation:

(a) the 'average salary method';

(b) the 'flat rate method';

(c) the 'money purchase method'; and

(d) the 'final salary method'. [*PSA 1993, s 84* and *Sch 3*].

The first step in revaluing a particular benefit is to decide which of these four methods is to apply.

The average salary method

6.34 The average salary method applies where the benefit is an average salary benefit (ie one whose rate or amount is calculated by reference to a member's average salary over the period of service on which the benefit is based) and the trustees consider it appropriate to use the average salary method. [*PSA 1993, s 84(2)*].

The average salary method itself is set out in *paragraph 3* of *Schedule 3* to *PSA 1993*. Average salary benefits are now relatively rare and so this method does not often apply in practice.

6.35 *Protection for early leavers*

The flat rate method

6.35 The flat rate method applies where the benefit is a flat rate benefit (ie one whose rate or amount is calculated by reference solely to the member's length of service) and the trustees consider it appropriate to use the flat rate method. [*PSA 1993, s 84(2)*].

Again, the flat rate method will rarely apply in practice. The method itself is set out in *paragraph 4* of *Schedule 3* to *PSA 1993*.

The money purchase method

6.36 Where the benefit is a money purchase benefit, the money purchase method must be used. This method is discussed in 6.38 below. [*PSA 1993, s 84(3)*].

The final salary method

6.37 In all other cases, the final salary method applies. This is described in 6.39 to 6.42 below. [*PSA 1993, s 84(1)*].

The money purchase method

6.38 The money purchase method is set out in *paragraph 5* of *Schedule 3* to *PSA 1993*. Effectively, the money purchase method requires the trustees to apply investment yield and bonuses arising from contributions paid by and on behalf of the member towards the provision of benefits, in the same way which would have applied had the member not left pensionable service.

The final salary method

General

6.39 The final salary method is set out in *paragraphs 1* and *2* of *Schedule 3* to *PSA 1993*. This method introduces the concept widely known as limited price indexation or 'LPI'. The effect of applying LPI to a benefit is to increase it in line with cost of living increases over a given period, subject to a maximum of five per cent per annum.

Precisely how LPI applies in this context is dealt with in the following paragraphs. Depending on the precise dates of the member's pensionable service, LPI will not always be applied in full (see 6.42 below).

The 'revaluation percentage'

6.40 *Paragraph 2* of *Schedule 3* of *PSA 1993* requires the Secretary of State, in each calendar year, by order to specify a 'revaluation percentage' for each period' which is a 'revaluation period' in relation to that order.

A 'revaluation period' is a period which:

(a) begins with 1 January 1986 or with an anniversary of that date falling before the making of the order; and

(b) ends with the next day after the making of the order which is 31 December.

The 'revaluation percentage' in relation to a given revaluation period is the lesser of:

(i) the percentage which appears to the Secretary of State to be the percentage increase in the general level of prices in Great Britain during that revaluation period; and

(ii) five per cent compound per annum.

Calculating the 'appropriate relevant percentage'

6.41   The 'appropriate relevant percentage' is the revaluation percentage (see 6.40 above) specified in the last calendar year before the date on which the member reaches normal pension age for a period of the same length as the number of complete years from the member's leaving pensionable service to his reaching normal pension age. [*PSA 1993, Sch 3 para 2(7)*].

Applying the 'appropriate revaluation percentage'

6.42   The final salary method of revaluation is to add to the amount that would otherwise be payable an amount equal to the whole or part of the appropriate revaluation percentage (see 6.41 above) of the benefit which has accrued on the date when pensionable service ends. [*PSA 1993, Sch 3 para 1*].

Where pensionable service ends on or after 1 January 1991 or all pensionable service falls on or after 1 January 1985 the whole amount is added. [*PSA 1993, Sch 3 para 1(1)(a)*]. In any other case, a proportionate amount is added. The proportion is calculated by reference to the proportion which the member's post-31 December 1984 pensionable service bears to his total pensionable service. [*PSA 1993, Sch 3 para 1(1)(b)*].

In either case, guaranteed minimum pensions are excluded from the benefit for the purpose of this calculation. These are revalued separately (see chapter 4).

TRANSFER VALUES – INTRODUCTION

6.43   Occupational pension schemes have always been able to offer a transfer payment as an alternative to providing benefits from the scheme.

6.44 *Protection for early leavers*

However, the *Social Security Act 1985* introduced legislation giving early leavers a statutory right to have the 'cash equivalent' of their benefits transferred to another pension arrangement. This statutory right overrides any inconsistent provisions in the scheme's governing documentation (other than those relating to the winding-up of the scheme), but this does not prevent a scheme from being more generous.

The legislation is now consolidated in *sections 93* to *101* of *PSA 1993* (as amended by *sections 152* to *154* of *PA 1995*) and the *Occupational Pension Schemes (Transfer Values) Regulations 1996 (SI 1996 No 1847)* ('the *Transfer Regulations*') as amended by the *Personal and Occupational Pension Schemes (Miscellaneous Amendments) Regulations 1997 (SI 1997 No 786)* and the *Occupational Pension Schemes (Transfer Values and Miscellaneous Amendments) Regulations 2003 (SI 2003 No 1727*.

THE RIGHT TO A CASH EQUIVALENT

When does a member acquire a right to a cash equivalent?

6.44   Broadly speaking, before 6 April 1997, a member of an occupational pension scheme acquired a statutory right to a cash equivalent if he terminated pensionable service after 1 January 1986 and at least one year before normal pension age (see 6.23 above). The ambit of the legislation was extended by *PA 1995* to include members who terminated pensionable service before 1 January 1986. [*PA 1995, s 152*]. However, the legislation does not apply to a member of a final salary scheme who terminated his membership before 1 January 1986, if all his pension benefits have been revalued by at least the rate of inflation. [*Transfer Regulations (SI 1996 No 1847), reg 2(b)*].

A major change introduced by *PA 1995* was the concept of a 'guaranteed cash equivalent'. As from 6 April 1997, the 'cash equivalent' of the benefits to which a member of a final salary occupational pension scheme is entitled must be guaranteed for a certain period. As a consequence of this change, the time at which a member acquires a right to a cash equivalent now differs depending on whether the scheme is money purchase or final salary.

A member of a money purchase occupational pension scheme acquires a right, when his pensionable service terminates, to the cash equivalent of any benefits which have accrued to or in respect of him under the rules of the scheme or any overriding legislation. [*PSA 1993, s 94(1)(a)*].

A member of a final salary scheme acquires the right to a 'guaranteed' cash equivalent if he has received a statement of entitlement (see 6.45 below) and has made a relevant application (see 6.52 below) within three months of the 'guarantee date'. [*PSA 1993, s 94(1)(aa)*].

Guaranteed statement of entitlement

6.45   On the application of a member of a final salary scheme, the trustees must provide him with a written statement, as at a 'guarantee date', of the amount of the cash equivalent of any benefits which have accrued to or in respect of him under the rules of the scheme or any overriding legislation. This statement is referred to in the legislation as a 'statement of entitlement'. [*PSA 1993, s 93A(1)*].

The guarantee date specified in the statement of entitlement must generally be within three months of the date of the member's application. However, this period can be extended for a reasonable period (of up to six months) if, for reasons beyond their control, the trustees are unable to obtain the information required to calculate the cash equivalent. [*Transfer Regulations (SI 1996 No 1847, reg 6(1))*].

The statement of entitlement must be given to the member within ten days (excluding weekends, Christmas Day, New Year's Day and Good Friday) of the guarantee date. [*Transfer Regulations (SI 1996 No 1847), reg 6(2)*]. For example, if a member terminates his pensionable service on 30 June 1997 and requests details of his cash equivalent on 18 October 1997, the trustees must supply him with a statement of his cash equivalent which has a guarantee date of no later than 17 January 1998. If the guarantee date chosen is, say, 15 January, the statement must be given to the member by 29 January; similarly if the guarantee date chosen were 10 December 1997, the statement would have to be given to the member by 23 December 1997.

A member cannot make more than one request for a statement of entitlement within any twelve month period unless the rules of the scheme specifically provide for this or the trustees otherwise allow it. [*Transfer Regulations (SI 1996 No 1847, reg 6(3))*]. Any trustee who fails to take all reasonable steps to provide a statement of entitlement to any member who requests it can be fined up to £1,000 in the case of an individual or £10,000 in any other case. [*PSA 1993, s 93A(4)* and the *Transfer Regulations (SI 1996 No 1847), reg 20*]. (See appendix I regarding penalties generally).

Partial cash equivalents

6.46 If a member leaves pensionable service but does not leave service (ie he ceases to be a member of his employer's scheme but remains an employee), he only acquires a right to that part of his cash equivalent which is attributable to his post-6 April 1988 pensionable service; it is only when he ceases to be an employee that he has a statutory right to the remaining part of his cash equivalent (assuming employment terminates at least one year earlier than what would have been the member's normal pension age). [*PSA 1993, s 98* and the *Transfer Regulations(SI 1996 No 1847), regs 3* and *4*].

In practice many schemes do not restrict a member's cash equivalent, preferring to avoid the unnecessary administration costs associated with providing two cash equivalent calculations; instead of relying on the statutory provision, the

6.47 *Protection for early leavers*

scheme's governing documentation will specifically allow a member to take a cash equivalent in respect of all of his pensionable service, even if he remains in service.

Losing the right to a cash equivalent

6.47 Section 98 of *PSA 1993* provides that the right to a cash equivalent is lost if:

(a) it is not exercised before the 'last option date', ie at least one year before the date on which the member attains normal pension age or, within six months of terminating pensionable service, whichever is the later; or

(b) the scheme is wound up. There is some doubt as to whether this means the commencement or the completion of the winding-up process, but the generally held view is that it is the latter.

CALCULATING THE CASH EQUIVALENT

The basic cash equivalent transfer value calculation

Final salary benefits

6.48 The cash equivalent transfer value of any final salary benefits must be calculated and verified in a manner approved by the scheme actuary (ie the actuary appointed in accordance with *section 47(1)(b)* of *PA 1995*), or, if the trustees are exempt from the requirement to appoint a scheme actuary, by a Fellow of the Institute or Faculty of Actuaries. [*Transfer Regulations, (SI 1996 No 1847), reg 7(1)*]. The methods and assumptions used must either be determined by the trustees or notified to them by the actuary. In either case, the methods and assumptions used must be certified by the actuary as:

(a) being consistent with the statutory requirements relating to the calculation of transfer values (as set out in *section 97* of *PSA 1993* and the *Transfer Regulations (SI 1996 No 1847)*;

(b) being consistent with the guidelines set out in the actuarial Guidance Note 'Retirement Benefit Schemes – Transfer Values' (GN11) issued by the Institute of Actuaries and the Faculty of Actuaries;

(c) being consistent with the methods and assumptions used when granting rights and benefits in respect of a transfer payment accepted by the scheme; and

(d) providing, as a minimum, the amount that would be provided if the methods and assumptions adopted in valuing liabilities for the purpose of the minimum funding requirement (see chapter 11) were used. [*Transfer Regulations, (SI 1996 No 1847), reg 7(3)*].

Money purchase benefits

6.49 A cash equivalent, or any portion of it, which relates to money purchase benefits must be calculated and verified in a manner approved by the trustees of the scheme and in accordance with methods consistent with the requirements of the legislation. [*Transfer Regulations, (SI 1996 No 1847), reg 67(5)*]. Generally the cash equivalent transfer value available in respect of money purchase benefits will simply be the accumulated value of the contributions made by and in respect of the member plus the investment growth of those contributions.

Requirement to take into account customary discretionary benefits

6.50 Unless the trustees decide otherwise, a cash equivalent transfer value must take account of any additional benefits customarily granted at the discretion of the trustees or the employer. [*Transfer Regulations (SI 1996 No 1847), reg 8*]. The trustees cannot decide to exclude such additional benefits unless, within the three months before making the decision, they have obtained the advice of their actuary. The advice must be in the form of a written report on the funding implications of making such a decision. In particular, the report must include the actuary's advice as to whether or not, in his opinion, there would be any adverse implications for the funding of the scheme if the trustees did not make a direction to exclude discretionary benefits. [*Transfer Regulations (SI 1993 No 1847, reg 8(3)*].

The requirement to obtain actuarial advice before deciding whether or not to include an allowance for discretionary benefits was introduced on 6 April 1997; before then it was solely a trustee decision which was, in practice, difficult to challenge. The introduction of the requirement for a funding report means that it will be difficult for trustees to exclude customary discretionary benefits unless they can justify doing so on the basis that the funding of the scheme will not permit them to do otherwise.

A common discretionary benefit for which allowance must be made is where early retirement is permitted without actuarial reduction but subject to employer consent. If it would be usual for the employer to consent to any such retirement after, say, age 62, there would be an established custom of granting the additional benefits. The calculation of any cash equivalent should therefore reflect this unless the trustees direct otherwise, taking into consideration the funding of the scheme.

Reduction of cash equivalents

6.51 If a scheme is subject to the minimum funding requirement (see 11.14 to 11.31 below), a cash equivalent may be reduced in certain circumstances. Where a scheme had, at the effective date of the actuary's last report to the trustees of the scheme in accordance with GN11 before the guarantee date, assets that were not sufficient to pay the full amount of the cash equivalent in

6.51 *Protection for early leavers*

respect of all members, the trustees may reduce each part of the cash equivalent as shown in that report by an amount that is no greater than the percentage by which the assets are shown in the actuary's report as being insufficient to pay the full amount of the corresponding part of the cash equivalent in respect of all members. This is provided that the amount of any cash equivalent after the reduction is not less than the minimum amount required under *regulation 7(3)(b)(iv)* to satisfy the liabilities referred in *section 73(3)* of the *PA 1995* (preferential liabilities on winding up) as modified by *regulation 3* of the *Winding Up Regulations* [*Transfer Regulations (SI 1996 No 1847), reg 8(4)*].

Further, in the case of a scheme which had, at the effective date of the last actuarial valuation before the guarantee date, assets that were not sufficient to pay the minimum amount of the cash equivalent in respect of the liabilities referred to in *section 73(3)* of the *PA 1995*, the trustees of the scheme may reduce each part of the minimum amount of the cash equivalent, as calculated under *regulation 7(3)(b)(iv)*, by a percentage that is no greater than the percentage which is the difference between:

(*a*) 100 per cent; and

(*b*) the percentage of the liabilities mentioned in the paragraph of *section 73(3)* of the *PA 1995 Act* corresponding to that part which the actuarial valuation shows the scheme assets as being sufficient to satisfy.

Although trustees are generally not obliged to reduce cash equivalents simply because the scheme is in deficit, they could be criticised for not doing so, particularly if a winding-up was at the time envisaged (or had even commenced) or where the remainder of members' benefits would be severely jeopardised if cash equivalents were not reduced. Indeed, it is arguable that *regulation 8(12)* of the *Transfer Regulations (SI 1996 No 1847)* does require such a reduction where winding-up has started before the guarantee date.

If the benefits to which a cash equivalent relates have been surrendered, commuted or forfeited before the trustees are required to comply with the member's request (see 6.55 below) the cash equivalent can be reduced or extinguished accordingly. Where a scheme is wound up, a cash equivalent can be reduced to the extent necessary to comply with the provisions of *PA 1995* relating to the benefits which must be secured on a winding-up (see chapter 12).

Once a cash equivalent has become a guaranteed cash equivalent it generally cannot be reduced unless either the scheme begins to be wound up or benefits have been surrendered, commuted or forfeited. [*Transfer Regulations (SI 1996 No 1847), reg 8(1)*]. The trustees could not, for example, make a direction that the cash equivalent will not allow for discretionary benefits after they have informed the member of his guaranteed cash equivalent. A guaranteed cash equivalent can be recalculated and either increased or reduced, as appropriate, if it transpires that it was not originally calculated in accordance with the statutory requirements. Where a guaranteed cash equivalent is reduced or increased a new 'guarantee date' will apply and the appropriate time limits will start again.

EXERCISING THE RIGHT TO A CASH EQUIVALENT

Making a relevant application

6.52 The right to a cash equivalent can be exercised at any time after termination of pensionable service; it does not have to be exercised coincident with, for example, the date on which the member leaves service. A member exercises his right to a cash equivalent by making a relevant application, ie an application, in writing, to the trustees requiring them to use the cash equivalent by transferring it to a specified arrangement. [*PSA 1993, s 95* and the *Transfer Regulations (SI 1996 No 1847), reg 12*]. The legislation provides that an application is taken to have been made if it is delivered to the trustees personally or sent by post in a registered letter or by recorded delivery. [*PSA 1993, s 95(9)*]. However, in practice this requirement is often waived.

Broadly speaking, in the case of an Inland Revenue approved arrangement, a member can ask for his cash equivalent to be paid to any other suitable Inland Revenue approved arrangement which is able and willing to accept a transfer. However some restrictions apply, particularly in relation to transfers from schemes contracted-out of the State earnings-related pension scheme. [*PSA 1993, s 95* and the *Transfer Regulations (SI 1996 No 1847), reg 12*]. Generally a transfer will be used to:

(*a*) acquire transfer credits under the rules of an occupational pension scheme which is exempt approved (or awaiting approval) by the Inland Revenue under *Chapter I* of *Part XIV* of *ICTA 1988*;

(*b*) acquire transfer credits under the rules of a personal pension scheme approved by the Inland Revenue under *Chapter IV* of *Part XIV* of *ICTA 1988*; or

(*c*) purchase an annuity from an insurance company chosen by the member.

The application must specifically identify the receiving arrangement. An application which does not do this will simply be treated as an enquiry (or possibly a request for a statement of entitlement) and not a relevant application.

In the case of a final salary scheme a member must make a relevant application within three months of the guarantee date. [*PSA 1993, s 94(1)(aa)*]. If the member makes a relevant application outside of this three month period, the application is treated as a request for a statement of entitlement. [*Transfer Regulations, (SI 1996 No 1847), reg 6(4)*]. As not more than one request for a statement of entitlement can be made within any twelve month period unless the rules of the scheme specifically provide for this (or the trustees otherwise allow it (see 6.45)), a member who fails to make a relevant application within the three month period could find that he cannot require the trustees to take any action for another nine months.

A member may withdraw an application for a cash equivalent at any time before the trustees are committed to complying with the member's request. [*PSA 1993, s 100*]. A member could not, therefore, withdraw his application if the trustees

6.53 *Protection for early leavers*

have already made a transfer or entered into a binding agreement with a third party, such as an insurance company. A member who withdraws an application is not prevented from making another application at some future date.

'Splitting' a cash equivalent

6.53 A cash equivalent can be 'split' between a number of arrangements. For example, a member can transfer part of his cash equivalent to an occupational pension scheme and part to a personal pension scheme. [*PSA 1993, s 96(1)*]. This is most commonly done where the transfer is from a contracted-out scheme to a contracted-in scheme which cannot accept assets representing the member's contracted-out rights (but due to changes in the contracting-out system (see chapter 4) this is likely to become less common in the future).

Although a cash equivalent can be split between different arrangements, a member must generally take his whole cash equivalent. [*PSA 1993, s 96*]. There are, however, two qualifications to this: firstly, where the member's cash equivalent is restricted because he terminated pensionable service without terminating service (see 6.46 above); and secondly, where his cash equivalent includes contracted-out rights which the receiving arrangement (not being contracted-out) is unable or unwilling to accept. [*PSA 1993 s 96(1)(b) and (2)*].

Benefits to be provided by the receiving arrangement

6.54 The benefit which the receiving arrangement provides in respect of a cash equivalent will depend on the rules of that arrangement. A final salary scheme may provide a fixed amount of pension, similar to a revalued preserved pension. Alternatively the money may be invested in the same way as a member's additional voluntary contributions, or it may be translated into 'added years'. In the case of a money purchase scheme a transfer value will usually simply be invested along with other contributions.

TRUSTEES' DUTIES AFTER MEMBER EXERCISES HIS RIGHT

Complying with the member's request

6.55 The trustees must do what is necessary to carry out the member's request, in the case of a final salary scheme, within six months of the guarantee date or (if earlier) the date on which the member reaches normal pension age. (*PSA 1993, s 99(2)*). As the six month period is from the guarantee date the trustees will have a minimum period of three months and a maximum period of six months in which to make the transfer payment (depending on how quickly the member requests the guaranteed cash equivalent).

In any other case, the necessary action must be taken within six months of the date on which the trustees received the application, or (if earlier), the date on which the member reaches normal pension age.

Trust busting

6.56 Concern by the Inland Revenue over the so-called practice of 'trust busting' has led to the amendment of the Practice Notes to impose new requirements in respect of transfers.

'Trust busting' arrangements, also known as 'Pension Liberation Schemes', are where a scheme member requests a transfer to a receiving scheme where he has become a 'share employee' on the books of a sponsoring employer. Once the transfer payment has been received by the receiving scheme, the member is given a lump sum representing that transfer payment minus the commission charged by the operation carrying out the 'trust busting'. Commission can often be as high as 30% of the transfer payment and if the Revenue discovers the payment the member may also suffer a tax charge of up to 40% of the transfer payment.

Since 1 July 2002 all schemes must implement the Inland Revenue's new requirements in respect of transfers.

Before meeting a transfer the trustees or administrator must satisfy themselves that the receiving scheme is a 'tax advantaged' scheme or arrangement that falls within 10.23(a)-(d) of the Practice Notes, these are:

(a) occupational schemes approved under *ICTA 1988, Chapter I, Part XIV*, including free standing additional voluntary contribution schemes;

(b) approved personal pension schemes,

(c) relevant statutory schemes and annuity contracts to which *ICTA 1988, s 431(B)(2)(d)* or (*e*) applies.

Where a transfer payment is requested, the trustees or administrator (or persons acting on their behalf) must, before making the transfer, ascertain the type of scheme or arrangement that the Member has asked the transfer be paid to. Different rules then apply depending on the type of scheme or arrangement to which it is going to be made.

The following table summarises the different new rules.

Receiving scheme	*Requirements*
Insured Scheme	Payment should only be made to the Life Office insuring the benefits.

6.56 *Protection for early leavers*

Receiving scheme	Requirements
SSAS	Before making the transfer, the transferring scheme must obtain written confirmation from the Pensioneer Trustee of the receiving SSAS that the transfer is to go ahead and the payment is to be made directly into a SSAS bank account of which the Pensioneer Trustee is a mandatory co-signatory. If the transferring scheme still has doubts about the transfer request then it is at liberty to make further enquiries of the Pensioneer Trustee. The prior written consent of the Inland Revenue must still be obtained before making a transfer payment of any kind to a SSAS.
Self-Administered Scheme (other than a SSAS)	The receiving scheme is required to give the transferring scheme written permission authorising the Inland Revenue to give the transferring scheme confirmation that the receiving scheme is/is not a tax approved self-administered scheme. If the transferring scheme has reason to believe the transfer request is suspect then it may write to the Inland Revenue (enclosing the authority) asking for confirmation of the receiving scheme's status.
Personal Pension Schemes	If the receiving personal pension scheme is underwritten by a Life Office than payment must be made to the Life Office only. If there is no Life Office or the receiving scheme is partly non-insured than if the scheme provider falls within ICTA 1988, s 632(1) then the transfer should be made to the Life Office or administrator as appropriate. If neither of these apply then the receiving scheme must provide the transferring scheme with written permission authorising the Inland Revenue to confirm its tax approved status to the transferring scheme. Again, if the transferring scheme has any doubts about making the transfer, it may write to the Inland Revenue (enclosing the authority) for confirmation of the tax approved status.

From 17 May 2002 transfers are no longer permitted to go through an independent broker.

The Inland Revenue may consider withdrawing approval from a scheme making a transfer to a 'trust busting' arrangement. Before approval is withdrawn, the trustees or administrator will be given an opportunity to demonstrate that they were acting in good faith.

If an approved scheme knowingly makes a suspicious transfer payment it may suffer an obligation to deduct tax under PAYE and additionally failure to comply with the PAYE Regulations may result in penalties and interest charges.

Variations and extensions of time limits

6.57 Under *section 99(4)* of *PSA 1993* and *regulation 13* of the *Transfer Regulations (SI 1996 No 1847)*, the Occupational Pensions Regulatory Authority (Opra) may grant an extension of the time limits for making the transfer payment in certain circumstances, including where:

(a)   the member disputes the amount of the cash equivalent;

(b)   the scheme is being wound up or is about to be wound up;

(c)   the scheme is ceasing to be a contracted-out scheme;

(d)   the interests of the members of the scheme generally would be prejudiced if the trustees acted on a member's request within the statutory time limit;

(e)   the trustees have not been provided with the information they reasonably require to carry out properly what the member requires.

An application for an extension must be made during the period within which the trustees should have complied with the member's request.

If disciplinary or court proceedings are brought against a member within twelve months of the termination of his pensionable service and there is a likelihood that his benefits may be forfeited as a result, the period within which the trustees are required to comply with the member's request is extended to three months after conclusion of the disciplinary or court proceedings. [*PSA 1993, s 99(3)*].

An application must still be brought under *regulation 13* where a transfer cannot be completed within the statutory time frame because of additional checks being made to avoid 'trust busting' but where this is the genuine reason Opra will look on the application sympathetically.

Consequences of delay

6.58 If the trustees fail to do what is needed to carry out the member's request within the appropriate time frame, and cannot establish grounds for an extension, they must notify Opra of the failure to comply. In making their notification to Opra the trustees should give an explanation, since Opra then has

6.59 *Protection for early leavers*

power to impose a financial penalty (of up to £1,000 in the case of an individual or £10,000 in any other case) if the trustees have failed to take reasonable steps to ensure compliance. [*PSA 1993, s 99(7)*].

A member's cash equivalent must be increased if the trustees delay implementing the member's request for more than six months. If there is a reasonable excuse for the delay, the cash equivalent must be recalculated, and increased as appropriate, as if the date on which the trustees carry out the member's request had been the guarantee date (in the case of a final salary scheme) or the date on which the trustees received the member's application for a cash equivalent (in any other case).

If there is no reasonable excuse for the delay, either the cash equivalent must be recalculated as above, or interest must be added to the original cash equivalent at one per cent above base rate (as defined in the *Local Government Pension Scheme Regulations 1995 (SI 1995 No 1019)*) if this would produce a greater amount. [*Transfer Regulations (SI 1996 No 1847), reg 10*].

Discharge of trustees

6.59 Once the trustees have done what is needed to carry out the member's request, they are discharged from any obligation to provide benefits to which the cash equivalent relates. [*PSA 1993, s 99(1)*].

DISCLOSURE REQUIREMENTS

6.60 Active members of any scheme and deferred members of money purchase schemes are entitled to certain information regarding cash equivalents and transfer values. [*Transfer Regulations (SI 1996 No 1847), reg 11* and *1 Sch*]. In particular, a statement of whether or not a cash equivalent or other transfer value is available, or would be available if the member terminated pensionable service, must be provided. Trustees must also supply the following information as soon as practicable and in any event within three months of the request being made:

(*a*) an estimate of the amount of the cash equivalent (calculated on the basis that the member's service terminated or will terminate on a particular date);

(*b*) details of the accrued rights to which the cash equivalent relates;

(*c*) details of how far discretionary or customary benefits have been taken into account and, if the trustees have exercised their right to direct that such benefits are not taken into account, the fact that the trustees have been obliged to obtain an actuary's report before excluding such benefits and that the member is entitled to ask for a copy of that report; and

(*d*) if the amount of the cash equivalent has been reduced, a statement of that fact and of the amount by which the cash equivalent has been reduced, an explanation of the reason for the reduction (which shall refer to the paragraph of *regulation 8* of the *Transfer Regulations (SI 1996 No 1847)* relied upon), an estimate of when an unreduced payment would be available and a statement of the member's right to obtain further estimates.

A member is only entitled to this information once in every twelve month period. Similar information must be given in respect of any non-statutory transfer value that may be available to the member.

When a member is given a statement of entitlement to a cash equivalent transfer value certain information must be given in addition to that referred to above. In particular, the member must be given a statement explaining:

(i) that the member can only request a statement of entitlement once in every twelve month period unless the trustees allow otherwise or the scheme rules permit more frequent requests;

(ii) that if the member wishes to exercise his right to take the guaranteed cash equivalent he must submit a written application to that effect so within three months of the guarantee date; and

(iii) in exceptional circumstances the guaranteed cash equivalent may be reduced and the member will be informed if his cash equivalent is reduced.

Any trustee who fails to take all reasonable steps to comply with these disclosure requirements can be fined up to £1,000 in the case of an individual or £10,000 in any other case. [*PSA 1993, s 93A* and the *Transfer Regulations (SI 1996 No 1847), reg 20*]. See appendix I regarding penalties generally.

HYBRID SCHEMES

6.61 The *Transfer Regulations (SI 1996 No 1847)* make special provisions for 'hybrid schemes', ie schemes which are final salary but under which some of the benefits which may be provided are money purchase benefits or vice versa. In relation to such schemes a member has a right to:

(a) a guaranteed cash equivalent in respect of his final salary benefits; and

(b) a cash equivalent which is equal to the money purchase benefits. [*Transfer Regulations, (SI 1996 No 1847), reg 19*].

In exercising his rights, the member must take the whole of his cash equivalent, ie both the guaranteed and non-guaranteed element.

TRANSITIONAL ARRANGEMENTS AND THE IMPLICATIONS OF *PA 1995*

6.62 The requirements relating to guaranteed cash equivalents apply from 6 April 1997. If a member of a final salary scheme made an application for the

6.63 *Protection for early leavers*

transfer of his cash equivalent before 6 April 1997, the provisions of the *Occupational Pension Schemes (Transfer Values) Regulations 1985 (SI 1985 No 1931)* apply. The main difference between the two regimes is the manner in which cash equivalents are calculated and the fact that cash equivalents are not guaranteed. The time limits for complying with the member's request are also different; under the old regime the trustees had twelve months within which to comply with the request.

Before the changes introduced by the *PA 1995*, for members of final salary schemes two calculations were usually made before a cash equivalent transfer value was paid; the first was made when the member requested details of his cash equivalent and the second was made when he decided to proceed with the transfer. As from 6 April 1997 only one calculation is necessary.

The practical implications of the current regime are unlikely to be overly burdensome for trustees; even before *PA 1995* came into force many schemes 'guaranteed' cash equivalents to a greater or lesser degree notwithstanding the lack of statutory requirements. However, the threat of penalties for non-compliance seems to have prompted trustees to be a little more careful about dealing with requests for cash equivalents, which in turn seems to have reduced the number of disputes relating to cash equivalents and transfers generally. (In the year 1995/1996, approximately 11 per cent of the cases dealt with by the Pensions Ombudsman related to transfer. In the year 2000/2001 this has dropped to approximately 6 per cent.)

SUMMARY OF GUARANTEED CASH EQUIVALENT PROCEDURE

6.63 It is proposed that a member of a pension scheme who has completed three months' pensionable service, but less than two years, will gain immediate vesting. This means that the member will have the option of a cash equivalent benefit which can be transferred to another pension scheme or a refund of his or her contributions to the pension scheme.

SUMMARY OF GUARANTEED CASH EQUIVALENT PROCEDURE

6.62

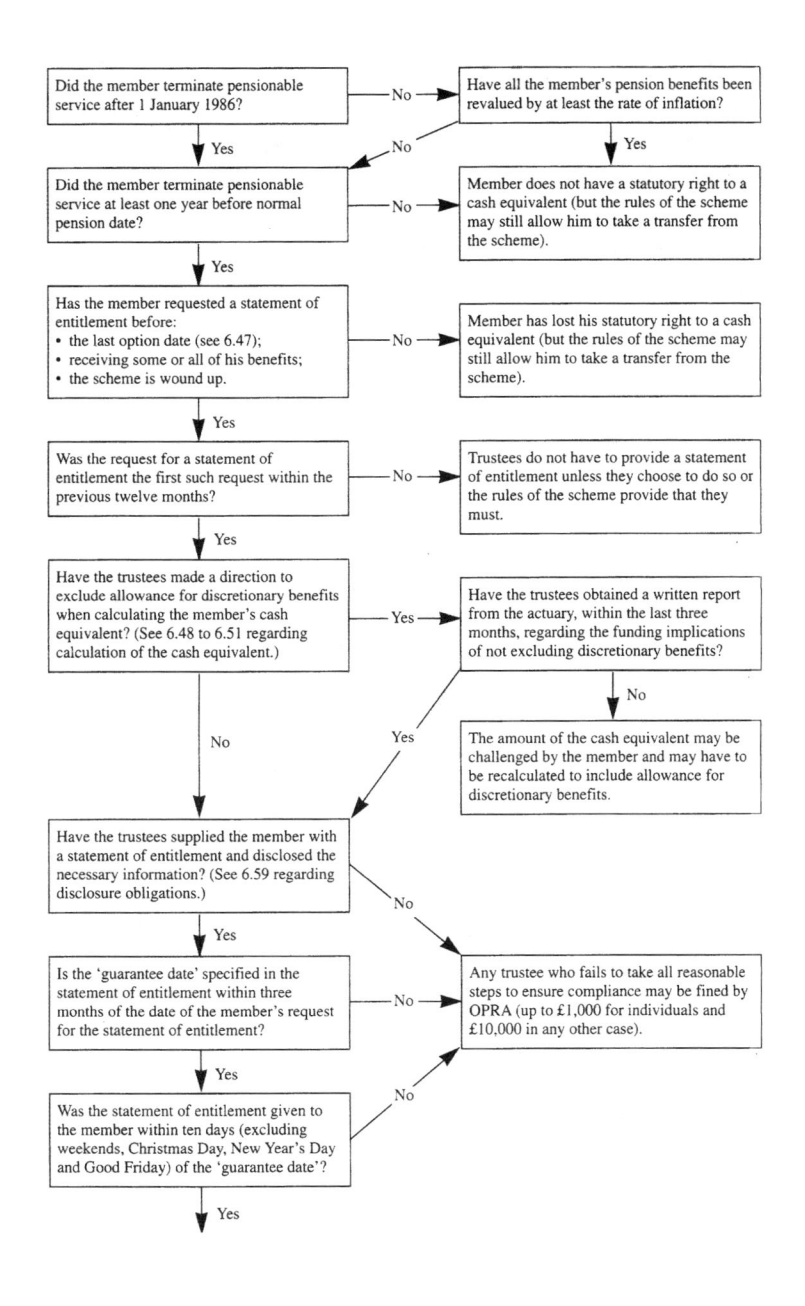

```
┌─────────────────────────────────┐                  ┌─────────────────────────────────────┐
│ Did the member terminate        │──── No ────▶    │ Have all the member's pension       │
│ pensionable service after 1     │                  │ benefits been revalued by at least  │
│ January 1986?                   │                  │ the rate of inflation?              │
└─────────────────────────────────┘                  └─────────────────────────────────────┘
            │ Yes              ◀──── No ────┐              │ Yes          │ No
            ▼                                │              ▼              │
┌─────────────────────────────────┐         │      ┌─────────────────────────────────────┐
│ Did the member terminate        │──── No ─┤      │ Member does not have a statutory    │
│ pensionable service at least    │         │      │ right to a cash equivalent (but the │
│ one year before normal pension  │         │      │ rules of the scheme may still allow │
│ date?                           │         │      │ him to take a transfer from the     │
└─────────────────────────────────┘         │      │ scheme).                            │
            │ Yes                            │      └─────────────────────────────────────┘
            ▼                                │
┌─────────────────────────────────┐         │      ┌─────────────────────────────────────┐
│ Has the member requested a      │         │      │ Member has lost his statutory right │
│ statement of entitlement before:│         │      │ to a cash equivalent (but the rules │
│ • the last option date (see     │──── No ───────▶│ of the scheme may still allow him   │
│   6.47);                        │                 │ to take a transfer from the scheme).│
│ • receiving some or all of his  │                 │                                     │
│   benefits;                     │                 │                                     │
│ • the scheme is wound up.       │                 │                                     │
└─────────────────────────────────┘                 └─────────────────────────────────────┘
            │ Yes
            ▼
┌─────────────────────────────────┐                 ┌─────────────────────────────────────┐
│ Was the request for a statement │                 │ Trustees do not have to provide a   │
│ of entitlement the first such   │──── No ────────▶│ statement of entitlement unless they│
│ request within the previous     │                 │ choose to do so or the rules of the │
│ twelve months?                  │                 │ scheme provide that they must.      │
└─────────────────────────────────┘                 └─────────────────────────────────────┘
            │ Yes
            ▼
┌─────────────────────────────────┐                 ┌─────────────────────────────────────┐
│ Have the trustees made a        │                 │ Have the trustees obtained a        │
│ direction to exclude allowance  │                 │ written report from the actuary,    │
│ for discretionary benefits when │──── Yes ──────▶ │ within the last three months,       │
│ calculating the member's cash   │                 │ regarding the funding implications  │
│ equivalent? (See 6.48 to 6.51   │                 │ of not excluding discretionary      │
│ regarding calculation of the    │                 │ benefits?                           │
│ cash equivalent.)               │                 └─────────────────────────────────────┘
└─────────────────────────────────┘                           │ No
            │ No               Yes                            ▼
            │                   │                  ┌─────────────────────────────────────┐
            │                   │                  │ The amount of the cash equivalent   │
            │                   │                  │ may be challenged by the member and │
            │                   │                  │ may have to be recalculated to      │
            │                   │                  │ include allowance for discretionary │
            │                   │                  │ benefits.                           │
            │                   │                  └─────────────────────────────────────┘
            ▼                   │
┌─────────────────────────────────┐
│ Have the trustees supplied the  │
│ member with a statement of      │
│ entitlement and disclosed the   │
│ necessary information? (See     │
│ 6.59 regarding disclosure       │
│ obligations.)                   │──── No ──┐
└─────────────────────────────────┘          │
            │ Yes                             │
            ▼                                 ▼
┌─────────────────────────────────┐          ┌─────────────────────────────────────┐
│ Is the 'guarantee date'         │          │ Any trustee who fails to take all   │
│ specified in the statement of   │──── No ─▶│ reasonable steps to ensure          │
│ entitlement within three months │          │ compliance may be fined by OPRA     │
│ of the date of the member's     │          │ (up to £1,000 for individuals and   │
│ request for the statement of    │          │ £10,000 in any other case).         │
│ entitlement?                    │          └─────────────────────────────────────┘
└─────────────────────────────────┘                    ▲
            │ Yes                                       │
            ▼                                           │
┌─────────────────────────────────┐                    │
│ Was the statement of entitlement│                    │
│ given to the member within ten  │──── No ────────────┘
│ days (excluding weekends,       │
│ Christmas Day, New Year's Day   │
│ and Good Friday) of the         │
│ 'guarantee date'?               │
└─────────────────────────────────┘
            │ Yes
            ▼
```

6.63 Protection for early leavers

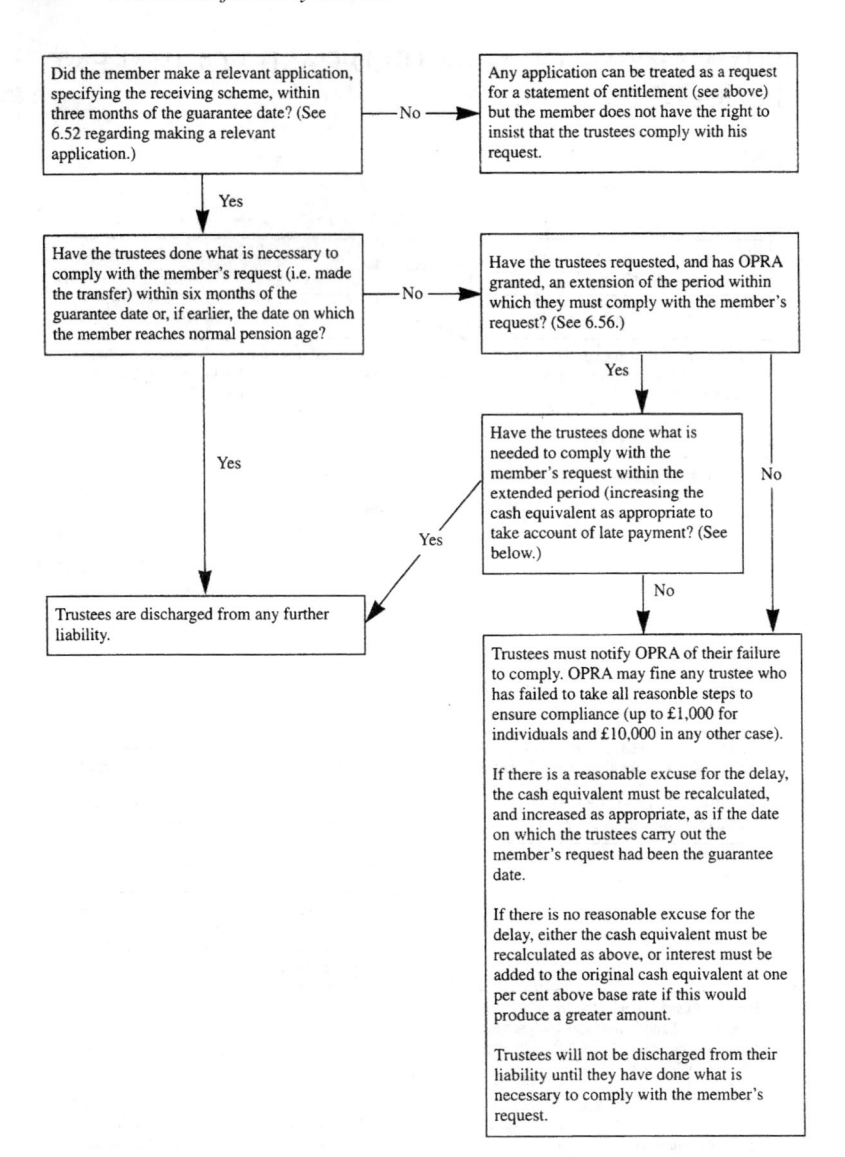

```
┌─────────────────────────────────┐                    ┌─────────────────────────────────┐
│ Did the member make a relevant  │                    │ Any application can be treated  │
│ application, specifying the     │                    │ as a request for a statement of │
│ receiving scheme, within three  │─── No ────────────▶│ entitlement (see above) but the │
│ months of the guarantee date?   │                    │ member does not have the right  │
│ (See 6.52 regarding making a    │                    │ to insist that the trustees     │
│ relevant application.)          │                    │ comply with his request.        │
└─────────────────────────────────┘                    └─────────────────────────────────┘
              │ Yes
              ▼
┌─────────────────────────────────┐                    ┌─────────────────────────────────┐
│ Have the trustees done what is  │                    │ Have the trustees requested,    │
│ necessary to comply with the    │                    │ and has OPRA granted, an        │
│ member's request (i.e. made     │─── No ────────────▶│ extension of the period within  │
│ the transfer) within six months │                    │ which they must comply with the │
│ of the guarantee date or, if    │                    │ member's request? (See 6.56.)   │
│ earlier, the date on which the  │                    └─────────────────────────────────┘
│ member reaches normal pension   │                                  │ Yes
│ age?                            │                                  ▼
└─────────────────────────────────┘                    ┌─────────────────────────────────┐
              │                                        │ Have the trustees done what is  │
              │ Yes                                    │ needed to comply with the       │
              │                                        │ member's request within the     │──── No ────┐
              │                                        │ extended period (increasing the │            │
              │                                        │ cash equivalent as appropriate  │            │
              │                         Yes            │ to take account of late         │            │
              │                         ◀──────────────│ payment? (See below.)           │            │
              │                                        └─────────────────────────────────┘            │
              ▼                                                      │ No                             │
┌─────────────────────────────────┐                                  │                                │
│ Trustees are discharged from    │                                  ▼                                ▼
│ any further liability.          │                    ┌─────────────────────────────────────────────────┐
└─────────────────────────────────┘                    │ Trustees must notify OPRA of their failure to   │
                                                       │ comply. OPRA may fine any trustee who has       │
                                                       │ failed to take all reasonble steps to ensure    │
                                                       │ compliance (up to £1,000 for individuals and    │
                                                       │ £10,000 in any other case).                     │
                                                       │                                                 │
                                                       │ If there is a reasonable excuse for the delay,  │
                                                       │ the cash equivalent must be recalculated, and   │
                                                       │ increased as appropriate, as if the date on     │
                                                       │ which the trustees carry out the member's       │
                                                       │ request had been the guarantee date.            │
                                                       │                                                 │
                                                       │ If there is no reasonable excuse for the delay, │
                                                       │ either the cash equivalent must be recalculated │
                                                       │ as above, or interest must be added to the      │
                                                       │ original cash equivalent at one per cent above  │
                                                       │ base rate if this would produce a greater       │
                                                       │ amount.                                         │
                                                       │                                                 │
                                                       │ Trustees will not be discharged from their      │
                                                       │ liability until they have done what is          │
                                                       │ necessary to comply with the member's request.  │
                                                       └─────────────────────────────────────────────────┘
```

Chapter 7

Employment issues

INTRODUCTION

7.1 Traditionally, lawyers attempted to keep pension schemes and employment issues entirely separate, but the distinction between pension rights deriving from a trust and contractual employment rights is becoming more blurred. In the past, pensions were seen as being provided by employers out of gratitude for the employee's long and dutiful service. The employer, as settlor, had absolute discretion as to what level or type of benefits were to be provided to the employee.

Pension schemes are now an integral part of the total remuneration package offered by employers (pension provision is often a key recruitment and retention issue) and the provision of pension benefits is heavily regulated by statute and secondary legislation.

There is currently no legislation requiring an employer to run a pension scheme (except in limited circumstances for ex-public sector employees, although such rights are statutory and not the norm). However, from 8 October 2001, employers of five or more employees are required to designate a stakeholder pension scheme which their employees may elect to join, and to arrange for salary deductions to be made and contributions paid directly to the provider on behalf of employees (*Welfare Reform and Pensions Act 1999, s 1*).

As a consequence of the *Social Security Act 1986* (now *section 160* of the *Pension Schemes Act 1993*), an employer can no longer make membership of a pension scheme compulsory. There is no minimum or maximum level of benefits that may or should by law be provided, except that a contracted-out scheme must provide certain minimum benefits required by statute (see chapter 4); an exempt approved scheme must not provide benefits which exceed Inland Revenue limits (see chapter 5) and final salary schemes must meet the minimum funding requirement (see chapter 11). None of the tax, preservation, revaluation or contracting-out legislation states that the contract of employment should contain any rights for the employee as against the employer; the employee's rights are ostensibly against the trustees of the pension scheme alone. Moreover, it is understandable that an employer would wish to exercise as much control as possible over a scheme which it operates and funds (particularly following the extension of the *Deficiency Regulations (SI 1996 No 3128)* and the introduction of the minimum funding requirement under the *PA 1995*.)

7.2 *Employment issues*

An employee does have specific rights against his employer but these are only in the areas of sex, race, religion of belief, sexual orientation and disability discrimination, equal pay, maternity absence and, as of 6 April 2003, paternity and adoption absence and even then these rights are statutory rather than contractual. It is true that *Barber v Guardian Royal Exchange [1990] 2 CMLR 513* (as subsequently clarified by *Coloroll Pension Trustees Ltd v Russell [1995] All ER (EC) 23*) confirmed that pensions are pay, but that is only in the context of the equality provisions of *Article 141 (formerly Article 119)* of the *Treaty of Rome*, as regards access to pension schemes and the benefits to be provided for men and women. In addition, although defined pension contributions and benefits were also recognised as pay by the Central Arbitration Committee, this was only in respect of trade union recognition for collective bargaining purposes (*UNIFI v Union Bank of Nigeria plc, [2001] IRLR 712*). Neither *Barber* nor *UNIFI* answer the more fundamental question of whether (and if so, to what extent) pensions are an employment right and neither does *PA 1995*.

WHAT IS THE EMPLOYEE PROMISED?

Wording of the employment contract

7.2 The wording of an employment contract generally provides little or no guidance as to the pension rights (if any) of the employee. *Section 1* of the *Employment Rights Act 1996 ('ERA 1996')* states that within two months of the commencement of employment, the employer must provide a written statement of the essential terms of the employment and must include any terms and conditions (see *ERA 1996 s 1(4)(d)(iii)*) relating to 'pensions and pension schemes'. Generally the information given will be limited, as *ERA 1996* in reality requires information to be given on access to a pension scheme, as opposed to the benefits which will be provided if an employee joins the pension scheme. Indeed it would be risky for an employer to give express commitments in the employment contract as to the benefits to be provided under a final salary scheme as, until the winding-up of a pension scheme and the crystallisation of its liabilities, an employer cannot be certain that there will be sufficient funds to meet the pension promise. There is less of a problem with money purchase arrangements.

Although the precise wording would have to be checked in any individual case, usually a contract will state that an employee may join the pension scheme if eligible to do so (for example upper and lower age limits may be imposed, or a requirement to have completed a year's service) and membership will be subject to the provisions governing the scheme from time to time, which are summarised in the scheme booklet. The contract may also reserve to the employer the right to amend or terminate the pension scheme, or alternatively an employer may rely on the reference to the scheme booklet (which should, if properly drafted, contain such a caveat). In most instances, and as clarified by the High Court in *ITN v Ward [1997] PLR 131*, the trust deed will override the booklet in cases of inconsistency.

When it comes to employing a senior executive, the employer is likely to take more time over the drafting of his particular service contract (which is less likely to follow a standard form) and one of the important clauses will usually deal specifically with the pension benefits to be provided (as opposed merely to access to the scheme).

In most cases the wording of the employment contract is unlikely to be of assistance in analysing pension rights, and it is designed to comply with statutory minimum requirements. The only employment 'right' is likely to be a right to join the scheme, if the employee satisfies the eligibility criteria.

In reality, an employee will obtain clearer information from the trustees of any occupational scheme, pursuant to the trustees' obligations under *PA 1995* disclosure requirements (for further details see chapter 3 and appendix II), than he will from his employer. Basic information about the scheme (*Disclosure Regulations* (*SI 1996 No 1655*), *reg 4*)) must be provided as a matter of course to each prospective member or, if this is not practicable, within two months of his becoming a member.

The pension scheme documentation

7.3 The explanatory booklet or announcement will usually be designed to comply with the disclosure requirements of *PSA 1993*, *PA 1995* and the *Disclosure Regulations* (*SI 1996 No 1655*). It will usually state that the scheme is established under a trust and is managed by trustees, that the booklet is explanatory only, and that the employees' rights are set out in the trust deed and rules, which is available for inspection or copies of which are available on application to the trustees. In practice it is uncommon for employees to exercise their rights to inspect the deed.

In addition, a statement will usually be incorporated saying that whilst the company has every intention of continuing the scheme it does reserve the right to modify or discontinue it at any time.

The application for membership will usually authorise the company to deduct any contributions payable by the employee from his remuneration and to remit these contributions to the trustees. This authority (which must be in writing and precede the first deduction) is required under *section 13* of *ERA 1996* (a consolidation of the *Wages Act 1986* provisions) and may not be specifically incorporated within the contract of employment. This is an important fact which must be remembered when considering the amalgamation of two or more schemes or the transfer of a group of employees into a new scheme. The authority to deduct contributions may be specific to the former scheme and may have to be renewed for the new scheme before any deductions are made.

The trust deed and rules will generally establish that the employee, if he joins the scheme and becomes a beneficiary of the trust, will become entitled to benefits in defined circumstances. The formal documentation will contain a

7.3 Employment issues

power of amendment, exercisable by the employer with the consent of the trustees, or vice versa, or (less commonly) by one party solely. Rights already accrued may also be expressly protected (see also 7.10 below).

The employer will usually have power to discontinue contributions, following which the scheme will normally be wound up, although the trustees may have power to continue it as a closed scheme (see chapter 12 for further details regarding winding-up of pension schemes). The benefits provided on winding-up will depend on the liabilities at that date, the value of the assets and the cost of purchasing annuities. Certain classes of member, starting with existing pensioners, will have priority. Employed members are often at the bottom of the list of priorities and, in cases of significant underfunding, may receive nothing, irrespective of their current age and length of pensionable service. It is at that stage that the employee will be looking to the employer to make good his loss, and the *Deficiency Regulations (SI 1996 No 3128)* will come into play. However, the *Deficiency Regulations (SI 1996 No 3128)* value benefits on different bases, depending on the date of winding up and the status of the employee and therefore, in certain circumstances, employees will not receive their full entitlement. In addition, the employer's debt under the *Deficiency Regulations (SI 1996 No 3128)* is an unsecured debt owed to the trustees from the employer, so if the employer is hopelessly insolvent the employee will potentially receive nothing. However, the employee does enjoy some security on an ongoing basis as a result of the minimum funding requirement (see chapter 11) and the statutory priorities on wind up (see chapter 12).

The Pensions Bill, introduced to Parliament in February 2004, has improved member security to an extent, introducing proposals for a Pension Protection Fund ('PPF'), which is designed to protect members of private sector defined benefits schemes in the event that their employer becomes insolvent with insufficient funds in the scheme. It is intended that members of the scheme who have reached retirement age will receive in full the pension originally promised to them and that members below retirement age will receive 90 per cent of the pension originally promised, subject to an overall cap, calculated on the basis of a number of criteria (including earnings and scheme rates). The PPF is expected to be financed by a levy on defined benefit schemes calculated on the basis of 'scheme factors' and 'risk factors'. In order to offset the cost of the levy, it is proposed to reduce the Limited Price Indexation cap on index-linked pensions to 2.5 per cent.

For a pension scheme established under trust, the employee's security therefore depends on a number of factors including the continued payment of contributions by the employer, to ensure sufficient funding, and investment performance. It is difficult to ascertain what the employee's 'rights' against an employer are. His pension entitlement is enforceable against the trustees, who will look to the employer for additional funding, if required. If the scheme is in deficit, the employee's enforceable rights against the employer are statutory, and statute does not guarantee that a full pension (ie as promised under the trust documentation) will be paid.

WHAT ARE THE EMPLOYER'S OBLIGATIONS?

General

7.4 The employer must comply with the rights and obligations set out in the trust deed and rules governing the scheme. However, these do not cover every eventuality, and it is often necessary to look to case law for guidance.

Fiduciary duties — Mettoy and Icarus

7.5 *Mettoy Pensions Trustees Ltd v Evans [1990] 1 WLR 1587* acknowledged (although the case did not hinge on this) that an employee's rights under a pension scheme trust are of a commercial and contractual origin; they derive from the contract of employment, with benefits being earned by virtue of service with the employer under those contracts and, where the scheme is contributory, by virtue of those contributions. Employees can therefore only benefit from a pension scheme by virtue of their employment, which in turn is governed by the employment contract. Similar issues were previously raised in *Kerry v British Leyland [1986] CA Transcript 286* and *Mihlenstedt v Barclays Bank International [1989] IRLR 522*, in which the judge stated that the scheme was 'established against the background of such employment and falls to be interpreted against that background'.

The judge in the *Mettoy* case concluded that the power apparently vested in the company to decide what to do with a surplus on winding-up was a fiduciary power (ie a power conferred on the employer as 'trustee' of the power, effectively being one which had to be exercised in the best interests of the members and putting the employer in the same position as a trustee as regards the duties owed to members).

A similar decision was made in *Icarus (Hertford) v Driscoll (1990) PLR 1*, where the employer remained as trustee of the scheme following its insolvency (this was prior to the legislation requiring an independent trustee to be appointed in such a situation). It is therefore logical that the judge held the employer to be in a fiduciary position, as the employer was the actual, as opposed to a quasi, trustee. There was held to be a fiduciary power which the employer had to exercise in good faith, 'in the sense that he cannot act for reasons which are irrelevant or perverse'.

Employers should, therefore, take care that the powers which they exercise are not powers which a court would consider to be fiduciary in nature.

Duty of good faith — the *Imperial case*

7.6 It is well established that under the contract of employment there exists a reciprocal duty of good faith on behalf of both employers and employees. As a consequence of the *Imperial* case this principle extends to the exercise of all the employer's powers and obligations under a pension scheme (*Imperial Group*

7.7 Employment issues

Pension Trust v Imperial Tobacco [1991] 2 All ER 597). In *Imperial* it was held that the company was under an implied contractual obligation of good faith in the exercise of its rights and powers under the pension scheme. The court also established the principle that the trust deed and rules were subject to the implied limitation that any rights or powers of the company should only be exercised in accordance with the obligation not to seriously undermine the relationship of trust and confidence existing between the employer and the employee. This duty of good faith is not the same as a fiduciary duty (see 7.5 above); the judge (Sir Nicholas Browne-Wilkinson V.C.) explained that the company can have regard to its own interests (financial and otherwise) but only to the extent that in doing so it does not breach the obligation of good faith to its employees.

The decision in *Imperial* can be seen as the judiciary importing employment law concepts into the pensions arena. Arguably, good faith means little more than the employer having to act in a reasonable manner and it remains to be seen how far this concept will be taken by the courts and by the Pensions Ombudsman. The duty of good faith must also be distinguished from a fiduciary duty which would require an employer to act in the beneficiaries' best interests.

Post *Imperial*

7.7 The rights and obligations of an employer were considered by the High Court in May 1996 in the case of *Engineering Training Authority v Pensions Ombudsman (1996) PLR 409*, this case being an appeal from a determination by the Pensions Ombudsman of maladministration on the part of the employer. The Ombudsman had jurisdiction at that time to consider the position of an employer's functions in relation to a pension scheme under the *Personal and Occupational Pension Schemes (Pensions Ombudsman) Regulations 1991 (SI 1991 No 588)* (which have subsequently been revoked and replaced by the *Personal and Occupational Pension Schemes (Pensions Ombudsman) Regulations 1996 (SI 1996 No 2475)*). The member was made redundant in May 1993. If he had been made redundant in September 1993, at age 50, he would have been entitled to an early retirement pension. In negotiations the employer agreed to keep the employee on its books until age 50 (agreeing that he could obtain an immediate pension without actuarial reduction) and the employee consented to this (by countersigning a letter to him from the employer). He then complained to the Ombudsman that the employer had not provided him with an enhancement (of six years' pensionable service) which was payable, at the employer's discretion, to employees retiring after age 47 and that he had been 'coerced' into signing away his pension enhancement rights. The court held that the Ombudsman does not have power 'to investigate complaints about the ordinary contractual relations between employer and employee', which are matters for an Employment Tribunal or a court. The Ombudsman's jurisdiction to investigate is confined to the employer's functions relating to the pension scheme.

Although this case deals essentially with the clarification of the jurisdiction of the Ombudsman, it is indicative of the uncertainty of the overlap between pension and contractual promises. Interestingly, in the appeal the Ombudsman tried to argue that even if the employer was not guilty of maladministration, the complaint should be upheld as the employer had breached the *Imperial* duty of good faith. The court was referred to the decision of the Court of Appeal in *Harris v Shuttleworth (1994) PLR 47* which stated that for an employer to dismiss an employee and thus deprive her of an ill-health pension 'might very well amount to a breach of good faith on the part of the employer, giving the employee a separate remedy'. The judge thought that these submissions were inappropriate in the context of the appeal (having not been considered by the Ombudsman in his determination). However, it is possible in situations such as this that the employee concerned could (time limits permitting) launch a separate action.

The *Imperial* duty continues to be an extremely important legal principle, in both High Court cases and in the Ombudsman's jurisdiction. For example, the judge (Knox J) in *Hillsdown Holdings plc v Pensions Ombudsman (1996) PLR 427* found that the employer had been in breach of the duty of good faith by threatening to suspend contributions and flood an overfunded scheme with new entrants if the trustees did not agree to merger proposals put forward by the employer. Similarly, the Ombudsman determined, in a complaint brought against the National Grid by two pensioners, that the power vested in an employer to distribute surplus had to be exercised in good faith and that, as the power was vested solely in the employer, the obligation approached a fiduciary duty, calling for the power to be exercised in the best interests of the scheme as a whole, without preferring the employer's interests. Inevitably, given the financial significance of the Ombudsman's determination, National Grid appealed the decision. The appeal (*1997 PLR 161*) was heard by the High Court simultaneously with a summons taken out by National Power, upon whom the *National Grid* determination would have impacted. Part of the appeal hinged on the Ombudsman's view of the duty to distribute surplus approaching a fiduciary duty. Walker J concluded that there is an essential distinction between the duty of good faith and a fiduciary duty, being the right of the employer to look at his own interests. He stated that the Ombudsman had 'lost sight of that essential distinction', and felt that if the *Imperial* case had been heard before the *Mettoy* case, the judge in *Mettoy* could have come to a different conclusion. Although the duty of good faith may have aspects in common with a fiduciary duty, Walker J saw no reason to blend them together; he concluded that no evidence had been put before the Ombudsman to suggest that the National Grid was in breach of its duty of good faith, and that the Ombudsman had therefore erred in law. The Ombudsman's directions were consequently set aside by the High Court, but this decision was reversed by the Court of Appeal judgement (*1999 PLR 37*) which in turn was reversed in the House of Lords in favour of the employers. However, the appeal was not concerned with the distinction between the duty of good faith and fiduciary duties, so the judgment of Walker J in that regard is still good law.

Later decisions emphasise the limits of the *Imperial* principle. In *University of Nottingham v Eyett [1999] IRLR 87* an employer was not obliged to warn an employee that he had not chosen the most advantageous course of action, where the employee was aware of his entitlement to a benefit and was taking a decision on ways to maximise it. In *Outram v Academy Plastics [2000] IRLR 499*, the Court of Appeal struck out a claim that an employer owed a duty of care to an employee who had resigned after 20 years' service and later re-joined the employer. Employers, it was held, do not owe a duty of care to advise scheme members faced with choices about pension matters, nor do they owe a wider duty in tort than in contract. If, however, an employer voluntarily undertakes to provide such advice, an implied duty not to give inaccurate, negligent or misleading advice may apply. *Outram* was cited in case *Wirral Metropolitan Borough Council v Evans and another [2001] OPLR 73* and that judgment followed. It was held that there was no duty on the administrators to give advice to Mr Evans which would have prevented him from transferring his pension benefits to the scheme on unfavourable terms.

Crossley v Faithful & Gould Holdings Limited [2004] EWCA Civ 293, [2004] All ER (D) 295 (Mar) is the most recent case on this matter and Dyson LJ, presiding, usefully analysed previous cases and concluded in paragraph 44 of the judgement that:

> 'The employer is not required to have regard to the employee's financial circumstances when he takes lawful business decisions which may affect the employee's economic welfare. There is no reason to suppose that he will even be aware of the details of those circumstances. Nor is it the function of the employer to act as his employee's financial adviser, that is simply not part of the bargain that is comprised in the contract of employment. There are no obvious policy reasons to impose on an employer the general duty to protect his employee's economic wellbeing. The employee can obtain his own advice, whether from his union or otherwise.'

Nevertheless, if an employer assumes the responsibility for giving financial advice to his employee, he is under a duty to take reasonable care in the giving of that advice. This principle was confirmed in the recent case of *Lennon v Metropolitan Police Commissioner [2004] EWCA Civ 130, [2004] 2 All ER 266*, and cited in the *Crossley* case.

Can an employer contract out of the *Imperial* duty?

7.8   This issue was considered by the Ombudsman in a determination issued in May 1998 (*Poole v Trustees of the Cytec Industries (UK) Limited*). The Interim Trust Deed of the Cytec Scheme contained a provision which stated that 'in exercising any discretion, or power, or giving its agreement or consent under the Plan, an Employer may act in its absolute unfettered discretion and in its sole and exclusive interests'.

The Ombudsman determined that this provision could not operate to nullify the implied obligation of good faith, particularly as it appeared in an agreement made between two parties (the employer and the trustees), to the exclusion of the complainant. Additionally the Ombudsman held that the provision cannot be allowed to operate so as to enable the employer to contract out of the

Ombudsman's jurisdiction in respect of injustice caused by maladministration. He also commented that the exclusion was unusual and oppressive.

Would the Ombudsman's decision have been different if the offending provision had been printed in the booklet? Probably not, for the reasons set out in paragraph 7.19 below, but there is a lesson for employers here: if you wish to rely on a provision, make sure that it is drawn to the employees' attention, in a booklet or other scheme literature distributed to employees.

To whom is the *Imperial* duty owed?

7.9 In the *National Bus* determination (*1997 PLR 1*) the Pensions Ombudsman stated that the duty of good faith was owed by the employer to the trustees as well as to the employees. The duty is therefore also enforceable by the trustees against the employer. It seems likely that a Court would hold that the duty is also owed to ex-employees and by implication, to those claiming through employees (ie spouses and dependants). This is yet to be tested.

In the words of Walker J, 'the scope and limits of the *Imperial Tobacco* duty will no doubt be worked out, on a case by case basis, in coming years'. Employers must therefore take care when exercising their powers.

Termination and reduction of benefits

7.10 In ascertaining the cross-over between pension and employment rights it is useful to focus on a scenario whereby the employer wishes to alter the level of benefits, either by terminating the pension scheme or by providing less beneficial benefits for future (or past) service. From a pure pensions viewpoint the employer would have to consider the power of amendment (which may be jointly vested in the trustees and the employer), and the limitations imposed by *PA 1995, s 67*. Additionally the employer would have to act in accordance with case law; in particular with the *Imperial* duty of good faith. From an employment perspective the situation is more complicated.

Termination

7.11 Arguably, termination of a pension scheme (other than cases of insolvencies, where a wind up would often be automatically triggered), is the real test as to how far an employee has contractual rights against the employer, in addition to the established rights against the trustees under the trust deed and the employee's statutory rights. There is no clear case law on this issue.

As a point of law the question is whether the employer would be in breach of contract by deliberately discontinuing the scheme, or whether he can rely on the express enabling power to terminate contained in the trust deed and (generally) the booklet. In practice an employer can terminate a pension scheme provided he acts in accordance with the termination procedures contained in the govern-

7.12 *Employment issues*

ing documentation. Employers must, however, act very carefully to minimise the risk of any claims by employees and must have a valid reason for wishing to terminate the pension scheme. The most compelling reason will be that the employer simply cannot continue to operate the scheme because of its cost (a reason which has become more commonplace due to the additional costs arising under *PA 1995*).

It would generally be impracticable for an employer to seek the consent of all of the employees who are active scheme members, although this option may sometimes be chosen where the scheme has very few members. Unless the scheme is in deficit, the position of the deferred members and pensioners will be unaffected. A period of consultation may be appropriate, as may negotiations with any Trade Unions. This will give an employer the opportunity to make the reason for the changes clear, and will also make it more likely that a court would consider that the employer had complied with the *Imperial* duty of good faith. (Consideration should also be given to consultation with employees who are eligible to join the scheme but have so far chosen not to do so.) At present, under the Pensions Bill, the Government is proposing to maintain an employer's flexibility as to consultation, to support the specific needs of the employer's organisation. Employers will have the choice to inform and consult employee members either through a recognised trade union; through a mechanism set up under the Information and Consultation Regulations (due to come into force in Spring 2005); via a specifically appointed Pensions Consultation Committee; or directly with the employees.

Alternatively the employer could terminate all existing contracts of employment (by giving the appropriate notice) and issue new contracts, reflecting the less favourable pension provision. There is a risk that, as this is a more aggressive tactic, employees may be able to argue that the unilateral change in their terms of employment constitutes a fundamental breach of contract by the employer which would entitle them to resign and claim constructive dismissal. Additionally, the employer must have a good and substantial reason for wishing to act in this way and the method of implementation must be fair. Also, if the employer has 20 or more employees at an establishment and their employment is terminated within a period of 90 days or less, it would have additional "collective" information and consultation obligations.

Reduction in benefits in an ongoing scheme

7.12 It has always been generally inadvisable to reduce an employee's past service benefits and in many instances this option will be precluded by the scheme's documentation. In addition, accrued rights and entitlements have been protected (from 6 April 1997) by *section 67* of *PA 1995* (see 12.18 below). The meanings of 'accrued rights' and 'entitlements' are considered in 12.1 and 12.20 below.

If an employer wishes to reduce benefits for future service, for example, by converting a final salary scheme to a money purchase basis, similar considerations to those in 7.9 above will apply. Generally, when a scheme's trust deed or rules are amended, an announcement will be issued to the members. In the context of a diminution of benefits, this course of action is probably not sufficient, and consultation with trade unions or employee representatives (if any) (or under the Information and Consultation Regulations, once in force) should be considered. It is vital that the impact of the changes is made entirely clear to the employees, to avoid any subsequent rejection of the new terms and conditions and any hostility and suspicion. To try to minimise friction within a workforce, open question and answer sessions or counselling from an external (ie independent) third party is often chosen by employers.

The Pensions Bill is also set to impose new consultation requirements on employers in relation to certain decisions made in relation to the scheme. Details will be set out in regulations as to which decisions will trigger the consultation requirements and how consultation should take place. Triggers for consultation are likely to cover proposals to wind up a scheme or cease future service accrual; closure to new members; amendments to future service benefits from defined benefit to defined contribution or hybrid benefits and reducing or removing an employer contribution to a defined contribution scheme.

This issue of accrued rights was considered by the High Court in *Lloyds Bank Pension Trust Corporation v Lloyds Bank plc [1996] PLR 263*. In that case the power of amendment was vested jointly in the trustee and the employer, but precluded (*inter alia*) alterations which would in the opinion of the actuary decrease 'the pecuniary benefits secured to or in respect of ... members under the scheme'. The trustee and company brought the court application to determine whether the trustee could agree to equalise benefits in accordance with a proposal put forward by the employer. The proposal effectively equalised male benefits up to the female level for the period 17 May 1990 to 30 April 2000 (at a cost of £100 million), but equalised female benefits down to the previous male level for the period 1 May 2000 onwards. The scheme also contained express provisions requiring member consent to any alterations. Although this case turns on its own facts and the peculiarity of the amendment power, the legal reasoning is of interest. The judge considered that, except with the requisite level of member consent, no amendment could be made either affecting accrued rights or future benefits and, accordingly, the court would not endorse the amendment.

Similar issues were considered by the Pensions Ombudsman in his determination in respect of the dissolution of the National Bus Company (*National Bus Company* – Determination of the Pensions Ombudsman, 6 September 1996 (*1997*) *PLR 1*). The power of amendment was, subject to trustee consent, vested in the company, and contained a proviso that accrued rights could not be affected without obtaining written member consent. As part of a package offered by the company the trustee agreed to alter the basis of indexation on wind up. The Ombudsman considered that the indexation changes affected 'at least some members' benefits' and that accordingly consent had been required. As the trustee, even if acting innocently, had altered benefits in contravention of the power of amendment, the trustee was under an obligation to recover surplus

7.13 *Employment issues*

monies paid to the Department of Transport, which inherited the rights and obligations of the company on its dissolution. On 1 June 1999, John Prescott, Deputy Prime Minister, announced that the Government had reached a settlement with the trustees and on 1 August 1999 paid over £355.77 million. What followed was the lengthy and difficult task of several court applications to assist the trustees to ensure the fair and equitable distribution of the returned monies. The final distribution to eligible members is now in progress.

Although it is now beyond doubt, following *Barber* and *Coloroll*, that pensions are deferred pay, whether the employer has obligations (whether fiduciary or contractual or arising from the duty of good faith) not to restrict, reduce or terminate the possibility of earning that future pay has yet to be tested in the courts. Given the wording of (or at least what could be considered to be the intention of) *PA 1995*, a successful challenge seems unlikely. However, in certain circumstances resulting from the particular drafting of scheme documents, such as highlighted in the *Lloyds Bank* case and the *National Bus Company* determination, nothing can be taken for granted. Both of these cases indicate how carefully scheme documents have to be drafted and construed by trustees and employers, as a narrow interpretation is likely to be imposed by a court or the Pensions Ombudsman in the event of a dispute.

HOW DO THE TRUSTEES FIT IN?

General

7.13 The trustees of a pension scheme have an overriding duty to act in the best interests of the beneficiaries, which usually means their best financial interests (see chapter 3). If the power of amendment is vested solely in the employer, the trustees cannot control the outcome, save to ensure that the amendment complies with the requirements of *PA 1995, s 67,* (except perhaps by way of court application in extreme circumstances, which could either be an injunction to prevent an amendment being made or an application for directions). When the power of amendment is vested in the trustees (or the trustees have to consent to the exercise of a power vested in the employer), the trustees must confine their considerations to the implications for the existing members (including deferred members and pensioners) only. Depending on the particular circumstances, the trustees may also wish to take into account the position of prospective beneficiaries (for example, if there was a waiting period before employees could join the scheme).

Whatever action the trustees take will depend very much on the circumstances; say, trustees are faced with a future reduction in benefits (for example, 60ths accrual to 80ths or final salary to money purchase). They may be persuaded that the amendment is in the interests of all members if the only other alternative is that the scheme will be discontinued because the employer cannot (for sound commercial reasons) afford to continue the current level of promised benefits. In all but the rarest of cases it must be in the beneficiaries' best interests to have an ongoing scheme. This was highlighted in *Re Courage Group Pension*

Schemes [1987] I AER 528 where the judge stated that 'it is important to avoid fettering the power to amend the provisions of the scheme, thereby preventing the parties from making those changes which may be required by the exigencies of commercial life'.

The trustees may often find themselves in the position of arbitrators between an employer and employee if a dispute over a pension issue arises. Often trust deeds confer upon the trustees the power to reach decisions on any matter of doubt arising under the scheme documentation. Since 6 April 1997, the trustees have had to put in place an internal dispute resolution procedure in accordance with *section 50* of *PA 1995* (for further details see chapter 3). This does not however, extend to disputes between a member and an employer. The trustees may delegate their obligations to deal with the initial query to another 'person' (this is not defined in *PA 1995* or the regulations made under *section 50* but could be one of the trustees). However, the trustees must take a final decision if the outcome of the initial investigation is not to the satisfaction of the employee.

In cases of dismissal or leaving service

7.14 When an employment contract is terminated, the leaving service rules of the scheme will apply and the employee will become a deferred member. The trustees will be obliged, if the ex-employee so requests, to provide details of his options under the trust deed in accordance with the requirements of the *Disclosure Regulations* (*SI 1996 No 1655*) and the *Preservation Regulations* (*SI 1991 No 167*). If the employee takes no action to exercise an option available to him he will simply continue to be treated as a deferred member.

Depending on whom the power to augment is vested in, the trustees may have to liase with an employer on dismissal or redundancy packages (see 7.15 below).

ENTITLEMENTS IN CASES OF DISMISSAL OR REDUNDANCY

Redundancy

7.15 If an employee is entitled to a statutory redundancy payment, such a payment will be based upon his age, length of continuous employment and his gross average weekly pay (subject to a maximum of £270 a week with effect from 1 February 2004). For the purposes of the *ERA 1996*, pay means either the remuneration payable under his contract or, alternatively, his pay based on his average hourly rate.

The *ERA 1996* definition of 'a week's pay' does not include any element relating to an employer's contributions to a pension scheme. Therefore, an employee's pension entitlement on redundancy will depend upon the wording of the scheme documentation. Generally, if the employee has been a member for less than two years he will be entitled to a return of his contributions (less

7.16 *Employment issues*

tax), otherwise he will become a deferred member. It is also worth bearing in mind that many schemes, particularly ex-public sector ones, retain beneficial redundancy/early retirement provisions.

The employer should also consider his rights under *section 158* of the *ERA 1996* and the *Redundancy Payments Pensions Regulations 1965 (SI 1965 No 1932)*, which in some circumstances enable the employer to reduce or extinguish a redundancy payment where a pension is payable immediately from the scheme.

Unfair dismissal

7.16 Unfair dismissal is the dismissal of an employee entitled to protection under *ERA 1996* without a potentially fair reason or without following a fair procedure.

If an employee establishes that he has been unfairly dismissed (the burden of proof being on the employee to establish dismissal and on the employer to establish the reason for the dismissal and, effectively, that it was fair) he will usually be awarded compensation comprising a basic award, based on his weekly pay (subject to the statutory cap), age and length of service, and also to a compensatory award. Other alternative remedies include reinstatement or re-engagement, but are less common. The effect of a reinstatement or re-engagement order is that the previous terms and conditions remain in force so, for pension purposes, the employer and employee will simply have to pay arrears of contributions. This, of course, pre-supposes that the rules of the scheme allow the employee to rejoin.

The maximum basic award for claims where the effective date of termination is on or after 1 February 2004 is currently £8,100 and does not include benefits in kind. Under *sections 123* and *124* of the *ERA 1996* the compensatory award is such an amount as the Employment Tribunal considers just and equitable in all the circumstances, having regard to the loss sustained by the complainant, including loss of any pension benefit, subject to a current maximum of £55,000. The above figures are normally adjusted on 1 February every year. The Tribunal has discretion to reduce any award if it feels that the complainant has caused or contributed to his dismissal or has failed to mitigate his loss by securing suitable alternative employment. An additional award is payable where reinstatement or re-engagement orders have not been complied with. This latter award does not include allowance for loss of pension benefits.

In practice, an employee may suffer loss of pension rights if he fails to find new employment or if his new employer does not operate a pension scheme or operates a less beneficial scheme. Compensation for loss of pension rights is often difficult to quantify, but until recently employment tribunals were happy to use as a starting point the guidelines prepared in 1990 by the Government Actuary's Department in consultation with three Employment Tribunal Chairmen ('Industrial Tribunals – Compensation for Loss of Pension Rights'). This publication recommends a 'rough and ready' style of calculation, viewing the loss in three stages, namely:

(a) between the date of the dismissal and the date of the hearing (being the actual loss sustained eg the difference between an old and a new employer's benefit provision or, if the complainant is unemployed, between the scheme benefits and State scheme benefits);

(b) the loss of future pension rights to the date of retirement (which is essentially speculation on the part of the Employment Tribunal – it may even conclude that the employee's future earnings and benefits will never match his old package, thus the loss may continue over the remainder of his working life); and

(c) the enhancement of accrued pension rights.

The report also provides guidance on how tribunals should reach a just and equitable sum for compensation. It allows the parties to adduce actuarial evidence and breaks down the calculation into three areas:

(i) when attempting to calculate the loss of rights which would have accrued between the date of dismissal and the hearing, reference should be made to the contributions which the employer would have made during that period (although the report admits that this method is not technically correct);

(ii) for the calculation of loss of future pension rights between the date of the hearing and the date of retirement, the Employment Tribunal should estimate how long it will take for the applicant to enter equivalent employment;

(iii) when calculating the loss of enhancement of the pension rights accrued to the date of dismissal, no enhancement should be granted where the applicant is in any public sector scheme, where he is within five years of retirement or where the employment would have been terminated within one year. Otherwise a multiple (as set out in the report) will be utilised and the Employment Tribunal may also, at its discretion, apply a withdrawal factor, based on the likelihood of the complainant leaving service, being made redundant or fairly dismissed.

The Employment Appeal Tribunal has ruled that there is no duty on Employment Tribunals to give precise effect to these guidelines (*Bingham v Hoboun Engineering Ltd [1992] IRLR 298*). Following the increase of the maximum compensatory award under all heads from £10,000 to £50,000 (£55,500 from 1 February 2004) (*ERA 1996, s 124(1)*), loss of earnings may now be less likely to be the major component of any compensatory award and arguably it is becoming more necessary for pension loss calculations to be precise.

Indeed, in *Clancy v Cannock Chase Technical College [2001] IRLR 331*, the Employment Appeal Tribunal noted that the Guidelines were drawn up at a time when the compensatory award was set at £10,000. In the EAT's opinion, the significant raising of the cap meant that an accurate compensation for loss of pensions will be relevant (rather than reliance on the guidelines) in many more cases in the future.

7.17 Employment issues

Wrongful dismissal

7.17 If an employer dismisses an employee without good cause in breach of an obligation to give notice (either statutory or contractual) and the employee suffers loss as a result he will be liable to pay to that employee damages for wrongful dismissal. The primary remedy is damages, normally equal to loss of earnings and other contractual benefits up to the earliest date upon which the contract could have been lawfully terminated by the employer. The aim of damages is to put the employee in the same position as he would have been had the contract been performed, although the employee is usually under a duty to mitigate his loss.

It is unlikely that an employer could successfully argue that he should not pay damages by reference to the pension scheme on the grounds that it could have been terminated by him at any time in accordance with the trust deed. However such a claim could be effective in respect of a single employee scheme such as a funded unapproved retirement benefits scheme (see chapter 14).

In practice, most compensation payments will be negotiated between the employer and employee. For example, if a fixed term contract was terminated two years before it could lawfully have been terminated, this period will be the starting point for the assessment of loss of pay and other benefits.

With a final salary arrangement, the employee would have been entitled to two years' additional pensionable service, perhaps taking into account an assumed pay rise if provision for this was made in the contract. If pay increases were not provided for in the contract, these will not be taken into account (ie the actual salary at the date of termination will be used), nor will any element of discretionary increases. The following three methods can be used to calculate the loss:

(*a*) The award of an additional two years' notional pensionable service to the employee under the rules of the scheme, dealing with the award under the augmentation provisions. The trustees would require payment of an additional contribution (generally a lump sum) by the employer to cover this (an actuary would be required to advise on the payment of this contribution, and, depending on the employee's age, it may not be simply a case of utilising the general scheme contribution rate as the nearer an employee is to normal retirement date, the more costly this becomes).

(*b*) The most straightforward way of calculating the damages to be paid directly to the employee would be by reference to the employer contribution rate over the two year period. This would not produce an accurate result (effectively younger employees may be over-compensated) and is more appropriate for money purchase arrangements. If it is used for the basis for calculating damages, it should be subject to grossing up and discounting for early receipt if it is paid directly to the employee.

(*c*) Loss can also be calculated by reference to the difference in capital value of the benefits accrued to the effective date of dismissal and the capital value of the benefits which would have been accrued up to the end of the notice period. This is the most accurate method and actuarial advice will be required.

In a money purchase arrangement, the compensation will be calculated on the basis of the employer contributions which would have been made in the two year period and an assumed investment return and (potentially) an allowance for salary increases. Similarly, discounting may apply.

Alternatively, an Inland Revenue concession permits the compensation for loss of pension rights to be paid as a contribution to the pension scheme. This may be more tax efficient for the employer (the Revenue could seek to disallow a proportion of a payment made directly to an employee on the grounds that it is not made wholly and exclusively for the purposes of the employer's trade). It may also be advantageous to the employee, if, for example, he is approaching retirement.

If the employee is over age 50 it may be worth considering early retirement, to be funded by an additional amount of the damages being paid into the scheme, subject to Inland Revenue limits (see chapter 5). This is tax efficient from both an employer and employee viewpoint (although care has to be taken to ensure that the employee does not become liable to tax on the payment into the scheme as a benefit in kind). However it may be less attractive if the augmentation does not compensate for the use of actuarial reduction factors. It would be necessary to involve the pension scheme trustees, as this would be an augmentation of the employee's pension benefits and in all likelihood either trustee or company consent would be required for the early retirement to go ahead (if there is not a consent mechanism and the employee is entitled to pension benefits as of right under the trust deed, *Hopkins v Norcross (1994) PLR 18* confirmed that pension payments cannot be deducted from a wrongful dismissal award, thus leading to an element of double compensation). The advice of an actuary on the scope of the augmentation will also be required.

The employer's aim should ultimately be to negotiate a settlement which should be full and final to preclude the bringing of further claims.

The express pension promise and GPPs

7.18 It is highly unusual for an employer to give an express contractual commitment to provide specified pension benefits in a contract of employment, except perhaps in the case of senior executives. If such a commitment is made, the employee's pension rights, in the event of dismissal or redundancy, will depend entirely on the wording of the pension promise. If, for example, the contract states that the executive shall be entitled to a pension of two thirds of his salary at the date he leaves the employer, the executive will have a contractual right against the employer if those precise benefits are not paid, and it may be necessary for an employer to provide partially unapproved benefits (see chapter 14) if Inland Revenue limits prevent the commitment being met out of the approved scheme.

7.19 *Employment issues*

It is, however, unlikely that a pension promise would be so widely drafted. Generally the promise will be contingent upon the executive remaining with the company until his normal retirement date, the benefits will be payable from his normal retirement date, they will often be subject to Inland Revenue limits and termination conditions will usually be incorporated. The lesson for employers is to take great care in drafting the contract of employment, and not to make any oral commitments.

A more common example of a contractual pension promise in today's climate is a Group Personal Pension, or GPP. This is a straightforward contractual arrangement between employer and employee. The employee joins the GPP, which will be administered by an insurance company. The employer's only commitment is to pay contributions on a fixed basis (for instance a stated percentage of pensionable salary) for so long as the employee is employed by the employer.

Exclusion in deed and rules

7.19 It is also worth considering a standard clause which many trust deeds contain, namely a statement that an employer has no liability to compensate employees for loss of pension rights on termination of employment. Case law makes it clear that the *Unfair Contract Terms Act 1977* (*'UCTA'*) applies to contracts of employment (eg *Brigden v American Express Bank Ltd [2001] IRLR 94*). This means that it is unlikely that such a clause will be effective, as either it is not a term of the contract of employment (being contained in the rules of the pension scheme only and not referred to in the employment contract) or, if it is part of the contract, it will fail the test of reasonableness under *section 3* of *UCTA 1977*.

In addition, *section 203* of *ERA 1996* provides that, subject to a number of exceptions, any agreement precluding an individual from making an unfair dismissal claim is void, (the most relevant exception to this – that a fixed term contract of one year or more can exclude an employee's right to bring an unfair dismissal claim – has been removed by *ERA 1999, s 18* with effect from 25 October 1999). Such a clause is therefore unlikely to afford any real protection to an employer.

Lump sum death in service benefits

7.20 Is an employer liable for the payment of a lump sum benefit if an employee dies following a dismissal which is wrongful or unfair? Providing death in service benefits can be costly and most insurance policies will lapse when an employee leaves service (although for larger schemes which self-insure, the provisions of the trust deed will apply).

In wrongful dismissal cases the employer would be liable if the employee died during the notice period, although it is likely that the duty to mitigate loss would apply. In certain cases the trustees of a scheme may also be liable, as the

Pensions Ombudsman ruled in the complaint by *Mrs E Richards* in connection with the Merchant Navy Ratings Pension Fund (May 1999). Consequently, an employee should make his own arrangements (and be compensated for the cost of so doing in his damages award) unless he is uninsurable as a single life (for example he may be unable to pass a medical). Any action would subsist for the benefit of the estate of the deceased.

The situation is less clear cut in cases of unfair dismissal. In such a situation the Tribunal will make an award which it considers to be fair and reasonable, but bearing in mind the limits on compensation a wise employee would arrange his own life cover following the dismissal.

If an employee obtains a reinstatement or re-engagement order his employer should double-check the policy or rules to ensure that life cover continues and that the free cover limit is not breached.

BUSINESS REORGANISATIONS

Purchase of a company with its own scheme

7.21 If a company purchases the entire issued share capital of another company, the employees' pension rights will not be affected if the latter company operates its own pension scheme, as the scheme will simply remain in place after the sale.

Purchase of a business

7.22 The situation is different if an employer purchases a business or part of a business, with the result that following the 'relevant transfer' the transferring employees become the employees of that purchasing employer. In such a scenario the *Transfer of Undertakings (Protection of Employment) Regulations 1981 (SI 1981 No 1794)* (*'TUPE'*) will apply. The employees' contracts are not terminated, and the rights and obligations under the contracts pass to the purchasing employer. As the law currently stands (but see below) *regulation 7* of *TUPE (SI 1981 No 1794)* states that 'supplementary pension schemes' are excluded from the operation of the regulations. *TUPE (SI 1981 No 1794)* was intended to implement the *Acquired Rights Directive (Council Directive 77/187)* which states that protection will not be granted to supplementary company pension schemes but nevertheless expressly requires Member States to adopt 'the measures necessary' to protect the scheme members. This has been reinforced by a new *Acquired Rights Directive (Council Directive 98/49/EC)*, adopted on 29 June 1998, which effectively gives member states the option of protecting pension rights under national legislation.

Following extensive consultation exercises since 1998, the Government is proposing to amend the *TUPE* pensions provisions to give protection where the transferring employer has an occupational pension scheme and such protection

7.22 *Employment issues*

to cover both scheme members and those eligible to join. The Pensions Bill proposes to introduce requirements so that the transferee employer must either:

(*a*) ensure that the employee is, or is eligible to be, an active member of an occupational pension scheme, and:

   (i) where the scheme is a money purchase scheme "relevant contributions" are made in respect of the employees; or

   (ii) where the scheme is not a money purchase scheme, the scheme satisfies *section 12A* of the *Pension Schemes Act 1993* (ie the reference scheme test) or complies with other requirements as may be prescribed by regulations

or

(*b*) make 'relevant contributions' into a stakeholder pension scheme.

'Relevant contributions' will be defined by regulations and are expected to require the transferee to match the employee's contributions up to 6 per cent.

It is interesting to note that the reference scheme test requirement may provide higher benefits than the transferring employer's scheme provided, and also there is no maximum member contribution stipulated. Also, unlike other *TUPE* protections, the employer and employee can agree that the above protections will not apply.

There have been a number of past cases on the scope of *TUPE*. In January 1992 in the case of *Warrener v Walden Engineering Co Ltd (1992) PLR 1*, the Hull Employment Tribunal was asked to consider employees' pension rights when, following a business sale the new employer decided to discontinue all pension arrangements. The Tribunal stated that the benefits provided by the scheme had been 'part of the contract of employment' and that if a pension scheme is terminated an employee has a contractual right to an equivalent scheme, providing benefits no less beneficial, being set up in its place. This case was based on the argument that, as the pension scheme was contracted-out of the State earnings-related pension scheme, it was not a supplementary pension scheme for the purposes of *regulation 7* of *TUPE (SI 1981 No 1794)*.

In December 1992 came the case of *Perry v Intec Colleges Ltd (1993) PLR 56* in the Bristol Employment Tribunal. The decision in the case was reached on a different interpretation of *TUPE*; the complainant argued that *TUPE* had failed to translate the aims of the *Acquired Rights Directive* into UK law (ie the subsidiary aim to protect employees). After the transfer no pension provision was to be made for the employees. It was held that the complainant was entitled to pension provision at least as beneficial as that which he had received prior to the transfer. It was suggested that to compensate the employee adequately, the employer should make an equivalent percentage contribution to a personal pension scheme and should also make a lump sum payment to compensate for lost opportunity to enhance accrued pension benefits. In effect, the Tribunal was advocating double recovery.

Employment issues **7.22**

In June 1993 the Employment Appeal Tribunal overturned the first instance decision in *Warrener (Walden Engineering Co Ltd v Warrener [1993] PLR 295)*; meaning that an employer does not have to maintain the pension benefits enjoyed by employees prior to a business sale. The Employment Appeal Tribunal stated that a contracted-out scheme is a supplementary scheme (ie supplementary to the basic State scheme) for the purposes of *TUPE*, and accordingly, the employer was protected under the *regulation 7* exclusion. In January 1996 this approach was sanctioned by the High Court in the case of *Adams & Ors v Lancashire County Council & Ors [1996] All ER 473*. The judge stated that *TUPE* required protection to be given to accrued rights only (which are protected as deferred benefits in the transferor employer's scheme by the preservation requirements now set out in the *1993 Act*). On 15 May 1997 the High Court Decision was upheld by the Court of Appeal (*[1997] IRLR 436*).

In *Hagen v ICI Chemicals and Polymers Ltd [2001] 64 PBLR, [2001] All ER (D) 273 (Oct)*, the High Court held that a transferor had made a negligent misrepresentation when persuading its employees to accept a *TUPE* transfer, when it stated that their pension rights after the transfer would be 'broadly comparable' to their pre-transfer rights. The Court held that 'broadly comparable' meant no more than 2 per cent difference whereas, in practice, some claimants would have been 5 per cent worse off. Liability for misrepresentations normally passes from transferor to transferee under *TUPE* (*regulation 5(2)(a)*). However, since the misrepresentation related to pension entitlement, and was caught by regulation 7, liability remained with the transferor only.

Some of the above issues will be clarified by the Pensions Bill, but an employer should always be cautious in situations where *TUPE* applies; if inferior pension provision is to be offered following a relevant transfer, providing the employees with alternative compensation is clearly the safest route and will go some way to forestalling industrial unrest. Transferor employers would be well advised to seek indemnity cover, although the judge in *Adams* confirmed that he did not believe that employees could claim against the transferor employer, this point has not yet been tested.

One important exception to the exclusion of pensions rights from *TUPE* comes under *regulation 7(2)* which attempts to implement *article 3(3)* of the *Acquired Rights Directive*. Article 3(3) excludes from the automatic transfer provisions 'employees' rights to old-age, invalidity or survivors' benefits under supplementary company or inter-company pension schemes …'. *Regulations 7(1)* and *7(2)* of *TUPE* stipulate that contractual provisions on occupational pension schemes do not transfer from the transferor to the transferee, except that 'any provisions of an occupational pension scheme which do not relate to benefits for old-age, invalidity or survivors shall be treated as not being part of the Scheme'. For many years, it was unclear whether certain benefits provided under occupational pension schemes (eg enhanced redundancy terms on early retirement, life assurance etc) fall within *regulation 7(2)*. This question has been dealt with, to some degree, by the ECJ in *Beckmann v Dynamco Whicheloe Macfarlane Ltd, Case C-164/00, [2002] 64 PBLR; [2002] All ER (D) 05 (Jun)*. The ECJ ruled

7.22 *Employment issues*

that the exceptions contained in *article 3(3)* of the *Directive* ought to be interpreted narrowly so as to apply only to old-age, invalidity or survivors benefits under occupational pension schemes falling due at the end of 'normal working life'. Other benefits, such as early retirement benefits and redundancy payments are excluded. (The decision in *Beckman* has recently been approved in *Martin and others v South Bank University C 4/01, [2004] 1 CMLR 472, [2003] All ER (D) 85 (Nov)*. See 16.15 for further elaboration on this topic.

Another notable exception to the exclusion of pension rights from *TUPE* relates to public service transfers. Until 14 June 1999 this exception covered, broadly, compulsory competitive tendering. On 14 June 1999 the Treasury issued a press release announcing the extension (with immediate effect) of the protection awarded to public service employees, also making it clear that the protection would apply to all Private Finance Initiative (PFI) and Public-Private Partnership (PPP) contracts.

Essentially the protection is two pronged, covering past and future service rights. In respect of future service, the purchaser must offer broadly comparable pension provision, which will be assessed by the Government Actuary's Department ('GAD'). In its guidance note to Government Departments and Agencies, (entitled 'A Fair Deal for Staff Pensions') the Treasury explains that this means that there shall be 'no identifiable employees who will suffer material detriment overall'. If an individual will suffer, that individual must be awarded compensation (eg a salary increase).

To protect past service, the purchaser's scheme must be prepared to accept a bulk transfer, and year for year transfer credits must be provided (or an equivalent basis as recommended by GAD shall apply).

In effect the outsourcing process has been tightened up, but there could be some unwelcome side effects for purchasers. Detailed pension information will have to be given to the contracting authority at the outset of the tendering procedure (this will be required before any shortlist of purchasers is drawn up) and the transfer terms (ie the credits to be awarded in the purchaser's scheme) will have to be settled at an early stage. This will have costs implications for purchasers. It is possible that delays will also occur further down the line. GAD will be required to provide a full analysis of the terms of the transferring and receiving schemes, which must be made available to Unions and employees. A reasonable period is to be allowed for discussion, and no contractual terms can be settled in that period.

A further, and more welcome, change to outsourcing was introduced on 13 January 2000. Where staff are members of the Local Government Pension Scheme, contractors now have a choice of either offering broadly comparable benefits or gaining admitted body status to the Local Government Pension Scheme, meaning that employees' pension provision is unchanged by the outsourcing.

The question of pensions and *TUPE* has been the subject of debate and consultation for a considerable time (including, most recently, the September

2001 *TUPE* consultation paper issued by the DTI) and there is now hope that the position has finally been settled following further consultation by the Government through the Green Paper 'Simplicity, Security and Choice: Working and Saving for Retirement' and publication of the Pensions Bill.

Purchase of a subsidiary participating in its parent's scheme

7.23 Similar considerations to those outlined at 7.22 above would apply on the sale of a company which participates in a holding company pension arrangement although *TUPE (SI 1981 No 1794)* itself would not apply. In practice if a new employer is unable to provide equivalent pension provision, alternative methods of compensation (for example, pay rises) should be considered.

EMPLOYER'S LIEN

7.24 Many pension schemes permit a lien to be placed on benefits payable where the employee or ex-employee owes money to the employer or the trustees of a scheme resulting from criminal, negligent or fraudulent acts or omissions. Liens are now governed by *sections 91* to *94* of *PA 1995*, and are an exception to the general rule that pension benefits can not be assigned or forfeited. However, a lien rule can only operate with the agreement of the employee unless a court or arbitrator has made an order or award in the employer's favour (*sections 91(5)(d)* and *93(3)*) of *PA 1995*. As an employee can insist on his statutory rights to payment of a guaranteed cash equivalent (see chapter 6), trustees may be forced to pay benefits out before a court or arbitrator has considered the lien issue unless they obtain a time extension for the payment of the cash equivalent.

It should be borne in mind that a lien cannot attach to benefits deriving from transfer credits (unless the transfer is attributable to employment with the same or an associated employer and the transferring scheme contained an appropriate lien rule), (*Occupational Pension Schemes (Assignment, Forfeiture, Bankruptcy etc) Regulations 1997 (SI 1997 No 785), reg 3*) and no part of a guaranteed minimum pension or protected rights may be subject to deduction. The amount that can be recovered is limited to the lesser of the actuarial value of the employee's actual or prospective benefits and the amount of the monetary obligation owed to the employer or trustees of a scheme (*section 91(6), PA 1995*).

Due to the restrictions referred to above, and in particular the need for consent or a court order or decision of an arbitrator, lien rules are often difficult to operate in practice.

DISCRIMINATION

Equality generally

7.25 The issue of sex equality is covered in detail in chapter 9, but it is worth

7.26 *Employment issues*

mentioning here the impact of *PA 1995*. *Section 62* of *PA 1995*(which came into force on 1 January 1996) implies overriding equality provisions into the rules of occupational pension schemes, to ensure that men and women are treated equally (in terms of both access to benefits and the benefits to be provided). The trustees are empowered, irrespective of the power of amendment contained in the trust documentation, to make whatever amendments are required to ensure compliance with *PA 1995* equal treatment requirements.

The position in respect of transsexuals has been unclear for some time, but much awaited ECJ guidance has recently been given. In December 2000, the Court of Appeal referred to the European Court of Justice the question of whether the exclusion of the female-to-male transsexual partner of a female member of the NHS Pension Scheme, which limits the material dependent's benefit to her widower, constitutes sex discrimination in contravention of *Article 141* of the *Rome Treaty* and the *Equal Treatment Directive* (*KB v National Health Service Pensions Agency and another ([2000] All ER (D) 2279)*. The ECJ has now ruled that it is unlawful under *Article 141* of the *Rome Treaty* to prevent a female-to-male transsexual from benefiting under the pension scheme of his female partner due to national legislation which prevents transsexuals from marrying.

It is important to note that the ECJ stated that the mere limitation on payment of benefits to married persons is not discriminatory under *Article 141*, as this would apply equally to men and women. The discrimination in the present case arose from the fact that, under the law, transsexuals, in contrast to heterosexuals, are prevented from getting married. However, it is up to the British courts to determine if a person in the applicant's position can rely on *Article 141* to ensure that she can nominate her partner as a beneficiary of her scheme.

It is now a matter for the Court of Appeal to decide how to implement the ECJ's judgment. Assuming that the Gender Recognition Bill, introduced in the House of Lords in November 2003, will become law, the issue may be resolved, in so far as future pension rights are concerned.

Part-time workers

7.26 Under the *Part-Time Workers (Prevention of Less Favourable Treatment) Regulations 2000 (SI 2000/1551)*, which came into force on 1 July 2000, part-time workers (not only employees) ought not to be treated less favourably than comparable full-time workers in their terms and conditions, unless a difference is objectively justified. In particular, this means that from 1 July 2000 part-time workers are entitled to have the same access to occupational pension schemes. The level of benefits offered also needs to be equal but pro-rated under general principles of equality law. For a difference in treatment to be objectively justifiable, the employer is likely to have to show that his policy corresponds to a real business need; is an appropriate method of achieving that objective; and is necessary in order to achieve that objective. Claims under the Regulations may only be made against an employer. The retrospective two year limit on the remedies which employment tribunals may award (currently *regulation 8*) has been declared incompatible with EU law in *Preston & others v Wolverhampton Healthcare NHS Trust [20001] 2 WLR 448* and has been removed with effect from 1 October 2002 by the *Part-time Workers (Prevention of Less Favourable Treatment) Regulations 2002 (SI 2002 No 2035)*. Full details are set out in Chapter 9. For claims to succeed, a part-time worker must establish that a comparable full-time worker was treated differently. Such a comparator may not be easily established *(Matthews and others v Kent and Medway Towns Fire Authority and others [2003] IRLR 732, [2003] All ER (D) 90 (Aug))*.

In respect of claims preceding 1 July 2000, the question of whether a part-time employee is entitled to be granted pension scheme access depends on whether or not denial of membership constitutes indirect sex discrimination (on the basis that most part-time employees are women). If not, there is no breach of the overriding equal treatment rule and if so, membership may still be denied if the exclusion can be objectively justified by factors unrelated to sex. If indirect discrimination is established, future pension benefits of affected employees will have to be calculated with reference to their periods of service from the latter of 8 April 1976, being the date of *Defrenne v Sabena (No 2) [1976] ECR 445* and the date of commencement of employment *(Preston & others v Wolverhampton Healthcare NHS Trust [2001] 2 WLR 448)*.

A number of other important principles continue to emerge in relation to the rights of part-time workers, as a result of the ongoing litigation in *Preston*. Thus in *Preston & Others v Wolverhampton Healthcare NHS Trust (No.3), [2004] All ER (D) 175 (Feb)*, the Employment Appeal Tribunal ('EAT') ruled that:

(i) the exclusion of a part-time employee from membership in a pension scheme, where such membership had been compulsory for full-time employees was unlawful;

(ii) however, *Article 141* of the *Rome Treaty* would not be breached where pension scheme membership is compulsory for full-time workers but only optional for part-time employees. A requirement that a part-time employee opts into the scheme does not contravene the requirement of equality;

(iii) there is no continuing breach of *Article 141* by an employer failing to inform a part-time employee of his/her entitlement to join the pension scheme, unless that failure was itself on discriminatory grounds. However, employees may have a breach of contract claim in such circumstances on the basis of the employer's implied obligation to inform employees of advantageous contractual terms *(Scally and others v Southern Health and Social Services Board, [1991] 4 All ER 563)*;

(iv) the six months time limit for bringing a claim under the *Equal Pay Act 1970*, in the context of 'stable employee relationships' begins to run when:

- either party indicates that further contracts will not be offered or accepted;

7.27 *Employment issues*

- either party acts in a manner which is inconsistent with the relationship continuing;
- the employer does not offer a new contract in circumstances where "the periodicity of the preceding cycle of contracts indicates that it should have been offered";
- either party stops treating the relationship as stable; or
- the terms under which work is to be done alter radically;

(v) since liabilities for occupational pension schemes do not transfer under *TUPE*, liability under the *Equal Pay Act 1970* and *Article 141* of the *Rome Treaty*, for the transferor's failure to provide equal access to a scheme, remains with the transferor; and

(vi) following a *TUPE* transfer, time for bringing a claim against the transferor begins to run from the date the employee's employment with the transferee comes to an end.

Inland Revenue Pension Update No. 131 confirms the Treasury's position that tax relief will only be available on employees' back contributions up to 15% of remuneration in the tax year in which the contribution is actually paid. Scheme rules may allow for higher contributions in excess of the 15% but they will attract no tax relief. Payments may, with the agreement of the trustees, be made in instalments to spread the tax relief. If the member has left the relevant employment but is being allowed to make retrospective contributions, no tax relief at all is given.

Employers' contributions to fund back service will be allowable for tax purposes in the normal way under *section 592(4), ICTA 1988*.

Lump sum compensation payments outside the pension scheme will not be taxable as income under Schedule E but may attract capital gains tax – the usual annual exemptions will apply.

Where a member has already retired and taken benefits an additional lump sum may not be paid but if a transfer payment has been made an additional supplementary transfer can be paid (see *PSO Update No. 40*).

Fixed-term (temporary) workers

7.27 EU *Council Directive 1990/70/EC* on *Fixed Term Work* prohibits employers from treating fixed-term workers less favourably than comparable permanent workers, unless a difference is objectively justified. The UK Government has implemented the Directive under the *Fixed-Term Employees (Prevention of Less Favourable Treatment) Regulations 2002 (SI 2002 No. 2034)*. The *Regulations* came into force on 1 October 2002. Essentially the *Regulations* require employers not to discriminate against fixed-term employees (not 'workers' as per the Directive) as compared with permanent employees, in the terms of their contract, unless the difference can be objectively justified. It needs to be borne in mind that employers are not obliged to offer an identical package of terms as long as, on the whole, the contract is no less favourable.

The Government was of the opinion that the Directive does not apply to pay and occupational pension schemes. The *Regulations* do cover pay and occupational pension schemes, however, and thus access to pension arrangements and level of benefits offered. In the pensions context, therefore, employers are required to offer fixed-term employees the same rights of entry to the pension scheme and the same benefits under it as they do for permanent employees. One difficulty is the two year vesting period. Many employees on contracts fixed for less than two years might well not want to contribute to the scheme if the only benefit will be a return of contributions. The administrative costs to the employer also might be disproportionate to the benefit (although balanced against this might be the death in service benefit). However, not to offer participation would be a high risk strategy. There may also be *Imperial* type issues which arise – would an employer inviting a fixed term employee to join a scheme, knowing that at the end of it all they would get back is their net contributions, be breaching its obligation of trust and confidence? Any employer opening its scheme to employees on contracts for less than two years should consider some form of disclaimer and issue a recommendation that the employee seeks independent advice before joining.

If an employer cannot offer entry to the main pension scheme for employees on fixed term contracts, it might consider offering to make equivalent contributions to a personal arrangement to allow for better portability. However, there may be a difficulty in showing that this benefit is 'at least as favourable' as that offered to permanent employees. A further alternative would be for fixed term employees, whom the employer does not want to admit to the pension scheme, to be paid a salary bonus equivalent to the value of the scheme membership, although this could give rise to industrial relations problems where permanent employees then ask for the bonus instead of scheme membership.

It should be noted that there is no direct claim under the *Regulations* by employees against trustees. However this is an issue which trustees of schemes excluding fixed term employees may wish to raise with the sponsoring employers.

Disability discrimination

7.28 In brief, the *Disability Discrimination Act 1995* makes it unlawful (with effect from 2 December 1996) for an employer with fifteen or more employees to discriminate without objective justification against disabled persons:

(*a*) in the arrangements made for deciding who should be offered employment; or

(*b*) in the employment terms; or

(*c*) by refusing to offer or deliberately not offering employment.

7.28 *Employment issues*

'Employment terms' include access to and benefits provided by a pension scheme. An employer discriminates against a disabled person if he treats that person less favourably than he treats (or would treat) others to whom that reason does not (or would not) apply (unless he can show that the treatment is objectively justified). The protection is diluted by the justification defence; unequal treatment may be justified if it is 'material to the circumstances of the case and substantial'. In respect of pension arrangements a justification may be that the cost of providing the disabled person with benefits (for instance, life assurance benefits) would be substantially greater than the cost for employees who do not have the disabling condition.

The *Disability Discrimination Act 1995* implies an overriding 'non discrimination rule' into pension schemes in respect of 'disabled people' (see *section 17, DDA 1995*). This is similar to the *Pensions Act 1995* equal treatment rule (see 7.25 above), and trustees or managers of pension schemes must not commit any acts or omissions which would amount to unlawful discrimination. This may cause trustees difficulties if there are costs involved in complying with the *Disability Discrimination Act 1995*, and it is not clear whether the trustees may also take advantage of the justification defence.

A person who believes that he has been discriminated against may bring a claim to an Employment Tribunal or, alternatively, against the trustees under the scheme's internal dispute resolution procedure (see chapter 3).

The *Equal Treatment 'Framework' Directive (Council Directive 2000/78/EC)* is designed to implement the equal treatment principle in the context of employment and training in relation to disability and other forms of discrimination. The disability discrimination provisions must be implemented in the UK by 1 October 2004 and the Government has now published the *Disability Discrimination Act 1995 (Amendment) Regulations 2003 (SI 2003 No 1673)* and the *Disability Discrimination Act 1995 (Pensions) Regulations 2003 ('Pensions Regulations')* *(SI 2003 No 2770)*. One of the major amendments introduced by the regulations is the abolition of the small employer exemption, following which the *DDA 1995* will apply to all employers, regardless of the number of employees they have.

Under the *Pensions Regulations* the *DDA 1995* is amended so trustees and managers of occupational pension schemes are prohibited from discriminating against or harassing disabled members or prospective members of the scheme in carrying out their functions under the scheme. Thus, a non-discrimination rule will be implied into every occupational pension scheme, and all the scheme's provisions will be read subject to that rule. However, the non-discrimination rule does not apply to rights accrued and benefits which are payable in respect of periods preceding the date the *Pensions Regulations* come into force (1 October 2004). Still, communications with members and prospective members about such rights and benefits are subject to the non-discrimination rule.

In addition, trustees and managers of occupational pension schemes have a duty to make reasonable adjustments in relation to provisions, criteria or practices (including scheme rules) which place a disabled member/prospective member at a substantial disadvantage compared with non-disabled members/prospective members. There is also a requirement, in such circumstances, to make any necessary reasonable adjustments to physical features of premises occupied by the trustees/scheme managers.

Breach of the *Pensions Regulations* can result in a complaint to the employment tribunal against the trustee/scheme managers (with the employer being joined as a party). A tribunal may make a declaration (except where the claim is brought by pensioner members) that the complainant has a right to be admitted to the scheme. The tribunal may not award damages, other than for injury to feelings or if there is a failure, without reasonable justification, to follow a recommendation made by the employment tribunal.

Maternity, paternity, adoption and parental absence

7.29 This issue is covered in detail at chapter 9. The provisions of the *Social Security Act 1989* have been in force since 23 June 1994. Briefly these provisions require that pension benefits for a woman who is on paid maternity leave must accrue in the same way as for a woman who is working normally. Death in service benefits must similarly remain in place. An employee who is absent on maternity leave is required to contribute, but on the basis of the actual statutory or contractual maternity remuneration received. Similar provisions are made under the Pensions Bill 2004 for employees on paid paternity or adoption leave (amending the *Social Security Act 1989, Sch 5*). The requirement for accrued pension rights does not apply in relation to statutory parental leave – which is unpaid leave and, thus, falls outside Article 141 of the EU Equal Pay and Equal Treatment Directives.

Same sex partners

7.30 The *Employment Equality (Sexual Orientation) Regulations 2003 (2003 No 1661)* (*'Sexual Orientation Regulations'*) implement the provisions of the *Equal Treatment 'Framework' Directive (Council Directive 2000/78/EC)*. The *Regulations*, which came into force on 1 December 2003, outlaw discrimination on the grounds of sexual orientation. This includes a prohibition on less favourable terms and conditions of employment based on an employee's sexual orientation. In the context of pensions, the *Regulations* (as amended by the *Employment Equality (Sexual Orientation) (Amendment) Regulations 2003 (SI 2003 No 2827)*) make it unlawful for trustees and managers of occupational pension schemes to discriminate against, or subject harassment to, any members or prospective members in carrying out their functions under the scheme (except in relation to rights accrued or benefits payable in respect of period of service preceding 1 December 2003). Every occupational scheme will thus be treated as including a non-discriminatory rule on the grounds of sexual orientation and trustees and scheme managers have the power to alter the scheme to ensure that it is non-discriminatory (regardless of the terms of the scheme).

7.31   Employment issues

Breach of the non-discrimination rule can result in a claim to the employment tribunal against trustees and scheme managers (and the employer may be joined as a party). If the claim is successful, a tribunal may make a declaration (except where the claim is brought by a pensioner member), eg that the complainant has a right to be admitted to the scheme. The tribunal may not award damages, however, other than for injury to feelings or in respect of a failure, without reasonable justification, to follow a recommendation made by the tribunal.

Finally, of particular importance is *Regulation 25* of the *Sexual Orientation Regulations* which allows discrimination on grounds of marital status (eg limiting payments under a pension scheme to the spouse of a member). This provision has now been the subject of judicial review proceedings on the ground that it contradicts EC Law. The High Court rejected this argument and held that the provision was lawful. It is not yet clear whether this decision will be appealed. It is also arguable that the *Regulation* contravenes *Articles 8* and *14*, European Convention of Human Rights and, on the basis of the decision in *KB v National Health Service Pensions Agency,[2004] All ER (D) 03 (Jan)* breaches *Article 141* of the *Rome Treaty*.

Religion or belief discrimination

7.31   The *Employment Equality (Religion or Belief) Regulations 2003 (SI 2003 No 1660)* (*'Religion or Belief Regulations'*) implement the provisions of the *Equal Treatment 'Framework' Directive (Council Directive 2000/78/EC)* on discrimination on grounds of religion or belief. The *Regulations*, which outlaw discrimination on these grounds, came into force on 2 December 2003. Like the *Sexual Orientation Regulations*, the *Religion or Belief Regulations* outlaw less favourable treatment, victimisation and harassment, in the employment context, on grounds of religion or belief.

In the context of pensions, the *Religion or Belief Regulations* introduce obligations on trustees and fund managers, identical to those which are contained in the *Sexual Orientation Regulations* (see 7.30 above). However, there is no equivalent provision to *Regulation 25* of the *Sexual Orientation Regulations*.

Age discrimination

7.32   The *Equal Treatment 'Framework' Directive (Council Directive 2000/78/EC)* also outlaws discrimination on grounds of age. The UK is not due to implement this aspect of the Directive until October 2006. A Government Consultation Paper ('Age Matters') was published in July 2003 in which views were sought on a number of proposals, including the abolition of mandatory retirement ages. In the context of pay and non-pay benefits, the Government proposed that legislation would allow employers to continue to provide such benefits on the basis of length of service and experience if this can be justified. The consultation ended in October 2003. Further consultation is expected in summer 2004, with draft Regulations expected to be published by mid 2005.

In October 2003 the EAT overturned an employment tribunal's decision that the statutory upper age which applies to complaints of unfair dismissal and for statutory redundancy pay was unlawful as being indirectly discriminatory on grounds of sex (*Rutherford v Secretary of State for Trade and Industry [2003] IRLR 858, [2003] All ER (D) 67 (Oct)*) As a result, until the Government introduces legislation outlawing age discrimination the current statutory age limit continues to apply.

Transsexual employees

7.33 In July 2002, the European Court of Human Rights found the UK to be in breach of *Article 8* of the ECHR in failing to deal with the legal implications which arise as a result of gender reassignment (*Goodwin v UK [2002] IRLR 664*). In *Goodwin*, a male to female transsexual brought various complaints, including that she had been refused a state pension at 60 as she was treated as a man for national insurance purposes contrary to *Article 8*. In the opinion of the ECHR the uncertain legal position of transsexuals in the UK was no longer sustainable. In *KB v National Health Service Pensions Agency [2000] All ER (D) 2279 (Jan)* the ECJ agreed with the UK Government that restricting access to certain benefits to married couples did not constitute discrimination on grounds of sex. However, the ECJ found *Article 141* of the *Rome Treaty* was nonetheless violated, since UK law, in breach of the ECHR, prohibited transsexuals from marrying. The Government is expected to introduce legislation in 2004 enabling transsexuals to marry a person of the opposite sex.

ADDITIONAL CHANGES

Time off for performance of duties and for training

7.34 Under *section 58* of *ERA 1996* (originally *section 42* of *PA 1995*), an employer must permit any employee who is a trustee of a scheme to take time off during working hours to allow him to perform all of his duties as a trustee or to undergo relevant training. The amount of time off, and any conditions imposed by the employer, must be reasonable having regard to the employer's business and the effect of the employee's absence. Any employee is entitled to be paid for any time taken off pursuant to this provision (*section 59* of *ERA 1996*). A common criticism of *PA 1995*, however, is that trustee training is not mandatory.

An employee can bring a complaint to an Employment Tribunal if he believes that his employer has failed to give him time off and failed to pay him (*section 60* of the *ERA 1996*). He has three months from the date when the failure occurred in which to present his complaint, but the Tribunal will have the power to extend this period if it is satisfied that it was not reasonably practicable for the complaint to be presented within the period.

If an employee's complaint is upheld, the Tribunal can award such compensation at it considers just and equitable.

Employment issues

Right not to suffer detriment or to be unfairly dismissed

7.35 Section 46 of ERA 1996 (previously *section 46* of *PA 1995*) states that an employer is not permitted to victimise an employee simply on the ground that he performed or proposed to perform his functions as a trustee of a scheme which relates to his employment.

Further, if an employee is dismissed and the reason (or the principal reason) for the dismissal is that the employee performed any functions as a trustee, the dismissal is to be regarded as automatically unfair and the employee may be entitled to compensation. [*ERA 1996, s 102*]

Any provision in the contracts of employment which purports to exclude or limit the right not to suffer detriment or to be unfairly dismissed is void. [*ERA 1996, s 203(1)*]

CONCLUSION

7.36 It is difficult to classify pension provisions or an entitlement to pension benefits as an employment 'right', as in most instances employers do not have to provide pension arrangements. There are certain exceptions to this (for example, ex-members of public sector arrangements have statutory 'protected person' status, meaning that on privatisation they must be offered membership of the mirror-image industry-wide schemes) but these rights are of a statutory nature and therefore uncommon. However, the Pension Bill provisions suggest that *TUPE* will be extended to cover pension rights on all business transfers, thus giving employees a degree of protection following a business transfer.

On becoming a member of a pension scheme, an employee does obtain rights and entitlements, but primarily against the trustees of the scheme. The only contractual 'right' of the employee is to join the pension scheme if eligible to do so. Otherwise, it is easier to classify the rights of a member as being either statutory (for example, not to be discriminated against on various grounds) or common law rights, for example, the *Imperial* duty of good faith. Some of the cases referred to in this chapter clearly indicate the difficulties of differentiating between pension and employment issues. However, the basis of pension provision is likely, in time, to move further towards a contractual as opposed to 'trusts' basis.

Chapter 8

Pensions and divorce

INTRODUCTION

8.1 The last few years have seen fundamental changes in the treatment of pension benefits in the context of divorce proceedings. These have arisen out of two different concepts for the treatment of pensions: earmarking and pension sharing, which have been introduced by *PA 1995* and *WRPA 1999* respectively. This legislation has not only increased the awareness of divorcing couples of the comparatively high value that pension benefits may have in the context of the matrimonial assets as a whole, but has introduced sufficient flexibility to enable a fair settlement to be reached, whatever the divorcing parties' general and financial circumstances.

It was not until the introduction of *PA 1995* that the family law courts were finally granted jurisdiction over pension schemes in the context of divorce settlements (*Brooks v Brooks [1995] All ER 257, HL* is the notable exception, but it is likely that this judgment is, in any case, confined to its own facts and has now been superseded by the legislation mentioned briefly above). That is not to say that the pension rights of parties to divorce proceedings were not taken into consideration prior to *PA 1995*, merely that the courts did not have the jurisdiction to make orders against pension schemes' trustees or scheme members, in respect of their pension benefits, when deciding how the parties' assets were to be split. This lack of options in law for the treatment of pension rights on divorce had long been a cause for dissatisfaction; the first report on this matter was given by the Law Commission as long ago as 1969. More recent milestones include the Pensions Management Institute report entitled 'Pensions and Divorce' produced in May 1993, and the Pension Law Review Committee's report 'Pension Law Reform', produced in September 1993 which endorsed the recommendations put forward in the PMI report. In essence, the recommendations were that courts should have the power to split the pension rights on divorce, thereby creating a separate entitlement for the ex-spouse.

So why, with this obvious desire for change, did it take so long for the legislation to appear on the statute books? The reason lies in the nature of pension schemes themselves. The majority of pension schemes are designed to be eligible for tax approval (see Chapter 5). The requirements for obtaining exempt approved status prevent benefits being paid to any person who is not a member or a 'dependant' (as defined in the Glossary to the Inland Revenue's Practice Notes, IR12 (2001)) of a member, and specifically prevent pensions from being

8.2 *Pensions and divorce*

assignable (subject to certain statutory exceptions) (IR12 (2001) PN 7.31). This has proved the main obstacle for the courts in the past because the governing trust deed of an exempt approved scheme will always contain a specific provision that benefits cannot be assigned. There was no mechanism to assign benefits to an ex-spouse so that they would become payable to the ex-spouse as of right, nor indeed to provide for the ex-spouse on the death of the scheme member unless, firstly, the ex-spouse fell within the definition of 'dependant' and, secondly, the trustees exercised their discretion to pay the benefits to him or her in that capacity.

These problems have now been overcome. However, it may still be appropriate for parties in some circumstances to leave the pension benefits intact and it is, therefore, useful to look at the issues which were relevant prior to the introduction of *PA 1995*.

POSITION PRIOR TO *PA 1995*

8.2 Prior to the introduction of *PA 1995* the treatment of property on divorce in England, Wales and Northern Ireland was governed by *sections 21* to *25* inclusive of the *Matrimonial Causes Act 1973* (as amended by the *Matrimonial and Family Proceedings Act 1994*) (*MCA 1973*).

Section 25A(1) of *MCA 1973* required the court to consider whether the financial obligations of each party towards the other can be terminated as soon after the grant of the decree as the court considers just and reasonable. This is known as a 'clean break'. It put the onus on the court to consider lump sum payments and property adjustment orders, rather than periodical payments orders (commonly known as maintenance payments), wherever possible and, if a maintenance payment order is made, to limit its duration if appropriate. A clean break will usually be appropriate where the couple is young, both are working and have no children or where the couple's assets are sizeable enough that they can be split in such a way that the ex-spouse will have sufficient resources on which to live.

Prior to amendment by *PA 1995, section 25(2)* of *MCA 1973* stated that the court should, when considering financial provision orders, have particular regard, amongst other matters, to the following:

'(*a*) the income, earning capacity, property and other financial resources which each of the parties to the marriage has or is likely to have in the foreseeable future, including in the case of earning capacity any increase in that capacity which it would in the opinion of the court be reasonable to expect a party of the marriage to take steps to acquire;

...

(*h*) in the case of proceedings for divorce or nullity of marriage, the value to each of the parties to the marriage of any benefits (for example, a pension) which by reason of the dissolution or annulment of the marriage, that party will lose the chance of acquiring.'

However, a problem of interpretation arose with the use of the words 'in the foreseeable future' in the then *section 25(2)(a), MCA 1973*. The approach adopted by the courts resulted in consideration being given only to those assets which a party could expect to acquire within the next ten years. Consequently, where a party to the divorce was more than ten years away from retirement, the value of his pension entitlements would not be taken into account. In any event, the court had no power over either the trustees or the assets of a pension scheme and so could not make an order re-allocating assets or obliging the trustees to make a payment to an ex-spouse. Therefore, even where pension rights fell within the definition of matrimonial property their value could only be taken into account in relation to the distribution of non-pension assets.

Under *section 25(2)(h)* of *MCA 1973* the court was required to have regard to the value of any pension that a party to a divorce loses the chance of acquiring. It was not clear, however, to which benefits these provisions referred, ie to the member's pension, any cash lump sum payable on retirement, a spouse's pension payable on the death of the member and/or lump sum on a member's death in service.

The courts' inability to divide pension assets was problematical, particularly where there were insufficient non-pension assets to provide for the ex-spouse's needs. A common result was that in the divorce settlement the ex-spouse would be allocated the matrimonial home whilst the scheme member retained the pension rights. This often created both long and short-term problems; the party with the matrimonial home had realisable assets but no income on retirement, whereas the scheme member retained pension rights, to which he could not gain access to set up a new home, but was guaranteed a certain level of future income. An even worse scenario was where the pension rights were the only or the largest asset and, consequently, the court was unable to make any order which would adequately compensate the ex-spouse. Therefore, in many cases, this was not satisfactory for either party. It was against this background that *section 166* of *PA 1995* was introduced.

EARMARKING – IMPACT OF *PA 1995*

General jurisdiction

8.3 The concept of earmarking was introduced by *section 166* of *PA 1995*. In general terms earmarking introduced a means by which pension benefits could be used to pay either maintenance or a capital sum from the pension scheme direct to the ex-spouse on the member's behalf, but which would only become payable when entitlement arose under the pension scheme in respect of the member.

The powers of the courts regarding financial provision on divorce are still contained in *MCA 1973* but *section 25* was amended to introduce a concept of earmarking. *Section 166, PA 1995* inserted new *sections 25B* to *25D* with effect from 1 August 1996 which applied to petitions presented on or after 1 July 1996.

8.3 Pensions and divorce

It should be noted that the *WRPA 1999* has subsequently made certain refinements to these sections which are acknowledged in this narrative. In the essence the amendments provided that the courts:

(*a*) must have regard to pension benefits which either party has or is likely to have or stands to lose the chance of acquiring because of the divorce and must ignore the words 'in the foreseeable future' contained in s*ection 25(2)(a)* of *MCA 1973* for this purpose (*section 25B(1), MCA 1973*);

(*b*) have jurisdiction to make orders against the person responsible for the pension arrangement for payment of financial provision from a member's pension benefits to the other party when payment of those benefits falls due to the member (*section 25B(4), MCA 1973*) The term 'person responsible' was introduced by s*ection 46(2)* of the *WRPA 1999* and means, in the case of occupational pension schemes or personal pension schemes, the trustees and managers of the scheme. In the case of a retirement annuity contract it means the provider of the annuity and, in the case of an insurance policy, the insurer. The term 'pension arrangement' was introduced by s*ection 46(1)* of the *WRPA 1999* and means an occupational pension scheme, personal pension scheme, retirement annuity contract, an annuity or insurance policy which is to give effect to the rights of an occupational pension scheme or a personal pension scheme or an annuity purchased for the purpose of discharging liability for a pension credit (as discussed in more detail under 8.12 below);

(*c*) have power to direct a member as to the extent to which he may commute payments, thereby reducing the pension benefits payable to him, and have power to order payment of any lump sum following commutation to be made to the ex-spouse (*section 25B(7), MCA 1973*);

(*d*) can direct trustees to exercise their discretionary powers in the event of the death of a member or pensioner in favour of the ex-spouse in whole or in part, and can also require a member to nominate his ex-spouse for all or part of a lump sum payable on his death (*section 25C, MCA 1973*).

Essentially, the type of order which the court was empowered to make was not changed by *PA 1995*, merely the source of the payment. The order is in the form of either a deferred periodical payments (or maintenance) order or a lump sum order. The member's pension benefits remain in the scheme and are still attributable to the member but a proportion is payable directly to the ex-spouse. No separate entitlement is created in the scheme for the ex-spouse so payments only become due to the ex-spouse when they become due to the member and will stop automatically on the death of the member. As with all periodical payment orders, either party can apply to the court to have the amount varied (*section 31, MCA 1973*) and payments will cease on the re-marriage or death of the ex-spouse.

The amount due to the ex-spouse must (since 1 December 2000) be expressed as a percentage of the total amount of pension due to the member (*section 25B(5), MCA 1973*). Such total amount can include the value of the member's GMP by virtue of the exclusion of the provisions relating to inalienability of GMPs (section 91, PA 1995) under sections 166(4) and (5) of PA 1995. Any lump sum payment made by the persons responsible for the pension arrangement shall discharge them of any liability to the member to the extent of the amount of the payment (sections 25B(6)(a) and 25C(3), MCA 1973) and, in the case of pension payments, any payments made by the person responsible for the pension arrangement shall be treated as a payment made by the member towards the discharge of his liability under the court order (section 25B(6)(b), MCA 1973).

The duty of the court to consider a clean break was not affected by the changes introduced by the PA 1995. In practice, therefore 'earmarking' orders against pension payments are likely only to be made where a clean break is not possible and a periodical payments order is appropriate. Such an order, however, gives the ex-spouse additional comfort and security because, instead of obtaining a deferred maintenance order payable by the member in retirement, the ex-spouse will now receive payments directly from the pension scheme. This removes direct dependency on the member for financial support and avoids the potential problems caused by non-compliance with an order by the member.

The amendments to MCA 1973 by PA 1995 (and the subsequent refinements by WRPA 1999) specified the schemes against which the court can make orders. As mentioned these are now called 'pension arrangements' and include not only occupational pension schemes (funded or unfunded, tax approved or unapproved) but also personal pension schemes, retirement annuity contracts, annuities and section 32 buy-out policies (section 25D(3),MCA 1973).

It is considered unlikely that any inheritance tax liability will attach where the court has made an order for a lump sum payment on death. The Inland Revenue statement of practice E3 relating to the provisions of the *Inheritance Tax Act 1984* states that pension scheme benefits will not be liable to IHT if the executors or administrators do not have a legally enforceable claim to the benefits. Therefore, whilst lump sum benefits which are subject to an earmarking order are no longer payable at the sole discretion of the trustees of the pension scheme, the lump sum payment nevertheless passes outside the will or intestacy of the deceased member.

Valuation of benefits for earmarking purposes

8.4 The question of the valuation of pension rights for earmarking was previously dealt with in the *Divorce etc. (Pensions) Regulations (SI 1996 No 1676)*. However, with the advent of the *WRPA 1999* these regulations have now been superseded by the *Divorce etc. (Pensions) Regulations (SI 2000 No 1123)* (although *SI 1996 No 1676* still applies in respect of divorce and nullity proceedings commenced before 1 December 2000). *Regulation 3* of the 2000 Regulations provides that, for the purposes of earmarking, benefits under a pension arrangement shall be calculated in the manner set out in *regulation 3* of the *Pensions on Divorce etc. (Provision of Information) Regulations (SI 2000 No 1048)*.

8.5   Pensions and divorce

Regulation 3 of the *Pensions on Divorce etc. (Provision of Information) Regulations (SI 2000 No 1048)* specifies that the basis of valuation depends on the category of member in question:

(*a*)   For active and deferred members of occupational pension schemes, members of personal pension schemes and a person with rights contained in a retirement annuity contact, the statutory cash equivalent transfer value basis (CETV) must be applied. Generally, the effective date for calculating the CETV is the date on which the request for the valuation was received by the person responsible for the pension arrangement. However, it should be noted that under *regulation 3* of the *Divorce etc. (Pensions) Regulations (SI 2000 No 1123)* the court can specify another date, if it considers it appropriate, such date not to be earlier than one year before the date of the petition and not later than the date on which the court is exercising its powers.

(*b*)   In any other circumstances *regulation 3 (SI 2000 No 1048)* specifies that the value of benefits shall be calculated and verified by a qualified actuary (*regulation 3(7), SI 2000 No 1048*) by adopting methods and making assumptions certified as being consistent with 'Retirement Benefit Schemes – Transfer Values (GN11)' as published by the Institute of Actuaries and the Faculty of Actuaries and current at the date on which the request for the valuation is received (*regulation 8, SI 2000 No 1048*). *Regulation 9 (SI 2000 No 1048)* provides for certain specific provisions to apply to money purchase benefits.

Transfers of, and notices in relation to, earmarked benefits

8.5   Given that the courts' powers enable orders to be made for deferred maintenance payments, payable at some date in the future, it was necessary to make provisions permitting the transfer of the orders on the transfer of the member's accrued benefits to a new scheme (*section 25D(1)(a), MCA 1973*). The *Divorce etc. (Pensions) Regulations (SI 2000 No 1123)* provide for the person responsible for the transferring arrangement to give notice to the person responsible for the receiving arrangement in circumstances where an earmarking order is in force against a member who wishes to transfer his pension benefits. The effect of this notice is that the earmarking order will attach to the transfer credits granted in the receiving scheme and will be enforceable against the trustees of the receiving scheme.

Regulation 4 (SI 2000 No 1123) sets out the content of the notices which must be given to the receiving arrangement and the ex-spouse and the period within which they must be given. Notice must be given within the period provided by *section 99* of the *PSA 1993* for the person responsible for the transferring arrangement to effect a transfer (usually six months) and before the expiry of 21 days after the person responsible for the transferring arrangement has made all required payments to the person responsible for the receiving arrangement (*regulation 4(5), SI 2000 No 1123*).

The notice to the ex-spouse must contain the following particulars:

(a) the fact that the pension rights of the member have been transferred;

(b) the effective date of the transfer;

(c) the name and address of the person responsible for the new arrangement; and

(d) the fact that the order made under *section 23* of the *MCA 1973* is to have effect as if it had been made in respect of the person responsible for the new arrangement.

The notice to the person responsible for the new arrangement shall consist of:

(i) every order made under the *MCA 1973* imposing a requirement on the person responsible for the transferring arrangement in relation to the rights transferred;

(ii) any subsequent orders varying the original order;

(iii) all information or particulars supplied by the ex-spouse under *rule 2.70* of the *Family Proceedings Rules 1991(as amended)* (*SI 1991 No 1247*) (eg address and bank details);

(iv) any notice given by the ex-spouse to the transferring trustees relating to a change of personal details or re-marriage; and

(v) where the rights of a member under the transferring scheme derive from a transfer from a previous scheme, any notices to the person responsible for the previous arrangement on the former transfer.

Under *regulation 5 (SI 2000 No 1123)* notice is also required to be given by the person responsible for the arrangement to the ex-spouse, within 14 days of the occurrence of an event, when:

(1) there has been a significant reduction in the benefits payable under the scheme in respect of the member (save where transfer of all benefits has been made or where market conditions have affected the value of the scheme's assets) (*regulation 5(1), SI 2000 No 1123*); and/or

(2) a partial transfer of the member's accrued benefits has been made (*regulation 5(3) SI 2000 No 1123*).

This notice shall state the nature of the event which has occurred and the extent of the reduction in benefits and, in the case of a partial transfer, the name and address of the person responsible for the receiving arrangement.

It should be noted that in the event of a partial transfer the order will remain with the original scheme and this may therefore give the member scope for the avoidance of the order. Nevertheless, because notice is given to the ex-spouse by the scheme, this gives the ex-spouse an opportunity to apply to the court for a variation of the original order.

8.6 *Pensions and divorce*

An ex-spouse is required to give notice (*regulation 6, SI 2000 No 1123*) within 14 days to the person responsible for the arrangement subject to a court order where the particulars supplied by her cease to be accurate; where the ex-spouse has remarried or where, for any other reason, the order has ceased to have effect. The person responsible for the arrangement will be discharged of any liability to the ex-spouse to the extent of a payment where, by reason of the inaccuracy of the particulars supplied by the ex-spouse or the ex-spouse's failure to give notice of a change in details, it is not reasonably practicable for the person responsible for the arrangement to make a payment as required by the order and a payment is therefore made to the member instead (*regulation 6(4), SI 2000 No 1123*).

Ambit of court orders

8.6 The courts were empowered to make deferred maintenance orders from 1 August 1996 where applied for in petitions presented after 1 July 1996, although any orders made could not take effect before 6 April 1997. In addition to making a deferred maintenance order from the pension arrangement the court can also require a member to commute his pension when he retires, with part or all of the lump sum being paid to the ex-spouse (*section 25B(7), MCA 1973*, see 8.3 above). Similarly in the case of benefits payable on the member's death, the court has the power to order the allocation of any lump sum and, even where payment of the lump sum is discretionary, the persons responsible for the pension arrangement can be ordered to pay all or part of it to the ex-spouse. In cases where the member himself has the power to nominate a beneficiary, the member can be required to nominate the ex-spouse.

As mentioned above the order must express the amount due to the ex-spouse as a percentage of the total amount due to the member. The order may also state the rate at which the payment is to increase annually and this may vary from the rates stated in the scheme rules. In relation to orders prior to 1 December 2000 which were made for a fixed amount, it would also be necessary to consider whether or not allowance would need to be made for re-valuation up to retirement and, further, to consider what the position would be were a member to retire and whether or not this earlier payment should be reflected in the ex-spouse's pension.

Charging for earmarking orders

8.7 Previously covered by *regulation 10* of the 1996 *Disclosure Regulations (SI 1996 No 1655)*, charges by pension arrangements in relation to earmarking orders are now covered by *section 24* of *WRPA 1999* by reference to *regulation 10* of the *Pensions on Divorce etc. (Charging) Regulations (SI 2000 No 1049)*. It is stated that the charges which a person responsible for a pension arrangement may recover in relation to an earmarking order are those charges which represent the reasonable administrative expenses which have been incurred or are likely to be incurred by reason of the order.

Regulation 3 (SI 2000 No 1049) deals with charges recoverable in respect of the provision of basic valuation information and provides that the persons responsible for the pension arrangement may also recover the reasonable costs of providing such information to the extent that they would not have been required to provide such information in the ordinary course of disclosure in accordance with the *Disclosure Regulations*.

Disclosure

8.8 The current provisions governing disclosure in relation to earmarking orders can be found under the *Pensions on Divorce etc. (Provision of Information) Regulations (SI 2000 No 1048)*. *Regulation 2* deals with the provision of the basic information which the person responsible for a pension arrangement can generally be required to disclose on request. These provisions apply equally to pension sharing and are set out in detail at 8.24 below.

Regulation 10 (SI 2000 No 1048) deals with the provision of information after receipt of an earmarking order. The person responsible for the pension arrangement must, within 21 days of receipt of the earmarking order, issue to both parties to the marriage a notice which includes the following, as appropriate:

(a) for an order in respect of pension rights not in payment, a list of the circumstances in respect of any changes of which the member or the ex-spouse must notify the person responsible for the pension arrangement;

(b) where the pension is in payment:
   (i) the value of the member's pension rights;
   (ii) the amount of those pension rights after the order has been implemented;
   (iii) the first date when a payment under the order is to be made; and
   (iv) the circumstances in respect of any changes of which the member or the ex-spouse must notify the person responsible for the pension arrangement;

(c) the amount of charges which remain unpaid by each party pursuant to regulation 3 of the *Pensions on Divorce etc. (Charging) Regulations (SI 2000 No 1049)* (see 8.7 above) and in respect of complying with the order;

(d) information as to how and when these charges will be recovered.

PENSION SHARING

Introduction

8.9 The concept of pension sharing was first introduced, but not imple-

8.9 Pensions and divorce

mented, by the *Family Law Act 1996*. A lengthy consultation process then followed which culminated in the provisions contained in the *Welfare Reform and Pensions Act 1999* (*WRPA 1999*).

In brief, the term pension sharing is used to signify a clean break approach towards dealing with pension rights. The aim is that the capital value of the pension will be divided between the parties with the effect that the rights of the member will be reduced by way of a 'pension debit' and the ex-spouse will be granted a 'pension credit' of the same amount. The primary advantage of pension sharing to an ex-spouse is that her rights are independent of those of the member and, in contrast with earmarking, will, therefore, continue beyond the death of the member and after the ex-spouse's remarriage.

The relevant sections of *WRPA 1999* came into force on 1 December 2000 and were in the form of insertions and amendments to *MCA 1973*, the provisions of *Part III* of *WRPA 1999*, and a number of statutory instruments.

Pension sharing is only available in proceedings commencing on or after 1 December 2000, the effective date for the new legislation (*Welfare Reform and Pensions Act 1999 (Commencement No 5) Order 2000 (SI 2000 No 1116)*). The provisions only apply to proceedings for divorce or nullity of marriage, and do not extend to judicial separation (*section 24B(1), MCA 1973*). Subsequent case law has made it clear that the question of whether a decree nisi could be rescinded, to allow new divorce proceedings to be issued after 1 December 2000 thus enabling a pension sharing order to be made, is one for judicial discretion. In *S v S [2002] All ER (D) 58 (Mar)* the court allowed rescission where both parties consented. However, in *Rye v Rye [2002] EWHC 956 (Fam)* the husband (who had the pension) successfully objected to rescission. The court held that the *WRPA 1999* provides a clear cut off date and in the absence of consent by both parties it would be an impermissible exercise by the court of its discretion to circumvent the statutory provision by rescinding the decree nisi.

The amendments made to the *MCA 1973* mean that the courts now have the option to consider the possibility of granting a sharing order, if deemed appropriate, when considering ancillary relief (*section 24B(1), MCA 1973*). Whilst it is open to the courts to make more than one sharing order in relation to a given set of divorce proceedings, the courts cannot make a pension sharing order in relation to a pension arrangement which is already the subject of a pension sharing order in relation to that marriage (*sections 24B(3) and (4), MCA 1973*). Moreover, the court cannot make a pension sharing order in respect of pension benefits which are already subject to an earmarking order.

Section 21A of the *MCA 1973* states that a sharing order involves the court ordering that the 'shareable rights' of the member be shared for the benefit of the ex-spouse, with the order specifying the value of those rights to be transferred as a percentage of the total rights attributable to the member.

Section 27(2) of the *WRPA 1999* sets out the definition of 'shareable rights' as any rights under a 'pension arrangement' other than non-shareable rights of a description specified in regulation*s*. As detailed above at 8.3 the *WRPA 1999* definition of 'pension arrangement' (*section 46(1)*) is broadly termed. Due to the adoption of the *PSA 1993* (*section 1*) definition of 'occupational pension scheme', benefits under unfunded and unapproved schemes are included as shareable rights, as are benefits under the state earning related pension scheme. Indeed, the only exceptions to date appear to be excepted public sector schemes (*section 27(1)(3), WRPA 1999*) by reference to the *Pension Sharing (Excepted Schemes) Order (SI 2001 No 358)* (being the schemes relating to the Prime Minister, Lord Chancellor and Speaker of the House of Commons) and the basic state pension.

Pension debits and credits

8.10 The person responsible for a pension arrangement is not required to implement the pension debit and pension credit until the pension sharing order has taken effect (*section 29(1)(a), WRPA 1999*). Pension sharing can also be provided under a 'qualifying agreement' between the parties to the marriage which takes effect on the dissolution of the marriage under the *Family Law Act 1996 (s 28(1)(b))*. (A 'qualifying agreement' has yet to be defined in regulations but, when it is, the sharing legislation will apply equally to it as to court orders).

A sharing order cannot take effect unless the decree pursuant to which it has been made has been made absolute (*section 24B(2), MCA 1973*). In addition s*ection 24C* (by reference to *regulation 9, Divorce etc. (Pensions) Regulations (SI 2000 No 1123)*) provides that the order cannot come into effect earlier than seven days after the end of the period for filing notice of appeal against the order.

Once the sharing order has become effective the member's shareable rights under the arrangement become subject to a 'debit' of the specified amount and the ex-spouse becomes entitled to a 'credit' of a corresponding amount, held as a right against the person responsible for the arrangement (*section 29(1), WRPA 1999*).

Pension debits

8.11 The pension debit operates by reducing the member's current and future benefits under the pension arrangement by a specified percentage (*section 31(1), WRPA 1999*) on the transfer day (ie the date on which the order takes effect). The benefits to be reduced must be 'qualifying benefits' (*section 31(3)*). A benefit is a qualifying benefit if the member's cash equivalent includes an amount in respect of it.

When a benefit is reduced by a pension debit each part of the benefit is reduced equally. Thus, for example, the GMP benefits of a member are reduced by the same percentage as the excess over GMP. *Section 31(2)* of the *WRPA 1999* clarifies how the percentage deduction rule applies for members who are in

8.12 Pensions and divorce

pensionable service on the transfer day. The debit is applied to the deferred pension to which the member would have been entitled had he left pensionable service on that day. The benefits of active members to be reduced by the pension debit therefore exclude any elements which would not be included in his deferred pension, such as a death in service lump sum.

Pension credits

8.12 The ex-spouse becomes entitled to the corresponding amount as a pension credit, made up of the same elements and in the same proportions as the benefits of the scheme member. An arrangement which is the subject of a pension sharing order may discharge its liability for the pension credit by conferring appropriate rights under that arrangement (an 'internal transfer') or by transferring the pension credit to another qualifying pension scheme or arrangement (an 'external transfer') (see 8.14 below).

Implementation period

8.13 The person responsible for the arrangement has a specified period within which to give effect to the provisions of the pension sharing order – this is known as the implementation period and is a period of four months beginning with the later of the day on which the pension sharing order takes effect, and receipt by the person responsible for the arrangement of certain matrimonial documents (eg the order itself and the order or decree of the divorce or annulment), and the information set out in the *Pensions on Divorce etc. (Provision of Information) Regulations (SI 2000 No 1048)* (this includes the names, addresses, dates of birth and National Insurance numbers of the divorcing couple) (*section 34(1), WRPA 1999*). A further pre-condition of implementing the sharing order may be the payment of any charges due from the divorcing couple (see 8.25 below).

In the event that the order has not been implemented by the trustees of an occupational pension scheme within the implementation period they shall be required to notify Opra within 21 days beginning with the day immediately following the end of the implementation period (*regulation 2, Pension Sharing (Implementation and Discharge of Liability) Regulations (SI 2000 No 1053)*) and *section 10* of the *PA 1995* shall apply. Opra may, therefore, impose civil penalties if the trustees failed to take all such steps as were reasonable to discharge liability for the pension credit before the end of the implementation period. On application by the trustees, Opra may extend the implementation period under certain circumstances (*section 33(4), WRPA 1999*). These circumstances are set out in *regulation 3* of the *Pension Sharing (Implementation and Discharge of Liability) Regulations (SI 2000 No 1053)* and include the scheme being in wind-up; ceasing to be contracted out or where an extension is in the financial interests of the members of the scheme generally. The implementation period may also be suspended or postponed where one of the parties has made an application for leave to appeal out of time (*regulation 4, SI 2000 No 1053*).

Discharging liability for the pension credit

General position

8.14 The main body of the pension sharing legislation is aimed at the means by which the liability of the person responsible for the pension arrangement which is subject to a pension sharing order can be discharged in respect of the pension credit created. The relevant provisions can be found in s*ection 35* of *WRPA 1999* by reference to *Schedule 5*, together with the *Pension Sharing (Implementation and Discharge of Liability) Regulations (SI 2000 No 1053)*.

Schedule 5 deals with funded (*paragraph 1*), unfunded (*paragraphs 2 and 3*) and 'other' (*paragraph 4*) pension arrangements. This chapter will concentrate on the description of 'funded' schemes in *Schedule 5 paragraph 1*, ie pension credits derived from a funded occupational pension scheme or a personal pension scheme.

Schedule 5 (paragraph 1(2)) states that the trustees or managers of these types of arrangements may discharge their liability in respect of the pension credit by conferring rights under the relevant scheme on the ex-spouse, with his or her consent or otherwise in accordance with regulations. This is known as the 'internal transfer' option. Alternatively, under *Schedule 5 paragraph 1(3)* the liability may be discharged by paying the amount of the pension credit to the person responsible for a 'qualifying arrangement' (defined widely in *Schedule 5 paragraph 6*) with the ex-spouse's consent or otherwise in accordance with regulations. This is known as the 'external transfer' option.

The *Pension Sharing (Implementation and Discharge of Liability) Regulations (SI 2000 No 1053)* set out the detail of these procedures under *regulation 7*. In summary, for internal transfers (*regulation 7(1)*) the consent of the ex-spouse must be obtained unless the ex-spouse has failed to provide this consent and has also failed to specify a suitable recipient scheme under the external transfer route.

An external transfer (*regulation 7(2)*) must be made with the ex-spouse's consent unless the ex-spouse fails to provide this consent and he or she has also failed to consent to an internal transfer or the trustees did not offer the internal transfer route as an option in the first instance.

Schedule 5 (paragraph 1(4)) specifies that any consent to be given by the ex-spouse to an internal transfer option will be invalid unless it is given after receipt of a written notice of an offer to discharge liability by way of an external transfer and the consent is not withdrawn within seven days of receipt of such notice.

Death of ex-spouse prior to discharge of liability

8.15 *Regulation 6 (SI 2000 No 1053)* specifies how a pension credit liability

8.16 *Pensions and divorce*

can be discharged when the ex-spouse dies after the liability has arisen but before it has been discharged. Essentially, any benefits the scheme provides must, subject to the rules of the scheme, be in the form of a lump sum payment; payment of a pension; payment of both a lump sum and a pension and/or the purchase of an annuity contract or insurance policy with a 'qualifying arrangement' (defined in *regulation 11(SI 1999 No 1053)*).

Small self-administered schemes

8.16 It should be noted that *regulation 2* of the *Retirement Benefits Schemes (Restriction on Discretion to Approve) (Small Self-administered Schemes) (Amendment) Regulations (SI 2000 No 1086)* confirms that, whilst an ex-spouse participant who is offered an internal transfer will count as a scheme member for general purposes, an additional member of this type in the scheme will, nevertheless, not count towards the total number of members for determining whether the scheme can qualify as a SSAS (ie less than 12 members).

Pros and cons of internal v external transfer options

8.17 There has been much debate amongst advisers about which option trustees should adopt as their policy for securing pension credits. Arguments against internal transfers are the added costs and the administrative burdens of an extra membership category; extended ongoing disclosure requirements and the need for extensive rule amendments to incorporate a new benefit structure and category of member. Moreover, the external option sits more easily with the 'clean break' motivation which gave rise to the pension sharing legislation in the first place.

The majority of funded occupational pension schemes have expressed a preference for the external transfer option, which avoids the problems outlined above. Concerns were, however, raised about the ability of trustees who were not authorised under the *FSA 1986* (now *FSMA 2000*) to select a default external transfer destination without contravening *section 191* of the *FSA 1986* (now *article 37* of the *Financial Services and Markets Act 2000 (Regulated Activities) Order 2001 (SI 2001 No 1544)*. However, the position has subsequently been clarified somewhat by the Financial Services Authority which, in a letter to the NAPF dated 2 February 2001, stated that, where trustees pay the pension credit to a designated default option provider, this will not amount to the purchasing of an investment which will be held for the purposes of the scheme and so falls outside the ambit of the definition of a specified activity for the purposes of the financial services legislation.

The question of the availability of a suitable 'qualifying arrangement' to receive external transfers (without the need for the ex-spouse's signature on a proposal form) remains, at the time of writing, a problem. In relation to the default option, generally the Department for Work and Pensions ('DWP') has clarified a few points that had arisen regarding the type of vehicle available for the default option.

1. The default option should not be available until the former spouse has been given adequate opportunity to make his or her choice or to make a further choice where payment cannot be made in accordance with his or her wishes. Where the default option, nevertheless, comes into play the only options available are either an internal transfer or the purchase of an annuity or insurance policy.

2. This gives rise to the question as to the type of annuity and insurance policy available for this purpose. A deferred annuity can be purchased but it is not clear what other 'insurance policy' can be used. It is not possible to transfer the credit to a personal pension scheme or stakeholder schemes without the consent of the former spouse.

3. *Section 32* buy-out contracts would also seem not to be an option. This is because only pension *benefits* can be transferred to a *section 32* buy-out contract (GN Practice Note 6A.21) so it would only be in the event that an ex-spouse were to acquire a 'pension credit benefit' in the scheme that this could then be transferred out – and even in that case the consent of the ex-spouse would be required. In most cases there will be no pension credit benefit, only a pension credit liability to be discharged by the trustees. This appears to leave the purchase of an annuity as the only available external default option.

In practice this issue seems to have posed less of a problem than anticipated. An ex-spouse who agrees to a pension sharing order as part of the divorce settlement will have been notified of the trustees' policy and, where only an external transfer option is offered, is likely already to have made suitable arrangements before agreeing to such an order.

Pension credit benefits

General benefits and transfers

8.18 Where the trustees of a scheme choose to offer ex-spouses an internal transfer option, and the ex-spouse does not elect to transfer the pension credit to another arrangement, the ex-spouse will become an ex-spouse participant and will become entitled to pension credit benefits in the scheme.

Section 37 of the *WRPA 1999* inserts new s*ections 101A to 101Q* in the *PSA 1993*, setting out the requirements relating to pension credit benefits under occupational pension schemes. The protection given to ex-spouses with pension credit benefits broadly reflects the existing provisions for early leavers from occupational pension schemes, including similar transfer rights to those of a deferred member. This legislation is supplemented by the *Pension Sharing (Pension Credit Benefit) Regulations (SI 2000 No 1054)*.

Pension credit benefits are payable at 'normal benefit age', which means the earliest date at which a person who has a pension credit right is entitled to receive a pension by virtue of those rights (disregarding provisions as to early payment on grounds of ill-health). Normal benefit age must be between 60 and

8.19 *Pensions and divorce*

65 and benefits cannot be taken in lump sum form before that age except in prescribed circumstances (*section 101C, PSA 1993* and *Part II of SI 2000 No 1054*). Essentially this is where the ex-spouse is suffering from serious ill health prior to normal pension age (ie a life expectancy of less than one year) or where the benefits can be trivially commuted.

Members with pension credit benefits are entitled under *section 101F* of the *PSA 1993* to request that their cash equivalent be transferred to another occupational pension scheme or personal pension scheme which satisfies the necessary criteria, or be used to purchase an annuity, subject to certain requirements and restrictions set out in *Part III of SI 2000 No 1054*. Section 101H of PSA 1993 provides, in relation to salary related schemes, that a statement of entitlement must be provided by the trustees or managers, on the application of an eligible member, following which the eligible member has three months within which to request a transfer (*section 101G(1)*). The exceptions to this general rule are that an eligible member may not take a transfer if there is less than a year remaining before the member reaches normal benefit age or where any part of the benefit attributable to the member's pension credit rights has or must become payable. Where the trustees receive a transfer notice (ie a request for transfer) from an eligible member *section 101J* of the *PSA 1993* requires the trustees to comply with the notice within six months of the valuation date or the date on which the member reaches normal benefit age, if earlier. *Regulation 26 (SI 2000 No 1054)* states that extensions may be applied for from Opra in similar circumstances to those referred to at 8.13 above in relation to the extension of the implementation period. Otherwise, failure to comply with the transfer notice must be reported to Opra within 21 days beginning with the day immediately following the end of the period for compliance (*regulation 25, SI 2000 No 1054*). Opra may then impose civil penalties under *section 10* of the *PA 1995* if the trustees failed to take all such steps as were reasonable to ensure that the notice was complied with.

Indexation

8.19 Regulations 32 to 35 of the *Pension Sharing (Pension Credit Benefit) Regulations (SI 2000 No 1054)* provide that occupational pension schemes must apply indexation to the pension credit benefit derived from safeguarded rights (see 8.27 below) and/or post-April 1997 rights excluding AVCs, at 5 per cent per annum or the increase in the retail prices index, whichever is lower. The proposed changes to *section 51* of *PA 1995* by the Pensions Bill are likely to be mirrored in amending regulations.

MNT legislation

8.20 Ex-spouse members with pension credit benefits under the scheme do not count as 'members' for the purpose of the statutory consultation procedures relating to MNTs or MNDs under *PA 1995* (*WRPA 1999, Sch 12 paragraphs 45 to 49*).

Section 67, PA 1995

8.21 *Paragraph 53* of *Schedule 12* of the *WRPA 1999* amended *section 67* of *PA 1995* to include pension credit benefits on the list of rights protected by that section. Any amendment of the scheme's rules, however, to give effect to the trustees' pension sharing policy and enable the application of a pension debit is excepted from *section 67* by virtue of *regulation 6(1)(a)* of the *Occupational Pension Schemes (Modification of Schemes) Regulations 1996* to the effect that *section 67(3)* of *PA 1995* does not apply.

The Pensions Bill proposes to amend the provisions of *section 67* of *PA 1995*. Current wording, contained in the definition of 'subsisting right', carries forward the current protection.

Treatment on winding-up

8.22 In the case of a scheme to which the Minimum Funding Requirement (MFR) applies and which is therefore subject to the provisions of *section 73 of PA 1995* (see Chapter 12), the statutory order of priorities on winding-up has been amended by *section 38* of *WRPA 1999*. Pension credit benefits already rank with other pensions in payment. The liability for safeguarded rights ranks alongside GMPs, EPBs, protected rights and *section 9(2B)* rights (excluding increases to pensions) into the order of priorities and pension credit benefits in excess of the contracted out benefits rank with other deferred benefits.

In the case of a scheme to which the MFR does not apply, pension credits are to be accorded the same treatment on winding-up as the rights of a pensioner member if they have come into payment and the rights of a deferred member if they have not come into payment (*section 38(2), WRPA 1999*). This section overrides the provisions of the scheme to the extent that they conflict with it.

Valuation

8.23 In creating pension debits and credits under *section 29* of *WRPA 1999* the pension sharing order is applied to the statutory cash equivalent of the member's benefits (*section 30, WRPA 1999*). The specified percentage for reduction of a member's benefits is therefore the percentage of his or her cash equivalent of the relevant benefits on the valuation day (*section 29(2), WRPA 1999*). 'Valuation day' is defined in *section 29(7)* of the *WRPA 1999* as such day within the implementation period for the credit as the person responsible for the arrangement may specify by notice in writing to the member and ex-spouse.

For active members of occupational pension schemes the statutory cash equivalent is calculated in respect of the benefits to which the member would have been entitled to had his pensionable service been terminated on the day immediately prior to the transfer day ie the day on which the pension sharing order takes effect (*section 29(4)*). *Section 30* of *WRPA 1999* provides for the

8.24 *Pensions and divorce*

calculation of the cash equivalent of these benefits to be carried out in accordance with the provisions set out in the *Pension Sharing (Valuation) Regulations (SI 2000 No 1052)*.

Regulation 4 (SI 2000 No 1052) provides that cash equivalents are to be calculated by a qualified actuary (*regulation 4(1)*) in accordance with the *GN11*. In the case of an active member his cash equivalent is required to be calculated on the assumption that the member had made a request for an estimate of cash equivalent as if his pensionable service were to terminate on the transfer day. The methods and assumptions used to calculate the cash equivalent of the benefits must not only comply with *GN11* but also be consistent the methods and assumptions use by the scheme for someone who is acquiring transfer credits under the scheme and, where a scheme is subject to *section 56* of *PA 1995*, provide a minimum amount, consistent with the MFR basis.

Regulation 5 (SI 2000 No 1052) provides for the possibility of increasing or, indeed, reducing cash equivalents in certain circumstances to provide, for example, for the inclusion of discretionary benefits, or conversely, the reduction of the cash equivalent where the scheme is in deficit on a MFR basis (following the usual principles applying to the reduction of statutory cash equivalent transfer values). It is important to note, however, that a reduction cannot be applied in circumstances where the pension credit liability is to discharged by way of internal transfer or by way of external transfer without the ex-spouse's consent.

Disclosure of information

8.24 *Section 23(1)(a)* of *WRPA 1999* provides for regulations to impose requirements on the person responsible for a pension arrangement to supply information to certain parties in connection with the power to provide financial relief under the *MCA 1973*. The *Pensions on Divorce etc. (Provision of Information) Regulations (SI 2000 No 1048)* set out the details of these requirements.

At the beginning of the divorce process the person responsible for the arrangement must, on the request of a scheme member, spouse or the court, ensure that the following information is provided in connection with the divorce in accordance with *Regulation 2*:

(a) a valuation of the pension rights or benefits accrued under the pension arrangement, if requested by the member or the court;

(b) a statement that, if a member or the court requests, a valuation of the member's accrued benefits will be provided to the member or the court;

(c) a statement summarising the way in which any such valuation of the benefits disclosed is calculated;

(d) a statement of benefits included the valuation;

(e) a statement as to whether the person responsible for the arrangement intends to offer membership of the scheme to a person entitled to a pension credit (ie internal transfer) and if so, the type of benefits available to the pension credit member under that arrangement;

(f) a statement as to whether the person responsible for the arrangement intends to discharge liability for a pension credit other than by offering membership to a person entitled to a pension credit (ie external option only);

(g) the schedule of charges to be levied by the person responsible for the arrangement;

(h) any other additional information relevant to the sharing order requested by the court.

Therefore the valuation of a member's accrued benefits can only be provided by the arrangement to a member or the court. Once requested it must be provided within three months beginning with the date of receipt of the request; or within six weeks of the date of receipt of the request if the member has notified the trustees that it is required in connection with financial relief in divorce proceedings; or within a shorter period if so ordered by the court.

All the other items of information set out above must be supplied within one month of receipt of the request (as long as the request makes it clear that this is a request in connection with divorce). These provisions are contained in *regulation 2* of the *Pensions on Divorce etc. (Provision of Information) Regulations (SI 2000 No 1048)*.

Regulation 4 sets out the information to be provided within 21 days of a notification that a pension sharing order or provision may be made, as follows:

(a) the full name and address of the pension scheme;

(b) whether the scheme is in winding up and, if so, the effective date of winding up and the contact details of the trustees or administrators;

(c) whether cash equivalents are subject to deductions;

(d) whether the trustees are aware of any other relevant court orders;

(e) any elements of the member's pension rights which are not shareable;

(f) details of how charges are to be paid;

(g) whether the member is a trustee of the scheme;

(h) whether the scheme may request details of the member's health from the member, if the order were to proceed;

(i) whether the scheme requires any further information before implementation of the order.

Regulation 5 sets out the information required by the person responsible for the pension arrangement before the implementation period begins, as follows:

8.25   *Pensions and divorce*

(i) In relation to the member – all names and former names; date of birth; address; NI number; name of scheme to which the order relates and membership/policy number.

(ii) In relation to the ex-spouse – all names and former names; date of birth; address; NI number; if the ex-spouse is also a member of the scheme from which the pension credit is derived, the membership/policy number.

(iii) Where the ex-spouse is transferring to another arrangement – the full name and address of that arrangement; the membership or policy number; details of the person able to discharge liability for the pension credit; in the case of rights transferring from an occupational pension scheme which is in winding up with a deficit, whether the ex-spouse has indicated she wishes to transfer the pension credit rights; and any further information the receiving arrangement may require.

Regulation 6 sets out the information to be provided after the death of the ex-spouse prior to liability having been discharged.

Regulation 7 sets out the information to be provided after receipt of the pension sharing order or provision and *regulation 8* the information to be provided after the implementation of a pension sharing order.

Charging

8.25   *Section 41 of WRPA 1999* and the *Pensions on Divorce etc (Charging) Regulations (SI 2000/1049)* provide for persons responsible for pension arrangements to recover charges in respect of pension sharing costs.

Costs are not recoverable unless the divorcing parties have been informed in writing by the person responsible for the pension arrangement of the intention to recover costs and a written schedule of the charges has been provided. Charges cannot, however, be recovered for the provision of basic information about pensions and divorce and for the provision of information in response to a notification that a pension sharing order may be made (*regulations 2* and *4* of the *Pensions on Divorce etc. (Provision of Information) Regulations (SI 2000 No 1048)*) unless that information has already been provided on the previous 12 month period; the member has reached normal retirement age or is within 12 months of normal retirement age. Charges also cannot be recovered for the provision of a cash equivalent which is provided in accordance with *section 93A* or *94* of *PA 1995* or in accordance with the *Disclosure Regulations*.

Where charges are recoverable they can only be for the reasonable administrative expenses the arrangement will incur in connection with the implementation of the pension sharing order or the provision of information in connection with the divorce proceedings and must be directly related to the individual case (*regulation 5, SI 2000 No 1049*). The legislation does not define, however, what is meant by 'reasonable'. The National Association of Pension Funds has issued guidance on this point to its membership (see 8.26 below).

Section 24D of *MCA 1973* has been introduced to give the courts power to include a provision in the order relating to the apportionment of charges between the parties. To the extent that the court is silent on the issue *section 41(3)(b)* of *WRPA 1999* provides that the charges shall be attributable to the scheme member.

Regulation 7 (SI 2000 No 1049) permits the postponement of the start of the implementation period for a sharing order until specified charges are paid, provided that appropriate notice has been given to the parties in accordance with that regulation.

Regulation 9 provides for certain methods of recovery of the charges by the person responsible for the pension arrangement. Where the charges are not paid in cash, recovery can be by way of deduction from the pension credit; deduction from the member's accrued rights; deduction from pension where the pension is in payment and deduction from payments of pension credit benefits (subject to certain conditions having been satisfied).

Reference should be made to the *Pensions on Divorce etc. (Charging) Regulations (SI 2000 No 1049)* for full details of the conditions and restrictions relating to the charging for information and pension sharing activities.

In relation to earmarking orders, charges for the provision of information are dealt with as described above. In relation to the costs associated with the implementation of an earmarking order *regulation 10* of *SI 2000 No 1049* provides that the person responsible for the pension arrangement recovers reasonable administrative expenses which have been or are likely to be incurred by reason of the order.

NAPF recommended scale of charges

8.26

Table A – Scheme member not yet retired – about to divorce

Procedure	Comments	Estimated cost
(i) Produce CETV quotation	Standard annual entitlement under disclosure of information regulations	£0
(ii) Additional CETV quotations		£150 per additional quotation
(iii) Provision of other information	If under disclosure of information regulations Otherwise, depending on nature of request	£0 minimum £25 maximum £75

8.27 *Pensions and divorce*

Procedure	Comments	Estimated cost
(iv) Receipt of pension sharing order or consent order	To cover all administration costs from receipt of pension sharing order to completion of pension payments	maximum £750
(v) Objections to order by scheme	Onus should be on the draftsman of the order to ensure that it is correctly drafted prior to issue.	Scheme to notify member/solicitor that costs for dealing with inoperable orders will be passed on

Table B – Scheme member retired – pension in payment – about to divorce

Procedure	Comments	Estimated cost
(i) Assess the value of the pension in payment, including any contingent benefits	Actual cost dependent on charges incurred for actuarial time	maximum £500
(ii) Administrative cost of collecting and interpreting medical evidence in respect of divorcing couple	It is assumed that the charges for supply of medical evidence will be met by the divorcing couple	Scheme to advise that payment for supply of medical evidence will be the responsibility of the member.
(iii) Establish a new pensioner record	To cover all administration costs from receipt of pension sharing order to completion of pension payments	maximum £750
(iv) Assuming all documentation is in place, settle a transfer out (instead of (iii) above)		maximum £300
(v) Establish a new member scheme record (record keeping/tracing reasons etc)		minimum £25 maximum £100

Safeguarded rights

8.27 Section 36 of *WRPA 1999* inserts new *sections 68A* to *68D* into *PSA 1993* with the effect that 'safeguarded rights' are created where rights to future benefits under the scheme are attributable to a pension credit which is or includes contracted-out (or safeguarded) rights. The safeguarded rights shall form the same percentage of the pension credit as the contracted-out (or safeguarded) rights form of the member's cash equivalent. Despite the different terminology, safeguarded rights are treated in broadly the same way as contracted-out rights. The detailed provisions can be found in the *Pension Sharing (Safeguarded Rights) Regulations (SI 2000 No 1055)*, including restrictions on the transfer or discharge of the safeguarded rights.

FAMILY PROCEEDINGS RULES

8.28 The procedures to be followed to obtain either an earmarking or sharing order are set out in *rule 2.70* of the *Family Proceedings Rules 1991 (as amended)* (*SI 1991 No 1247*).

The rule applies to applications for ancillary relief and sets out the obligations of the parties with regard to the provision of information relating to benefits which a party has or is likely to have under a pension scheme. For both earmarking and pension sharing the order must be specifically applied for on Form A or Form B. The court will then fix an appointment and, within seven days after receiving notification of the date of that appointment, the member must request that the person responsible for the pension arrangement(s) under which the member has or is likely to have benefits provides basic information set out in *regulation 2(2)* and *2(3)(b)* to *(f)* of the *Pensions on Divorce etc. (Provision of Information) Regulations (SI 2000 No 1048)* (see 8.24 above).

Within seven days of receiving this information the member shall send a copy of it to the other party together with the name and address of the person responsible for the pension arrangement(s). *Rule 2.70(4)* states that, where the member is already in possession of, or has requested, a relevant valuation of his benefits under the pension arrangement in question, then this request for disclosure need not be made (for these purposes a relevant valuation is one which has been furnished to the member within the preceding 12 months).

If notice is given of intention to proceed with an application for a pension sharing order, the applicant must send a copy of Form A to the person responsible for the pension arrangement (*Rule 2.70(6)*). In the case of an application for an earmarking order the applicant must send the person responsible for the pension arrangement a copy of Form A; an address for the service of any notices on the applicant by the person responsible for the pension arrangement; an address to which payments can be remitted and, if that address is a bank, sufficient details to enable payment to be made into the applicant's account (*rule 2.70(7)*).

Within 21 days after service of a notice of application for an earmarking order under *rule 2.70(7)*, the person responsible for the pension arrangement has the right under *rule 2.70(8)* to require a copy of the statement in Form E supporting the application to be provided and they may provide to the applicant, respondent and the court a statement in answer. *Rules 2.70(8) and (9)* provide the relevant

8.29 *Pensions and divorce*

time limits. If the earmarking order is being applied for by way of consent order the relevant information, together with a copy of the draft order, must be provided to the persons responsible for the pension arrangement and the order shall not be made until 21 days have elapsed without objections being made or the court has considered any objections (*rule 2.70(11)* and *(12)*).

Under *rule 2.70(13)* any order for ancillary relief, whether by consent or not, which includes either a provision for pension sharing or for earmarking must:

(*a*)   in the body of the order state that there is to be provision by way of pension sharing or earmarking in accordance with the annex to the order; and

(*b*)   be accompanied by an annex setting out specified information in relation to each of the pension arrangements under consideration.

Rule 2.70(14) specifies the annexed information for pension sharing and *rule 2.70(15)* specifies the information needed for earmarking. In general terms the type of information that is specified is as follows:

(i) the name of the court making the order together with the case number and title of proceedings;

(ii) the type of order (ie sharing or earmarking);

(iii) the names of the parties;

(iv) national insurance details of the member;

(v) details sufficient to identify the pension arrangement concerned;

(vi) percentage deduction from the member's pension rights;

(vii) any apportionment of charges (pension sharing).

There are also certain statements which are required to be made and which are specific to either type of order. The detailed requirements can be found under *Rule 2.70(14)* and *Rule 2.70(15)*, as appropriate.

On being asked to review the contents of either a pension sharing or earmarking order it is *Rule 2.70* of the *Family Proceedings Rules 1991* (as amended) to which reference should be made and, in particular to *rules 2.70(13)*, *(14)*, *(15)*.

SCHEME DOCUMENTATION

8.29   *PSO Update 62* and the Inland Revenue's model rules cover pension sharing on divorce. Any new scheme which is seeking Inland Revenue approval after 10 May 2000 will need to provide for pension sharing on divorce, although in most cases the model rules will need significant tailoring in order to fit in with any particular provisions of the scheme (the Revenue has confirmed that this was the intention when issuing the model rules). For any schemes fully approved before 10 May 2000 *PSO Update 62* states that pension sharing legislation is overriding but there is an expectation that schemes will take the opportunity to incorporate the pension sharing provisions as soon as reasonably practicable and, in any case, when submitting a deed of amendment on another topic to the Inland Revenue, the scheme's examiner will wish to ensure that provisions for pension sharing have been included.

OVERLAP BETWEEN EARMARKING AND PENSION SHARING

8.30   *Section 24(B)(5)* of *MCA 1973* states that a pension sharing order may not be made in relation to the rights of a person under a pension arrangement if there is in force an earmarking order in relation to any of the member's benefits under the relevant schemes.

Section 25B(7B) of *MCA 1973* states, similarly, that the power to make an earmarking order may not be exercised in relation to a pension arrangement which is the subject of a pension sharing order in relation to the marriage in question or has been the subject of a pension sharing between the parties to the marriage. In addition, *section 25C(4)* also extends this prohibition on to lump sum orders where the pension arrangement is subject to a pension sharing order in relation to the marriage or has been the subject of pension sharing between the parties to the marriage.

TAXATION

8.31   For earmarking purposes any benefits paid out under an earmarking order will be treated as if they are the benefits of the member despite the fact that they are paid directly to the ex-spouse.

In relation to pension sharing, *section 79* of and *Schedule 10* to the *Finance Act 1999* set out the tax treatment. Full detail of the Schedule is beyond the scope of this chapter. It should be noted, however, that the Inland Revenue has taken steps to ensure that tight control is maintained. Pension credits must, where derived from an approved source, remain in an approved environment and pension credit benefits must be relevant benefits for the purposes of *ICTA 1988*. Pension payments derived from pension credits will be chargeable to tax under Schedule E and lump sum retirement benefits will be tax free, as is the case with the pension benefits of the scheme member.

In relation to a member's ability to rebuild his pension after a pension sharing order, this is only possible to the extent that the member can increase his benefits by contributing AVCs, and the Revenue has not granted any concession allowing members to contribute more than the normal maximum 15 per cent. Also, unless the member is a 'moderate earner' (ie earns less than 25 per cent of the earnings cap at the date of divorce) then the value of the pensions credit (or 'negative deferred pension') will be taken into account for Revenue maxima purposes. Further detail is contained in *PSO Update 62*.

8.32 *Pensions and divorce*

THE FUTURE

8.32 The Pensions Bill sets out the treatment of pension credits and debits in the new regime post A Day.

There are provisions addressing the situation where an individual has received a pension credit prior to A Day (6 April 2006). The effect of this would be that the individual can protect his or her pre-A Day pension credit rights or benefits from the recovery charge by registering those rights/benefits with the Inland Revenue. It is understood that the Inland Revenue will then issue a certificate showing that the individual has an increased personal lifetime allowance, ie increased by the value of the pension credit rights or benefits.

A pension share post A Day under the new provisions will be treated differently to the current regime. Currently a pension credit does not count for the purposes of the ex-spouse's benefit and contribution limits and, correspondingly, a pension debit is disregarded for the purposes of the member's benefit and contribution limits. This position is reversed post A Day to the effect that for a pension shared after 6 April 2005 the pension credit will now count towards the ex-spouse's lifetime allowance and not towards the member's. The exception to this is in relation to a pension share of a crystallised pension already in payment after 6 April 2006. To avoid double counting, and because the pension will already have been tested against the lifetime allowance of the member on retirement, the ex-spouse's lifetime allowance will be increased by a pension credit factor, to reflect the increased benefits resulting from the pension sharing order. It is also intended that neither pension debits nor pension credits will count towards an individual's annual allowance.

Chapter 9

Sex equality

INTRODUCTION

9.1 In the UK, differential pension provision for men and women was, prior to the 1990's, the norm rather than the exception. Two main factors contributed to this situation; the differing life expectancies of men and women, and the work patterns of men and women in paid employment. A further contributing factor in the UK has been the discriminatory retirement ages in the State scheme, although this is now in the process of being equalised.

The effect of European Community (EC) law in prescribing requirements for equal treatment in pension schemes could no longer be ignored in the UK when the Court of Justice of the European Communities (ECJ) confirmed in the *Barber* case (*Barber v GRE Assurance Group [1990] ECR I–1889*) that pensions were 'pay' for the purposes of the equal pay requirements of *Article 141* of the *Treaty of Rome* (formerly *Article 119* but renumbered by the *Treaty of Amsterdam* with effect from 1 May 1999).

Article 141 of the *Treaty of Rome* provides that:

'1. Each Member State shall ensure that the principle of equal pay for male and female workers for equal work or work of equal value is applied.

2. For the purpose of this Article, "pay" means the ordinary basic or minimum wage or salary and any other consideration, whether in cash or in kind, which the worker receives, directly or indirectly, in respect of his employment from his employer.

Equal pay without discrimination based on sex means:

(*a*) that pay for the same work at piece rates shall be calculated on the basis of the same unit of measurement;

(*b*) that pay for work at time rates shall be the same for the same job.'

The action in *Barber* was against the employer, not the pension scheme, as it was founded on the equal pay concept. In brief, Mr Barber was made redundant at the age of 52, and received various cash benefits, but was only entitled to a deferred pension payable from his normal retirement date. A woman in the same position as Mr Barber would have been entitled to an immediate retirement pension in addition to redundancy pay. The total value of the benefits payable to a woman in these circumstances exceeded the amount paid to Mr Barber.

9.1 Sex equality

Mr Barber claimed successfully in the European Court that pensions should be treated as pay under *Article 141* and that, in consequence, he should be entitled to the same benefits as a woman of the same age. However, the European Court's decision was not retrospective and persons were not permitted (unless legal proceedings had already begun) to claim entitlement to a pension effective from a date prior to the date of judgment ie 17 May 1990.

The Maastricht Protocol (No 2) ('the Maastricht Protocol') annexed to the Treaty of European Union (7 February 1992) was ratified by the Member States in October 1993 and amended *Article 141* but constrained its application only to benefits accrued after 17 May 1990.

Although ECJ decisions are not legislative in nature, they are binding upon those to whom they are addressed (see *Article 249 (formerly Article 189)*). Where EC law has direct effect, it will generally override UK law. The principle that *Article 141* had direct effect was established on 8 April 1976 by the *Defrenne (No 2)* case which stated that 'direct effect' means that the protections given under *Article 141* apply directly to UK law without the need for any further national or European legislation. This was confirmed in the *Coloroll* case, which also made it clear that *Article 141* can be relied upon by both employees and their dependants against trustees who are bound to observe the principles of equal treatment.

The *Pensions Act 1995* ('*PA 1995*') incorporates the general requirements for equal treatment in pension schemes (see *sections 62* to *66*). These cover not only the terms on which scheme members are treated but also the terms on which employees are admitted to membership. Thus *section 62(3), PA 1995* provides that in relation to such a 'term' that is '… less favourable to the woman than it is to the man, the term shall be treated as so modified as not to be less favourable'. These provisions came into force on 1 January 1996, but their operation is to some extent retrospective, as explained later. These requirements are overriding so schemes must comply with them, irrespective of the actual provisions in their governing documentation. *Section 65, PA 1995* also empowers trustees of schemes with inadequate amendment powers in their governing documentation to make whatever rule amendments are necessary to ensure compliance with the equal treatment requirements without employer consent.

The Pensions Bill was first published on 12 February 2004. Although no date has been given for its implementation, it is understood at the time of writing that the Government is aiming for April 2005, but that some aspects may not come into force until April 2006. Clause 162 of the 21 May 2004 version of the Bill [HL Bill 73] provides in relation to the 'payment function' of the Board of the Pension Protection Fund for the equal treatment of men and women where a woman has been employed on like for like work, work rated as equivalent, work that is equivalent in terms of demand made on effort, skill and decision, where service in that employment was pensionable under an occupational pension scheme.

Clause 162 states, broadly, that if any payment functions relating to pensionable service under a scheme on or after 17 May 1990 in respect of the scheme are or become less favourable to either the man or the woman then modifications will be made to ensure that the payment function is no less favourable.

A 'payment function' is a function of the Board of the Pension Protection Fund relating to 'pension compensation', 'duty to pay scheme benefits unpaid at assessment date' and the 'discharge of liabilities in respect of money purchase benefits' (see Chapter 2).

There has been no clear policy or decision of principle underlying the development of UK law in this area. Indeed, it had been thought that the implementation of sex equality in pension schemes was simply not practicable. The cost issue alone was a significant deterrent to equalisation. Pension matters were expressly excluded from the equal pay and sex discrimination legislation passed in the 1970s and 1980s. Thus, the law has grown in fits and starts, very much in reaction to developments in Europe. It is an area of law in which most of the major issues have now been resolved, although a few anomalies remain.

A summary of relevant legislation and case law (UK and European) is set out at the end of the chapter.

ACCESS/ELIGIBILITY

General

9.2 The principle of equal access to pension scheme membership was established by the *Social Security Act 1973*, with detailed provision contained in regulations made under that Act (the *Occupational Pension Schemes (Equal Access to Membership) Regulations 1976 (SI 1976 No 142)*). These regulations were subsequently superseded by the *Occupational Pension Schemes (Equal Treatment) Regulations 1995 (SI 1995 No 3183)* (the *'Equal Treatment* Regulations'). Occupational pension schemes were required to provide equal access to membership for both men and women, but at that time there was no requirement for equal contributions or benefits. The relevant provisions of the *SSA 1973* were re-enacted in the *PSA 1993* (see *section 118*, now repealed), and are now covered in *sections 62* to *66* of *PA 1995*, and associated regulations.

The ECJ, in the 1994 judgments of *Vroege v NCIV Instituut C-57/93 [1994] ECR I–4541* and *Fisscher v Voorhuis Hengelo BV [1994] C-128/93 ECR I–4583*, unequivocally stated that the right to join an occupational pension scheme falls within the scope of *Article 141* of the *Treaty of Rome*, and is therefore covered by the prohibition on sex discrimination laid down by that Article. Therefore, this means that the direct effect of *Article 141* could be relied upon to claim (retrospectively) equal treatment from 8 April 1976 (the date of the *Defrenne Case* when it was established that *Article 141* had direct effect). In these two judgments the ECJ confirmed the earlier decision in *Bilka-Kaufhaus GmbH v Weber von Hartz C-170/84 [1986] ECR 1607* that discriminatory entry conditions which could not be objectively justified on grounds that related to the needs of the business, and not to the gender of the employee, were in breach of *Article 141*.

9.3 Sex equality

Part-time employees

Exclusion from membership – general

9.3 The exclusion of part-timers from scheme membership may infringe *Article 141* if it can be shown that there has been indirect sex discrimination.

There are two types of sex discrimination: direct and indirect. Direct sex discrimination occurs where, for example, women are denied entry to pension schemes but men are not. Indirect sex discrimination occurs where, for example, the pension scheme eligibility requirements are such that they are to the detriment of a significantly greater proportion of women than men because considerably fewer women can comply with them. By applying such restrictions (without objective justification not dependent on sex), women are being indirectly discriminated against on grounds of sex because considerably more women than men are being detrimentally affected.

It has generally been the case that considerably more women than men work part-time and, thus, may suffer indirect discrimination. Unfortunately, the ECJ did not expand on what it meant by 'a much greater number', nor did it specify a minimum number of hours that a part-timer must work in order to qualify for membership. Some light was shed on the latter point by the ECJ decision in *Nolte v Landesversicherungsanstalt Hannover C-317/93 [1996] All ER (EC) 212*, where it was decided that it was permissible to avoid granting pension benefits to employees who work less than 15 hours per week, where the reason is to achieve a social policy unrelated to any discrimination on grounds of sex. Here, the ECJ agreed that the fostering of 'minor' employment, for which there was a social demand, was practicable only if it was excluded from the relevant compulsory insurance provisions.

In the case of *Regina v Secretary of State for Employment ex parte Seymour-Smith and Another (case C-167/97 [1999] I.C.R. 447)*, the Advocate General considered among other questions the test for determining whether a measure adopted by a member state had 'such a disparate effect as between men and women as to amount to indirect discrimination'. The Advocate General opined that the best approach to this issue was to compare statistical evidence of the proportion of men able to satisfy the condition at issue and those unable to do so and to compare those proportions. If the statistics indicated that a 'considerably smaller percentage' of women than men was able to satisfy the condition, there was indirect sex discrimination unless the measure was justified by objective factors. He also said that a lesser but persistent and relatively constant disparity over a long period between men and women who satisfied the particular condition at issue could also amount to indirect sex discrimination.

Exclusion from membership with justification

9.4 Even if the workforce statistics suggest that there might be discrimination, a scheme will not have to admit part-timers if the employer can demonstrate that the exclusion can be explained by objectively justified factors unrelated to any discrimination on grounds of sex. In the *Bilka-Kaufhaus* case, the first case to consider the issue of part-timers becoming members of an occupational pension scheme, it was accepted that a rule that incidentally adversely affects more women than men may nevertheless be lawful. It is for national courts to decide whether a particular rule is or is not justifiable, but guidelines laid down by the ECJ suggest that the onus is on the employer to show that:

(*a*) the grounds put forward do not relate to the employee's sex;

(*b*) the grounds put forward relate to a real need of the employer; and

(*c*) the measures taken are appropriate and necessary to achieve the desired end.

An employer who can show, for example, that there is a genuine need to encourage full-time working patterns because they increase productivity or that part-timers will gain very little or nothing by joining a scheme that is contracted-out instead of remaining with the State Second Pension, may be able to exclude part-timers without infringement of *Article 141*.

Part-timers' claims

9.5 The *Equal Treatment Regulations (SI 1995 No 3183)* came into force on 1 January 1996 to supplement the requirements for equal treatment relating to occupational pension schemes provided for in *sections 62* to *66 of PA 1995*. The regulations extend the scope of the *Equal Pay Act 1970* to cover pensions as well as remuneration and apply the maximum arrears under the *Equal Pay Act 1970* to claims for indirect discrimination resulting from exclusion from an occupational pension scheme.

Thus, employees may, after 31 May 1995, claim under the *Equal Pay Act 1970*, providing that they bring the claim within six months from the date of leaving service (see *section 63(4)(c)* of *PA 1995*). This means that any part-timer still in employment will be able to bring a claim, whereas anyone who has left employment will have to claim, in respect of that employment, within six months of the date of leaving. Until 1 October 2002 the claim would have been limited to two years' backdated membership, but this has since been overruled by the *Preston* case as implemented by the *Part-time Workers (Prevention of Less Favourable Treatment) Regulations 2000 (Amendment) Regulations 2002 (SI 2002 No 2035)* (see 9.7 below). The *Equal Treatment Regulations (SI 1995 No 3183)* impose the full cost of funding the excluded employee's benefits after 31 May 1995 on the employer. Thus, the employee cannot be required to contribute in respect of benefits accrued after that date.

The European Court of Justice reviewed the validity of these time limits in *Preston v Wolverhampton Healthcare NHS Trust [2000] All ER (EC) 714*. This was followed by a referral to the House of Lords *Preston (No 2) [2001] 3 All ER 947*. The House of Lords confirmed that any national legislation was unlawful if

9.5 Sex equality

it prevented any service from being taken into account that was earlier than two years before the date of the claim. Therefore, pension benefits payable after the date of claim now have to be calculated by reference to all periods of service for which the employee should have been a scheme member (or, if later, from 8 April 1976). The significance for employees of this decision is that claims must, at the latest, be filed within six months of leaving employment. Employers also have to be aware that claims may arise not only from current part-time workers, but also from those who have ceased employment within the last six months or those who left employment more than six months previously but filed their claims within the six month period. The House of Lords made it clear that a series of short-term contracts can amount to a stable employment relationship and therefore employment does not terminate at the end of each individual contract. Further, time starts to run for bringing a claim only when that relationship is broken.

A Directions hearing was subsequently held in November 2001 in which further issues relating to the *Preston* decision were raised and test cases were selected for a full hearing. These hearings took place in June and July 2002 and the decision of the Employment Tribunal was published on 5 August 2002 (*Preston v Wolverhampton Healthcare NHS Trust (No.3) [2002] PLR 389*). A number of aspects of the Employment Tribunal's decision were appealed to the Employment Appeal Tribunal and the decision of the Employment Appeal Tribunal has now been reported (*Preston v Wolverhampton Healthcare NHS Trust (No.3) [2004] IRLR 96*).

The Employment Appeal Tribunal ('EAT') made the following determinations.

1. There is a breach of the *Equal Pay Act 1970* where a part-time worker is excluded from membership of a scheme, such membership is compulsory for full-time workers and, but for the exclusion, part-time workers would have been compulsory members of the scheme.

2. There is no breach of *Article 141* of the *Treaty of Rome* where membership of the scheme is compulsory for full-time workers but part-time workers are given the option of joining or not joining the scheme.

3. There is no continuing breach of *Article 141* by an employer failing to inform a part-time employee of his/her entitlement to join the pension scheme, unless that failure was itself on discriminatory grounds. However, employees may have a breach of contract claim in such circumstances on the basis of the employer's implied obligation to inform employees of advantageous contractual terms.

4. The six month time limit for bringing a claim under the *Equal Pay Act 1970*, begins to run when:

    (i) either party indicates that further contracts will not be offered or accepted;

    (ii) either party acts in a manner which is inconsistent with the relationship continuing;

Sex equality **9.5**

    (iii) the employer does not offer a new contract in circumstances where the periodicity of the preceding cycle of contracts indicates that it should have been offered;

    (iv) either party stops treating the relationship as stable;

    (v) the terms under which work is to be done alter radically;

    (vi) since liability for occupational pension schemes does not transfer under *TUPE*, liability under the *Equal Pay Act 1970* and *Article 141* for the transferor's failure to provide equal access to a scheme remains with the transferor; and

    (vii) following a *TUPE* transfer, time for bringing a claim against the transferor begins to run from the date the employee's employment with the transferee comes to an end. Although the EAT commented that an employee may be advised to take action shortly after a relevant transfer to lessen the risk of the transferor going out of business and 'disappearing'.

The last finding relating to *TUPE* is being appealed.

A settlement model has been agreed between HM Treasury and six public sector trade unions for the calculation of backdated employee contributions. This model may be used by employers and trustees to assist them in calculating the appropriate contribution required in order for part-time service to be reinstated. There is no requirement for the model to be followed. It can be accessed at www.employmenttribunals.gov.uk/england/ptsettlement.html.

In *Deutsche Telekom v Schroder [2000] ECR I-743* the ECJ confirmed that the *Defrenne* time limit does not prevent more favourable national legislation which may allow even further back-dating of periods of service, ie prior to 8 April 1976, thereby going further than European legislation itself.

The Department for Work and Pensions ('DWP') launched a consultation in July 2003 on amendments to the law governing claims from part-time workers. Draft Regulations (*The Pensions Act 1995* and the *Occupational Pension Schemes (Equal Treatment) (Amendment) Regulations 2003*) seek to amend *section 63* of the *PA 1995*, the *Equal Pay Act 1970* and the *Equal Treatment Regulations* by removing the two year time limit on backdating successful claims and permitting Court and Tribunal orders for retrospective admission back to April 1976 (see 9.7 below where the Department for Trade and Industry has made similar changes to *the Part-time Workers (Prevention of Less Favourable Treatment) Regulations (SI 2000 No 1551)*). The draft Regulations also deal with the issue of 'stable employment relationships' where breaks in employment do not necessarily frustrate claims. At the time of writing, the Regulations have not been implemented.

The right of access to a pension scheme for contract workers arose in the case of *Allonby v Accrington and Rossendale College [2001] IRLR 364 (CA))*. In 1996 the college terminated Mrs Allonby's part-time contract and employed her

9.5 Sex equality

services through an employment agency instead. Mrs Allonby complained, inter alia, that she was no longer eligible for membership of the Teachers' Superannuation Scheme and that this amounted to discrimination. The Court of Appeal held that by virtue of *section 1(2)(a)* of the *Equal Pay Act 1970*, Mrs Allonby was in a contract of employment for occupational pension purposes. The appeal was allowed on the ground that the Employment Tribunal had not adopted the correct approach to the questions whether the impact of the condition for continuous employment was proportionate and justifiable, and the case was remitted back to the Employment Tribunal for a further hearing on whether the employer had discriminated against the employee as a contract worker. The Court of Appeal also referred certain questions to the ECJ and on 13 January 2004, the ECJ gave its judgment in *Allonby v Accrington and Rossendale College (Case C-256/01 [2004] IRLR 224)*. The ECJ considered and gave judgment on the questions referred to it by the Court of Appeal as outlined below.

1. The first question concerned whether Mrs Allonby could bring an equal pay claim identifying a male full-time employee as her comparator (Mr J). The ECJ held that Mr J could not be a comparator for Mrs Allonby. Mr J was paid by the college and Mrs Allonby by an employment agency. There was no basis on which the differences in pay between Mrs Allonby and Mr J could be attributable to a single source. There was therefore no single body responsible for the inequality.

2. The ECJ considered whether Mrs Allonby was entitled to the right to equal pay conferred by *Article 141*. The ECJ held that the right extends to all 'workers' but does not cover an independent provider of services who is not in a relationship of subordination with the person who receives those services.

3. Where an equal pay claim relates to a private occupational pension scheme a 'worker' must identify, in the same undertaking, workers of the opposite sex who perform or have performed comparable work.

4. Where the pension scheme is statutory, an equal pay claim could be pursued where the statistics support it, even in the absence of an actual comparator. This is on the basis that the legislation is the sole source of the unequal treatment, ie there is no requirement for the comparator.

5. In order to succeed, Mrs Allonby would have to show that, among teachers who are 'workers' and fulfil all of the scheme's membership conditions except that of being employed under a contract of employment, there is a much higher percentage of women than men. It would be open for the college to objectively justify the difference in treatment.

In the recent case of *Brook Street Bureau (UK) Ltd v Dacas [2004] EWCA Civ 217*, Mrs D worked for a local authority through an agency. She claimed unfair dismissal against both the agency (Brook Street) and the local authority. Brook Street appealed the EAT's decision that it was her employer. The Court of Appeal held that Brook Street was not Mrs Dacas' employer. It went on to say that there might be an implied contract of employment between Mrs Dacas and the local authority. If the local authority had been a party to the appeal then that question would have been remitted to the Employment Tribunal for decision. The importance of this decision for pensions is that the Court of Appeal is indicating that agency workers could be employees of the organisation they provide their services to. This is a move away from the previously generally held view that the individual's only contractual relationship was with the agency. If such workers can establish implied contracts of employment then they may well also, as employees, have rights to membership of pension schemes.

It may be possible for employees who are excluded from schemes and who are outside the statutory time limits to complain to the Pensions Ombudsman, meaning that longer time limits may therefore apply. The Ombudsman has indicated that such exclusion could constitute maladministration and, consequently, he may investigate equal access complaints and indeed took this view in his determination of *Mrs D Copnall (Case No F00828, 28 September 2000)*. He determined that failure to admit part-timers retrospectively to a pension scheme was maladministration. However, this finding was overturned on appeal to the High Court in *Glossop v Copnall [2001] PLR 263* on 5 July 2001 when Sir Andrew Morritt held that a trustee's failure to comply with the requirements of legislation is not of itself maladministration (in fact, Mrs Copnall had not complained of the matter which the Ombudsman held to be maladministration). The High Court held that trustees acted properly in waiting for the relevant decisions by the European Court before granting backdated benefits.

The benefit of making a complaint to the Pensions Ombudsman is that the more generous limitation period of three years applies. The Ombudsman can also extend the three year limitation period in exceptional cases where the complainant was unaware of the event giving rise to the complaint or if it was not reasonably practicable for the complaint to be made or referred within the three year time limit. However, the Ombudsman is precluded from investigating complaints if proceedings have already been brought before the courts, and this includes Employment Tribunal claims (*PSA 1993, s 146(6)*).

With regard to the backdating of employee contributions where retrospective membership of a scheme has been granted, the Inland Revenue has indicated (see IR SPSS update No 26 March 1997) that in the case of schemes approved before 27 July 1989, if prescribed circumstances are satisfied, any employee granted back-dated membership of a pension scheme who is required to pay a contribution to purchase past service benefits, may pay contributions in excess of 15 per cent of remuneration. The same treatment applies to schemes approved on or after 27 July 1989 under the IR SPSS's discretionary powers. Tax relief for the contributions will be limited to 15 per cent of the individual's earnings for the tax year in which the payment is made. The Occupational Pensions Board (before it was dissolved) confirmed that National Insurance contributions may be refunded to both employers and employees where retrospective contracted-out membership has been granted. Pension Update No 131 dated 23 April 2002 noted the position on the tax treatment of pension contributions of part-time employees who are given rights following the decision in *Preston*. This Update confirms the Treasury's position that tax relief will only

9.6 *Sex equality*

be available on employees' back contributions up to 15 per cent of remuneration in the tax year in which the contributions were actually paid. The Update also provides that, where a member has already retired and taken benefits, an additional lump sum may not be paid, but if a transfer payment has been made an additional supplementary transfer can be paid. The Inland Revenue subsequently announced that Update 131 would be amended to permit pensioners to take a second lump sum and this announcement was given effect to in Pensions Update No 135 'Lump Sums' dated 20 December 2002.

The Government published its proposals for simplifying the pensions regime in its paper 'Simplifying the taxation of pensions: the Government proposals' and published the Finance Bill on 8 April 2004. In the context of the limits on employee contributions mentioned above, it is worth noting that from April 2006, when it is intended that the new regime will be implemented, the current limits on contributions will disappear (see Chapter 5).

Membership conditions

9.6 Some schemes/employers may impose membership conditions that indirectly discriminate against part-timers. An example of this type of practice was challenged in the complaint of Mrs E M Shillcock which was determined by the Pensions Ombudsman (*No F00317, 30 October 1997*). In that complaint, the scheme rules required the lower earnings limit for national insurance contributions (LEL) to be deducted when determining pensionable salary. Employees who earned less than the LEL were not eligible to join the scheme.

The Pensions Ombudsman ruled that this practice amounted to indirect discrimination against part-time employees earning less than the LEL. He said that only part of the LEL should have been deducted, representing the proportion that the employee's part-time hours bore to full-time hours. The decision was appealed to the High Court and the decision was overturned. It was held that the Pensions Ombudsman did not have jurisdiction to entertain a complaint regarding death in service benefits. In addition, the LEL offset was not discriminatory and had it been so, the intention to provide integration with the State scheme would have been sufficient objective justification (*Uppingham School v Shillcock [2002] EWHC 641 (Ch), [2002] 2CMLR 39*).

The Part-time Workers Regulations

9.7 The *Part-time Workers (Prevention of Less Favourable Treatment) Regulations 2000 (SI 2000 No 1551)* came into effect on 1 July 2000 and implemented *Directive 97/81/EC* as extended to the UK by *Directive 98/23/EC*. The Regulations require employers to treat part-time workers no less favourably than they treat full-time workers in respect of the same type of employment contract. In addition, employers may not treat less favourably an employee who, having worked full-time, returns to work on a part-time basis after absence, compared with the way the employee was treated when he/she worked full-time. This is subject to the defence of objective justification. It will not be necessary for a part- timer to prove indirect sexual discrimination in order to claim entitlement to the same benefits as full-time workers. So for example, part time workers cannot be excluded from a pension scheme which full-time workers are entitled to join unless this exclusion can be objectively justified. Employers will have to ensure that there are no restrictive conditions relating to access to, and benefits under, the pension scheme for part-time workers.

However, treating part-timers less favourably than full-timers can be justified on objective grounds provided that it can be shown that the less favourable treatment is (*a*) to achieve a legitimate objective (eg genuine business objective); (*b*) necessary to achieve that objective; and (*c*) an appropriate way to achieve that objective.

To reflect the ruling in *Preston* (see 9.5 above), the *Part-time Workers (Prevention of Less Favourable Treatment) Regulations 2000 (Amendment) Regulations 2002 (SI 2002 No 2035)* came into force 1 October 2002. The *2000 Part-time Regulations (regulation 8(8))* had limited the backdating of a claim to two years from the date upon which the complaint was presented. *Regulation 2(3)* of the *Amendment Regulations* removes this restriction. In addition, the distinction between fixed-term and permanent contract employees has been removed with the result that part-time workers on a fixed-term contract can now compare themselves with full-time workers on a permanent or fixed-term contract.

The first case under *the Part-time Workers (Prevention of Less Favourable Treatment) Regulations 2000 (SI 2000 No 1551)* to reach the Court of Appeal, is at the time of writing, currently being heard (*Matthews v Kent & Medway Towns Fire Authority [2003] IRLR 732*). Mr Matthews worked as a part-time fire-fighter and complained that he was discriminated against compared with full-time fire-fighters, in particular by not being granted access to the pension scheme. The EAT had held that part-time fire-fighters were not employed on the same contracts as full-time fire fighters, could not establish an appropriate comparator and therefore failed to establish unfavourable treatment.

The Fixed-term Employees Regulations

9.8 The *Fixed-term Employees (Prevention of Less Favourable Treatment) Regulations 2002 (SI 2002 No 2034)* came into force on 1 October 2002. The *Regulations* require employers to treat fixed-term employees no less favourably than permanent employees of the same employer who are doing similar work, unless there is an objective justification for the difference in treatment. The *Regulations* also provide that if a fixed-term employee is employed on a number of successive contracts for four years or more then their contract has the effect of a permanent contract unless the employer can objectively justify continuing employment on a fixed-term basis. The *Regulations* cover all employees under a fixed-term contract with the exclusion of apprentices, agency workers, the armed forces and those employed under a Government training scheme. It is worth noting that under *Regulation 8*, continuous employment can commence

9.9 *Sex equality*

(under a new or renewed contract) from 10 July 2002 for the purpose of calculating the four year period of a fixed-term contract (this is because the *Regulations* had to be implemented in the UK by 10 July 2002).

The *Regulations* cover, in addition to other contractual terms, pay and occupational pension schemes and thus access to pension arrangements and levels of benefits offered. However, the *Regulations* do not require term-per-term equality, providing the overall package offered is broadly comparable. Therefore, whilst in principle employers are required to offer fixed-term employees the same rights of entry to the pension scheme and the same benefits under it as they do for permanent employees, it may, however, be possible, in certain circumstances, to offer access on different terms, providing that the overall package of rights is comparable (see Chapter 7).

BENEFITS

General

9.9 Although the matter of equal access to pension schemes has presented many difficulties, many more questions have been raised over the issue of equality in benefits and contributions. This arises, in the main, by the fact that benefit design and computation have been dictated by actuarial science which takes into account, among other matters, the differing mortality rates of the sexes. The *Barber* decision (17 May 1990) meant that immediate action had to be taken, and various measures were adopted to implement equalisation. Many, but not all, of the issues raised by the *Barber* decision were clarified in subsequent ECJ decisions (notably, the 1994 *Coloroll* decision (*Coloroll Pension Trustees Ltd v Russell C-200/91 [1994] ECR I–4389*)). It had been feared by employers that the equalisation of benefits would have to be fully retrospective, although the ECJ in the *Coloroll* case confirmed that retrospection is only required in relation to benefits payable for periods of service from 17 May 1990. This is known as the 'accruals' basis. The reason for this limitation on equalisation of benefits for men and women is because it was held that Member States could argue that they had been led to believe that such discrimination was acceptable because of parallel EU legislation. In the case of *Quirk v Burton Hospital [2002] 24 PBLR* the Court of Appeal upheld the judgment of the Employment Appeal Tribunal which held that the limitation is correct and equal treatment under Article 141 in relation to scheme benefits does not apply to service prior to 17 May 1990.

The ECJ required employers and trustees to consider three time periods in respect of measures to equalise benefits under their schemes:

(*a*) the period up to 17 May 1990, when benefits need not be equalised;

(*b*) the period from 17 May 1990 to the date when scheme benefits are equalised, when benefits must be 'levelled up' (ie increased to the level enjoyed by the advantaged sex); and

Sex equality **9.11**

(c) the period after the date when scheme benefits are equalised. Although *Article 141* itself permits benefits to be 'levelled up' or 'levelled down' in respect of this period, the UK decision in the *Lloyds Bank* case should be noted at this point. (*Lloyds Bank Pension Trust Corporation Ltd v Lloyds Bank plc [1996] OPLR 181*) In this case, the High Court decided that future accrual rates could not be reduced to meet equalisation objectives. This may be a decision turning on the particular facts of the case (summarised in the table of cases at the end of this chapter), and certainly flows against the tide of the other main cases, notably *Smith v Advel Systems Ltd C-408/92 [1994] ECR I–4435*.

Derived rights

9.10 The requirement for equality in pay and pensions applies also to spouses, survivors, dependants and others who are entitled to claim benefits through an employee's membership of a scheme. In *Ten Oever v Stichting Bedrijfspenioenfonds voor het Glazwenwassers-en Schoonmaakbedrijf [1993] ECR I-4879* the ECJ confirmed that a survivor's pension falls within the scope of *Article 141*. Thus, any scheme benefit provided for the wife of a male member must also be provided for the husband of a female member. The ECJ in the *Coloroll* case confirmed that, as for members' benefits, this requirement for equal treatment only applies in relation to service from 17 May 1990, except for those claims brought before this date.

Transfers

9.11 Schemes which accept transfer payments in respect of benefits accrued since 17 May 1990 will bear the burden of equalisation as a consequence of any inadequacy in the transfer payments received. The ECJ considered (in *Coloroll*) that the rights accruing to an employee from *Article 141* cannot be affected by the fact that he changes his job and has to join a new scheme, with his accrued pension rights being transferred to the new scheme. However, in the event of an inadequate transfer payment being made, the ECJ envisaged the receiving scheme making a claim (under national law) against the transferring scheme for the additional sums required to equalise the benefits to be paid. In practice trustees of the receiving scheme will also obtain an indemnity from the transferring scheme to cover such additional sums as may be required.

It may be that transferring employees have a claim against both the trustees of the transferring scheme and of the receiving scheme. The *Acquired Rights Directive* (77/187 EEC) was designed to safeguard employees' rights and ensure continuing employment following a transfer of a business undertaking. However, provisions contained in a contract of employment or collective agreement relating to an occupational pension scheme are specifically excluded. There have been a number of challenges to this pensions exclusion over the years. The case of *Beckmann v Dynamco Whicheloe Macfarlane Ltd, Case C-164/00, [2002] 64 PBLR; [2002] All ER (D) 05 (Jun)* held that benefits

9.12 *Sex equality*

payable on redundancy do transfer under the Acquired Rights Directive. The effect of this judgment appears to be that redundancy benefits payable under an occupational pension scheme and other benefits payable before normal retirement date may transfer. The decision in *Beckmann* has recently been approved in the case of *Martin v South Bank University [2004] IRLR 74* where it was decided that only benefits paid from the time when an employee reaches the end of his normal working life can be classified as 'old age' benefits within the meaning of *Article 3(3)* and are thus excluded from automatic transfer under *TUPE*. The UK Government is proposing to amend the *TUPE* provisions relating to pensions (see Chapter 7).

The position of money purchase schemes which receive unequalised transfer payments is uncertain. Clearly, there would be serious practical difficulties in complying with the obligation to equalise, possibly entailing the re-allocation of funds in individual members' accounts. Arguably, the *Coloroll* decision does not encompass money purchase schemes (see 9.15 below) but pending clarification of the issue, the trustees of such schemes should act with great caution. For example, trustees should consider very carefully whether this would be an appropriate circumstance in which they should exercise any discretion (in the provisions of the scheme) to refuse transfers.

Bridging pensions

9.12 Bridging pensions aim to achieve a form of equality between men and women in the pensions received where men have retired before State pension age, by taking into account the earlier date from which women are eligible to receive the State pension. Thus, bridging pensions could be paid to both men and women who take early retirement at, say, age 55, and stop at age 60 for women, but to continue to age 65 for men. In *Birds Eye Walls v Friedl M Roberts [1993] PLR 281*, the pension for a female ex-employee was reduced when she reached age 60, whereas a man would have received a full pension to age 65. The ECJ was asked whether bridging pensions where in breach of *Article 141*. The ECJ held that bridging pensions were not discriminatory because they were designed to remove an existing inequality arising as a consequence of the different ages that State pension commences for men and women. This decision can be criticised, however, in that it allows employers to reduce a pension on the assumption that a woman is in receipt of a full State pension, whether or not that is in fact the case. It is to be noted that *section 64(2) of PA 1995* and the *Equal Treatment Regulations (SI 1995 No 3183)* exclude bridging pensions paid in these circumstances from the ambit of the equal treatment rule contained in *section 62, PA 1995*.

The decision in *Birds Eye* is difficult to consider against the decision in *Bestuur van het Algemeen Burgerlijk Pensioenfonds v Beune [1995] All ER (EC) 97* where the ECJ held that it was unlawful for a scheme to make deductions in respect of the State pension where it had the effect of producing a lower pension for men but not women from the scheme. In the Netherlands, the Dutch state scheme gives married men a higher pension than married women.

Actuarial factors

9.13 The use of actuarial factors in funded final salary occupational pension schemes which vary according to sex was held by the ECJ in *Coloroll* not to fall within the scope of *Article 141*. This was so even though the amount of transfer value for a man would be lower than for a woman in consequence of the actuarial factors used in the assessment of the capital sum transferred that are based on life expectancy which differs between men and women. (It should be noted, however, that the European Commission has made proposals for a Directive on equal treatment in the supply of goods and services. This would impact on annuity rates if it were to become law. Moreover, it is considered likely that a change in law would not result in higher annuities for women, but rather that the more conservative, female rates would be applied to both sexes.)

The issue of unequal transfer values had previously been considered in *Neath v Hugh Steeper Ltd [1993] ECR I–6935*, in which the ECJ decided that lump sum payments and transfer values were not 'pay' within *Article 141*. It considered that it is only the employer's commitment to the payment of a periodic pension at a particular level which constitutes pay within the meaning of *Article 141*. It decided that the funding arrangement by which the pension was to be secured falls outside the scope of *Article 141*. (Although this was confirmed in the *Coloroll* decision, the ECJ has made the position clear only in relation to final salary schemes.)

It was confirmed in *Neath* that as employees' contributions were deducted from salaries, employees' contribution rates must be the same for both men and women as they constitute an element of pay within *Article 141*. Thus, although contributions made by employees must be equal as between men and women, as these contributions are an element of their pay, employers' contributions are pitched to ensure the adequacy of the funds necessary to secure the future payment of periodic pensions and may be unequal due to the use of sex-based actuarial factors. Inequalities in the amounts of capital benefits or substitute benefits (eg where a dependant's pension is payable in return for surrender of part of the member's annual pension or where a reduced pension is paid on early retirement) whose value can be determined only on the basis of the arrangements chosen for funding the scheme, were likewise considered to be outside the scope of *Article 141*.

Additional voluntary contributions

9.14 Equality principles apply to all pension benefits under a scheme and it is irrelevant whether they are attributable to employers' or employees' contributions. However, where the scheme does no more than provide the necessary arrangements for the management of contributions and payments of the resulting benefits (in relation to money purchase additional voluntary contributions) those resulting benefits are not covered by *Article 141*. Consequently additional benefits deriving from contributions paid by employees on a voluntary basis are not covered by *Article 141*, as these additional contributions are to secure

9.15   *Sex equality*

benefits over and above those which they are entitled to expect by reason of their employment and cannot, therefore, be regarded as pay within the meaning of *Article 141*.

Money purchase benefits

9.15   In money purchase schemes, the pension commitment of the employer is an obligation to pay a defined level of contribution. The ECJ has not directly decided how the principle of equal treatment is to be applied to money purchase schemes. What has been established is that the commitment or 'promise' to the employee, which must be equal between men and women, is to be distinguished from the funding considerations, which are not covered by *Article 141*.

Whilst it is clear that employee contributions must be equal as between men and women, the position in relation to employer contributions is less certain. It is generally accepted that, as the employer in a money purchase scheme does not promise any particular level of benefit, the commitment is the contribution, and as such these must be equal. In schemes which use sex-based actuarial factors, it is not possible to have both equal contributions and equal benefits. If the *Neath* case applies to money purchase schemes, women are most likely to be the disadvantaged sex. This is because the capital sum built up will not secure the same amount of pension for a woman as for a man. Her periodic pension will be lower as it will take account of the expectation that she will live longer. *Article 6* of the *Equal Treatment Directive* specifically allows a differential where the ultimate aim is to achieve equality.

PA 1995 (*section 64(3)(b)*) seems to allow schemes to operate on the basis of equal employee contributions and unequal benefits. In contrast, the DSS directed that where trustees have been responsible for providing or securing a pension, this must be equal. Where a member exercises an open market option provided under the provisions of the scheme, the DSS considered the benefit to be the capital sum, which again must be equal. This appears to be a distinction without a difference, but until unisex actuarial factors are an accepted norm in the insurance domain, it would be safer for schemes to make the open market option available to members and let them make the arrangements for securing their benefits with the insurer of their choice. The member is not subject to the same constraints on trustees in securing a pension. On taking his capital sum from the scheme, the trustees are released from any further liability to the member, and it is for the member to buy the best pension he can in the annuity marketplace.

Retirement ages

State pension age and contractual retirement age

9.16   State pension age is being equalised over a ten year period commencing in the year 2010. The new pension age of 65 for women will apply to those born on or after 6 March 1955. The public sector has had to offer equal pension

Sex equality **9.16**

ages since the coming into effect of *Directive 76/209* in 1979, as the ECJ in *Marshall v Southampton & SW Hampshire Area Health Authority [1986] ECR 723* held that the Directive had direct effect on the employer in that case as the employer was an 'emanation of the State'. This decision did not affect pension rights, as this Directive permitted inequality founded on unequal State pension provision.

Ascertaining the contractual retirement age is not as straightforward as it seems. If the contract of employment is silent on the retirement age the established custom and practice will be looked at to determine when employees have retired in the past in relation to that particular position. However, the contractual retirement age must not be different for men and women doing the same job.

The *Equal Treatment 'Framework' Directive (2000/78/EC)* outlaws discrimination on the grounds of age, although the UK is not due to implement this aspect of the Directive before 2006. A Government Consultation Paper 'Equality and Diversity: Age Matters' was published in July 2003 and further consultation is due to take place in Spring 2004 with draft regulations to be published by the end of 2004 (see Chapter 7). The *Directive* is limited to employment and occupation and does not apply to the State pension scheme. In addition, *Article 6(2)* of the *Framework Directive* provides a specific exemption for certain aspects of pension scheme rules including ages for admission, entitlement to retirement and invalidity benefits and allows fixing of different ages for employees or groups of employees. However, *Article 6(2)* states explicitly that age discrimination which amounts to sex discrimination will be prohibited.

In the ECJ case, *Kutz-Bauer v Freie und Hansestadt Hamburg [2003] All ER (D) 327 (Mar)*, provisions allowing workers over 55 to work part-time applied only until the date on which the worker became entitled to a statutory old age pension. For most women this was 60 and for most men it was 65. It was held that this was capable of breaching the *Equal Treatment Directive* and it was for the national court to determine whether there was in fact indirect discrimination which could not be objectively justified.

In October 2003, in the case of *Secretary of State for Trade and Industry v Rutherford, Bentley and Harvest TownCircle Limited EAT [2003] 78 PBLR*, the Employment Appeal Tribunal overturned a tribunal's decision that the statutory upper age limit which applies to complaints of unfair dismissal and for statutory redundancy pay was unlawful for being indirectly discriminatory on grounds of sex. As a result, until the Government introduces legislation outlawing age discrimination the current statutory age limit continues to apply.

It is possible (and permissible) for employers to have differing retirement ages for different positions, as long as the demarcation of positions is not sex discriminatory (whether direct or indirect). This principle was upheld in *Bullock v The Alice Ottley School [1992] IRLR 564* in which the Court of Appeal decided that a school's grounds and maintenance staff (who had a retirement age of 65) could have a different retirement age from its domestic staff (who had

9.17 *Sex equality*

a retirement age of 60). However, where different groups of employees are treated in this way, the court will look very closely at the reasons given to justify the difference.

Retirement age under the pension scheme

9.17 Although the *Barber* case established beyond doubt that pensions were 'pay' and, in consequence, that pensions had to be equal for men and women, the questions as to how and from which date equalisation was to be implemented were not answered until later. These issues were addressed by the ECJ in the *Coloroll* and *Smith v Avdel* cases. In the *Smith v Avdel* case, the employer proposed to implement the *Barber* decision by raising the retirement age of women to that of the men, and including the period prior to the date of the *Barber* decision. The ECJ held that until equalisation measures had been taken, the only proper method of compliance with *Article 141* was to confer upon the disadvantaged sex those advantages enjoyed by the favoured sex, in respect of service after 17 May 1990.

Thus, from 17 May 1990 until the date of the equalisation of retirement ages, the pension rights of the men had to be enhanced to correlate with the lower retirement age of the women, ie 60. For the period prior to the date of the *Barber* decision, the ECJ determined that there was no requirement to equalise benefits.

With regard to the period following the date of equalisation, the ECJ stated that *Article 141* did not preclude equalisation measures which had the effect of reducing the benefits of the (previously) advantaged sex. *Sections 62 to 66 of PA 1995* (which aim to bring into statute the effect of *Barber* and the subsequent cases) do not preclude this either. However, neither *Article 141* nor *PA 1995* overrides trustees' duties to act in their members' best interests (or an employer's duty of good faith) and so these duties must still be borne in mind.

The equal treatment requirement was not, therefore, a victory for women. Where retirement ages have been equalised upwards, women will have to work for longer or face the risk of a reduction in their pensions if they still wish to retire at age 60. Further, as the decisions in *Coloroll* and *Neath* confirm, sex-based actuarial factors may be applied which could further reduce the amount of pension received. This would affect transfer values, which on transfer to a money purchase scheme would lead to unequal benefits. However where a prospective pensionable service factor is used, for example on ill-health early retirement, this can increase the resultant pension.

CONCLUSIONS AND PRACTICAL ISSUES

General

9.18 Although most of the equality issues raised by the *Barber* case have now been settled, a few anomalies remain. There is also an increasing realisation that equalisation does not necessarily lead to equity. The main difficulty which has confronted many employers and trustees is how to implement the equal treatment requirement in their schemes.

Employers and trustees

9.19 It was unclear from the *Barber* decision whether *Article 141* imposed an obligation both on the trustees and the employer in respect of equal treatment. Whilst the primary obligation to implement equalisation falls upon the employer, the position of trustees was clarified by the ECJ in the *Coloroll* case. The ECJ confirmed that trustees in the exercise of their powers and in the performance of their obligations are also bound to observe the principles of equal treatment. Although the ECJ decisions are overriding, *PA 1995* clearly envisages schemes being able to be amended so as to comply with the equal treatment provisions. *Section 65, PA 1995* empowers trustees or managers of occupational pension schemes to make amendments by resolution where either they do not have the necessary amendment powers to implement the equal treatment requirements, or they do have powers available but the procedure for implementation is 'liable to be unduly complex or protracted' or 'involves the obtaining of consents which cannot be obtained, or can only be obtained with undue delay or difficulties'.

Review of scheme documentation

9.20 In as much as the equal treatment cases are overriding, clarity and consistency in the day to day application of the equal treatment principles is only likely to be achieved when scheme documentation is brought into line with the current law. Areas requiring careful consideration include:

(*a*) conformity of the (equalised) normal retirement age under the scheme and the contract of employment;

(*b*) equality in early retirement terms, survivors' benefits, and transfer arrangements; and

(*c*) allowing trustees the discretion to grant enhanced benefits in individual cases.

Scheme amendments

9.21 As stated above (see 9.9 and 9.17 above), employers and trustees must consider three time periods in respect of measures to equalise benefits under their schemes:

(*a*) the period up to 17 May 1990, when benefits need not be equalised;

(*b*) the period from 17 May 1990 to the date equalisation takes place, when benefits must be 'levelled up'; and

(*c*) the period after the date equalisation takes place, when benefits can be levelled up or down.

9.22 *Sex equality*

Careful scrutiny of the power of amendment will be necessary to ensure that any changes made are a valid exercise of that power. Amendment powers often contain an express restriction that accrued rights cannot be reduced without members' consent. Even in the absence of specific wording to that effect, such a restriction is consistent with a trustee's fiduciary duty to act in the best interests of the members and it is generally accepted to be consistent with the employer's duty of good faith towards its employees. Further, *PA 1995, section 67* imposes restrictions on scheme amendments which reduce the accrued rights or entitlements of members.

Where there is no amendment power, or inadequate provision, the power conferred by *PA 1995, section 65* must be used to implement the equal treatment requirements. The exercise of the statutory power may place the employer in a vulnerable position, as it is a power to be used by the trustees alone, and not, as is usually found in scheme provisions, either an employer's power or a joint power of the employer and the trustees.

The power of amendment is a fiduciary power and, as mentioned above, its exercise is, therefore, subject to a duty of good faith to the beneficiaries of the scheme. Thus, in seeking to amend the scheme to comply with the equal treatment requirements, the best interests of the whole membership must be considered. Following the decision in *Van den Akker v Stichting Shell PF [1994] ECR I–4527*, it is not possible to 'red circle' groups of members, ie to apply preferential benefits to a group of members who were exclusively women or men, unless the group delineation was objectively justified and, thus, not sex discriminatory.

Employment law considerations

9.22 In considering how to implement the equal treatment requirements, careful review must be made of the employees' contracts of employment and the precise wording of the 'pension promise' (if any) contained in it. Changes made by an employer to contracts (for example, amending the normal retirement date from 65 to 60), could give rise to a claim of breach of contract by the employee, although loss would have to be shown to substantiate a claim for damages. Where possible, and particularly where terms of employment are clearly worsened, the consent of the employees should be sought.

New employees

9.23 Employers are not constrained to deal with new employees in the same way as existing employees. Thus, new employees may be employed on terms differing from those of current employees, including a different (but equal between men and women) retirement age. However, once the UK enacts legislation prohibiting discrimination on the grounds of age in compliance with the *Framework Directive*, such differentials may amount to age discrimination.

Ill-health early retirement

9.24 Where the provisions of a scheme calculate ill-health pensions as inclusive of prospective service to normal pension age, a lowered normal pension age will operate to reduce the amount of pension payable. It is to be noted that in respect of the 'levelling up' period described at 9.9(b) above, benefits calculated by reference to a member's prospective service to normal retirement age must be calculated by reference to the higher normal retirement date.

Single sex schemes

9.25 The *Coloroll* case confirmed that *Article 141* does not apply to schemes which have at all times had members of only one sex nor could *section 62* of *PA 1995* give rise to a claim in such a case. However, it is not permitted to establish a scheme open to only one sex.

Transfers

9.26 The ECJ in *Coloroll* stated that benefits on transfer must be equalised by the receiving scheme if the transfer value does not take into account any inequality for service from 17 May 1990 to the date of transfer. This applies to group transfers and individual transfers alike, and the ECJ has confirmed that, if necessary, a claim can be made by a receiving scheme against the transferring scheme under national law in respect of any additional liability. In the case of individual transfers, it is unlikely that a discharge form signed by a member in favour of a transferring scheme will constitute an effective defence, unless it can be shown that the member fully understood that he was waiving any claim he might have following the *Barber* decision. Unequalised transfer values should not be accepted by a scheme.

Actuarial issues

9.27 The use of unisex actuarial factors is permitted. Unisex tables appear to be logical, and the aim of achieving equal contributions and equal benefits would seem to be desirable. However, as long as insurance companies remain outside the constraints of *Article 141* in their assessments of risk, this disparity with company pension schemes would distort the market.

Unisex annuity rates are already required in securing the protected rights element of contracted-out money purchase schemes and personal pension schemes (see chapter 4). Similarly, the Inland Revenue has introduced unisex commutation rates to ascertain the maximum benefits available from exempt approved schemes (see chapter 5 as concerns Inland Revenue limits). In respect of pre-Finance Act 1989 Continued Rights members, schemes are permitted to switch to or, indeed, keep, unisex rates provided these do not exceed either 12:1

9.28 *Sex equality*

or the existing permitted rates for male members. For other members, the maximum 12:1 commutation factor applies to both male and female members (see 5.6).

Inland Revenue requirements

9.28 The IR SPSS produced an update (No 27) on Equal Treatment dated 2 May 1997 which had immediate and, if desired, retrospective effect. Where a member has different normal retirement ages for different periods of service, as envisaged by the ECJ, the IR SPSS will only take into account the current normal retirement age and apply this age to all services.

This is likely to be of particular concern to members subject to the pre-1989 tax regime who are treated as taking early retirement (for example, where a woman retires at age 60 in a scheme which has now equalised retirement ages at age 65, but which preserves a previous right to retire at age 60 with unreduced benefits). This is due to the fact that the IR SPSS would normally calculate maximum benefits by reference to the higher retirement age which, in applying the usual N/NS formula (ie the ratio of completed to potential service) would reduce the maximum approvable benefits under the scheme. However, in circumstances like these, the IR SPSS Update contains an easement which would allow potential service to be calculated and paid on the basis that the unequalised normal retirement date still applied to that member. Men would have to be treated in the same way, at least in respect of service after 17 May 1990, so as to comply with the equal treatment requirements.

Update No 27 also allows, where despite the application of the easements unequal benefits are still yielded in respect of equal service, the benefits of the disadvantaged sex to be calculated on the same basis as the advantaged sex even if normal revenue limits related to the old or new normal retirement age would be exceeded for that member.

From a procedural viewpoint, the IR SPSS has confirmed that advance clearance of changes to effect an equalised normal retirement age is not required, provided that the new normal retirement age is not less than 60. Once the change has been made, the IR SPSS will need to be notified.

Update No 27 was clarified by Update No 68 dated 29 August 2000, which provides that the easements apply to members with continued rights in schemes where the normal retirement ages for males and females have been equalised. This includes all members with continued rights and members who joined after equalisation and those still to join an equalised scheme.

Contracted-out schemes/Guaranteed Minimum Pensions (GMPs)

9.29 The issue of equalisation of GMPs (see chapter 4) is fraught with difficulty, and the relevant provisions of *PA 1995, section 126* deal only with the future equalisation of the contracting-out arrangements. Neither the ECJ nor the

Government have addressed all the difficulties that arise as a result of the fundamental design of GMPs correlating to the State scheme with its discriminatory pension ages. Specifically, the difficulties arise out of the methods of calculation and revaluation applied to the GMP element of a pension before and after State pension age is attained. The *Equal Treatment Regulations* permit pension increases to be paid at different rates on GMPs and pensions in excess of GMPs, insofar as the difference does not exceed the SERPS increase for the same period. The *Equal Treatment Regulations* do not, however, legalise the differences in benefits caused by the contracting-out legislation.

The determination by the Pensions Ombudsman in *Williamson* dated 7 January 2000 (*No: H00177*) restated the requirement to equalise GMPs. The Pensions Ombudsman directed that the trustee and the company equalise GMPs in compliance with the equal treatment rule under *section 62* of the *PA 1995*. However, he did not make any directions as to how this should be done and noted that:

> 'Parliament apparently concluded that salary-related schemes should have the flexibility and freedom to make their own arrangements as to how equalisation should be achieved.' (paragraph 37).

Furthermore he expressed the view that the method of equalisation chosen should not be one that could lead to some members of the scheme being adversely affected.

The *Williamson* determination was subsequently overturned in the High Court in *Marsh Mercer Pension Scheme v Pensions Ombudsman [2001] 16 PBLR (28)* on the basis that the Ombudsman cannot make a direction relating to the equalisation of GMPs and compliance with the equal treatment rules in *section 62* of *PA 1995* as the question was too wide ranging and the nature and effect of the Ombudsman's direction was so uncertain that he was in error making it. The Ombudsman's jurisdiction did not extend to his making a decision on the question of equalisation of GMPs as this matter had an impact on other members of the scheme without allowing them the opportunity to put their case. Rimer J added that GMPs in isolation did not have to be equalised on the basis that they are not a distinct part of a pension scheme. However, the position as to whether total benefits should be equalised was undecided. Therefore, the issues as to the application of *Article 141* and the method of equalisation of GMPs remain undetermined and trustees currently attempting to wind up contracted-out final salary schemes are left with little guidance as to how to proceed.

In its Update 3 'Winding Up' dated August 2003, Opra recognised that trustees have concerns regarding GMP equalisation. The Update states that, although Opra does not endorse any particular approach taken to resolving the question of GMP equalisation, it expects trustees to consider the funding position of their scheme and the costs to the fund of equalising benefits, and comments that 'the cost and time involved in devising and implementing a methodology for equalisation may well outweigh the value in terms of benefits to members'.

9.30 *Sex equality*

The rulings of the European Court in *Bestuur van het Algemeen Burgerlijk Pensioenfonds v Beune [1995] All ER (EC) 97* and *Birds Eye Walls v Friedl M Roberts Case C [1993] PLR 203* (see 9.12) appear contradictory in deciding whether a scheme may provide unequal benefits to men and women to remove an existing inequality as a result of the different ages that State pension commences for men and women. These two cases were considered by the High Court in *Uppingham School v Shillcock [2002] EWHC 641 (Ch), [2002] 2CMLR 39* in its ruling that an LEL offset to integrate with the State scheme was not indirect sex discrimination and, had it been so, that it would have been objectively justified. This case would appear to support the argument that unequal GMPs are objectively justifiable if the intention is to integrate with the State scheme.

In the recent case of *Leadenhall Independent Trustees v Welham [2004] All ER (D) 423 (Mar)*, the scheme was winding up with a surplus and the trustee sought directions as to whether it had the power to allocate funds in such a way as to neutralise the gender discrimination of GMPs. The court said that the trustee could augment deferred benefits as there was express power in the governing documentation to do so. In the case of existing pensioners (for which there was no express power of augmentation) the court was not willing to say whether or not the trustee could augment benefits, nor was it prepared to state whether overriding EC equal treatment law could be applied. The court suggested that if the trustee did decide to go ahead and augment benefits for pensioners, it should consider taking out trustee insurance.

Alan Pickering's review of pension schemes, the Pickering Report ('A Simpler Way to Better Pensions') published July 2002 recommended a new, simpler reference scheme test (RST) for contracted-out salary-related schemes and that schemes should be able to convert all benefits including GMPs to RST benefits, thereby removing equalisation issues. The Pensions Bill, introduced in the House of Commons on 10 February 2004, contains modifications to the payment of contracted-out benefits but the general simplification of these benefits previously put forward by the Government has not been included.

Same sex partners

9.30 The legal position of same sex partners was examined in the case of *Grant v South West Trains Limited [1998] All ER (EC) 193*. This was an employment case involving the granting of travel concessions. South West Trains refused to give travel concessions to Ms Grant's same sex partner when she was promoted to a post at South West Trains previously occupied by an employee whose opposite sex partner had obtained such concessions. The ECJ found that the refusal of the employer to grant the travel concessions in this case did not constitute discrimination prohibited by *Article 141* of the *EC Treaty* or *Council Directive 75/117/EEC* of 10 February 1975. The ECJ said that Community Law as it stands at present does not cover discrimination based on sexual orientation. If the ECJ had decided in favour of the plaintiff, this would have had

Sex equality **9.30**

implications for pension benefits provided for unmarried couples which would have to be the same for all such couples irrespective of gender.

The European *Equal Treatment 'Framework' Directive (2000/78)*, establishing a general framework for equal treatment in employment and occupation, requires Member States to enact legislation to prohibit discrimination on the grounds of religion, belief, disability, age and sexual orientation. The time limit for compliance was December 2003 for discrimination on the grounds of religion or belief or sexual orientation, October 2004 for discrimination on grounds of disability and 2006 for discrimination on the grounds of age. In the context of sexual orientation discrimination, the Directive provides that pension schemes which recognise unmarried heterosexual partners will be required to recognise same sex partners. However, a loop hole in the Directive allows pension schemes which recognise married couples only to continue to do so.

The *Employment Equality (Sexual Orientation) Regulations 2003 (SI 2003 No 1661)* are designed to implement the Directive in respect of sexual orientation discrimination and outlaw discrimination in employment and vocational training on grounds of sexual orientation. The *Regulations* came into force on 1 December 2003 and protect heterosexuals, homosexuals and bisexuals.

The *Regulations* prohibit direct discrimination (ie treating people less favourably than others on grounds of sexual orientation) and indirect discrimination (ie applying a provision, criterion or practice which disadvantages people of a particular sexual orientation and which is not justified in objective terms) (*regulation 3*). The *Regulations* also prohibit unwanted conduct that violates people's dignity or creates an intimidating, hostile, degrading, humiliating or offensive environment (harassment) (*regulation 5*) and the treatment of people less favourably because of action they have taken under or in connection with the new legislation (victimisation) (*regulation 4*).

As with other anti-discrimination legislation, the *Regulations* cover the terms of a person's employment. As is established law, this extends to the field of occupational pensions. The primary target of the *Regulations* as they apply to pension schemes would seem to be to prevent discrimination in respect of dependant's pensions (ie where the scheme rules provide that a pension may be paid to an unmarried opposite sex partner but not to a partner of the same sex). If a scheme provides benefits to opposite sex unmarried partners but not same sex partners, then this would constitute direct discrimination.

If the scheme provides benefits to married partners but not unmarried opposite sex partners then there would be no actual discrimination as *regulation 25* states that it will not be unlawful discrimination if access to benefits is prevented or restricted by reference to martial status. This 'loophole' arises out of the Government's interpretation of the Directive's provision that it is without prejudice to national laws on marital status and benefits dependant thereon.

However, six unions sought a judicial review of the *Regulations* backed by the Trades Union Congress ('TUC'). The most significant aspect of the legal

9.31 *Sex equality*

challenge is centred on *regulation 25*. The unions stated that because it allows UK pension schemes to continue to discriminate in favour of married people, *regulation 25* is allowing indirect discrimination against homosexuals as they are not able to marry their partners. The unions argued that apart from a misinterpretation of the *EU Framework Directive*, the proposed *regulation* may also be a breach of the *Human Rights Act 1998*. A further aspect of the challenge related to *regulation 7(3)* which allows for sexual orientation discrimination where someone works for an organised religion. The unions argued that the law may allow employers to stop gay, lesbian or bisexual people from working at church groups and other religious organisations. Irrespective of this challenge, the introduction of civil partnerships with effect from 2010 may mean that a spouse's pension rule will need to be amended. It was reported on the 26 April 2004 that the trade unions lost both aspects of their challenge. The High Court upheld the legality of the *Regulations* and refused to condemn them as 'incompatible' with European law.

It should also be noted that it has been reported that the Pension Protection Fund (see Chapter 2) may face legal challenge on the basis that the Government has decided to exclude survivor benefits for unmarried partners.

The *Employment Equality (Sexual Orientation)(Amendment) Regulations 2003* (*SI 2003 No 2827*) have amended the *Regulations* to extend their provisions to the trustees and managers of occupational pension schemes. The amended *Regulations* make provision for every occupational pension scheme to be treated as including a 'non-discrimination' rule prohibiting discrimination contrary to the *Regulations*.

Civil partnerships

9.31 The Civil Partnerships Bill was published on 31 March 2004. The Bill provides for same-sex couples to obtain legal recognition of their relationship by registering as civil partners. Registered civil partners will have access to rights and responsibilities including, for example;

- employment and pensions benefits;
- the duty to provide maintenance for a civil partner;
- the duty to provide maintenance for children of the partnership; and
- recognition under intestacy rules.

At the time of writing, the pensions provisions (clause 245 and schedule 24 of HL Bill 79 (25 May 2004)) are brief and will no doubt be clarified by regulations. Clause 245 gives the power to Ministers to amend pensions legislation for the 'purpose of, or in connection with, making provision with respect to pensions, allowances or gratuities for the surviving civil partners or dependants of deceased civil partners'. Contracted-out defined benefit schemes will be required to provide survivor benefits from the protected rights accrued after commencement of the Bill if the Member is in a registered civil partnership at retirement. Also, specific references to 'spouse' or 'marriage' will be extended to refer also to 'civil partners' and to 'civil partnership'.

Gender Recognition Bill

9.32 Case law and, more recently, the publication of the Gender Recognition Bill have developed the law relating to transsexuals. In the case of *Goodwin v United Kingdom [2002] IRLR 664*, the European Court of Human Rights held that UK law was in breach of the European Convention of Human Rights in not allowing Ms Goodwin to marry or enjoy the benefits and burdens of her new gender. In particular, it was held that Ms Goodwin was entitled to the pension rights available to members of her new gender.

In its judgment of 10 April 2003 in *Bellinger v Bellinger [2003] UKHL 21, [2003] 2 All ER 593* the House of Lords considered the position of Mrs Bellinger, a transsexual woman who had undergone a marriage ceremony to a man in 1981. The Court of Appeal had declined to grant a declaration that the marriage was valid. The House of Lords held that the marriage was not a valid marriage but declared that the non-recognition of gender reassignment for the purposes of allowing transsexuals to marry was incompatible with the right to respect for private and family life and the right to marry guaranteed by *Articles 8* and *12* of the *European Convention on Human Rights*.

Also, in the case *KB v National Health Service Pensions Agency [2004] All ER (D) 03 (Jan)*, the ECJ confirmed that national legislation which prevents marriage (and therefore the enjoyment of certain pension benefits) to individuals who have undergone a sex change is in breach of EU law.

The Gender Recognition Bill was introduced into the House of Lords on 27 November 2003 and it is anticipated that the Bill will come into force in 2005.

Under the Bill, a person over 18 may make an application to a Gender Recognition Panel for a gender recognition certificate on the basis of living in the other gender, or having changed gender under the law of a country outside of the UK. Where a gender recognition certificate is granted, then the applicant's gender becomes for all purposes the acquired gender. The Bill will allow transsexuals on acquiring a gender recognition certificate to marry in their acquired gender and be given birth certificates that recognise the acquired gender.

Temporary workers

9.33 On 28 November 2002 the European Parliament amended its proposal for a Directive on working conditions for temporary (agency) workers.

The aim of the Directive is to provide a protective framework for temporary workers engaged via employment agencies which does not impede the develop-

9.34 *Sex equality*

ment and creation of small businesses. It is stated that 'The basic working and employment conditions applicable to temporary workers should be at least those which would apply to such workers if they were recruited by the user undertaking to occupy the same job.'

It is uncertain at present as to what extent pensions will be covered, although the Directive does make reference to 'pay' and as mentioned above, *Barber* held that pensions should be treated as pay under *Article 141*. Agreement has not yet been reached on the Directive's provisions.

MATERNITY PROVISIONS

General

9.34 Some form of favourable treatment is afforded to women in the area of maternity provision. The requirements for the equal treatment of women on maternity leave, contained in the *Third Equal Treatment Directive (86/378)*, led to the passing of the *Social Security Act 1989*, the relevant provision of which came into effect on 23 June 1994. These provisions provide for benefits under occupational pension schemes to accrue for women on paid 'ordinary' maternity leave in the same way as for women working normally, and by reference, therefore, to their full remuneration. Members pay contributions based upon their actual pay received.

Generally, all pregnant employees who satisfy certain conditions (mainly in relation to notifications) are entitled to a period of 'ordinary' maternity leave. During this period, most employees will be entitled to statutory maternity pay from their employer (depending on their earnings and period of continuous employment) or to Maternity Allowance, paid by the State. The right to 'ordinary' maternity leave applies regardless of the number of hours a woman works or her length of service (except that they must give notice, and thus be employed, by the 15th week before the expected week of childbirth) (see *section 71* of *ERA 1996*.)

The *Employment Act 2002* has introduced measures designed to enhance and simplify the rules on maternity leave and pay. The *Act*'s regime applies to employees whose expected week of childbirth began on or after 6 April 2003. Thus, from 6 April 2003, 'ordinary' maternity leave was increased from 18 weeks to 26 weeks and the period in respect of which statutory maternity pay is payable was also extended to 26 weeks (see 9.35 below).

In the case of *Boyle & others v Equal Opportunities Commission (C411/96) [1998] All ER (EC) 879*, it was stated that a condition limiting accrual of pensionable service to periods of paid 'ordinary' maternity leave was contrary to *Article 12* of the *Pregnant Workers Directive (EU Directive 92/85)*. The Court said that the Directive required that the period of 'ordinary' maternity leave was to be pensionable regardless of whether the woman concerned is in receipt of pay. This means that the pensionable service of any woman who is a pension scheme member but who is not entitled to either contractual or statutory maternity pay (perhaps because she has recently become an employee) must continue during this minimum period (see *section 71(4), ERA 1996*). It remains the case, however, that pension rights do not continue to accrue during 'additional maternity leave'.

Under *ERA 1996*, those employees with one year's continuous service are entitled to an 'additional maternity leave period' which lasts up to the 29th week following the week of birth. Under the *Employment Act 2002*, from 6 April 2003 the qualifying period for 'additional maternity leave' was reduced to 6 months and the period of leave was increased to 26 weeks.

Under the *Employment Relations Act 1999* which implements the European Directive on parental leave, qualifying employees with one year's continuous service have a right to take up to 13 weeks unpaid leave in respect of a child for whom they have parental responsibility, provided the child was born or adopted on or after 15 December 1994. This right must be exercised before the child's fifth birthday (18th if the child is disabled).

The *Employment Act 2002* and regulations made under it give certain qualifying employees (of either sex) the right to two weeks' paid paternity leave in respect of a child born, or whose expected week of birth begins, on or after 6 April 2003, and in respect of a child matched for adoption, where the adopter was notified of the match or the placement took effect on or after 6 April 2003. Continuity of employment will be preserved during this period of leave.

The *2002 Act* also provides a new right for adoption leave (some of which is paid) for certain qualifying employees. This right is similar to the right to maternity leave and, thus, pension contributions may have to be maintained during absence on ordinary adoption leave (but not periods of unpaid additional adoption leave).

Clause 254 of the Pensions Bill [HL Bill 73, 21 May 2004] proposes to add two new paragraphs into *schedule 5* of the *Social Security Act 1989*. These new paragraphs relate to periods of paid paternity leave and paid adoption leave. The new provisions provide that in respect of any period of paid paternity leave or paid adoption leave, a member shall only be required to pay pension contributions on the amount of contractual remuneration or statutory pay actually paid to or for him in respect of that period. Employer pension contributions during periods of paid paternity or adoption leave should be made as if the member were working normally.

Maternity pay

9.35 Statutory maternity pay ('SMP') is only payable where an employee has completed six months' continuous service with the same employer by the 15th week before the expected week of childbirth. This requirement continues to apply under the *Employment Act 2002*. Employees with an expected date of

9.36 *Sex equality*

childbirth falling on or after 6 April 2003 will receive SMP for a maximum of 26 weeks. The payment of contractual remuneration, ie payment under the employee's contract of employment, affects pension rights only in respect of maternity leave in excess of 26 weeks or if the contractual pay is higher than SMP.

Contractual remuneration

9.36 Although the protection of pension rights during maternity absence can depend upon the payment of 'contractual remuneration', it is not clear what this includes. Employment legislation defines remuneration as comprising cash payments, whereas tax legislation includes benefits in kind within the definition. The safer approach is to treat remuneration as including all benefits in kind, for example, a company car. What has been confirmed, in the case of *Gillespie v Northern Health & Social Services Board [1996] AER (EC) 284*, is that bonuses or pay increases granted during paid maternity absence, but which are backdated to the relevant pre-absence period, are to be reflected in the remuneration of those on paid maternity leave. SMP will also have to be recalculated if a backdated pay increase affects the average earnings which underlie the calculation of SMP.

Essentially the *Gillespie* case, underlines the requirement in the *Social Security Act 1989* that pension rights accruing during a period of paid maternity absence reflect any increase to 'normal pay'.

Final salary schemes

9.37 The *Social Security Act 1989* provides for periods of paid 'ordinary' maternity absence to count as pensionable service as if the woman was working normally, and for the accrual of benefits to continue on the basis of the pre-absence level of remuneration. As the employee's contributions are based upon actual pay and full final salary benefits accrue during the periods of paid absence, the employer will incur an additional cost to fund those benefits to compensate for any reduction in the amount of contribution paid by the employee. In respect of women with six months continuous service who have the right to 'additional maternity leave', *ERA 1996* provides for continuity of employment but the period of absence on 'additional maternity leave' does not count.

Money purchase schemes

9.38 The position here is less certain, but money purchase schemes are not excluded from the scope of the legislation. Although the employee can only be required to contribute on the basis of actual pay received, the employer has to contribute at the full rate appropriate to the employee's pre-absence remuneration. It is also arguable that, as with the final salary schemes, the employer has to make good any shortfall in contributions (ie the difference between the contributions actually paid by the employee and those that would have been paid by her if she had been working normally) but this point is far from certain.

Death benefits

9.39 Benefits on death are treated in the same way as pension benefits, in that they must be continued during periods of paid maternity absence. On the death of an employee during such absence, death benefits will be calculated by reference to full pre-absence remuneration as if the employee had been working normally.

All of the requirements for equal treatment are clearly subject to the special provisions relating to paid maternity and family leave.

TABLES OF RELEVANT LEGISLATION AND CASE LAW

9.40 The following tables list relevant UK and European legislation and its main effect. The table of cases lists the main issues decided.

UK legislation	
Legislation	*Main effect*
Equal Pay Act 1970	Did not encompass pension schemes; *section 6(1A)* provides 'An equality clause …shall not operate in terms related to death or retirement …'. (Amended by the *Occupational Pensions Schemes (Equal Treatment) Regulations 1995, (SI 1995 No 3183)*, see below.)
Social Security Act 1973	Required schemes to provide equal access to membership for both men and women (re-enacted in the *Pension Schemes Act 1993* and now covered by *PA 1995*).
Employment Protection (Consolidation) Act 1978	Preserved contractual terms and conditions of employment during the maternity leave period (but did not confer right to remuneration). (Re-enacted in the *Employment Rights Act 1996*).
Sex Discrimination Act 1986	Removed the exemption from the *Sex Discrimination Act 1975* relating to occupational pension schemes, and required equal retirement ages for men and women in contracts of employment.
Social Security Act 1989	This was designed to implement the requirements of *Directive 86/378* on equal treatment (see below).

9.40 *Sex equality*

UK legislation	
Legislation	*Main effect*
Pension Schemes Act 1993	Consolidated previous pensions legislation (*Social Security Act 1973*, *Social Security (Pensions) Act 1975*, *Social Security Act 1990*).
Pensions Act 1995	Imposes equal treatment requirements on scheme provisions in relation to pensionable service after 17 May 1990, and covers both access to schemes and benefits under schemes. It also empowers trustees to make changes unilaterally for the purpose of implementing equal treatment.
Occupational Pensions Schemes (Equal Treatment) Regulations 1995 (SI 1995 No 3183)	The *Regulations* supplement the requirements for equal treatment relating to occupational pension schemes provided for in *sections 62* to *66 of PA 1995*.
Employment Rights Act 1996	Consolidated previous employment legislation.
Part-time Workers (Prevention of Less Favourable Treatment) Regulations 2000 (SI 2000 No 1551) (implementing *Directive 97/81/EC*)	The *Regulations* give part-time workers the right not to be treated less favourably than full-time workers working for the same employer under the same type of employment contract. Workers who change from full-time to part-time are also protected as they are to be treated no less favourably than they were before going part-time. The *Regulations* apply where the less favourable treatment is applied to a part-time worker which cannot be justified on objective grounds.
Part-time Workers (Prevention of Less Favourable Treatment) Regulations 2000 (Amendment) Regulations 2002 (SI 2002 No 2035)	The *Regulations* remove the provision which had limited the backdating of a claim to two years from the date on which the complaint was presented. Additionally, provisions for comparators have been amended, removing the distinction between fixed-term and permanent contracts.
Fixed-term Employees (Prevention of Less Favourable Treatment) Regulations 2002 (SI 2002 No 2034)	The Regulations give fixed-term employees the right not to be treated less favourably than permanent employees of the same employer who are doing similar work unless there is an objective justification for the difference.
Employment Act 2002	The *Act* provides a number of family friendly provisions including measures designed to simplify maternity leave and pay, a right to paid adoption leave, a right to paid paternity leave, improvements to the Employment Tribunal process, introduction of an equal pay questionnaire and provisions to implement the Fixed-term Workers Directive.

Sex equality **9.40**

UK legislation	
Legislation	*Main effect*
The Employment Equality (Sexual Orientation) Regulations 2003 (SI 2003 No 1661)	The *Regulations* are designed to implement the Directive in respect of sexual orientation discrimination and outlaw discrimination in employment and vocational training on grounds of sexual orientation. The *Regulations* came into force on 1 December 2003 and protect heterosexuals, homosexuals and bisexuals.
The Employment Equality (Sexual Orientation) (Amendment) Regulations 2003 (2003 No 2827)	These *Regulations* extend the provisions of the *Sexual Orientation Regulations* to the trustees and managers of an occupational pension scheme. The *Amendment Regulations* make provision for every occupational pension scheme to be treated as including a 'non-discrimination' rule prohibiting discrimination contrary to the *Regulations*.
Pensions Bill	The Bill was published on 12 February 2004 and, although no date is given for implementation, it is understood that the Government is aiming for 6 April 2005. Many of the Bill's provisions will require regulations to clarify its detailed requirements.
The Gender Recognition Bill	Under the Gender Recognition Bill, a person over 18 may make an application to a Gender Recognition Panel for a gender recognition certificate on the basis of living in the other gender, or having changed gender under the law of a country outside of the UK. Where a gender recognition certificate is granted, then the applicant's gender becomes for all purposes the acquired gender.
The Civil Partnerships Bill	The Civil Partnerships Bill provides for same-sex couples to obtain legal recognition of their relationship by registering as civil partners.

European legislation	
Legislation	*Main effect*
Treaty of Rome 1957 – Article 141 (formerly 119)	'Each Member State shall …ensure and subsequently maintain the application of the principle that men and women should receive equal pay for equal work.'
Directive 75/117 on equal pay	Requires Member States to introduce equal pay laws.
Directive 77/187 on acquired rights	Ensures continuing employment following a transfer of the business undertaking (but excludes pension rights).

9.40 *Sex equality*

European legislation	
Legislation	*Main effect*
Directive 76/207 on equal treatment	Requires Member States to prohibit sex discrimination in employment, but made no specific reference to pensions or social security (made under *Article 235*).
Directive 79/7 on statutory benefits	Requires Member States to implement equal treatment in statutory social security schemes but excludes retirement ages, survivors' benefits, derived rights and maternity provisions.
Directive 86/378 on equal treatment	Requires Member States to implement equal treatment in pension schemes and includes access, calculation of contributions and of benefits, retirement ages and maternity provisions. [N.B. following the various ECJ decisions on equal treatment, a revised directive has been issued – see below.]
Directive amending *Directive 86/378* (above)	Transposes the ECJ decisions on equal treatment onto the *1986 Directive*. Thus, those parts of the *1986 Directive* which provide for derogations from the principle of equal treatment are invalid as far as paid employees are concerned. However, the provisions of the *1986 Directive* relating to self-employed workers remain valid.
Directive 98/50 on acquired rights	Reinforces *Directive 77/187* and effectively gives member states the option of protecting pension rights under national legislation.
Directive 2000/78/EC on equal treatment.	This Directive, establishing a general framework for equal treatment, requires Member States to enact legislation prohibiting discrimination on grounds of religion or belief, disability, age or sexual orientation.
Directive 2001/23 on acquired rights	Codified and replaced previous acquired rights directives.
Directive 2002/73 on equal treatment	Amends *Directive 76/207* in respect of sex discrimination and introduces two new definitions of harassment.

Sex equality **9.40**

Cases		
Decision	*Date*	*Main issues decided*
Defrenne v The Belgian State *Case No 80/70 [1971] ECR 445*	1971	Distinguished between statutory pension provision and private occupational pension schemes, in that the former did not come within the scope of *Article 141*. Payments from the latter were not, in principle, to be excluded from the concept of 'pay' for the purposes of *Article 141*.
Defrenne v Sabena (No 2) *Case No 43/75 [1976] ECR 455*	1976	Determination that *Article 141* had direct effect, and consequently could be enforced by individuals in Member States without the need for further legislation to implement it.
Bilka-Kaufhaus GmbH v Weber von Hartz *Case No 170/84 [1986] ECR 1607*	1986	Exclusion of part-timers from scheme membership is unlawful where the reason for exclusion is discriminatory on grounds of sex. Here, the exclusion affected ten times as many women as men and could not be explained by any reason other than one based on sex discrimination ie it was not 'objectively justified'.
Marshall v Southampton & SW Hampshire Area Health Authority *Case No 152/84 [1986] ECR 723*	1986	State employers were required to have equal contractual retirement ages (as the *1976 Directive* had direct effect on 'emanations of the state'), but discriminatory normal pension ages were not outlawed.
Barber v GRE Assurance Group *Case No C–262/88 [1990] ECR I–1889*	17 May 1990	Decided that a pension paid from a UK occupational pension scheme was 'pay' for the purposes of *Article 141* which requires equal pay for equal work. Also decided that the same retirements benefits 'package' available to a woman who is made compulsorily redundant, should also be available to a man in like circumstances, and that each element (as opposed to the totality) of a pay package must be equal.
Bullock v The Alice Ottley School *[1992] IRLR 564*	1992	Employers are permitted to have a variety of normal retirement ages for different types of workers, provided that the reason for the differences is not based upon direct or indirect sex discrimination.

9.40 Sex equality

Cases		
Decision	Date	Main issues decided
Ten Oever v Stichting Case No C–109/91 [1993] ECR I–4879	6 Oct 1993	Temporal limitations of the *Barber* judgment clarified in that the direct application of *Article 141* can only substantiate a claim in respect of benefits (in this case, a widower's pension) relating to periods of employment on or after 17 May 1990, unless the claim is brought before that date.
Birds Eye Walls v Friedl M Roberts Case No C–132/92 [1993] PLR 203	9 Nov 1993	'Bridging' pensions do not infringe *Article 141*, as they are designed to remedy inequality (in this case, in taking into account the differing ages at which State pensions became payable).
Neath v Hugh Steeper Ltd Case No C–152/91 [1993] ECR I–6935	22 Dec 1993	Under a final salary scheme, it is the employer's commitment (ie the amount of pension promised) that must be equal, even though the use of sex-based actuarial factors may require unequal contributions from the employer to meet the funding requirements of the scheme.
Coloroll Pension Trustees Ltd v Russell Case No C–200/91 [1994] ECR I–4389	28 Sept 1994	Determined that: • both employees and their dependants may rely on the direct effect of Article 141 against a scheme's trustees (who are required to observe the principles of equal treatment); • equal treatment may be implemented by the 'levelling down' of benefits (ie reduction of the advantages enjoyed by one group of members to the level received by a less advantaged group) from the date of scheme equalisation; • retrospection is only in relation to benefits (including survivors' benefits) for periods of service after 17 May 1990; • the receiving scheme must make good any inadequacy in respect of an unequalised transfer payment made to it; and • AVC's and single sex schemes do not fall within the scope of Article 141.

Sex equality **9.40**

Cases		
Decision	*Date*	*Main issues decided*
Smith v Avdel Systems Ltd Case No C–408/92 *[1994] ECR I–4435*	28 Sept 1994	Retirement ages for women could not be raised to that of men for the period from 17 May 1990 to the date of equalisation, although this measure would not infringe *Article 141* in respect of service completed after the date of the change.
Van den Akker v Stichting Shell PF Case No C–28/93 *[1994] ECR I–4527*	28 Sept 1994	*Article 141* does not allow a uniform retirement age to be set whilst maintaining an advantage for women members. Equality can only be achieved by the 'levelling up' of benefits ie for men to enjoy the same advantages of women members, for service after *Barber* to the date of equalisation.
Algemeen Burgerlijk PF v Beaune Case No C–7/93 *[1994] ECR I–4471*	28 Sept 1994	Civil service pension schemes do come within the scope of *Article 141*.
Vroege v NCIV Instrituut Case No C57/93 *[1994] ECR I–4541*	28 Sept 1994	The right to join an occupational pension scheme is covered by *Article 141*, but falls outside the temporal limitations of the *Barber* judgment. This right continues to be governed by the *Bilka-Kaufhaus* judgment.
Fisscher v Voorhuis Hengelo BV Case No C–128/93 *[1994] ECR I–4583*	28 Sept 1994	As for *Vroege*, but also decided that administrators must comply with *Article 141*. Further, it confirmed that employees can claim retrospective membership although they cannot avoid paying backdated contributions.
Nolte v Landesversicherungsanstalt Hannover Case No C–317/93 *[1996] All ER (EC) 212*	14 Dec 1995	Exclusion of part-timers from membership is permissible, even where to do so affects more women than men, where the reason is to achieve a social policy unrelated to any discrimination.
Lloyds Bank (EC) Pension Trust Corporation Ltd v Lloyds Bank plc *[1996] OPLR 181*	24 Apr 1996	The rules of the scheme provided that 'pecuniary benefits secured' for members could not be reduced without their consent. The court refused to permit the trustees to amend the rules to reduce future benefits.

9.40 *Sex equality*

Cases		
Decision	*Date*	*Main issues decided*
Gillespie v Northern Health & Social Services Board Case No 342/93 [1996] AER (EC) 284	13 Feb 1996	Where maternity pay is calculated by reference to the pre-absence salary, it must include pay rises (if backdated to the relevant pre-absence period) during the period of maternity absence.
Regina v Secretary of State for Employment ex parte Seymour-Smith and Another case C-167/97 [1999] ICR 447	9 February 1999	The Advocate General considered, among other questions, the test for determining whether a measure adopted by a member state had 'such a disparate effect as between men and women as to amount to indirect discrimination'. The Advocate General opined that the best approach to this issue was to compare statistical evidence of the proportion of men able to satisfy the condition at issue and those unable to do so and to compare those proportions. If the statistics indicated that a 'considerably smaller percentage' of women than men were able to satisfy the condition, there was indirect sex discrimination unless the measure was justified by objective factors.
Grant v South West Trains Limited, [1998] All ER (EC) 193	17 February 1998	This was an employment case involving the granting of travel concessions. South West Trains refused to give travel concessions to Ms Grant's same sex partner when she was promoted to a post at South West Trains previously occupied by an employee whose opposite sex partner had obtained such concessions. The ECJ said that Community Law as it stood did not cover discrimination based on sexual orientation.

Sex equality **9.40**

Cases		
Decision	*Date*	*Main issues decided*
Preston v Wolverhampton Healthcare NHS Trust Case No C78/98 [2000] All ER (EC) and [2001] 3 All ER 947	16 May 2000 and 8 February 2001	Claims by part-timers in respect of unlawful exclusion from scheme membership have to be made within six months of leaving service as required under national UK law. However, the maximum of two years' backdated benefits that can be awarded under the UK legislation is not valid and backdated benefits can be claimed going as far back as of April 1976. However, Member States are permitted to require that individuals making a claim pay any past contributions which they would have had to pay had they belonged to the scheme throughout the relevant period.
Deutsche Telkom v Schroder [2000] ECR I-743	10 Feb 2000	The *Defrenne* time limit of 8 April 1976 (backdated benefits can be claimed as far back as this date) does not prevent national legislation being even more generous and backdating claims even further.
Marsh Mercer Pension Scheme v Pensions Ombudsman 2001 16 PBLR 28)	23 Feb 2001	The Pensions Ombudsman could not make a direction relating to the equalisation of GMP's and compliance with equal treatment rules in *section 62* of *PA 1995* as the matter was too wide ranging for determination in such a manner. The Ombudsman was wrong to determine that the dispute was one affecting the scheme and all the members generally and also his direction requiring the rewriting of the scheme affected all the members. It was not within the jurisdiction of the Ombudsman to purport to decide equalisation of GMPs on behalf of all the other members of the scheme.

9.40 *Sex equality*

Cases		
Decision	Date	Main issues decided
Allonby v Accrington & Rossendale College [2001] IRLR 364	23 March 2001	Claim brought by a part-time lecturer who was no longer eligible for membership of the scheme by virtue of change in employment status – the lecturer's services were changed by the employer from being employed on a one year renewable contract with the employer to being employed through an employment agency while doing the same work. It was held by the Court of Appeal that the part-time lecturer was in a contract of employment for occupational pension purposes. As there could be a possible conflict with *Article 141 Allonby* has been referred to the ECJ.
Glossop v Copnall [2001] PLR 263	5 July 2001	The Pensions Ombudsman's determination that the trustees failure to comply with Article 141 amounts to maladministration was incorrect. A mere error of law could not amount to maladministration.
Quirk v Burton Hospital [2002] 24 PBLR	12 February 2002	Mr Quirk, a male nurse, had been excluded by scheme rules from rights available to female nurses. Mr Quirk complained that the decision in *Barber* should be retrospective. It was held that the reason for the limitation on equalisation of benefits to 17 May 1990 was because Member States could reasonably have believed that such discrimination was lawful on the basis of parallel EU legislation. Therefore the limitation in *Barber* is correct and equal treatment under *Article 141* in relation to scheme benefits does not apply to service prior to May 1990.
Uppingham School v Shillcock [2002] EWHC 641 (Ch), [2002] 2CMLR 39	19 April 2002	The case overturned the decision of the Pensions Ombudsman and held that an LEL offset to integrate benefits with the State scheme was not indirect discrimination and, had it been so, it would have been objectively justified.

Sex equality **9.40**

Cases		
Decision	*Date*	*Main issues decided*
Beckmann v Dynamco Whicheloe Macfarlane Ltd, Case C-164/00, [2002] 64 PBLR; [2002] All ER (D) 05 (Jun)	4 June 2002	This case held that benefits payable on redundancy under the NHS Compensation for Early Retirement Regulations transfer under *TUPE* and the *Aquired Rights Directive* despite the fact that they are calculated by reference to the same rules used to calculate normal pension benefits. Early retirement benefits and benefits intended to enhance the conditions of such retirement, paid before the end of a 'normal working life' in the event of dismissal for redundancy are not 'old age, invalidity or survivors' benefits' within the meaning of Article 3(3) of the ARD and thus are not subject to exclusion from transfer.
Goodwin v UK [2002] IRLR 664	11 July 2002	The European Court held that the UK was in breach of Article 8 (right to respect for private and family life) and Article 12 (right to marry and to found a family) of the European Convention of Human Rights. The UK had failed to legally recognise that Ms Goodwin who underwent 'gender re-assignment' surgery was female. Ms Goodwin was therefore required pay NICs until age 65. Had her sex change been legally recognized, NICs would have ceased at age 60.
Bellinger v Bellinger [2003] UKHL 21, [2003] 2 All ER 593	10 April 2003	The House of Lords held that the marriage was not a valid marriage but declared that the non-recognition of gender reassignment for the purposes of allowing transsexuals to marry was incompatible with the right to respect for private and family life and the right to marry guaranteed by *Articles 8* and *12* of the *European Convention on Human Rights*.

303

9.40 Sex equality

Cases		
Decision	Date	Main issues decided
Kutz-Bauer v Freie und Hansestadt Hamburg [2003] [2003] All ER (D) 327 (Mar)	20 March 2003	Provisions allowing workers over 55 to work part-time applied only until the date on which the worker became entitled to a statutory old age pension. For most women this was 60 and for most men it was 65. It was held that this was capable of breaking the *Equal Treatment Directive* and it was for the national court to determine whether there was in fact indirect discrimination which could not be objectively justified.
Preston & Others v Wolverhampton Healthcare NHS Trust (No.3) [2002] PLR 389	24 July 2002	Decision of the Employment Tribunal on test cases selected for a full hearing following the 2001*Preston* decision mentioned above.
Allonby v Accrington and Rossendale College [2004] IRLR 224	13 January 2004	The ECJ's judgment on matters referred to it by the Court of Appeal following the 2001 *Allonby* case.
Martin v South Bank University [2003] [2004] IRLR 74)	6 November 2003	It was decided by the ECJ that only benefits paid from the time when an employee reaches the end of his or her normal working life can be classified as 'old age' benefits within the meaning of *Article 3(3)* and are thus excluded from automatic transfer under *TUPE*.
Secretary of State for Trade and Industry v Rutherford, Bentley and Harvest TownCircle Limited EAT [2003] 78 PBLR	2 October 2003	The Employment Appeal Tribunal overturned a tribunal's decision that the statutory upper age limit that applies to complaints of unfair dismissal and for statutory redundancy pay was unlawful as being indirectly discriminatory on grounds of sex. As a result, until the Government introduces legislation outlawing age discrimination, the current statutory age limit continues to apply.
Preston v Wolverhampton Healthcare NHS Trust (No. 3) [2004] IRLR 96	19 December 2003	Decision of the Employment Appeal Tribunal on a number of part-timer issues raised by the 2002 *Preston* case.
KB v National Health Service Pensions Agency [2004] [2004] All ER (D) 03 (Jan)	7 January 2004	The ECJ confirmed that national legislation which prevents marriage (and therefore the enjoyment of certain pension benefits) for individuals who have undergone a sex change is in breach of EU law.

Sex equality **9.40**

Cases		
Decision	*Date*	*Main issues decided*
Leadenhall Independent Trustees Ltd v Welham [2004] [2004] All ER (D) 423 (Mar)	19 March 2004	The trustee of a scheme in surplus sought directions as to whether it had the power to augment benefits to neutralise the gender discrimination of GMPs.
Brook Street Bureau (UK) Ltd v Dacas [2004] EWCA Civ 217	19 March 2004	Court of Appeal decision indicating that agency workers could be employees of the organisation they provide services to.
Matthews v Kent & Medway Towns Fire Authority [2003] [2003] IRLR 732	Judgment of Court of Appeal still awaited at the time of writing.	Case brought before the Court of Appeal under the *Part-time Workers (Prevention of Less Favourable Treatment) Regulations.2000 (SI 2000 No 1551)* The EAT had held that a part-time fire fighter had not suffered less favourable treatment than full-time fire fighters despite being excluded access from the pension scheme.

Chapter 10

Investment

INTRODUCTION

10.1 One of the fundamental duties of any trustee is to invest the monies under his control so as to produce income for his trust. In doing so a trustee must act within the boundaries imposed on him by the trust instrument, by statutory restrictions and by case law. The duties and obligations are onerous and consequently many trustees prefer to delegate their powers to professional fund managers.

This chapter deals with the powers of trustees regarding the investment of the funds for which they are responsible and the duties imposed on them when exercising those powers. It considers how, and to whom, trustees may delegate their powers and briefly discusses the implications of the *Financial Services and Markets Act 2000* (FSMA 2000). Finally it examines the protection afforded to trustees in respect of investment decisions. This chapter is particularly relevant to trustees of self-administered schemes, whether large or small, who will be more directly involved with investment activities than trustees of insured schemes.

Following the publication, on 6 March 2001 of the report by Paul Myners, 'Institutional Investment in the United Kingdom: A Review', the Government issued a voluntary code of best practice on 2 October 2001, containing ten or so key principles which relate to the setting of investment objectives, and the method by which pension trustees should take investment decisions.

Although the Code of Practice is voluntary, the Myners review recommended that there should be a subsequent review, to be commenced in March 2003, to establish how effective the voluntary code had been in bringing about change. The Government said that, if change has not occurred in the methods by which trustees reached investment decisions by March 2003 on a voluntary basis, the Government would legislate.

This chapter considers the Myners' Code of Practice at 10.51 below.

THE MEANING OF INVESTMENT

10.2 The classic statement of the legal meaning of the words 'invest' and 'investment' was given in the case *Re Wragg* in which Mr Justice Lawrence said that:

'Without attempting to give an exhaustive definition of the words 'invest' and 'investment' I think that the words 'to invest' when used in an investment clause may safely be said to include as one of its meanings 'to apply money in the purchase of some property from which interest or profit is expected and which property is purchased in order to be held for the sake of the income which it will yield'.' (*Re Wragg [1919] 2 Ch 58* at page 64.)

On a strict interpretation, an asset purchased for some reason other than deriving an income would therefore not be an investment; for example, land that is purchased for the financial gain it will produce when it is sold will not be an investment unless it is let for a rent or produces some other income.

In recent years there have been indications of greater flexibility in the definition of investment. In *Marson v Morton* Sir Nicolas Browne Wilkinson VC recognised that in the modern financial arena 'new approaches to investment have emerged putting the emphasis in investment on the making of capital profit at the expense of income yield'. (*Marson v Morton [1986] 1 WLR 1343* at page 1350.) He gives the purchase of short-dated stocks (which give a capital yield but no income) and works of art as examples of common ways of investing and concludes that the mere fact that land is not income-producing should not be decisive on the question of whether it was bought as an investment.

The Pension Law Review Committee used the term investment to mean 'any application of assets, whether or not investments in the technical sense, and thus [including], for example, stock lending and borrowing' (Report of the Pension Law Review Committee, page 342). Unfortunately this approach was not adopted in the *PA 1995*, which does not define 'investment'. Consequently there remains doubt as to the modern meaning of the term. The cautious approach must be to adopt the strict interpretation set out in *Re Wragg* in the absence of a more definitive modern definition.

TRADING OR INVESTING?

10.3 Broadly speaking, exempt approved schemes are not liable for income tax or capital gains tax on the investments they make. [(See 5.25 to 5.27 above for details of the taxation of pension schemes.)] However, in certain circumstances, the Inland Revenue may argue that trustees are not investing but are in fact trading. If a pension scheme is found to be trading, rather than investing, the transaction will fall outside the scope of the statutory tax exemptions and the trustees will be liable for the appropriate income tax. It is, therefore, important to determine whether the proceeds of the sale of an asset constitute the realisation of an investment, or are the profits of a trade.

Badges of trade

10.4 The 1954 Royal Commission (Cmnd 9474, paragraph 116) identified

10.5 Investment

'six badges of trade' as being relevant in deciding whether a transaction is, or is not, to be treated as a trading transaction. These 'badges' are discussed below.

The subject matter of the realisation

10.5 Generally property which does not yield an income is more likely to have been acquired for the purpose of trading rather than as an investment. A one-off transaction of the purchase of a type of property which yields no income followed by a profit on a sale has been held to be trading. (*IRC v Fraser (1942) 24 TC 498.*) However, dealing with an asset which does not produce an income, does not of itself necessarily imply trading; an asset can quite legitimately be purchased solely for the capital profit it will yield. (*Marson v Morton [1986] 1 WLR 1343.*) Some forms of property, such as manufactured articles, are usually purchased for trading and can only very exceptionally be an investment.

The length of the period of ownership

10.6 There is an inference of trading where property is realised within a short time of acquisition. However, if trustees can show a good reason for their actions the presumption that the trustees are trading may be rebutted. There is no doubt, however, that a quick sale helps to support the finding of trading, especially where other indications of trading are present. (*Turner v Last (1965) 42 TC 517; Eames v Stepnell Properties Ltd (1966) 43 TC 678.*)

The frequency or number of similar transactions by the same person

10.7 If there are repeated instances over a period of the same type of activity being carried out by trustees then the number of transactions may in itself give rise to a presumption of trading. In some cases it may be conclusive proof. (*Pickford v Quirke (1927) 13 TC 251.*) However, much will depend on the reasons for the sale.

Supplementary work on or in connection with the property realised

10.8 If land is purchased and then developed for sale there is often a suggestion that the trustees are to sell the property soon and thus enter into a transaction in the nature of trade. However, this is not necessarily the case; trustees may well refurbish a property simply in order to retain its marketability in the long term, which most prudent investors would, and probably should, do.

The circumstances that were responsible for the realisation

10.9 There are many situations that may arise which call for an asset to be sold very shortly after its purchase, for example, changes in market conditions or the payment of a large cash benefit. In such a situation it would be sensible for the trustees or their investment advisers to record in writing the reason for the sale so that any suggestion of 'trading' can be rebutted.

It should be remembered that one of the prime duties of a trustee is to exercise his duty of investment with diligence and prudence. Even if there may be a potential tax charge on grounds of trading, trustees should realise an asset, where appropriate, if not to do so would be a breach of trust. The duty of a trustee to invest prudently can be a very powerful weapon against allegations of trading.

Motive

10.10 The intention or motive of the trustees can be an important factor. There are cases in which the purpose of a transaction is clearly discernible, but where this is not so it may be sensible for the trustees or their investment advisers to note the reason for the purchase or the sale of an asset. In the absence of direct evidence of the trustees' intentions, motive can be inferred from the surrounding circumstances.

Application of the badges of trade

10.11 The 'badges of trade' are of general application to all types of transactions, where tax mitigation may be in question; they were not drawn up to apply solely to trustees or to pension schemes, and so may not always be relevant to dealings by pension scheme trustees. The onus of proving trading is, in reality, on the Inland Revenue, as far as occupational pension schemes are concerned (*Salt v Chamberlain (1979) 53 TC 143*) and there are presumptions to assist trustees who are accused of trading.

Presumption against trading

10.12 It is common practice for frequent changes to be made in a scheme's portfolio of Stock Exchange securities. Normally no inference of trading would be drawn from such changes. However, if there is evidence of a large turnover of a scheme's holdings, which appears to have been carried out pursuant to a deliberate and organised plan of buying and selling with a view to profit-making, it may be possible to infer that trading has taken place. (*Cooper v C & J Clarke Ltd (1982) 54 TC 670.*)

In the case of *Clark v British Telecom Pension Scheme [1999] 06 PBLR 21*, Lightman J overturned the earlier decision of the Commissioners of the Inland Revenue that profits received from the sub-underwriting of share issues by the trustees were not profits from trade rather than gains from investments and hence were not subject to tax. Lightman J found instead that the trustees had been involved in operations of a 'commercial character' for a period of years and the activity had all the hallmarks of trade being 'frequent (or habitual) and organised as well as extensive, business-like and for profit' (Paragraph 31).

10.13 *Investment*

However, the trustees of British Telecom Pension Scheme appealed and the Court of Appeal *[2000] 21 PBLR 13* held that the sub-underwriting activities of the trustees were an integral and indissoluble part of their investment activities. Income from the sub-underwriting was not therefore trading income and was exempt from tax by virtue of *ICTA 1988, s 592*. Lightman J's decision was therefore reversed. Appeal to the House of Lords was refused.

Powers given under the trust instrument

10.13 The majority of trust deeds governing pension schemes contain wide powers permitting investments in many areas. Trustees may also be given power to trade, but when such a power is missing there is a very strong argument against any allegation of trading; it is unlikely that a trustee will knowingly commit a breach of trust in order to trade.

POWER OF INVESTMENT

10.14 A trustee's power of investment will derive from two sources; statute and the trust instrument.

Statutory power to invest

10.15 Prior to 6 April 1997, statutory powers of investment were conferred on trustees by the *Trustee Investments Act 1961* (*TIA 1961*), and to a small extent, the *Trustee Act 1925*. Even before *PA 1995* it was rare for a pension scheme to rely solely on the powers conferred by these Acts as they are very restrictive in the types of investments they permit. So far as pension scheme trustees are concerned, the provisions of *TIA 1961* have largely been replaced or superseded by the provisions of *PA 1995* and so are no longer generally relevant.

Section 34(1) of PA 1995 confers a wide power of investment on trustees by providing that they have the same power to 'make an investment of any kind as if they were absolutely entitled to the assets of the scheme; subject only to any restriction imposed by the scheme'. This provision, which takes effect as if it was contained in the scheme's governing documentation, was intended to aid trustees who were prevented from making some types of investment by an overly restrictive power of investment. However, the wording of the provision causes problems which were not intended. If the term 'investment' is narrowly construed then certain traditional assets including, for example, group life policies, are not investments under *PA 1995,* so *s 34* alone would not permit trustees to purchase them. Consequently, trustees still need a carefully drafted investment power, allowing them specifically to undertake transactions, or to purchase assets, which fall outside the meaning of investment used in *Re Wragg 1919] 2 Ch 58.*

Investment **10.18**

The trust instrument

10.16 It is common for trustees to be given power to invest, or otherwise apply the monies under their control in any manner which they could do if they were absolutely and beneficially entitled to the assets of the scheme and in any manner which they could do as trustees of a pension scheme. The second limb is necessary to allow trustees to invest in those investments, such as exempt unit trusts which are only available to trustees of funds which are not liable for income or capital gains tax. The ability to 'apply' the fund allows trustees to purchase assets which are not, perhaps, technically investments.

Trustees will generally be given specific power to purchase certain assets such as traded options, financial futures, life assurance contracts and assets which are to be held for capital growth rather than the income they produce. Trustees may also be given power to underwrite new issues on the Stock Market and possibly the power to engage in stock lending. Trustees are sometimes given specific power to trade, but this is less common (see 10.13 above).

Trustees may also be given the power to commingle the assets of their scheme with the assets of one or more other schemes in a common investment fund, which will usually be set up under an independent trust. In order to continue to benefit from the tax advantages available to 'exempt approved schemes', all schemes participating in such a fund must themselves be exempt approved schemes.

It is also advisable to have express power in the trust deed to lease, charge and otherwise deal in and conduct the management of real property, and to have a general power to give indemnities and guarantees.

Notwithstanding the supposedly wide power of investment given in *PA 1995*, the investment provisions contained in most trust deeds will probably continue to spell out the powers of the trustees, since, if they do not, there is the possibility of the trustees exceeding their powers by inadvertently purchasing an asset which is not an investment and which cannot, therefore, be purchased under the power given by *section 34* of *PA 1995*.

DUTIES OF TRUSTEES WHEN EXERCISING THEIR INVESTMENT POWER

10.17 When exercising their investment power, trustees must consider the duties imposed on them under the trust instrument, by statute and by case law. The main duties are set out in 10.18 to 10.22 below.

The duty to act in the best interests of the beneficiaries

10.18 One of the fundamental duties of a trustee is to exercise his powers in the best interests of the beneficiaries of the scheme and to act fairly between

10.19 *Investment*

different classes of beneficiaries. In the context of an investment power, a beneficiary's best interests will generally mean his best financial interests. Consequently an investment power must generally be exercised so as to produce the best return possible, having regard to the level of risk involved. (*Cowan v Scargill [1984] 2 All ER 750.*)

The prudent man test

10.19 The basic duty of a trustee, when exercising his investment power, is to choose investments which are within the terms of his trust and, in selecting those investments, to 'take such care as an ordinary prudent man would take if he were minded to make [an investment] for the benefit of other people for whom he felt morally bound to provide'. (*Re Whiteley (1886) 33 Ch D 347.*)

The House of Lords decision in *Learoyd v Whiteley* sets out the principles which trustees must consider when exercising their investment power as follows:

> 'As a general rule the law requires of a trustee no higher degree of diligence in the execution of his office than a man of ordinary prudence would exercise in the management of his own private affairs. Yet he is not allowed the same discretion in investing the money of the trusts as if he were a person *sui juris* dealing with his own estate. Business men of ordinary prudence may, and frequently do, select investments which are more or less of a speculative character; but it is the duty of a trustee to confine himself to the class of investments which are permitted by the trust, and likewise to avoid all investments of that class which are attended with hazard.' (*Learoyd v Whiteley (1887) 12 AC 727*, Lord Watson at page 733.)

Sir Robert Megarry has reiterated and clarified the standard required of a trustee in exercising his powers of investment, making it clear that, in addition to the above, the duty 'includes the duty to seek advice on matters which the trustee does not understand, such as the making of investments, and on receiving that advice to act with the same degree of prudence'. (*Cowan v Scargill [1984] 2 All ER 750* at page 762).

The Pensions Bill, as introduced in the House of Commons on 10 February 2004, contains provisions concerning the 'requirement for knowledge and understanding' of trustees and introduces more specific and onerous requirements for trustees of occupational pension schemes. This is dealt with further at 10.51.

However wide the provisions of an express investment power may be, the trustees are not absolved from their duty to consider whether a proposed investment is such that it is prudent and right for them, as trustees, to make it. The mere fact that a certain type of investment is authorised by the trust instrument or by statute does not mean that it is necessarily proper to invest in it. Even though under *PA 1995* trustees have power to invest at their absolute discretion and as if they were absolute owners, they should remember that they must act as trustees in exercising that power. Moreover, the Pensions Bill proposes to amend *section 36* of *PA 1995* to ensure compliance with *Article 18(1)* of the *European Pensions Directive [2003/41/EC]*. This directive requires investments to be carried out in accordance with the 'prudent person principle' as defined in the directive. Further detail is expected to be set out in regulations

When exercising their investment power, *section 36* of *PA 1995* requires trustees (and any fund manager to whom a discretion has been delegated) to consider the need for diversification (see 10.20 below) and the suitability of the investments proposed. *Section 36, PA 1995* also requires trustees to obtain and consider 'proper advice' before making any investment in order to ascertain whether the investment is suitable, having regard to the need for diversification (see 10.20 below) and whether it is in accordance with the statement of investment principles (see 10.23 below). Broadly speaking, proper advice is advice from a person authorised under the *Financial Services and Markets Act 2000* in relation to investments covered by that Act. In any other case proper advice must be obtained from a person whom the trustees reasonably believe to be qualified by his ability in, and practical experience of, financial matters and to have the appropriate knowledge and experience of the management of the investments of pension schemes. Trustees must ensure that they obtain confirmation of the 'proper advice' given in writing in order to comply with the requirements of *PA 1995*.

Failure to comply with the requirements set out in *section 36, PA 1995* could result in a trustee being fined and/or removed or, in extreme cases, disqualified from acting as a trustee (see appendix I).

The duty to diversify

10.20 Before exercising any investment power, trustees (and any fund manager to whom the trustees' discretion has been delegated) must 'have regard to the need for diversification of investments, in so far as appropriate to the circumstances of the scheme'. This duty to diversify is contained in *section 36(2)* of *PA 1995*.

The requirement imposed on the trustees to diversify is also important from the actuary's standpoint, particularly in mature schemes. Although the actuary does not advise between one investment and another he may, and frequently does, become involved in deciding investment policy and asset allocation of the scheme. The actuary will ascertain the liabilities of a scheme and will advise on the short, medium and long term liabilities. He should then be able to advise on the various types of investment and, for example, how they should be split to allow the trustees sufficient cash funds to provide lump sum and pension benefits for the beneficiaries as they fall due.

The trustees, or more likely the fund managers, will look at the strategy for the short, medium and long term cash needs which the actuary has mapped out and

10.21 *Investment*

should select investments that suit the aim. Not only must they look at diversification from that standpoint but they must also look at diversification on a second level. Clearly if a certain percentage of the fund has to be put in short term investments, they would not put all of the fund designated for such purpose into one investment; they would spread the risk amongst a group of investments.

Moral and ethical considerations

10.21 There has been much discussion on the ability of trustees legitimately to consider moral and ethical considerations in preference to financial return on any particular investment.

Decided case law indicates that trustees cannot invest other than on the usual criteria (financial returns, security and diversification) but there is no reason why they cannot consider other factors, including social and moral criteria. If, for example, trustees wish to make an ethically acceptable investment which will produce a financial return that is at least as good as that produced by any other suitable (although perhaps not so ethically sound) investment, there is no reason why they cannot do so. Essentially they must act with the standard of care and prudence required by the law. What the trustees cannot generally do is subordinate the interests of the beneficiaries to ethical or social demands (see *Cowan v Scargill [1984] 2 All ER 750*; *Bishop of Oxford v Church Commissioners (1991) PLR 185*; *Martin v The City of Edinburgh District Council (1989) PLR 9*). In some circumstances trustees 'may even have to act dishonourably (though not illegally) if the interests of their beneficiaries require it'. (*Cowan v Scargill [1984] 2 All 750* at page 761.)

However, although trustees cannot allow their own political, social and moral views to override financial considerations when making investments, they can in some circumstances be influenced by the views of the beneficiaries of the scheme. If all the beneficiaries are known to hold strong moral views on a matter '... it might not be for the 'benefit' of such beneficiaries to know that they are obtaining rather larger financial returns under the trust by reason of investments in those activities than they would have received if the trustees had invested the trust funds in other investments'. (*Cowan v Scargill [1984] 2 All ER 750* at page 761.) The circumstances where this principle could apply in relation to a pension scheme must be very limited due to the inevitable divergence of opinions of a large number of beneficiaries.

The debate over whether trustees can, or even should, invest in so-called ethical or socially-responsible investments has moved on. The *Occupational Pension Schemes (Investment, and Assignment, Forfeiture, Bankruptcy etc.) Amendment Regulations 1999 (SI 1999 No 1849)* amended the *Occupational Pension Schemes (Investment) Regulations 1996 (SI 1996 No 3127)* (the *'Investment Regulations'*) and came into force on 9 August 1999, except for the provisions relating to ethical/social/environmental investment policies and voting which came into force on 3 July 2000. These require the trustees to state in their Statement of Investment Principles (a) the extent (if at all) social, environmental or ethical considerations are taken into account in the selection, retention and realisation of investments; and (b) their policy (if any) in relation to the exercise of the rights (including voting rights) attaching to investments.

Duty to review investments

10.22 A trustee's responsibility does not stop once he has made an investment; trustees have a duty to review the investments of the scheme from time to time. Although this is a continuing duty it will be particularly relevant in a scheme which is close to winding-up as it may be advisable to match the investments of the fund with the liabilities of the scheme. Even where a scheme is wholly insured trustees should still review the position from time to time as it may be sensible for the trustees to consider changing the insurance company or to become self-administered.

Under *section 36* of *PA 1995* trustees must consider at what intervals they should obtain 'proper advice' in respect of investments they retain and must then obtain and consider such advice accordingly (see 10.19 above regarding the meaning of 'proper advice'). In determining the appropriate intervals the trustees must consider the circumstances of the case and, in particular, the nature of the investment. It might, for example, be appropriate to review the scheme's gilt portfolio less frequently than its equity portfolio as equities are a more volatile investment than gilts.

STATUTORY OBLIGATIONS

Statement of investment principles

10.23 Under *Section 35* of *PA 1995* trustees must ensure that there is prepared, maintained and from time to time revised, a written statement of the principles governing their decisions about investments. Trustees (or the fund manager acting on their behalf) must then exercise their investment power with a view to giving effect to the principles contained in the statement, so far as reasonably practicable. [*PA 1995, s 36(5)*].

The statement must cover, among other matters, the trustees' policy for securing compliance with *section 36* of *PA 1995* (see 10.19 and 10.20 above), the provisions of *PA 1995* relating to the minimum funding requirement (see 11.13 to 11.31) and their policy about:

(*a*)   the kinds of investments to be held;

(*b*)   the balance between different kinds of investments;

(*c*)   risk;

(*d*)   the expected return on investments; and

(*e*)   the realisation of investments.

10.23 Investment

The agreed investment strategy set out in the statement of investment principles must accord with the general law discussed in 10.17 to 10.22 above and be devised to reflect the liability position of the scheme in question. Schemes approved under *section 615(6)* of the *Income and Corporation Taxes Act 1988*, small self-administered schemes, wholly insured schemes, unapproved schemes and schemes whose solvency is guaranteed by a Minister of the Crown are exempt from having a statement of investment principles. [*Investment Regulations, reg 10*].

Before a statement of investment principles is prepared or revised, trustees must:

(i) obtain and consider the written advice of a person whom they reasonably believe to be qualified by his ability in, and practical experience of, financial matters and to have the appropriate knowledge and experience of management of the investments of pension schemes; and

(ii) consult the scheme's sponsoring employer.

Where a scheme has more than one sponsoring employer, all the participating employers may nominate a person to represent them, in which case the trustees need only consult that person. Where the employers do not nominate a representative, each employer must be consulted individually unless all the employers notify the trustees to the contrary. [*Investment Regulations, reg 11*].

The Act does not define what is meant by 'consult'. Consultation does not mean consent; in fact *PA 1995* specifically prohibits the exercise of any investment power being subject to the consent of the employer. To comply with their duty to consult trustees should allow the employer sufficient time to make representations and should ensure that they consider suggestions put forward by the employer with an open mind. If the trustees are obliged to consult all the employers they may specify a reasonable period (which cannot be less than twenty eight days) within which the employers must make representations regarding the statement of investment principles; any representations made after the specified date can be ignored by the trustees. [*Investment Regulations, reg 11*].

The extent of the requirement to consult was considered in the recent case of *Pitmans Trustees v the Telecommunications Group plc [2004] PBLR 32, [2004],All ER (D) 143*. The Vice Chancellor ('VC') confirmed the above views, namely that to comply with the consultation requirements in *section 35(5)(b)* of *PA 1995* trustees must go further than simply giving notice to the employer of the proposed changes to the statement of investment principles. Although no timeframe is prescribed in *section 35(5)(b)* it was held that it is necessary to give adequate time for the employer to obtain and consider advice of its own on the proposals and to comment on the proposals. The VC held that prior consultation is a pre-condition to the existence and exercise of the trustees' powers in *section 35* of *PA 1995* and, therefore, if prior consultation has not taken place then this pre-condition has not been satisfied, the power has not yet arisen and a purported exercise of it will be of no effect. The adoption of any revised statement of investment principles will be invalid as a result.

Investment **10.24**

Trustees must confirm in their annual report whether they have produced a statement of investment principles in accordance with *section 35* of *PA 1995* and must also include a statement providing details of any investments which were not made in accordance with the statement of investment principles giving the reasons why and explaining what action has been or will be taken to resolve the position. A copy of the statement of investment principles must be provided to any member or beneficiary who requests it. [*Occupational Pension Schemes (Disclosure of Information) Regulations 1996 (SI 1996 No 1655), reg 6*].

A failure to take all reasonable steps to prepare or maintain a statement of investment principles or to take advice from an appropriately qualified person could result in a trustee being fined and/or removed [*s 35(6), PA 1995*]. See appendix I.

The Pensions Bill introduces new provisions for the preparation of a statement of investment principles which will replace the existing *section 35* of *PA 1995*. The provisions of the Bill restate the requirement for trustees to have a statement of investment principles but most of the detail is left to the *Regulations*. For example, the frequency with which it is to be reviewed, the requirements before preparation or revision of the statement and the areas that must be covered in the statement. The Bill contains a clear statement that 'Neither a trust scheme nor a statement of investment principles may impose restrictions (however expressed) on any power to make investments by reference to the consent of the employer'.

Restrictions on employer-related investment

10.24 Trustees are under a statutory duty to ensure that not more than 5 per cent of the current market value of the resources of the scheme are invested in employer-related investments. Furthermore, none of the resources of a scheme may be invested in an employer-related loan or in any employer-related investment if it would involve the trustees entering into a transaction at an undervalue (see *section 40* of *PA 1995* and *regulation 5* of the *Investment Regulations (SI 1996 No 3127)*).

Employer-related investments are defined under *section 40* of *PA 1995* as:

(*a*) shares or securities referred to in *section 22* of and *Schedule 2* to the *Financial Services and Markets Act 2000* issued by the employer or by any person who is connected with, or an associate of, the employer (for definition of connected employers see table 13.3 and for associated employers see diagram 13.10);

(*b*) land which is occupied by, or used by, or subject to a lease in favour of, the employer or by any person who is connected with, or an associate of, the employer;

(*c*) property (other than land) which is used for the purposes of any business carried on by the employer or by any person who is connected with, or an associate of, the employer;

10.25 *Investment*

(d) loans to the employer or any person who is connected with, or an associate of, the employer.

In addition, regulation 4 of the Investment Regulations (SI 1996 No 3127) sets out additional employer-related investments including:

- the obligations of any employer, or any person who is connected with, or an associate of, the employer, to the extent that they have been guaranteed or secured by the trustees;
- loans to any person where repayment depends on the employer's actions (unless the trustees did not intend to financially assist the employer);
- the appropriate proportion of any collective investment scheme which would have counted as an employer-related investment had it been made by the scheme directly.

If any sums due and payable by a person (including, but not limited to, an employer) to the trustees of a scheme remain unpaid they are to be regarded, for the purposes of *section 40* of *PA 1995*, as a loan made to that person by the trustees and may consequently be treated as an employer-related investment.

The provisions under *PA 1995* relating to employer-related investments do not apply to unapproved schemes. Nor do they apply to small self-administered schemes if the rules of the scheme provide that before any investment is made in an employer-related investment, each member must agree in writing to the making of that investment. (See chapter 13 for details of restrictions on investment for small self-administered schemes.)

Certain insurance policies and additional voluntary contributions may be invested in an employer-related investment with the written agreement of the member who paid the contributions. [*Investment Regulations (SI 1996 No 3127), reg 6*].

Regulation 7 of the *Investment Regulations (SI 1996 No 3127)* sets out transitional provisions for existing loans and employer-related investments. Generally, so long as any conditions relating to the loan or investment remained unchanged, the transitional period lasted until 5 April 2002.

If the resources of a scheme are invested in employer-related investments in excess of the maximum allowed, sanctions, in the form of a fine and/or removal, could apply to any trustee who fails to take all reasonable steps to ensure compliance with the Act. Further, a trustee who agrees to make an employer-related investment is guilty of an offence and may be liable, in extreme cases, to imprisonment (see appendix I).

THE FINANCIAL SERVICES AND MARKETS ACT 2000

10.25 The *Financial Services and Markets Act 2000 (FSMA 2000)* came into effect on 1 December 2001. Its purpose is to provide for the regulation of the whole of the UK financial services and banking industry by a single regulator, the Financial Services Authority (FSA). The FSA has assumed responsibility for banking supervision from the Bank of England and HM Treasury, and for the admission of securities to the official List from the London Stock Exchange. With effect from 1 December 2001 the FSA took over the regulatory duties of IMRO, SFA and PIA and those of the Building Societies Commission and the Friendly Societies Commission.

Transitional arrangements were in force until 30 June 2002 to enable the business rules operated by the previous regulatory bodies to be harmonised with the new conduct of business rules made by the FSA. The purpose of the transitional provisions was to assist firms to achieve a smooth transfer from one regulatory regime to another.

Professional firms (solicitors accountants and actuaries) who do not undertake FSA regulated activities such as providing investment advice will be exempt from direct regulation by the FSA.

Such firms will also be exempt if they only carry out certain restricted activities arising out of, or incidental to the provision of professional services.

It should be noted that in February 2004 the Government published a Consultation Paper entitled 'Financial Services and Markets Act two year review: Changes to secondary legislation – Proposals for Change'. The deadline for submissions was 28 May 2004. This document, published by HM Treasury, reviews the *FSMA 2000* and includes proposals to ease investment restrictions on trustees and to increase an employer's ability to advise on pensions matters.

Objectives of the FSA

10.26 The FSA has four principal objectives under the Act:

(*a*) maintaining market confidence;

(*b*) promoting public understanding of the financial system;

(*c*) the protection of consumers; and

(*d*) reducing financial crime ie by the regulation of investment activities and persons authorised to carry on such activities.

Investment managers

10.27 From 1 December 2001, investment managers providing financial services to pension scheme trustees have re-classified their trustee clients as 'Intermediate Customers' under the new regime, instead of 'non-private clients' under the FSA 1986 regime. Such clients no longer have access to the complaints handling ombudsman, but are required to take up their complaints with an independent senior executive within the investment house.

10.28 *Investment*

Prohibited activities

10.28 It is a criminal offence under *FSMA 2000, s 24* to carry out a 'regulated activity', without authorisation or exemption from authorisation.

What constitutes a regulated activity?

10.29 *FSMA 2000* and specifically the *Financial Services and Markets Act 2000 (Regulated Activities) Order 2001 (SI 2001 No 544)* ('*Regulated Activities Order*') specify a wide range of regulated activities which include the following activities, namely:

(*a*) dealing in investments;

(*b*) arranging deals in investments;

(*c*) managing investments;

(*d*) giving investment advice;

(*e*) establishing, operating or winding up a collective investment scheme or a stakeholder pension scheme; and

(*f*) safeguarding and administering investments.

Specified investments, for the purposes of *FSMA 2000*, include shares and stocks, debentures, Government and public securities, certificates representing securities, units in collective investment schemes, rights under a stakeholder pension scheme, options, futures, contracts for differences and rights under contracts of insurance (*Part III* of the *Regulated Activities Order*). Land and cash are not investments for the purposes of *FSMA 2000*.

The position of the trustees

10.30 Ordinarily, where trustees deal, arrange deals or give advice in relation to investments, they are likely to benefit from the exclusions contained in the *Regulated Activities Order*. However, *Article 4* of the *Financial Services and Markets Act 2000 (Carrying on Regulated Activities by Way of Business) Order 2001 (SI 2001 No 1177)* ('the *Business Order*') provides that trustees will be treated as carrying out the activity of managing investments by way of business, where assets are held for the purposes of an occupational pension scheme. An exception to this is where all 'routine or day-to-day' decisions in the carrying on of that activity (except for certain exclusions in *Article 4(6)* of the *Business Order*) relating to assets, securities or contractually based investments are taken by an authorised or exempted person or an overseas person who does not require authorisation. Most commonly trustees seek to benefit from this provision by delegating investment management activities to duly authorised fund managers. However, it should be noted that this provision is reconsidered in the February 2004 Consultation Paper referred to in 10.25 above – see further on this below.

Where a trustee undertakes investment management activities himself, he will need to be authorised under *FSMA 2000* and regulated by the FSA. The rules of the FSA are intended to ensure that those managing pension scheme assets are adequately trained and supervised and meet competence thresholds; that adequate records are kept; that proper investment contracts are entered into and that adequate procedures exist to safekeep assets.

In supervising a fund manager (see 10.34 below), trustees must ensure that they do not inadvertently end up taking routine or day-to-day investment decisions which would require them to be authorised under *FSMA 2000*. The Securities and Investments Board issued a guidance note 'Pensions Advice and Management under the Financial Services Act 1986' in March 1988, confirming that if the trustees limit their investment to the strategic level, for example by deciding on an overall investment plan but not specific investments, they will not be regarded as taking any day-to-day (now routine or day-to-day) decisions and, therefore, would be exempt. It is anticipated that a similar position will prevail under *FSMA 2000* and the FSA is currently updating its guidance on investment activities relating to pension schemes. The publication of this guidance has been delayed and is now expected in the last quarter of 2004. The involvement of most trustees extends to deciding on an investment policy, which will generally be reflected in the statement of investment principles required under *section 35 of PA 1995* (see 10.23 above), and monitoring the performance of the fund manager against the market generally. This will not constitute routine or day-to-day decision making but if, for example, the trustees direct the fund manager to purchase specific investments, they may have to be authorised. The Government's February 2004 Consultation Paper proposes that the word 'routine' should be removed from *Article 4* of the *Business Order*. The Consultation Paper proposes this change on account of the uncertainty surrounding the scope of 'routine' and 'day-to-day' decisions and concern that the combination of these two elements imposes tougher regulations on trustees than under the predecessor legislation which only referred to 'day-to-day' decisions.

Certain exemptions apply in relation to small self-administered pension schemes where all of the scheme members are trustees (see also 13.14 below).

Trustees should also beware of breaching the provisions of section *98* of *FSMA 2000* which prohibits the issuing of investment advertisements unless their contents are approved by an authorised person.

Care should also be taken when investing in common investment funds. These are usually established where an employer operates more than one pension scheme and it is decided to place all of the schemes' investments in one vehicle. Usually such arrangements are established to enable the participant schemes to benefit from the additional purchasing power, reduction in costs and wider market-exposure that a larger investment arrangement may offer. However, it is most likely that such arrangements would constitute collective investment schemes for the purposes of *FSMA 2000* and therefore require authorisation.

10.31 *Investment*

THE SELECTION AND SUPERVISION OF INVESTMENT ADVISERS

10.31 Quite apart from the *FSMA 2000* implications discussed in 10.25 to 10.30 above, many trustees will lack either the time or skill to manage directly their scheme's portfolio, and so will delegate their investment power to a professional fund manager. Although it is a fundamental rule of trust law that a trustee cannot delegate his powers and discretions, there are statutory exceptions to the rule and it can be overridden by the trust documents.

Position before *PA 1995*

10.32 *Section 23* of the *Trustee Act 1925* (now repealed) allowed trustees to employ and pay an agent to transact any business required in the execution of a trust. However, this provision did not allow a trustee to delegate the exercise of a discretion. The trustees still had to decide on the investments to be sold and purchased; the agent simply implemented the decisions made.

Section 23 of the *Trustee Act 1925* has now been replaced by *section 11* of the *Trustee Act 2000*, which allows trustees to authorise any person to exercise any or all of their 'delegable functions' as their agent. Trustees may delegate any function other than:

(a) a function relating to the distribution of the assets of the trust;

(b) a power to decide whether payments from the trust funds should be made out of income or capital;

(c) a power to appoint trustees; or

(d) a power conferred by any other enactment or the trust instrument which permits the trustees to delegate their functions or to appoint a person to act as a nominee or custodian.

Section 25 of the *Trustee Act 1925* allows trustees to delegate the exercise of their discretions for a period of up to one year under a power of attorney but does not explicitly allow for the remuneration of the person to whom the discretion has been delegated.

Due to the constraints of the statutory power to delegate, trustees are generally given power to delegate investment decisions and to appoint and remunerate advisers and agents, including investment advisers and fund managers, in their scheme's documentation.

Position after *PA 1995*

10.33 The statutory power allowing trustees to appoint agents and delegate the exercise of their investment power has been significantly extended from 6 April 1997 by *PA 1995*.

Section 34 of *PA 1995* effectively permits delegation of investment decisions by the trustees where the delegation is:

(*a*)   to a fund manager who is authorised under *FSMA 2000*;

(*b*)   to a fund manager who is not authorised under *section 19* of *FSMA 2000* so long as any decisions made by that fund manager would not constitute activities of a specified kind under *FSMA 2000*;

(*c*)   to a sub-committee of two or more trustees;

(*d*)   in accordance with *section 25* of the *Trustee Act 1925* (see 10.32 above).

Trustees cannot otherwise delegate any investment decision. [*PA 1995, s 34(2)(b)*]. As the provisions of *PA 1995* are overriding in this regard, even if the trust instrument permits delegation in other circumstances, it appears that the trustees cannot delegate outside of the four situations referred to above. In the case of (*c*) and (*d*) above, the trustees' ability to delegate may be further restricted by the requirements of *FSMA 2000* (see 10.25 to 10.30 above).

Section 34(2) of *PA 1995* permits trustees to delegate any discretion to make any decision about investments to a fund manager who is authorised under *FSMA 2000*. Provided that the trustees take all reasonable steps to satisfy themselves that the fund manager has the appropriate knowledge and experience for managing the investments of the scheme and is carrying out his work competently and complying with *section 36* of *PA 1995*, they will not be responsible for the acts or defaults of the fund manager. (See 10.19 above regarding the requirements of *section 36,* and see 10.34 below regarding supervision of a fund manager.)

Section 34(5) provides that, subject to any restrictions imposed by the scheme, trustees may delegate investment decisions to a sub-committee of two or more of the trustees. However, in practice, the requirements of *FSMA 2000* may restrict the circumstances in which such a delegation would be appropriate. The trustees, or a person on their behalf, may also delegate decisions which do not constitute carrying on a regulated activity (within the meaning of *FSMA 2000*) to a fund manager who is not authorised under the *FSMA 2000*. Trustees will remain liable for any acts or defaults of the sub-committee or the fund manager to whom the discretion has been delegated. However, if the trustees or the person who delegated the discretion on their behalf, take all reasonable steps to ensure that such a fund manager is an appropriate person to appoint, the trust documents can exclude or restrict the liability of the trustees for the acts and defaults of the fund manager. (See 10.50 below for discussion on restricting liability of trustees.)

Although *section 34* of the *PA 1995* gives trustees a power to delegate investment decisions, it does not give trustees explicit authority to remunerate any fund manager to whom such decisions have been delegated. The cautious approach is to ensure that the trust instrument contains power to remunerate fund managers although, arguably, there is an implicit statutory power to do so. Although the statutory power to delegate investment discretions has certainly been widened by *PA 1995*, most trust deeds will probably continue to include some form of express powers of delegation. The relationship between the trustees and the fund manager they appoint is, and will continue to be, governed to a large extent by the terms of the agreement entered into between them.

Section 47 of *PA 1995* requires an individual or a firm to be appointed by or on behalf of the trustees as fund manager if the assets of the scheme consist of or include investments (within the meaning of the *FSMA 2000*) (see 10.29 above). The appointment of the fund manager must be made in writing and must specify the date on which the appointment is due to take effect, to whom the fund manager is to report and from whom the fund manager is to take instructions. [*Occupational Pension Schemes (Scheme Administration) Regulations 1996 (SI 1996 No 1715), reg 5*].

Neither the Act nor the regulations made under *section 47, PA 1995* impose any requirements or restrictions regarding the qualifications or experience required of a person to be appointed as a fund manager. He does not, for example, have to be authorised under the *FSMA 2000*. In reality trustees are likely to appoint the person to whom they have delegated their investment decisions but this is not a requirement of the Act. Indeed, on a literal reading of *PA 1995*, a fund manager appointed under *PA 1995, section 47* need play no role in the scheme whatsoever.

Supervision of a fund manager

10.34 Trustees have a general duty to supervise and monitor the performance of a fund manager. In particular, trustees should ensure that the fund manager is carrying out his work competently and complying with the requirements of *PA 1995* if they wish to benefit from the statutory exoneration provision contained in *section 34(4)* which is applicable where an FSA authorised manager is appointed (see 10.33 above and 10.50 below). Supervising does not imply that the trustees should continually check-up on their fund manager but it does impose an obligation to review his appointment from time to time. If the fund manager is regularly performing below the market performance or is outside the benchmark set by the trustees, the trustees should ask why this is and, if appropriate, consider whether they wish to continue their arrangement with that fund manager.

THE LIABILITY OF INVESTMENT ADVISERS

Duties arising from the agreement

10.35 As a matter of general contract law, a fund manager is obliged to act in accordance with the terms of his contract and must not exceed his authority or he will be liable for a breach of contract even if he acted in his client's best interests. (*Fray v Voules [1859] 1 E&E 839*.) A fund manager may be required to follow the trustees' instructions, but he cannot be obliged to commit an illegal act. It is not enough for the fund manager simply to follow the trustees' instructions and to observe to the letter the terms of his written agreement, he is in addition contractually bound to act with due care and skill. As a fund manager is remunerated for his services he must perform his duty exercising the care, skill and diligence which it is usual, necessary and proper for professional fund managers to employ.

The *FSA 1986* and now *FSMA 2000* have, to an extent, dictated the terms of the contractual relationship between fund manager and trustees. Under the FSA Rules a fund manager cannot generally manage the investments of trustees on a discretionary basis unless there is in place an investment management agreement regulating the rights and liabilities of the trustees and the investment manager. 'Standard' terms and conditions for discretionary fund management are now published by the Investment Management Association ('IMA'). The most recent edition of the standard terms was published in March 2004 (IMA 1). Many fund managers do, however, prefer to use their own 'standard' terms and conditions. The fact that such contracts are described as 'standard', however, should not dissuade trustees from questioning their terms or seeking additional protections.

The agreement will also contain a schedule setting out specific investment guidelines agreed upon by the fund manager and the trustees. Some of the 'standard' terms deal specifically with the fiduciary duties imposed upon fund managers and, where appropriate, these are considered in 10.42 to 10.47 below. The following provisions in the standard terms are examples of provisions which could cause concern for trustees, particularly in light of *PA 1995*.

Investment discretion

10.36 The fund manager and the trustees must agree on any restrictions or objectives to be imposed on the fund manager. Trustees should consider supplying the fund manager with a copy of the investment power they are delegating to ensure that the fund manager does not inadvertently make an investment which is outside the scope of the power. Trustees may also wish to clarify the details of their statement of investment principles with the fund manager and to append it to the written agreement to seek to ensure that he exercises the investment power with a view to giving effect to the principles contained in the statement of investment principles. (See 10.23 above and *section 36(5)* of *PA 1995*.)

Liability

10.37 Typically fund managers will attempt to limit their contractual liability. In particular they will look to exclude liability for indirect or consequential loss (even where they have had prior notice of special circumstances concerning the possibility of such loss arising). It is not uncommon for managers to attempt also to avoid responsibility for the acts and omissions of delegates and agents. Trustees should be concerned to obtain protection in respect of these 'third

10.38 *Investment*

parties' given that they will have little involvement in their selection and may have no direct contractual relationship with them.

Uninvested cash

10.38 The IMA's standard terms allow a fund manager to hold uninvested cash in a bank account. Trustees should ensure that in doing so, the fund manager is obliged to comply with the requirements of *PA 1995* relating to the retention of money in a bank account. [*PA 1995, s 49* and the *Occupational Pension Schemes (Scheme Administration) Regulations 1996 (SI 1996 No 1715), reg 11*]. Consideration should also be given to the application of the 'FSA's Conduct of Business Rules' concerning the treatment of client money. These rules were formerly contained in the *Financial Services (Client Money) Regulations 1991*).

Voting

10.39 The IMA's standard terms refer to the way in which a fund manager may exercise any voting rights attaching to investments. Trustees should consider whether they should impose any specific conditions on the fund manager in light of their possible duties to exercise voting rights (see 10.49 below).

Valuation and reports

10.40 Trustees will need to consider when they require reports to be made regarding the valuation of investments. In agreeing on a suitable timeframe they should bear in mind their duty to supervise the fund manager and in particular whether the timing is appropriate to ensure that they are satisfied that the fund manager is carrying out his work competently and complying with *section 36* of *PA 1995* (see 10.19 above). It may also be appropriate to require the fund manager to disclose other documents and information in his possession on the reasonable request of the trustees and to allow auditors or other advisers to inspect these documents. Trustees should also take care over clauses which provide that, following a specified period after the trustees have received a valuation or report, they may no longer bring an action against the manager for any breach which occurred during the period to which the valuation or report relates.

Custodianship

10.41 If the fund manager is to make use of the services of a custodian (who may or may not be a party to the investment management agreement), the trustees should ensure that they have formally appointed that custodian (ie in accordance with *section 47* of *PA 1995* and *regulations 4* and *5* of the *Occupational Pension Schemes (Scheme Administration) Regulations 1996 (SI 1996*

No 1715)) as otherwise they will not be able to rely on his skill or judgement without the risk of incurring sanctions in the form of a fine and/or removal (see appendix I).

The debate as to whether trustees must also appoint sub-custodians was closed as a result of the publication of the *Occupational Pension Schemes (Scheme Administration) Amendment Regulations 1998 [SI 1998 No 1494]* which relieve trustees of this obligation and enable them to rely on the skill and judgment of sub-custodians appointed by the custodian provided that written disclosure of the extent to which (if any) the custodian accepts liability for its sub-custodians' actions is made in the Custody Agreement. Any changes to the liability position must be immediately notified to the trustees by the custodian. The trustees should also check that the custodian they appoint has the appropriate *FSMA 2000* authorisation.

Where the custodian is not a party to the investment management agreement, it is likely that there will be a separate 'global custody agreement'. Whether custody is dealt with in the investment agreement or otherwise, it will be necessary to deal with a number of key areas in addition to core custody, including: settlement of transactions (contractual or actual), cash management, liability for sub-custodians and foreign exchange transactions.

Investment management and custody agreements should always be carefully reviewed by trustees and their advisers before being entered into, as some of their terms (for instance, the extent to which the agreement seeks to exempt the fund manager or custodian from liability) can expose the scheme to considerable liabilities.

Fiduciary duties

10.42 Because the fund manager is handling trust monies, it may be argued that his duties are not only contractual, but also fiduciary, ie they may have to be exercised in the best interests of the members. In effect, this means that the following duties may be implied.

Duty not to delegate

10.43 The general duty not to delegate applies not only to trustees but also to their agents. An agency relationship is based on the confidence one person has in another, and so an agent is in principle prohibited from delegating his authority to another person or even appointing a sub-agent. (See *Allam & Co Ltd v Europa Poster Services Ltd [1968] 1 All ER 826*) Delegation is, however, permitted in certain circumstances. For example, where the employment of a sub-agent is usual in managing a client's investments and is not unreasonable or inconsistent with the express terms of any written agreement; or where the act delegated is purely administrative and one which does not require or involve confidence or discretion.

10.44 *Investment*

Usually the investment management agreement will expressly permit a fund manager to delegate or appoint sub-agents, often without the consent of the trustees. Fund managers will often include a provision to the effect that they are not liable for the actions of their sub-agents unless they are 'connected companies'. As trustees may have no direct contractual relationship with the sub-agent it is advisable for them to ensure that, if the fund manager is to be allowed to delegate or appoint agents, he remains liable to the trustees for their acts or defaults.

The fund manager must not put himself in a position where his duties to the trustees conflict with his own interests

10.44 This is no more than the application of the equitable maxim that a person in a position of trust must not put himself in a situation in which his interest and his duty would be in conflict. An extreme example is where a fund manager seeks to buy an asset from the trustees. He would be attempting to achieve the impossible; trying to achieve the highest price for the trustees and at the same time endeavouring to pay the lowest possible price himself.

The FMA's standard terms specifically address potential conflicts of interest. They allow the fund manager to effect transactions where conflicts arise but provide that the fund manager must ensure that such transactions are effected on terms which are not materially less favourable to the trustees than if the potential conflict had not existed. Despite this there may be situations where the fiduciary duty should, and does, override the contractual provision.

A fund manager appointed under *section 47(2)* of *PA 1995* must, on being appointed, confirm that he will declare any conflict of interest affecting his relationship with the trustees immediately he becomes aware of it or, if he is regulated under *FSMA 2000*, in accordance with the rules of the FSA. However, many managers will interpret the rules to allow them to give generic style disclosures in the investment management agreement, thus avoiding the impracticality of making prior disclosure on a case by case basis.

Duty not to accept bribes

10.45 This duty is self explanatory. If a fund manager accepts a payment which could constitute a bribe and conducts himself in the way proposed by the person offering the bribe, it will be presumed that he has been influenced by the bribe and has breached his duty to the trustees. This presumption is not rebuttable and the trustees' loss is considered to be at least the amount of the bribe.

The person offering the bribe, as well as the fund manager who receives it, will be criminally liable. The fund manager will have to repay or forego any commission, profit or remuneration to which he would otherwise have been entitled from the trustees. (*Andrews v Ramsey & Co [1903] 2 KB 635.*) The trustees will be able to dismiss the fund manager without notice (*Bulfield v*

Fournier [1895] 11 TLR 282) and claim for the amount of the bribe plus interest from the date upon which the bribe was received.

The fund manager has a duty not to take advantage of his position or the trustees' property in order to acquire a benefit for himself

10.46 An investment manager is liable to account to the trustees for any profits he makes using confidential information acquired in the course of his appointment. (*Peter Pan Manufacturing Corporation v Corsets Silhouette Ltd [1963] 3 All ER 402.*) The provisions relating to insider dealing contained in the *Criminal Justice Act 1993* may also be relevant. Broadly speaking, dealings in securities of a company by an individual who holds unpublished price-sensitive information in respect of that company by virtue of his connection with the company are prohibited. There are similar provisions with regard to advising others to deal in the shares or debentures of the company, and in respect of the communication of unpublished price-sensitive information to others where that person might reasonably be expected to make use of it for the purpose of dealing.

Ultra vires

10.47 If trustees make an investment which under their investment power is barred or outside its scope they are acting *ultra vires*. *Hazell v Hammersmith and Fulham London Borough Council [1990] 2 WLR 17*, raised the concept of *ultra vires* in connection with a local authority's funds as certain of the activities were beyond those permissible by the relevant Local Government Act. An act which is *ultra vires* is generally void and may not be ratified. Fund managers should be made aware of the powers of the trustees on whose behalf they are acting as otherwise they may enter into *ultra vires* arrangements. Equally, trustees are advised to ensure that they restrict fund managers from inadvertently acting outside the trustees' powers by ensuring that the investment management agreement contains appropriate investment restrictions.

Liability for breach of trust by agents

10.48 It is possible for an agent of trustees to be held liable in respect of a breach of trust committed by the trustees for whom he is acting, and which he, as agent, has facilitated. To be liable, the fund manager would have to knowingly commit a wrongful act in relation to the scheme's assets; in effect, he would have to know that the trustees did not have authority to give the instructions he followed or take the action he took. A fund manager may also be liable where he turns a blind eye to what is an obvious breach of trust where an honest and reasonable man would have considered it such.

Unless fund managers are either aware that a breach of trust is being committed by the trustees concerned, or the situation is such that it is, or should be, obvious to any competent fund manager that this is the case, they are entitled to assume

10.49 *Investment*

that the instructions given are bona fide and within the powers of the trustees. If a fund manager follows an investment policy which he knows to be outside the powers of the trustees he renders himself liable to an action for breach of trust.

The most crucial factor on which liability of a fund manager depends is the precise terms of the investment powers given to the trustees and whether the fund manager is aware of them. Consequently trustees should ensure that the fund manager is fully apprised of any restrictions on their powers of investment and appropriate restrictions should be built into the investment management agreement.

VOTING RIGHTS AS A CONSEQUENCE OF SHARE OWNERSHIP – IS IT A TRUST ASSET?

10.49 In the UK approximately a third of all shares in publicly quoted companies are held by pension funds. Trustees have traditionally exercised their voting rights only in exceptional cases but the sheer size of their voting power begs the question: are trustees and any fund managers to whom they have delegated their discretions in some way responsible for the actions of the companies in which they invest?

The Cadbury Committee recommended that institutional investors should make positive use of their voting rights and should also disclose their policies on the use of voting rights. The National Association of Pension Funds has recommended that trustees should decide on their voting policy and that voting policy should be made public. Trustees should then exercise their votes prudently and in the interests of scheme beneficiaries.

There is no doubt that in the United States this idea has progressed further than in the UK. Pension funds in the United States have been obliged to exercise their voting rights since 1988 in respect of US companies. This duty was extended in 1994 to include overseas companies and the effect of this duty is being felt in the UK. (See 10.51 below.)

The legislators in the UK have, to date, resisted attempts to impose a similar obligation on trustees. The previous Government successfully resisted an attempt by the then opposition to include such a duty in *PA 1995*. Although it was felt that imposing a mandatory duty to exercise voting rights was contrary to the general aim of deregulation and would be too difficult to enforce, it was accepted that trustees, or fund managers on their behalf, should be encouraged to exercise their voting rights.

Even in the absence of a statutory duty to exercise voting rights, there is a strong case for arguing that some form of duty exists. Trustees have a clear duty to act in the best interests of their members and this includes protecting the value of, and the income derived from, an investment. There may be circumstances where this can only be achieved by voting for or against certain proposals and in such situations trustees may be open to attack if they simply make no voting decision whatsoever. It should be remembered that positively abstaining from voting can be a legitimate voting decision. The duty is perhaps not necessarily to vote but to consider whether, and if so how, to vote.

Arguably, fund managers to whom discretionary investment responsibilities have been delegated have fiduciary responsibilities similar to the responsibilities of trustees. Accordingly, if trustees have a duty to consider exercising voting rights, it follows that fund managers must also concern themselves with the running of companies in whom they invest trustees' monies.

In 2002, the Government gave its response (its 'Consultation Document') to the Myners Review in which it stated at Principle 6 on Activism:

> 'The mandate and trust deed should incorporate the principle of the US Department of Labor Interpretative Bulletin on activism. Trustees should also ensure that managers have an explicit strategy, elucidating the circumstances in which they will intervene in a company; the approach they will use in doing so; and how they measure the effectiveness of this strategy'.

In October 2002, the Institutional Shareholders Committee (which consisted of the Investment Management Association, the Association of British Insurers, the National Association of Pension Funds and the Association of Investment Trust Companies) unveiled the publication of a new statement of principles entitled, 'The Responsibilities of Institutional Shareholders and Agents – Statement of Principles'. It develops the principles set out in its 1991 statement 'The Responsibilities of Institutional Shareholders in the UK' and expands on the Combined Code of Corporate Governance of June 1998. It sets out best practice for institutional shareholders and/or agents in relation to their responsibilities in respect of investee companies. The Statement comments in relation to intervention, that if boards do not respond constructively when institutional shareholders and/or agents intervene, then institutional shareholders and/or agents will consider on a case-by-case basis whether to escalate their action. The Government said that it welcomed the publication of the statement of principles and that it would review their impact after two years to see 'whether this non-legislative approach has been successful in delivering change'.

TRUSTEE LIABILITY AND PROTECTION

10.50 The ultimate responsibility for investment decisions lies firmly with the trustees. The duties placed on trustees regarding investment are onerous, and becoming more so, not only in terms of the legal principles governing the propriety of their actions, but also in terms of the types of investment vehicles now available. It would be a foolish trustee who did not take specialist advice regarding the exercise of his investment power. However, taking advice will not, on its own, necessarily protect the trustee; he must still act honestly with reasonable care and prudence. The increased responsibilities of trustees proposed in the Pensions Bill should also be noted (see further at 10.51 below). The

10.51 *Investment*

fiduciary duties and liability of fund managers are discussed at 10.42 and 10.48 above but the following particular points arise in relation to investment decisions.

Trustees will be liable for the acts or defaults of the fund manager if they fail to take reasonable care in choosing the fund manager or in fixing or enforcing the terms of his engagement. (*Steel v Wellcome Trustees Ltd [1988] 1 WLR 167.*)

Section 23 of the *Trustee Act 2000* gives trustees some protection by providing that a trustee is not liable for any act or default of an agent, nominee or custodian, or a permitted substitute, when entering into or reviewing the arrangements under which that person acts, unless the trustee has failed to comply with the applicable duty of care.

Case law considers 'wilful default' to include both positive acts and a 'want of ordinary prudence'. (*Speight v Gaunt (1883) 22 Ch D 727; Re Chapman (1896) 2 Ch 763.*) There have been cases to the effect that 'wilful default' should be interpreted in the company law context so that it includes a deliberate or reckless breach of duty but not a negligent breach of duty. (*Re Vickery [1931] 1 Ch 572.*) However, the safer and the generally more acceptable view of trustees' responsibilities is the former definition.

It is common sense that trustees should take care when selecting their advisers and agents, as would any man or woman with common prudence, and further exercise reasonable and responsible supervision.

Many trust deeds attempt to mitigate trustees' responsibilities by widely drafted exoneration clauses. However, *section 33* of *PA 1995* limits the extent to which liability in respect of investment decisions may be excluded by providing that liability for breach of an obligation to take care or exercise skill in the performance of any investment functions exercisable by the trustees (or by a person to whom that function has been delegated under *section 34, PA 1995*) cannot be excluded or restricted by any instrument or agreement. *Section 33, PA 1995* does not prevent trustees being exonerated under the provisions of the trust deed from liability for the actions of a fund manager to whom the trustees have delegated an investment discretion under *section 34(5)* of *PA 1995* (see 10.33 above).

However, *PA 1995* also offers some exoneration for trustees who delegate their investment discretion to a fund manager authorised under *FSMA 2000* in accordance with *section 34(2)* of *PA 1995*. The trustees will not be liable under *PA 1995* for the acts or defaults of such a fund manager provided they have taken all reasonable steps to satisfy themselves that he has the appropriate knowledge and experience and is acting competently and complying with the requirements of *section 36* of *PA 1995* (see 10.19 and 10.20 above). [*PA 1995, s 34(4)*].

MYNERS' REPORT: VOLUNTARY CODE OF PRACTICE

10.51 A brief summary is set out below of the proposed principles which the

Investment **10.51**

Myners' Report suggests should be adopted on a voluntary basis by the trustees of defined benefit schemes when taking investment decisions. There is a separate set of principles applicable to defined contribution schemes. The Government allowed schemes two years to comply with Myners (or explain why they could not) and it stated that it intended to conduct an 'audit' of Myners compliance in 2003. The Department for Work and Pensions published a report on compliance with Myners in autumn 2003 which set out the extent to which 14 schemes have voluntarily complied with Myners. Voluntary compliance is most visible in relation to quantifiable targets, such as asset allocation and performance measurement, and there has been less progress towards effective decision making, shareholder activism and socially responsible investment. Larger schemes seem more compliant than smaller ones.

- Effective decision making

Trustees should have sufficient expertise and appropriate training to be able to evaluate critically any investment advice they may receive. They should also ensure that they have sufficient in-house staff to support them in their investment responsibilities. It is good practice to have an investment sub-committee to provide focus. Trustees should adopt a forward looking business plan and arrange to conduct a self-assessment of their skills and their investment processes to ensure that they carry out their role effectively. Myners' view is that trustees should be paid.

- Clear objectives

Trustees should set investment objectives which take into consideration the trustees' view of what is necessary to meet the fund's liabilities taking account of the fund's overall income, and the trustees' attitude to risk (and, specifically, their willingness to accept under performance by their fund manager due to market conditions). Investment objectives set by trustees must relate to the fund's specific liabilities, not in relation to peer group performance.

- Focus on asset allocation

Trustees should pay significant attention to strategic asset allocation, and recognise its importance in helping the trustees to achieve the fund's investment objectives. Trustees should take advantage of the full range of investment opportunities available to them to meet their objectives, including investment in private equity.

- Expert advice

Contracts for actuarial and investment advice should be open to separate competition.

- Explicit mandates

Trustees should agree explicit written mandates with their fund managers, covering topics such as objectives, benchmarks, risk, the manager's investment approach and the timescales for measurement and evaluation of the manager's performance. Myners' does not believe that a fund manager's mandate should be terminated before its term expires for under performance

10.51 *Investment*

alone, at least where such underperformance results from adverse market conditions. No financial instruments should be excluded from the fund manager's mandate without clear justification. Trustees must seek to understand how transaction related investment costs including commissions are incurred and should put in place controls to monitor investment costs. Trustees should not permit soft commissions to be paid in respect of their investment transactions.

- Activism

The US Department of Labor Interpretative Bulletin on activism (ie the investor's policy on proxy voting, or guidelines) should be incorporated into the fund manager's mandate and the scheme's trust deed. Trustees and their fund managers should agree explicitly the circumstances in which the manager will be required to intervene in a company which the trustees hold as an investment.

- Appropriate benchmarks

Trustees and their fund managers should agree appropriate benchmarks, avoiding sub-optimal investment strategies. Trustees should consider, in relation to each asset class, whether active or passive management is more appropriate and allow managers to pursue active strategies (if chosen) to achieve higher investment returns.

- Performance measurement

Trustees must arrange to measure their fund's performance regularly and carry out a regular formal assessment of their own investment procedures and decisions together with a review of the procedures and investment decisions delegated to their advisers and fund managers.

- Transparency

Trustees should produce a more detailed Statement of Investment Principles than the existing SIP, showing:

- who takes investment decisions and why the investment structure used by the Scheme has been selected;
- the fund's investment objectives;
- the fund's asset allocation strategy, and how this has been reached;
- details of the mandates agreed with each of the fund's *advisers* and managers;
- the fee structures agreed with managers and with *advisers* and managers and, why these fee structures have been selected.

- Regular reporting

The fund's Statement of Investment Principles should be published, together with the results obtained from monitoring the performance of advisers and fund managers. A summary of key information taken from the Statement of Investment Principles and the performance results of the Scheme's managers should be sent to scheme members, together with an explanation of why the fund has decided to depart from any of the key principles set out above.

Given the increasingly complex investment decisions which trustees are required to make, it seems entirely sensible that trustees should seek to increase their knowledge and understanding of how investment markets work, and in particular, how charges operate in relation to investment decisions made by the trustees.

However, it seems equally valid that, where investment managers, with a full discretionary mandate involve pension scheme trustees in complex financial transactions, or instruments, they should clearly communicate the value of entering into such transactions in relation to their trustees' particular circumstances.

In the light of the Government's threat to legislate to incorporate Paul Myners' principles into trustees' investment decision making, it would be advisable for pension scheme trustees to meet to debate the issues raised with their advisers, and to decide which (if any) Myners principles to adopt.

The Pensions Bill includes provisions introducing a new standard of care for trustee conduct. Trustees will be expected to be 'conversant' with the relevant scheme documentation and to have 'knowledge and understanding of':

- pensions and trust law; and
- principles relating to funding of occupational pension schemes and the investment of the assets of schemes.

The degree of knowledge and understanding required is that appropriate for the purposes of enabling the individual properly to exercise the function in question. It is envisaged that codes of practice will be issued by the Regulator by way of guidance on how trustees are expected to comply with this new requirement.

Chapter 11

Funding, deficits and surpluses

INTRODUCTION

11.1 Most private sector occupational pension schemes in the United Kingdom are funded; assets are set aside, in advance, to provide a fund to meet the benefits ultimately payable (although it is not uncommon for death in service benefits to be insured). Public sector schemes are often unfunded or partially funded as they are, instead, backed by a Government guarantee. It has become increasingly common for higher-paid employees to be provided with benefits from an unapproved top-up scheme (which may be unfunded) (see chapter 14). However, new changes to simplify the tax treatment of pension schemes (see chapter 5) may well affect their popularity. In general, unfunded occupational schemes are the exception rather than the rule even though, before *PA 1995* came into force, there was little in the way of legislation relating to funding.

The first part of this chapter deals with the legal requirements imposed on trustees and employers regarding funding and, in particular, it considers the minimum funding provisions first introduced by *PA 1995* and the proposed changes to them in the Pensions Bill, as introduced in the House of Commons on 10 February 2004. The second part of this chapter considers the implications of excessive funding and discusses the ways in which a 'surplus' can be reduced.

PRE-PA 1995 REQUIREMENTS RELATING TO FUNDING

11.2 Until *PA 1995* there was no legislation which specifically required an employer to fund a pensions promise in advance. An employer could, quite legitimately, promise a pension to an employee and then make no financial provision for the benefit until it became payable. However, there were several controls which had implications in respect of funding which are discussed in 11.3 to 11.5 below.

Inland Revenue requirements

11.3 The IR SPSS will not grant an occupational pension scheme exempt approved status unless that scheme has some element of employer funding. Although the IR SPSS has no hard and fast rules, it looks for at least ten per cent of the total contributions to be provided by the employers, unless of course there is an employer contribution holiday in place (11.41(b) below).

At the other end of the scale, the Inland Revenue aims to restrict funding by limiting the tax reliefs available in respect of overfunded schemes (see 11.38 to 11.43 below).

Subject to these points, the Inland Revenue's view is that 'the amount and timing of the employer's contributions are matters for the employer' (IR12 (2001) PN 5.3).

Contracting-out requirements

11.4 Before the changes introduced by *PA 1995*, contracted-out final salary schemes were required to obtain an actuarial certificate at least once every three years which confirmed that, in the actuary's opinion, the assets would be sufficient to ensure that members' guaranteed minimum pensions would be paid in full if the scheme were to be wound up during the following three and a half years. This requirement was intended to ensure that contracted-out schemes were sufficiently funded to provide at least guaranteed minimum pensions and any benefits which, on the winding-up of the scheme, would have to be secured in priority to guaranteed minimum pensions. (For the later position see 11.23 below)

Disclosure requirements

11.5 Under the *Occupational Pension Schemes (Disclosure of Information) Regulations 1986 (SI 1986 No 1046)*, trustees of Inland Revenue approved schemes were required to produce an annual report which had to include an actuarial statement. The statement had to set out information on long term funding, including:

(*a*)   whether members' accrued benefits were covered by the assets held;

(*b*)   the long term contributions required to provide the benefits; and

(*c*)   the key assumptions adopted by the actuary.

Where the assets were not sufficient to cover the accrued benefits, the statement had to indicate what percentage of the benefits were covered and when the assets were expected to be sufficient to cover all of the accrued benefits.

The disclosure requirements and the contracting-out requirements have now been superseded by the requirements of *PA 1995*. The Inland Revenue's controls on funding are largely unaffected by *PA 1995*.

FUNDING PRACTICE

11.6 Generally employees prefer not to rely on their employer having the

11.7 *Funding, deficits and surpluses*

financial resources available to meet the pension commitment by the time benefits become payable. With an unfunded scheme, an individual could find that, when he comes to retire, the employer he worked for 20 years previously and who had promised him a pension, has gone out of business. A funded scheme alleviates this concern and ensures members will (or should) receive the pension due to them at retirement.

From the employer's perspective, making provision for future benefits as they accrue (as opposed to when they fall due) means that the employer can control his cash flow more easily and plan ahead; he is not faced with having to provide a costly benefit when his financial position may be such that he can ill afford it. Also, in the case of exempt approved schemes, the tax advantages available in respect of contributions to the scheme and income and capital gains on assets held by the scheme (see chapter 5) mean that the overall cost of providing benefits is reduced.

Most occupational pension schemes are funded in a way that aims to ensure that, by the time each member reaches retirement, there are sufficient funds to provide the benefits that have been promised. A scheme's governing documentation will normally contain rules specifying how the contributions payable by both the employer and the employees are to be determined. In most final salary schemes employees' contributions are fixed, with the employer meeting the balance required to pay the benefits promised (a 'balance of cost' scheme). The question of who determines the contribution rates (the trustees, the employer or, in some cases, the actuary) generally depends upon the scheme rules. Typically, no matter who has the responsibility under the trust deed to decide the contribution rate, the advice of an actuary will be sought and generally followed.

Contribution rates are significantly affected for the time being, however, by the minimum funding requirement ('MFR') (see 11.20 below).

ACTUARIAL VALUATIONS

Types of actuarial valuations

11.7 At regular intervals, an actuary must conduct an investigation to determine the value of a scheme's assets and liabilities as at a certain date. This enables the actuary to advise on the relative solvency of the scheme and also to estimate the rate of contributions required to provide the benefits promised. The various methods by which assets and liabilities can be valued, and funding assessed, are described in the actuarial Guidance Note, 'Pension Fund Terminology', GN26, which was first issued in May 1986 (as a paper entitled 'Pension Fund Terminology: Specimen Descriptions of Commonly Used Valuation Methods') and revised in March 2001.

The types of actuarial valuation which must be carried out in relation to a particular scheme depend on whether the scheme is a final salary scheme or a money purchase scheme.

Final salary schemes

11.8 Trustees of final salary schemes are generally required to obtain three types of actuarial valuations:

(a) an ongoing valuation to determine the appropriate contribution rate and funding level (see 11.10 to 11.12 below);

(b) a minimum funding requirement valuation to determine whether the scheme complies with the minimum funding requirement (see 11.13 to 11.19 below);

(c) a *'Schedule 22* valuation' to determine whether the scheme is funded in excess of the levels permitted for full tax advantages (see 11.38 to 11.43 below).

Some final salary schemes are exempt from the requirement to obtain a minimum funding requirement valuation (see 11.14 below). Such schemes are also exempt from the requirement to obtain an ongoing valuation (*regulation 30* of the *Occupational Pension Schemes (Minimum Funding Requirement and Actuarial Valuations) Regulations 1996 (SI 1996 No 1536)* (the *'MFR Regulations'*)) as amended by the *Occupational Pension Schemes (Minimum funding Requirement and Miscellaneous Amendments) Regulations 2002 (SI 2002 No 380)*.

In practice, the actuary will prepare one valuation report which encompasses all three valuations. Both the minimum funding requirement valuation and the *Schedule 22* valuation must be made in accordance with the methods and assumptions set out in legislation and actuarial guidelines. The aim is to ensure that two actuaries making the same valuation will arrive at the same result. More flexibility is permitted with the ongoing valuation, although there are still guidelines which must be complied with (see 11.10 below).

Money purchase schemes

11.9 Trustees of money purchase schemes are only required to obtain a *Schedule 22* valuation (see 11.38 to 11.43 below).

Ongoing actuarial valuations

11.10 Ongoing valuations are required under *section 41* of *PA 1995* and *regulation 30* of the *MFR Regulations*. They must be prepared in accordance with the guidelines set out in the actuarial Guidance Note, 'Retirement Benefit Schemes – Actuarial Reports', GN9 and any material departure from those guidelines must be indicated. The valuation must be accompanied by a statement made by the actuary (in the form set out in *Schedule 6* to the *MFR Regulations*) commenting on the security of prospective rights under the scheme, the contributions payable and the methods and assumptions adopted. The periods within which trustees must commission ongoing valuations and

11.11 *Funding, deficits and surpluses*

within which they must be signed, mirror those relating to the minimum funding requirement (see 11.16 to 11.18 below).

Depending on the approach taken by the actuary, and the method and assumptions he uses, the results of an ongoing valuation will vary significantly. The two main bases on which the actuary will usually make a valuation are the discontinuance basis and the past service reserve basis.

Discontinuance basis

11.11 On this basis the actuary will assume that the accrual of benefits and the payment of contributions are to cease at the date of the valuation. He will be able to calculate the exact value of the liabilities because they will, for the purpose of the valuation, have crystallised. No actuarial assumptions will have to be made as to future events; what is compared is the current realisable value of the scheme's assets as compared to its liabilities. From March 2004, actuarial guidance requires the actuary to assess, on a full buy out basis, the level of benefit cover for each priority if the scheme were to commence winding up on the valuation date.

Until 6 April 1997, an ongoing valuation, prepared in accordance with GN9, had to include a statement by the actuary regarding the funding position on a discontinuance basis. This requirement has been superseded in respect of schemes which are subject to the minimum funding requirement. A valuation of an ongoing scheme solely on a discontinuance basis will not give a true indication of the funding position of the scheme.

Past service reserve basis

11.12 Using this basis the actuary will have to make certain assumptions as to future events. The current salaries of existing members will be projected forward to a suitable date (usually normal retirement date, with some allowance being made for a certain percentage of members leaving before that date) using assumptions anticipating future salary growth and mortality rates. Future liabilities will then be predicted on the basis of existing service, but using the projected salaries.

How the actuary values the assets of the scheme will depend on the type of assets. Where the value of an asset fluctuates relatively frequently over a period of time, the actuary will generally use a 'smoothed' value that allows for those fluctuations. For example, the value of a particular holding of shares will not simply be the market value on the valuation date, it will be the average value over a period of time and will take into account the expected income from the shares. Assets which are relatively static in value will generally be given their market value. The future value of the fund will also have to be predicted and so the actuary will have to make assumptions about future interest rates and the investment return on the scheme's assets.

By comparing the projected liabilities with the projected value of the fund, the actuary will be able to determine the contribution rate required to ensure that the value of the fund will be sufficient to meet the future liabilities as they fall due. It must be remembered that, as the actuary is making assumptions about future events, the result of his valuation can only ever be a best estimate. The assumptions used will be derived from data collected over a lengthy period of time. It is possible that all the assumptions used by the actuary will be borne out in the future, but this is unlikely.

The differential between certain assumptions is often more significant than the assumptions themselves. If, for example, the assumptions include a low increase in salary growth but high investment growth, the valuation will tend to make the scheme appear to be well-funded. However, in reality if investment growth is high, salary growth may also be high so this valuation result may be a misleading guide to the true funding position of the scheme. By using a different set of assumptions the actuary can significantly alter the results of his valuation and consequently the rate of contributions required. The more conservative the assumptions, the less well funded a scheme will appear. Actuaries will often discuss their assumptions with the trustees before signing off a report.

THE MINIMUM FUNDING REQUIREMENT

The need for a solvency standard

11.13 The Goode Committee considered the issue of funding in some detail and concluded that a statutory funding requirement was desirable. After discussing the arguments put forward both for and against a minimum solvency standard, the Committee concluded:

> 'In assessing these various arguments we have taken as our basic premise the need to ensure that scheme members are not faced with a reduction in their accrued benefits. We take the view that the purpose of a funded pension scheme is that, no matter what happens to the sponsoring employer, the scheme members' accrued rights will be inviolate. We have therefore concluded that the introduction of a statutory minimum solvency requirement is necessary to provide security for the accrued pension rights of scheme members.' (Report of the Goode Committee, paragraph 4.4.16.)

During the passage of *PA 1995* through Parliament, the 'minimum solvency requirement' became the 'minimum funding requirement' but the change in name was not the only alteration. Many of the proposals put forward by the Committee were adopted in principle, but the test itself became less stringent. The minimum funding requirement does however, play a pivotal role in the working of many of the provisions of *PA 1995*.

The minimum funding requirement

11.14 The *Pensions Act 1995* introduced a requirement that 'the value of the

11.15 *Funding, deficits and surpluses*

assets of the scheme is not less than the amount of the liabilities of the scheme'. This requirement is referred to in *PA 1995* as the minimum funding requirement ('MFR').

Details of the MFR are contained in *sections 56 to 61* of *PA 1995*, the *MFR Regulations* and a professional Guidance Note, 'Retirement Benefit Schemes – Minimum Funding Requirement', GN27, issued by the Institute and Faculty of Actuaries and revised most recently in January 2003.

Compliance with the MFR, however, will not always guarantee that the assets of the scheme will be enough to meet its liabilities. This is because there will be timing differences between applying the MFR test and taking action in response to the results of the test. Also, the test does not seek to guarantee that schemes will always have sufficient funds to provide for benefits by purchasing annuities from an insurance company.

The MFR does not apply to all occupational pension schemes, the main exemptions being:

(*a*) money purchase schemes (which for the purposes of *PA 1995* includes a money purchase scheme which also provides salary related death benefits (*Personal and Occupational Pension Schemes (Miscellaneous Amendments) Regulations 1997 (SI 1997 No 786), reg 2*));

(*b*) certain public service pension schemes and government guaranteed schemes;

(*c*) unapproved schemes;

(*d*) schemes established in the UK under trust in respect of non-UK businesses which provide benefits in respect of individuals employed outside the UK;

(*e*) schemes with less than two members; and

(*f*) schemes which provide only death benefits.

[1995 Act, s 56(2) and the MFR Regulations, reg 28].

The MFR is a cyclical process consisting of three components: valuations, contribution schedules and annual certification. Trustees have an important role to play in the process. There are penalties (see 11.31 below) for failure to comply with the requirements.

Minimum funding valuations

11.15 Trustees of schemes which are subject to the MFR are required to obtain MFR valuations at regular intervals (see generally *section 57* of the *1995 Act* and *regulation 10* of the *MFR Regulations*). Any MFR valuation must be signed by the scheme actuary within one year of the effective date. (The scheme actuary is the actuary appointed by the trustees in accordance with *sec-*

tion 47(1)(b) of PA 1995.) The trustees are obliged to ensure that a copy of each MFR valuation is made available to the employer within seven days of the trustees receiving it.

Each MFR valuation must contain a statement made by the scheme actuary (in the form set out in *Schedule 1* of the *MFR Regulations*) which confirms the value of the scheme's assets as a percentage of its liabilities and the extent to which the liabilities of the scheme are met. [*MFR Regulations, reg 14*]. A copy of the latest statement and the latest actuarial valuation must be disclosed to any member, potential member, the spouse of any member or potential member, any beneficiary or any recognised Trade Union who requests it. [*Occupational Pension Schemes (Disclosure of Information) Regulations 1996 (SI 1996 No 1655), reg 7*].

First MFR valuation

11.16 The effective date of the first MFR valuation depends on when the scheme commenced, when it first became subject to the MFR and when the latest valuation required under the *Occupational Pension Schemes (Disclosure of Information) Regulations 1986 (SI 1986 No 1655)* was obtained (*regulation 10 of the MFR Regulations*). The possibilities are set out in the following table.

Status of scheme	Latest effective date for first MFR valuation
Schemes in existence on 6 April 1997 and subject to the MFR at that date.	Third anniversary of the effective date of the latest valuation obtained under the *Occupational Pension Schemes (Disclosure of Information) Regulations 1986 (SI 1986 No 1046)*.
Schemes in existence on 6 April 1997 but not subject to the MFR until a later date.	First anniversary of the date on which the scheme first becomes subject to the MFR.
Schemes which commence after 6 April 1997.	First anniversary of the date on which the scheme commenced.
Schemes in existence on 6 April 1997 and subject to the MFR at that date but which have not obtained a valuation under the *Occupational Pension Schemes (Disclosure of Information) Regulations 1986 (SI 1986 No 1046)* before that date.	The date after 6 April 1997 that is the earlier of the first anniversary of: (a) the date on which the scheme commences; or (b) the date on which the scheme is first subject to the MFR.

The signed valuation must be obtained by the trustees within one year of the effective date.

11.17 *Funding, deficits and surpluses*

Subsequent valuations

11.17 Trustees must obtain subsequent MFR valuations within three to four years of the signing of the previous MFR valuation. The exact time scale will depend on the effective date of the MFR valuation (*regulation 10 of the MFR Regulations*):

If the effective date of MFR valuation is to be:	The MFR valuation must be obtained by the trustees within:
On or before the third anniversary of the effective date of the previous MFR valuation.	Four years of the effective date of the previous MFR valuation.
After the third anniversary of the effective date of the previous MFR valuation.	Three years of the date on which the previous MFR valuation was signed.

Generally all MFR valuations must be signed within 12 months of the effective date of the valuation. If trustees intend to instruct their actuary to prepare an MFR valuation with an effective date later than the third anniversary of the effective date of the previous MFR valuation, they should bear in mind that, depending on when the previous valuation was signed, the actuary may have considerably less than 12 months within which to finalise the valuation. If, for example, an MFR valuation was prepared with an effective date of 1 April 1999 and signed on, say, 27 December 2000, the next MFR valuation must be obtained by:

(*a*)   26 December 2002 if the trustees choose an effective date later than 2 April 2002 (ie more than three years after the effective date of the previous valuation); or

(*b*)   31 March 2003, if the effective date of the valuation is on or before 1 April 2002.

In practice it is likely that the period between effective dates will usually be three years.

MFR valuations in exceptional circumstances

11.18 Trustees may have to obtain an MFR valuation outside of the regular pattern if doubts arise about the funding of the scheme. Three possible scenarios are specified in the *MFR Regulations*:

(*a*)   Occurrence of an event which has a significant effect on funding (*regulation 11*) – If it appears to the trustees, having obtained the scheme actuary's opinion, that, due to an event which has had a significant effect on the value of the scheme's assets or liabilities, there is a serious risk that the MFR will not be met throughout the schedule period (see 11.20 below), the trustees have six months from the date on which the actuary gives his opinion within which they should either obtain an MFR valuation or revise the schedule of contributions (see 11.23 below). However, this *regulation* only applies where the actuary gives that opinion on or after 1 January 2005.

The *MFR Regulations* give no indication of what would constitute an 'event' or what is a 'significant effect'. Examples of events that could have an effect on funding include the receipt of a substantial bulk transfer into the scheme, a significant drop in the performance of a substantial investment or the implementation of a redundancy programme which includes enhanced early retirement pensions. Trustees should consult their professional advisers and seek the scheme actuary's opinion whenever they become aware of any likely 'event'. They will then be able to consider the actuary's opinion before deciding on the level of the risk of not meeting the MFR and whether or not they should obtain a valuation or revise the schedule of contributions.

(b) New serious underfunding suspected (*regulation 12*) – If, as part of the annual certification process (see 11.27 below), the scheme actuary forms the opinion that an MFR valuation would disclose a serious shortfall (see 11.28 below), he or she must include a statement to that effect in his certificate. The trustees will then have six months from the date of the certificate in which to obtain an MFR valuation. However, this regulation only applies where the date of the certificate falls on or after 1 January 2005.

(c) Debts in multi-employer schemes (*regulation 13*) – If a situation arises where an employer owes a debt to the trustees under *section 75* of *PA 1995* (see 12.76 to 12.81 below) and the latest MFR valuation shows that the MFR has not been met or the latest annual certificate (see 11.27 below) shows that contributions have been insufficient to meet the MFR, the trustees must obtain an MFR valuation (normally) within three months.

Basis of valuation

11.19 Details of the liabilities and assets to be taken into account, and the way in which their amount and value are to be determined, calculated and verified, are set out in the *MFR Regulations* and in GN27.

For the purposes of an MFR valuation, the liabilities to be taken into account are those liabilities a scheme would have to make provision for under *PA 1995* on a winding-up, namely:

(a) benefits deriving from additional voluntary contributions;

(b) pensions in payment and contingent pensions;

(c) the accrued rights to pensions of members and deferred pensioners (or a refund of contributions in the case of individuals with less than two years' pensionable service); and

(d) increases to the pensions mentioned above.

11.19 Funding, deficits and surpluses

In addition, if the scheme is contracted-out, the liability for contributions-equivalent premiums will have to be taken into account for all members in respect of whom such premiums could be paid (*regulation 7, MFR Regulations*).

It is a moot point as to whether the liabilities to be taken into account are those specified in *PA 1995, s 73* as modified by *regulation 3* of the *Occupational Pension Schemes (Winding-Up) Regulations 1996 (SI 1996/3126)* and whether, therefore, for valuations having an effective date before 6 April 2007, the transitional priority order should apply. However, the DWP has expressed the view that the liabilities to be taken into account should be those for an on-going scheme and therefore the post April 2007 priorities should apply.

The MFR test assumes that the scheme meets its liabilities by the payment of cash equivalents (ie the minimum transfer value which the trustees would be obliged to pay in respect of a member who leaves the scheme and requests a transfer) rather than by the buying out of benefits through the purchase of annuities. Details of how the value of these liabilities are to be calculated are specified in GN27. Liabilities for pensions in payment must generally be valued by reference to the yield on gilt-edged securities. Liabilities for the accrued rights of other members, up to ten years before normal pension age, must be valued by reference to the yield on equities. It is assumed that, during the ten years before normal pension age, there is a progressive switch from equities to gilts.

Schemes which have a liability in excess of £100 million for pensions in payment in the 12 years following the effective date of the valuation can assume that the excess will be met from investment in equities.

The value of any asset is the market value, assuming an open market and an arm's length transaction. Generally the value used will be the audited market value. Information is given on the valuation of various types of assets in GN27. As a consequence of using market value, rather than a 'smoothed value' which allows for recent fluctuations, the MFR is a relatively volatile test. A sudden dip in the equities market could mean that a scheme fails the MFR test, even though on an ongoing valuation basis it is well funded.

This is particularly true of more mature schemes with a high percentage of pensioners. In such schemes, the liabilities for MFR purposes will be measured against gilts but it is not always the case that the statement of investment principles prepared in accordance with *section 35* of *PA 1995* will set out a policy of matching those liabilities by holdings of gilts. Some trustees face the dilemma of considering investing heavily in gilts, but knowing that in doing so they would probably be reducing the investment return on the fund as equities over the long term have outperformed gilts. Reducing the return in this way increases the chance that the employer will be asked for increased contributions.

Employer-related investments, in excess of the permitted level (5 per cent of total fund), are excluded for the purposes of calculating a scheme's assets.

Funding, deficits and surpluses **11.20**

The consequences of the abolition of dividend tax credits in the July 1997 budget led to a revision in the MFR basis with effect from 15 June 1998. The effect of the change is to reduce the value of certain liabilities. Subsequent to this change, further discussion has taken place regarding the appropriateness of the MFR test in the light of changes in investment circumstances. In March 2001 the Government published its proposals for replacing the MFR with a long-term, scheme-specific funding standard in conjunction with a number of other measures aimed at protecting scheme members (see 11.33 et seq below).

Schedule of contributions

Time limits and content of schedule

11.20 The signing of the first MFR valuation triggers the requirement under *section 58* of *PA 1995* for a schedule of contributions. The trustees and the employer have eight weeks from the signing of the MFR valuation in which to agree on the matters to be shown in the schedule (*MFR Regulations, reg 15(3)*). The schedule of contributions must show separately the rates and due dates of:

(*a*)   all contributions other than voluntary contributions payable by or on behalf of active members of the scheme;

(*b*)   the contributions payable by or on behalf of each employer;

(*c*)   if made separately, the contributions payable to cover the total expenses which are likely to be payable by the trustees in the period covered by the schedule. [*MFR Regulations, reg 17(1)*].

Within these parameters trustees and employers are free to agree the exact details of what the schedule of contributions is to show. If they fail to reach an agreement the trustees can unilaterally decide on the matters to be shown, but the contributions required to meet the MFR must be covered [PA 1995, s 58(4)].

Opra has produced a guide, last revised in April 2000, entitled 'Paying Pensions Contributions on Time', which gives an outline of the details required, and sets out a specimen schedule of contributions. The guide is available from Opra free of charge by telephoning 01273 627600.

The schedule of contributions, certified by the scheme actuary, must be obtained by trustees within 12 weeks of the date on which the actuary signs the MFR valuation (*MFR Regulations, reg 15*). The schedule must cover a period of five years, beginning with the date on which the rate of contributions shown in the schedule is certified. (This period is referred to in this chapter as the schedule period.) If during the period 6 April 1997 to 5 April 2002 an MFR valuation shows that the MFR is not met, the trustees can extend the schedule period so that it ends on 5 April 2007. [*MFR Regulations, regs 16(1), (2)*].

As the schedule of contributions, which generally covers five years, is tied into the signing of an MFR valuation, which will happen at least every four years, there will be overlap between successive schedules. Trustees may find them-

11.21 *Funding, deficits and surpluses*

selves receiving contributions in accordance with two schedules simultaneously or may choose to 'revise' (see 11.22 below) the earlier schedule so that no contributions are payable under it, if appropriate. The schedule of contributions is applicable from the date of the signing of the schedule and not from the effective date of the MFR valuation. As a consequence, a schedule of contributions will not have to be in place until, potentially, 15 months after the effective date of the MFR valuation. Some sort of adjustment may therefore be necessary in respect of any difference between the contributions which were actually paid, and the contributions which the MFR valuation indicates should have been paid during the intervening period.

Certification by the actuary

11.21 The schedule showing the rates of contributions must be certified by the scheme actuary. [*PA 1995, s 58(4)*]. The actuary cannot certify the schedule unless he is of the opinion that the rates are adequate for the purpose of securing that the MFR will be met, or will continue to be met, throughout the schedule period. [*PA 1995, s 58(6)*].

Where an MFR valuation discloses that the scheme is less than 90 per cent funded, the schedule of contributions must provide for the deficit to be met by:

(*a*) additional contributions, of equal or decreasing amounts, made at least annually; or

(*b*) increasing contribution rates by a percentage that either remains the same throughout or decreases during the schedule period (*MFR Regulations, reg 17*).

In either case the additional payments must total in aggregate the amount which, in the opinion of the actuary, is necessary to secure that the MFR will be met by the end of the schedule period. This requirement ensures that an employer cannot postpone increasing the scheme's assets until the end of a schedule period.

The following table summarises the requirements described above relating to the certification of the schedule of contributions.

Percentage funded on MFR basis	Before certifying the schedule of contributions, the actuary must be of the opinion that the rates shown in the schedule are adequate to:
100% or more funded.	secure that the MFR will continue to be met throughout the schedule period.

Percentage funded on MFR basis	Before certifying the schedule of contributions, the actuary must be of the opinion that the rates shown in the schedule are adequate to:
90% to 100% funded.	secure that the MFR will be met by the end of the schedule period and are such that the shortfall will be reduced by either: (a) additional contributions of equal or decreasing amounts made at least annually; or (b) increasing contribution rates by a percentage that either remains the same throughout or decreases during the schedule period.
less than 90% funded.	secure that the MFR will be met by the end of the schedule period and are such that they satisfy the uniform funding requirement, ie during the schedule period: (a) additional contributions of equal or decreasing amounts are made at least annually; or (b) contribution rates are increased by a percentage that either remains the same throughout or decreases during the schedule period; so as to ensure that the aggregate amount of such payments is the amount which is necessary, in the actuary's opinion, to secure that the MFR will be met by the end of the schedule period.

Contracting out

11.22 Where a scheme is contracted out on the 'reference scheme' basis, the scheme must either satisfy the MFR test, or must be on track to satisfy the test by reference to the schedule of contributions [*Occupational Pension Schemes (Contracting-Out) Regulations 1996 (SI 1996 No. 1172), reg 18*]. There are transitional provisions dealing with the period up to 5 April 2007.

Revision of schedule

11.23 The trustees and the employer may agree to revise a schedule of contributions from time to time. [*PA 1995, s58(3)(b)*]. Any revision in the rate of contributions must be certified by the scheme actuary. The revised schedule must show the rates of contributions payable during the remainder of the schedule period that is current on the date on which the revised rates are certified.

In any event, the schedule of contributions must be revised within the appropriate time limit following the signing of each subsequent MFR valuation. [*PA 1995, s 58 (3)(c)*].

11.24 *Funding, deficits and surpluses*

Record keeping

11.24 As part of the MFR procedure, under *regulation 19* of the *MFR Regulations*, trustees are required to keep records of:

(*a*) all contributions made to the scheme, showing separately:

  (i) the aggregate of the contributions paid by or on behalf of active members and the dates on which they were paid;

  (ii) the voluntary contributions paid by each member; and

  (iii) the aggregate of the contributions paid by or on behalf of each employer and the dates on which they were paid;

(*b*) all contributions and payments made to secure any increase required to meet a serious shortfall (see 11.27 below);

(*c*) any action taken by trustees to recover:

  (i) any contributions which are not paid on the date on which they are due;

  (ii) any debt which has arisen as a result of any failure to deal with a serious shortfall within the required time frame; and

  (iii) any debt that has arisen as a consequence of an employer's insolvency.

Extension of schedule period

11.25 Opra has a discretion to extend the schedule period if it is satisfied that the circumstances justify it. Exact details of the requirements which will have to be met are set out in *regulations 25* to *27* of the *MFR Regulations*.

Supervision by Opra

11.26 If the contributions due in accordance with a schedule of contributions are not paid, trustees must give notice of that fact to Opra within 30 days of the due date (unless payment has been made within ten days beginning with the due date, and the default is only the first or second such default in the period of 12 months ending on and including the due date) (*MFR Regulations, reg 23*). Notice must then be given to members within 90 days of the due date (unless payment has been made within 60 days of the due date). Any contributions which remain unpaid become a debt due from the employer to the trustees (*PA 1995, s 59(2)*) for which the trustees may choose to sue the employer if the funding of the scheme is at risk. Opra's published policy is that they will only expect reports from trustees of late payment of contributions where there is:

- a significant risk to the security of scheme assets; or
- a significant detrimental impact on the members;

Funding, deficits and surpluses **11.28**

and (in either case) the contributions remaining overdue for 90 days. However, trustees complying with the 90 day report will not be penalised by Opra for failing to report strictly in accordance with legal requirements.

Annual certification

11.27 After obtaining the first MFR valuation trustees must obtain an 'annual certificate' not earlier than 21 days before, and not later than 21 days after, each anniversary of the signing of the schedule of contributions (*MFR Regulations, reg 18*). In the certificate the scheme actuary must state whether or not, in his opinion, the contributions payable are adequate for the purpose of securing that the MFR will continue to be met throughout the schedule period. He must also indicate any relevant changes that have occurred since the last MFR valuation was prepared.

Trustees must forward a copy of the certificate to the employer within seven days. The exact form of the actuary's statement and actuary's certificate is set out in *Schedule 3* of the *MFR Regulations*.

If the actuary certifies that, in his opinion, the contributions payable are not adequate to ensure that the MFR is, or will be, met throughout the schedule period, and the value of the scheme's assets is less than 90 per cent of its liabilities, the trustees must either obtain an MFR valuation or revise the schedule of contributions within six months of the date on which the certificate was signed. In practice it is likely that the scheme actuary will notify the trustees of any potential problems before issuing a negative certificate. This will give the trustees an opportunity to take remedial action, if appropriate, before the certificate is issued.

Serious underprovision

11.28 Where an MFR valuation shows that the value of a scheme's assets is less than 90 per cent of the amount of its liabilities, the employer must increase the value of the assets within a set period to a level which (taken with any contributions paid) reaches the 90 per cent level. This can be done either by the employer making an appropriate payment to the trustees or (if the trustees so decide within 12 weeks of the signing of the valuation) by one of the following 'prescribed' methods:

(*a*) a guarantee, in writing, from a bank or building society that it will meet the shortfall should the employer become insolvent or the scheme wind up;

(*b*) the payment of the required sum into a deposit account held in the names of the trustees and designated as an account that complies with the regulations made under the *1995 Act*;

(*c*) a charge over any assets which are otherwise free from any encumbrance,

11.29 *Funding, deficits and surpluses*

provided that the charge is registrable under a statutory provision. [*PA 1995, s 68; MFR Regulations, reg 22*].

Schedule 4 of the *MFR Regulations* specifies conditions relating to each of the above methods for securing the required increase.

If the required increase is to be secured by the making of an appropriate payment, the payment must be made within 12 months of the signing of the MFR valuation. In all other cases the employer has three months within which to secure the increase. Opra has the power to extend these periods if circumstances justify such action.

If the employer fails to secure the required increase, the shortfall becomes a debt on the employer and the trustees are obliged to notify Opra and members of the scheme within 14 days. [*PA 1995, s 60(4), (5)*].

If the MFR is not met and between MFR valuations the funding of the scheme deteriorates the trustees must prepare a report stating the reasons for the failure to meet the MFR and for the deterioration in the funding of the scheme. Such a report must be made available to any member or prospective member and their spouses, any beneficiary or prospective beneficiary and any independent trade unions recognised for the purposes of collective bargaining in relation to the scheme. [*MFR Regulations, reg 21*].

Modifications in respect of certain schemes

Multi-employer schemes

11.29 Where a scheme has several employers and each employer effectively operates a distinct section of the scheme, for the purposes of the MFR, each section is treated as a separate scheme. [*MFR Regulations, Sch 5 paras 1 and 2*].

Frozen or paid-up schemes

11.30 Where there are no active members, references to the employer are taken as references to the person who was the employer on the date on which there was last an active member. [*MFR Regulations, Sch 5 para 3*].

Shared cost scheme

11.31 Shared cost schemes are defined as schemes where, if there is a shortfall, the rates of both employer and employee contributions are increased by the same proportion. In such a scheme, in the case of serious under provision, both the employer and the employees are required to meet any shortfall. [*MFR Regulations, reg 24*].

Consequences of non-compliance

11.32 If trustees fail to take all reasonable steps to secure compliance with the various requirements of the MFR legislation summarised above, they face being fined (maximum of £5,000 for an individual or £50,000 for a company) and/or removed as a trustee. The sanction on the employer is that if contributions are not paid within a certain time frame they become a debt due to the trustees for which the trustees could sue the employer. The burdens placed on trustees are fairly onerous, but they have few statutory powers if the employer does not co-operate. They are responsible only to the extent that they have not taken 'all reasonable steps'.

Trustees and employers alike should remember that, in its current form, the MFR is intended to provide only a minimum level of funding. If, instead, the legislation had based the MFR on the cost of securing benefits by the purchase of annuities, the test would have been considerably stricter in terms of funding, but would provide members with greater security.

Proposals for replacement

Initial reforms

11.33 Until the new primary legislation implements the Government's proposals for replacement of the MFR (see 11.34 below), the current regime will remain in place. However, the Government has already made a number of amendments to existing regulations as the first stage of the reform of the MFR by the *Occupational Pension Schemes (Minimum Funding Requirement and Miscellaneous Amendments) Regulations 2002 (SI 2002 No 380)* which came into force on 19 March 2002. The amendments include:

(*a*) an extension of the periods within which any deficit in funding must be made good – to three years for schemes where there is serious underprovision (see 11.28 above) for them to reach the 90 per cent MFR funding level and to ten years for schemes to reach the 100 per cent MFR funding level (this applies only to new schedules of contributions certified after the effective date);

(*b*) the removal of the requirement for annual re-certification of schemes that are 100% funded (see 11.27 above);

(*c*) the extension of the 'transitional period', as defined in the *MFR Regulations, reg 1* to 31 December 2004;

(*d*) a change in the MFR equity market value adjustment from 3.25 per cent to 3 per cent; and

(*e*) the introduction from 19 March 2002 of stricter conditions in cases where the pension scheme of a solvent employer is voluntarily wound up, so that

11.34 *Funding, deficits and surpluses*

the debt on the employer includes the actual costs of winding up, the purchase of immediate annuities for pensioners and the provision of cash equivalent transfer values for non-pensioner members.

Pensions Bill

11.34 On 7 March 2000, the Government announced its intention to abolish the MFR. The Pensions Bill broadly follows the proposal laid down by Myners in his November 2000 report, taking account of responses it received to the consultation exercise (see 10.51 above).

The Pensions Bill (sections 178–188) will replace the MFR with a statutory funding requirement. Much of the detail will be provided by regulation but, in principle, the new funding requirement will move from a generic basis to a scheme specific basis. Actuarial valuations will still be required, but there will be a new requirement for the scheme's trustees or managers to maintain a statement of funding principles, setting out their policy for securing that the statutory funding objective is met. This will include the actuarial methods and assumptions and their policy as to how and when any shortfall below the statutory funding objective is to be remedied. Actuarial valuations will have to include a certificate stating that the prescribed requirements of the statutory funding objectives have been met. If they have not, the actuary must report that fact to the Regulator. As with MFR, there is to be a statutory provision for scheme recovery where the statutory funding objective is not met (section 183). The detailed provisions are to be set out in regulation but it is clear that the recovery plan will need to be submitted to the Regulator, together with a copy of the schedule of contributions. Both the statement of funding principles (including methodology) and any recovery plan must be agreed between the trustees and the employer. If agreement cannot be reached, the Regulator must be notified, but there is no provision for the trustees to impose a unilateral decision on the employer. However, *the* trustees and employer may instead amend the scheme as regards future benefit accrual, thereby reducing prospective scheme liabilities.

Actuarial advice must be taken when deciding on the methodology and assumptions, preparing or changing the statement of funding principles, any recovery plan which may be needed and preparing or changing the schedule of contributions.

If the trustees and employer cannot agree or if the trustees or the employer have failed in their scheme funding duties, the Regulator may amend the scheme for future accrual or give directions as to the funding objectives (including actuarial methods and assumptions), any recovery plan and the schedule of contributions.

The Pensions Bill will also create a new compensation scheme (see 2.29 above so that the level of compensation is increased to cover not simply the MFR liability as at present, but the cost of the members' accrued benefits (or the amount of the loss, whichever is the lesser).

WHAT IS A SURPLUS?

11.35 Although the expression 'surplus' is widely used, it is not a legally defined term and often has misleading connotations. By way of a general definition, a surplus is said to exist when the actuarially estimated value of a scheme's assets at a certain date exceeds the actuarially estimated value of its liabilities at that date.

When a scheme is winding-up, a surplus is easy to identify as the cost of securing the liabilities of the scheme in a given manner will ultimately be known, as will the value of the assets of the scheme. On a winding-up, a surplus will exist if there are any funds remaining after all the benefits have been secured.

The position is different with an ongoing scheme as the actuary will have to make certain assumptions as to future events. Depending on the method adopted and the assumptions used for the valuation, a scheme could be either in deficit or in surplus at any given time. A 'surplus' in an ongoing scheme is therefore simply the actuary's prediction, based on a given method and on a certain set of assumptions that the scheme will have more than sufficient assets to cover its liabilities over a certain period. Unlike the MFR provisions, there is no statutory basis or method required to assess a surplus, except in the limited circumstances of Revenue limits on over-funded schemes (see 11.40 et seq below).[it means 'and an unspecified number of following paragraph numbers']

An employer may tend to see a surplus in an ongoing scheme as representing past overfunding. Trustees may see it as representing a reserve fund, providing security in the event of the cost of the benefits being more than the actuary anticipated or the investments of the scheme failing to perform to the level hoped for. Members on the other hand will sometimes regard a surplus in an ongoing scheme as 'spare' money that could be used for immediate benefit increases. However, arguably there can be no certainty of a surplus unless and until the scheme is wound up and all benefits secured. Any surplus in an ongoing scheme is notional as any number of events could happen which would totally eradicate it.

WHY SURPLUSES ARE AN ISSUE

11.36 During the 1980s a huge growth in the value of investments, coupled with a reduction in the workforce, led to many schemes having substantial surpluses. Where these forces combined to produce a large surplus in a scheme, even the suspension of contributions by employers and employees was sometimes insufficient to eliminate it over a foreseeable period. Many employers began to look for ways to extract what appeared to be unrequired assets in their pension schemes.

At the same time, the Government became concerned that the tax advantages conferred on occupational pension schemes meant that it was losing valuable

11.37 *Funding, deficits and surpluses*

tax revenue from the assets in these overfunded schemes. The *Finance Act 1986* removed some of the tax advantages available to schemes with excessive surpluses by imposing tax on the income and gains arising from scheme assets in excess of a certain prescribed limit (see 11.40 below). Some employers saw the introduction of the legislation as a mandate to remove a surplus from a scheme. Others were encouraged to take contribution holidays or improve scheme benefits to eradicate surplus.

The combination of the factors outlined above caused some members and trustees of pension schemes to become increasingly concerned that employers were unjustly appropriating part of their schemes' funds, resulting in the reduction of scheme security and the loss of any possibility of increased benefits. Consequently the treatment of a surplus in an ongoing scheme gave rise to controversy and continues to do so.

WHO OWNS A SURPLUS?

Ongoing schemes

11.37 Although a surplus in an ongoing scheme may be considered notional, the debate over the ways in which such a surplus can be used is very real. In most final salary schemes the employer's contribution will be the balance of the cost of providing the benefits promised. One of the easiest ways of dealing with a surplus is, therefore, simply to adjust the employer's contribution rate. However, trustees and beneficiaries may argue that if there is a surplus in a scheme it will not necessarily have arisen because the employer has paid excessive contributions; it could be due to high investment growth on the assets purchased by both the employer's and members' contributions or to members leaving a scheme at a faster rate than that assumed by the actuary for the purposes of his valuation. In such a situation the issue of who owns the surplus is inevitably raised.

There have been a number of cases in which the courts have been asked to consider the use of a surplus and, in particular, the members' right to share in the surplus. These cases have generally recognised that, in a final salary scheme where an employer would be required to meet any deficit it would be inequitable for the employer not to benefit at all from any surplus. There has, however, been a gradual shift away from the proposition that any surplus belongs solely to the employer while the scheme is ongoing.

In *Re Courage Group's Pension Schemes [1987] 1 All ER 528* the view of Millet J (as he then was) was that although members did not have an absolute legal right to participate in the surplus in their scheme, they were entitled to have the surplus dealt with by consultation and negotiation between them and the employer. He rejected the argument that members were entitled, as of right, to a contributions holiday, directing that any surplus arising from past overfunding in a balance of cost scheme did not arise from the employer and members pro rata, but arose primarily from the employer. The judge did, however, draw a distinction between the employer using a surplus to fund a contributions holiday and it requiring a payment out of the scheme. In the latter situation the trustees could, and should, press for generous treatment of members and the employer could be expected to be influenced by the desire to maintain good industrial relations with its workforce.

When considering how to deal with a surplus, it should be remembered that an employer can have regard to its own interests (financial and otherwise) but only to the extent that in doing so it does not breach the obligation of good faith to its employees (*Imperial Group Pension Trust Ltd v Imperial Tobacco Ltd [1991] 2 All ER 597*). (See chapter 7 for discussion of the employer's obligations in this regard.)

The issue of who owns a surplus continues to be subject to debate. The starting point should of course be the terms of the trust deed and rules of the particular scheme. The position would currently seem to be that members may have a legitimate expectation of benefit improvements, particularly where the trustees have a discretion as to the use of a surplus and there is a possibility of a payment to the employer, but this is not to say that they have an absolute right to any surplus. When considering the use of a surplus the employer is, however, obliged to keep an open mind and consider arguments put forward on behalf of the members. (See *Stannard v Fisons Pension Trust Ltd [1992] 1 PLR 27* and *LRT Pension Fund Trustee Co Ltd v Hatt [1993] PLR 227*.) Much will depend on the respective powers of the trustees and the employer under the scheme's governing documentation and the relative bargaining position of the parties.

The Goode Committee Report (paragraph 4.3.3X) pointed out 'if employers were to be debarred from taking contribution holidays, they might well feel impelled to freeze the scheme or wind it up altogether and, in relation to new schemes, to fund at a level designed to avoid a surplus arising'. This point was accepted by the Judge in *The National Grid Company plc v Laws [1997] PLR 157*, who said '... any general exclusion of employers from surplus would tend to make employers very reluctant to contribute to their pension schemes more than the bare minimum that they could get away with. That would be unfortunate, and it would be even more unfortunate if employers were driven to abandon final salary, balance of cost schemes and were instead to turn to money purchase schemes which may in the long term prove less advantageous to the beneficiaries'.

Since 1997 the *National Grid* case has progressed to the Court of Appeal and, in 2001, to the House of Lords. The Court of Appeal best summarised the current law on the matter with the words:

> 'The solution lies within the terms of the scheme itself, and not within a world populated by competing philosophies as to the true nature and ownership of actuarial surplus.'

This view was supported by the Court of Appeal in the *Stevens v Bell (British Airways) [2002] PLR 247* case. The judgement again explored the use of surplus although the emphasis was again placed on the specific construction of the relevant trust documentation.

11.38 *Funding, deficits and surpluses*

Interestingly, despite Myners suggestion that the Law Commission should review the issues involved in the ownership of surpluses, the Government, in the Green Paper 'Simplicity, Security and Choice: Working and Saving for Retirement', has concluded that for the time being there will be no steps made towards legislation. This may, in part, be due to the fact that in the current economic climate surpluses have become less of a concern.

Schemes which are winding-up

11.38 A scheme's trust deed and rules will generally include a rule setting out how the fund is to be distributed on a winding-up. This rule should include a provision relating to how any assets remaining after all the liabilities have been secured are to be used. Usually there will be a power to increase benefits up to Inland Revenue limits and/or make a payment to the employer. It is important to check whether this power is given to the employer, or to the trustees, or to both jointly. In some instances the provision will simply provide that all assets remaining should be paid to the employer.

If the rules do not contain provisions regarding the use of a surplus, perhaps because the scheme is being wound up whilst still governed by interim documentation, the general principles of trust law will have to be considered. Essentially, where funds are transferred to a trust and it subsequently transpires that those funds are not needed for the purposes of the trust, the trustees hold those funds for the benefit of the person who provided them on a 'resulting trust'. A resulting trust does not arise where the person who provided the money never intended to receive any of it back, so if the rules of the scheme specifically provide that no payment can be made to an employer (on a winding-up or otherwise) a resulting trust cannot arise.

How a surplus should be dealt with in the absence of a valid rule was considered by Scott J in *Davis v Richards Wallington Industries Ltd [1991] 2 All ER 563*. A resulting trust in favour of the members of the scheme was excluded largely on the grounds that, as the scheme provided salary related benefits, two members who paid in the same monetary amount in contributions could be entitled to benefits of a different value. A resulting trust was therefore unworkable as between the different groups of beneficiaries. A resulting trust in respect of transfer payments was also excluded; it was clear that the transferring schemes were divesting themselves once and for all of the transferred funds and had not intended to receive any of it back. Consequently any resulting trust had to be in favour of the employer.

Consideration was also given by Scott J as to how much of the surplus derived from employer contributions, how much from the contributions of members and how much from transfer values. In his opinion, it was wrong to consider that the surplus was attributable to all three sources proportionately. The employer's obligation was to pay whatever was necessary to fund the benefits over and above that provided from other sources. It was, therefore, logical to treat the benefits as being funded first by the contributions made by members and by the transfer payments and only secondly by the employer's contributions. Consequently any surplus was to be treated as being provided first and foremost by the employer's contributions.

INLAND REVENUE REQUIREMENTS RELATING TO THE REDUCTION OF SURPLUSES

11.39 Considerable tax advantages are available in respect of exempt approved occupational pension schemes. An employer is entitled to deduct contributions made to such schemes before calculating its profits for tax purposes, and the income and gains of such a scheme are generally not taxable. When large surpluses arose during the 1980s, the Government, concerned at the loss of potential tax revenue, introduced measures to ensure that the tax advantages available to pension schemes with large surpluses were restricted. These measures are now consolidated in *sections 601* to *603* of, and *Schedule 22* to, the *Income and Corporation Taxes Act 1988* and the *Pension Scheme Surpluses (Valuation) Regulations 1987 (SI 1987 No 412)* ('the *Surplus Regulations*').

Schemes to which the legislation applies

11.40 *Regulation 3* of the *Surplus Regulations (SI 1987 No 412)* applies to all exempt approved schemes other than:

(*a*) small self-administered schemes (ie schemes with less than 12 members whose assets are not invested exclusively in insurance policies) unless there is an intention to make a payment to the employer;

(*b*) insured schemes where the policy requires the level of contributions to take account of surpluses or which provide only lump sum death in service benefits;

(*c*) simplified defined contribution schemes.

Schedule 22 valuations

11.41 The administrator of a scheme which is subject to the legislation must submit an actuarial valuation of the assets and liabilities of the scheme, or a certificate stating whether or not the assets of the scheme exceed the permitted maximum, to the Inland Revenue:

(*a*) whenever a valuation (including an MFR valuation) of the assets and liabilities of the scheme is made; and

(*b*) in any event, not later than three and a half years after:

    (i) the effective date of the last valuation or certificate; or

    (ii) the date on which the scheme was established.

11.42 *Funding, deficits and surpluses*

The valuation or certificate must be signed by a Fellow of the Institute or Faculty of Actuaries or a person with an approved actuarial qualification. It is likely that the actuary signing the certificate will be the scheme actuary appointed under *section 47(1)(b)* of *PA 1995*, but this is not currently a requirement.

The *Surplus Regulations (SI 1987 No 412)* set out the method the actuary must use in valuing liabilities, the assumptions as to rates of interest and investment yield which must be adopted and the methods that may be used to value assets. The assumptions and requirements laid down are generally considered to be conservative so a valuation made under these requirements is likely to show a smaller surplus than a valuation conducted for the purpose of determining the contribution rate.

Although a certificate can be submitted rather than a valuation, the Inland Revenue can require the administrator to provide a full written valuation within 60 days. The Revenue also has power to require the submission of further information regarding a certificate or valuation. [*ICTA 1988, 22 Sch 4*]. If a valuation or further information is required, the Revenue may reject the findings submitted and instead serve a notice stating its own estimate of the liabilities and assets of the scheme. In such a case, the estimate made by the Inland Revenue will take the place of the valuation or certificate.

Consequences of overfunding

11.42 Where a valuation discloses that the value of the assets of a scheme exceeds 105 per cent of the value of its liabilities when calculated in accordance with the prescribed assumptions, the administrator of the scheme must submit proposals for eliminating the excess; these proposals must be submitted within six months of the date on which the valuation was signed. The permitted ways in which the excess can be reduced or eliminated are any one or more of the following:

(*a*) making a payment to the employer;

(*b*) suspending or reducing the employer's obligation to contribute to the scheme for a period of five years or less;

(*c*) suspending or reducing the employees' obligation to contribute to the scheme for a period of five years or less;

(*d*) improving existing benefits;

(*e*) providing new benefits.

These permitted ways are set out in *paragraph 3(3)* of *Schedule 22* to *ICTA 1988*; provision is made for other methods to be prescribed but, to date, this power has not been used.

The Revenue will not sanction any payment to an employer if the proposed payment would result in the assets of the scheme being less than 105 per cent of

Funding, deficits and surpluses **11.44**

the liabilities, calculated on the prescribed basis. A surplus may be reduced to below this level if the proposals do not include a payment to the employer.

Once the Revenue have accepted proposals for reducing a surplus, the administrator is obliged to implement them so as to ensure that the excess is eliminated within a specified time. [*Surplus Regulations (SI 1987 No 412), reg 10*]. If the excess is to be reduced by a payment to the employer or by benefit enhancements, the administrator has six months in which to take the necessary action. A contributions holiday may last for five years unless a shorter period is agreed with the Inland Revenue. These time limits start to run 30 days after the date on which the Inland Revenue notifies the administrator of acceptance of the proposals.

In some situations a surplus may be reduced over a longer period. These are set out in *regulation 11* of the *Surpluses Regulations (SI 1987 No 412)* and include:

(i) where the scheme has been in existence for less than 15 years, the excess surplus may be eliminated within the longer of five years or 15 years from commencement of the scheme;

(ii) where a scheme has ceased to admit new members, the excess may be reduced over the period until the last member leaves service; and

(iii) where a scheme is the employer's only scheme and has less than 30 members, the excess may be reduced over the period until the last member leaves service.

Consequences of making a payment to the employer

11.43 A payment cannot be made to an employer pursuant to proposals approved under *Schedule 22* until all pensions payable under the scheme have been increased, in respect of both past and future service, by the appropriate percentage, being the lesser of five per cent per annum and the increase in the retail prices index.

Where a payment is made to any employer as a result of proposals submitted under *Schedule 22*, the payment is subject to a 35 per cent tax charge. [*ICTA 1988, s 601*]. The administrator is responsible for deducting the tax before the payment is made to the employer and must make a return to the Revenue within 14 days of making the payment to the employer. [*Pension Scheme Surpluses (Administration) Regulations 1987 (SI 1987 No 352), reg 3*].

Sanctions for non-compliance

11.44 A scheme which has assets in excess of the 105 per cent of its liabilities which fails to submit or implement acceptable proposals, will lose all tax relief in respect of income and gains deriving from assets in excess of that 105 per cent threshold. Tax relief is lost for the period from the effective date of the valuation

11.45 *Funding, deficits and surpluses*

(or certificate) which disclosed the surplus, until the Inland Revenue is satisfied that the excess surplus is less than the permitted level.

TRUST LAW REQUIREMENTS RELATING TO THE REDUCTION OF SURPLUSES

Powers under the trust instrument

11.45 Although the Inland Revenue permits some flexibility in respect of how a surplus is reduced, the ways in which a reduction may be achieved can be restricted by the terms of a scheme's trust deed and rules. Usually a scheme's governing documentation will be wide enough to let the employer and the trustees decide on benefit improvements or a contributions holiday. However, the trust deeds of many schemes established before 1970 include a restriction on the power of amendment to the effect that no amendment can be made which would permit scheme funds to be paid to the employer. It is debatable whether such a restriction can be validly removed so as to allow a payment to be made to the employer, much will depend on the circumstances of the case and the exact wording of the power of amendment. Before agreeing to a payment to the employer, trustees should carefully check all previous trust deeds to ensure that the power of amendment has not been inappropriately amended in the past.

Even if the amendment is possible, trustees must consider whether, in agreeing to the amendment, they are acting in the best interests of the beneficiaries. Trustees may be faced with the offer of benefit improvements for the beneficiaries in return for making the amendment and subsequently making a payment to the employer. In such a situation, trustees must balance the security of members' interests in the fund against the benefit improvements on offer when deciding whether to agree to the amendment. The decision is not easy and trustees must consider carefully the propriety of making the amendment when the benefit improvements on offer are relatively small.

In some circumstances the trustees of a scheme may make an application to Opra for an order authorising the modification of the scheme with a view to permitting the reduction or elimination of an excessive surplus (*section 69 of PA 1995*). Before 6 April 1997 it was possible to make a similar application to the Occupational Pensions Board. The granting of a modification order can enable the trustees to make a payment to the employer as part of the proposals for reducing a surplus, in circumstances where the power of amendment under the trust deed cannot be used to permit such a payment. A modification of the trust deed of a scheme, authorised by Opra, has the same effect in law as if the change had been made under powers conferred under the trust deed [PA 1995, s 71(2)].

Exercise of trustees' powers

11.46 Before agreeing to a payment of surplus to the employer (or, where the trust deed requires their agreement, to an employer's contributions holiday) trustees should obtain independent legal advice and should also consider whether they are subject to any conflicts of interest. For example, a trustee who is also a director of the employer may have difficulty maintaining his impartiality and fulfilling his duties as a trustee. In some circumstances it may be necessary to appoint independent trustees.

In exercising their powers, trustees must act in the best interests of the beneficiaries and must act impartially between the different groups of beneficiaries. If, for example, an agreement was reached between the employer and the employees' representatives, it would indicate that active members find the proposal satisfactory, but the trustees would still have to consider the interests of deferred members and pensioners. Trustees have a duty to negotiate the best bargain they can in the circumstances, taking into consideration the relative balance of power between themselves and the principal employer (see *Re Courage Group's Pension Scheme [1987] 1 All ER 528*). The employer also has obligations to the membership; it must ensure that it is not acting in breach of its implied obligation of good faith (see *Imperial Group Pension Trust Ltd v Imperial Tobacco Ltd [1991] 2 All ER 597*). In practice it is difficult to see how the trustees can justify making any payment to the employer unless they have also secured some clear advantage (usually benefit improvements) for the beneficiaries.

LEGISLATIVE REQUIREMENTS RELATING TO THE REDUCTION OF SURPLUSES AND PA 1995

Ongoing schemes

11.47 The *Pensions Act 1995* provides that if a scheme's rules contain a power to make payments to any person, including the employer, that power can only be exercised by the trustees, irrespective of what the rules provide. [*PA 1995, s 37* and the *Occupational Pension Schemes (Payments to Employers) Regulations 1996 (SI 1996 No 2156), regs 4* to *6*]. However, any restriction imposed by the rules on the exercise of the power also applies to its exercise by the trustees so far as it is capable of doing so. [*PA 1995, s 37*]. If, for example, a rule provides that, with the consent of the employer, the trustees may reduce a surplus by making a payment to the employer, the restriction (ie the consent of the employer) will continue to apply. Conversely, if the rule vests the power in the principal employer, subject to the consent of the trustees, under *PA 1995* the power would be exercisable by the trustees alone. *PA 1995* only affects a power to make a payment out of the scheme. It does not affect the exercise of a power vested in an employer to reduce a surplus by any other means.

Under *section 37* of *PA 1995*, any power to make a payment to a person out of the assets of the scheme cannot be exercised unless the following requirements are satisfied:

(*a*) the power is to be exercised in pursuance of proposals approved by the IR Savings, Pensions, Share Schemes of the Inland Revenue under *paragraph 6(1)* of *Schedule 22* to *ICTA 1988* (see 11.41 above);

11.47 *Funding, deficits and surpluses*

- (*b*) the trustees are satisfied that it is in the interests of the members that the power be exercised in the manner proposed;
- (*c*) where the power is conferred by the scheme rules on the employer, the employer has asked for the power to be exercised or has consented to it being exercised, in the manner proposed;
- (*d*) the annual rates of pensions payable under the scheme are increased by the 'appropriate percentage' ie the revaluation percentage by which accrued pension benefits must be revalued in accordance with *paragraph 2* of *Schedule 3* to the *Pension Schemes Act 1993*, being the lesser of five per cent per annum and the increase in the retail prices index); and
- (*e*) notice has been given regarding the proposal to exercise the power to all members of the scheme, in accordance with prescribed requirements.

The prescribed requirements are set out in the *Occupational Pension Schemes (Payment to Employers) Regulations 1996 (SI 1996 No 2156)*. To comply the trustees must take all reasonable steps to ensure that each member is given two written notices. The first notice must be given after proposals to reduce or eliminate the surplus have been approved by the Inland Revenue. The notice must:

- (i) inform the member of the proposed method of reducing or eliminating the surplus, by reference to the ways permitted under *Schedule 22* of *ICTA 1988* and state whether the requirements of *PA 1995* are satisfied;
- (ii) invite the member, if he wishes, to make written representations regarding the proposals to the trustees before a specified date (which cannot be earlier than two months from the date on which the notice is given); and
- (iii) advise the member that a second notice will be given to him if the trustees intend to proceed with the proposal and that no payment may be made to the employer until at least three months after the date on which the second notice is given.

The second notice must be given after the last date for making representations, as specified in the first notice, and at least three months before the power is exercised. The second notice must:

- (*a*) inform the member once again as to how it is proposed that the surplus is to be reduced or eliminated and whether the requirements of *PA 1995* are satisfied, noting any modifications made to the original proposals; and
- (*b*) advise the member that he may make written representations to Opra before a specified date (which cannot be earlier than three months from the date on which the notice is given) if he considers that any of the requirements of *PA 1995* are not satisfied.

A notice is validly given if it is sent to the member at his last known address, or, in the case of an active member, to the address at which he is currently employed. Notices do not have to be given where a member has no known address, or where correspondence sent to the last known address has been returned.

Funding, deficits and surpluses **11.48**

A payment cannot be made to an employer without the authority of Opra if written representations have been made to Opra by a member or if Opra receives information from any source and, in either case, there is sufficient doubt as to whether all the requirements of *PA 1995* are satisfied. If concerns are raised, Opra will notify the trustees, in writing, that no payment should be made to the employer until Opra has confirmed, in writing, that it is satisfied that the all the requirements have been met.

If at the end of the expiry of the notice period given in the second notice the trustees have not received information from Opra regarding representations made to it, the trustees must obtain written confirmation from Opra that it has not received any representations or information which would necessitate Opra's approval to the exercise of the power.

Schemes which are being wound up

11.48 If an exempt approved scheme commences winding-up on or after 6 April 1997, any power which is conferred on the employer or the trustees to distribute assets to the employer on a winding-up, cannot be exercised unless the requirements set out in *sections 76* and *77* of *PA 1995* and *regulations 7* to *10* of the *Occupational Pension Schemes (Payments to Employers) Regulations 1996 (SI 1996 No 2156)* are satisfied. These can be summarised as follows:

(*a*) the liabilities of the scheme must have been fully discharged;

(*b*) where there is any power under the scheme to distribute surplus assets to any person other than the employer, that power must have been exercised or a decision must have been made not to exercise it;

(*c*) the annual rate of pensions payable under the scheme (excluding any guaranteed minimum pension or any money purchase benefits) must have been increased by the appropriate percentage (see 11.46(d) above); and

(*d*) notice must have been given, in accordance with the prescribed requirements, to members of the scheme of the proposal to exercise the power.

The notice requirements in respect of a scheme which is winding-up are similar to those for ongoing schemes. The same time limits and the same restrictions regarding the consent of Opra apply. The first notice must:

(i) inform the member of the trustees' estimate of the value of the assets remaining after the scheme's liabilities have been discharged and the persons to whom it is proposed they should be distributed and state whether the requirements of *PA 1995* (as set out in (*a*) to (*d*) above) are satisfied;

(ii) invite the member, if he wishes, to make written representations regarding the proposals to the trustees before a specified date (which cannot be earlier than two months from the date on which the notice is given); and

(iii) advise the member that a second notice will be given to him if the trustees

11.49 *Funding, deficits and surpluses*

intend to proceed with the proposal and that no payment may be made to the employer until at least three months after the date on which the second notice is given.

The second notice must be given after the last date for making representations, as specified in the first notice, and at least three months before the power is exercised. The second notice must:

(a) inform the member again of the trustees' estimate of the value of the assets remaining after the scheme's liabilities have been discharged and the persons to whom it is proposed they should be distributed and state whether the requirements of *PA 1995* (as set out in (a) to (d) above) are satisfied noting any modifications made to the original proposals; and

(b) advise the member that he may make written representations to Opra before a specified date (which cannot be earlier than three months from the date on which the notice is given) if he considers that any of the requirements of *PA 1995* are not satisfied.

The position is slightly different where a scheme contains a prohibition on the distribution of assets to the employers on a winding-up (see *section 77* of *PA 1995*). If such a scheme has assets remaining undistributed after all the liabilities have been fully discharged, and after any power to distribute assets has been either exercised or a decision has been made not to exercise it, the trustees must use the remaining assets for the purposes of providing additional benefits or increasing the value of the benefits up to Inland Revenue limits. Only then may the trustees distribute any remaining assets to the employer. There are no notice requirements.

Schemes with more than one employer

11.49 Where a scheme has more than one employer and is divided into two or more sections and the provisions of the scheme are such that:

(a) different sections of the scheme apply to different employers or groups of employers;

(b) contributions payable to the scheme by an employer or by his employees are allocated to that section; and

(c) specified part or a proportion of the assets of the scheme is attributable to each section and cannot be used for the purposes of any other section;

the requirements of the Act relating to payments to the employer for both ongoing schemes and schemes which are winding-up apply as if each section of the scheme were a separate scheme. [*Occupational Pension Schemes (Payments to Employers) Regulations 1996 (SI 1996 No 2156), reg 12*].

Impact of *PA 1995*

11.50 Neither the *PA 1995* nor the Pensions Bill addresses perhaps one of the most fundamental issues relating to surpluses, namely that of who owns a surplus. The *PA 1995* applies only when proposals are put forward to reduce a surplus by way of a payment to the employer. It does not restrict the ability of an employer to reduce a surplus by other means, for example, by an employer contributions holiday or the inclusion of new employees, and so does not necessarily ensure that the members benefit from a surplus either by greater security or by improved benefits.

The impact of the *PA 1995* on payments to employers has not been great, not least because such payments are no longer common. Although *PA 1995* gives members the opportunity to make representations to the trustees, it does not require the trustees to act on those representations. A member's recourse against the trustees will therefore continue to be through an application to the Ombudsman or the courts. Opra have power to prevent a payment to the employer only where the requirements of *PA 1995* have not been satisfied; they seemingly do not have power (although the courts and the Ombudsman do) to question the propriety of making the payment on the grounds that it is not in the members' best interests.

The notice requirements do, however, offer members a greater opportunity to voice their opinions. Trustees must act in the best interests of their beneficiaries and it is hoped that any representations made by members to trustees regarding the payment of a surplus will help trustees in deciding if they are fulfilling this duty.

PENSIONS BILL

11.51 The Bill proposes to amend *PA 1995* in relation to any repayment of surplus to an employer. The intention is that payments to an employer may not be made from a defined benefit scheme unless it is funded to a level sufficient to purchase annuities and deferred annuities securing the rights of all members and beneficiaries. Further details are expected to be set out in regulations.

Chapter 12

Reconstruction and winding-up

INTRODUCTION

General

12.1 In this chapter the word 'reconstruction' is used to denote some significant change in the nature or structure of an employer's pension arrangements. Such a reconstruction will typically involve:

(a) a scheme amendment;

(b) a bulk transfer of assets and liabilities between different schemes operated by the same employer (or by employers within the same group); and/or

(c) the winding-up of a scheme.

Amendments

12.2 Examples of scheme amendments which are significant enough to be regarded for the purposes of this chapter as reconstructions include:

(a) converting a final salary scheme into a money purchase scheme;

(b) closing a scheme to future entrants;

(c) amending a scheme so that no further benefits accrue under it; or

(d) amending a scheme as part of a wider exercise, so as to enable the parties to make bulk transfer payments to other schemes (see 12.3 below) and/or wind up the scheme (see 12.4 below).

Scheme amendments are dealt with further in 12.8 to 12.31 below.

Bulk transfers

12.3 Bulk transfers of assets and liabilities between schemes operating within the same group of employers have become increasingly common in recent years. Typical cases include:

(a) bulk transfers from a final salary scheme to a money purchase arrangement; or

(b) bulk transfers between final salary schemes operating within the same group of employers, so as to replace two or more final salary schemes with a single, larger final salary scheme. Some of the advantages of having a single, larger scheme are that:

(i) it avoids the inefficiency for employers of operating some over-funded schemes and some underfunded schemes;

(ii) administrative costs for a single scheme should be lower owing to economies of scale;

(iii) a single, larger fund may justify the trustees in pursuing some investment opportunities which might be considered too risky in relation to a smaller fund; and

(iv) less time and resources overall need be spent on compliance with statutory requirements as there will be only one scheme (rather than several) in relation to which these requirements need to be met.

Bulk transfers are considered further in 12.32 to 12.50 and 12.85 to 12.90 below.

Winding-up

12.4 A winding-up occurs when a scheme is terminated and its assets are used to secure the scheme's benefits through other means (typically, by purchasing annuities or making transfer payments to other schemes).

The circumstances in which schemes go into winding-up are varied, but some examples are:

(a) where the purpose of the winding-up is to make a bulk transfer to another scheme, often for one of the purposes referred to in 12.3 above;

(b) where the employers can no longer afford to run the scheme. The employment law implications of this are considered in chapter 7 above; or

(c) where a scheme (perhaps with few, if any, remaining active members) has become too small to justify the cost of continuing to operate it as a separate scheme.

Winding-up is dealt with in more detail in 12.51 to 12.89 below.

Before dealing further with these areas, it is worth looking at some of the key considerations which will determine how far it is possible to achieve a scheme reconstruction.

KEY CONSIDERATIONS

Powers

12.5 The trustees and the employers need to be certain that they have the

12.6 *Reconstruction and winding-up*

necessary powers to carry out any proposed reconstruction. If, for example, the trustees were to accept a bulk transfer from another scheme in circumstances where they had no power under their trust deed to do so, they could subsequently be challenged by the members and held liable for resulting losses even though the trustees had at the time taken all available steps to ensure that the arrangement was in the members' best interests.

The question of whether the parties have the necessary powers will be determined primarily by the scheme's trust deed and rules. If therefore it is intended, for instance, to amend a scheme, it should be checked that the governing documentation does not impose restrictions on the power of amendment which the proposed alteration would infringe.

PA 1995 has a further bearing on whether the parties have the necessary powers. The effect of the Act in some areas is to restrict the exercise of certain powers which a scheme's rules (when read in isolation) appear to confer, and in other areas the effect is to give wider powers to the trustees. For instance:

(*a*) section 67 of *PA 1995* introduces certain restrictions on the exercise of the power of amendment (dealt with further in 12.18); and

(*b*) where an approved final salary scheme begins to be wound up after 5 April 1997, any power in the trust deed to apply the assets in respect of pensions or other benefits becomes exercisable by the trustees (even if the trust deed confers that power on another party, such as the employer) (*section 73(5), PA 1995* – see 12.71 below).

It is not sufficient, however, for the employers and the trustees simply to have the necessary powers to carry out the reconstruction; they must ensure that in exercising those powers they act in a manner consistent with their duties as employers (see 12.6 below) and trustees (see 12.7 below) respectively.

Employers' duties

12.6   Many scheme reconstructions are initiated by employers, often prompted by funding concerns. An employer should ensure that its proposals do not contravene its contractual commitments towards its employees in relation to pensions. These commitments will be set out primarily in employees' written terms and conditions of employment (although references to pensions in such documents are usually brief). There will, in addition, be written announcements or booklets issued to the employees explaining the scheme, which the courts are increasingly inclined to regard as contractually binding. (The legal nature of these written particulars is considered further in 7.2.)

Employers are also under an implied contractual duty of good faith (*Imperial Group Pension Trust Ltd v Imperial Tobacco Ltd [1991] 1 WLR 589*). The nature of this duty is that both employers and employees are obliged to act in a manner which is consistent with a relationship of mutual trust and confidence between them. Failure to do so can amount to a breach of contract.

This implied duty of good faith (unlike the more onerous duties placed on trustees) does not require the employer to act solely in the best interests of those to whom the duty is owed; an employer is entitled also to take its own commercial interests into account. It is not possible to give a definitive statement as to what would and would not amount to a breach of that duty. However, the following instances, which can be expected to amount to a breach of the duty of good faith, may be useful as guidelines:

(a)   a refusal by the employer even to consider (as opposed to considering and then rejecting) alternative proposals put forward by the trustees;

(b)   putting forward proposals which discriminate between employees (or groups of employees) without justification;

(c)   threatening to suspend contributions unless the trustees agree to the proposals (*Hillsdown Holdings plc v Pensions Ombudsman (1996) PLR 427*); or

(d)   threatening never to grant further pension increases unless the parties agree to the proposals (*Imperial Group Pension Trust Ltd v Imperial Tobacco Ltd [1991] 2 All ER 597*).

Chapter 7 considers the duty of good faith in further detail (from 7.6).

Trustees' duties

12.7   Trustees' powers are of a fiduciary nature, which means that they must exercise them in the best interests of the persons for whose benefit those powers were conferred. In most cases, this will be the scheme's present and past members (and any of their family or dependants who may have an interest in the scheme as a consequence of their membership).

Trustees may also owe a duty towards the employer when exercising certain of their powers. For instance, if the scheme rules give the trustees a discretion to pay surplus assets to the employer on winding-up, they must at least take the employer's interest into account. However, their duties towards scheme members are undoubtedly more onerous than an employer's duty of good faith towards its employees (described in 12.6 above).

This mis-match between the trustees' duties and those of the employer can give rise to a potential conflict of interests between the two sides and trustees should, therefore, seek separate advice wherever such a conflict exists. In the absence of separate advice, trustees may find themselves vulnerable to criticism if their decisions are subsequently called into question by scheme members; even if the trustees have acted entirely in their beneficiaries' best interests, it may be harder to convince the Pensions Ombudsman (or a court) of this if independent advice has not been obtained.

The terms of the trust deed (as qualified by *PA 1995* – see 12.5 above) will be relevant, in that any conflict is likely to be less of an issue if the trustees simply have no power to do anything other than implement the employer's proposals;

12.8 *Reconstruction and winding-up*

however, such instances are rare (and will become even more so in the future as the Pensions Bill proposes to shift the balance of power further from the employer to trustees).

Conflicts can arise not only as between employers and trustees, but also as between the trustees of separate schemes. This may happen where a bulk transfer of assets and liabilities from one scheme to another is under consideration, as the trustees of the two schemes will owe their duties to different groups of beneficiaries. Again, where there is a conflict, separate advice should be sought.

AMENDMENTS

General

12.8 Scheme reconstructions very often involve amending a scheme, either because the reconstruction itself takes the form of a fundamental change to the scheme's rules, or because an amendment is required to enable the employers or the trustees to make (or receive) a bulk transfer and/or wind up the scheme.

The main ways in which an occupational pension scheme may be amended are:

(a) in accordance with a power of amendment contained in the scheme's trust documents;

(b) by a court order;

(c) by means of a modification order granted by Opra; or

(d) by a trustees' resolution passed under a specific provision in *PA 1995*.

The first of these methods is by far the most common, but it is worth summarising the others before considering the scheme's own power of amendment in more detail.

Court order

12.9 A court order to vary the terms of a trust may be available in the following limited circumstances:

(a) on application by the trustees (or, less likely, a beneficiary) under *section 57* of the *Trustee Act 1925*. The basis for any such application must be that the trustees do not have the necessary investment or administrative powers which they need to deal in some particular way with the trust property. The court will need to be convinced that the proposed transaction is expedient;

(b) on application to the court under the *Variation of Trusts Act 1958*. This Act (which is not normally used in relation to pension schemes) enables the court to approve amendments on behalf of beneficiaries; or

(c) under the court's inherent jurisdiction to vary trusts. The court will generally only exercise this jurisdiction in circumstances where some matter concerning the scheme has in any event come before the court.

Modification orders

12.10 Opra has powers under *sections 69* to *71* of *PA 1995* and the *Modification Regulations* (*SI 1996 No 2517*) as amended by the *Occupational Pension Schemes (Winding up Notices and Reports etc) Regulations 2002* (*SI 2002 No 459*) (the '*Winding up Notices and Reports* Regulations') to grant orders for the modification of occupational schemes (other than public service schemes) in certain circumstances.

There are three purposes for which Opra may grant an order in this context (*section 69* of *PA 1995*), as illustrated in the following table.

	Who may apply for order	Orders which may be granted
Where the purpose is to reduce a surplus in an exempt approved scheme where the Inland Revenue requires this (and all relevant requirements for that reduction are met).	The trustees.	• Order authorising the trustees to modify the scheme; or • order modifying the scheme.
Where the purpose, in the case of an exempt approved scheme which is being wound up, is to enable assets remaining after the liabilities have been fully discharged to be distributed to the employer (and all other relevant requirements for that distribution have been met).	The trustees.	• Order authorising the trustees to modify the scheme; or • order modifying the scheme.
Where the purpose is to enable the scheme, for the period from 6 April 1997 to 5 April 1999, to be so treated that an employment to which it applies may be contracted-out (see chapter 4).	The trustees, the employer or any person other than the trustees who has power to alter the rules of the scheme.	• Order authorising such persons (not restricted to parties to the application) as Opra thinks appropriate to modify the scheme; or • order modifying the scheme.

Opra may only make such an order if it is satisfied that the desired result cannot be achieved without one, or that it can only be achieved in accordance with a procedure which is liable to be unduly complex or protracted (or involves the obtaining of consents which cannot be obtained without undue delay or difficulty) (*section 70, PA 1995*).

There is provision for such a modification to be retrospective. The modification order may be made or complied with even if the scheme rules or other legal requirements would otherwise prevent it (*section 71, PA 1995*).

12.11 *Reconstruction and winding-up*

Where an application is made to Opra under the *Winding up Notices and Reports Regulations* such application will be subject to the following conditions:

(a) it must set out the modification required and specify what effect (if any) it may have on benefits;

(b) specify the reasons for the modification;

(c) identify any previous application for a modification order made to a court or to Opra;

(d) confirm that the employer is subject to an insolvency procedure;

(e) specify whether the modification order will reduce the value of the assets;

(f) contain a statement that notices have been given to members of the scheme and any other relevant persons together with the relevant date(s) where such notice is given.

A member of the scheme in respect of which a notice has been given has the right to make representation to Opra within one month of any notice to request a modification order. Before Opra considers any application for a modification order it will require:

(i) a copy of the documents which govern the scheme;

(ii) a copy of any actuarial advice on the effect or otherwise of the modification order on the scheme's assets;

(iii) a copy of any legal advice in relation to the application for a modification order;

(iv) a copy of any court determination in relation to the application for a modification order or any similar order;

(v) a copy of any determination by trustees or managers to wind up the scheme.

Trustees' statutory power to amend

12.11   Subject to limited exceptions (primarily public service schemes) (*regulation 7* of the *Modification Regulations*), trustees now have power under *section 68* of *PA 1995* to amend a scheme by resolution with a view to achieving any of the following purposes:

(a) (subject to the consent of the employer) to extend the class of persons who may receive benefits in respect of the death of a member;

(b) to enable the scheme to conform with arrangements required by *PA 1995* in respect of the appointment of member-nominated trustees or member-nominated directors (see chapter 3);

(c) to enable the scheme to comply with requirements imposed by the Pensions Compensation Board in relation to any payment to be made by that body; or

(d) to enable the scheme to conform with certain other specified provisions of *PA 1995*.

There are further sections of *PA 1995* and its accompanying regulations which enable the trustees to modify the scheme by resolution for specific purposes. For example, *section 65, PA 1995* enables trustees to alter the scheme in line with the requirements for equal treatment as between men and women (see chapter 9).

Scheme's own power of amendment – general

Need for power

12.12 An occupational pension scheme may well continue in operation for several decades. During that time, it will almost certainly need to be adapted to cater for circumstances which could not reasonably have been predicted at the outset. For this reason, it is essential that the documents governing the scheme contain a power of amendment.

If no amendment power is included in the interim deed, it may still be possible to adopt a suitable power in the scheme's definitive deed, to take effect retrospectively to the date of the interim deed. (*Re Imperial Foods Ltd Pension Scheme [1986] 2 All ER 802.*)

The consequences of omitting the power from the definitive deed will be more serious and render it unlikely that a power of amendment can validly be inserted into the documents at a future date. It may still be possible subsequently to adopt a power of amendment, if it can clearly be shown that it had always been intended to include the power but that it was omitted by mistake; however, this would involve a court application.

Exercise of power

12.13 The exercise of any power of amendment must be carried out by the persons, and in accordance with any requirements (for instance, that there be a deed), specified in the provision conferring that power. The vast majority of amendment powers require some involvement by both the principal employer and the trustees before the scheme may be amended.

To the extent that an employer is involved in the exercise of the power, it must act in accordance with its implied duty of good faith towards its employees (see 12.6). In the rare cases where an employer has power to amend without requiring the agreement of the trustees, the courts can be expected to scrutinise the exercise of that power particularly strictly.

12.13 Reconstruction and winding-up

The trustees' duties are more onerous, as mentioned earlier in 12.7 above. Some examples of the sorts of amendments which trustees may and may not properly agree to are considered in 12.25 to 12.31 below. At this point, however, it is enough to say that trustees must not, as a matter of trust law, agree to amendments which reduce benefits earned before the amendment power is exercised (whether or not immediately payable), and only in exceptional circumstances may they agree to reductions in the future accrual of benefits.

Whoever exercises the power of amendment must do so for the purpose for which it was conferred, namely (unless the trust deed indicates otherwise) to promote the purposes of the scheme. Any statement in the trust deed as to the scheme's main purpose may therefore be relevant to the validity of a subsequent amendment. However, this purpose need not remain fixed indefinitely, and it was recognised in the *Courage* case that a scheme's underlying purpose may change gradually as a scheme evolves over a period of time. (*Re Courage Group's Pension Schemes [1987] 1 WLR 495.*)

The *Courage* case itself provides an example of scheme amendments which were successfully challenged in court as not promoting the schemes' purposes. There were three schemes involved, whose principal employer had recently been acquired by a new owner. The aim of the amendments was to enable the new owner (who had no genuine relationship with the members and was already negotiating to sell the existing principal employer) to be substituted as the schemes' new principal employer, and so gain some benefit from the schemes' surplus funds. This conflicted with the purpose for which the schemes had been established, which was the provision of retirement benefits. The judge specifically commented upon the fact that the new owner was not recognisably the successor to the business or workforce of the company for which it was intended to be substituted.

The case of *Harwood-Smart v Caws [2000] PLR 101* arose following the compulsory liquidation of the employer. The trustees asked the Court to determine whether they had to use any surplus to increase benefits to Revenue maxima prior to making any repayment to the employers. It was found in favour of the beneficiaries rather than the employers. The original trust provisions on winding-up had required any surplus to be used to enhance benefits to Revenue maxima prior to making any payment to the employers. The power of amendment contained a specific prohibition on paying any part of the fund back to the employers. However, the power of amendment had itself been subsequently amended and been used to amend the winding-up provisions to permit refunds to be paid to the employers without increasing members' benefits in excess of their entitlement. The Court found that this power of amendment was invalid.

In the other recent case of *Bestrustees v Stuart [2001] PLR 283*, the BAI pension scheme amended its normal retirement age to 65 for all members following the case of *Barber v GRE [1990] ECR I-1889* in the European Court of Justice in 1990. This case arose around the ambiguity of how and when the decision was made to amend the Rules to effect equalisation. As the employer was also trustee, the issue of consent by the other party did not arise. The amendment to the rules was found to be of limited effect. The scheme was in deficit and in the process of being wound-up while its assets were used to apply for a decision in circumstances where it was suggested that the professional trustees should have exercised their discretion.

Effect of winding-up

12.14 It is unlikely that a power of amendment can be exercised once winding-up has started, unless the terms of that power and the other provisions of the scheme rules indicate a contrary intention. (*Thrells v Lomas (1992) PLR 233.*) However, a power of amendment can probably be exercised (unless the scheme rules indicate otherwise), after an employer has given notice to wind up a scheme, but before that notice has expired (*Municipal Mutual v Harrop [1998] PLR 149*).

Many trust deeds include wording to the effect that the trusts of the scheme will cease once winding-up begins, and this can be taken to include any amendment power. Others include a provision to the effect that amendments may be made during the winding-up stage, in which case the power will continue to be exercisable.

If a scheme's winding-up rule has not been triggered, but the scheme has become closed to new entrants or benefits have ceased to accrue, the power of amendment remains exercisable unless the scheme rules suggest that it does not.

Retrospective amendments

12.15 A power of amendment may be worded so as to permit scheme amendments to take effect from a date earlier than the date on which they are made. Retrospective amendments may validly be made under such a power, although the requirements of *section 67* of *PA 1995* will usually apply (see 12.18 below).

If the power of amendment does not expressly allow retrospective alterations, the position is less certain. In reality, a court's decision on the validity of a purportedly retrospective amendment in these circumstances may depend on the nature of the change. A retrospective amendment made simply to ensure compliance with some statutory requirement would probably be upheld; a more controversial alteration might not.

Not surprisingly therefore, the judge in *Municipal Mutual v Harrop [1998] PLR 149* disallowed a retrospective amendment which would have taken away vested rights. He also decided that the amendment could not be upheld on the grounds that its purpose was to correct an error in the scheme rules.

12.16 *Reconstruction and winding-up*

Restrictions

12.16 An amendment will not be valid if it infringes restrictions written into the amendment power under which it is made. Some of the more common restrictions found in amendment powers are as follows:

(a) that no amendment may be made which would alter the main purpose of the scheme. This reflects the general law on scheme amendments (see 12.13 above);

(b) that no amendment may be made which would result in surplus assets being returned to the employers. Such restrictions were built into some older trust deeds in order to comply with requirements of tax approval which no longer apply. *PA 1995* has introduced provisions to overcome restrictions of this nature in certain circumstances (see 12.10 above and 12.69 below);

(c) that no amendment may reduce pensions in payment or accrued benefits. This adds nothing to existing trust law principles; the position is now reinforced by *PA 1995* (see 12.18 below); or

(d) that amendments (or amendments of a certain nature) may be made only with the members' consent. Sometimes the members concerned are simply not contactable; *PA 1995* helps to relieve this problem (see 12.24 below).

Of course, an amendment will not be valid if it infringes overriding legislation.

Amending a power of amendment

12.17 The presence of unwanted restrictions in an amendment power raises the question of whether those restrictions can be removed by amending the power of amendment.

If the trust deed states that the amendment power can itself be amended, then this should be possible. However, if the restriction being removed is one which can only serve to protect members' interests, the change may be hard for the trustees to justify.

If there is no express power to amend the power of amendment, it will generally not be possible (without a court order or modification order) to remove restrictions which have been there since the scheme was established; widening the amendment power in this way would be like introducing an amendment power where none had previously existed.

However, removing a restriction which did not exist at the scheme's inception but was introduced at a later date may present less of a problem. The nature of the restriction being removed, how it arose, and how long it has been in place, are likely to be relevant.

It is not usual for the parties to wish to introduce restrictions where none previously existed. Were the trustees to do so, they would be in breach of the general trust law duty not to fetter their own discretion (although it is possible for that duty to be excluded by an express provision in the trust deed).

Statutory protection of entitlements and accrued rights

General

12.18 Under *section 67, PA 1995*, any power conferred by an occupational pension scheme (other than a public service pension scheme) to modify the scheme cannot be exercised 'in a manner which would or might affect any entitlement, or accrued right, of any member of the scheme acquired before the power is exercised' unless the following requirements are satisfied:

(*a*) the trustees must be satisfied that:

    (i) the 'certification requirements' (see 12.21 below); or

    (ii) the 'consent requirements' (see 12.22 below);

are met in respect of that member; and

(*b*) (where the power is exercised by a person other than the trustees) the trustees must have approved the exercise of the power in that manner on that occasion.

The circumstances where the legislation excludes an amendment from the impact of *section 67, PA 1995* are extremely narrow (*Modification Regulations 1996 (SI 1996 No 3127), reg 6*). One example, however, would be an amendment creating an employer's lien over benefits where permitted by PA 1995.

The fact that an amendment 'would or might affect' an acquired entitlement or accrued right is enough for this section to apply. An amendment to alter a member's accrued rights without reducing their value (or even, to improve a member's accrued rights) will, therefore, be subject to these requirements.

The application of *section 67, PA 1995* to benefit improvements may appear anomalous, given that the purpose of *section 67* is to protect members' interests. However, there could be circumstances where a court might decide that a benefit improvement is invalid for non-compliance with *section 67*. This could happen, for instance, if an underfunded scheme were being wound up and a member (whose own benefits had not been improved and whose pension was being reduced because of the deficit) challenged the improvement. It is proposed that *section 67* is amended by the Pensions Bill. Details of the proposed changes are set out in 12.96 below.

Meaning of 'member'

12.19 For this purpose, the term 'member' includes any active member,

12.20 *Reconstruction and winding-up*

pensioner, deferred pensioner or postponed pensioner and, if any such person has died, his widow or widower or (if there is no widow or widower) any other person entitled to a payment under the scheme in respect of the deceased (*regulation 2* of the *Modification Regulations (SI 1996 No 2517)*).

Meaning of 'accrued rights' and 'entitlement'

12.20 A member's 'accrued rights' at any time are defined in *section 124(2)* of *PA 1995* so as to be the rights which have accrued to or in respect of him at that time to future benefits; for this purpose, the accrued rights in relation to an active member are to be determined as if he had opted, immediately before that time, to leave pensionable service.

'Entitlement' by contrast, is not defined (although it must at the very least include pensions in payment). The issues which this gives rise to are considered in 12.23(b) below).

The 'certification requirements'

12.21 Despite the wording of *PA 1995*, there is only one certification requirement. This is that an actuary certifies to the trustees that, in his opinion, the proposed amendment would not adversely affect any member (without his consent) in respect of his entitlements, or accrued rights, acquired before the power of amendment is exercised. [*PA 1995, s 67(4)(a)* and the *Modification Regulations (SI 1996 No 2517), reg 3*].

This certification is to be given by the scheme actuary appointed under *section 47(1)(b), PA 1995* (see 2.4) or, where the requirement to appoint an actuary under that section does not apply, by any actuary.

The 'consent requirements'

12.22 Again, there is only one consent requirement (even though *PA 1995* uses the word 'requirements'), which is that members who are affected consent to the proposed amendment in writing. [*PA 1995, s 67(4)(b)* and the *Modification Regulations (SI 1996 No 2517), reg 4*].

Practical issues

12.23 Some of the more difficult points raised by these provisions are as follows:

(a) *'Modification'*. *Section 67* of *PA 1995* is stated to apply specifically to a power 'to modify the scheme'. This may have been intended only to cover amendments to the wording of the scheme's trust deed and rules, but it is certainly possible to interpret the phrase more widely. An exercise of the scheme's augmentation power, for instance, does not usually involve an amendment to the scheme's governing documents, but it is, at least arguably, a modification of the scheme. (The fact that an augmentation will of course be a benefit improvement does not take it out of *section 67* – see 12.18 above).

As another example, it may be decided to change a scheme's actuarial early retirement factors (including in relation to past service) for future retirements. If the scheme rules specify the factors to be applied, then the change will clearly require those rules to be amended and so be subject to the *section 67* requirements. However, many schemes' rules simply state that actuarial factors are to be decided by the trustees having considered the advice of the actuary. This will not require an amendment to the rules, but whether *section 67* applies depends on how widely the phrase 'modify the scheme' is interpreted.

(b) *'Entitlement'*. The word 'entitlement' is not defined, but there can be little doubt that it includes pensions in payment. Whether it includes future mandatory pension increases payable under the scheme rules, however, is uncertain.

It is reasonable to assume that any right which a member is unconditionally entitled to exercise (for instance, to take an immediate early retirement pension without requiring the trustees' or any employer's consent) counts as an 'entitlement'. What is less certain is whether a member's right to exercise such a right subject to his employer's consent is also covered. Arguably, such a member has acquired an entitlement (albeit a qualified one).

(c) *Increases in deferment.* Another question which the legislation does not address is whether future statutory increases to deferred pensions (particularly where those increases exceed the statutory minimum) are protected by *section 67*.

(d) *Security of benefits.* The generally held view is that modifications which would or might affect the security of benefits (as opposed to the benefits themselves) are not covered by *section 67*. The point has not, however, been tested in court.

Because of the nature of issues, the safest course of action for employers and trustees will be to obtain legal advice before committing themselves to a course of action.

Consent required by scheme rules

12.24 Where the scheme's own amendment power requires a member's consent, *PA 1995* recognises that this consent may not always be obtainable (perhaps because the member's whereabouts are unknown). *Section 67(6)* of *PA 1995* and *regulation 5* of the *Modification Regulations* (*SI 1996 No 2517*) therefore allow this consent to be treated as having been given following two notifications (at least two months apart) sent to the member's last known address, with no response having been received one month after the second notification.

12.25 *Reconstruction and winding-up*

This applies only to consent requirements contained in the scheme rules; if *section 67, PA 1995* applies (see 12.18 above), the actuary's certificate will be required in relation to any member whose consent is unobtainable.

Examples

12.25 The following examples consider some of the scheme amendments which an employer might wish to make, and whether the trustees could properly agree to them.

It is assumed for this purpose that the scheme's amendment power is wide enough to allow the amendments proposed but that agreement between the employer and the trustees is required.

(Whether the employer's decision to make these amendments accords with its contractual obligations is not dealt with here, but will be governed by the principles outlined in 7.6 to 7.10 above.)

Reduction of past service benefits

12.26 As mentioned earlier, trustees must not agree to an amendment which reduces any benefit earned before the amendment power is exercised (whether payable immediately or from some time in the future). To do so would be a clear breach of trust (quite apart from the requirements, summarised in 12.18 to 12.23 above, of *section 67* of *PA 1995*).

Sometimes an employer will propose a method of re-calculating all past service benefits which appears to represent a general benefit improvement but, on closer examination, disadvantages a small number of members. The trustees should not agree to the proposals unless they are revised to remove that detriment; it is no defence to a breach of trust action brought by a disadvantaged minority that the arrangements benefit the majority.

Reduction of future service benefits

12.27 Trustees should not agree to a reduction in future benefit accrual without compelling reasons. For example, if the likely outcome of the trustees refusing to agree to the reduction is that the employer will arrange for the scheme to be wound up, the trustees may take the view that they are acting in the best interests of their members by agreeing to the change. Trustees do also owe a duty to the employer (see chapter 3), and are not required to push the company into paying more than it can genuinely afford.

Amending the scheme so that no further benefits will accrue in the future

12.28 This is simply a more drastic version of 12.27 above, and so the same principles apply.

Closing the scheme to future entrants

12.29 The proposal here will be that an amendment is made to the scheme's eligibility rule so that no further members may join the scheme in the future. This will not necessarily cause the trustees significant problems as the main effect of the amendment will be to exclude individuals who have never belonged to the scheme and to whom the trustees will, therefore, not normally owe a duty.

However, some schemes impose a 'waiting period' for membership, so that an employee has to complete, say, six months' service before he is allowed to join the scheme. Individuals currently serving this 'waiting period' can be regarded as being contingently entitled to benefits from the scheme, and the trustees would usually, therefore, be well advised (unless the scheme is seriously underfunded) to insist that the closure to new entrants does not affect these particular individuals.

Introduction of different benefits for future joiners

12.30 The concern here is very often that the new benefits package is (or is capable of being) less generous than the one for current members. The issues which this raises for trustees are similar to those in 12.29 above, in that the individuals to be affected by the amendment will not yet be scheme members. The same considerations as regards anyone serving a 'waiting period' will apply.

Conversion to money purchase

12.31 An employer may continue to operate its final salary scheme on the existing basis for current members, but decide that future joiners should be admitted to membership on a money purchase basis only. This is an example of the sort of amendment described in 12.30 above.

The trustees will face harder decisions if they are asked to agree to an amendment which will convert the current final salary members to a money purchase basis for future accrual (and possibly also for past service benefits).

The trustees, acting on actuarial advice, should not hesitate where appropriate to seek from the employer improvements in the money purchase benefits being offered. This might take the form of:

(*a*) a more generous method of conversion (if it is proposed to convert past service benefits);

(*b*) an increase in the employer's future contributions; or

(*c*) possibly even some form of 'final salary underpin' for the members involved, so that their eventual benefits will not dip below a given level.

12.32 *Reconstruction and winding-up*

The employer may be prepared to compromise on at least some of these points in order to see the conversion go ahead. The improvements will also make the exercise easier for the employer to justify to its employees.

The trustees should seek actuarial advice as to how the employer's proposals will compare with the existing final salary basis. Applying the principles set out in 12.26 and 12.27 above, the position will normally be as follows:

(i) The trustees should have no difficulties in agreeing to the proposals in relation to any member whom those proposals will clearly benefit

(ii) The trustees should not agree to the proposals in relation to any member for whom the risks or other disadvantages of those proposals outweigh any advantage.

(iii) If neither of the above applies in relation to a member, the trustees should generally be reluctant to permit the conversion to take place without his consent. In seeking his consent, the position should be explained fully to him in terms which he can understand and which clearly draw his attention to any risks involved. He should also be advised to seek independent financial advice. If he decides to consent, he should be asked to sign a consent form which states that the decision reached is his own and that the trustees will not be held responsible for it.

In some circumstances, the trustees may justifiably go further than this towards accommodating the employer's proposals (for instance, if the future service benefits offered are genuinely the best which the employer can afford). However, in no circumstances should the trustees allow a reduction in the value of a member's accrued benefits. The conversion of past service final salary benefits to a money purchase basis will also be subject to *section 67* of *PA 1995* (see 12.18 above).

BULK TRANSFERS – GENERAL

Background

12.32 Some of the reasons for making bulk transfers of assets and liabilities between schemes operating within the same group of employers were outlined in 12.3 above. The matters that arise in relation to bulk transfers vary to some extent according to whether or not the transferring scheme has begun to be wound up before the time of the transfer (see 12.48 to 12.50 and 12.85 to 12.91 below). Here, however, some general issues are considered.

Members' consents to transfer

12.33 An advantage of obtaining members' consents to the transfer is that, if matters have been properly and clearly explained to the members, they are less likely to feel aggrieved about the transfer arrangements later on.

Reconstruction and winding-up 12.33

However, the fact that members' consents are being sought in no way relieves the trustees of the responsibility to ensure that the arrangements are in the members' best interests. The consent form which members are asked to sign may contain a statement discharging the transferring trustees from any further liability, but it may not be possible for trustees to rely on this discharge if it is later shown that they did not take proper steps to protect their members.

In seeking consents, care should be taken not to give unauthorised investment advice contrary to the *Financial Services and Markets Act 2000* (explained further in 10.25 above) and members should be encouraged to seek independent financial advice before taking a decision.

In reality, however, obtaining the consent of the entire membership will often be impractical, particularly in relation to deferred pensioners, some of whom are likely to have moved house and not advised their former employer or the trustees of their new address. Transfers to other occupational pension schemes (but not to personal pension schemes) are therefore permissible without the need for members' consents, but only if:

(*a*) either:

   (i) the scheme rules expressly permit transfers to be made without consent; or

   (ii) the transferring scheme is an approved final salary scheme, the transfer follows the commencement, after 5 April 1997, of the winding-up of that scheme and the requirements dealt with in 12.74 are met; and

(*b*) either:

   (i) both schemes apply to employment with the same employer (which is generally taken to mean that the two schemes must have at least one participating employer in common); or

   (ii) it is a bulk (as opposed to an individual) transfer, either resulting from a financial transaction between the employers or where the employers are 'connected' for the purposes of the legislation (*regulation 12(2)* of the *Preservation Regulations (SI 1991 No 167)*);

(*c*) an actuarial certificate (often called a 'GN16', this being the number of the Guidance Note issued by the Institute and Faculty of Actuaries regulating the preparation of such certificates) is given to the effect that:

   (i) the transfer credits in the receiving scheme for each member are broadly no less favourable than the rights being transferred; and

   (ii) there is good cause to believe that the award of discretionary benefits (or discretionary benefit increases) in the receiving scheme will be broadly no less favourable than any established custom of awarding discretionary benefits (or discretionary benefit increases) in the transferring scheme (*regulation 12(3)* of the *Preservation Regulations (SI 1991 No 167)*). For this purpose, the actuary may

12.34 *Reconstruction and winding-up*

> make an allowance for any amount by which the transfer credits under the receiving scheme are more favourable than the rights to be transferred; and

(*d*) in relation to contracted-out arrangements (see chapter 4) the transfer is not of such a kind that members' consents are required as set out in 4.33 above. These requirements are particularly onerous in relation to protected rights. At the time of writing, it is arguable (but by no means certain) that these requirements do not apply so long as the transferring scheme is an approved final salary scheme, the transfer follows the commencement, after 5 April 1997, of the winding-up of that scheme and the requirements dealt with in 12.74 below are met.

Where a transfer is to be made without consent, information about the proposed transfer and details of the value of the rights to be transferred (including rights in respect of death in service benefits and survivors' benefits) must be given to each member affected not less than one month before the proposed transfer is due to take place (*regulation 12 (4B)* of the *Preservation Regulations (SI 1991 No 167)*).

The ability to transfer without consent in these circumstances applies only to past service benefits. Future service benefits cannot accrue without consent in the receiving scheme; this would amount to compulsory scheme membership contrary to *section 160* of *PSA 1993*.

Even where all the above conditions are met, the trustees may not exercise a discretion to make a transfer unless they are satisfied that it is in their members' best interests.

Issues for trustees to consider

12.34 The matters to be borne in mind by the trustees in deciding whether they are doing the best for their members will vary according to the circumstances, but the following issues are amongst those which will most commonly arise. It is assumed here that the trustees have some discretion as to whether the transfer takes place.

Benefits

12.35 The employers may offer benefit improvements in order to encourage the trustees to agree to the transfer. If improvements are not offered, the trustees should seek them (particularly if, without any, there is no advantage for their members in the transfer going ahead). This is potentially an issue for both the transferring and receiving trustees.

The transferring trustees should examine closely the benefits which are offered in respect of the transfer and guard against the possibility of agreeing to proposals which result in any person's benefits being reduced. Trustees' duties in relation to changes in benefits were considered in 12.25 to 12.31 above in the context of scheme amendments. The same principles apply in relation to transfers, so that trustees will be in breach of trust if they agree to a transfer which reduces any person's past service benefits, and only exceptionally may they agree to a transfer which reduces future benefits (for instance, in the circumstances outlined in 12.27).

Funding disparity

12.36 Another issue is the comparative funding levels of the transferring and receiving schemes. If, for example, the trustees of an ongoing scheme are considering whether to make a bulk transfer, they should seek advice as to the solvency of both the transferring and receiving schemes respectively. If the transferring scheme is significantly better funded than the receiving scheme, the transferring trustees should question whether they can justify making a transfer which would, in effect, put their members into a worse funded scheme than the one to which they presently belong.

How much of an issue this is will depend not only on the extent of the funding disparity but also on other factors. For instance, both schemes might be well funded, but the receiving scheme only slightly less so than the transferring scheme. In these circumstances the transferring trustees could properly take the view that the modest funding disparity was outweighed by any more significant advantages of the transfer, such as:

(*a*) better benefits to be provided by the receiving scheme;

(*b*) provisions in the receiving scheme's rules creating greater scope than under the transferring scheme for surplus assets to be used for benefit improvements; or

(*c*) a likelihood of the receiving scheme's future investment performance significantly outstripping that of the transferring scheme (perhaps because the receiving scheme is much larger – see 12.38 below).

If the funding disparity remains an issue, the transferring trustees should impose conditions upon the employers (and, where appropriate, the receiving trustees) before agreeing to make the transfer. These conditions might typically include one or both of the following:

(i) that a benefit improvement be granted in respect of the members to be transferred; and/or

(ii) that any surplus to be transferred from the transferring scheme be subject to some measure of 'ringfencing' in the receiving scheme. The aim of ringfencing is to ensure that assets transferred from the transferring scheme are subject to safeguards for the benefit of the transferring members in the receiving scheme. This is done by amending the rules of the receiving scheme, so as (in this context) to give the transferring members prior rights over other members as regards the transferred assets in relation to such matters as:

- any use of surplus assets to grant benefit improvements;

12.37 *Reconstruction and winding-up*

- the calculation of future transfer values paid from the receiving scheme; and/or
- the distribution of assets on a winding-up of the receiving scheme. However, such an amendment may be partly or wholly ineffective if the receiving scheme subsequently goes into winding-up with insufficient assets to meet all its liabilities. This is because of the winding-up requirements in *PA 1995* which, at least to some extent (as explained further in 12.67 below), override the scheme's rules.

The employer may well insist that any 'ringfencing' provisions only remain effective for a specified period of time. In agreeing to a suitable period, the trustees should consider actuarial advice as to how long the surplus might otherwise have lasted in the transferring scheme.

The transferring trustees are likely to have less negotiating power, however, if their scheme has gone into winding-up.

If, conversely, the receiving scheme is better funded than the transferring scheme, then similar considerations in reverse will have to be borne in mind by the receiving scheme's trustees before they exercise any discretion under the terms of their trust deed to accept the transfer.

Comparison of balance of powers

12.37 The trustees of an ongoing scheme ought also, before agreeing to make a transfer, to consider the 'balance of powers' (as between the employers, on the one hand, and the trustees, on the other) under the provisions of their own scheme and compare it with the corresponding balance in the receiving scheme. If the receiving scheme's balance of powers is overall less favourable towards the trustees (and therefore the beneficiaries) than under the transferring scheme, then the transferring trustees should again question whether they can properly make the transfer.

An unfavourable shift in the balance of powers may be compensated for by other factors; for instance, if the receiving scheme is significantly better funded than the transferring scheme, provides better benefits, or (as mentioned in 12.38 below) has better prospects for future growth. If this is not the case, however, then the trustees should consider obtaining from the employer some benefit or safeguard for their members before agreeing to the transfer. This might take the form of:

(*a*) an immediate benefit improvement in respect of the transferring members; or

(*b*) amendments to the receiving scheme to make its balance of powers more favourable to the trustees, at least insofar as that scheme will ultimately relate to the transferring members. Where surplus assets are being transferred, any such amendment will be another form of 'ringfencing' as referred to in 12.36(ii) above. The difference here, however, is that the purpose of the ringfencing will be to protect the transferring members' interests against those of the employers (rather than against those of the other members).

The issue will not be as acute for the transferring trustees if their scheme is already in winding-up.

Long term future of schemes

12.38 It is increasingly difficult to predict the long term stability and growth of any pension scheme, but it is nevertheless an issue which trustees should bear in mind. The overall financial circumstances of a scheme's sponsoring employers may give a clue as to the scheme's future. Another factor is the scheme's size.

Many transfers of the sort discussed in this chapter are from smaller schemes to larger schemes. Larger funds tend to bear proportionately lower administrative costs (owing to economies of scale) and may be able to pursue a successful investment strategy which might not realistically be available to a smaller scheme. However, trustees should be wary of relying too heavily on this to justify a transfer which would not otherwise be in their members' best interests.

It is comparatively rare for trustees to be asked to agree to a transfer to a smaller scheme within the same group of employers. The trustees should make certain that there is a clear advantage for their members (most probably in the form of benefit improvements) should this happen.

Of course, if the transferring scheme is already being wound up, that scheme will not have any long term future for the trustees to consider.

Other ways of securing benefits on a winding-up

12.39 If the transferring scheme is in the course of being wound up, some of the issues mentioned above may be less relevant, as members will not have the alternative simply of remaining in the transferring scheme. Instead, the transferring trustees should satisfy themselves that any bulk transfer will be on terms which serve their members at least as well as the other courses of action available (such as transfers to personal pension schemes or purchasing annuities).

Inland Revenue approval

12.40 The Inland Revenue's permission should be sought in respect of the transfer if the scheme is approved (IR12 (2001) PN 10.36). The application is to be made to the IR SPSS, using Form PS295.

Few schemes now have such large surpluses that the Inland Revenue require them to be reduced (as described in 11.36 above). However, where the transfer-

12.41 *Reconstruction and winding-up*

ring scheme is such a scheme, there may be difficulty in obtaining Revenue agreement to a transfer of that surplus. This is because *Schedule 22* to *ICTA 1988* specifies a number of 'permitted ways' in which such a surplus may be reduced; transferring the surplus to a replacement scheme is not one of those ways.

Contracted-out schemes

12.41 Further requirements apply in relation to contracted-out schemes and these are particularly restrictive where a transfer of protected rights is concerned. These requirements are dealt with in 4.33 above, but the legislation can be read as suggesting that they will not apply so long as it is unclear whether they will apply in full where the transfer follows the commencement, after 5 April 1997, of the winding-up of an approved final salary transferring scheme, where the requirements explained in 12.71 below are met. (In any event, separate requirements continue to apply in relation to the buying-out of protected rights (*section 32A* of *PSA 1993*).)

Transfer agreement

12.42 It is advisable for the parties involved to enter into a formal transfer agreement where the terms of the arrangement which has been entered into can be clearly set out. The parties will usually be the trustees of the two schemes and each scheme's principal employer. The terms of any such agreement will vary enormously depending on the circumstances, but 12.43 to 12.47 below describe the provisions which will most often be included.

Some of these are in reality scheme amendments. The parties could, as an alternative, deal with these areas in separate deeds of amendment relating to the two schemes, but it is often more convenient to deal with all matters relating to the transfer in a single document. Care should be taken to ensure that, if the transfer agreement is to amend either of the schemes, it complies with all the relevant requirements of that scheme's power of amendment (for instance, by being in the form of a deed).

The agreement will typically cover the following areas:

Amendments to the transferring scheme

12.43 Amendments to the transferring scheme may be necessary to:

(*a*) permit the parties to make the transfer; and/or

(*b*) grant any benefit improvements which the transferring trustees require as a condition of their making the transfer.

Transfer amount

12.44 This may be stated as a specific sum (subject to a market value adjustment and/or increase for late payment) or the agreement may simply set out the method by which the amount is to be calculated (perhaps by reference to an actuary's letter appended to the agreement). If the agreement provides for the transferring scheme's entire assets to be transferred, then the precise calculation of the amount becomes less of an issue.

Past service benefits

12.45 The benefits to be provided in the receiving scheme in relation to the transfer payment should be clearly stated.

Amendments to the receiving scheme

12.46 Amendments may be required in relation to the receiving scheme, for instance to:

(*a*)   permit the parties to accept the transfer;

(*b*)   incorporate any special future service benefits in relation to the transferring members which have been agreed;

(*c*)   grant any benefit improvements for the receiving scheme's existing members which the receiving trustees require as a condition of their accepting the transfer; and/or

(*d*)   incorporate any 'ringfencing' provisions (as referred to in 12.36(ii) and 12.37(b) above) which have been agreed between the parties as a condition of the transfer being made.

Indemnity

12.47 The transferring trustees may seek an indemnity from the receiving trustees in relation to any claims which might be brought against them in relation to the transferring members. The receiving trustees should of course consider how this might affect their own members' interests. Any such indemnity will normally exclude matters where there has been an element of bad faith or dishonesty by the transferring trustees and be limited, for instance, to that part of the receiving scheme's assets which is attributable to the transfer payment.

To the extent that these assets may be insufficient fully to indemnify the transferring trustees, one or more of the employers may agree to indemnify the transferring trustees for the difference; however, care should be taken not to infringe the provisions in *section 310* of the *Companies Act 1985* (referred to further in chapter 3) regarding companies indemnifying their own officers.

12.48 *Reconstruction and winding-up*

BULK TRANSFERS – SPECIFIC ISSUES WHERE WINDING-UP HAS NOT COMMENCED

Background

12.48 The questions of whether there is power to make a bulk transfer, and how any transfer payment is to be calculated, will attract different answers depending on whether or not the transferring scheme has gone into winding-up at the time of the transfer. The date on which a scheme commences to be wound up for this purpose is governed by *regulation 2* of the *Winding-up Regulations* (*SI 1996 No 3126*) the effect of which is illustrated in the flowchart at the end of the chapter.

Where winding-up has not commenced (or is not even expected to happen), the position is as set out in 12.49 and 12.50 below. (The corresponding position where winding-up has commenced is dealt with in 12.85 to 12.89.)

Power to make bulk transfers

12.49 Whether there is power to make a bulk transfer out of a scheme which is not in winding-up depends upon the terms of that scheme's trust deed and rules. If there is power to make the transfer, much will depend on whether the trust deed and rules place that power primarily with the employers or with the trustees. For instance:

(*a*)   the principal employer might have power to direct the trustees to make a transfer, with the trustees having no right of refusal;

(*b*)   the principal employer might have power to request the trustees to make a transfer, with the trustees having a discretion as to whether or not they act on that request;

(*c*)   the trustees might have power to initiate a transfer, subject only to the employer's consent. This gives the trustees a greater degree of control than in (b) above since, in putting their proposals to the employer, the trustees are effectively requiring the employer to consider those proposals in a manner consistent with its implied duty of good faith (see 12.6 above);

(*d*)   the trustees might have power to make a transfer, subject only to consultation with the employer. So long as a genuine consultation procedure is carried out, this does not require the trustees actually to obtain the employer's consent; or

(*e*)   the trustees might have power to make a bulk transfer without any form of reference to the employer being required.

Amount to be transferred

12.50 Similarly, the calculation of the transfer amount is governed by the trust deed and rules, subject to members' statutory entitlements to a minimum of the cash equivalents of their accrued benefits (see 6.44 above) (although underfunding in the transferring scheme may justify a reduction of cash equivalents – see 6.51 for further details on the reduction of cash equivalents).

Trust deeds vary considerably as to how the transfer amount is to be calculated. Some examples are as follows:

(a) the matter might be left entirely to the discretion either of the principal employer or of the trustees, often subject to the requirement that they first consider the advice of the actuary (which advice the trust deed may or may not require them to accept, but in practice may be hard to reject without good reason);

(b) more commonly, the deed will leave the decision as to the amount to one of the two parties – either the principal employer or the trustees – subject to the consent of the other;

(c) the trust deed might (particularly if it is an older one) have the effect of requiring that the transfer payment represent a share of the overall fund in respect of the members being transferred. In an underfunded scheme, this would mean the transferring members bearing a proportion of the brunt of any overall deficit in the transferring scheme. In an overfunded scheme, by contrast, the transfer payment would have to include a share of any surplus; or

(d) the trust deed might (especially if it is a relatively modern one), seek to give the employers maximum control in relation to active members by specifying that the transfer payment be the lesser of:

   (i) their statutory cash equivalents; and

   (ii) the amount which would be available to be applied in respect of them were the scheme to be wound up;

(which is, effectively, the minimum which the law will allow) subject to the principal employer's sole discretion to direct a greater amount.

Schemes are seldom overfunded when valued on the basis used by the Inland Revenue for determining if the scheme has a statutory surplus, but there may be difficulties in transferring a share of the surplus in the rare cases where this is so (see 12.40 above).

The position with regard to these issues will be rather different where the transfers take place after winding-up has commenced. Before looking at this further (see 12.85 below), however, it is necessary to consider the winding-up procedure as a whole.

TRIGGERING A WINDING-UP

Triggering events

12.51 The events which will trigger a winding-up of a scheme will depend upon the scheme's governing trust deed and rules. These might typically provide for a winding-up of the scheme to be triggered upon the earliest of:

(a) the expiry of a notice to the trustees by the principal employer, requiring that the scheme be wound up;

(b) the trustees resolving to wind the scheme up and notifying the principal employer accordingly;

(c) the principal employer being in arrears in its contributions to the scheme and failing to rectify the position within a specified period of the trustees formally requesting it to do so;

(d) the principal employer going into liquidation; and

(e) the expiry of a specified period from the date on which the scheme was established.

Many trust deeds and rules will, in some of these circumstances, give the trustees a discretion to continue operating the scheme (with a new principal employer, where appropriate) rather than wind it up immediately; this is dealt with further in 12.53 below.

Application to Opra or to court

12.52 In the unlikely event of the employer or the trustees wishing to wind up a scheme and there being no power in the trust deed enabling them to do so, Opra may, under *section 11* of *PA 1995*, authorise or direct a winding-up if:

(a) the scheme (or any part of it) ought to be replaced by a different scheme;

(b) the scheme is no longer required; or

(c) it is necessary in order to protect the interests of the generality of the scheme members.

It should only rarely be necessary to resort to an application to Opra, and Opra is unlikely to make such an order without a compelling case being made to it. Alternatively, it may in exceptional circumstances be necessary to apply to the court for directions to wind up a scheme.

Disclosure requirements

12.53 The intention of Opra's disclosure requirements is to shorten the time between the instigation of terminating a pension scheme and its completion. An outline of Opra's requirements is as follows:

(a) the trustees must notify Opra where a scheme has been in the process of winding-up for more than three years;

(b) the trustees must notify Opra in writing every 12 months about current progress;

(c) the trustees must provide a member of the scheme with a copy of any report sent to Opra within two months of a request being made;

(d) Opra is expected to have the power to speed up the winding-up process of a scheme, where it deems it appropriate;

(e) the scheme's sponsor or administrator must notify Opra in the absence of an independent trustee where an independent trustee is required;

(f) an independent trustee must be appointed by the official receiver or insolvency practitioner where relevant within three months of the date such appointment was required;

(g) the trustees must notify Opra within one month in the absence of an independent trustee where an independent trustee is required;

(h) the administrator must notify Opra within one month where the scheme has no trustees;

(i) the trustees and the employer (if appropriate) must keep a written record of any decisions to wind-up a scheme;

(j) the trustees can seek a modification order from Opra to wind-up a scheme.

Where the trustees have not complied with the requirements to wind-up a scheme, they will have to provide justified reasons to Opra for not doing so. This may include copies of statements from the scheme's actuary or auditor. Delays in winding-up which are allegedly caused by awaiting information from the Inland Revenue on contracting-out issues are expected to be reduced. Trustees may be fined by Opra in the event of unjustified delays in winding-up a scheme.

DEFERRAL OF WINDING-UP BY TRUSTEES

Power under scheme rules

12.54 Some scheme rules give the trustees power, even after the winding-up rule has been triggered, to defer winding the scheme up. Examples of circumstances where the trustees might wish to defer winding-up are:

(a) where annuity rates are low at the time when the winding-up rule is triggered and the trustees wish to wait for them to rise, so placing the fund in a better position to secure the benefits with an insurance company;

(b) where the trustees are awaiting a clarification of the law without which winding-up may prove risky (the initial uncertainty over the European Court's *Barber* decision – see chapter 9 – being an example); or

(c) where the scheme's winding-up rule has been triggered by the principal employer going into receivership and the trustees expect the business to be sold to a new owner who is committed to the continued funding and operation of the scheme.

12.55 *Reconstruction and winding-up*

A scheme rule enabling the trustees to defer winding-up in these circumstances may or may not permit the trustees to take steps during the deferral period (for example, requiring further employers' contributions) which would create further liabilities for the employers.

Statutory power

12.55 Where winding-up has not commenced before 6 April 1997, there is in some circumstances a statutory power to defer winding-up for those trustees who do not have such a power under their scheme rules. (See the flowchart at the end of this chapter to ascertain the date on which winding-up commences for this purpose.)

This statutory power is conferred by *section 38(1)* of *PA 1995* and is available only where (in particular):

(*a*) there is no power to defer winding-up in the scheme's trust deed and rules (*section 38(1)*);

(*b*) it is not a money purchase scheme (*section 38(3)(a)*);

(*c*) the scheme:

- has at least two members;

- is approved (or formerly approved) or a relevant statutory scheme; and

- is not a tax approved (or formerly tax approved) small self-administered scheme (see chapter 13) [Winding-up Regulations (SI 1996 No 3126), reg 10 (1)]; and

(*d*) a 'relevant insolvency event' has occurred in relation to any of the scheme's employers and that event is, under the scheme rules, an event triggering a winding-up of the scheme. A 'relevant insolvency event' is defined in *section 75* of *PA 1995* and its meaning is considered further in 12.80, but in broad terms it means the commencement of an employer's bankruptcy or an employer going into liquidation. If the scheme has no active members, anyone who was an employer in relation to the scheme when the scheme last had active members will count as an employer for this purpose. [*Winding-up Regulations (SI 1996 No 3126), reg 10(1)(a) and (2)*].

Where trustees exercise this new power, they may not allow new members to join the scheme during the deferral period. However, *section 38(2), PA 1995* does allow them to decide:

(i) that contributions will not continue to be payable; or

(ii) that benefits will not continue to accrue;

during deferment, but not to stop increases to accrued rights.

Winding-up priorities

12.56 Whilst winding-up is being deferred, some active members are likely to become deferred pensioners, others to become pensioners, and so on. These changes of status are important because, should the scheme be wound up with insufficient assets to secure all the benefits, some membership categories (such as pensioners) will usually have preferential rights over others. (See 12.65 and 12.67.)

Trustees who defer winding-up now have a limited degree of scope under *regulation 5* of the *Winding-up Regulations (SI 1996 No 3126)* for deciding the date at which membership status (for instance, whether a person is an active member or a pensioner) is to be determined for this purpose.

Disclosure requirements

12.57 Any decision to defer winding-up (whether reached under the scheme rules or under *section 38* of *PA 1995*) or to fix a date for determining winding-up priorities (whether reached under the power referred to in 12.56 above or under any other power) must be recorded and members must be informed of the decision within one month. [*Winding-up Regulations (SI 1996 No 3126), reg 11*].

If the trustees do not defer winding-up, or when any period of deferral comes to an end, the winding-up process will start.

THE WINDING-UP PROCESS

Overview

12.58 The application of scheme assets where a scheme is being wound up varies according to whether winding-up began before 6 April 1997 or begins after 5 April 1997. (See the flowchart at the end of the chapter to ascertain the date on which winding-up commences for this purpose.)

The following table provides an overview of these two regimes, which are described further in 12.59 to 12.74 below:

	Where winding-up started before 6 April 1997	Where winding-up starts after 5 April 1997
Do the trustees have power to purchase annuities and make transfer payments to other schemes?	Depends on scheme rules.	In an approved final salary scheme, yes, subject to certain requirements (see 12.74). Otherwise depends on scheme rules.

12.58 *Reconstruction and winding-up*

	Where winding-up started before 6 April 1997	Where winding-up starts after 5 April 1997
May the employers force the trustees to exercise those powers?	Depends on scheme rules.	In an approved final salary scheme, it is uncertain as to whether any such right of the employer under the scheme rules may be exercised (see 12.87). Otherwise, depends on scheme rules.
Will any surplus be used to increase benefits?	Depends on scheme rules (subject to Inland Revenue limits where scheme is approved).	In an approved final salary scheme, it is arguable (but unlikely) that any power in the scheme rules of a person other than the trustees to decide the matter becomes exercisable only by the trustees (see 12.71). Otherwise, depends on scheme rules (subject to Inland Revenue limits where scheme is approved).
Will any surplus be paid to the employers?	Only if: (*a*) scheme rules permit it; and (*b*) certain requirements are met (see 12.64).	As for pre-6 April 1997, except that: (*a*) if the scheme is exempt approved, a further requirement (requiring members to be notified and enabling them to make representations to Opra) must be met; and (*b*) in certain circumstances, surplus may be paid from an exempt approved scheme to the employers even though the scheme rules prohibit it (see 12.72).
If the scheme is underfunded, will scheme expenses take priority over liabilities for benefits?	Depends on scheme rules in each case.	
How will any underfunding be borne amongst beneficiaries?	Depends on scheme rules.	In an approved final salary scheme, scheme rules are subject to a new statutory order of priorities (see 12.67). Otherwise, scheme rules will continue to apply.
Do the employers become liable to the trustees for any underfunding?	Depends on extent of underfunding; applicable mainly to final salary schemes (see 12.78).	

	Where winding-up started before 6 April 1997	Where winding-up starts after 5 April 1997
Do the trustees receive a statutory discharge from liability following completion of winding-up?	No statutory discharge.	In an approved final salary scheme, yes, but only if they wind up in accordance with certain requirements (see 12.74). Otherwise, no statutory discharge.

Application of assets where winding-up starts before 6 April 1997

12.59 Where winding-up commences before 6 April 1997, the winding-up process will be governed primarily by the scheme rules. These will, of course, vary from one scheme to another, but the following matters will usually be covered.

Expenses

12.60 Most schemes' rules will first provide for an amount to be set aside out of the assets to cover scheme expenses.

The case of *Kemble v Hicks [1999] PLR287* was heard to determine issues following the liquidation of the employer in 1991 with a final salary scheme with assets of £8 million. The two issues raised were whether the trustees could apply the assets of the scheme to purchase insurance cover to protect themselves against any claim for breach of trust and whether they could apply any surplus assets in the final salary scheme to increase the value of the new money purchase scheme. The Court found that trust moneys could not be used in either case.

The first issue is referred to in paragraph 12.77(d).

In relation to the application of the surplus from the final salary scheme to increase the value of the money purchase scheme, the judgement was made on the grounds that the two schemes had to be looked at separately and the latter was not a continuation of the same overall scheme.

Purchase of annuities

12.61 From the remaining assets, the rules will normally provide for the trustees to secure the benefits by purchasing annuities from an insurance company. An order of priorities (see 12.65 below) will usually be specified in the event of there being insufficient assets.

Transfers out

12.62 As an alternative to purchasing annuities, most schemes will allow the

12.63 *Reconstruction and winding-up*

trustees to transfer benefits to other tax-approved retirement benefits schemes or personal pension schemes. In the context of bulk transfers, this is considered further in 12.86 and 12.88 below.

Surplus – power to increase benefits

12.63 The trustees may or may not have power (or even an obligation) under the rules to use any surplus assets remaining after the liabilities have been secured to provide further benefits. Where the trustees do have this power, the rules will often require them to obtain the principal employer's consent before exercising it. In other schemes, the rules may simply require the trustees to follow the principal employer's directions in relation to the matter.

In the case of an exempt approved scheme, those further benefits should be limited to the most that are permitted by the Inland Revenue (although it is rare for a scheme to be so overfunded that there is a risk of exceeding those limits).

Surplus – payment to employers

12.64 The vast majority of schemes' rules will provide for any ultimate surplus remaining to be paid (net of 40 per cent tax where the scheme has had exempt approval for tax purposes) to the employers. Before such a payment may be made:

(a) the scheme's liabilities must have been fully discharged;

(b) where there is a power to augment benefits, the power must either have been exercised or a decision made not to exercise it;

(c) where it is a final salary scheme, 'limited price indexation' (ie increases equal to the lesser of five per cent per annum and increases in the index of retail prices) must have been applied to pensions in payment (*PSA 1993, s 108*); and

(d) the agreement of the Inland Revenue must be obtained if the scheme is approved. If there is to be a replacement scheme for the one being wound up, the Revenue will only allow the surplus to be paid to an employer to the extent that (valuing the scheme on the Revenue's own basis) the scheme's assets exceed 105 per cent of its liabilities (IR12 (2001), PN 13.31).

Deficits

12.65 If an underfunded final salary scheme goes into winding-up, the employers may become liable to the trustees for the deficit. Until 5 April 1997 this debt would have arisen under *section 144* of *PSA 1993*. Since 6 April 1997, however, any such debt arises under *section 75* of *PA 1995* (unless the scheme commenced winding-up before 19 December 1996). *Section 75, PA 1995* is considered further in 12.78 below. The debt arises regardless of the terms of the trust deed.

If there are still insufficient assets to provide all the benefits, the deficit will be borne amongst the scheme's beneficiaries in accordance with its rules. Certain benefits are required by law to be given priority in the scheme rules over others, but as these requirements have been superseded where winding-up starts after 5 April 1997 (see 12.67 below), they are not considered further here.

The position is more complex in relation to a winding-up commencing after 5 April 1997.

Application of assets where winding-up starts after 5 April 1997

12.66 Where winding-up starts after 5 April 1997, *sections 73* to *77* of *PA 1995* introduce new provisions which will often prevail over the particular scheme's trust deed and rules. The following differences will apply as compared with a winding-up commencing before 6 April 1997 (see 12.59 to 12.65 above).

New order of priorities prior to 10 May 2004

12.67 Where there are insufficient assets to secure all the liabilities, a new statutory order of priorities is introduced by *section 73, PA 1995* (as amended by *regulation 3* of the *Winding-up Regulations (SI 1996 No 3126)*). *Sections 73* and *74, PA 1995* apply to all schemes which are subject to the 'minimum funding requirement' ('MFR'). This covers practically all approved final salary schemes (see 11.14).

The new statutory order of priorities operates as summarised in the following table, with liabilities headed 'First' taking precedence over those headed 'Second', and so on. The amounts which the Act requires to be applied in this order towards each of these groups of liabilities are:

(*a*) in relation to the liabilities headed 'Second' and 'Third', the amounts actually needed to secure them (*Winding-up Regulations, reg. 4(5)*); and

(*b*) in relation to the other liabilities in the table, the lesser of the amounts actually required to secure them and amounts representing the sums required to satisfy the MFR in respect of them (*reg 4(4)*):

New statutory order of priorities where winding-up starts after 5 April 1997	
Where winding-up starts during the transitional period*	Where winding-up starts after the transitional period*
First: AVC benefits.	**First**: AVC benefits.
Second: Where:	**Second**: Where:

12.67 *Reconstruction and winding-up*

New statutory order of priorities where winding-up starts after 5 April 1997	
Where winding-up starts during the transitional period*	*Where winding-up starts after the transitional period**
(a) the trustees are entitled to benefits under an insurance contract entered into: • before 6 April 1997; and • in order to secure all or part of the scheme's liability for any benefit payable in respect of one particular person whose entitlement to payment of a benefit has arisen (and for any benefit which will be payable in respect of him on his death); and (b) either: • the contract may not be surrendered; or • the surrender value does not exceed the liability secured (excluding liability for pension increases); the liability secured.	(a) the trustees are entitled to benefits under an insurance contract entered into: • before 6 April 1997; and • in order to secure all or part of the scheme's liability for any benefit payable in respect of one particular person whose entitlement to payment of a benefit has arisen (and for any benefit which will be payable in respect of him on his death); and (b) either: • the contract may not be surrendered; or • the surrender value does not exceed the liability secured (excluding liability for pension increases); the liability secured.
Third: Liability for benefits to which entitlement to payment has arisen and benefits which will be payable in respect of the person so entitled upon his death (excluding pension increases).	**Third**: Liability for benefits to which entitlement to payment has arisen and benefits which will be payable in respect of the person so entitled upon his death (excluding pension increases).
Fourth: Liabilities for:	**Fourth**: Liabilities for:
(a) equivalent pension benefits and benefits arising from being contracted-out of SERPS (excluding pension increases); and (b) (for members with less than two years' pensionable service not entitled to accrued rights) the return of contributions.	(a) benefits accrued to or in respect of members (excluding pension increases); and (b) (for members with less than two years' service) the return of contributions.
Fifth: Liabilities for increases to pensions referred to in 'Second' and 'Third' above.	**Fifth**: Liabilities for increases to pensions referred to in 'Second', 'Third' and 'Fourth' above.
Sixth: Liabilities for increases to pensions referred to in 'Fourth' above.	
Seventh: Other liabilities for accrued benefits (including pension increases).	
*The transitional period runs from 6 April 1997 and generally ends on 5 April 2007 (subject to exceptions – see *regulation 3(2)* of the *Winding-up Regulations* (*SI 1996 No 3126*)).	

The order of priorities in this table will partially override the order set out in the scheme rules, but not entirely. This is because (as described just before the table) the amounts to be allocated towards the liabilities listed in the above order

Tolley's Pensions Law Handbook, 6th Edition
Erratum

Dear Subscriber,

Due to a publishing error, Chapter 12 of Tolley's Pensions Law Handbook, 6th edition, should be read in conjunction with the following information.

The wording of paragraph 12.68 should appear as set out below:

"*New Order of Priorities from 10 May 2004*

12.68

The *Occupational Pension Schemes (Winding up) (Amendment) Regulations 2004 (SI 2004 No 1140)* came into effect on 10 May 2004. There will be a new statutory priority order as follows:
- expenses and third party liabilities;
- AVCs;
- pre-April 1997 insurance policies;
- pensions in payment or where entitlement has arisen, excluding increases;
- accrued pension, excluding increases;
- future pensions or other benefits in respect of pension credits, excluding increases;
- refund of contributions;
- increases on pre-April 1997 insurance policies and pensions in payment or where entitlement has arisen; and
- increases on accrued pensions.

Contracted-out benefits will no longer be prioritised over other benefits.

These Regulations only apply in the case of a defined benefit occupational pension scheme which commenced winding-up on or after 10 May 2004.

The *Occupational Pension Schemes (Winding Up and Deficiency on Winding Up etc) (Amendment) Regulations 2004 (SI 2004 No 403)* came into force on 15 March 2004. Where a scheme commences winding-up on or after 11 June 2003 where the employer is not insolvent and the date on which the assets and liabilities are valued falls on or after 15 March 2004, the deficit will be the full buy out cost. This means the scheme must have sufficient assets to purchase immediate and deferred annuities for all members to provide the full benefits promised under the scheme together with the full costs of winding-up the scheme. In the case of insolvent employers, the scheme will only have to be funded in accordance with minimum funding requirements or, presumably, with the new scheme specific funding requirement once it comes into effect. Once the Pensions Protection Fund ('PPF') comes into effect it will assume responsibility for the assets of the scheme and payment of benefits.

In view of the definition of insolvency used in pensions legislation, which refers to a relevant insolvency event as described in *section 75* of the *PA 1995*, companies in members' voluntary liquidation are regarded as insolvent. This means that if a company is in a members' voluntary liquidation prior to the commencement of winding-up of its sponsored occupational pension scheme, there is no requirement to provide full buy out benefits for those persons who were active members or deferred pensioners at the date the scheme commenced winding-up."

The publishers wish to apologise for this error and for any inconvenience caused.

Yours faithfully

Andrew Trinder
<u>Managing Editor</u>

may well be less than the sums actually needed to secure them. Any assets remaining after allocating these amounts in this way must then be used to satisfy any remaining liabilities, in the order of priorities set out in the scheme's own rules (*section 73(4), PA 1995*).

The new statutory order does not override a scheme rule which provides for the payment of scheme expenses to prevail over the securing of benefits on a winding-up.

New Order of Priorities from 10 May 2004

12.68 The *Occupational Pension Schemes (Winding up)(Amendment) Regulations 2004 (SI 2004 No 1140)* came into effect on 10 May 2004. There will be a new statutory priority order as follows:

- expenses and third party liabilities;
- AVCs;
- pre-April 1997 insurance policies;
- pensions in payment or where entitlement has arisen, excluding increases;
- accrued pension excluding increases;
- future pensions or other benefits in respect of pension credits, excluding increases;
- refund of contributions;
- increases on pre-April 1997 insurance policies and pensions in payment or where entitlement has arisen; and
- increases on accrued pensions.

Contracted-out benefits will no longer be prioritised over other benefits.

Accrued Pension and Priority Table		
Service (years)	**Priority**	**Postponed**
Less than 2	0	Refund
2	5%	95%
3	7.5%	92.5%
4	10%	90%
5	12.5%	87.5%
6	15%	85%
7	17.5%	82.5%
8	20%	80%
9	22.5%	77.5%
10	25%	75%
11	27.5%	72.5%

12.68 *Reconstruction and winding-up*

Accrued Pension and Priority Table		
Service (years)	Priority	Postponed
12	30%	70%
13	32.5%	67.5%
14	35%	65%
15	37.5%	62.5%
16	40%	60%
17	42.5%	57.5%
18	45%	55%
19	47.5%	52.5%
20	50%	50%
21	52.5%	47.5%
22	55%	45%
23	57.5%	42.5%
24	60%	40%
25	62.5%	37.5%
26	65%	35%
27	67.5%	32.5%
28	70%	30%
29	72.5%	27.5%
30	75%	25%
31	77.5%	22.5%
32	80%	20%
33	82.5%	17.5%
34	85%	15%
35	87.5%	12.5%
36	90%	10%
37	92.5%	7.5%
38	95%	5%
39	97.5%	2.5%
40	100%	0

~~Contracted-out benefits will no longer be prioritised over other benefits.~~

The purpose of the table is that, where there is a deficit on winding-up, the degree of protection will reflect the length of time the member has been contributing to the scheme. The *Regulations* also give priority to non pensioners over the indexation of pensions in payment. However, pensions in payment will still be the first priority.

These *Regulations* only apply in the case of a defined benefit occupational pension scheme which commenced winding-up on or after 10 May 2004.

The *Occupational Pension Schemes (Winding Up and Deficiency on Winding Up etc) (Amendment) Regulations 2004*([SI 2004 No 403) came into force on

15 March 2004. Where a scheme commences winding-up on or after 11 June 2003 where the employer is not insolvent and the date on which the assets and liabilities are valued falls on or after 15 March 2004, the deficit will be the full buy out cost. This means the scheme must have sufficient assets to purchase immediate and deferred annuities for all members to provide the full benefits promised under the scheme together with the full costs of winding-up the scheme. In the case of insolvent employers, the scheme will only have to be funded in accordance with minimum funding requirements or, presumably, with the new scheme specific funding requirement once it comes into effect. Once the Pensions Protection Fund ('PPF') comes into effect it will assume responsibility for the assets of the scheme and payment of benefits.

In view of the definition of insolvency used in pensions legislation, which refers to a relevant insolvency event as described in *section 75* of the *PA 1995*, companies in members' voluntary liquidation are regarded as insolvent. This means that if a company is in a members' voluntary liquidation prior to the commencement of winding-up of its sponsored occupational pension scheme, there is no requirement to provide full buy out benefits for those persons who were active members or deferred pensioners at the date the scheme commenced winding-up.

Purchase of annuities

12.69 The *PA 1995* confers upon the trustees of approved final salary schemes which commence winding-up after 5 April 1997 a power to purchase annuities (*section 74(3), PA 1995*). For other schemes, a specific power in the trust documents is required.

The new statutory power may be exercised only in accordance with the requirements dealt with in 12.73 below.

Transfers out

12.70 The trustees of approved final salary schemes which commence winding-up after 5 April 1997 now have statutory powers (under *section 74(3), PA 1995*) to make transfers to other arrangements. The trustees of other schemes may only make transfers if their trust documents give them power to do so. The bulk transfer position on winding-up is considered further in 12.85 and 12.89 below.

Again, the new statutory powers may be exercised only in accordance with the requirements summarised in 12.74 below.

Surplus – power to increase benefits

12.71 The general principle remains that (subject to any Inland Revenue limits which apply) the use of surplus to increase benefits is governed by the scheme rules.

12.72 *Reconstruction and winding-up*

However, under *section 73(5)* of *PA 1995*, if the rules of an approved final salary scheme which is being wound up confer a power on any person other than the trustees (for instance, the employers) 'to apply the assets of the scheme in respect of pensions or other benefits', that power can no longer be exercised by that person but may be exercised by the trustees instead.

The intention behind *PA 1995* appears to be that the word 'apply' here should have the narrowest meaning necessary to enable the trustees to wind up the scheme in accordance with the other provisions of the Act. On this basis, a power under the scheme rules of the employers to decide whether surplus assets are used to increase benefits should not be affected.

Surplus – payment to employers

12.72 Where the winding-up of an exempt approved scheme starts after 5 April 1997, *PA 1995* adds a further requirement to those listed in 12.64 above. *Section 76* provides that members be notified before a repayment can be made to an employer and enables dissatisfied members to make representations to Opra before the payment is made. [*Occupational Pension Schemes (Payment to Employers) Regulations 1996 (SI 1996 No 2156), regs 7* to *9*].

For the very few exempt approved schemes which prohibit payments to employers on winding-up, *section 77, PA 1995* enables trustees to make such payments (subject to their first meeting certain requirements, including augmentation of benefits up to Inland Revenue limits).

When the trustees of a centralised 'industry-wide scheme' are considering the implications of a surplus or a deficit on winding up the case of *BEC Pension Trustee Ltd v Sheppeck [2002] EWHC 101 (Ch)* should be taken into account. It was held that, for the purposes of *section 108* of *PSA 93*, each section of a centralised scheme is treated as a separate 'qualifying scheme'. Any surplus in a particular section of a centralised scheme should therefore only be applied for the benefit of members in that section or refunded to the relevant employer (if appropriate) of that section.

The provisions summarised here are considered in more detail in chapter 11 (see 11.45).

Deficits

12.73 Where the scheme has insufficient assets to secure all its liabilities, the assets available must be allocated amongst the liabilities as summarised in 12.67 above. The deficit may also give rise to a debt owed by the employers to the trustees. This is considered in 12.78 below.

Trustees' discharge

12.74 Trustees of approved final salary schemes which begin to be wound up after 5 April 1997 are treated under *section 74* of *PA 1995* as having discharged any liability in respect of scheme benefits, so long as they have:

(*a*) arranged for the discharge of that liability (or, if the scheme's assets are insufficient to meet fully that liability, applied assets towards it as required by the new statutory order of priorities (see 12.67 above)) in one or more of the following ways:

   (i) by making transfer payments to other occupational pension schemes (*section 74(3)(a), PA 1995*);

   (ii) by making transfer payments to personal pension schemes (*section 74(3)(b), PA 1995*);

   (iii) by purchasing annuities from insurance companies (*section 74(3)(c), PA 1995*);

   (iv) by transferring the benefits of an annuity contract or insurance policy to the member concerned (or to a person entitled to benefits in respect of him) (*regulation 8(4)* of the *Winding-up Regulations (SI 1996 No 3126)*); or

   (v) in certain limited circumstances relating to insolvent contracted-out schemes, paying sums to the Department for Work and Pensions (DWP) (*regulation 8(5)* of the *Winding-up Regulations (SI 1996 No 3126)*);

(*b*) given to the member to whom the liability relates (or, if he has died, each beneficiary who is entitled to benefits in respect of him) notice in writing ('a discharge notice') of the proposed discharge of that liability (*Winding-up Regulations (SI 1996 No 3126), reg 6(2)(a)*; and

(*c*) complied with the requirements set out in the following table (which vary according to the proposed method of discharge) relating to:

   (i) the contents of the discharge notice (column 1) (*Winding-up Regulations (SI 1996 No 3126), reg 7*); and

   (ii) other requirements, such as whether the individual's consent is required (column 2) (*Winding-up Regulations (SI 1996 No 3126), regs 6 and 8*):

	1. Information to be included in discharge notice	2. Other requirements
A. All cases.	• The sum available.	(Depends on method proposed.)

	1. Information to be included in discharge notice	2. Other requirements
	• (If the amount required to satisfy the statutory order of priorities in respect of that liability (see 12.67) exceeds the sum available), the amount so required and the reason for the difference.	
	• The proposed way(s) of discharging the liability.	
B. Where the individual is to be given the option to choose another method of discharge.	• That, if he wishes to elect that, instead of the method proposed, one or more of the other permitted ways be used to discharge the liability, he must notify the trustees to that effect in writing, specifying:	(Depends on method proposed.)
	(*a*) the way(s) in which he wishes it to be discharged; and	
	(*b*) the name of the scheme trustees, personal pension provider or insurance company (as appropriate)	
	• That he must give this notice within three months of the notice given to him.	
	• That he should obtain independent financial advice before deciding.	
C. Where the individual's consent is required.	• That his consent is required.	(Depends on method proposed.)
	• The period within which he may consent, being at least three months from when the notice is given.	
	• The way or ways in which it is proposed to discharge the liability if he does not consent.	
	• That he should obtain independent financial advice before deciding.	
D. Where a transfer to an occupational pension scheme is proposed.	• The matters set out in A above.	• The individual's consent is required unless the requirements set out in 12.33(b) to (d) are met.

	1. Information to be included in discharge notice	2. Other requirements
	• (If other options are to be made available) the matters set out in B above.	• The receiving scheme must be one to which a cash equivalent could be paid (*PSA 1993*, s 95(2)(*a*)).
	• (If the individual's consent is required (see column 2)) the matters set out in C above.	
	• The name of the trustees of the occupational pension scheme proposed and the scheme address.	
E. Where a transfer to a personal pension scheme is proposed.	• The matters set out in A above.	• The individual's consent is required.
	• (If other options are to be made available) the matters set out in B above.	• The receiving scheme must be one to which a cash equivalent could be paid (*PSA 1993*, s 95(2)(*b*)).
	• The matters set out in C above.	
	• The name of the proposed personal pension provider and (if different) the scheme administrator and scheme address.	
F. Where the purchase of an annuity from an insurance company is proposed.	• The matters set out in A above.	• The annuity must be one which could be purchased with a cash equivalent (*PSA 1993*, s 95(2)(*c*)).
	• (If other options are to be made available) the matters set out in B above.	
	• The name and address of the insurance company.	
	• (If different) the name and address of the person from whom information about the terms of the annuity contract can be obtained.	
	• (If the annuity contract has not yet been made) whether information about its terms will be given on the strength of a quotation.	

12.75 *Reconstruction and winding-up*

	1. Information to be included in discharge notice	2. Other requirements
G. Where transferring to the individual the benefit of an annuity contract or an insurance policy is proposed.	• The matters set out in A above.	• Annuity must:
	• (If other options are to be made available) the matters set out in B above.	(*a*) be one which could be purchased with a cash equivalent (*PSA 1993, s 95(2)(c)*); and
	• The name and address of the insurance company.	(*b*) be provided by an insurance company which consents to the transfer.
	• (If different) the name and address of the person from whom information about the terms of the annuity contract can be obtained.	• Insurance policy must meet the requirements of *section 19(4)* of *PSA 1993*.
	• (If the annuity contract has not yet been made) whether information about its terms will be given on the strength of a quotation.	

Regulation 9 of the *Winding-up Regulations (SI 1996 No 3126)* confirms that these requirements are in addition to (and do not replace) certain requirements of *section 32A* of *PSA 1993* in relation to the discharge of protected rights on winding-up and any scheme rules reflecting those requirements.

Disclosure requirements during winding-up

12.75 The disclosure requirements of the winding-up process fall into the following categories:

(*a*) *Within one month of commencement of winding-up:* By the end of this period (and sooner if practicable) the trustees must:

    (i) inform members and beneficiaries that they have commenced winding-up, stating:

        • the reasons why; and

        • a name and address for future enquiries;

    (ii) inform members and beneficiaries of any statutory requirement there may be to have an independent trustee (see 3.6 above);

    (iii) inform all active members whether death in service benefits will continue to be payable; and

Reconstruction and winding-up 12.75

- (iv) provide members and beneficiaries with the information referred to in (b)(i) to (iii) below (*regulation 5(10)* of the *Disclosure Regulations (SI 1996 No 1655)*).

(b) *At least once in every twelve months until winding-up is complete:* At these times, the trustees must provide members and beneficiaries with the following information:

- (i) what action is being taken to establish the scheme's liabilities and to recover any assets;
- (ii) when it is anticipated that final details will be known; and
- (iii) (where the trustees have enough information) an indication of any extent to which the actuarial value of that person's accrued rights or benefits are likely to be reduced (*regulation 5(10)(d)* of the *Disclosure Regulations (SI 1996 No 1655)*).

(c) *Before discharging liabilities:* Before applying the assets towards the discharge of scheme liabilities, 'discharge notices' must be provided, as set out more fully in 12.74 above.

(d) *Within three months after the trustees have done what they can to discharge their liabilities in relation to a member or beneficiary:* During this period (or sooner if practicable), the trustees must:

- (i) if that person is entitled to payment of benefits, provide to him the following information:
  - the amount of the benefit payable to him; and
  - if a benefit is payable periodically, any conditions subject to which payment will be continued and any provisions under which the amount payable will be altered;
- (ii) if (except in relation to money purchase benefits) that person is not entitled to payment of benefits, provide to him an estimate of the amount of his and of his survivors' benefits expected to be payable from normal pension age or death; and
- (iii) in either of the above cases, inform that person:
  - whether (and if so by how much) the benefits concerned are reduced due to insufficient scheme resources; and
  - who has or will become liable for payment of those benefits (*regulation 5(12)* of the *Disclosure Regulations (SI 1996 No 1655)*).

(e) Section 72A of *PA 1995* and *regulation 10* of the *Occupational Pension Schemes (Winding up Notices and Reports etc) Regulations 2002 (SI 2002 No 459)* require trustees or managers of a scheme in winding up to report to Opra within certain prescribed timescales and to give members and beneficiaries the right to a copy of such winding-up report within two months of any request. The initial report should contain the information prescribed in the regulations, including the following:

12.76 *Reconstruction and winding-up*

(i) details of the scheme including its name and the date winding-up commenced;

(ii) details of the scheme filed with the Pension Schemes Registry;

(iii) an outline of the type of benefits provided by the scheme;

(iv) details of the scheme actuary, if relevant;

(v) details of any administrator;

(vi) a statement setting out what stage of the winding-up process has been reached, if any potential problems have arisen and when the winding process is expected to be completed.

Further reports to Opra must be made on an annual basis in accordance with *regulation 10(2)* and must contain an update on the status of winding up, as prescribed in that regulation.

The requirements relating to the winding-up report for submission to Opra do not apply to the following schemes:

- schemes with less than two members;
- SSAS schemes (see Chapter 13);
- schemes where all members are trustees;
- life assurance only schemes; and
- schemes which do not provide accrued rights.

Notifying regulatory bodies

12.76 Following the completion of the winding-up of an approved scheme, the IR SPSS should be notified of the winding-up using Form PS199. The Pensions Registry should also be informed that the scheme has been wound up. If the scheme was contracted-out, it will be necessary to surrender its contracting-out certificate (see chapter 4).

Missing or unknown beneficiaries

12.77 Some schemes have more complete records than others, and it is frequently a matter of concern to the trustees of a scheme which is being wound up as to whether they have sufficient information of all benefits for which the scheme may in due course become liable. Even where the records have been well kept, deferred pensioners may have moved house since they left the scheme and not kept the company or the trustees advised of their new addresses. These beneficiaries may prove difficult to trace.

The following points are relevant in these circumstances:

(a) *Advertising. Section 27* of the *Trustee Act 1925* confers some level of protection on trustees who, before distributing trust funds, advertise for beneficiaries in the London Gazette and other newspapers. At least two months' notice is required.

Care should be taken in following the *section 27* route, particularly as the legislation is unclear about which newspapers will suffice. More fundamentally, however, *section 27* was not drawn up with modern pension schemes in mind. Its wording (which appears only to cover distribution among the beneficiaries themselves) may well not cover such matters as the purchase of annuities or the making of transfer payments to other schemes.

That said, appropriate advertising is still worthwhile if it reveals beneficiaries whose details would otherwise have remained unknown. Even if the protection of *section 27* does not apply in a particular case, a court is likely to be more sympathetic towards trustees who have taken all suitable steps to find their beneficiaries than towards those who have not.

(b) *DWP Tracing Service.* This can be used to enable trustees and administrators to establish contact with beneficiaries whose addresses they do not know. The individuals are traced by the DWP by reference to their National Insurance numbers and the system is therefore most appropriate for finding missing (as opposed to unknown) beneficiaries.

(c) *Exemptions and indemnities.* Aside from whatever protections may be available to the trustees under the scheme rules, they would be well advised to seek an indemnity from the employer against any risks in relation to the scheme arising in the future. This assumes, of course, that the employer is still solvent (and will remain so). Where the winding-up is effected by means of a bulk transfer to the trustees of another scheme, it is sensible also to seek an indemnity from the receiving scheme.

(d) *Insurance. Kemble v Hicks (1999) PLR 287* confirms the principle that in the absence of a specific power in the scheme rules, the trustees may not charge the cost of trustee indemnity insurance to the scheme. (Even where there is such a power, *section 31* of *PA 1995* prevents the trustees from using the fund to pay premiums to insure against fines and civil penalties incurred under that Act).

Whether a scheme can properly be amended to introduce such a power will depend on whether the amendment is in the best interests of the scheme's beneficiaries; this will of course depend on the particular circumstances. In any case, there may well be difficulties in amending a scheme so as to introduce such a power once winding-up has commenced, for the reasons mentioned in 12.14. None of this, of course prevents the employer from bearing the costs of such insurance in connection with the termination of the scheme.

EMPLOYER'S DEBT

General

12.78 In certain circumstances involving the winding-up of a scheme or the

12.79 *Reconstruction and winding-up*

insolvency of an employer, employers can become liable to the trustees for a debt in respect of any deficit in the scheme. A debt can also arise when an employer ceases its participation in a multi-employer scheme.

The position is presently governed by *section 75* of *PA 1995* and the *Deficiency Regulations (SI 1996 No 3128)*. *Section 75, PA 1995* replaces *section 144* of *PSA 1993*. The old *section 144* still applies where winding-up started before 19 December 1996, or the debt arose before 6 April 1997. However, only the current *section 75* of *PA 1995* is dealt with here.

Schemes affected

12.79 *Section 75, PA 1995* is capable of applying to most schemes providing final salary benefits except, for example, where:

(*a*) the scheme has less than two members;

(*b*) the scheme provides only death benefits and no member has accrued rights; or

(*c*) the scheme provides relevant benefits but has never been (and is not seeking to be) tax approved and is not a 'relevant statutory scheme' as defined in *section 611* of the *Income and Corporation Taxes Act 1988* (*regulation 10* of the *Deficiency Regulations (SI 1996 No 3128)*).

(A debt can also arise in a money purchase scheme, where the underfunding results from a crime involving dishonesty. The legislation works rather differently in relation to money purchase schemes (*regulations 7, 8* and *9* of the *Deficiency Regulations (SI 1996 No 3128)*) and only the final salary position is considered here.)

'Relevant insolvency events'

12.80 The circumstances in which a debt arises will often be linked to a 'relevant insolvency event' happening in relation to an employer. The following table illustrates when such an event will occur (*PA 1995, s 75(4)*):

	In England and Wales	In Scotland
Where the employer is a company	When the employer goes into liquidation (within the meaning of *section 247(2)* of the *Insolvency Act 1986*).	At the commencement of the employer's winding-up (within the meaning of *section 129* of the *Insolvency Act 1986*).
Where the employer is an individual	At the commencement of the employer's bankruptcy (within the meaning of *section 278* of the *Insolvency Act 1986*).	Where the employer is a debtor (within the meaning of the *Bankruptcy (Scotland) Act 1995*), on the date of sequestration (as defined in *section 12(4)* of *B(S)A 1995*).

When the debt arises

12.81 If, at any time indicated in the following table, the value of the scheme's assets is less than the value of its liabilities, the difference becomes a debt due from the employer to the trustees (*section 75(1)* and *section 75(3)* of *PA 1995* as amended by *regulation 4(3)* of the *Deficiency Regulations* (*SI 1996 No 3128*) and *regulation 2* of th*e Occupational Pension Schemes* (*Winding Up and Deficiency on Winding Up etc*) (*Amendment*) *Regulations 2004* (*SI 2004 No 403*)). The time at which this happens is as follows:

	Scheme being wound up	*Scheme not being wound up*
Scheme with one employer	Any time when a scheme is being wound up before a relevant insolvency event occurs in relation to the employer.	Immediately before a relevant insolvency event occurs in relation to the employer.
Scheme with more than one employer	Any time: ● after the start of winding-up; and ● before a relevant insolvency event occurs in relation to each of the employers.	(In relation only to any employer who ceases to employ persons in the description or category of employment to which the scheme relates whilst at least one other employer continues to do so) immediately before that employer so ceases. (In relation only to any employer in relation to whom a relevant insolvency event occurs) immediately before that event.

The impact of these provisions on a sale of a subsidiary company or business is considered in chapter 16.

Where the scheme has more than one employer:

(*a*) there are provisions for the amount of the debt to be apportioned between them (*section 75(1A), PA 1995*) (see chapter 16); and

(*b*) (if the scheme is divided into different sections for different employers, with no cross-funding between different sections) *section 75(1B), PA 1995* provides for those separate sections to be treated as separate schemes.

Meaning of 'employer'

12.82 In most instances, the term 'employer' covers any employer of persons in the description or category of employment to which the scheme relates (*section 124(1), PA 1995*).

12.83 *Reconstruction and winding-up*

However, there are some special cases, so that:

(a) where the scheme has no active members, the employers are taken as being those persons who were employers in relation to the scheme when the scheme last had active members (*regulation 5(1)* of the *Deficiency Regulations* (*SI 1996 No 3128*));

(b) where after 5 April 1997 an employer ceases to employ persons of the description or category of employment to which the scheme relates, he may in some circumstances be treated as remaining an employer (*regulation 5(2)* and *(3)* of the *Deficiency Regulations* (*SI 1996 No 3128*)). These circumstances are considered further in chapter 16, in the context of commercial transactions; and

(c) where during the period from 19 December 1996 to 5 April 1997, at a time when the scheme was not being wound up and had active members, an employer ceased to employ persons in the description or category of employment to which the scheme relates, he is treated (subject to some exceptions) as remaining an employer (*regulation 6(2)* of the *Deficiency Regulations* (*SI 1996 No 3128*)).

Valuation of assets and liabilities

12.83 The valuation of the scheme's assets and liabilities is carried out by reference to the basis used for the 'minimum funding requirement' (see 11.14 above). Where this valuation reveals a deficit, the scheme actuary is required to complete a certificate in the form scheduled to *regulation 3* of the *Deficiency Regulations* (*SI 1996 No 3128*). (The certificate is often referred to as a 'GN19', this being the number of the Guidance Note issued by the Institute and Faculty of Actuaries, relating to the method of valuation.) This deficit (subject to apportionment where there is more than one employer (see 12.81(a)) becomes the amount of the employer's debt.

With effect from the dates mentioned below, changes have been introduced to the MFR valuation basis (see GN27); these impact on the calculation of the employer's debt on winding up, and are as follows:

- from 7 March 2002, the market value adjustment for non pensioner benefits decreases from 3.25 per cent to 3 per cent. This will result in lower liabilities for active and deferred members and a smaller deficit;

- from 19 March 2002, schemes winding up where the employer is not insolvent will have to take account of both the full cost of winding up the scheme and the full buy-out costs for pensioners in calculating the employer's debt. This will result in a larger deficit where existing pensioners are paid from the scheme before the winding up commences;

- from April 2002, the revaluation cost of GMP's for members leaving pensionable service after this date will be lower, resulting in a smaller deficit.

With one exception, however, the legislation placed no absolute obligation on the trustees to have such a valuation carries out. (The exception is relevant primarily to commercial transactions, and so is considered separately in Chapter 16 – see 16.64.)

In the absence of such an obligation, the trustees may, in some circumstances, decide against having a valuation carried out. This would be an entirely proper decision if, for example, the employer was insolvent and the claims of the other creditors were such that the trustees stood no chance of recovering any debt. The trustees would similarly be justified in avoiding the costs of a valuation if the actuary were to advise them that such a valuation was likely to reveal no deficit (or a deficit which was less than the actuarial fees that would be incurred).

In the event that a scheme is winding-up without being replaced the normal requirements of the Valuation Regulations relating to the preparation of an actuarial valuation report may be waived by the IR SPSS. The circumstances where such concession will apply are set out in Pensions Update No. 83.

Impact of employer's debt

12.84 Whilst *section 75, PA 1995* confers a measure of protection for members of underfunded schemes, its impact, in practice, will often be limited. If, for example, the debt has arisen upon an employer's insolvency, there will inevitably be doubts as to the trustees' ability to recover the debt, particularly as the trustees will not rank as preferential creditors (*section 75(8), PA 1995*).

Even if the debt can be recovered in full, the basis of valuation described above will tend to result in the amount of the debt being less than is actually required to secure the scheme's benefits.

The question of recoverability of a *section 75* debt on the employer was considered recently in the case of *Bradstock Group Pension Scheme Trustees Ltd v Bradstock Group plc and others [2002] All ER (D) 109 (Jun)*. The facts of the case are that the actuarial valuation of the scheme revealed a deficit on a MFR basis and the trustees were required to serve a MFR schedule on the employers under which a payment of £1.7 million fell due. The employers claimed that they were unable to pay such amount and that the group would be forced into liquidation. The trustees and the employers sought to agree a compromise whereby the scheme would be wound up and monies would be

12.85 *Reconstruction and winding-up*

paid into the scheme in respect of the debt which would arise under *section 75* by way of an immediate cash payment plus deferred consideration, suitably secured and guaranteed. The amount received would be less than the *section 75* debt but more than the scheme would receive as an unsecured creditor on liquidation of the employers. The trustees sought the approval of the court to the proposed compromise and it was held that the trustees had a power under *section 15(f)* of the *Trustee Act 1925* to compromise a statutory debt under *section 75* and that to do so in the circumstances did not amount to contracting out of the *MFR Regulations* nor the provisions of *section 75*. On the second question, as to whether the compromise was one which a reasonable and properly advised trustee would enter into, arguments were held in private but the judgment noted that the compromise reached was in the best interests of the members and that the scheme would receive significantly less if the employers went into liquidation.

The Pensions Bill proposes to introduce protection for scheme members on the insolvency of an employer by the establishment of the Pension Protection Fund ('PPF') (see 12.95 below and 1.3 above)

BULK TRANSFERS – SPECIFIC ISSUES WHERE WINDING-UP HAS COMMENCED

Preliminary

12.85 It is now appropriate to return to the subject of bulk transfers and address the questions of whether there is power to make a bulk transfer, and how any transfer payment is to be calculated, from a scheme which has commenced to be wound up. (The corresponding position where the transferring scheme has not gone into winding-up is dealt with in 12.48 to 12.50 above. See also the flowchart at the end of this chapter for the date on which winding-up commences for this purpose.)

Power to make bulk transfers on winding-up

Winding-up started before 6 April 1997

12.86 In these circumstances, the existence of a power to make bulk transfers on winding-up, and the question of who may exercise that power, is governed by the scheme's trust deed and rules.

Care should be taken to check whether any bulk transfer out power under those documents may be exercised during the winding-up stage. A transfer out power which is intended for use whilst the scheme is ongoing may well cease to be exercisable after winding-up has commenced, depending on the exact wording of the scheme documents.

Winding-up started after 5 April 1997

12.87 Section 74 of *PA 1995* gives the trustees of approved final salary schemes which commence winding-up after 5 April 1997 power to make bulk transfers even if there is no power to do so in the scheme rules (so long as the requirements in 12.74 above are met). Whether trustees have power to make a transfer from a scheme to which *section 74, PA 1995* does not apply will continue to depend upon the trust deed and rules.

Many schemes' rules give the principal employer a power to direct the trustees to make a bulk transfer. Any such power in an approved final salary scheme where winding-up has started after 5 April 1997 needs to be considered in the context of *section 73(5), PA 1995*. If it amounts to a power 'to apply the assets of the scheme in respect of pensions or other benefits', then, under that section, the power will no longer be exercisable by the principal employer and will be exercisable by the trustees instead.

Amount to be transferred on a winding-up

Winding-up started before 6 April 1997

12.88 The amount to be transferred in these circumstances will depend upon the trust deed and rules. However, a minimum of the statutory cash equivalents of members' accrued benefits (see 6.44 above) must be transferred (although cash equivalents may be reduced to take account of underfunding – see 6.51 for further details on the reduction of cash equivalents).

In the unlikely event of the transferring scheme being regarded by the Revenue as overfunded, there may be difficulties in transferring the surplus to another scheme (see 12.40 above).

Winding-up started after 5 April 1997

12.89 The position as set out in 12.88 above is subject to two further points in relation to approved final salary schemes where winding-up instead commences after 5 April 1997:

(*a*) if the scheme is underfunded, the amount of the transfer payment in respect of any given person must be consistent with the sums required to be allocated towards the scheme's various liabilities under the new statutory order of priorities (*section 73* of *PA 1995*, summarised in 12.67 above); and

(b) again, *section 73(5)* of *PA 1995* becomes relevant. Under that section, any power given by the scheme's rules to a person other than the trustees (the principal employer, for instance) 'to apply' scheme assets during winding-up 'in respect of pensions or other benefits' will become exercisable by the trustees and not by that person. This raises the question as to whether an employer's power to direct the trustees as to how much to transfer would fall within *section 73(5), PA 1995*. The most likely answer is that *section 73(5)* prevents an employer from directing the trustees to transfer less than the amounts required under the new statutory order of priorities (see 12.67 above) but does not affect an employer's power under the scheme rules to decide whether the transfer amount should include any surplus.

BULK TRANSFERS – OVERVIEW

12.90 The following table provides an overview of the requirements governing bulk transfers as described in this chapter.

	1. Where the transferring scheme has not gone into winding-up.	2. Where the transferring scheme has gone into a winding-up which commenced before 6 April 1997.	3. Where the transferring scheme has gone into a winding-up which commenced after 5 April 1997.
A. Issues for trustees.	Before exercising any discretion enabling the transfer to go ahead, issues which the trustees should consider may include: • the effect of the transfer on members' benefits (issue for transferring trustees and receiving trustees – see 12.35); • any disparity between the funding position of the transferring scheme and that of the receiving scheme (issue for transferring trustees and receiving trustees – see 12.36); • the 'balance of powers' in the receiving scheme as compared with that in the transferring scheme (issue for transferring trustees – see 12.37); • the long term futures of the transferring and receiving schemes (issue for transferring trustees – see 12.38); and • if the transferring scheme is already being wound up, the comparative merits of other ways of securing benefits (issue for the transferring trustees – see 12.39).		

		1. Where the transferring scheme has not gone into winding-up.	2. Where the transferring scheme has gone into a winding-up which commenced before 6 April 1997.	3. Where the transferring scheme has gone into a winding-up which commenced after 5 April 1997.
B.	Members' consents.	Members' consents are required unless: • scheme rules permit non-consent transfers; • either: 　(a) both schemes relate to employment with the same employer; or 　(b) it is a bulk transfer either resulting from a financial transaction between the employers or where the employers are 'connected'; • actuarial certificate GN16 is given; • members are notified at least one month before transferring; and • contracting-out requirements do not require members' consents (see 12.33).		Member's consents are required unless: • either: 　(a) both schemes relate to employment with the same employer; or 　(b) it is a bulk transfer either resulting from a financial transaction between the employers or where the employers are 'connected'; • actuarial certificate GN16 is given; • members are notified at least one month before transferring; and • either: 　(a) scheme rules permit non-consent transfers; or 　(b) the transferring scheme is an approved final salary scheme and the requirements mentioned in 12.74 are met; and • any contracting-out requirements for members' consents are met (see 12.33).
C.	Revenue approval.	Revenue permission should be sought in advance of transfer. If the transferring scheme is overfunded on the Inland Revenue basis, the Revenue may refuse to agree to the transfer of that surplus to another scheme (see 12.40).		

	1. Where the transferring scheme has not gone into winding-up.	2. Where the transferring scheme has gone into a winding-up which commenced before 6 April 1997.	3. Where the transferring scheme has gone into a winding-up which commenced after 5 April 1997.
D. Contracting-out.	Further requirements may apply if either the transferring scheme or the receiving scheme is contracted-out, depending on the circumstances (see 4.33)).		As for columns 1 and 2, except that, if the transferring scheme is an approved final salary scheme, it may be sufficient to meet the requirements mentioned in 12.76. At the time of writing, however, this point is not beyond doubt.
E. Do trustees have power to make a bulk transfer?	Depends on scheme rules.	Depends on scheme rules.	If transferring scheme is an approved final salary scheme, yes (see 12.87). Otherwise, depends on scheme rules.
F. Can the employer(s) *require* the trustees to make a bulk transfer?	Depends on scheme rules.	Depends on scheme rules.	Depends on scheme rules *except* that, if any such power of the employer (in an approved final salary scheme) amounts to a power 'to apply the assets of the scheme in respect of pensions or other benefits', that power becomes exercisable by the trustees and not by the employer(s) (see 12.87).

Reconstruction and winding-up 12.90

	1. Where the transferring scheme has not gone into winding-up.	2. Where the transferring scheme has gone into a winding-up which commenced before 6 April 1997.	3. Where the transferring scheme has gone into a winding-up which commenced after 5 April 1997.
G. How is the transfer payment calculated?	As set out in the scheme rules, but subject to: ● H below where the transferring scheme is in deficit; and ● C above where the transferring scheme has a Revenue surplus.	As set out in the scheme rules, but subject to: ● H below where the transferring scheme is in deficit; and ● C above where the transferring scheme has a Revenue surplus.	As set out in scheme rules, but subject to: ● H below where the transferring scheme is in deficit; ● C above where the transferring scheme has a Revenue surplus; and ● the fact that, if an approved final salary scheme's rules give to any person other than the trustees (eg the employers) power 'to apply the assets of the scheme in respect of pensions or other benefits', that power ceases to be exercisable by that person and becomes exercisable instead by the trustees (see 12.87).
H. Deficit: may the scheme rules provide for the transfer payment to be reduced to take account of underfunding in the transferring scheme?	Yes, so long as members are not denied their statutory cash equivalents. Some reduction of cash equivalents is, however, permissible in cases of underfunding (see 6.51).	Yes, so long as members are not denied their statutory cash equivalents. Some reduction of cash equivalents is, however, permissible in cases of underfunding (see 6.51).	Yes, subject: ● (in relation to an approved final salary scheme) to complying with the statutory order of priorities (as explained in 12.67 and 12.87); and ● (in relation to other schemes) as set out in column 2.

12.91 *Reconstruction and winding-up*

	1. Where the transferring scheme has not gone into winding-up.	2. Where the transferring scheme has gone into a winding-up which commenced before 6 April 1997.	3. Where the transferring scheme has gone into a winding-up which commenced after 5 April 1997.
I. Surplus: may the scheme rules provide for the transfer payment to include a share of any surplus in the transferring scheme?	Yes, but see C above where there is a Revenue surplus.	Yes, but see C above where there is a Revenue surplus.	Yes, but subject to: • C above where there is a Revenue surplus; and • the fact that, if an approved final salary scheme's rules give to any person other than the trustees (eg the employers) power 'to apply the assets of the scheme in respect of pensions or other benefits', that power ceases to be exercisable by that person and becomes exercisable instead by the trustees (see 12.89).

The flowchart below illustrates whether (and on what date) a scheme has gone into winding-up for the purpose of the above table. This flowchart illustrates the effect of *regulation 2* of the *Winding-up Regulations* (*SI 1996 No 3126*).

SANCTIONS AGAINST TRUSTEES UNDER PA 1995

12.91 Trustees who disregard provisions of *PA 1995* as summarised in this chapter may be subject to prohibition orders and civil penalties. Further details appear in the table set out in appendix 1.

PENSIONS BILL

Additional voluntary contributions

12.92 It is proposed that occupational pension schemes will no longer have to provide facilities for members to pay additional voluntary contributions. The absence of such a facility in respect of new schemes established after the Pensions Bill has been enacted may simplify the order of priorities rules on winding-up. However, in the case of existing occupational pension schemes, the removal of such a facility to pay voluntary contributions, even where members are not currently making such contributions, would require amendment to the scheme's trust deed and rules.

TIME AT WHICH WINDING-UP COMMENCES

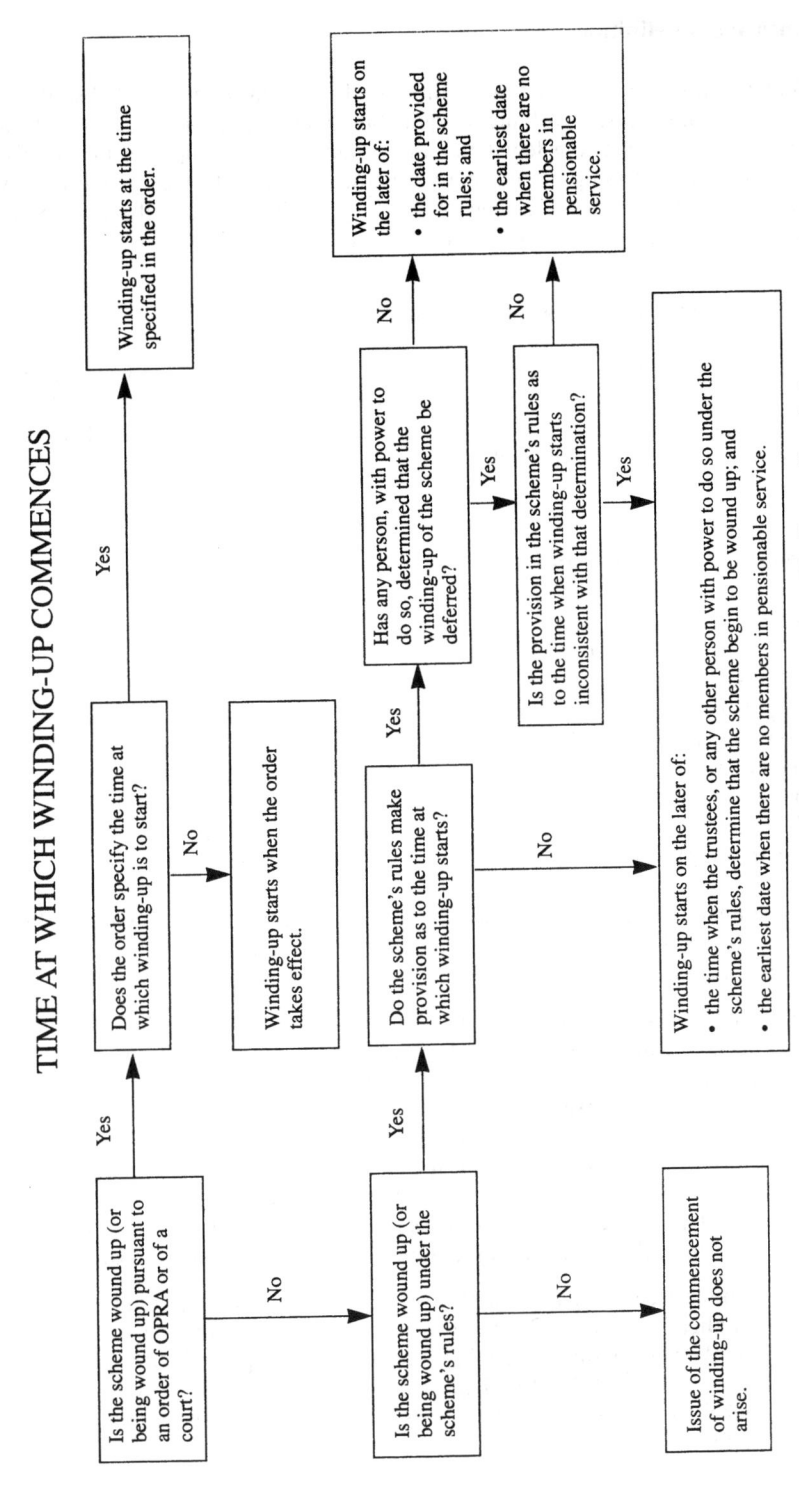

Is the scheme wound up (or being wound up) pursuant to an order of OPRA or of a court?

— Yes → **Does the order specify the time at which winding-up is to start?**
  - Yes → Winding-up starts at the time specified in the order.
  - No → Winding-up starts when the order takes effect.

— No → **Is the scheme wound up (or being wound up) under the scheme's rules?**

  — Yes → **Do the scheme's rules make provision as to the time at which winding-up starts?**

    — Yes → **Has any person, with power to do so, determined that the winding-up of the scheme be deferred?**
      - No → Winding-up starts on the later of:
        - the date provided for in the scheme rules; and
        - the earliest date when there are no members in pensionable service.
      - Yes → **Is the provision in the scheme's rules as to the time when winding-up starts inconsistent with that determination?**
        - No → Winding-up starts on the later of:
          - the date provided for in the scheme rules; and
          - the earliest date when there are no members in pensionable service.
        - Yes → Winding-up starts on the later of:
          - the time when the trustees, or any other person with power to do so under the scheme's rules, determine that the scheme begin to be wound up; and
          - the earliest date when there are no members in pensionable service.

    — No → Winding-up starts on the later of:
      - the time when the trustees, or any other person with power to do so under the scheme's rules, determine that the scheme begin to be wound up; and
      - the earliest date when there are no members in pensionable service.

  — No → Issue of the commencement of winding-up does not arise.

This flowchart illustrates the effect of *regulation 2* of the *Winding-up Regulations*.

12.93 *Reconstruction and winding-up*

Insolvency definition

12.93 It is proposed that the definition of insolvency be amended so that a company in members' voluntary liquidation would be regarded as solvent for the purposes of pensions legislation in the same way as companies in administration or receivership are currently regarded as solvent. A company is only insolvent if there is no certificate of solvency for the purposes of *section 89* of the *Insolvency Act 1986* (see Chapter 18 on insolvency).

Scheme specific funding requirement

12.94 A scheme specific funding requirement is expected to be introduced in place of the minimum funding requirement for the purposes of calculating liabilities on winding-up (see Chapter 11 on funding in general). This new calculation basis is expected to apply where the full buy-out cost is not stipulated.

Pension Protection Fund

12.95 It is proposed that a Pension Protection Fund ('PPF') will be introduced from April 2005 and will assume responsibility for defined benefit schemes where a relevant insolvency event has occurred in relation to an employer. A relevant insolvency event would include entering into administration and passing a resolution for voluntary winding-up. If a scheme is unable to secure benefits at the protected liabilities level and pay all other scheme liabilities, including winding-up costs, the PPF will assume responsibility for the scheme. The scheme's assets will be transferred to the PPF and the trustees and the employer will be discharged from further responsibility.

In summary, there are three routes by which a scheme can arrive with the PPF Board, ie notification by an insolvency practitioner; application by the trustees/managers of a scheme or notice from the new Regulator.

1. In the case of notification by an insolvency practitioner, the notification period will be a prescribed period beginning with the later of the insolvency date or the date on which the insolvency practitioner becomes aware of the existence of the scheme. It should be noted that a members' voluntarily liquidation (which does not subsequently convert into a creditors' voluntary liquidation) is not an insolvency event for these purposes. In the event that no 'scheme rescue' (as yet undefined) is possible the insolvency practitioner must issue a notice to that effect or, failing a notice by the insolvency practitioner, the PPF Board must do so.

2. The trustees or managers of an eligible scheme are required to make an application to the PPF Board if it appears to them that the employer is unlikely to continue as a going concern and other prescribed requirements are met. The PPF Board must, on receiving an application, consider whether a scheme rescue is possible and, if not, issue a notice to that effect.

3. Where the Regulator becomes aware that an employer in relation to an eligible scheme is unlikely to continue as a going concern and other requirements are met it must give notice to the PPF Board. Again, the PPF Board must consider whether a scheme rescue is possible and if not, issue a notice to that effect.

The PPF Board will assume responsibility for a scheme where a qualifying insolvency event has occurred in relation to an eligible scheme and the following conditions are met:

- the value of the assets is less than the 'protected liabilities' immediately before the insolvency date;
- the insolvency practitioner has issued a notice that scheme rescue is not possible;
- the PPF Board has not ceased to be involved ie because a scheme rescue has occurred; and
- the PPF Board is not required to refuse responsibility (either because the scheme was not an eligible scheme throughout the prescribed period or because the scheme was established with a view to benefiting from the PPF where it previously would not have done).

Where the PPF Board issues a 'transfer notice' the Board will assume responsibility for the scheme. In that event property, rights and liabilities of the scheme transfer to the PPF with effect from the date that the trustees receive the transfer notice. The trustees are then discharged from their pension obligations and the Board will assume responsibility for ensuring that compensation is paid in accordance with the pension compensation provisions. Pension compensation may take the form of periodic compensation, lump sum compensation and annual increases to periodic compensation. Both periodic compensation and lump sum compensation will be subject to a cap. The level of compensation payable where the PPF Board has assumed responsibility for an eligible scheme is as follows:

- pensioners and postponed pensioners over normal pension age, ill health and survivors' pensions – 100 per cent of benefits; and
- non-pensioners (and pensioners below normal pension age including those members who have retired early other than due to ill health) – 90 per cent of accrued benefits determined in accordance with scheme specific factors such as accrual rate, pensionable service and salary.

The initial cap on pension payments is likely to be £25,000 per annum.

Up to 25 per cent of the periodic compensation may be taken as a lump sum and pensions relating to service after 6 April 1997 will be increased at LPI capped at 2.5 per cent. Pensions in deferment will be revalued at RPI capped at 5 per cent. It is intended that *section 75* of the *PA 1995* will be amended to clarify the date on which a debt is calculated. This will depend on whether the debt is triggered by the winding-up of the scheme or the insolvency of the employer(s). If the

12.96 *Reconstruction and winding-up*

employer is solvent but the scheme has commenced winding-up then the trustees will determine the date on which the assets and liabilities must be valued. If there is a deficit in the funding, the debt is due to the trustees from the employer. Where the employer is insolvent, the debt arises immediately before the insolvency event.

There will be restrictions on winding-up during an 'assessment period'. This period will start with an insolvency date and end when the trustees of the occupational pension scheme receive a withdrawal notice from the PPF board, receive a transfer notice or receive an order to wind-up.

It is proposed that amendments will be made to *section 11* of the *PA1995* so that the PPF may direct a defined benefit scheme to be wound-up if the PPF is satisfied that:

(*a*) the scheme or any part of it might be replaced;

(*b*) the scheme is no longer required; and

(*c*) it is necessary to protect the interests of the members.

An order may not be made unless they are satisfied that the winding-up:

(*a*) cannot be achieved otherwise; and

(*b*) can only be achieved by unduly complex or protracted procedures.

The PPF will be funded by a new levy which initially will be calculated on the basis of scheme membership. In subsequent years, the Board of the PPF may introduce a risk based levy. The Board of the PPF will also administer a Fraud Compensation Fund which will replace the existing pensions compensation fund. This will be funded by a separate levy which will cover all occupational pension schemes. Further details are contained in Chapter 2.

Section 67 of PA 1995 and scheme modifications

12.96 The Pensions Bill proposes to amend the provisions of *section 67* of the *PA 1995*. The essential change is in relation to the current certification requirement (see 12.21 above). The current requirement makes it difficult for schemes to make sensible restructurings because it is practically impossible to assess whether a particular restructuring would or might adversely affect accrued rights. It is therefore proposed that *section 67* be amended so that, although schemes will not be able to reduce the value of members' accrued rights, they will be able to make changes to those rights provided that the overall actuarial value of those rights is not reduced. Once the Pensions Bill is enacted trustees will need to consider whether or not a 'regulated modification' is being made. Regulated modifications are defined as being either 'protected modifications' or 'detrimental modifications' or both:

(*a*) protected modification: is a modification which would or might result in the reduction of any pension in payment or involve the conversion of defined benefit rights into defined contribution rights.

(b) detrimental modification: is a modification which would or might adversely affect the 'subsisting rights' of any member of the scheme or any survivor of a member of the scheme.

The exercise of a power to make a regulated modification will be voidable unless certain conditions are satisfied. In summary all regulated modifications must satisfy the trustee approval requirement, the reporting requirements and either the consent or actuarial equivalence requirement. However, in the case of protected modifications the consent requirement must always be satisfied. The consent requirement will have been satisfied if the trustees have given information to members explaining the proposed modification and notified members that they may make representations to the trustees about the modification; members are notified that the consent requirements apply; members subsequently give their consent to the proposed modification in writing and the modification takes effect within a reasonable period after the giving of the consent.

The actuarial equivalence requirement applies in relation to detrimental modifications that are not protected modifications and where the trustees determine that the test is to apply. To satisfy the actuarial equivalence test, the trustees must firstly provide information in relation to the proposed modification in writing to members and allow them to make representations to the trustees. Secondly, the trustees must take steps to secure that actuarial value will be maintained. Thirdly, an actuarial equivalence statement must be obtained from the scheme actuary, certifying that the actuarial value has been maintained. The Pensions Bill provides that actuarial value is maintained if the actuarial value, immediately after the time at which the modification takes effect, of the members' subsisting rights is equal to or greater than the actuarial value of his subsisting rights immediately before that time.

It can be seen that the change in terminology has taken place from 'accrued rights or entitlements' to 'subsisting rights'. It remains to be seen whether or not the issues surrounding the definition of accrued rights and entitlements will have been resolved by the new terminology. 'Subsisting right' is defined in the Pensions Bill as any right which is accrued to or in respect of a member to future benefits under the scheme rules; any other entitlement to benefits under the scheme rules; and, in relation to a survivor of a member, any entitlement to benefits, or right to future benefits, which he or she has at that time under the scheme rules in respect of the member.

Where the Regulator determines that the requirements under *section 67* have not been complied with an order may be made that the modification is void to the extent specified in the order.

Chapter 13

Small self-administered schemes

INTRODUCTION

13.1 Small self-administered schemes ('SSASs') were first developed by the pensions industry in the early 1970s as a result of the decision to change pensions policy and permit private company directors to join occupational pension schemes (*Finance Act 1973*). SSASs were promoted as a flexible means of providing directors of small companies with their own pension fund whilst, at the same time, allowing some of the money in the fund to continue to work for the business by way of loans and leasebacks.

The Inland Revenue estimated in April 2004 that there were almost 38,000 SSASs then in existence, with almost 90,000 members.

SSASs are occupational money purchase schemes. Very few are operated on a final salary basis. SSASs operate under a legal and regulatory structure which differs in a number of respects from larger schemes, eg:

(*a*) one trustee must be a pensioneer trustee (see 13.4 below);

(*b*) the investment rules are different (see 13.14 to 13.27 below);

(*c*) some Pensions Act provisions do not apply, particularly if (as is usual) all members are appointed trustees (see 13.34 below);

(*d*) the requirements for reporting to the Inland Revenue are stricter.

This Chapter aims to focus on those issues which arise most in practice.

The rules are, of course, set to change significantly as a result of the proposals in the Government's two consultation documents on 'Simplifying the Taxation of Pensions'. These were published in December 2002 and December 2003, and primary legislation to enact the changes was published in April 2004 in the Finance Bill. The intention is to have a single set of rules applying to all kinds of tax-privileged pension schemes from 6 April 2006, and the result of this will be that the requirement for separate rules for SSASs will largely become redundant. However, this chapter deals with the current, pre-April 2006 position.

Currently there are six main sources of information for those involved with advising on SSASs:

(i) statutes, particularly *Part XIV* of the *Income and Corporation Taxes Act 1988* and the *Pensions Act 1995*;

(ii) a number of statutory instruments, referred to below;

(iii) *Part 20* of 'Occupational Pension Schemes Practice Notes', booklet IR12 (2001) ('PN') published by the Inland Revenue;

(iv) the Inland Revenue's internal manual 'SSAS Guidance Notes' published under the Open Government rules;

(v) regular Inland Revenue practice statements, formerly called Joint Office Memoranda and Pension Schemes Office ('PSO') Updates, and now (as a result of the Revenue reorganisation in 2001) called Pensions Updates; and

(vi) regular Newsletters published for members by the Association of Pensioneer Trustees (the 'APT').

All the above (except the SSAS Guidance Notes and the APT Newsletters) are publicly available online.

DEVELOPMENT OF THE REGULATORY FRAMEWORK

Background

13.2 Typically, the directors (and shareholders) of the sponsoring company, and the members and trustees of the SSAS, will all be the same people. This close identity of interests provided some scope for abuse, prompting the Inland Revenue's concern that SSASs may in some cases be operated other than for the sole purpose of the provision of benefits on retirement. This concern led to the Revenue's first attempt to regulate SSASs as a specific group, codified in their Memorandum No 58 (issued in February 1979). This Memorandum represented a general guide to the exercise of Revenue discretion in approving SSASs.

The *Retirement Benefits Schemes (Restriction on Discretion to Approve) (Small Self-Administered Schemes) Regulations 1991 (SI 1991 No 1614)* now set out a regulatory framework within which SSASs must be administered on a day to day basis. These SSAS Regulations were, amended in 1998 by two sets of regulations, the *Retirement Benefits Schemes (Restriction on Discretion to Approve) (Small Self-Administered Schemes) (Amendment) Regulations 1998 (SI 1998 No 728);* and the *Retirement Benefits Scheme (Restriction on Discretion to Approve) (Small Self-Administered Schemes) (Amendment No 2) Regulations 1998 (SI 1998 No 1315)*. The main aim of the changes was to tighten up on the role of the Revenue's 'watchdog', the Pensioneer Trustee. The Regulations have been further amended by the *Retirement Benefits Scheme (Restriction on Discretion to Approve (Small Self Administered Schemes) Regulations (Amendment) Regulations 2000 (SI 2000 No 1086)*.

13.3 Small self-administered schemes

The *Retirement Benefits Schemes (Information Powers) Regulations 1995 (SI 1995 No 3103)* (recently amended by the *Retirement Benefits Schemes (Information Powers) (Amendment) Regulations 2002 (SI 2002 No 3006)*) introduced a requirement for reports to be made to the Revenue of certain investment transactions by SSASs. For reporting requirements generally, see Appendix VII to IR12 (2001).

PSO Update No 69 published on 29 August 2000, enhanced the role of the Pensioneer Trustee in relation to SSASs (see 13.15 below).

Changes affecting pension schemes generally may also affect SSASs – as for instance the introduction of self-assessment tax returns, changes in data protection legislation, and changes resulting from the *Financial Services and Markets Act 2000 (FSMA 2000)*.

As regulation continued to develop, practitioners saw the need to come together to negotiate jointly with the Revenue, the Department of Social Security (now the Department for Work and Pensions) and other official bodies. As a result, the APT was formed in the early 1980s. It is the practice of the Revenue to consult with the APT on many proposals for changes relating to SSASs, with a view to ensuring that the changes will be clear and workable in practice.

Formal definition of a SSAS

13.3 A SSAS is defined (under *regulation 2* of the *SSAS Regulations (SI 1991 No 1614)*) as a scheme:

(*a*) with some or all of its income and other assets invested otherwise than in insurance policies;

(*b*) where the number of active members is below twelve (although there are a few instances where the IR SPSS may treat a scheme as a SSAS where there are more than twelve members); and

(*c*) where at least one scheme member is 'connected' to:

- another member; or
- a trustee of the scheme; or
- a person who is an employer in relation to the scheme.

'Scheme member' here broadly means an active member, not a deferred, or pensioner member (IR12 2001 PN 20.1).

Table 13.4 below sets out what is meant by the term 'connected'.

Pensioneer trustee

13.4 Currently a SSAS must have a pensioneer trustee (*regulation 9* of the *SSAS Regulations (SI 1991 No 1614)*). It is expected that this will not be a

Small self-administered schemes **13.4**

requirement after April 2006. Approval criteria for pensioneer trustees were restated in PSO Update 69. A pensioneer trustee is an individual or body recognised by the IR SPSS as:

(*a*)   being widely concerned with SSAS's;

(*b*)   having evidenced that knowledge in relation to at least 20 SSASs; and

(*c*)   having given confirmation to the Revenue in the form set out in PSO Update 69, and summarised in IR12 (2001) PN 20.4. The pensioneer trustee must agree not to consent to any action that he considers infringes any approval requirement in relation to a SSAS, and not to consent to the termination of the SSAS otherwise than in accordance with the approved terms of the winding-up rule. A company which is a pensioneer trustee must demonstrate that a person with the required experience and knowledge (see (*a*) and (*b*) above) is in a position of authority with the company, so that the company is able to comply with its obligations to the Revenue (IR12 (2001) PN 20.6).

Pensioneer trustee status can in extreme circumstances be withdrawn – see IR12 (2001) PN 20.12.

In practice the pensioneer trustee (or another company in the same group) sometimes carries out administrative, consultancy, actuarial, investment management and legal work in relation to the SSAS. Different arrangements are adopted by different practitioners. The *Income and Corporation Taxes Act 1988* places certain responsibilities on the 'administrator' of a pension scheme – see IR12 (2001) PN 16. It is worth remembering that the administrator for Taxes Act purposes is not always the administrator for the purposes of the SSAS – the Trust Deed and Rules should make the position clear.

Since 1998 the pensioneer trustee has been prohibited from terminating his appointment to a given scheme, unless he dies, is removed by a court order, the Revenue withdraws his pensioneer trustee status, an Opra order is made, or (most significantly) someone else is willing and able to be appointed as pensioneer trustee in his place. This removing of the pensioneer trustee's freedom to resign stirred up much concern, and continues to be an ongoing part of wider discussions between the APT and the Revenue about the role of the pensioneer trustee and the terms of his Revenue undertaking. Many consider that this 'lock-in' is unfair.

Where it is proposed that one pensioneer trustee replaces another, the appointment must be effective at the same time as the termination.

In the other instances listed above the Revenue requires 30 days for an appointment to be notified to them.

In certain circumstances a pensioneer trustee must be appointed to act in respect of a personal pension scheme – see Pensions Update 118, 25 February 2002.

13.4 Small self-administered schemes

The names of all approved pensioneer trustees are published on the Revenue website. There are around 280 at present. Most active pensioneer trustees are members of the APT.

A pensioneer trustee should not act as such for any scheme of which he is a member. Nor must the pensioneer trustee be connected with a member, trustee or participating employer of that scheme (IR 12 (2001) PN 20.10). (See the Table below for the definition of 'connected'.)

Table 13.4

Definition of 'connected'

Individuals: Individuals

an individual is considered 'connected' to his:	– husband (or wife);
	– relatives;
	– relatives' husband(s) (or wife/wives);
	– husband's (or wife's) relatives.
an individual who is also a scheme member is considered 'connected' with an employer participating in a scheme if the employer:	– is a partnership and he is 'connected' to one of the partners; – is a company and he (or anyone 'connected' to him) has been a controlling director of that company within the last ten years.

Companies: Companies

a company is considered 'connected' with another company if:	– the same person has control of both companies
	– one person has control of one company and persons 'connected' with him have control of the other;
	– a group of two or more persons has control of both companies.

Companies: Individuals

a company is considered 'connected' to an individual if:	– the individual has control of the company;
	– the individual and persons 'connected' with him together have control of the company.

Control of a Company

any two or more persons acting together to secure control of a company are 'connected' (in relation to that company) with:	– one another; – any person acting on their directions to secure 'control' of the company.

> **'Control' means**
> the power of a person to secure by means of:
> - a shareholding;
> - voting power; or
> - specific powers in the company's constitution:
>
> – that the affairs of the company are conducted in accordance with his wishes.
>
> N.B. if the company has five or fewer members (a 'close company') the definition of 'control' also takes in any right to acquire the highest percentage of share capital if it were to be distributed.

Practice

13.5 The relevant provisions of the *SSAS Regulations* (*SI 1991 No 1614*) must be incorporated in all SSAS trust documentation. IR12 (2001) PN 20 contains guidance on other provisions that should be incorporated, for instance relating to the winding up of the employer (PN 20.84 to 20.86).

FUNDING SSASS AND PAYMENT OF BENEFITS

13.6 SSASs are currently subject to the usual funding principles which apply to all approved schemes (see chapter 10). For instance, employers must be under an obligation to contribute, and contributions must be actuarially justifiable. New maximum funding rules for SSASs came into effect on 1 June 1996. Although many consider that these do not reflect current financial conditions. Limited revisions were introduced by Pension Update 137 of 11 March 2003.

Spreading

13.7 Given that many SSASs are established by relatively small companies, whose ability to make consistent contributions will often be limited, the Revenue's previous insistence that tax relief on special contributions (that is, contributions in excess of the amount set out in the most recent actuarial valuation report), should be spread into future tax years, seemed harsh.

As from 1 June 1996 this requirement fell away, ensuring increased flexibility for companies with variable yearly cash flow. Basically, any special contribution below £500,000, once actuarially justified, is permissible. The IR SPSS still reserves the right to spread contributions in excess of £500,000.

Deferred annuities

13.8 The Revenue has, for some time, required that pensions coming into payment under SSASs should be secured as soon as possible by the purchase of an annuity from a life office, with a maximum long-stop period of five years from retirement. Investment restrictions apply during this five-year period.

13.9 *Small self-administered schemes*

However, scheme rules may provide for the purchase of the annuity for members and widows and dependants alike to be deferred for longer (up to age 75), and for the pension to be paid in the meantime from the scheme's resources (Memorandum 119; PSO Update No 14 (26 March 1996); IR12 (2001) PN 20.38 et seq). The trustees might choose to use this facility if, for example, annuity rates at the time of a member's retirement are unfavourable, or if they prefer for the time being not to pay a capital sum to an insurance company.

The deferral of an annuity is subject to the conditions set out below.

Note that annuities generally may now be purchased in the name of the member or beneficiary, rather than the names of the trustees (Pensions Update 126, 4 March 2002).

Actuary's certificate

13.9 For annuity deferral, the actuary must at the time when the payment of the pension begins and the annuity purchase is to be deferred, certify the amount of pension under the scheme rules which the scheme is capable of providing.

The certificate must compare the pension provided from the scheme with an annuity that could be secured on the open market on the same terms at the time the funds are available. Any difference in excess of 10 per cent between the two amounts must be explained by the actuary.

A copy of the certificate must be filed with the IR SPSS at the same time as the next actuarial report is submitted. A renewal certificate must then be submitted with each three-yearly report thereafter.

Difficulties sometimes occur when the value of the scheme's assets declines, and as a result the amount of pension is felt to be too high. In deciding whether the pension should be reduced, *section 91* of the *Pensions Act 1995* should be considered.

Loans, share purchases and borrowing

13.10 Where a pension is being paid directly from the scheme, the actuary must ensure that the portion of the fund nominally underpinning the deferred annuity is excluded when calculating the maximum sum available for loans to the employer or associated employers (see 13.21 and 13.22 below regarding loans made by SSASs), or with which to purchase shares in the employer or 'associated' employers (see the diagram below for a definition of Associated Employers).

As with the calculations for loans and share purchases the retired member's fund must be excluded during the deferral period from the scheme assets in calculating the maximum available borrowing limit. There is a five-year transitional period enabling the trustees to reduce existing borrowings to the acceptable level in the event that a member retires.

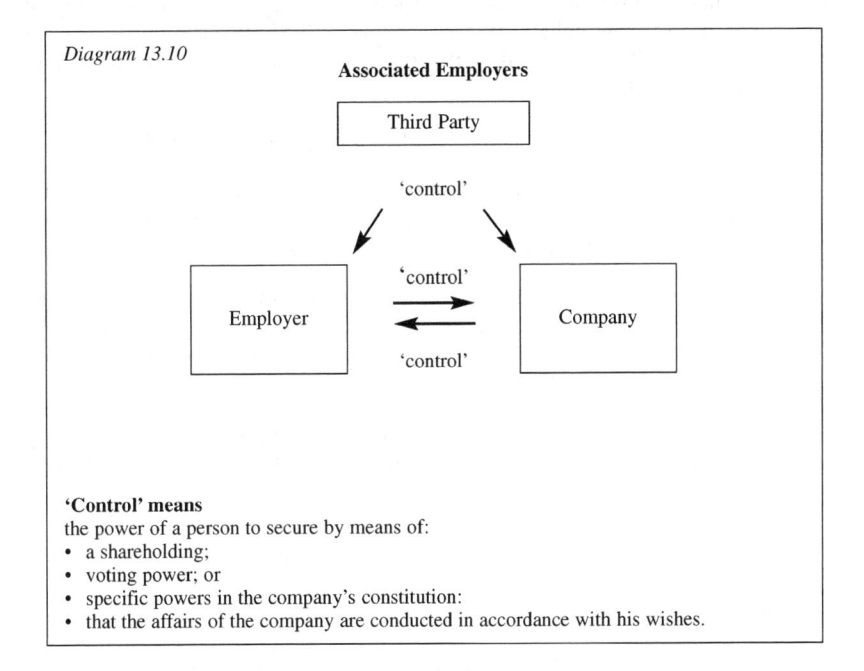

```
Diagram 13.10
                    Associated Employers

                        ┌─────────────┐
                        │ Third Party │
                        └─────────────┘
                             'control'
                           ↙         ↘
                              'control'
    ┌──────────┐           ─────→           ┌──────────┐
    │ Employer │           ←─────           │ Company  │
    └──────────┘                            └──────────┘
                              'control'

'Control' means
the power of a person to secure by means of:
• a shareholding;
• voting power; or
• specific powers in the company's constitution:
• that the affairs of the company are conducted in accordance with his wishes.
```

If all scheme members (or their survivors) are in receipt of a pension, no new loans to, or share purchases in, the employer or an associated employer are permitted nor any share purchase in any other unquoted company. There is then a five year transitional period during which all existing loans must be repaid and/or relevant shares sold.

Investment in property

13.11 The trustees are still able to invest in property during the deferral period provided sufficient readily realisable assets are available to purchase the annuity from age 70 onwards. This avoids a forced sale situation when the member who has deferred the purchase of an annuity is between 70 and 75 years old and an annuity needs to be purchased.

Drawdown

13.12 On 30 June 1999, the Revenue introduced a more flexible facility allowing scheme rules of approved SSASs that provide only money purchase benefits to defer the purchase of an annuity and in the meantime pay pensions by income drawdown (PSO Update No 54 (30 June 1999)). Income drawdown is subject to the conditions in IR12 (2001) Appendix XII.

13.13   *Small self-administered schemes*

BORROWING BY SSASS

13.13   There is a restriction on the amount of money which trustees may, at any time, borrow on behalf of the scheme. (*SSAS Regulations (SI 1991 No 1614), reg 4*). The current rule is that the total amount borrowed must not, in aggregate, exceed the total of:

(*a*)   three times the ordinary annual contribution paid by the employer;

(*b*)   three times the annual amount of basic or contractual contributions paid by the scheme members in the year of assessment ending immediately before the date on which the borrowing takes place; and

(*c*)   45 per cent of the market value of the investments then held for the purposes of the scheme, (excluding funds notionally underpinning benefits in payment and any outstanding sum borrowed to purchase those investments) IR 12 (2001) PN 20.62 et seq).

One aspect of this calculation to bear in mind is the interpretation of 'ordinary annual contributions' in the SSAS Regulations (*SSAS Regulations (SI 1991 No 1614), reg 4*).

Ordinary annual contributions are defined as the smaller of:

(i)   the amount found:

- where the scheme has been established for three years or more at the time of any borrowing, by dividing the amount of the contributions paid by the employers in the period of three years which ended at the end of the previous accounting period of the scheme by three; or

- where the scheme has been established for less than three years at the time of borrowing, by dividing the amount of the contributions paid by the employers in the period since the scheme was established ending at the time of that borrowing by the number of years falling within that period (a part of a year being counted as one year); and

(ii)   the amount of annual contributions which, within the period of three years immediately preceding the date of the borrowing, an actuary has advised in writing would be necessary to secure the benefits payable under the scheme.

The pensioneer trustee must be a party to borrowings (IR 12 (2001) PN 20.28) although lenders will often agree to exclude the personal liability of the pensioneer trustee to repay the sums borrowed, and interest (see 13.15(d) below).

All borrowings must be used to benefit the scheme, and must be reported to the IR SPSS within 90 days on Form PS7015. (Small short-term borrowings however need not be reported – IR12 (2001) PN 20.66).) The 90 day limit is strictly enforced.

Where borrowings from a company are proposed, and the trustees are directors of that company, consideration should be given to the *Companies Act 1985* restrictions on loans to directors.

From 6 April 2006, the borrowing limit is expected to be 50% of the value of the assets of a scheme.

INVESTMENTS BY SSASS – GENERAL

Financial services regulation

13.14 One preliminary point to make about investment by SSAS trustees concerns the application of the *Financial Services and Markets Act 2000 (FSMA 2000)*.

For self-administered schemes in general it is common for trustees to delegate the exercise of their investment powers to a person authorised under the *FSMA 2000*. (In the case of a SSAS, this may be the pensioneer trustee, or an associate of the pensioneer trustee, if in either case he is authorised.) This is so that the trustees do not 'carry on a regulated activity …by way of business' in contravention of the *FSMA 2000, ss 19 and 22*.

Trustees of SSASs, may however want to rely on a specific exemption from the *FSMA 2000*. The *(Carrying on Regulated Activities by Way of Business) Order 2001 (SI 2001 No 1177), reg 4,)* follows on from the similar exemption that used to apply under *section 191* of the *Financial Services Act 1986*. The exemption provides that a person is not treated as 'managing investments' for the purposes of the *FSMA 2000* if he is a member-trustee of a SSAS, or he is a trustee who takes no part in day to day investment management decisions. For the exemption to apply, all members (including for instance deferred and pensioner members) must be trustees, and day to day investment decisions must be taken by all (or a majority) of the members, if of course they are not taken by a person who is authorised under the *FSMA 2000*.

The FSA has published a detailed guidance note covering the application of the *FSMA 2000* to pension scheme trustees generally.

Further regulation is likely to come into effect in January 2005, as a result of the *Insurance Mediation Directive (2002/92/EC)* and the *Financial Services and Markets Act 2000 (Regulated Activities) (Amendment) (No 2) Order 2003 (SI 2003 No 1476)*. Among other things, these changes appear likely to affect a pensioneer trustee who, for payment, arranges for SSAS trustees (including him or herself) to enter into an insurance policy, to be held as an investment of the SSAS.

Co-ownership and co-signatory requirements

13.15 The Revenue brought in new rules in August 2000, in PSO Update 69.

13.15 Small self-administered schemes

They are now incorporated in IR12 (2001), largely in PN 20.17 to 20.33. The objective of the new rules is to encourage greater compliance with the Revenue's requirements. The general principles are that 'where it is legally possible' the pensioneer trustee should be a registered co-owner (along with the other trustees) of all the assets; and that the pensioneer trustee's signature should be required to move any funds out of SSAS bank, building society and other types of investment accounts.

As to co-ownership, there are detailed rules. Some assets acquired before 1 October 2000 are not affected. The precise requirements depend on the nature of the asset. For shares, the pensioneer trustee's name must appear on the company's share register. For investment management arrangements entered into by the trustees, shares may be registered instead in the name of the investment manager's nominee company, but only if the shares cannot be transferred out of the investment manager's control without the pensioneer trustee's written approval. (IR 12 (2001) PN 20.23 and 20.24)

For loans made by the SSAS, the pensioneer trustee must be a party to the loan agreement, and similarly with insurance policies the pensioneer trustee's name should appear on the policy.

Particular rules apply for land. The situation is complex for four reasons:

(a) England and Wales, Scotland and Northern Ireland each have different land laws, and within each area there are further differences depending on whether or not the title to the land is registered at a Government land registry.

(b) with registered land, in England and Wales, an alternative to the pensioneer trustee becoming a registered owner is for a 'restriction' to be registered, to the effect that the land cannot be disposed of without the written consent of the pensioneer trustee.

(c) ownership of land may bring with it certain liabilities, such as duties in respect of any asbestos, and liability for clearing up costs in the event of contaminated land. The pensioneer trustee will want to avoid taking on such liabilities.

(d) often land is purchased by a SSAS with the aid of a bank loan (see 13.13 above). The pensioneer trustee must be a party to the borrowing, but will want to avoid becoming personally liable to repay it. The Revenue has confirmed, in the answers to the 'frequently asked questions' on PSO Update 69, that 'the Update does not require the pensioneer trustee to enter into any covenants in favour of the lender to, say, repay the sum borrowed, or to pay interest on that sum. The Update does not require the pensioneer trustee to put itself in a position where it could be sued by the lender.'

As to the co-signatory requirements, the pensioneer trustee must be a mandatory signatory (not merely an optional signatory) on bank current and deposit accounts which hold scheme assets. There is of course a requirement in the

Pensions Act 1995 for there to be a scheme bank account. Contributions, transfers-in and proceeds of sale of scheme assets must be paid into an account on which the pensioneer trustees is a co-signatory (IR (2001) PN 20.30). All movements of money out of SSAS bank accounts must be authorised by the pensioneer trustee, except:

(i) regular payments previously authorised by the pensioneer trustee and covered by direct debit or standing order arrangements – examples are given in IR12 (2001) PN 20.31;

(ii) payments out of loan or overdraft accounts (IR12 (2001) PN 20.31); and

(iii) transfers between SSAS current and deposit accounts, where the transfer arrangements have been agreed in general by the pensioneer trustee (IR12 (2001) PN 20.29).

From 6 April 2006, since there will be no need for a pensioneer trustee, these co-ownership and co-signatory arrangements (and the protection for the Exchequer which they bring) will no longer be required by tax law. Where SSASs wish to remove the pensioneer trustee as a co-owner and as co-signatory, new instructions are likely to have to be given in respect of each asset. Holdings of land and of investments will need to be re-registered, re-negotiations with lenders may be required, and new signing instructions will have to be given to banks. Whilst welcoming simplification in general, the APT has commented that the new rules will be 'reversing all the good work achieved by PSO Update 69'.

Prohibited investments

Personal chattels

13.16 There is currently a total prohibition on personal chattels falling within the 'pride in possession' category (*SSAS Regulations (SI 1991 No 1614), reg 5*). This includes works of art, jewellery, vintage cars, yachts and gold bullion. (IR12 (2001) PN 20.75).This prohibition is likely to become redundant as from 6 April 2006, although the 'benefits in kind' charge is intended to catch members who enjoy a 'non-commercial use' of a scheme asset.

Residential property

13.17 There is also currently a ban on all investments 'directly or indirectly' in residential property. This is to prevent schemes from providing members with benefits which are not retirement or death benefits.

There are limited exceptions where employees need to occupy residential premises as a condition of employment (for instance, as a caretaker), or as a direct result of occupation of business premises. There are regulations preventing any such permitted occupant being a member or being connected with a member or the employer company (IR 12 (2001) PN 20.72). (See table 13.4 for definition of connected.)

13.18 *Small self-administered schemes*

Further exemptions cover holdings in authorised property unit trusts, and investments in ground rents and similar interests, where there is no member occupation (IR12 (2001) PN 20.73).

Developments and commercial property should be viewed very carefully to ensure no residential element becomes involved, notably developments involving changes of use of the premises. Holiday property is highlighted as a specific exclusion (IR 12 (2001) PN 20.74).

Substantial shareholdings

13.18 Investments are prohibited in shares in unlisted companies which carry with them in excess of 30 per cent of the voting power or dividend rights of the company (*SSAS Regulations (SI 1991 No 1614), reg 5*). This is intended to guard against trustees setting up trading companies or acquiring a controlling interest in a trading company, directly or indirectly, in order to convert the non-tax exempt trading profits into tax exempt dividends (IR12 (2001) PN 20.80).

Some specific classes of investments are considered generally in the IR's manual 'SSAS Guidance Notes'.

Transactions between approved and non-approved schemes

13.19 Many transactions between tax-approved schemes and non-approved schemes are prohibited. This prohibition catches shared investments, preventing (for instance) a SSAS and a funded unapproved retirement benefit scheme ('FURBS') buying a property jointly, particularly where a member of the SSAS (or a person connected with him) has an interest in the FURBS. It also catches sale purchase and lease transactions between a SSAS and a FURBS. For details it is necessary to refer to PS Update 102, and IR12 (2001) PN 20.77 to 20.79, before any proposed transaction is entered into.

Transactions with members or connected persons

13.20 Purchase, lease or sale transactions directly, or indirectly, with a scheme member or someone 'connected' with that member are also banned (*SSAS Regulations (SI 1991 No 1614), reg 8*).

The ban on transactions with scheme members (or persons 'connected' with them) applies so that the trustees cannot purchase property which has, at any time in the last three years, been owned by a member or 'connected' person. Similarly the trustees should not sell property which will in the next three years be sold on to a member or 'connected' person (IR 12 (2001) PN 20.67 and 20.69).

Loans to members or 'connected' persons are prohibited (*SSAS Regulations (SI 1991 No 1614), reg 6*). This prevents the amount available for pensions being artificially reduced, and any attempt to circumvent this ban by means of a back-to-back arrangement would result in scheme approval being withdrawn.

'Members' has a wide meaning here, and can include deferred and pensioner members, ex-spouse members and even former members if they are still in the service of a participating employer.

The IR SPSS reviews transactions in order to satisfy itself that they do not involve a member or 'connected' person. Note however that by the *SSAS Regulations (SI 1991 No 1614, reg 11)*, the restrictions on assets held by a SSAS in 1991 are looser in some respects than the restrictions affecting subsequently – acquired assets.

LOANS BY SSASS

Permitted loans

13.21 Loans by SSASs are generally permitted, subject to the ban on loans to members and persons 'connected' with them (see 13.20 above), and subject to the overall requirement of prudence. In particular, loans are permitted to employers and other 'associated' employers for the purpose of the borrower's business, subject to the restrictions in 13.22 below and the self-investment restrictions. (See Diagram 13.10 above for the meaning of 'associated'.) Interest on loans can now be paid gross (*Finance Act 2002, s 94*).

It should be noted that if a company is 'associated' with an employer, a loan to that company would be permitted regardless of the fact that the company was at the same time also 'connected' to one of the members. (See table 13.4 for definition of 'connected'.)

Requirements for loans to employers and associated employers

13.22 All loans to employers (or 'associated' employers) must be notified to the IR SPSS on Form PS7013 with a copy of the loan agreement. The terms of any such loan must provide that:

(*a*) the loan is for a fixed term. It is possible to roll the loan over into a fresh agreement, but the IR SPSS will not permit a loan to be rolled over more than twice and no rollover may include any unpaid interest;

(*b*) a loan should not be for long periods as the scheme's funds should not be with the employer for longer than necessary;

(*c*) loans should not be arranged on such a frequent basis as to raise the suggestion that the employer is only partly funding the scheme whilst claiming tax deductions for the total cost of pensions;

13.23 *Small self-administered schemes*

(*d*) a commercial rate of interest must be paid, and in general this requires a figure of at least 3 per cent above the Clearing Banks' Base Rate, whether the loan is secured or not; and

(*e*) the loan must be for the genuine purpose of the employer's business, in order to maintain Revenue approval. Loans to help an ailing business, or to assist employers who are technically insolvent, or in arrears on previous loans, are not appropriate. Nor are loans 'for the purpose of making and managing investments by the employer'; and

(*f*) the loan should be made on an ongoing repayment basis, with capital and interest being repaid quarterly (although this is not an absolute requirement in all cases).

The IR SPSS requires the trustees to take all available steps to ensure that a loan is repaid if the employer breaks its agreement, ceases business or becomes insolvent. The trustees must approach any proposed loan to an employer or 'associated' employer purely as a commercial investment decision. Due to their likely knowledge of the company's financial position it should be clear to them whether they are making a good or bad investment. The loan must not be 'injudicious'. The IR SPSS tightened up the rules relating to loans in March 2003, and is covered in Pension Update 143. Reference should be made to this Update, and in particular to the new requirements in paragraphs 11 and 23 of the Update.

Any loan to an employer which is written off represents a payment to that employer and so can be subject to tax at 35 per cent. This would not, however, be the case where the company has gone into liquidation (*SSAS Regulations (SI 1991 No 1614), reg 6*). The pensioneer trustee must be a party to the loan agreement, and loan repayments and interest must be paid into an account of which the pensioneer trustee is a signatory. [IR12 (2001) PN 20.22].

There is a requirement for trustees to pursue the payment of any arrears promptly, and to notify the IR SPSS in writing within 90 days of any default. Within a further 90 days, the IR SPSS should be notified of steps taken to recover the debt.

INVESTMENT IN SHARES

13.23 Form PS7014 must be submitted to the Revenue on the sale or purchase of shares in an unlisted company (and it may be prudent for the trustees to obtain a share valuation in these circumstances). This reporting requirement does not apply to listed shares or OEICS, but it does apply to shares listed on the Alternative Investment Market.

Dealings in shares between the trustees and members (or someone connected with a member) are prohibited due to the close interests of the parties (*SSAS Regulations (SI 1991 No 1614), reg 6*).

Subject to the 30 per cent limit on investment in all unquoted shares (see 13.18), dealings in shares are permitted between the trustees and employers and 'associated' companies on the condition that the trustees first seek written independent professional advice as to price and act in accordance with that advice. (*SSAS Regulations, reg 8*). Best practice also requires that in appropriate cases clearance is obtained from the Revenue under *section 707* of the *Income and Corporation Taxes Act 1988*.

The IR SPSS will require a copy of the written advice to be submitted with the notification of the sale or purchase on Form PS7014.

The self-investment limits detailed in 13.24 below will also apply.

See 13.15 above for the 'co-ownership' requirements in respect of investments in shares and other securities.

SELF-INVESTMENT

13.24 Both loans to, and the purchase of shares in, an employer or 'associated' employer, are subject to Inland Revenue limits on self-investment (*SSAS Regulations (SI 1991 No 1614), reg 7*). The requirements are that:

(*a*) for the first two years of a scheme's life self-investment does not exceed 25 per cent of the market value of the scheme assets derived specifically from contributions from the employer and employee since the date of establishment; and

(*b*) from two years onwards self-investment must not exceed 50 per cent of the market value of all the scheme assets. (The key difference, therefore, apart from the percentage increase, is that for the first two years transfers-in cannot be taken into account.)

It should also be noted that the IR SPSS applies these self-investment limits to loans to and shares in other persons and companies connected with the scheme via a member, trustee or employer. 'Connected' is defined separately for this purpose – see table 13.24 below.

Table 13.24

'Connected' in this context means:

(*a*) business associates of:
- a member;
- an employer; } of the scheme
- an employer;

(*b*) a partnership where one of the partners is connected via a business associate with:
- a member;
- a trustee;

13.25 *Small self-administered schemes*

> - an employer;
> (c) a company where a director or influential shareholder (ie with excess of 20% of votes) is connected via a business association with:
>   - a member;
>   - a trustee;
>   - an employer.

An exemption from the five per cent limit on employer-related investments is available to SSASs under the *Investment Regulations 1996 (SI 1996 No 3127)* – see chapter 10.

Employer-related investments are defined to include not only loans to and shares in the employer but also land occupied by, or leased to, an employer and property other than land which is used for the purposes of the employer's business. Trustees of SSASs are permitted to exceed the general limit of 5 per cent of the scheme's resources by investing in these ways if:

(a) all members are trustees;

(b) the prior agreement, in writing, of each member is first obtained; and

(c) the scheme rules permit the investment.

From 6 April 2006, there is likely to be a fixed limit of 5% on the value of the scheme assets which can be invested in shares in an employer.

INVESTMENT IN REAL PROPERTY

Prohibitions

13.25 There is currently a general prohibition on investment in residential property (see 13.17 above). The ban against transactions with members and 'connected' persons also applies (see 13.20 above) (*SSAS Regulations (SI 1991 No 1614), reg 8*).

Permitted investments

13.26 Commercial property transactions with the employer or an associated company are permitted provided that an independent written professional opinion is obtained and the trustees act in accordance with it. (*SSAS Regulations (SI 1991 No 1614), reg 8*). The IR SPSS require a Form PS7012 with a copy of the valuation within 90 days of the sale or purchase. The limit is strictly enforced.

Purchases or sales with third parties must also be notified to the IR SPSS on Form PS7012.

The IR SPSS views investment in real property as an acceptable long term investment but it becomes less appropriate as retirement draws nearer due to the difficulty of realising the asset at short notice (IR12 (2001) PN 20.51).

Any involvement, no matter how indirectly, with property development must be approached with caution. The trustees may face tax charges for trading (see 13.32 below), and changes in use of the property could inadvertently contravene the residential property provisions (see 13.17 above). If the trustees are in any doubt they should obtain an IR SPSS view in advance.

With commercial properties, trustees need to be aware of the obligations placed on a 'duty-holder' under *The Control of Asbestos at Work Regulations 2002* (*SI 2002 No 2675*).

With property investments, the 'co-ownership' requirements must be followed – see 13.15 above.

Leasing

13.27 Despite the prohibition on leases to members or persons connected to members, (*regulation 8* of the *SSAS Regulations* – see 13.20 above) it is permitted for property owned by the trustees to be leased to the employer or an 'associated' company. The trustees must seek independent advice as to rent (*regulation 8* of the *SSAS Regulations*) and a copy of the lease and valuation must be submitted to the IR SPSS together with Form PS7012 within 90 days of the lease commencing. Again, liquidity considerations arise if members are approaching retirement.

The lease must be at arm's length and at a commercial rent. In considering this issue, the trustees should ask themselves whether they would enter into such an arrangement with a totally independent third party.

Rent must be paid into the Scheme bank account (see 13.15 above).

The trustees must take all available steps to collect rent due; otherwise they risk loss of the scheme's tax approval for failing to consider the members' best interests. Any rent which is written off may be treated as a refund to the employer and so be taxed at 35 per cent. (Similar tax considerations apply to loans – see 13.22 above).

TAX AVOIDANCE AND THE BONA FIDES OF THE SCHEME

General

13.28 The IR SPSS will generally only interfere with the trustees' exercise of their power of investment where:

13.29 *Small self-administered schemes*

(*a*) tax avoidance is suspected; or

(*b*) scheme investments seem irreconcilable with the bona fide sole purpose of the scheme being to provide retirement benefits (IR12 (2001) PN 20.51).

The IR SPSS has expressed concern about investment by SSASs in certain overseas arrangements which appear to be promoted with tax avoidance in mind, and which (in return for a large fee) promise that members can receive assets from the SSAS tax free. Serious doubts have been expressed about whether these schemes work, and the Inland Revenue has issued Pensions Update 132 (17 May 2002). See also the guidance on Opra's website (www.opra.gov.uk) relating to 'pension liberation'.

Tax avoidance

13.29 Possible tax avoidance is a major issue in the IR SPSS's review of transactions between the trustees and the employer (or an 'associated' company) to ensure that nothing conflicts with the scheme's approval. The IR SPSS may well consult with the relevant Inspector of Taxes to decide whether tax avoidance is involved and whether the transaction could be seen to fall foul of *section 703* of *ICTA 1988*, as part of a transaction in securities. In practical terms, in this context *section 703* legislates against company profits being routed into the pension scheme in order to avoid tax bills on sums that might otherwise be paid out in the form of dividends.

All proposed transactions with securities should be discussed with professional advisers in order to verify that *section 703* will not bite. There is a clearance procedure available under *section 707* of *ICTA 1988* so that trustees may apply in advance to the Inland Revenue.

Bona fides

13.30 It is a condition of approval under *section 590(2)(a)* of *ICTA 1988* that a scheme should be bona fide established for the sole purpose of providing relevant benefits. The concern of the IR SPSS is that tax-exempt investments held for the provision of the scheme benefits should not be of such a kind or used in such way as to produce a non-relevant benefit for the beneficiaries or the employer (IR12 (2001) PN 20.45).

In general the trustees must look primarily to the members' interests; concerns as to the operation of the employer company and how it may benefit from the permitted flexibility of SSAS investments should not feature in this consideration.

Trustees should be wary of artificially dressing up questionable investments (and the methods by which they are achieved) so that they appear to be in the members' best interests. The IR SPSS could investigate matters and either require the action taken to be reversed or simply withdraw approval.

WITHDRAWAL OF APPROVAL

13.31 The Revenue's power to withdraw the approval of a scheme (*section 591B(1)* of *ICTA 1988*) is operated on a purely discretionary basis. Recently forty-two SSASs have had approval withdrawn, for various reasons.

Approval may be withdrawn for serious rule breaches. In addition, in certain instances the IR SPSS has set specific time limits for regulatory changes in scheme documentation. Failure to comply with these deadlines could now have serious effects. *Section 61* of the *Finance Act 1995* introduced a 40 per cent tax charge on the market value of a scheme's assets if the scheme loses approval for any reason. This penalty includes non-deliberate failings of the trustees, for example, to keep the trust documentation up to date in line with Inland Revenue regulations.

The so called 'trust busting' provisions, introduced by the *Finance Act 1995*, should also be borne in mind. A 40 per cent tax charge will result if SSASs are used as a method of tax avoidance. The general consequences of approval being withdrawn are:

(*a*) lump sum benefits paid will generally not be tax free;

(*b*) employees become liable to tax on any subsequent contributions by the employers;

(*c*) from the date of withdrawal all applicable exemptions or reliefs cease;

(*d*) the capital gains tax exemption is withdrawn on any capital gains realised on or after withdrawal of approval (IR 12 (2001) PN 19.3.)

It is also worth remembering that one of the most common reasons for withdrawal of approval is the failure to comply with the obligation to obtain an actuarial valuation report on inception and then at three year intervals from then on, and to file the report with the IR SPSS within one year of the effective date (IR12 (2001) PN 20.35). However, the Revenue have conceded that for SSASs in wind-up, if the wind-up is completed within one year of the 'as at' date of the valuation, the IR SPSS will be prepared to dispense with the report (PSO Update No 53 (28 May 1999)). See generally Pensions Updates 113 (21 January 2002) and 129 (5 March 2002).

Arrangements for compliance are expected to change from 6 April 2006. There is to be a self-assessment approach with, in most instances, a 'process now, check later' regime. There will be tax-geared penalties for non-compliance, the amount of which will depend on the size and gravity of the matter, and on the willingness of those concerned to co-operate with enquiries. Withdrawal of tax-privileged status will be limited to the most serious cases only.

TRADING

13.32   *Section 592(2)* of *ICTA 1988* exempts income from investments and

13.33 *Small self-administered schemes*

deposits held for the purposes of the scheme from income tax. Any income which is considered by the Revenue to be derived from trading does not, however, benefit from this exemption. (See chapter 10 for a general discussion on what constitutes trading.)

The issue of trustees' trading is something which concerns not only the IR SPSS but the Revenue generally. Trading by the trustees will result in a tax bill.

What actually constitutes trading is not something which the Revenue has outlined in regulations. There are restrictions on trustees setting up or controlling a trading company (IR 12 (2001) PN 20.80), but other than this the Revenue will simply step in when it perceives trading is occurring.

If in any doubt trustees should seek professional advice at the earliest point.

VAT

13.33 SSASs receive the same VAT treatment as all other occupational schemes. However, when on 30 November 1994 the *VAT (Buildings and Land) Order (SI 1994 No 3013)* was introduced as an anti-avoidance measure in order to counter VAT avoidance schemes on land and buildings, the most common schemes hit were those involved in the aggressive marketing of leases and leasebacks. Due to the frequent use of the purchase and leaseback arrangements by SSASs they found themselves caught by the Order and subject to VAT liability. The Government initially declined to permit any extra statutory concessions across the board for SSASs. However, this stance has now fortunately been relaxed, with an extra-statutory concession specifically for SSASs.

THE PENSIONS ACT 1995

13.34 Generally speaking *PA 1995* is limited in its application to SSASs as SSASs are specifically exempted from many of the provisions. Practice since the advent of *PA 1995* has illustrated that the bulk of its protective requirements are largely unsuitable for SSASs where there is such community of interest between members, trustees and employers.

The Green Paper, 'Partnership in Pensions' published by the Government in December 1998, looked in detail at the relevance of *PA 1995* to SSASs. It acknowledges that application of the legislation to SSASs is complex, inconsistent, confusing and generally inappropriate and recommends a widening of the exemptions. No legislation has to date resulted from this, although draft regulations have been produced.

However, those areas of *PA 1995* specifically exempting SSASs or treating them differently from other schemes are as set out in the table below.

APPLICATION OF PA 1995 TO SSASS

Subject	Position for SSASs	Authority
Advisers	An auditor and actuary must be appointed in accordance with requirements of *PA 1995* and the *Scheme Administration Regulations* (*SI 1996 No 1715*) unless the scheme is?a money purchase SSAS (where for the auditor exemption all members are trustees and all decisions made by unanimous agreement or the scheme?only has one member). N.B. Even if the scheme is exempt, it must still have an actuary for Inland Revenue purposes. If this actuary is appointed by the trustees, he must be appointed in accordance with the requirements of *PA 1995* and the *Scheme Administration Regulations* (*SI 1996 No 1715*). Actuary may be a pensioneer trustee. Whistle-blowing mandatory by auditor or actuary where their appointment is *required* and is permissible by any other professional adviser.	*PA 1995, ss 47* and *48* and the *Scheme Administration Regulations 1996* (*SI 1996 No 1715*).
Compensation scheme	Exempt where only one member or all members are trustees and their decisions can (by the rules) only be made by unanimous agreement.	*PA 1995, s 81(1)* and *Compensation Regulations* (*SI 1997 No 665*)
Disclosure	Exemption where one member only, and trustees have no disclosure obligations to members where all members are trustees.	*Disclosure Regulations* (*SI 1996 No 1655*).
Disputes	Exempt where either only one scheme member or all members are trustees.	*Dispute Regulations* (*SI 1996 No 1270*).
Equal treatment	No exemption unless one member only.	*PA 1995 ss 62 to 66* and *Equal Treatment Regulations* (*SIs 1995 No 1215 and No 3183*).

13.35 *Small self-administered schemes*

Subject	Position for SSASs	Authority
Independent trustee appointment	Exempt from appointing independent trustee if a money purchase scheme. In final salary schemes, appointment required where not all members are trustees.	*Independent Trustee Regulations* (*SI 1997 No 252*).
Indexation of pensions	No exemption (but indexation applies only from 6 April 1997).	*PA 1995, s 51(1)*
Investment	Exempt from self-investment restrictions under *PA 1995*, but different restrictions apply. Statement of investment principles not needed if all members are trustees and scheme's rules require written agreement of all members before making an investment.	*PA 1995, ss 34* and *35*, *Investment Regulations* (*SI 1996 No 3127*).
Member-nominated trustees	Exempt.	*MNT Regulations* (*SI 1996 No 1216*).
Minimum funding requirement	Inapplicable if money purchase scheme. Generally applies to approved final salary schemes unless one member only.	*PA 1995, s 56(2)(a)*. *PA 1995 s 87(2)*. *PA 1995 s 56(1)* and *MFR Regulations* (*SI 1996 No 1536*).
Schedule of payments	Exempt if only one member or if all members are trustees and all decisions are made by unanimous agreement.	*MFR Regulations* (*SI 1996 No 1536* and *SI 1996 No 1715*)
Opra	Trustees may be liable to suspension, disqualification, fines and imprisonment.	Various. *PA 1995 ss 6, 9* and *10*.
Pensions Ombudsman	No exemption from Pensions Ombudsman's jurisdiction.	*PA 1995 ss 156* to *160*. *SI 1991 No 588*.
Transfers	No exemption.	*PA 1995 ss 152* to *154*. *SI 1996 No 1847*.
Winding-up	Inapplicable where money purchase scheme. Approved final salary schemes are generally covered unless there is only one member.	*PA 1995 s 75*. *PA 1995 ss 73, 74, 76* and *77*.

TRANSFERS AND CONVERSIONS

13.35 Generally the Inland Revenue permits transfers of a member's benefits between tax approved pension schemes. For SSASs, reference should be made to Pensions Update 134 (20 December 2002) for the approval and reporting requirements. For transfers from SSASs to personal pension schemes, PSO Update No 85 (22 January 2001) introduced new requirements which may limit the amount that can be transferred. Reference should be made to IR12 (2001) Appendix XI for the details. Scheme rule amendments may be necessary, before a transfer can be made in respect of a member who is not permitted by the new requirements to transfer out the full value of his benefits. Where a member's benefits are greater in value than the amount that can be transferred, the excess may in certain circumstances be reallocated (Pensions Update 121, 25 February 2002).

Pensions Update 127 (16 March 2002) deals with the requirements which apply where a scheme originally approved under *Chapter I* of *Part XIV, ICTA 1988* is to be converted so that it is approved instead as a personal pension scheme under *Chapter IV*.

THE FUTURE

13.36 Very radical changes are expected to take effect from 6 April 2006. SSASs are likely to cease to form a separate category of schemes for tax purposes, although there will be transitional arrangements covering matters such as existing investments. There will be a single tax regime for 'registered' (now known as 'approved') schemes. The current regulatory system for SSASs, based on pensioneer trustees, detailed limits on contributions and pensions, separate investment rules and detailed reporting, will become redundant. Primary legislation to put these changes in place was contained in the 2004 Finance Bill, which is expected to become law in July/August 2004. There will be consultation on secondary legislation during 2004, and guidance is due to be published by the IR SPSS early in 2005.

Chapter 14

Unapproved arrangements

INTRODUCTION

14.1 Unapproved schemes are a relatively recent phenomenon. Before 27 July 1989, the date on which the *Finance Act 1989* received Royal Assent, all schemes relating to a particular class of employees were considered in conjunction with each other and the total benefits had to be within Inland Revenue limits for any of the schemes to be approved. In his 1989 budget speech, Nigel Lawson, the then Chancellor of the Exchequer, effectively severed the links between pension schemes, paving the way for employers to operate approved and unapproved schemes in tandem.

It was, however, another aspect of the Chancellor's proposals which provided the main impetus for establishing unapproved schemes. As a quid pro quo for relaxing Inland Revenue practice towards approved schemes, the Chancellor introduced a limit or cap on the earnings of an employee which may be taken into account when determining the benefits that can be paid from an approved scheme. (This cap applies to any individual who became a member of an occupational pension scheme on or after 1 June 1989 or if the scheme was established after 14 March 1989, who became a member of the scheme after that date. There are exceptions to this general rule, for example, a member may be deemed to have joined a scheme from an earlier date by virtue of his membership of his employer's previous scheme. For the tax year 2004/2005 the earnings cap is £102,000.)

To compensate employees who are subject to the so called 'earnings cap' many employers have chosen to provide unapproved 'top-up' schemes.

Although most unapproved schemes will be aimed at individuals who are subject to the earnings cap, funded unapproved schemes can be a tax efficient way of remunerating highly paid employees. However, following the changes to liability for National Insurance Contributions (NICs) with effect from 6 April 1998 (see 14.36 below) and changes to the capital gains tax regime (see 14.18 below) following the March 1998 Budget, the attractiveness of funded unapproved schemes has been reduced for employers and highly paid employees. Moreover, the treatment of such schemes under the forthcoming 2006 tax regime (see 14.38 to 14.40 below) will further reduce their attraction.

TYPES OF UNAPPROVED ARRANGEMENTS

14.2 There are no restrictions on the benefits that may be paid from an unapproved scheme, either in amount or type (although the tax implications will differ depending on what type of benefits are provided). Most unapproved schemes will be designed to compensate employees for loss of benefits due to the imposition of the earnings cap, but how this is achieved will depend on a number of issues. An employer will have to decide whether he wishes to provide money purchase or final salary benefits; whether the benefits are to be provided through a group or an individual arrangement; and whether he wishes to fund the benefits in advance or not.

Funded or unfunded?

14.3 Unapproved schemes can be either funded or unfunded or a mixture of both (eg unfunded except that death benefits are insured). In the case of a funded unapproved retirement benefits scheme (a 'FURBS') contributions are paid by the employer and accumulated, usually within a trust, until the benefits become payable. Such arrangements are usually non-contributory for the employee (see 14.16 below). With an unfunded unapproved retirement benefits scheme (an 'UURBS') no provision is made for benefits until they become payable, at which point the whole benefit is usually paid directly by the employer. When deciding whether to follow the funded or unfunded route an employer will need to consider the fiscal and commercial implications, whilst the employee will generally be concerned with the issue of security (see 14.6 below).

Tax considerations

14.4 The tax treatment of funded and unfunded arrangements differ in several key respects.

Assuming the arrangement is correctly structured, the investment growth of a FURBS will be taxed at the basic rate of income tax (see 14.17 below). If the employer were to provide the same net benefit through an UURBS, he could use the capital he would otherwise have paid into a FURBS to produce income for the company. This income would be taxed at the applicable rate of corporation tax. For a large employer paying corporation tax at the standard rate, providing a targeted benefit through a FURBS can be attractive. As the standard rate of corporation tax is higher than the basic rate of income tax to which a FURBS is charged, less capital has to be expended to achieve the same net result. Arguably an employer may achieve a better rate of return by continuing to utilise the capital itself, but this is unlikely to offset the tax advantage.

An employee is liable for income tax on the contributions paid by his employer into a FURBS in respect of him (see 14.16 below). Financing this tax charge can place a heavy financial burden on the employee who, as a consequence, may prefer an UURBS. Many employers will attempt to mitigate the liability by 'grossing-up' the contributions paid. A grossing-up arrangement will usually result in additional salary being paid to the employee, on which the employer will have to pay National Insurance contributions. This additional tax and National Insurance liability may make a FURBS unattractive to the employer.

14.5 Unapproved arrangements

With an UURBS, the tax liability arises when the benefits are paid out so the payment can simply be reduced to take account of the tax charge. Grossing-up is therefore not an issue.

Commercial considerations

14.5 The advance funding of an unapproved arrangement allows the employer to regulate its cash flow and so plan ahead.

Although provision for an UURBS may be made in the form of a reserve in a company's accounts, there is still the possibility of an unexpected payment having to be made (for example, the employee may have to retire early due to ill-health) which could place a strain on the employer's cash flow.

Security

14.6 A funded pensions promise, which is usually provided through a trust, offers a far greater degree of security for the employee than an unfunded contractual promise.

In the case of an UURBS, the employee is relying on the employer honouring its promise when he comes to retire, which could be some time after leaving his employer. If an employee is to be paid a pension (rather than a lump sum) directly from his former employer, the lack of security will continue throughout retirement. If the employer runs into financial difficulties there may be little prospect of the employee receiving his pension as in the event of the employer's insolvency the employee would only rank as an ordinary creditor. It is this inherent lack of security with an UURBS which prompts many employees to prefer a FURBS, notwithstanding the immediate tax liability.

In a survey conducted by William M Mercer in May 2001 on the impact of the pensions earnings cap and the various methods available to compensate highly paid executives for this restriction on retirement benefits, FURBs proved to be the most popular, used by 34 per cent of employers with UURBs being used by 24 per cent. UURBs had fallen in popularity from 30 per cent in 1998, largely as a result of concerns over lack of funding and security.

The security issue can be addressed by the employer granting a charge over some of its assets. This raises the separate question of whether the purchase of an asset by the employer (to grant a charge over it) could itself be regarded by the Revenue as a payment of a sum and therefore be charged to tax under *section 386* of *ITEPA 2003* (previously *section 595* of *ICTA 1988*). In the Revenue's 1991 Booklet 'The Tax Treatment of Top-Up Pension Schemes' the following statements are made at paragraphs 2.2.12 and 2.2.13 on this point:

'2.2.12

One example of a borderline case is the creation of a fixed or floating charge on some of the employer's assets. The purpose of such a charge would be to provide security for an unfunded benefit promise. Normally the charge will be called in only if the employer became insolvent or failed to pay the benefits when due. In these cases, the value of the charge would not count as the employee's taxable income when it is created.

2.2.13

On the other hand, if the charge should at any time be called in, that will involve a payment by the employer that could lead to a *section 595* charge (even if the employee is then retired or no longer in service). In practice, the tax treatment may depend upon what happens to the funds realised ...'.

More recently, it has been confirmed at a meeting of the Occupational Pension Schemes Joint Working Group in November 1998 (as noted in the minutes of the Joint Working Group) that the Revenue had been advised that, in law, where it could not be disputed that the intention of the employer was to pay the benefits from sources other than the charged assets, a charge to tax could not be levied under *section 595* (now *section 386* of *ITEPA 2003*). This approach has not, however, been formally published or announced.

There may also be other difficulties in granting security to one group (the higher paid employees) ahead of other creditors. The charge may also contravene banking covenants because of negative pledges.

Group or individual arrangement?

14.7 Group arrangements can reduce administration expenses and may be more convenient to manage. Generally a group arrangement can also replicate an approved scheme more closely, both in terms of benefit structure and administration, which in some instances may be an advantage.

Many employers prefer individual arrangements so that if and when the employee leaves the service of the employer he can simply take the scheme with him and the employer can step out of the picture. It is possible to provide for an employee to keep his benefits within a group arrangement, but take responsibility for the assets representing his benefits, by diverting part of the fund into a sub-trust for which the employee takes responsibility. However, this would probably result in increased administration costs and would not necessarily ensure that the employer's involvement was terminated.

Finally, although unapproved arrangements are exempted from most of the requirements of *PA 1995*, an individual arrangement will be able to obtain additional exemptions on the ground that it has less than two members (see 14.12 below).

Final salary or money purchase?

14.8 An unapproved arrangement may provide either final salary or money purchase benefits, or a combination of both. However, the provision of final

14.9 *Unapproved arrangements*

salary benefits via a FURBS can be difficult as funding cannot be predicted with total certainty. If a FURBS is slightly underfunded when the benefits become payable a large contribution may be necessary, which will result in a large tax charge for the employee. Care would also have to be taken to ensure that a FURBS is not overfunded. For tax reasons, it is inadvisable for an employer to retain any interest in an unapproved arrangement (see 14.15 and 14.17 below) so overfunding could result in a windfall for the employee. If final salary benefits are provided through a group FURBS, problems also arise in respect of the liability for tax on the contributions paid by the employer (see 14.34 below for further discussion on final salary FURBS).

An UURBS is a more natural vehicle for providing a final salary benefit as the problems relating to the level of funding do not arise.

However it would also be possible to provide a final salary benefit to the employee by setting up a FURBS on a money purchase basis and topping it up with an UURBS which would only provide a benefit in the event that the funds built up in the FURBS were insufficient to provide the benefit promised.

ESTABLISHING UNAPPROVED ARRANGEMENTS

General

14.9 Having decided on the type of unapproved arrangement to provide, the next issue to consider is how to establish it. Whatever type of arrangement is proposed, a formal board resolution of the employer will almost always be required to implement it. An explanatory letter should also be issued to the employee or employees who will benefit from the arrangement. The employer must report the existence of an unapproved arrangement to the Inland Revenue tax office dealing with its accounts within three months of the date on which the scheme first comes into operation for any employee, ie when a contribution or benefit is paid. [*ICTA 1988, s 605(3)(a)*]. The Inland Revenue have power to request further information either from the employer or the administrator. [*ICTA 1988, s 605(3)(b) and (4)*].

Unfunded arrangements

14.10 An UURBS can be established either within the employee's contract of employment or by separate documentation.

If an UURBS is established through a provision in a contract of employment, careful consideration must be given as to the precise details of the arrangement. Care should be taken that the explanatory letter does not, in itself, create an UURBS (see also 14.10 below). An employer will want to retain a degree of flexibility to allow for legislative changes in the future, including possible relaxation of Inland Revenue requirements. Retaining this flexibility can be difficult as a contract of employment can usually only be amended with the employee's agreement.

If the UURBS is to be established by separate documentation, this will normally take the form of a contract or, in some cases, a trust deed. A trust deed is more likely if certain benefits are funded; for example, death benefits may be insured via a suitable life insurance policy, the policy itself being the asset of the trust. If the arrangement is entirely unfunded, a contractual arrangement is generally the preferable route. If a trust were utilised, its only asset would be the promise to pay benefits. It is questionable whether such a trust would be valid or whether it would offer any advantage over a contractual arrangement.

Alternatively, the terms of the UURBS could simply be recorded in a board minute or by deed poll instead of a trust deed. A deed poll will (like a trust deed) give the employee the assurance that the benefit will be paid (as long as the employer remains solvent) and will give his or her dependants a right to receive any death benefit which may become payable.

If the UURBS is to be established in a separate document, the employee's contract of employment should contain a reference to the arrangement. However, care must be taken to ensure that the reference does not in itself constitute an unapproved occupational pension scheme.

The importance of ensuring that the parties fully understand and properly record the pensions promise cannot be over estimated.

In *Royal Masonic Hospital Appeal and Another v Pensions Ombudsman and another [2001] 3 All ER 408*, the High Court reversed the Pensions Ombudsman's determination and ruled that preservation requirements under the Pensions Schemes Act 1993 do not apply to UURBS. It was also held that deferred rights to a pension for early leavers could not apply in the case of an UURBS. The case highlights the need for employees to scrutinise closely the terms of any benefit promise given in relation to an UURBS to ensure that it includes a commitment to provide benefits for early leavers, and conversely, for employers to ensure that any commitment as to early leaver benefits go only so far as it intends.

Although there is no actual funding by the employer of the benefits promised during the course of the employee's employment, accounting standard FRS17 requires the employer to account for the costs in its accounts.

Funded arrangements

14.11 Although there is no legal requirement for a FURBS to be established under trust, the majority of FURBSs are. If a FURBS is not established under trust, one of its key advantages, that of security, would be lost. Usually a trust deed will be executed which sets out the provisions of the trust, including the obligations and powers of the trustees and the employer. Suitable investment arrangements will have to be made for a FURBS and the trustees will usually have to open a bank account. Life insurance to cover death benefits may have to be put in place.

14.12 *Unapproved arrangements*

An individual's contract of employment should also contain reference to any FURBS applicable to him, with care being taken to ensure that the reference does not in itself constitute an UURBS.

APPLICATION OF PENSIONS LEGISLATION

14.12 Unapproved arrangements generally fall within the definition of an 'occupational pension scheme' as set out in *section 1* of *PSA 1993* and as such are, *prima facie*, subject to many of the same statutory controls as approved schemes. Unapproved arrangements are, however, specifically exempt from some statutory requirements relating to occupational pension schemes, including most of the provisions of *PA 1995*. In addition, although not exempt as an unapproved scheme *per se*, they will often be exempt from *PA 1995* due to their status as money purchase schemes and/or the fact that they have less than two members.

The following table summarises the extent to which major pieces of pensions legislation apply to unapproved arrangements:

Legislation relating to:	Applicability to unapproved arrangements	
	Pre-*1995 Act*	Post-*1995 Act*
Preservation, transfers and revaluation (see chapter 6)	The DWP take the view that legislation relating to preservation, transfers and revaluation applies to all occupational pension schemes, including unapproved schemes. There are, however, practical problems, particularly in relation to transfers.* The extent to which the legislation applies is under consideration.	Unchanged (but see 14.10 above).
Equal treatment (see chapter 9)	The Equal Access requirements set out in *section 118* of *PSA 1993* applied.	Sections 62 to 66 of PA 1995 apply with effect from 1 January 1996 (*section 118* of *PSA 1993* has been repealed).
Independent trustee (see chapter 3)	The requirement for an independent trustee where the employer became insolvent applied to all occupational pension schemes established by a trust deed (*sections 119 to 122* of *PSA 1993*). Money purchase schemes were exempt (*Occupational Pension Schemes (Independent Trustee) Regulations* (SI 1990 No 2075).	Sections 22 to 26 of PA 1995 (which replace *sections 119 to 122* of *PSA 1993*) apply to all occupational pension schemes established under trust, but unapproved schemes are exempt (*Occupational Pension Schemes (Independent Trustee) Regulations* (SI 1997 No 252), reg 5(1)(f)).

Unapproved arrangements 14.12

Legislation relating to:	Applicability to unapproved arrangements	
	Pre-*1995 Act*	Post-*1995 Act*
Debt on the employer (see chapter 12)	A debt on the employer could arise in respect of any occupational pension scheme which was not a money purchase scheme (*section 144* of PSA *1993*).	Section 75 of PA *1995* (which replaces *section 144* of the *1993 Act*) applies to any occupational pension scheme which is not a money purchase scheme but regulations exempt unapproved schemes (*Occupational Pension Schemes (Deficiency on Winding-Up etc) Regulations* (*SI 1996 No 3128*) reg 10(1)(c)).
Disclosure (see chapter 3)	The *Occupational Pension Scheme (Disclosure of Information) Regulations* (*SI 1986 No 1046*) did not apply to any occupational pension scheme which had not been approved or had not been the subject of an application for approval. A scheme that was unapproved because it had lost approval would still be caught.	The *Occupational Pension Schemes (Disclosure of Information) Regulations* (*SI 1996 No 1655*) provide that trustees of unapproved schemes must provide every member and prospective member with details of which benefits are, and which are not, funded and the manner in which funded benefits are secured, together with a statement to the effect that the provisions of *PA 1995*, subject to certain exceptions, are not applicable. *Reg 2(1)* applies this limited disclosure in reg 8 to unapproved schemes. *Reg 2(2)* exempts schemes with one member only. Details of Opra, OPAS and the Ombudsman must also be given.
Limited price indexation (see chapter 6)	Indexation potentially applied to any occupational pension scheme which was not a money purchase scheme (*section 102* of PSA *1993*) but this provision was not brought into effect.	Indexation applies only to approved schemes or schemes for which approval has been applied for and has not been refused (*section 51* of *PA 1995*).
Self-investment restrictions (see chapter 10)	Unapproved schemes were exempt from restrictions relating to self-investment (*Occupational Pension Schemes (Investment of Scheme's Resources) Regulations* (*SI 1992 No 246*)).	Unapproved schemes continue to be exempt from the restrictions relating to self-investment (*Occupational Pension Schemes (Investment) Regulations* (*SI 1996 No 3127*)). *Reg 10(3)(a)* exempts unapproved schemes from the requirement to produce a statement of investment principles.

14.12 Unapproved arrangements

Legislation relating to:	Applicability to unapproved arrangements	
	Pre-*1995 Act*	Post-*1995 Act*
Contracting-out (see chapter 4)	It was possible to contract-out of the State Earnings-Related Pension Scheme via a funded unapproved scheme but in reality it was not practicable.	It is not possible to contract-out via an unapproved scheme (*Occupational Pension Schemes (Contracting-Out) Regulations (SI 1996 No 1172)*, reg 29(*a*) and 40(*h*)).
Voluntary membership (see chapter 7)	Membership of an unapproved scheme cannot be compulsory.	Unchanged.
Voluntary contributions (see chapter 5)	Unapproved arrangements do not have to allow members to pay voluntary contributions (*Pension Schemes (Voluntary Contributions Requirements and Voluntary and Compulsory Membership) Regulations (SI 1987 No 1108)*, reg 2(3)).	Unchanged.
Levy/registration (see chapter 2)	Unapproved schemes were not required to register with the Registrar of Occupational and Personal Pension Schemes (*Register of Occupational and Personal Pension Schemes Regulations 1997 SI 1997 No 371* and were not required to pay a levy (*Occupational and Personal Pension Schemes (Levy) Regulations (SI 1995 No 524)*).	The *Register of Occupational and Personal Pension Scheme Regulations 1990* were replaced with effect from 1 April 1997. However, *reg 4* of the *Register of Occupational and Personal Pensions Schemes Regulations 1997*, (*SI 1997 No 371*) operates so that the same exemption to register with the Registrar applies as unapproved schemes are not 'registrable' as defined under the regulations. The *Occupational and Personal Pension Schemes (Levy) Regulations 1995* were revoked with effect from 1 April 1997. However, *reg 2* of the *Occupational and Personal Pensions Schemes (Levy) Regulations 1997* (*SI 1997 No 666*) applies so that unapproved schemes are not required to pay a levy as they are not 'registrable' as defined under the regulations.

Unapproved arrangements **14.12**

Legislation relating to:	Applicability to unapproved arrangements	
	Pre-*1995 Act*	Post-*1995 Act*
Pensions Ombudsman and Dispute resolution (see Chapters 2 and 3 respectively)	Disputes arising in connection with unapproved arrangements can be investigated by the Pensions Ombudsman (*PSA 1993 section 146*).	Trustees must put in place a dispute resolution procedure in accordance with *section 50* of *PA 1995* unless all members are also trustees or there is only one member (the *Occupational Pensions Schemes (Internal Dispute Resolution Procedure) Regulations 1996, reg 8*). The Ombudsman still has jurisdiction but cannot investigate a complaint that has not gone through the internal dispute resolution procedure unless he believes there is no prospect of a decision being made within a reasonable time (*Personal and Occupational Pension Schemes (Pensions Ombudsman) Regulations (SI 1996 No 2475, reg 3)*).
Pension Sharing on Divorce (see Chapter 8)	–	The provisions of *Welfare Reform and Pensions Act 1999* (WRPA) relating to pension sharing on divorce apply to unapproved schemes. In the case of unfunded schemes (whether approved or unapproved), other than public service schemes, *paragraph 3 of Schedule 5* to WRPA 1999 provides that the trustees or managers of the scheme may discharge their liability in respect of a pension credit by conferring rights on the former spouse within the member's scheme without obtaining the consent of the former spouse – ie no requirement to make available a transfer payment to another suitable scheme/arrangement.

*It will often be difficult to find a scheme willing to accept a transfer as approved schemes cannot accept transfers from unapproved schemes. In the case of an UURBS, the question of how to calculate a cash equivalent is also problematic. Legislation allows cash equivalents to be reduced in the event of insufficient assets in a scheme. As an UURBS will not have any assets, the cash equivalent could, in theory, be reduced to nil.

14.13 *Unapproved arrangements*

TAXATION ASPECTS OF A FURBS

14.13 Guidance on the Inland Revenue's approach to the tax treatment of unapproved schemes can be found in their booklet 'The Tax Treatment of Top Up Pension Schemes'. Although unapproved schemes do not receive the tax advantages that exempt approved schemes do (see chapter 5), there are certain advantages to be gained by structuring an unapproved scheme in a tax-efficient way. As a consequence, the design of unapproved schemes has, to a large extent, been driven by taxation legislation. A summary of the tax treatment of a typical money purchase FURBS is given below.

Money and assets going into the FURBS

14.14 A FURBS will generally be funded by contributions made solely by the employer as it is inadvisable for an employee to make contributions to a FURBS (see 14.16 below). There is no limit on the amount of money that may be paid into a FURBS or on the emerging benefits. Contributions may be made as and when the employer deems it appropriate; generally contributions will be regular, for example, monthly or annually, but there is no requirement for them to be. Contributions may take the form of a cash payment or a transfer of assets.

Employer's tax position

14.15 Contributions made to a FURBS by a company will generally be deductible for corporation tax purposes. *Section 74* of *ICTA 1988* permits a deduction if the expenditure can be classified as an income expense incurred wholly and exclusively for the purposes of the trade, profession or vocation of the employer.

(*a*) An income expense — Whether or not a payment is classified as an income or capital expense will depend on the circumstances of the payment. Case law suggests that where expenditure brings into existence an asset for the benefit of the company, the expenditure is of a capital nature. A one-off payment of a lump sum which is sufficient to provide the entire benefit promised is a capital expense (*Atherton v British Insulated & Helsby Cables Ltd (1925) 10 TC 155*) but a series of payments, with no specific target, either in concept or amount, would be income expenses (*Jeffs v Ringtons Ltd (1985) 58 TC 680*). If the company can, at its own volition, recover the payments it makes, for example on winding-up the FURBS, the payments will probably not be deductible as they are effectively being used to build up a capital sum which the company can recover (*Rutter v Charles Sharpe & Co Ltd (1979) 53 TC 163*).

(*b*) Incurred for purposes of the trade, profession or vocation — A payment into a FURBS can be treated in the same way as the payment of salary or employee benefits and such expenditure is generally accepted as being capable of benefiting the company's trade. A deduction may not be allowed if the company making the payment does not actually employ the person in respect of whom those payments are made as the expenditure will not be benefiting the appropriate company's trade.

(c) Relevant statutory provisions — The *Finance Act 1989* introduced new rules affecting the availability of a deduction for corporation tax purposes by making the right to a deduction dependent on whether the payments to the unapproved arrangement are chargeable to tax. Under *section 76* of the *Finance Act 1989*, a deduction cannot be made in respect of the expense of providing benefits from a FURBS unless either:

   (i) those benefits are subject to income tax on receipt; or

   (ii) the payment is treated as the member's taxable income by virtue of *section 386* of *ITEPA 2003* (see 14.16 below).

The Inland Revenue currently interpret this as providing that contributions to a FURBS are deductible for corporation tax purposes so long as either of these conditions are satisfied. This is a somewhat generous interpretation of *section 76, FA 1989*, which does not expressly allow such deductions but rather does not prevent them.

The Revenue's liberal interpretation of *section 76, FA 1989* does not cover the making of payments by the company to cover establishment and administration costs as these are not an expense of providing benefits. However, the Revenue have stated that such payments may still be deductible on the general principles set out above.

Section 76, FA 1989 also provides that expenses cannot be deducted unless payments have actually been made. A company could not, for example, make provision for benefits solely in the form of a book-keeping entry and claim a deduction on that basis.

Employee's tax position

14.16 A summary of the employee's tax position is as follows:

(a) Employee's contributions — Generally it is inadvisable for an employee to make contributions to a FURBS for two reasons. First, any contributions would be made from taxed income as there is no tax relief available in respect of employee contributions. An employee would therefore be better advised to make voluntary contributions to his employer's approved scheme (if there is sufficient scope to do so within the Inland Revenue limits applicable to approved schemes). Secondly, any contributions made by an employee might be regarded as providing funds for the purpose of a settlement. The consequence of this would be that the income of the FURBS would be treated as the employee's income and so taxed at his highest marginal rate (see also 14.17 below). [*ICTA 1988, s 660A*].

(b) Employer's contributions — Contributions to a FURBS by an employer are deemed to be the income of the employee in respect of whom they are made, and are assessed to income tax at the employee's marginal rate,

14.16 *Unapproved arrangements*

which is likely to be the highest marginal rate, (*ITEPA 2003, s 386(1)*) as unapproved arrangements tend to be established only for the highly paid. If the FURBS is self-administered, only the contributions used towards providing relevant benefits are chargeable to income tax. For the purposes of this provision, 'relevant benefits' include benefits payable to an employee's spouse, children, dependants or personal representatives. [*ITEPA 2003, s 386(6)*]. Separately identifiable contributions made to meet establishment and administration expenses are not deemed to be the employee's income as they are not paid with a view to providing relevant benefits. If the FURBS is insured, the whole of the premium is chargeable to tax; the Revenue do not allow premiums to be 'split' so as to distinguish administration expenses for tax purposes.

In the case of a group FURBS, *section 388* of *ITEPA 2003* requires each contribution paid to be apportioned between the employees in respect of whom it is paid in accordance with their respective benefit entitlement. For a money purchase scheme this is relatively simple as each member will generally have his own 'pot' to which contributions are made. The scheme administrator should inform the Revenue as to how contributions are to be split and the tax charge will generally be based on those figures. The position regarding group final salary schemes is more complex (see 14.34 below).

Whether the arrangement is a group or an individual FURBS, the employer should notify the employee of the payments which are chargeable under *section 386* of *ITEPA 2003* These notices may be required when benefits are paid out of the FURBS in order to show that income tax has been paid on the contributions.

(*c*) 'Grossing-up' — An employer may decide to meet the employee's tax liability on the contributions it pays to a FURBS by grossing-up the contributions. It is possible for the employer to pay the employee's tax directly to the Revenue. In such a case the Revenue will treat the payment as having been made by the employee. Alternatively, the employer may increase the employee's pay sufficiently to cover the extra tax due. If a grossing-up arrangement is in operation, the grossed-up equivalent of the chargeable contribution and the tax figure should be included on the employee's pay record (Form P11) for the pay period in which the contributions are paid. The employer will also have to notify the relevant tax office at the end of each tax year on Form P9D or P11D so that the Revenue can assess the employee for any resulting tax liability.

If the employee is a director of a UK incorporated company, a direct grossing-up arrangement will not be possible as it is unlawful for a company to pay a director remuneration which varies with the amount of his income tax. [*Companies Act 1985, s 311*]. It may be possible indirectly to gross-up the director's pay by means of a discretionary bonus, paid on the clear understanding that the company is not committed to adjusting the director's remuneration in the event of a change in tax rates. In a consultation paper issued by the Law Commission in August 1998, it was provisionally recommended that *section 311* be repealed. (See para 9.32 of the Joint Consultation Paper on 'Company Directors: Regulating Conflicts of Interest and Formulating a Statement of Duties'.)

Taxation of the income and gains of a FURBS

Income tax

14.17 The taxation of the income and gains of a FURBS will, to an extent, depend on the structure the arrangement takes. Generally, if the FURBS is a trust where the trustees have discretion as to the accumulation of the income there will, potentially, be a liability for basic rate income tax and an additional rate applicable to trusts. However, if the FURBS is established for the sole purpose of providing 'relevant benefits' the additional rate applicable to trusts will not apply. [*ICTA 1988, s 686(2)(c)(i)*]. The expression 'relevant benefits' is defined in *section 612* of *ICTA 1988* as 'any pension, lump sum, gratuity or similar benefit which is, or will be, given when a person retires or dies, in anticipation of retirement, after a person has retired or died (if given in recognition of past service) or as compensation for any change in the conditions of a continuing employment'. If a FURBS provides any other benefits, for example, private health care, it would be unlikely to qualify for the exemption as it would not have been established for the sole purpose of providing relevant benefits.

The income tax position may be different if the employer retains an interest in the FURBS. Under *section 660A* of *ICTA 1988*, income arising under a settlement (in this case the FURBS) is treated as the income of the settlor (in this case the employer) if the settlor retains an interest in the trust property (in this case the assets of the FURBS). Any provision under a FURBS which could result in the employer receiving a payment from the FURBS means that the income of the FURBS may be treated as the income of the employer. In such a situation, income tax is chargeable under Case VI of Schedule D and so, if the employer is a company, would be charged at the rate of corporation tax. The employer would be entitled to recover the amount of the tax paid from the trustees so effectively the trustees would end up paying income tax at a higher rate. [*ICTA 1988, s 660D*].

Income of the FURBS will not be treated as the income of the employer if a payment can be made only in the event of the bankruptcy of the beneficiary or an assignment or charge being made or given by a beneficiary. [*ICTA 1988, s 660A(4)*]. However, the Revenue may argue that even retaining the possibility of a payment in these limited circumstances means that the FURBS is not established for the sole purpose of providing relevant benefits. As a consequence the additional rate of tax applicable to trusts would be payable.

If an employee pays contributions to a FURBS, he may be treated as a settlor. If he were entitled to receive a benefit from the FURBS (which he almost certainly would be) a proportional part of the income would be treated as the employee's income and taxed at his marginal rate. The employee would be entitled to recover the tax he pays from the trustees so the trustees would end up paying income tax at the employee's marginal rate.

Capital gains tax

14.18 Trustees will be liable for capital gains if a majority of them are, or are

14.19 *Unapproved arrangements*

ordinarily, resident in the UK and the general administration of the trust is ordinarily carried on in the UK. If either of these conditions is not met, the trustees will not be liable for capital gains tax under *section 69* of the *Taxation of Chargeable Gains Act 1992* (but see 14.33 below for special conditions relating to off-shore arrangements).

Trustees used to be liable for Capital Gains Tax ('CGT') at the same rate as they were liable for income tax. [*Taxation of Chargeable Gains Act 1992, s 5*]. However a significant change was made to this in the March 1998 Budget. *Section 5* of the *Taxation of Chargeable Gains Act 1992* was repealed by the *Finance Act 1998* with effect from 1998–99 and all subsequent years of assessment. The *Finance Act 1998* added a new Schedule A1 to the *Taxation of Chargeable Gains Act 1992* to reflect the change in the CGT.

The rate of CGT payable on disposals by trustees was, from 6 April 1998, changed to 34 per cent subject to a tapering relief, reducing the amount of CGT payable on assets held over the longer term. This tapering relief replaced the previous indexation relief (which now applies only to the gain made up to 6 April 1998). For disposals from 6 April 2004, the rate of CGT payable by trustees was increased to 40 per cent bringing the rate into line with that payable by an individual.

Trustees are entitled to one half of the personal annual exemption. [*Taxation of Chargeable Gains Act 1992, Sch 1*]. So for the tax year 2004/2005, the first £4,100 of gains will be exempt.

Inheritance tax

14.19 The current inheritance tax regime imposes a charge to inheritance tax on the value of all 'relevant property' on each tenth anniversary of the establishment of a trust and on the value of any payment made out of a trust. However, under *section 58* of the *Inheritance Taxes Act 1984*, assets held by a FURBS will not be 'relevant property' if the FURBS is a 'sponsored superannuation scheme' as defined in *section 624* of *ICTA 1988*. To fall within the definition, the FURBS:

(*a*) must relate to service in particular offices or employments;

(*b*) must be intended to make provision for retirement or death benefits; and

(*c*) part of the cost of providing the benefits must be borne by someone other than the person who receives the benefits.

At first sight, most FURBS would appear to fit easily within the definition of a sponsored superannuation scheme. However, as contributions made by an employer for the purposes of providing relevant benefits are deemed to be the income of the employee (see 14.16(b) above) the employee is treated as having borne the cost of providing the benefits. The third limb of the definition will be satisfied if the costs of setting up and/or running the FURBS are separately identifiable. The Revenue consider such costs to be part of the cost of providing the benefits and, as the employee will not be taxed on them, they will be borne by someone other than the person who receives them. A FURBS should, therefore, be exempt from the potential inheritance tax charge if the administration and/or establishing costs are separately identifiable and the employee does not pay income tax on them. Where several employers participate in a FURBS it does not matter how they allocate the costs.

Reporting requirements

14.20 The administrator of the FURBS should prepare accounts for submission to the relevant tax office so that the appropriate assessments to income tax and capital gains tax may be made. The Revenue may request any additional information it requires regarding the FURBS. The administrator is under a duty to give the information required within any time limit specified in the notice requesting the information. [*ICTA 1988, s 605(4)*].

Money and assets coming out of the FURBS

Benefits on retirement

14.21 *Prima facie*, any benefit provided by an unapproved arrangement is taxable in the year of receipt. [*ITEPA 2003, s 394(1)*]. However, under *section 396* of *ITEPA 2003* (read with *sections 395(2)* and *(4)* of the *Act*), income tax is not payable if:

(*a*) the benefit takes the form of a cash lump sum;

(*b*) the employer has made payments to the scheme with a view to the provision of relevant benefits;

(*c*) the employee has been assessed to tax in respect of the sums paid;

(*d*) all of the income and gains accruing to the Scheme are brought into charge to tax; and

(*e*) the lump sum is paid to the employee or to the employee's spouse, children, dependants, personal representatives, ex-spouse or any individual designated by the employee.

If a pension is provided from the FURBS, either directly or by the purchase of an annuity, income tax will be payable on the full amount of each instalment. If an annuity is required, it is more tax efficient for the employee to receive a lump sum from the FURBS and then purchase an annuity himself. Under *section 656* of *ICTA 1988*, tax is only payable on the interest element of a 'purchased life annuity'. An annuity purchased by an individual falls within the definition of a purchased life annuity but an annuity purchased by a sponsored superannuation scheme does not.

If the provisions of *section 396* of *ITEPA 2003* do not apply (for example, because the benefit is paid to an organisation or trust rather than an individual, or to an individual who does not fall within one of the permissible categories)

14.22 *Unapproved arrangements*

income tax will be payable. If the benefit is paid to an individual, that individual is liable to tax, chargeable by virtue of *Chapter 2* of *Part 6* of *ITEPA 2003* (employment income), on the amount received or on the cash equivalent of the benefit if it is not paid in cash [*ITEPA 2003, s.394(1)*]. If the benefit is not paid to an individual, the administrator of the FURBS is liable to tax under Case VI of Schedule D at the rate of 40 per cent. [*ITEPA 2003, s 394(2)*]. Authority for deducting this tax from the payment must be included in the rules of the FURBS as there is no statutory authority for doing so.

It is considerably more tax efficient for an individual to receive his benefits from a FURBS in the form of a cash lump sum rather than by way of a pension through the purchase of an annuity. The employee should retain the notices he has been given by his employer regarding the contributions which are chargeable to income tax under *section 386* of *ITEPA 2003* (see 14.16 above) in order to show that he has been assessed to tax and so is not liable to tax on the lump sum benefit he receives.

Benefits on death

14.22 If a FURBS provides a benefit on the death of the employee, it will usually take the form of a cash lump sum equal to the value of the accrued benefit or, possibly, a multiple of earnings (or earnings in excess of the earnings cap). The payment of a lump sum that has been funded in advance (either by way of contributions from the employer or by the payment of an appropriate insurance premium) will not attract an income tax liability provided the conditions of *section 396* of *ITEPA 2003* (read with *sections 395(2)* and *(4)* of that *Act*) are met (see 14.21 above).

Unless the trustees are obliged to follow the employee's direction as to the way in which the lump sum should be paid, the lump sum should not form part of the employee's estate for inheritance tax purposes as he did not have an absolute entitlement to the benefit. [*Inheritance Taxes Act 1984, s 5*]. Consequently, inheritance tax will not be payable. However, the employee's estate should be excluded from the class of potential beneficiaries to avoid the possibility of any dispute with the Revenue.

TAXATION ASPECTS OF AN UURBS

14.23 The tax position of an UURBS is considerably more straightforward than that of a FURBS. As there is no advance funding, the only tax consequences arise when benefits are paid out.

Retirement benefits

Employer's position

14.24 A payment made to an employee under the provision of an UURBS may be deductible for corporation tax purposes on normal principles (see 14.15 above). The payment made must not be excessive, having regard to the service of the employee.

Section 76 of the *Finance Act 1989* will not prevent a deduction as the benefits paid to the employee will be taxable. A corporation tax deduction can only be claimed when the benefits are actually paid; no deduction is, therefore, permissible in respect of a notional payment to a book reserve scheme.

Employee's position

14.25 If the benefit payable from an UURBS takes the form of a pension, the pension will be taxed as employment income at the employee's highest marginal rate. [*ITEPA 2003, s.394*].

If the benefit payable from an UURBS takes the form of a lump sum paid to an individual, the recipient will be liable to income tax, chargeable on the amount received, or if the benefit is not paid in cash, on the cash equivalent of the benefit. [*ITEPA 2003, s 394(1) and s 398*]. If the lump sum is not paid to an individual, the administrator of the arrangement will be liable to tax under Case VI of Schedule D at the rate of 40 per cent. [*ITEPA 2003, s 394 and s 398*]. Authority for deducting this tax from the payment must be included in the documentation governing the UURBS as there is no statutory authority for making the deduction.

Death benefits

14.26 If an UURBS provides a benefit on the death of the employee, it is likely to take the form of a multiple of earnings (or earnings in excess of the earnings cap). If the recipient of the death benefit is determined at the discretion of someone, for example, the employer, the payment will not normally form part of the employee's estate and so will not be subject to inheritance tax. [*Inheritance Taxes Act 1984, s 5*]. The employee's estate should be excluded from the class of potential beneficiaries to avoid the possibility of any dispute with the Revenue.

The payment of the lump sum will probably attract an income tax liability. Unless the lump sum benefit has been insured, the exemption contained in *section 396* of *ITEPA 2003* will not apply as the employee will not have been assessed to tax on the sum paid by the employer. If the death benefit has been insured the UURBS is, in effect, treated as though it is a FURBS. The employee will have been assessed to income tax in respect of the insurance premiums paid, so income tax should not be payable provided the lump sum is paid to the employee's spouse, children dependants, personal representatives, ex-spouse or any individual designated by the employee (see 14.21, 14.22 above and 14.27 below).

14.27 *Unapproved arrangements*

INSURING DEATH BENEFITS

14.27 Many unapproved schemes aim to provide the benefits an employee would have received had he not been subject to the earnings cap. In the case of a benefit on the death of an employee, this will usually be a multiple of his earnings above the earnings cap. Many employers choose to effect an insurance policy on the employee's life in such circumstances, particularly if the sums involved are substantial. In the case of a FURBS, the policy premiums can be paid by the trustees out of the fund. In the case of an UURBS, the employer may pay the premiums directly or may establish a trust, paying contributions which are sufficient to meet the premiums. In either case the tax position is similar.

Tax position of the employer

14.28 Whether premiums are paid directly by the employer, or via contributions to a trust should have no effect on the tax position of the employer. The expenditure will be deductible on normal principles so long as the expenditure is an income expense incurred wholly and exclusively for the purposes of the trade, profession or vocation of the employer. Essentially the position will be the same as if the employer were contributing to a FURBS (see 14.15 above).

Tax position of the employee

14.29 The payments made by the employer to cover the cost of the insurance premiums will be deemed to be the income of the employee under *section 386(1)* of *ITEPA 2003*. The employee will be taxed at his marginal rate on the payments made.

Beneficiary's tax liability on the payment of the policy proceeds

14.30 Again, the tax position in relation to the beneficiary will be very similar to the position under a FURBS. The payment of the policy proceeds should not attract an income tax liability provided the conditions of *section 396* of *ITEPA 2003* (read with *sections 395(2)* and *(4)* of that *Act*) are met (see 14.21 above).

Unless the trustees are obliged to follow the employee's direction as to the way in which the lump sum should be paid, the lump sum should not form part of the employee's estate for inheritance tax purposes. [*Inheritance Taxes Act 1984, s 5*]. Consequently, inheritance tax will not be payable. However, the employee's estate should be excluded from the class of potential beneficiaries to avoid the possibility of any dispute with the Revenue.

14.33
Employer's tax liability on the payment of the policy proceeds

Proceeds paid to the employer

14.31 If the proceeds of the policy are payable to the employer on the employee's death they may be taxable on general principles as a trading receipt. The Revenue treat each case on its own merits so it is not possible to state with absolute certainty that a tax liability will arise.

If the lump sum death benefit is paid out directly by the employer, and not via any intervening trust, the expenditure will probably be deductible for corporation tax purposes on normal principles (see 14.15 above). The overall tax position should therefore be neutral; the policy proceeds will be a trading receipt but will also be deductible.

Prior to changes introduced by the *Finance Act 2003*, tax was chargeable on any policy 'gains' arising. Under *s .540–547* of *ICTA 1988*, a gain arises on a death, giving rise to a benefit under a life insurance policy. The gain is calculated as the surrender value of the policy immediately before the death plus the value of any benefits previously paid out, less the premiums paid. As the surrender value of a policy is likely to be negligible, the 'gain' is also likely to be negligible in most cases. However, if the insurance policy covers more than one life, the 'gain' on the second death could be substantial as it will include the value of the death benefit paid out on the first death. For this reason, even if there is a group arrangement in place, death benefits have usually been insured on an individual basis. From 9 April 2003, the *Finance Act 2003* amended the relevant provisions of *ICTA 1988* to remove the tax charge on gains arising under certain group life assurance policies, referred to in the legislation as 'excepted group life policies'. In order to qualify as an excepted group life policy, the policy must satisfy a number of specified conditions, including a condition that potential beneficiaries are limited to individuals and charities and a condition that the policy must not be used for tax avoidance. These conditions numbering seven in total, are detailed in *s 539A* of *ICTA 1988*. The *Finance Act 2003* also provided that the tax charge would no longer apply to policies providing benefits solely on death or disability ('pure protection group life policies') before 9 April 2003 and that an existing policy which was amended prior to 6 April 2004, in order to satisfy the new conditions, would qualify for the exemption retrospectively from 9 April 2003.

Proceeds paid to trustees

14.32 If the policy has been effected by trustees, the proceeds of the policy will be paid to trustees rather than the employer, and the employer's tax position will be neutral; he will not have any tax liability and will not be able to claim any deduction.

OFFSHORE ARRANGEMENTS

14.33 In the early 1990s many advisers were advocating the use of offshore arrangements to maximise investment growth on the basis that non-UK resident trustees would not be liable to income tax on their non-UK income nor would

14.34 *Unapproved arrangements*

they be liable to UK capital gains tax. Anti-avoidance legislation is generally not applicable to a FURBS and so offshore arrangements seemed an attractive option.

In his 1993 budget speech, the Chancellor indicated that he intended to close this 'loophole' by taxing beneficiaries on the difference between benefits paid out and contributions paid in. The *Finance Act 1994* amended *ICTA 1988* in relation to benefits paid out from any FURBS which was established (or varied so as to allow the payment) after 1 December 1993. As a consequence, the recipient of a benefit from an offshore FURBS is liable to income tax, at his highest marginal rate, on any income and gains of the FURBS which have not already been taxed. [*ITEPA 2003, s 397(1)*]. As the employee's marginal rate is likely to be higher than the rate UK-resident trustees would have paid, offshore FURBS are no longer an attractive option in most cases.

Care should be taken before amending any offshore arrangements established prior to 1 December 1993 so as not to fall inadvertently within the ambit of the legislation referred to above.

FINAL SALARY FURBS

14.34 Although a FURBS is not a natural vehicle for providing final salary benefits, it is possible to have a final salary FURBS. If the pensions promise is such that on his retirement an employee will be entitled to the same benefits he would have been entitled to had he not been subject to the earnings cap, the FURBS will usually be 'integrated' with any approved scheme. Thus the payment from the FURBS will be calculated by deducting the benefits provided by the approved scheme from the total benefit the employee would have received if he were not subject to the earnings cap. This will give the amount of notional pension which the FURBS must provide. As it is more tax efficient to provide a lump sum than a pension, the notional pension will have to be converted into a lump sum. This conversion can be left to the discretion of an actuary, or can be tied into annuity rates at the date of retirement, although if the latter approach is adopted, the problems of funding will be exacerbated due to possible changes in annuity rates. Finally, an adjustment will have to be made to allow for the tax free nature of the lump sum.

In such a scenario, benefits from the approved scheme should be augmented up to Inland Revenue limits for maximum tax efficiency and the FURBS should be funded accordingly. If the FURBS provides a greater benefit than is required, the benefits payable from the approved scheme could be adjusted rather than providing the employee with the windfall. For this reason it is advisable to augment benefits from the approved scheme on retirement rather than on establishment of the FURBS.

The main problem with providing final salary benefits via a FURBS is that funding can be difficult to predict. As it is inadvisable for an employer to retain an interest in a FURBS (see 14.15 and 14.17 above) any surplus will have to be paid to the employee or retained within the FURBS. The problem can, to an extent, be overcome by adjusting the benefits payable from the approved scheme. At the other end of the spectrum, if the FURBS is underfunded the employer may have to make a large payment to top-up the arrangement which, in turn, will result in a large tax charge on the employee. To an extent this problem could be overcome by the employer providing most of the benefit through a FURBS with the balance being paid via an UURBS. As it is important to minimise the potential for either a surplus or a deficit, overly cautious assumptions should not be used and regular reviews of funding should be conducted.

If a group final salary FURBS is to be used, problems with funding may be smoothed out to an extent as any surplus generated when benefits are paid out to one employee can be used to provide benefits for another employee. However, the tax position can be quite complicated. Separate calculations will have to be made in respect of each member to ascertain the appropriate contributions and it is on these contributions that each individual will be charged to income tax under *section 386* of *ITEPA 2003*. If the employee is meeting the tax liability, he will obviously want the full contributions on which he has paid tax to be used for his benefit; in short, he will want the benefit of any surplus contributions himself rather than see them be used for someone else. If a group final salary FURBS is to be used successfully, the employer will almost certainly have to operate some form of grossing-up arrangement to ensure that an employee does not end up paying tax in respect of contributions ultimately used to provide benefits for someone else.

INVESTMENT AND IMPLICATIONS OF THE FINANCIAL SERVICES AND MARKETS ACT 2000

14.35 There are no statutory restrictions placed on trustees of FURBS in terms of what type of 'investments' they can invest in. However, as trustees they will still be subject to general trust law principles regarding investment (see chapter 10). The trust deed establishing the FURBS should give the trustees a power of investment which is sufficiently wide to allow for the investments intended. When establishing the trust, the employer could restrict the investment power if he wished to prevent the trustees from investing in certain types of investment.

Trustees may find themselves carrying on investment business within the meaning of the *Financial Services and Markets Act 2000* (*'FSMA 2000'*). Under *FSMA 2000*, a person is treated as carrying on investment business if he manages assets held for the purposes of an occupational pension scheme and those assets include investments (as defined in FSMA 2000). However, this provision will not apply where all decisions, or all day to day decisions, are taken on behalf of the trustees by an authorised person. A further exemption applies if the FURBS is constituted under trust, has twelve or fewer members all of whom are trustees and requires all day-to-day decisions to be taken by all or a majority of the member-trustees. In such a situation, a trustee will not be treated

14.36 *Unapproved arrangements*

as carrying on investment business if he is a beneficiary or potential beneficiary or he takes no day-to-day decisions relating to the management of investments. A FURBS should, therefore, be structured to ensure that all day to day investment decisions are made by authorised persons or by trustees who are also beneficiaries or potential beneficiaries.

NATIONAL INSURANCE CONTRIBUTIONS

14.36 The position of National Insurance contributions ('NICs') in relation to FURBS changed with an announcement by the Secretary of State for Social Security in July 1997. At that time it was announced that it was intended to bring payments into FURBS into the NIC 'net' with effect from April 1999. It was indicated that the Government would be introducing legislation to that effect. The Secretary of State noted that FURBS were being heavily marketed as NIC avoidance devices by paying large NIC-free lump sum bonuses. The proposal would bring NI liability on contributions to FURBS into line with tax liability – they are liable to income tax Schedule E on the member concerned – and bring in extra revenue of £50 million a year.

However, later in 1997, the then Department of Social Security ('DSS') received legal advice that most payments into FURBS were already within the NIC 'net ' (whether or not they were intended as an NI avoidance device). This seems to be based on a wide definition of the term 'earnings' as defined in *section 3(i)(a)* of the *Social Security Contributions and Benefits Act 1992*. Therefore the DSS announced in November 1997 (Contributions Agency Press Release 17 November 1997) that all payments into FURBS on or after 6 April 1998 would be subject to NICs, with no amending legislation being put in place. Despite initial concerns, the DSS did not make NICs retrospective prior to April 1998 unless the FURBS was clearly being used for tax avoidance.

This action by the DSS was rather controversial. A payment into a pension scheme is not normally considered as earnings. If contributions to unapproved pension schemes are 'earnings' that would mean that contributions to approved schemes are also subject to NI.

Primary legislation has not been enacted to bring FURBS into the NI 'net'. Instead Regulations have been enacted clarifying that payments into approved schemes (and generally payments out of both approved and unapproved schemes) are not subject to NI. The relevant regulations are the *Social Security (Contributions) Regulations 2001 (SI 2001 No 1004) (as amended)*. These regulations amend the underlying principal contributions regulations (ie the *Social Security (Contributions) Regulations 1979*).

Therefore, as employers now have to pay NICs on any FURBS contributions, a payment into a FURBS is as expensive for the employer and employee as a direct payment of remuneration. In other words, there are no initial tax or NI advantages into paying into a FURBS instead of paying additional remuneration.

The situation is, however, still not entirely clear. In October 2002 the Inland Revenue indicated in correspondence that it was still reviewing the position but that its view at that time was that payments into a FURBS are 'earnings' for NIC purposes.

When benefits are paid out of the FURBS they should not constitute earnings. Pension payments are expressly excluded from the definition of earnings by the *Social Security (Contributions) Regulations 2001 (SI 2001 No 1004), Sch 3, Part VI, para 1*. If a lump sum payment is made to a member who has retired from gainful employment there will be no National Insurance contributions because the retired employee is not an 'employed earner'. [*Social Security Contributions and Benefits Act 1992, s 2(i)(a)*]. Some FURBS may need to be amended to make it clear that the cash lump sum benefit is commuted pension.

Subject to satisfying certain conditions payments under an UURBS are treated as payments by way of pension and thus not subject to NICs. As no contributions are made to the UURBS prior to payment of benefit, NICs cannot apply before then.

COMPANY LAW IMPLICATIONS

14.37 The Memorandum and Articles of Association of a company which proposes to make voluntary contributions to a FURBS must include a power to make such contributions.

If an employer intends to 'gross-up' contributions to a FURBS by giving the employee the money to pay his tax liability, care should be taken if the employee is a director. This is because a company cannot pay a director remuneration calculated by reference to or varying with the amount of his income tax (see 14.16 above). [*Companies Act 1985, s 311*].

SIMPLIFICATION OF THE TAX TREATMENT OF PENSIONS

14.38 An overview of the new taxation regime for pensions to be introduced from 6 April 2006 can be found in Chapter 5 (see 5.42). The introduction of this regime will have a significant impact on unapproved arrangements (or 'non-registered schemes' as they will be referred to under the new legislation). In view of the flexibility of the new regime to allow for unlimited pensions within registered schemes, with the only limit being on how much tax relief is given, the Government's view is that unapproved arrangements as separate top-up vehicles to provide benefits are no longer essential, unless the aim is to provide benefits that would not be allowed under a registered scheme. Consequently, under the new taxation regime, although unapproved arrangements will be allowed to continue, they will not receive any particular tax-favoured status. Summarised in 14.39 to 14.40 below is the post 5 April 2006 position relating to

14.39 *Unapproved arrangements*

the taxation of unapproved arrangements as it is understood to be from the provisions contained in the Finance Bill published by the Treasury on 8 April 2004.

FURBS

14.39 A summary of the intended post 5 April 2006 taxation position is set out below.

1. The value of an individual's FURBS benefits will not be taken into account for the purpose of the annual and lifetime allowances.

2. Benefits under a FURBS that were accrued before 6 April 2006 may still be payable as a tax-free lump sum provided that the employee was taxed on the contributions paid into the arrangement. If contributions continue to be made to an existing FURBS after 5 April 2006, the emerging lump sum will be apportioned between the pre-6 April 2006 (tax-free) and post 5 April 2006 (taxable) elements.

3. From 6 April 2006, any contributions to a FURBS will be taxed as if made to an employee benefit trust. This means that there will be no income tax or NI contributions payable when contributions are made, but also no corporation tax relief for the employer on those contributions. When the benefits are paid, income tax will be charged and relief from corporation tax given.

4. So long as the employment relationship between employer and employee has ceased, it would appear that there will be no NI charge on the benefits paid under the FURBS, provided that the benefits are within the limits of benefits that can be paid under a registered scheme. As registered schemes will only be able to pay a lump sum of up to a maximum of 25 per cent of the value of the scheme benefits (see 5.42), this means that, in order to avoid any NI charge, no more than 25 per cent of a FURBS fund which has accrued after 5 April 2006 may be paid as a lump sum.

5. The taxation of investment income under trusts (including FURBS) will be aligned with the rate paid by higher rate taxpayers.

UURBS

14.40 A summary of the intended post 5 April 2006 taxation position is set out below.

1. The value of the promise under an UURBS to pay a pension on retirement will not be taken into account for the purpose of the annual and lifetime allowances.

2. The NI position on the payment of benefits will be the same as for a FURBS (see 14.39(4) above).

3. Suitable security for an UURBS will continue to be permissible (see 14.6

above), subject to the individual paying a benefit in kind tax charge on the cost to the employer of providing the security.

4. It will be possible for an UURBS to be consolidated and rolled into a registered scheme. If this is done within three months of 6 April 2006, the increase in the value of benefits in the registered scheme will not count towards the annual allowance, although it will count towards the lifetime allowance.

Chapter 15

Personal pension and stakeholder schemes

INTRODUCTION

15.1 This Chapter describes personal pension schemes, self-invested personal pension schemes and stakeholder schemes. Unless stated otherwise, the descriptions given in this Chapter with regard to personal pension schemes (with the exception of self-invested personal pension schemes) also apply to stakeholder schemes.

The forerunner of the personal pension scheme was the 'retirement annuity contract' ('RAC'). RACs were first introduced in the 1950s. They subsequently became governed by *section 226* of the *Income and Corporation Taxes Act 1970* and consequently are often referred to as *section 226* policies. The most significant distinctions between RACs and personal pension schemes are:

(*a*)   RACs were only available to the self-employed and those in non-pensionable employment (ie broadly speaking, employment where the employer did not provide a pension scheme); an individual could not leave an occupational pension scheme and take out an RAC if he remained employed by the sponsoring employer of that occupational scheme;

(*b*)   an individual's employer is not permitted to contribute to an RAC but can contribute to a personal pension scheme (*ICTA 1988, s 620*); and

(*c*)   insured personal pension schemes allow individuals to contract-out of the Second Tier State Scheme ('S2P') (formerly the State Earnings Related Pension Scheme ('SERPS') via an 'Appropriate Personal Pension Scheme' ('APPS') – there was no such facility under an RAC. [*PSA 1993, s 43(1)*].

Although RACs are still in existence and contributions can still be made to them, it has not been possible to establish a new RAC since 1 July 1988.

Personal pension schemes first became available on 1 July 1988, although the concept of personal pensions was originally brought in by the *Social Security Act 1986*. The main reason for the introduction of personal pensions was to allow individuals who did not have access to a company sponsored group scheme (or who wanted to leave such a scheme whilst still employed by the sponsoring employer ie to 'opt out') the opportunity of building up their own pension entitlement. The power of an employee to leave their occupational scheme whilst remaining an employee was one of the major factors in the pensions mis-selling scandal and has resulted in many Providers of personal pension schemes having to pay substantial compensation in order to re-instate those individuals' mis-sold personal pensions back into their previous occupational schemes. Personal pension schemes were also designed to give individuals the opportunity (at their own volition) to contract-out of SERPS on an individual basis.

The introduction of the concept of the Self-Invested Personal Pension Scheme ('SIPP') in the 1989 Budget has led to individuals having even more choice in retirement provision by giving the member the opportunity to become involved in decisions about the investment of contributions. SIPPs have tended to attract higher earners because of the higher costs of administration and membership and the general complexity of such arrangements. SIPPs are not suitable vehicles for contracting-out and, therefore, if a SIPP member wishes to contract-out of S2P this should be achieved by taking out a separate APPS for this purpose. (Originally, the requirements for a SIPP (in addition to those personal pension requirements already set out in the Revenue Practice Notes) were outlined in Memorandum No. 101 published in October 1989. However, this Memorandum has now been superseded by new Personal Pension Schemes Practice Notes IR76 (2000) and in particular by the *Personal Pension Schemes (Restriction on Discretion to Approve) (Permitted Investments) Regulations 2001 (SI 2001 No 117)* which came into force on 6 April 2001. For more details regarding this Statutory Instrument see 15.51 below.

Personal pension schemes must, like occupational pension schemes, be approved by the IR SPSS if they are to benefit from the full range of tax advantages. The *Finance (No 2) Act 1987* introduced legislation governing the approval and tax treatment of personal pension schemes. This legislation is now consolidated in *sections 630* to *655* of *ICTA 1988*. Although, for many years, it was anticipated that the Inland Revenue would publish a separate set of Practice Notes that would deal specifically with the requirements relating to SIPPs this has not happened. However, the new Practice Notes IR76 (2000) describe in much greater detail than previously the Revenue's specific requirements in relation to SIPPs. Previously, the Personal Pension Schemes Practice Notes were drafted very much from the perspective of insured personal pension schemes. This anomaly has been largely addressed in the current version.

Stakeholder schemes were introduced by the Government in an attempt to considerably increase pension coverage for the UK working population. One of the main driving forces was that stakeholder schemes were to be low cost personal pension schemes. They were originally introduced by the *Welfare Reform and Pensions Act 1999* and the first stakeholder schemes were available from April 2001. It is a requirement that a stakeholder scheme, in order to be recognised as such, has to be registered with Opra and approved by the Inland Revenue. Stakeholder schemes are also approvable under *Chapter IV Part XIV* of *ICTA 1988* in the same way as personal pension schemes. Stakeholder schemes were registrable from 1 October 2000 but they could only commence from 6 April 2001

15.2 *Personal pension and stakeholder schemes*

In order that the Government's objective for stakeholder schemes is met, the *Welfare Reform and Pensions Act 1999* stated that, in many cases, an employer must offer access to a stakeholder pension scheme. This is known as the 'Employer Access Requirement'. Unless exempt, an employer has to select a stakeholder pension scheme that the employees could join if they so wish. Membership of the scheme is not compulsory. In addition an employer does not have to contribute on behalf of the employee. The following is a list of exemptions whereby, if one of them is satisfied, there is no obligation upon the employer to arrange access to a stakeholder scheme:

(*a*) The employer already offers an occupational pension scheme that all staff are eligible to join within one year of commencing work for the employer.

(*b*) The employer employs less than five people. In determining this all employees must be counted which may include company directors (but does not include any self-employed persons). If the employer has five or more employees but fewer than five meet the conditions to have access then these employees must be given access to a stakeholder scheme.

(*c*) If the employer already offers a personal pension scheme providing that the scheme:

   (i) is receiving a contribution from the employer of at least 3 per cent of the employee's basic pay (please note that an employer does not have to count overtime, commission or bonuses when calculating this figure);

   (ii) does not penalise members for ceasing contributions or transferring their entitlements;

   (iii) is offered to every employee who would in law have access to a stakeholder scheme (ignoring anyone under age 18).

This chapter deals with Inland Revenue approved personal pension and stakeholder schemes and many of the conditions and restrictions referred to are as a consequence of the tax legislation.

REVENUE APPROVAL OF THE SCHEME

Personal pension scheme providers

15.2 A personal pension scheme will currently only be approved by the IR SPSS if it is established by a permitted 'Provider' (*ICTA 1988, s 632*). The list shown below applies from 6 April 2001. It also applies to stakeholder schemes established under contract.

   '(*a*) a person who has permission under *Part 4* of the *Financial Services and Markets Act 2000* to effect or carry out contracts of long-term insurance or to manage unit trust schemes authorised under *section 243* of that Act;

   (*b*) an EEA firm of the kind mentioned in paragraph 5(d) of Schedule 3 to the Financial Services and Markets Act 2000 which:

(i) has permission under paragraph 15 of that Schedule (as a result of qualifying for authorisation under paragraph *12* of that Schedule) to effect or carry out contracts of long-term insurance; and

(ii) fulfils any one of the requirements under subsections (5), (6) or (7) of section 659B of ICTA 1988;

(c) a firm which has permission under paragraph 4 of Schedule 4 to the Financial Services and Markets Act 2000 (as a result of qualifying for authorisation under paragraph 2 of that Schedule) to manage unit trust schemes authorised under section 243 of that Act;

(d) a person who qualifies for authorisation under Schedule 5 to the Financial Services and Markets Act 2000;

(e) a building society within the meaning of the Building Societies Act 1986;

(f) a person falling within section 840A(1)(b) of ICTA 1988;

(g) a body corporate which is a subsidiary or holding company of a person falling within section 840A(1)(b) of ICTA 1988, or is a subsidiary of the holding company of such a person;

(h) an institution which

(i) is an EEA firm of the kind mentioned in paragraph 5(a), (b) or (c) of Schedule 3 to the Financial Services and Markets Act 2000;

(ii) qualifies for authorisation under paragraph 12(1) or (2) of that Schedule, and

(iii) has permission under that Act to manage portfolios of investments.

(1) The Board may approve a personal pension scheme established by any person other than a person mentioned in subsection (1)(a) to (h) if the scheme is established under a trust or trusts.

(2) In subsection (1)(a) above "contracts of long-term insurance" means contracts which fall within Part II of Schedule 1 to the Financial Services and Markets Act 2000 (Regulated Activities) Order 2001.

(3) In subscription (1)(g) above "holding company" and "subsidiary" are to be construed in accordance with section 736 of the Companies Act 1985 or Article 4 of the Companies (Northern Ireland) Order 1986.

(4) Subsection (1) above shall not apply in relation to a scheme approved by the Board by virtue of section 620(5) of the Income and Corporation Taxes Act 1988 if it was established before 1 July 1998.

(5) The Treasury may by order amend this section as it has effect for the time being.

(i) an EEA firm of the kind mentioned in paragraph 5(d) of Schedule 3 to the Financial Services and Markets Act 2000 which

    (i) has permission under paragraph 15 of that Schedule (as a result of qualifying for authorisation under paragraph 12 of that Schedule) to effect or carry out contracts of long-term insurance; and

    (ii) fulfils any one of the requirements under subsections (5), (6) or (7) of section 659B of the Income and Corporation Taxes Act 1988;

(j) a firm which has permission under paragraph 4 of Schedule 4 to the Financial Services and Markets Act 2000 (as a result of qualifying for authorisation under paragraph 2 of that Schedule) to manage unit trust schemes authorised under section 243 of that Act;

(k) a person who qualifies for authorisation under Schedule 5 to the Financial Services and Markets Act 2000;

(l) a person who has permission under Part 4 of the Financial Services and Markets Act 2000 to accept deposits other than

    (i) a building society within the meaning of the Building Societies Act 1986,

    (ii) a friendly society within the meaning of section 116 of the Friendly Societies Act 1992,

    (iii) a society registered as a credit union under the Industrial and Provident Societies Act 1965 or the Credit Unions (Northern Ireland) Order 1985, or

    (iv) an insurance company within the meaning of section 659B(1)

or a body corporate which is a subsidiary or holding company of such a permitted person

(m) an institution which

    (i) is a European institution within the meaning of regulation 3(1) of the Banking Co-ordination (Second Council Directive) Regulations 1992, and

    (ii) in conformity with the conditions and requirements of those Regulations, carried on in the United Kingdom, through a branch established in the United Kingdom for that purpose, or by the provision of services, any activity falling within item 1, 7 or 11 of the list of activities contained in Schedule 1 to those Regulations.

(n) In the case of a personal pension scheme established under a trust or trusts, a person not falling within any of the above categories.' [*ICTA 1988, s 632*]

The Administrator

15.3 In addition, the IR SPSS also require there to be a person resident in the United Kingdom who is responsible for the management and administration of the scheme. [*ICTA 1988, s 638(1)*]. This person, known as the administrator, can be any corporate body or individual appointed for the purpose, including the Provider, an employee of the Provider or the trustees of a scheme established by trust.

Applying for approval

Personal pension schemes

15.4 The Provider of a personal pension scheme must apply to the IR SPSS on the appropriate form (PSPP101) to have the scheme approved. Approval is granted under *Chapter IV* of *Part XIV* of *ICTA 1988*.

In order to obtain IR SPSS approval, it is necessary (under *section 633* of *ICTA 1988*) to satisfy the IR SPSS that the sole purpose of the scheme is the provision of benefits on retirement or death (see 15.10 below) and to comply with the IR SPSS's requirements relating to how these benefits are provided. The IR SPSS has published new Model Rules (coded IMR 2003) for personal pension schemes and, if these are incorporated in full without amendment, the scheme will usually be granted approval very quickly.

There are four versions of IMR 2003. These are:

(*a*) IMR 2003 (this covers all types of schemes);

(*b*) IMR 2003 PP (abridged version – cannot be used for contracted-out personal schemes or stakeholder schemes);

(*c*) IMR 2003 CO (to be used by contracted-out personal pension schemes (but not stakeholder));

(*d*) IMR 2003 SHP (to be used by contracted-out personal pension schemes that are also stakeholder schemes).

If a SIPP is being established the documentation will need to include the relevant additional provisions for conditions applicable to SIPPs in addition to the Model Rules. A version of IMR 2003 should be adopted and in place by 6 April 2004 if, for no other reason, to demonstrate compliance with the *Personal Pension Sharing (Restriction on Discretion to Approve) (Permitted Investments) Regulations 2001 (SI 2001 No. 117)*. However, the "concession" given in Update 144 for schemes already operating with IMR 2000 (ie that IMR 2003 did not have to be adopted by 6 April 2004) appeared to be withdrawn by Update 146. Providers and trustees should, if operating on IMR 2000 seek legal advice regarding the requirement to adopt IMR 2003.

Schemes still operating on the 1995 Model Rules must have adopted a version of IMR 2003 by 6 April 2004.

15.5 *Personal pension and stakeholder schemes*

Various documents have to be prepared when establishing a tax approved personal pension scheme. The IR SPSS has relaxed the amount of documents it requires to review when making application for tax approval but, of course, the IR SPSS expects that the rest of the documentation used in connection with the personal pension scheme fully satisfies the requirements of IR76 (2000). The following list indicates the documents required for a personal pension scheme being established on or from 6 April 2001:

(a) the instruments showing the arrangements between the Provider and the member (including any master trust deed adopting the Model Rules IMR 2000);

(b) a Contributions Payment Certificate ('CPC') for self-employed members and employed earners;

(c) the member's application form (please note this no longer needs to include a Certificate of Eligibility providing the first contribution is made on or after 6 April 2001). It should be noted that the IR SPSS has increased its requirements with regard to the wording of the Application Form and the new Practice Notes IR76 (2000) include Appendix 19, which is a checklist of the basic requirements of the Form and Appendix 20, which is a checklist for a transfer-in Application Form;

(d) the member's booklet or other form of member literature;

(e) the member's transfer application form if appropriate.

If anyone knowingly makes a false statement on making an application for approval of a personal pension scheme or for the purpose of obtaining relief from or repayment of tax, a penalty not exceeding £3,000 may be imposed. [*ICTA 1988, s 653*].

Stakeholder schemes

15.5 Unlike personal pension schemes, a stakeholder scheme can be considered to be either an occupational scheme (where, as a consequence, the majority of the *Pensions Act 1995* would then apply) or a personal pension scheme. This is because a stakeholder scheme can either be established on a contract basis or a trust basis. If a trust basis is selected then most of the *Pensions Act 1995* applies. Where a stakeholder scheme has been established purely for a specific employer or group of employers then occupational pension scheme rules will apply. In the majority of cases stakeholder schemes will be established under contract and, because the majority of individuals and employers are likely to be joining a scheme already set up by a financial institution (eg an insurance company) the scheme will be governed by a Deed (as is sometimes also the case for personal pension schemes where the Provider is an insurer and the investments under the scheme consist purely of insurance products) or a Board Resolution. Careful consideration would need to be given when establishing a stakeholder scheme under trust because much of the regulatory framework that some employers will be trying to avoid by not establishing a pure occupational pension scheme will, in fact, apply equally to a trust based stakeholder scheme. For example, a trust based stakeholder scheme needs to appoint a scheme auditor and the requirement to ensure that there is suitable diversification of investments as described in the *Pensions Act 1995*. Industry wide stakeholder schemes must be established under trust.

When making an application for a stakeholder scheme the applicant needs to obtain the standard application pack for 'Establishing a Stakeholder Pension Scheme' from the IR SPSS (this is also available on their web site). If the stakeholder scheme is also to be used for the purposes of contracting-out then the appropriate forms for this also need to be obtained. As stated previously registration for stakeholder schemes commenced from 1 October 2000 but the effective date of approval could not have been earlier than 6 April 2001. The IR SPSS had discretion to issue approval notices before 6 April 2001 but this did not mean that the stakeholder scheme could be operated before 6 April 2001. There is also a standard stakeholder registration application that the applicant needs to complete and send to Opra. The governing rules for stakeholder schemes are, as with personal pension schemes, IM3 2003.

Once the registration forms to both the IR SPSS and Opra have been submitted, if the IR SPSS decides that the scheme is approvable they will then consult with Opra and then either confirm to the applicant that the scheme qualifies as a stakeholder scheme or, alternatively, that it does not and refuse the application. In the event of the application being refused it is not a question of simply amending the application already made – a fresh application for registration would have to be submitted in these circumstances. As with personal pension schemes if the scheme is approved the IR SPSS will inform FICO (the Financial Intermediaries and Claims Office). FICO will then issue the appropriate tax repayment claims forms to the administrator. The IR SPSS will also inform the appropriate Tax Offices for both the Provider and the administrator that approval has been granted.

MEMBERSHIP OF A PERSONAL PENSION SCHEME AND STAKEHOLDER SCHEME

Conditions for membership

15.6 An individual may become a member of a personal pension scheme or stakeholder scheme only if he has not attained age 75. With effect from 6 April 2001 it is no longer essential that an individual always has 'net relevant earnings' in order to make contributions to a personal pension scheme (IR76 (2000) PN 3.7). This means that any individual who is under age 75 and is either:

(*a*) resident and ordinarily resident in the UK at sometime in the relevant tax year; or

(*b*) a Crown Servant; or

(*c*) the spouse of a Crown Servant.

15.7 Personal pension and stakeholder schemes

may, subject to requirements relating to a person who is also accruing benefits under a tax-approved occupational personal pension scheme, contribute up to what is known as the 'earnings threshold'. The 'earnings threshold' is defined in *section 630(1)* of *ICTA 1988* and, for the tax year 2002/2003 is £3,600. This figure may be amended each year by a Treasury Order. If the individual does not have any 'relevant earnings' or does not fall under the concession described above, he may become a member of a personal pension scheme so that it can receive a transfer payment, but in this situation, no contributions can be made to the scheme by or in respect of the individual until he has 'relevant earnings'.

Concurrency

15.7 With effect from 6 April 2001, there are provisions (IR76 (2000) PN 3.16g) in force relating to what is known as 'concurrency'. ie where a person accrues benefits under an occupational pension scheme and, at the same time, is permitted to pay contributions to a personal pension scheme. The individuals that are permitted to do this must fall under at least one of the following categories.

The individual:

(a) is being provided with death in service benefits only under the occupational pension scheme; or

(b) is joining the personal pension scheme solely for the purpose of contracting-out of S2P; or

(c) can satisfy all of the following requirements in relation to the year in question:

  (i) at some time in the year, the individual is either resident and ordinarily resident in the UK, or is overseas, a Crown Servant or the spouse of a Crown Servant;

  (ii) is not, and has not been a 'controlling director' of a company at any time in the year or in any of the five tax years preceding it (note: tax years prior to 2000/2001 do not count); and

  (iii) in at least one of the five tax years preceding the year in question, the individual has had an 'aggregate grossed up remuneration' not exceeding the 'remuneration limit' for that earlier year (again, tax years prior to 2000/2001 do not count). (The 'remuneration limit' is described in *section 632B(4)* of *ICTA 1988* and is currently equal to £30,000. As with the earnings threshold this figure may be amended by Treasury Order).

An individual who satisfies the above conditions is then permitted to contribute to a personal pension scheme up to the earnings threshold. Another important concession here is that where concurrent membership takes place in accordance with these provisions then the individual's personal pension scheme benefits can be ignored when assessing his or her maximum benefits (in accordance with Inland Revenue limits) under the occupational scheme. A member of a personal pension scheme must immediately notify the scheme administrator if they join an occupational pension scheme. If this notification is not given at the time of joining it must be given the next time they make a contribution to the personal pension scheme.

In relation to a new stakeholder scheme the following employees are not entitled to access to a stakeholder scheme even where the employer has a basic obligation to provide a stakeholder scheme for certain of its employees, ie where that employee:

(a) is already a member of the employer's occupational pension scheme; or

(b) has worked for the employer for less than three months in a row; or

(c) has not been able to join the occupational scheme of the employer solely because the scheme does not permit employees under the age of 18 or where the employee is already within five years of that scheme's normal pension age; or

(d) has earnings that have fallen below the National Insurance lower earnings limit for a period of one or more weeks within the last three months; or

(e) would have been eligible to join the occupational pension scheme but has opted not to; or

(f) is not eligible to join a stakeholder scheme because an Inland Revenue condition means he is not eligible.

The employer is obliged to discuss with eligible employees and any representative organisations the employer's plans for the stakeholder pension scheme. There is flexibility here in how this is achieved, for example, by way of a meeting or by giving details in writing and then asking for feedback. Once the consultation process is completed it is the employer who makes the final decision. The employees may, despite the employer setting up a stakeholder scheme, decide to join a different stakeholder scheme. Of course, if an employee already contributes to another pension scheme that can continue or they may choose to transfer to the employer's new stakeholder scheme.

'Relevant earnings'

15.8 Relevant earnings are defined in *section 644* of *ICTA 1988* as any earned income which is chargeable to income tax for the year of assessment in question and which falls within one of the following categories:

(a) emoluments chargeable under Schedule E from an office or employment held by the individual;

(b) income from any property which is attached to, or forms part of, the emoluments of an office or employment held by him or her;

(c) income chargeable under Schedule D immediately derived from the carrying on or exercise of a trade, profession or vocation (either as an individual or as a partner acting personally or in a partnership);

15.9 *Personal pension and stakeholder schemes*

(d) income from patent rights which is treated as earned income by virtue of *section 529* of *ICTA 1988*.

However, certain elements of remuneration are specifically excluded from the definition of 'relevant earnings', including:

(i) anything arising from the acquisition or the disposal of shares or an interest in shares or from a right to acquire shares or from payments on termination of employment such as redundancy payments or golden handshakes;

(ii) pension benefits in payment;

(iii) benefits paid by the State;

(iv) earnings above the level of the so called 'earnings cap';

(v) earnings from international organisations which are exempt from UK income tax.

Miscellaneous membership requirements

15.9 With the exception of the concurrency rules described above (effective from 6 April 2001) it has always been possible for an individual to be a member of more than one personal pension scheme in respect of the same source of income. However, the additional establishment and administration costs which may be incurred usually do not make this an attractive or viable option. The maximum percentage limit of contributions (see 15.26 below) must be adhered to irrespective of the number of schemes.

If an individual has more than one source of income he may be a member of a personal pension scheme in respect of one source and a member of an occupational pension scheme in respect of another source. Similarly, the individual could enter into several personal pension arrangements, having a separate one for each source of income. In this situation a separate maximum percentage limit of contributions will then apply to each separate occupational/personal pension arrangement.

BENEFITS PAYABLE FROM A PERSONAL PENSION SCHEME

General

15.10 A personal pension scheme is a money purchase scheme (sometimes also known as 'cash accumulation'). The benefits it can provide are determined by the level of contributions paid to it and the amount of investment growth achieved on those contributions. The only control on funding is the level at which contributions may be paid (see 15.25 below). No actuarial calculations and recommendation as to the funding of a personal pension scheme are

Personal pension and stakeholder schemes **15.11**

required. The value of the assets of the scheme at the time of payment of benefits determines the level of benefits to be paid.

The only benefits which a personal pension scheme could provide were, until May 1995, annuities payable to the member on his retirement, annuities payable to his spouse and/or dependants on his death or a lump sum payable on the retirement of the member or on his death. The Inland Revenue impose conditions on the type of annuity which may be provided and on the amount of cash lump sum which can be taken (see 15.12 to 15.15 below). Since May 1995 it has been possible for a member to defer purchasing an annuity and instead make income withdrawals (known as 'income drawdown' or 'income withdrawal') from the scheme (see 15.18 below).

Pension date

15.11 The scheme rules of a personal pension scheme will usually allow the member to choose the date on which he retires but the date must generally not be before age 50 nor after age 75 (*ICTA 1988 s 634*). The date on which a member chooses to receive his benefits is referred to as his 'pension date'. The Inland Revenue will allow a pension date earlier than age 50 if they are satisfied that the member's occupation is one in which people usually retire before age 50. For example, if the IR SPSS are satisfied that a member is a professional athlete, the rules of the scheme may allow the member to choose a pension date of age 35. The following is a list of occupations where the Inland Revenue permit a pension date to be set that is lower than age 50. Certain other conditions do also apply (see Appendix 10 of IR76 (2000)).

PROFESSION OR OCCUPATION	RETIREMENT AGE
Athletes	35
Badminton players	35
Boxers	35
Cricketers	40
Cyclists	35
Dancers	35
Divers (saturation, deep sea and free swimming)	40
Footballers	35
Golfers	40
Ice hockey players	35
Jockeys – flat racing	45
Jockeys – national hunt	35
Members of the reserve forces	45
Models	35
Motor cycle riders (motocross or road racing)	40

15.12 *Personal pension and stakeholder schemes*

PROFESSION OR OCCUPATION	RETIREMENT AGE
Motor racing drivers	40
Rugby league/union players	35
Skiers (downhill)	30
Snooker/billiards players	40
Speedway riders	40
Squash players	35
Table tennis or tennis (including real tennis players)	35
Trapeze artists	40
Wrestlers	35

Annuity payable to a member

15.12 Before his pension date a member will need to take advice about annuity rates and decide how much of the fund he wishes to take as tax-free cash (see 15.13 below). The remaining fund will be used to purchase an annuity (*ICTA 1988 s 634*; see also IR76 (2000) PN 9.2–PN 9.8) The annuity purchased for the member must satisfy the following conditions:

(*a*) it must be payable by an authorised insurance company situated within the European Union which may be chosen by the member. (The member is not obliged to choose the Provider of the scheme (assuming, of course, the Provider is an insurance company) as the insurance company which provides the annuity, although the rules of a scheme may require this);

(*b*) from September 2002 members of a personal pension scheme or stakeholder scheme must be told of the existence of an Open Market Option as well as the general advantages and disadvantages of exercising the option, how the option is exercised and the advisability of seeking professional advice; this is not pertinent to a Self Invested Personal Pension Scheme;

(*c*) it must commence on the member's pension date, although it may commence earlier if the member retires due to ill-health, and must be payable for life;

(*d*) it may be guaranteed for a specified term not exceeding ten years (although it is more usual for a five year period to be selected), so that it continues to be paid at the full rate in the event of the member's death during that term or the equivalent of that amount is paid as a lump sum upon the death of the member;

(*e*) it must not be capable of assignment or surrender; the only exception to this is that an annuity which has a guarantee period may be assigned on the death of a member by his will;

(*f*) it may increase in line with the retail prices index or at a fixed percentage per annum or remain at the same level ie 'static' throughout the period of payment; and

Personal pension and stakeholder schemes **15.13**

(g) it may be payable in advance or in arrears and may be of any frequency of payment.

Tax free cash lump sum payable to the member

15.13 A member may elect to receive part of his benefit in the form of a tax-free cash lump sum, (IR76 (2000) PN 9.41–PN 9.56) If a member wishes to receive a lump sum he must make an election to that effect before his pension date. A cash lump sum is payable subject to the following conditions:

(a) it must be paid at the same time as the balance of the fund is used to provide the annuity;

(b) it must not exceed 25 per cent of the total value of the fund, and in this regard there is a distinction depending on when the scheme was established; in respect of schemes established before 27 July 1989:

- if the arrangement includes separate provision for a spouse's or dependant's annuity, the fund accumulated to provide these benefits must be excluded from the total value of the fund; and

- the total amount of lump sum available is restricted to £150,000 (*FA 1989, Sch 7*); and

- if the scheme is an APPS the protected rights provided by the scheme may be included in the value of the fund for the purpose of calculating the amount of the lump sum available, but only that part of the fund which does not constitute protected rights may be used to provide the lump sum (consequently a member who has an APPS which is used solely for the purpose of contracting-out will not be able to take a cash lump sum from it);

- a smaller maximum amount than 25 per cent may be imposed if a transfer payment has been made to the personal pension scheme from an occupational pension scheme and a controlling director or high earner has been subject to the certification requirements of the *Personal Pension Schemes (Transfer Payments) Regulations 1988 (SI 1988 No 1014*, now covered under the *Personal Pension Schemes (Transfer Payments Regulations 2001(SI 2001 No 119)*. This Statutory Instrument limits the amount of tax free cash available under the personal pension scheme to the amount of cash that would have been available to the individual under the occupational pension scheme

(c) in respect of schemes established after 27 July 1989, if the scheme is an APPS, the protected rights provided by the scheme cannot be used for the purposes of calculating the amount of the lump sum. (See *ICTA 1988, s 635* and IR76 (2000));

(d) Pensions Update Number 135 (20 December 2002) allows, in limited circumstances, more than one lump sum to be paid under the same personal pension scheme; this can occur where:

15.14 *Personal pension and stakeholder schemes*

(i) there has been pensions mis-selling; or

(ii) where it is necessary to comply with a Court order.

The IR SPSS allow, as a result of a second lump sum being paid, a realignment or adjustment of the annuity or income drawdown already in payment.

Annuity payable after the death of the member

15.14 If a member dies before electing to take his benefits from the scheme, annuities may be provided by the scheme for the member's spouse and/or dependants (*ICTA 1988, s 636* and IR76 (2000) Part 10). Alternatively, when a member reaches his pension date he may choose to make provision for the payment of an annuity to his spouse and/or dependants. In either case an annuity payable after the death of the member is subject to the following conditions:

(*a*) it must be payable by an authorised insurance company situated within the European Union which may be chosen by the member or the person in respect of whom the annuity is being purchased ('the annuitant');

(*b*) the annuitant must be the member's spouse or a person who was a 'dependant' of the member at the date of the member's death (a 'dependant' need not be a relative but he or she must be regarded as being financially dependent on the member; a child of the member who is under age 18 or undergoing full-time education or vocational training will always be considered to be a dependant);

(*c*) if the member dies before his pension date, the aggregate annual amount of all annuities payable to the spouse and any dependants must not exceed the highest amount of annuity that would have been payable to the member if his pension date had been the date of his death;

(*d*) where the member dies after his pension date, the aggregate annual amount of all annuities payable to the spouse and any dependants must not exceed the annual amount of the annuity that was being paid to the member at the date of his death;

(*e*) it may be guaranteed for a specified term not exceeding ten years so that it continues to be paid at the full rate in the event of the annuitant's death during that term;

(*f*) it must not be capable of assignment or surrender; the only exception to this is that an annuity which has a guarantee period may be assigned on the death of an annuitant by his will;

(*g*) it may increase in line with the retail prices index or at a fixed percentage per annum or remain at the same level ie 'static' throughout the period of payment;

(*h*) it may be payable in advance or in arrears and may be of any frequency of payment;

(*j*) it must generally be payable for life but, in the case of an annuity payable to a spouse, payment may cease on the re-marriage of the annuitant (this is becoming increasingly less common); if the annuity is payable to a child, payment should cease when the child reaches 18 or ceases to be in full-time education or vocational training.

A spouse who, whilst under age 60, becomes entitled to an annuity on the death of a member may elect to defer purchasing the annuity until, at the latest, she or he reaches age 60. This facility is particularly useful where the spouse is relatively young when the member dies and the annuity that could be purchased at that time would produce little income. Where the purchase of the annuity is deferred under this provision income withdrawal is not permitted (see 15.18 below).

Lump sum payable on the death of the member

15.15 When entering into a personal pension scheme, an individual should decide what element (if any) of his contributions he wishes to use to purchase term assurance (ie life cover). (*ICTA 1988, s 637* and IR76 (2000) PN 4.8) The amount allowable is described in 15.29 below. Any sum assured under a contract purchased from an authorised insurance company can be paid as a lump sum in the event of his death before age 75.

In any event, on the death of a member, any part of the fund not used to purchase an annuity may be paid as a lump sum. The amount of the lump sum must represent no more than a return of the contributions paid by the member (and, where relevant, the member's employer) together with interest at a reasonable rate. However, if the contributions are invested in units under a unit trust scheme the lump sum may represent the sale price of units.

A lump sum can be paid to the member's personal representative, to a beneficiary nominated by the member or at the discretion of the scheme administrator. The conditions relating to a discretionary payment are similar to those which apply in respect of approved occupational pension schemes (see chapter 5).

Clustering

15.16 Annuity rates move in line with changes in yield on medium term gilts. People retiring in early 1999 faced an annuity income of approximately 40 per cent less than those retiring four or five years earlier with the same size of fund and, currently, the position continues to worsen. To minimise these problems it is possible to write a personal pension as a cluster of policies, colloquially known as 'clustering' or 'segmentation'. The vast majority of both insured personal pension schemes and SIPPs offer this feature. Usually, but not always, the number of segments offered is 1,000. This works by allowing segments of the pension policy or slices of the fund in the insured personal pension scheme or SIPP to be encashed each year to provide a combination (if selected) of a tax-free cash lump sum and income withdrawals whilst leaving the remainder to roll-up gross, free in most usual circumstances from inherit-

15.17 *Personal pension and stakeholder schemes*

ance tax should the member die. Using clustering in this way increases the tax efficiency of the whole arrangement and the potential return of capital on death of the member.

INCOME WITHDRAWAL

Background

15.17 Until May 1995, once a member of a personal pension scheme decided to draw his benefits, an annuity had to be purchased at that time from a life office. If annuity rates were low at that time, his resulting pension would be lower (in some cases much lower) than he could have hoped for. This inflexible approach had obvious disadvantages, especially compared with small self-administered schemes (see chapter 13) where the purchase of the annuity could be deferred until age 75. As annuity rates are progressively worsening this difference becomes increasingly more important and, without the introduction of income drawdown, would have meant 'switching' to a personal pension scheme from a small self-administered scheme would have, in all likelihood, become considerably less popular.

The life offices introduced what is known as 'staggered vesting' and managed annuities to get round the problems only to be thwarted by the Inland Revenue. Subsequent lobbying induced the Chancellor to make proposals in his 1994 budget that would allow members of personal pension schemes to defer the purchase of an annuity when they retired to age 75 and withdraw amounts during the period of deferral. These proposals were eventually enacted in *section 58* of, and *Schedule 11* to, the *Finance Act 1995* and came into effect on 1 May 1995.

Since May 1995 those personal pension schemes (including SIPPs) which have adopted suitable rules to offer the facility to defer annuity purchase until, at the latest, age 75 and in the interim permit income withdrawal. Those personal pension schemes which have not adopted rules allowing income withdrawal may only pay the benefits outlined in 15.10 above and so must purchase an annuity on the retirement of the member. Part 9 of IR76 (2000) contains considerable information in relation to all aspects of operating income drawdown. The paragraphs below describe the main points of these conditions.

Income withdrawal by the member

15.18 Income withdrawal is defined as payment of income from a personal pension scheme otherwise than by way of an annuity. [*ICTA 1988, s 630*]. A member's pension date is still the date the member's annuity first becomes payable between age 50 and 75. The link between the cash lump sum benefit and the commencement of the annuity is totally severed permitting the lump sum to be taken, but the purchase of the annuity to be deferred. The lump sum is, however, only payable on the date on which the election to defer the purchase of the annuity takes effect; it may not be taken later.

Personal pension and stakeholder schemes **15.19**

If a member elects to defer purchasing an annuity he must withdraw income from the funds during the period of deferral although not, if he so chooses, in the year the annuity is purchased or in which the member dies. All amounts withdrawn are taxable under Schedule E and the administrator is obliged to deduct payment through the PAYE system.

The amounts withdrawn are subject to maximum and minimum limits. [*ICTA 1988, s 634A*]. The maximum is broadly equivalent to the payments which would be made from a level single life annuity and is calculated by reference to tables provided by the Government Actuary's Department (GAD) for each age and sex. The minimum level of income withdrawal is 35 per cent of the maximum permitted. The calculations take account of the amount of the member's fund available for annuity purchase at pension date with a deduction in the first year for any lump sum benefit paid or to be paid. (*Section 634A(4)* of *ICTA 1998* sets out further conditions.)

Within the maximum and minimum limits, members may choose the level of income withdrawal and vary the amounts from year to year. The scheme administrator is responsible for ensuring withdrawals remain within the limits each year. The initial maximum and minimum withdrawal limits originally applied for the first three years and then were subject to further reviews every three years. The scheme administrator needs to make a fresh calculation (employing the GAD tables) at each specified review date. The calculation is based on the remaining value of the member's fund at that date. The timing of this review is effectively set by what is known as the 'relevant reference date'. There are new provisions in force from 1 October 2000 (known by the Inland Revenue as the 'new rule'), which allow greater relaxation on how the relevant reference date is timed. What is known as a '60 day window' was also brought in from that date. Any personal pension scheme approved on or after 1 October 2000 is allowed to choose whether to operate the old or the new income drawdown rules. Alternatively a combination of these rules can be used.

The Practice Notes IR76 (2000) set out in considerable detail the further requirements relating to income drawdown and, in particular, where income withdrawals are taking place from two or more arrangements at the same time (IR76 (2000) PN 9.21–PN 9.33).

In addition, for the first time, with effect from 14 February 2001, the *Personal Pension Schemes (Transfer Payments) Regulations 2001 (SI 2001 No 119)* permit transfers to be made to and from personal pension schemes where income drawdown has already been triggered under the paying scheme.

Death of a member on or after pension date

Death where an annuity has already been purchased

15.19 Where an annuity has already been bought by a member and the member then dies, an annuity can be paid to a 'survivor'. The Inland Revenue definition of 'survivor' is:

15.20 *Personal pension and stakeholder schemes*

'... a widow, widower or dependant of a member who has died'.

'Dependant' is defined as:

> 'a person who is financially dependent on the member or dependent on the member because of disability or who was so dependent at the time of the member's death or retirement. An ex-spouse of the member who was in receipt of payments from the member up to his or her death in respect of, for example, a financial provision order under the Matrimonial Causes Act 1973 may be regarded as financially dependent on the member. An adult relative who is not, or was not, supported by the member is not that member's dependant.'

IR76 (2000) (within the definition of 'dependant') then continues to describe the Inland Revenue conditions with regard to children and states that, in most circumstances, a pension paid to an adult dependant who '... qualifies on grounds of financial dependency or disability ...' may continue indefinitely.

It is a matter for the Scheme administrators to determine whether a person satisfies the definition of 'dependant'.

In these situations the Revenue do not permit a survivor to request income drawdown. This is not surprising as the annuity has already been purchased by the member.

Death where income drawdown had started

15.20 Where the member has died after receiving income drawdown under an arrangement (there may, of course, be other arrangements under the scheme where no such drawdown has commenced) there are four basic options available. These options are available to the 'survivor'. The options are to:

(*a*) leave purchasing any annuity until a later date (the maximum age for this purchase is age 75);

(*b*) buy an annuity immediately on the open market;

(*c*) take income withdrawals in the interim period and then purchase an annuity at a later date (but no later than age 75 under current rules);

(*d*) take an immediate lump sum from the arrangement. It should be noted that this will be subject to a tax charge of 35 per cent and the lump sum must be paid within two years of the member's death. The only exception to this would be where the lump sum has arisen as a result of a survivor's death where that survivor had been making income withdrawals. It is the responsibility of the scheme administrator to deduct the 35 per cent tax charge. The administrator would then provide for this within the annual tax return. No reclamation of this tax can be made by any of the survivor's beneficiaries.

The same maximum and minimum limits apply to income withdrawal by a spouse or dependant, but the calculations take account of the amount of the fund available at the death of the member. Again the withdrawal limits apply for the first three years from the death of the member and fresh calculations must be made as at the first day of each subsequent three year period.

Even if a spouse's entitlement ceases on remarriage or a dependant's entitlement ceases at age 18 or on cessation of full-time education, he or she may still opt for income withdrawal during the intervening period.

If a spouse or dependant who has chosen to receive income withdrawals dies within two years of the member's death, provided no annuity has been purchased, the remaining balance in the survivor's fund can be paid as a lump sum if the scheme rules permit this. If the spouse or dependant dies more than two years after the member died and an annuity has not been purchased, the balance in the survivor's fund is forfeit and must be used to meet administration expenses of the scheme.

Any lump sum payable to a spouse or dependant following the death of the member is liable to a tax charge of 35 per cent which is payable by the administrator. [*ICTA 1988, s 648B*].

Death of a member before pension date

15.21 In these circumstances, as with death following pension date, there are varying permutations of potential benefit payable. The main factors which cause these variations will be:

- Were there any protected rights under the arrangement?

- Was there provision for a survivor's annuity?

- Was there a survivor?

- Had the arrangement received a transfer from what the Inland Revenue term a 'designated scheme'? The definition of 'designated scheme' encompasses a Retirement Benefits Scheme approved under *Chapter I Part XIV* of *ICTA 1988*, a relevant statutory scheme under *section 611A* of the *ICTA 1988* or a 'Section 32' buy-out policy that holds benefits deriving from an occupational pension scheme.

- Have contributions been paid for term assurance which provides a lump sum on death?

Parts 10.3, 10.4, 10.5, 10.6, and 10.7 of IR76 (2000) describe in full the various benefits that can be paid in the circumstances described above and these are summarised below.

15.22 Personal pension and stakeholder schemes

Was there provision for a survivor's annuity?

15.22 If the answer to this is 'yes' and the member dies leaving a survivor (and where no transfer-in from a designated scheme has been received) a survivor's annuity can be bought using the whole value of the arrangement at the date of death. This is true even if there are protected rights under the arrangement as well. In addition, any term assurance benefits would be paid as a lump sum under a discretionary trust (in most circumstances) on top of the annuity.

Death with survivor but no specific provision for survivor's annuity

15.23 Where no transfer has been received and there is no specific provision for survivor's annuity (for whatever reason) the benefits can be paid in complete lump sum form (subject to conditions described in IR76 (2000) PN 10.3 and PN 10.4). However, this can only be done where:

(a) if there are protected rights there is no 'qualifying survivor' for the purposes of the contracting-out requirement, or there is a 'qualifying spouse' but the maximum pension payable to that spouse amounts to less than £260 per annum;

(b) there are no protected rights;

In the same circumstances as above but where there happens to be an annuity payable to a qualifying survivor with the protected rights, the entire fund can be used to buy a survivor's annuity or can be used for the purposes of income drawdown). 'Entire fund' means the whole of the fund that the member could have used had he survived.

In addition any lump sum life cover can also be paid subject to the terms of the scheme's governing rules.

Had the transfer been received from a designated scheme?

15.24 In these circumstances the basic choices available are that the scheme administrator must, with that part of the member's fund representing a transfer in from a designated scheme, use it either entirely to buy an annuity or annuities for a survivor or survivors (or survivor's income withdrawal) or pay up to one quarter of the transfer amount as a lump sum and use the remainder to buy a survivor's annuity or to be used for the purposes of the survivor receiving income drawdown. In addition there are further detailed requirements set out in the *Personal Pension Schemes (Transfer Payments) Regulations 2001 (SI 2001 No 119)*.

CONTRIBUTIONS

General

15.25 Both a member and his employer may make contributions to a personal pension scheme, but unlike occupational pension schemes, the employer contributing is purely an option not an obligation (this also applies to stakeholder schemes)(IR76 (2000) PN 4.1).

Unless the 'concurrency' rules apply (see 15.6 above), if the personal pension scheme is an APPS and the member is also a member of an occupational pension scheme which is not contracted-out of the S2P the only contributions that can be made are the 'minimum contributions' paid by the NI Contributions Office (see 15.41 below).

When a member's benefit becomes payable either by the purchasing of an annuity or commencing income withdrawal, no further contributions may be paid to the personal pension scheme. [*ICTA 1988, s 638*]. The only exception to this is where the member is under State Pension Age in which case 'minimum contributions' may continue to be paid to accrue further 'protected rights' until the member reaches State Pension Age (see 15.42 below). [*Personal Pension Schemes (Deferred Annuity Purchase)(Acceptance of Contributions) Regulations 1996 (SI 1996 No 805)*].

Maximum contributions

15.26 The position described here applies from 6 April 2001.

Contributions up to the 'earnings threshold'

15.27 Any member can contribute up to the earnings threshold (see 15.6 above) irrespective of their age (providing they are under age 75), whether they have earnings or whether they are currently in an occupational pension scheme (although the conditions as described earlier still have to be met).

Contributions higher than the 'earnings threshold'

15.28 Where more than the earnings threshold is to be paid to a personal pension scheme, the aggregate amount of contributions paid into an approved personal pension scheme by a member and his employer (if applicable) must then not exceed the appropriate percentage of 'net relevant earnings' for the year of assessment as determined in accordance with the table set out below. [*ICTA 1988, s 640(4)*].

15.28 Personal pension and stakeholder schemes

Age on 6 April	Percentage of net relevant earnings
35 or less	17.5
36 to 45	20
46 to 50	25
51 to 55	30
56 to 60	35
61 or more	40

'Net relevant earnings' is defined in *section 646(1)* of *ICTA 1988*. Essentially, it is the amount of an individual's relevant earnings (see 15.8 above) for the tax year in question less certain deductions including any necessary expenses incurred by the individual as part of his job (for example, travelling expenses, subscriptions to professional bodies).

A partner's 'net relevant earnings' are calculated after necessary business expenses and allowances have been deducted from his share of partnership income.

From 6 April 1989, the 'net relevant earnings' of a member are restricted to the 'permitted maximum' or, as it is colloquially known, the 'earnings cap', imposed by *section 590C* of *ICTA 1988*. This is set at £97,200 for the tax year 2002/2003, and is generally increased in line with the retail prices index each year. Any earnings above the earnings cap must be disregarded for the purposes of calculating net relevant earnings. [*ICTA 1988, s 640A*].

From 6 April 2001 there has been a new principle introduced for the purposes of an individual determining their 'net relevant earnings'. This involves the member selecting the 'basis year' for the purposes of calculating their net relevant earnings. The 'basis year' can be the current tax year or any of the previous five tax years. An important point to note here is that the 'basis year' can occur in a year where the member did not have a personal pension scheme but that individual must be able to show that he did have net relevant earnings in that selected year.

This basis can then be used for calculating what can be paid by way of contributions to the personal pension scheme. Once the basis year has been selected that, naturally, is the year that has to be used for determining the net relevant earnings applicable. Their age must be the age on 6 April of the current tax year that the contribution is being paid. Clearly this new mechanism gives a potential advantage to those who have earned more in one of the five previous tax years and, therefore, they are able to pay more by allowable contribution to the personal pension scheme than would have ordinarily be the case. Importantly, this figure can then be used for the purposes of contributions in the following five tax years – not just the first tax year that contributions were paid. A member is permitted to change the basis year where, for example, their net relevant earnings are higher than they were by using the original basis year.

In stakeholder schemes where the employee has asked the employer to make payments by way of the employer's payroll the employer must explain within two weeks and in writing how the payroll deductions will be administered. This would include such things as how often the employer can accept changes (this must be available at least once every six months), how the employee can ask for these contributions to be stopped and how notifying changes in the rate of contribution should be communicated to the employer. If the employer cannot accept a request for a change then the employee must be told in writing. An explanation for the refusal should be given and the employee should be reminded that the employee can cancel the deduction from payroll at any time.

The employee has a variety of choice in relation to how he or she pays ie the basis by which contributions are deducted from their pay. This can be on the basis of a fixed monetary sum that has been agreed between the parties involved or on a percentage of pay. Where the contribution is to be on the basis of a percentage of pay it obviously needs to be determined in advance on what basis 'pay' is to be calculated. This is very similar, of course, to an occupational pension scheme that would contain a clear definition of, for example, 'pensionable salary' so that the employee clearly understands what elements of pay are being counted for contribution purposes and what elements are being ignored.

Application of contributions

Purchase of life assurance

15.29 Before 6 April 2003 contributions of up to five per cent of a member's 'net relevant earnings' for the tax year in question may be used to purchase a term assurance contract to pay a lump sum benefit in the event of the member's death before age 75 (This will often, but not always, be written under discretionary trust so as to mitigate any inheritance tax liability by ensuring that the lump sum does not form part of the member's estate (see also 15.15 above). From 6 April 2001 the position has been altered so that now the amount of life cover that can be bought can not exceed 10% of what the Revenue term 'relevant pension contributions', ie the amount of pension contributions made by the member during the scheme year in question. Further details are given in IR76 (2000) PN 4.14.

Insurance against incapacity – after 6 April 2001

15.30 From 6 April 2001 no individual will be allowed to use any element of contributions to insure against their incapacity where this may lead to a loss of earnings and, therefore, the member would be unable to make contributions. However, if an arrangement to do this was already in place before 6 April 2001 this can continue. This insurance is usually known as 'waiver of contribution'. From 6 April 2001 although it is not possible to provide such insurance within the context of the personal pension scheme itself this can still be arranged but has to be completely separate from the personal pension scheme. Where a pension contract has an option to take out waiver in existence pre 6 April 2001

15.31   *Personal pension and stakeholder schemes*

this option can be exercised after 6 April 2001 but the Revenue will not allow the scheme to exercise the option – only the member will be permitted to do so.

Insurance against incapacity – pre 6 April 2001

15.31   Scheme rules may allow a member to elect that not more than 25 per cent of his contributions shall be applied as a premium under a contract of insurance which provides that:

(*a*)   his contributions and those of an employer will be waived for any period during which, by reason of incapacity, he is unable to work and for the value of benefits to be maintained as though those contributions have been paid;

(*b*)   an annuity payable to a member whose vesting date has been brought forward because of incapacity will not be reduced on that account.

This means that the scheme may include a lifetime or permanent disability insurance which may be paid in the event of permanent and total incapacity. Any contributions used in this way will not qualify for tax relief (see 15.33 below).

Contributions paid in error whilst a member of an occupational pension scheme

15.32   Some individuals may have contributed unwittingly to a personal pension scheme at the same time as being members of an occupational pension scheme (unless the concurrency rules apply) being unaware that they were ineligible to make retirement provision via a personal pension scheme in respect of the same source of earnings. Strictly speaking, any contributions paid to personal pension schemes in these circumstances should be refunded. If an occupational scheme provides only modest lump sum benefits (less than £400 for each year of service), an extra-statutory concession (small lump sum retirement benefits schemes: Extra Statutory Concession A95, 11 October 1996) allows the contributions to remain with the personal pension scheme without affecting the tax reliefs if the following conditions are satisfied:

(*a*)   the member waives entitlement to the lump sum retirement benefit; or

(*b*)   no lump sum retirement benefits accrue; and

(*c*)   the arrangement under the personal pension scheme is not cancelled.

The concession applies only where the occupational schemes rules provide for no such lump sum to accrue in respect of any period during which the member has paid contributions to the personal pension scheme.

From 6 April 2001 if the total contributions paid are greater than the higher of the earnings threshold and the permitted maximum percentage contribution (please see the table in 15.28 above) then all contributions which are not eligible for relief have to be repaid.

TAX TREATMENT

Tax relief for member's contributions

15.33 The position stated here applies from 6 April 2001.

A member can obtain tax relief, at his highest marginal rate, on the contributions he makes to a personal pension scheme. (*ICTA 1988, s 639*) It now does not matter whether the member is an ordinary or higher rate tax payer, all permitted contributions to a personal pension scheme are now treated as being paid net of basic rate tax (*ICTA 1988 s 639(2)(a)*). The administrator of the personal pension scheme must accept the amount paid after this deduction in full discharge of a member's liability and can then recover the amount deducted by making a claim to the Inland Revenue.

If the member is a higher rate tax payer he must claim the remaining amount of relief due to him from his local Inspector. A claim for this relief must be made on Form PP120 or it can be done on the individual's tax return. PP120 can be completed at any time during the tax year.

Employers are permitted to contribute to personal pension schemes (subject to the appropriate limits) and they can claim their tax relief by showing such contributions in their accounts which, as it will be shown in calculating taxable profits will usually be permitted as a deduction under Schedule D. The procedures here are not automatic in the same way as they would be for employee contributions and the employer would need to liaise with his Tax Office in assessing what relief would be made available.

Carrying forward tax reliefs – pre 6 April 2001

15.34 If, in any tax year, the amount of contributions made to all personal pension schemes is less than the allowable maximum, then the balance may be carried forward as 'unused relief' (*ICTA 1988 s 642*). This can then be set off against contributions paid by the individual to personal pension schemes in any of the following six tax years which would otherwise exceed the maximum applicable. Relief will be given for an earlier year before being given for a later year. The ability to carry forward tax relief is not available:

(*a*) in respect of contributions made by an employer of the member; or

(*b*) in any tax year after the member attains age 75.

Carrying forward tax reliefs – after 6 April 2001

15.35 The carrying forward of tax relief is not available after 6 April 2001 although in some situations this may still be possible in limited circumstances. This is discussed in more detail in IR76 (2000) PN 6.41.

15.36 *Personal pension and stakeholder schemes*

Carrying back contributions

15.36 This section discusses the position as applicable from 6 April 2001.

It was also permissible for a member to 'carry back' contributions by electing to have a contribution or part of a contribution treated as having been paid in the tax year immediately preceding that in which it was actually paid (or, if there are no 'net relevant earnings' in that year, in the previous year). (*ICTA 1988 s 641* and IR76 (2000) PN 6.30.) Contributions paid by an employer may not be carried back. If contributions are carried back, it is not possible to exceed the maximum allowable percentage of contributions in the year to which they are carried back. Carry back was abolished by *section 17* of the *Finance Act 2000* after 6 April 2001.

Applications to carry back or carry forward contributions must be submitted to the Inland Revenue on the specified form PP43. Scheme administrators should keep a supply of the forms as members have a right to request them. The wording of PP43 should not be varied unless prior consent from FICO has been obtained (see IR76 (2000) PN 6.38). An election to carry back the contribution must be made not later than three months after the end of the tax year in which the contribution was paid.

Where an individual is electing for a contribution to be treated as if it had been paid in the previous tax year, this can only be done where the contribution had been paid between 6 April and 31 January and the person confirmed that he or she wished to carry back at the time that contribution was paid.

One major advantage of the option to carry back is that tax relief may be obtained more quickly than if the relief is claimed against the tax year in which the contribution is actually paid. However, care must be taken to ensure that carrying back does not, in fact, lead to relief at a lower rate.

Tax relief for employer's contributions

15.37 Contributions paid by an employer on behalf of a member will not be regarded as taxable emoluments of the employee and will not therefore be subject to income tax. [*ICTA 1988, s 643(1)*].

Taxation of the fund

15.38 Personal pension schemes which are approved by the Inland Revenue are exempt from tax on the income from investments or deposits held for the scheme (*ICTA 1988, s 643(2)*) and capital gains tax on gains arising from disposals of investments. A scheme established by an insurance company for the issue of insurance policies or annuity contracts does not obtain relief in this way, but claims an exemption from income tax, corporation tax and capital gains tax, as this is referable to the 'pension business' of the insurance company. [*ICTA 1988, s 438(1)*].

Taxation of benefits

15.39 An annuity paid under a personal pension scheme is chargeable to income tax under Schedule E. [*ICTA 1988, s 648A*]. The tax is collected through the PAYE system via the administrator.

No general exemption from income tax is given by the UK tax legislation to recipients of pension who are resident abroad. However, it may be possible to obtain an exemption if there is a double taxation agreement in force in relation to the overseas country involved.

A lump sum paid under a personal pension scheme to a member is not liable to income tax, provided it is within the Revenue's limit of 25 per cent of the fund at the date the lump sum is being paid (and assuming no lesser amount has had to be paid as a result of certification (see 15.13 above). The lump sum must be paid at the same time as the balance of the fund is used to provide an annuity (see also 15.13 above).

CONTRACTING-OUT OF THE STATE EARNINGS RELATED PENSION SCHEME

Appropriate personal pension schemes (APPS)

15.40 The rules of an APPS may provide for the payment of contributions in addition to 'minimum contributions' (see 15.31 below). An APPS may be used as a vehicle for transfers-in and, if the member has 'relevant earnings' (see 15.8 above) it can also receive ordinary contributions to build up benefits in excess of those provided by protected rights. An individual who is a member of an occupational pension scheme which is not contracted-out of the State earnings-related pension may contract-out via an APPS. Such an APPS can then only accept 'minimum contributions'(see 15.41 below).

A properly constituted APPS must have a current 'Appropriate Scheme Certificate' in force. Such a certificate can only be issued once a scheme complies with the statutory requirements. [*PSA 1993, s 9(5)*].

An APPS may take the form of any one of the following:

(*a*)   an arrangement for the issue of insurance policies or annuity contracts; or

(*b*)   an authorised unit trust scheme (set up solely for the purpose of providing personal pension schemes); or

(*c*)   a building society deposit; or

(*d*)   a bank account.

Providers of an APPS may be insurance companies, friendly societies, suitably authorised banks or building societies.

15.41 *Personal pension and stakeholder schemes*

There are detailed requirements relating to the continuing supervision of APPSs by NISPI. These include, the need to submit an annual return, the need to notify NISPI in writing of any changes in scheme details and the requirement to give members certain information.

Minimum contributions

15.41 Minimum contributions equate to the contracted-out rebate and the age-related rebate paid by the Department of Work and Pensions (DWP). The contracted-out rebate is the difference between the full rate of National Insurance contribution and the reduced, contracted-out rate, payable on 'band earnings' ie earnings between the lower earnings limit and the upper earnings limit. Since 6 April 1997 only an age-related rebate has been payable. No 'flat-rate' rebate is available.

Protected rights benefits

15.42 Unless the rules of the scheme provide otherwise, the whole of the fund will be treated as 'protected rights'. This is inadvisable as it would mean that all the stringent provisions relating to protected rights would then have to apply to all the rights in the scheme. Consequently the rules of the scheme will usually contain a specific definition of what constitutes protected rights. (For a general discussion on protected rights, see chapter 4.)

When a scheme's rules define protected rights, they must include all or any of the following:

(*a*)   minimum contributions;

(*b*)   protected rights transferred from another personal pension scheme or occupational pension scheme;

(*c*)   guaranteed minimum pensions transferred from an occupational pension scheme;

(*d*)   any 'incentive payments' made by the DWP;

(*e*)   payments representing basic rate relief from income tax on the member's share of minimum contributions. [*PSA 1993, s 10*].

Protected rights benefits become payable as a pension through the purchase of an annuity at state pension age. This benefit may not be drawn before state pension age and may only be taken in the form of pension. It may not be commuted to a cash lump sum. Payment of the protected rights pension annuity must be monthly unless the member agrees to a longer interval. The scheme rules must provide for the protected rights pension to be revalued in respect of the amount of protected rights attributable to contributions made before 6 April 1997, in line with the retail prices index or three per cent (whichever is less), and in respect of contributions remitted on or after 6 April 1997, in line with the retail prices index or five per cent (whichever is less).

Protected rights cannot be assigned, suspended or forfeited.

Death of member and protected rights pension

15.43 In the event of the death of the member, either before or after taking protected rights pension benefits, a spouse's pension will be payable.

If the member dies after the pension has commenced, the spouse's pension will equate to 50 per cent of the pension the member was receiving at his or her death. If the member dies before the pension has commenced, the spouse's pension will equate to 50 per cent of the pension that would have been payable to the member at death.

The spouse's pension must generally be payable until he or she dies or re-marries while under state pension age (but see also chapter 4).

Transfer of protected rights

15.44 Protected rights may be transferred to another pension arrangement which is permitted to accept such a transfer, including:

(*a*) another APPS; or

(*b*) a contracted-out or previously contracted-out occupational pension scheme; or

(*c*) an overseas occupational pension scheme.

The member must at all times consent to the transfer and the transfer payment must be at least equal to the cash equivalent value of the member's protected rights.

In the case of a transfer of protected rights to a contracted-out money purchase scheme, the transfer payment must be applied by the receiving scheme and be used to provide protected rights under the scheme for that member. In the case of a transfer of protected rights to a contracted-out salary related scheme, the receiving scheme must provide for the member and the member's spouse to be entitled to guaranteed minimum pensions in respect of pre-April 1997 service and benefits calculated on the same basis as for other scheme members for post-April 1997 service.

A transfer from a contracted-out salary related scheme is made to an APPS, and pre-April 1997 accrued guaranteed minimum pension rights and any post-April 1997 contracted-out rights must be treated as protected rights in the receiving APPS.

Personal pension protected rights premium

15.45 If an APPS ceases to be contracted-out or if the member wishes to

15.46 *Personal pension and stakeholder schemes*

cease being in contracted-out employment, the member may regain the entitlement from the State Earnings Related Pension Scheme by the payment of a Personal Pension protected rights Premium ('PPRP') to the DWP. The PPRP will be calculated according to the accumulated protected rights fund or, if necessary, by an objective actuarial calculation. The ability to pay a PPRP is not available post-6 April 1997 so the scheme must either retain the protected rights in deferred form, or buy them out by purchasing a suitable annuity.

TRANSFER VALUES

The right to a cash equivalent

15.46 A personal pension scheme will not be approved unless it includes provisions for transfer payments to be made, accepted and applied in accordance with the statutory provisions. (See *sections 93* to *101* of *PSA 1993* and the *Personal Pension Schemes (Transfer Payments) Regulations 2001 (SI 2001 No 119)* and IR76 (2000) Part 12). Transfers to a personal pension scheme from an (tax approved) occupational pension scheme in respect of a controlling director or an individual whose remuneration exceeds the earnings cap may be restricted to prevent transfers being used to maximise the tax free lump sum from a personal pension scheme.

The right to a cash equivalent (ie the value of all the benefits accrued under the scheme to or in respect of the member) is exercised by the member requiring the administrator to acquire transfer credits for him under an occupational pension scheme or rights under another personal pension scheme.

A transfer payment between schemes must be made from scheme administrator to scheme administrator either directly or through an independent broker. In no circumstances must any transfer payment be made via a member or his employer.

A transfer need not be in cash: it may be made by a transfer of assets such as stocks and shares or property. This is commonly known as a 'transfer in specie'. It is also (usually) possible to assign a policy from one personal pension scheme to another.

Transfers made to a personal pension scheme

15.47 A personal pension scheme may, on the written request of the relevant member, accept transfer payments from any of the following:

(*a*)   another approved personal pension scheme; or

(*b*)   a retirement benefits scheme approved or being considered for approval under *Chapter I, Part XIV* of *ICTA 1988*; or

(*c*)   a scheme established by statute (for example, a local authority scheme)(see *section 611A* of *ICTA 1988*; or

(d) an RAC; or

(e) a deferred annuity contract securing benefits which have accrued to the individual by virtue of membership of a retirement benefits scheme or scheme established by statute; or

(f) a Section 608 fund.

A personal pension scheme is not permitted to accept monies from any other source unless the prior consent of the IR SPSS has been obtained. In addition, if the personal pension scheme is accepting 'minimum contribution' only then it can only receive a transfer consisting of protected rights from another source.

There are further requirements where a 'regulated individual' has requested the transfer from a 'designated scheme'. The meaning of designated scheme is discussed in 15.21 above, but a 'regulated individual' is a person who:

(i) is or was in any period 10 years prior to the transfer a controlling director; or

(ii) was a person earning above the 'earnings cap' in any one year falling in whole or in part during a six year period prior to the date the transfer took place *and* was aged 45 or over at the date of transfer.

In these circumstances it is a requirement that the administrator of the transferring scheme has signed a certificate in accordance with *regulation 8(3)* of the *Personal Pension Schemes (Transfer Payments) Regulations 2001 (SI 2001 No 119)*. It should be noted that this regulation does not apply to any Section 32 contracts established before 6 April 2001. In this case there is an Inland Revenue concession in place described in IR76 (2000) PN 12.14.

In addition, 'regulated individual' will have controls in relation to the maximum tax free cash available at pension date and this means that no more than the certified amount of tax free cash available from the 'designated scheme' can be paid by the personal pension scheme at pension date. This will often, but not always, have the effect of reducing the usual 25 per cent tax free cash (ie 25 per cent of the accumulated fund value of the personal pension scheme) to a lesser amount. If the certified amount is greater than 25 per cent of the non-protected rights fund then the 25 per cent limit prevails.

Nil certificates

15.48 Some transfers may be subject to what is known as a 'nil certificate'. This simply means that the transfer either derived from a source which was non-commutable (for example an FSAVC Contract or an AVC Scheme where AVC's were commenced on or after 8 April 1987). This is designed so that a transfer from such a source (a full list is given in IR76 (2000) PN 12.17) cannot become commutable simply because a transfer to a personal pension scheme has taken place. If the nil certificate is only certifying a proportion of the transfer monies coming across then only that portion is subject to the nil

15.49 *Personal pension and stakeholder schemes*

certificate and the excess can be commutable in accordance with the usual 25 per cent personal pension scheme limit for tax free cash transfers made from a personal pension scheme.

Transfer made from a personal pension scheme

15.49 On the written request of the member, the administrator of a personal pension scheme must, if the statutory procedures are complied with, make the requested payment (IR76 (2000) PN 12.3). The transfer can be to any of the following:

(*a*) another personal pension scheme;

(*b*) a retirement benefit scheme approved under *Chapter I, Part XIV* of *ICTA 1988* (including a free-standing additional voluntary contributions scheme (FSAVC) or a separately approved AVC scheme) but not a scheme awaiting approval;

(*c*) a relevant statutory scheme (*section 611A* of *ICTA 1988*);

(*d*) an overseas scheme, if:

  (i) all the conditions in Appendix 22 of IR76 (2000) are satisfied; and

  (ii) where necessary the prior consent of the IR SPSS has been obtained.

A transfer payment made from an approved personal pension scheme must represent the whole fund accumulated under that arrangement except:

(i) it need not include any assets which represent protected rights; and

(ii) if a member requests a transfer but does not leave the service of his employer, then he only has an automatic right to a transfer of benefits accrued from 6 April 1988 (although, in practice, it is unlikely that holding partial deferred benefits would in this manner be in anyone's interest).

If a cash equivalent is being paid to a contracted-in occupational scheme, or to a personal pension scheme that is not an APPS, the assets representing the member's protected rights cannot be transferred. In such a situation the protected rights element will generally remain in the scheme as a deferred benefit.

Further detailed control, when making transfer payments from a personal pension scheme to prevent 'improper transfers' (ie to sources involved in trust busting) came in with effect from 1 July 2002 under Pensions Update 132 published by the IR SPSS.

DISCLOSURE OF INFORMATION

15.50 The trustees (or the Provider) are responsible for disclosing certain information to the member. In particular they must provide certain basic information about the scheme to every new member within thirteen weeks of joining. [*Personal Pension Schemes (Disclosure of Information) Regulations 1987* (as amended) (*SI 1987 No 1110*)].

Information relating, in particular, to the amount of contributions credited to the member, the value of the member's protected rights, and the value of the member's accrued rights other than those protected rights must be given to the member annually. In addition, further information must be given to each member before his retirement.

In relation to each scheme year commencing on or after 1 October 1987, the trustees must make available to every member a copy of an annual statement containing specified information.

INVESTMENT

Personal pension and stakeholder schemes in general

15.51 In order to ensure that the sole purpose of a scheme is the provision of benefits on retirement or death (*ICTA 1988, s 633*) (see 15.10 above) restrictions are placed on the investment activities of an approved scheme. The purpose of these restrictions is to ensure the member does not receive benefits from the scheme other than in the prescribed form. The main restrictions are that:

(*a*) scheme funds must not be used to provide loans to a member or any persons 'connected' with the member;

(*b*) there must be no investment transaction with a member or persons 'connected' with the member;

(*c*) schemes must not hold residential property or land directly as an investment. Commercial property which is leased to a business or partnership 'connected' with a member can form part of the assets of the scheme provided that an independent professional valuation is carried out and the terms of the lease are to be termed on a commercial basis. (IR76 (2000) PN 11).

With stakeholder schemes the investment choice is likely to be more restricted than that available under general insured personal pension schemes and, much more restricted than the choice available to SIPPs. This is because of the much stricter control placed on costs with the main control being that the annual management charge levied on a stakeholder scheme cannot exceed 1 per cent of the member fund per year. This will inevitably lead to a limited range on offer. However, that said, stakeholder schemes will be operating in a very competitive market and, as such, Providers have been looking to provide innovative ways of attracting stakeholder contributions whilst, at the same time, being imaginative with what is on offer regarding investments under stakeholder schemes. Lifestyle funds, tracker and various types of flexible funds are being made available. It should be noted, however, that members cannot be required to select an investment choice so a stakeholder scheme will need a fallback investment

15.52 *Personal pension and stakeholder schemes*

policy to cover those members. Of course, all investment transactions must comply (from 6 April 2001) with the *Personal Pension Schemes (Restriction on Discretion to Approve) (Permitted Investments) Regulations 2001 (SI 2001 No 117)*. All stakeholder schemes are obliged to have a Statement of Investment Principles. Therefore, proper advice must be taken by the trustees or managers to ensure diversification and the appropriateness of the investments selected. Further requirements related to with profits funds (that can be offered under stakeholder schemes) which include the ring fencing of those with profit funds so those funds are only available to stakeholder schemes. No investments are permitted in collective investment schemes or unitised funds which operate on a bid/offer spread basis.

SIPPs

Member directed investments

15.52 For Self-Invested Personal Pension Schemes (this does not apply to stakeholder schemes) the range of permitted investments has been adapted to provide an opportunity for members to become directly involved in decisions about the investment of contributions. The original requirements relating to the types of investments which members could make were set out in Memorandum No 101. These have subsequently been extended and clarified by the *Personal Pension Schemes (Restriction on Discretion to Approve) (Permitted Investments) Regulations 2001 (SI 2001 No 117)*)so that a member of a SIPP may choose to invest the fund in any of the following:

(*a*) Stocks and shares traded on any recognised stock exchange (including the AIM), including:
- equities;
- fixed interest securities issued by governments or other bodies;
- debenture stock and other loan stock;
- warrants (for equities);
- permanent interest bearing shares;
- convertible securities.

(*b*) Futures and options traded on any recognised stock exchange whether currency, equity or bonds and either long or short positions or options.

(*c*) Unit trusts:
- resident in the UK and authorised under *Financial Services and Markets Act 2000 (FSMA 2000)*;
- tax exempt unauthorised trusts.

(*d*) Stocks and shares in investment trusts purchased and held through investment trust savings schemes or investment plans operated by persons:

- resident in the UK and authorised for that purpose under *FSMA 2000*;
- resident outside the UK but subject to regulation for that purpose in terms of the *FSMA 2000*.

(e) Open ended investment companies (OEICs).

(f) Insurance company managed funds and unit-linked funds, investment policies or unit linked funds of a UK insurance company or insurance company within the EEC authorised under *Article 6* of the *First Life Insurance Directive 79/267/EEC*.

(g) Endowment policies traded by a *FSMA 2000* regulated person (TEPs).

(h) Deposit accounts with any authorised institution in any currency.

(i) Commercial property (including land whether development land, farmland or forestry) in or outside the UK.

(j) Borrowing to finance the purchase or development of a commercial property, or to pay for VAT liability arising from the purchase of any such property.

(k) Undertaking for Collective Investment Schemes in Transferable Securities (UCITS).

(l) Ground rents.

(m) Foreign currency deposit accounts.

(n) Public houses.

(o) Depository interests (including CREST Depository Interests).

(p) Individual Pension Accounts (IPAs).

(q) Hotels, motels and guest houses.

(r) Nursing homes.

For the first time (within IR76 (2000)) the Inland Revenue also gave a list (in Appendix 25) of prohibited investments and these are as follows:

(i) Premium Bonds.

(ii) Loans to any party.

(iii) Milk quotas.

(iv) Fishing quotas.

(v) Residential property.

(vi) Gold bullion.

(vii) Shares traded on OFEX.

(viii) Unlisted shares (except in a site maintenance property, for the necessary extent needed to purchase a commercial property).

(ix) Leisure property (eg golf courses) or property with an affiliated leisure interest such as sporting rights.

(x) Any land or property directly adjacent to any land or property owned by the member or any party connected with the member.

(xi) Personal chattels (eg paintings, antiques, fine wine and jewellery).

(xii) Borrowing other than that specified in IR76 (2000) Appendix 25 Part 11 paras 11.24, 11.26 or 11.27.

SIPP INVESTMENT REQUIREMENTS

15.53 For the first time IR76 (2000) contains (in Part 11) specific details relating to the Inland Revenue requirements for SIPP investments. The main principle behind a SIPP is that the member must retain control as to how contributions are to be invested. The members can choose the type of investments (subject, of course, to Inland Revenue requirements (see 5.51 above)), when those investments are disposed of etc. Although there is currently debate within the industry as to the regulatory position of SIPPs, there are usually two basic choices available to a SIPP member:

(*a*) he or she makes all day to day investment decisions unilaterally; or

(*b*) investment decisions are made on behalf of the member by an appointed, appropriately regulated, investment manager.

It is a requirement of IR76 (2000) PN 11.4 that the member normally has no legal ownership over the investments (although separate trusts with the member acting as co-trustee are permitted by IR76 (2000) PN 11.5). Where IR76 (2000) PN 11.4 applies the Practice Notes envisage that the investments are held by the scheme administrator although, in practice, legal title to those investments would be held by the Trustee of the SIPP on behalf of the member. An important point to note is that, unlike the Inland Revenue concession for personal pension schemes where the assets comprise of purely insured assets (ie the Revenue allows such schemes to be governed by Deed) such a concession is not available to a SIPP. A SIPP is required to have assets governed under an irrevocable trust and it follows that, to achieve this, a trustee is required!

IR76 (2000) PN 11.7 makes it clear that the Inland Revenue require trustees of a SIPP to act in a fiduciary manner on behalf of the scheme members ie to act in their best interest (case law indicates this would mean best financial interest). The trustee should not be attempting to act in the interest of other parties – to do so is likely to threaten the removal of Inland Revenue approval to the SIPP.

STAMP DUTY

15.54 In relation to property, Stamp Duty was a document based tax charged voluntarily up to 30 November 2003.

If a property situated in the UK was purchased by the trustees of a tax approved occupational or personal pension scheme or retirement annuity contract (RAC) Stamp Duty was payable on the purchase/sale price or open market value of the property, which ever was higher, at the relevant percentage rate subject to any de minimis exception. If the property was subject to a mortgage, Stamp Duty was still payable on the equity value and the amount of the debt assumed by the purchaser (Statement of Practice 6/90, 27 April 1990).

Stamp Duty may also have been payable on the taking of a lease by the trustees as lessee of any tax approved pension scheme on both the premium and rent payable with the rate varying according to the length of the lease (*section 55* of the *Finance Act 1963* and *section 55* of the *Stamp Act 1891*).

It can be seen from the second and third paragraphs above that the trustees of a SIPP were liable to pay Stamp Duty in the relevant circumstances.

In specie transfers

15.55 If a property in the UK is owned by the trustees of a tax approved pension scheme and is transferred in specie for no consideration other than the liability of the receiving trustees of another tax approved pension scheme to pay the retirement benefits represented by the value of the property concerned, the value of the property being transferred is exempt from Stamp Duty (*Category F* in the Schedule to the *Stamp Duty (Exempt Instruments) Regulations 1987 (SI 1987 No 516)* ('*Stamp Duty Exemption Regulations*'). However, the document evidencing the transfer is only subject to the fixed rate of Stamp Duty of £5.00.

If the property being transferred in specie is subject to a mortgage or legal charge, the mortgage/legal charge value is not exempt from Stamp Duty as the consideration passing on the transfer comprised 'other consideration', so far as the Inland Revenue is concerned, and attracts Stamp Duty at the relevant percentage rate. Any remaining equity value in the property is exempt from Stamp Duty in accordance with *Category F* in the *Schedule* to the *Stamp Duty Exemption Regulations*.

If the trustees of a SIPP received a transfer in specie of a property in the UK as part of or the whole of the retirement benefits of the member from:

(*a*) any tax approved occupational pension scheme; or

(*b*) another SIPP; or

(*c*) from a retirement annuity contract;

or they transferred in specie a property in the UK as part or the whole of the retirement benefits of the member to:

(*d*) any tax approved occupational pension scheme; or

(*e*) another SIPP;

15.56 *Personal pension and stakeholder schemes*

the value of the property forming part of the transfer is exempt from Stamp Duty (*Category F* in accordance with the *Schedule* to the *Stamp Duty Exemption Regulations 1987*.

The legal title of a property, which comprised an asset of an occupational or personal pension scheme (including a SIPP) or a RAC, could also have changed in any of the following circumstances:

(i) a change of name or death of individual trustee;

(ii) a change of name of a sole corporate trustee;

(iii) a commercial acquisition by a corporate trustee of a portfolio of SSAS and/or SIPPS from another corporate pension trustee;

(iv) the divorce of a SSAS/SIPP/RAC member where a separate SSAS or SIPP is established to receive the pension credits.

In (i), (ii) or (iii) above, as the trust vehicle is likely to remain the same, no transfer of property takes place therefore Stamp Duty does not apply except for the £5.00 fixed duty charge where appropriate and the mortgage element of any property involved. At (iv) the exemption at *Category F* in the *Schedule* to the *Stamp Duty Exemption Regulations*) applies subject to the £5.00 fixed duty charge where appropriate and subject to the mortgage element of any property involved.

STAMP DUTY LAND TAX (SDLT)

15.56 Stamp Duty Land Tax ('SDLT'), which came into effect on 1 December 2003, is transaction based and no longer a voluntary tax like Stamp Duty.

Stamp Duty, in respect of UK property acquisitions, was abolished with effect from 1 December 2003 and replaced by SDLT (*section 42* of the *Finance Act 2003*). Purchases of property by the trustees of occupational and personal pension schemes and retirement annuity contracts are liable to SDLT at the appropriate percentage rate subject to any de minimus exemptions. If the property is subject to a mortgage, SDLT is payable on the equity value and the amount of the debt assumed by the purchaser (*FA 2003, Sch 4, para 8*).

Stamp Duty on the taking of a lease was also abolished with effect from 1 December 2003 and replaced by SDLT (*s 56* and *Sch 5* of the *FA 2003*). The basis of valuation of the lease to arrive at the SDLT payable is different from Stamp Duty and the amount of SDLT payable is likely to be greater than the former Stamp Duty.

The trustees of a SIPP are liable to pay SDLT in the circumstances outlined in the second and third paragraph of 15.56.

In specie transfers

15.57 Where a property in the UK owned by the trustees of a tax approved pension scheme forming part or the whole of an in specie transfer of a member's retirement benefits is transferred between tax approved occupational and personal pension schemes and RACs from 1 December 2003, the value of the property is not liable to SDLT. This is because the assumption by the trustees of the receiving pension scheme to provide retirement benefits does not constitute chargeable consideration for the property transaction in the Inland Revenue's view.

If the property being transferred in specie is subject to a mortgage or legal charge, the mortgage/legal charge is not liable to SDLT. This is because the Inland Revenue, as a concession, will not treat the assumption of the outstanding debt as chargeable consideration. Any remaining equity value in the property is not liable to SDLT as referred to in the first part of this paragraph 15.57.

If the trustees of a SIPPS receive a transfer in specie of a property in the UK as part or the whole of the retirement benefits of the member from:

(a)   any taxed approved occupational pension scheme; or

(b)   another SIPP; or

(c)   from a retirement annuity contract;

or they transfer in specie a property in the UK as part or the whole of the retirement benefits of the member to:

(a)   any tax approved occupational pension scheme; or

(b)   another SIPP;

the value of the property forming part of the transfer is not liable to SDLT in accordance with the first paragraph of this section.

The legal title of a property, which is an asset of an occupational or personal pension scheme (including a SIPPS) or a RAC, may also change in any of the following circumstances:

(i)   change of name or death of individual trustee;

(ii)   change of name of a sole corporate trustee;

(iii)   acquisition commercially by a corporate trustee of a portfolio of SSAS and/or SIPP from another corporate pension trustee; or

(iv)   divorce of a SSAS/SIPP/RAC member where a separate SSAS or SIPP is established to receive the pension credits.

In all of these circumstances, including any such case where a mortgage or legal charge is secured on the property concerned, a charge to SDLT will not arise.

15.58 *Personal pension and stakeholder schemes*

Property transactions covered by (i) to (iv) above do not have to be notified to the Inland Revenue, but must be self-certified if registration of the change of title is needed.

The Inland Revenue's interpretation of the SDLT legislation as it applies to pension schemes was not made public until after 1 December 2003. It is contained in its own internal SDLT Manual which is available publicly via Open Government. It can be relied upon as a statement of the Inland Revenue's policy on SDLT and pension schemes in relation to transfers in specie and related mortgages/legal charges effective from 1 December 2003. It should be noted, however, that transfers between non-trust based arrangements has yet to be resolved.

The taking of a lease by the trustees of any tax approved pension scheme from 1 December 2003 is liable to SDLT.

WITHDRAWAL OF REVENUE APPROVAL

15.58 The IR SPSS has the power to withdraw the approval from a personal pension scheme if the circumstances warrant it. [*ICTA 1988, s 650* and Part 13 of IR76 (2000)]. Approval will be withdrawn from the date when the facts were such as not to warrant the continuance of approval. In such circumstances a notice of withdrawal of approval will be sent to the administrator. The notice must state the grounds on which, and the date from which, approval is withdrawn.

Approval is only likely to be withdrawn where there is a serious breach of legislation or the IR SPSS guidelines, such as where securing the provision of appropriate benefits was not the sole purpose of the member. Unacceptable amendments may also lead to loss of approval, as could payment of excessive lump sum benefits, transactions with connected persons or the acquisition of prohibited investments. Withdrawal of approval would effectively reverse the tax reliefs afforded to personal pension schemes.

The IR SPSS also has the power to refuse to approve a personal pension scheme. The grounds for a refusal are likely to be those which would also involve withdrawal of approval. If approval is either withdrawn or refused the decision may be appealed against. The appeal must be in writing, stating the grounds for the appeal and must be made within 30 days of the original decision. [*ICTA 1988, s 651(1)*]. Other adverse decisions of the IR SPSS relating to personal pension schemes should be pursued by representations to the officer concerned or to a more senior officer. Unresolved problems or complaints may be taken to the Inland Revenue Adjudicator.

PENSIONS BILL

15.59 The Pensions Bill is intended to amend the definition of an occupational pension scheme to exclude death benefit only schemes. This is intended to make it clear that employers will not be able to use a death benefit only scheme after 5 April 2005 to avoid establishing or providing access to a stakeholder scheme (see 15.7).

Chapter 16

Commercial transactions

INTRODUCTION

General

16.1 This chapter considers the pensions implications of buying or selling a company or business. The value of the pension liabilities concerned can be very substantial and in some cases may exceed the value of the company or business itself, particularly where there is a final salary scheme involved. It is therefore essential that the main pensions issues arising from such a transaction are considered and addressed at an early stage in the negotiations.

Type of scheme

16.2 Inevitably, much will depend upon the type of scheme involved. However, pensions will tend to feature most prominently in the negotiations where the employees affected by the sale belong to a final salary scheme. Most of these schemes are approved under *Chapter I, Part XIV* of *ICTA 1988* and will also frequently be contracted-out (see chapter 4).

This chapter is therefore primarily concerned with those transactions where the employees concerned belong to an approved, contracted-out, final salary occupational pension scheme. The implications for other types of scheme are considered at the end of the chapter.

Type of sale

16.3 The course of the pensions negotiations will depend largely upon:

(*a*) whether the sale is of shares or of assets (see 16.14 below); and

(*b*) whether or not the sale will require a transfer of assets and liabilities between schemes. The circumstances which will typically give rise to such a transfer are described further in 16.19 below.

Funding

16.4 A preliminary point to establish, which will set the tone of subsequent negotiations, is the funding position of the scheme providing benefits for the employees of the company or business which is being sold.

Where employees' benefits are to be transferred from the vendor's scheme to a scheme of the purchaser following completion (see 16.19 below), the funding level is likely to affect the sum which is transferred from the vendor's scheme and consequently the level of past service benefits to be granted in the purchaser's scheme following the transfer (unless the purchaser can negotiate a shortfall clause – see 16.44 below).

Where instead the purchaser is to take over the entire scheme (see 16.20 below), the funding level may impact on the profitability of the company or business being purchased. For example, a well-funded scheme may reduce future liability for the company to contribute (so boosting profits) but, conversely, an underfunded scheme may require an immediate injection of cash to raise its funding level.

These situations are likely to affect the negotiation of the contract wording and, of course, the purchase price itself. They are dealt with in more detail below.

Warranties and indemnities

16.5 It is common in a sale and purchase agreement for both warranties and indemnities to be agreed to deal with specific issues of concern to the parties, often points which have arisen during the course of negotiations and the due diligence exercise.

A *warranty* is a statement of fact made by one party to the contract (usually the vendor). An example of this may be that the benefits provided by the scheme have been fully equalized as between men and women as required by law (see Chapter 9). This statement may then be disclosed against in the disclosure letter (see 16.12 below) to negate the effect of the statement to some extent, for example by the disclosure that guaranteed minimum pensions have not yet been equalized. In such a circumstance the purchaser may seek to obtain an *indemnity* to the effect that the vendor will indemnify the purchaser for the costs of equalizing benefits, should this cost be incurred by the purchaser after completion.

The main difference between a warranty and an indemnity is the level of protection given to the party for whose benefit it is given and the method by which each is enforced. To enforce a warranty, the party seeking to benefit must take steps to enforce the contract. Unless a breach of warranty is agreed by both the parties, this is likely to involve proceedings, incurring costs and delays.

By contrast, an indemnity requires the party who granted the indemnity to reimburse the other party for specified losses which have been incurred. There is no requirement for the indemnified party to mitigate his loss or to take steps to prove any wrongdoing by the indemnifying party. Consequently an indemnity offers not only more protection than a warranty to the purchaser but also considerably less inconvenience in obtaining a remedy.

Due diligence

16.6 Due diligence is the name given to the fact-finding exercise which takes place before and during negotiation of the contract. The purchaser will be concerned to find out as much information as possible about the company or business it is seeking to acquire, to ascertain not only what potential liabilities there are but also to ensure that these are quantifiable and that protection, in the form of warranties and indemnities, is sought from the vendor where appropriate.

In the context of pensions, the purchaser will wish to see, for example, a copy of the trust deed and rules, the scheme's booklet and full details of employees (including salary levels). Where a company with its own scheme is being purchased, as opposed to a transfer payment being received, more extensive information will be sought, as the purchaser will effectively be inheriting the whole scheme. The results of the due diligence exercise may result in re-negotiation of the purchase price or the seeking of further warranties and indemnities. Due diligence is considered in further detail below.

THE SALE DOCUMENTS

The sale agreement

Parties

16.7 The distinction between share sales and assets sales is considered in 16.14 below, but in either case the main parties to the agreement will be the vendor and the purchaser respectively.

The important point to bear in mind, therefore, is that the trustees of the respective pension schemes will not be parties to the agreement and, consequently, there will be no contractual relationship between them. In any event, trustees may not under normal circumstances fetter a future exercise of their discretion and so making them a party to the agreement would be of little comfort to either the vendor or the purchaser when the calculation of the transfer payment and the granting of past service benefits take place a few months after completion of the agreement. [*Stannard v Fisons Pension Trust Ltd [1992] 1 PLR 27*].

This is relevant when the pensions schedule is negotiated. It may be impossible for a party to agree to procure that a certain event occurs, because the scheme rules place that event in the hands of the trustees. An example of this would be where the rules of the purchaser's scheme provide that past service benefits are granted entirely at the trustees' discretion. Where this is the case, the principal company or an adhering employer cannot guarantee that a certain level of past service benefits will be granted. The most the purchaser is likely to agree to in such circumstances is that it will use its best endeavours to procure that the specified event will take place.

The extent to which the parties can hold out for a greater commitment will therefore generally depend on who has the relevant power under the trust deed and rules and (if it is the trustees) the extent to which the principal employer or an adhering employer (subject to any overriding legislation) has control over the trustees' actions. An exception to this, however, is the transfer payment. In the context of transfer payments, the purchaser should seek to place the vendor in such a position that, should the trustees pay less than the contractually defined transfer payment, the vendor will be bound to make up any shortfall – see 16.44 below.

Warranties

16.8 The pensions warranties will usually appear in the part of the agreement which sets out all the warranties (not just those relating to pensions) being given by the vendor. Sometimes, however, where there is a schedule to the agreement dealing with other pensions issues (typically a transfer payment – see 16.9 below) the pensions warranties may appear in that schedule instead. Where this happens, the vendor should take care to ensure that any clauses in the agreement that limit the scope of the warranties also extend to the warranties in that schedule.

It is common for parties to enter into a 'disclosure letter' of the same date as the main agreement (see 16.12 below). To the extent that a warranty is disclosed against, this will negate the effect of the warranty. An example of this has already been given in 16.5 above.

The warranties that a purchaser requires will vary considerably according to the nature of and the circumstances surrounding the transaction and are dealt with later on in this chapter in the contexts in which they arise.

Pensions schedule

16.9 Where the transaction involves a transfer of assets and liabilities from a scheme operating within the vendor's group to one to be set up (or already established) by the purchaser, its holding company or one of its subsidiaries, there will normally be detailed provisions specifying how this is to happen. In the vast majority of cases, these will be set out in a schedule to the agreement, dealing specifically with pensions.

Other provisions

16.10 Other provisions may be included either in the pensions schedule (where there is one) or in the main body of the agreement.

16.11 Commercial transactions

These might include indemnities (see 16.5 above), for instance in relation to equalisation issues (see Chapter 9). Another example might be a provision which seeks to adjust the purchase price for any past overfunding or underfunding that may emerge where the purchaser is to inherit the scheme in its entirety (see 16.27 to 16.28 below).

Consistency with scheme rules

16.11 Any action to be taken in connection with the transfer of benefits from one scheme to another will need to be carried out in accordance with the respective scheme's rules. It is therefore important that both parties are aware of the provisions in the schemes' rules governing each particular issue. One example of this is where the transaction involves a transfer payment and the scheme rules require a different method of calculation from that specified in the sale agreement. Other examples are given in the course of this chapter.

The disclosure letter

16.12 As mentioned briefly above, the disclosure letter documents the agreement between the parties on the information which has been provided during the due diligence exercise and acts to limit or negate the effect of the warranties given in the sale and purchase agreement. The disclosure letter is a letter from the vendor to the purchaser which is likely to set out first certain general statements of agreed information (such as records at Companies House) and will then go on to set out specific disclosures against specific warranties.

Purchasers should seek to ensure that the wording of disclosures is specific and to the point. From the perspective of the vendor, by contrast, it will often be desirable to make general disclosures, or make reference to a bundle of documents (thereby making an effective disclosure without drawing attention to specific areas about which the purchaser should be concerned or, at least, aware). From the purchaser's point of view, it is important to receive as much specific information as possible to ensure that it is informed of all potential and actual liabilities and can take these into account when negotiating the sale and purchase agreement.

Actuary's letter

16.13 It will be seen later in this chapter that, particularly where the transaction involves a transfer payment from the vendor's scheme, it may be necessary to agree a calculation method and assumptions for valuing the scheme's liabilities. Although there is no reason in principle why these assumptions cannot be set out in the agreement itself, they will usually be covered separately in a letter from the vendor's actuary to the purchaser's actuary and countersigned by the purchaser's actuary by way of agreement. The letter should be clearly identified in the pensions schedule and referred to where relevant.

SHARES OR ASSETS

The distinction

16.14 For the purposes of this chapter, a share sale takes place when the vendor is selling all of the issued share capital of a company. In such a situation the identity of the company remains the same; it is the underlying ownership of the company which has changed. The purchaser inherits through its ownership of the company all the company's pre-existing contracts including (of particular relevance to pensions) contracts of employment and deeds which the company has entered into in relation to a pension scheme.

An asset sale takes place when all or part of a business is being sold to the purchaser. In such a transaction the purchaser will take on only specific contracts, premises and employees of the company selling the business and will only assume those liabilities specified in the agreement.

Practical implications

Employment aspects

16.15 Following a sale of shares there is no change in the employment relationship between the company and its employees. The employment contracts will stay intact and the employees therefore will enjoy the ongoing benefit of any contractual provisions, including any that relate to pensions.

This contrasts with the position of employees on an asset (or business) sale where their employment contracts are transferred to a new employer. Whilst the *Transfer of Undertakings* (*Protection of Employment*) *Regulations 1981* (*SI 1981 No 1794*) (*'TUPE'*) contains provisions to transfer contractual employment rights to the purchaser, *regulation 7* makes an exception in relation to 'so much of a contract of employment ...as relates to an occupational pension scheme'.

However, any provisions of an occupational pension scheme which do not relate to benefits for old age, invalidity or survivors are excluded from the exception described above, and will therefore pass to a purchaser. The first case in which the status of such benefits was raised in the Courts was the case of *Frankling v BPS Public Sector Ltd [1999] IRLR 212, [1999] ICR 347, EAT*. The Employment Appeal Tribunal refused the employee's claim that the previous entitlements to early retirement pensions and compensation on redundancy were not part of the scheme and therefore transferred under *TUPE*. The Employment Appeal Tribunal considered that the rights still related to old age, they were just triggered by redundancy. The employee's leave to appeal was granted but the action was settled before it reached appeal.

This was followed by the case of *Beckmann v Dynamco Whicheloe Macfarlane Ltd, Case C-164/00, [2002] 64 PBLR; [2002] All ER (D) 05 (Jun)*. Katia

16.15 *Commercial transactions*

Beckmann was a former NHS employee whose employment transferred to Dynamco Whicheloe Macfarlane under *TUPE*. She was subsequently dismissed on redundancy grounds and claimed entitlement to an early retirement pension and other lump sum benefits, on the basis that these had transferred under *Article 3* of the 1977 *Acquired Rights Directive* (now repealed). *Article 3(3)* excludes the provision of 'employees' rights to old-age, invalidity or survivors' benefits under supplementary company or inter-company pension schemes outside the statutory social security schemes in member states'. A reference was made to the European Court of Justice, and the ECJ decided that 'it is only benefits paid from the time when an employee reaches the end of his normal working life as laid down by the general structure of the pension scheme ... that can be classified as old age benefits, even if they are calculated by reference to the rules for calculating normal pension benefits'. As a result, the right to an early retirement pension on redundancy was held to transfer. The judgment was short and has given rise to concerns amongst pensions professionals.

Beckmann is considered further at 16.50 below.

A new case was subsequently referred to the ECJ in which additional questions were posed. In *Martin v South Bank University[2004] 1 CMLR 472, [2003] All ER (D) 85*, Martin and Others transferred into a private pension arrangement following the transfer of their employment from the NHS to South Bank University. The claimants subsequently opted to take early retirement and claim an early retirement redundancy pension.

Nine questions were referred to the ECJ on the assumption that rights contingent upon both dismissal and premature retirement pass under TUPE. These included:

(*a*) Is an employee's right to the payment of early retirement benefits and lump sum compensation:

- on redundancy;
- in the interests of the efficiency of the service;
- on organisational change;
- a right to 'old age, invalidity or survivors' benefit'?

(*b*) May an employee agree to waive benefits if the purchaser's scheme does not entitle the employee to the same benefits if:

- the employee joins the purchaser's scheme; or
- joins the purchaser's scheme and transfers his past service pension rights to the purchaser's scheme?

(*c*) Where a purchaser and employee agree that the employee will take premature retirement on less generous terms than under the vendor's scheme, what criteria should a national court use to establish if the transfer is the reason for that agreement (a reconsideration of *Tellerup v*

Daddy's Dance Hall [1988] ECR 739 – employment terms can be varied, provided that the transfer is not the reason for the variation)?

When the Advocate-General's opinion was handed down it was dubbed 'Beckmann revisited'. Early retirement benefits and benefits intended to enhance the conditions of such retirement, paid in the event of dismissal to employees who have reached a certain age, did not relate to 'old-age, invalidity or survivors' benefits'. The right did therefore transfer.

On the *Daddy's Dance Hall* issue, rights cannot be waived, but could be varied within the parameters of that case – whether the transfer is the reason for the variation can only be answered on all the facts of the case. However, changes in the law or in the purchaser's economic position may suggest that the reason is something other than the transfer.

The Advocate-General did not give a view on the impact of a transfer of past service rights.

The ECJ gave its decision on 6 November 2003. It upheld the Advocate-General's opinion, but gives no guidance on the issue of in what circumstances the transfer may not be considered to be the reason for the change.

However, as regards waiving rights, the ECJ considered that as the protection was imposed as a matter of public policy, an employee could not waive his rights.

So what will transfer under *TUPE*? It is likely that redundancy benefits payable under an occupational pension scheme will transfer, and it is certainly arguable that other benefits payable before normal retirement date may transfer. The matter will undoubtedly give rise to further litigation, as the issues are clarified in the courts. In the meantime, there are a number of interesting issues raised by the case law.

1. Must benefits be replicated in a purchaser's scheme to in all respects? *French v Mitie Management Services Limited [2002] IRLR 513, [2002] All ER (D) 150 (Sep)* provides some authority for not having to replicate unjust, absurd or impossible features. Replacement benefits, for example salary increases, may need to be offered instead.

2. When is the transfer going to be considered to be the reason for the change? Can it be argued that an employee agreeing to join the purchaser's scheme post transfer constitutes a variation of terms by mutual consent as opposed to a waiver?

3. Does it make a difference whether past rights are transferred? What happens if an employee is told that if his or her past service benefits are not transferred, any benefits will be limited to future service?

4. Can *Beckmann/Martin* be distinguished? The *Beckmann* pension was only payable to normal retirement age – the rights under a private sector scheme may be payable for life.

16.16 *Commercial transactions*

The Pensions Bill has modified the above position somewhat. It does not currently contain any provisions dealing with *regulation 7* type issues, but it does introduce a limited requirement upon purchasers to provide pensions for employees transferring on an asset (or business) sale. Under the Bill, where before the transfer an employee was a member of an occupational pension scheme to which the employer contributes, or was entitled to be a member, or would have been entitled to be a member if he or she had been employed for longer, the purchaser must ensure that after the transfer the employee becomes eligible to be a member of an occupational or stakeholder pension scheme.

Where the purchaser's scheme provides money purchase benefits the purchaser will have to make 'relevant contributions' in respect of the employee (to be set out in regulations; but in the Department for Work and Pensions (DWP) paper 'Simplicity, security and choice: Working and saving for retirement Action on occupational pensions' June 2003, it was envisaged that employer contributions would match the employees' contributions up to six per cent of pensionable salary). Where the employer's scheme provides final salary benefits, the new scheme must at least satisfy the current reference scheme test – see chapter **4**, and such other requirements as may be included in regulations.

Employer's debt

16.16 We shall see later in this chapter (see 16.62 onwards) that, where the vendor's scheme is underfunded, the sale may give rise to a statutory debt payable to the trustees by the purchaser or by the company that it is buying. It will be seen, however, that the extent of this problem will normally be less on an asset purchase than on a purchase of shares (see 16.66 below).

Deed of substitution

16.17 Circumstances may arise where an asset sale results in the employment contracts of all of the scheme's active members being transferred to the purchaser. In such a situation it may be appropriate for the entire scheme to become the purchaser's responsibility. This will typically require the execution of a deed substituting the purchaser as the scheme's new principal employer. In most cases, the execution of such a deed will be entirely consistent with *Re Courage Group's Pension Schemes [1987] 1 WLR 495* (outlined in 12.13 above).

A share sale is generally less likely to give rise to a deed of substitution. However, one example of where this might be appropriate would be where the vendor is the scheme's principal employer but the subsidiary being sold employs all of the scheme's active members.

WHETHER THE SALE WILL GIVE RISE TO A TRANSFER PAYMENT

General

16.18 The scope, nature and extent of the contractual provisions required in the sale and purchase agreement will generally depend on whether or not a transfer payment is anticipated. In most cases, the question of whether there is to be a transfer will be dictated largely by the structure of the pension arrangements and of the sale (see 16.19 and 16.20 below) but the parties may nevertheless be able to agree some alternative approach (see 16.21 below).

Circumstances involving a transfer

16.19 The following circumstances will normally give rise to a transfer payment:

(*a*) where a company being sold is one of a number of companies which participate in the vendor's scheme; or

(*b*) on an asset sale, where some but not all of the scheme's active members are to have their employment transferred to the purchaser.

Transactions such as these are discussed further in 16.30 to 16.61 below. Where the scheme is funded below the statutory minimum funding requirement, the sale (particularly if it is a share sale) may give rise to an employer's debt, and this aspect is considered further in 16.62 to 16.66 below.

Circumstances not involving a transfer

16.20 The following circumstances will not usually give rise to a transfer payment:

(*a*) the sale of a company with its own scheme; or

(*b*) an asset sale, where all of the scheme's active members are to have their employment transferred to the purchaser and the purchaser is to be substituted as the scheme's new principal employer (see 16.17 above).

In these cases, the purchaser will effectively be taking over the whole of the scheme, as it will be buying (or, alternatively, becoming) its principal employer. This is considered further in 16.22 below.

Other approaches

16.21 The general principles outlined in 16.19 and 16.20 may sometimes be overridden if the parties agree to structure matters differently.

One example of this would be where the vast majority of the active members were to be affected by the transaction, but not all of them. In these circum-

16.22 *Commercial transactions*

stances, rather than provide for a transfer payment to be made in respect of most the scheme's active members, the parties might decide instead to arrange for the purchaser to be substituted as the scheme's principal employer (and then for a transfer payment to be made back to another scheme within the vendor's group in respect of the minority of active members whose employment was to remain with the vendor).

The parties will need to satisfy themselves that the course of action proposed will be one which can be achieved under the terms of the scheme rules (particularly as the co-operation of the trustees, who will not be parties to the agreement, may be required). Even if the scheme rules themselves do not appear to present a problem, the agreement may still fail if it is inconsistent with the purposes of the scheme; the *Re Courage Group's Pension Schemes [1987] 1 WLR 495* (see 12.13 above) is perhaps the best known example of this happening.

In some cases, the purchaser may refuse to accept any responsibility for past service benefits at all, so that the employees concerned simply become deferred pensioners in the vendor's scheme. The industrial relations consequences of such a step do of course need to be borne in mind and the employment law position carefully considered in all the circumstances (see Chapter 7); in this respect, there may be a difference depending on whether it is a share or asset sale, in view of the employment law distinction mentioned in 16.15 above.

TRANSACTIONS WHERE THE PURCHASER TAKES OVER THE WHOLE SCHEME

Protection of purchaser

General

16.22 Where the purchaser is, in effect, to take over the whole of the vendor's scheme (see 16.20 above), its main concern will be to obtain as much protection as possible from any liabilities associated with it which arose prior to completion. This is especially the case because the scheme will relate not only to those current employees being acquired by the purchaser, but also to past employees with benefits (whether deferred or in payment) under the scheme.

This protection will take the form of thorough due diligence, warranties and, in relation to areas of particular concern, indemnities.

Due diligence

16.23 The purchaser should seek to ensure that its advisers have the opportunity to examine as much as possible of the scheme's documentation at an early stage.

At the very least, this should cover the scheme's governing trust documents, the latest actuarial valuation report (and any subsequent actuarial advice), booklets and announcements issued to members (as well as references to pensions in contracts of employment and service agreements), recent annual reports and accounts and sufficient membership data to enable the purchaser's advisers to take a view on the costs of the scheme's ongoing liabilities.

The purchaser should also seek to obtain copies of the Inland Revenue approval letter and any contracting-out certificates. Other relevant matters are trustees' minutes, copies of investment management agreements (and other advisers' appointment letters), insurance policies, transfer agreements with the trustees of other schemes, the statement of investment principles, the schedule of contributions, documentation relating to member-nominated trustee arrangements and details of the scheme's internal dispute resolution procedure. The aim should be to build up a full picture of the scheme including funding levels, liabilities, the balance of powers between the employers and the trustees and compliance with the *PA 1995*.

Warranties

16.24 The more comprehensive the warranties that the purchaser is able to obtain from the vendor, the safer he will generally be. For maximum protection, the agreement may stipulate that the warranties apply not only as at the date of the agreement but also (if later) the date of completion. Even if the vendor gives warranties but then discloses against them, the purchaser will at least be in a better position to know where any problems lie.

Some examples of the warranties that a purchaser should seek are:

(*a*) that there are no schemes or similar commitments (whether legally binding or not) relating to the employees, except those that have been disclosed;

(*b*) that the documents provided to the purchaser are true and complete;

(*c*) that the scheme is an exempt approved scheme and there is no reason why that approval might be withdrawn;

(*d*) that the scheme is contracted-out (where appropriate) (see chapter 4)and the necessary contracting-out certificates have been issued;

(*e*) that the scheme complies with all legal requirements for the equalisation of benefits as between men and women;

(*f*) that the scheme, its trustees and the employers have complied with all applicable statutory requirements;

(*g*) that the information contained in the latest actuarial valuation report is complete and accurate in all respects and that nothing has happened since its effective date which would have an adverse affect on its conclusions;

16.25 *Commercial transactions*

(*h*) that none of the employers being acquired is, or may become, liable in respect of any underfunding under *sections 59, 60* or *75* of *PA 1995*;

(*i*) the rate of employers' contributions;

(*j*) that all contributions due have been paid in accordance with the trust deed and rules and as required by the scheme's schedule of contributions;

(*k*) that no changes have been made (or proposed or announced) to the scheme's eligibility requirements, contribution rates or benefits;

(*l*) that all risk benefits are validly insured with an insurance company of good repute on normal terms for persons in good health; and

(*m*) that there are no court proceedings and no complaints (whether under the scheme's internal dispute resolution procedure, or to OPAS or to the Pensions Ombudsman) in progress, pending, threatened or anticipated.

The purchaser may seek more extensive warranties than these and the vendor, conversely, will often aim to limit their scope. For instance, the vendor may wish to restrict the warranties to matters of which it is aware, which in turn may lead to negotiations as to what extent of knowledge the contract should deem the vendor to have. The vendor will be particularly cautious with regard to any funding warranty, as a breach of this can prove extremely expensive.

Indemnities

16.25 Either party may seek indemnity protection from the other in respect of matters where there is some particular risk involved.

Purchasers therefore frequently require indemnities against the costs of benefits not having been equalised as between men and women in respect of past service (see Chapter 9). Another area which may give rise to an indemnity is the possibility of an employer's debt becoming payable under *section 75* of *PA 1995* (see 16.62 to 16.66 below).

Funding

General

16.26 The importance to a purchaser of having a funding warranty has already been mentioned in 16.24.

A separate (but related) issue arises where the scheme is understood to be overfunded or underfunded on an ongoing basis and it is agreed that there should be some payment between the parties following the sale (usually as an adjustment to the purchase price) to compensate. Where this happens, the respective parties' actuaries will normally negotiate a method and assumptions for determining the amount of overfunding or underfunding; the calculation itself is then carried out after completion.

(It is common for these issues instead to be dealt with at an earlier stage, as part of the purchase price negotiations. The most likely reason for dealing with the matter by means of a post-completion adjustment would be that there was insufficient information as to the scheme's funding position at the time of sale.)

Underfunded scheme

16.27 Where the scheme is underfunded on an ongoing basis, the purpose of the compensating payment will, in effect, be to relieve the purchaser of the costs of bringing the funding up to that level.

The sum which the *scheme* will require, therefore, will be the amount by which the scheme's assets fall short of the value calculated in accordance with the agreed actuarial method and assumptions. The vendor, however, will be reluctant to pay more than is necessary to achieve this, and so (instead of paying the sum directly into the scheme) may propose to pay it to the purchaser net of the standard rate of corporation tax, on the basis that corporation tax relief will become available to the purchaser's group when it is remitted to the trustees. (The vendor may be particularly concerned that the payment should be used to restore the scheme's funding position rather than to benefit the purchaser, and so expressly require that the purchaser pay the sum into the scheme as soon as it is received.)

The purchaser will not necessarily be satisfied with this approach. For instance, the purchaser's group may prove not to be making profits when the time comes, in which case it will derive no benefit from the theoretical availability of corporation tax relief. Alternatively, even if the purchaser is making profits, the sum involved may be treated by the Inland Revenue as a special contribution (see Chapter 5), in which case the tax relief would have to be spread over a period of years.

A compromise position would be for the payment to be made to the purchaser gross of corporation tax, on condition that the purchaser take steps to avail itself of corporation tax relief on paying the sum into the scheme and account to the vendor for the value of that relief.

Overfunded scheme

16.28 Where the scheme has a surplus on an ongoing basis, the purpose of a compensating payment (which would instead be from the purchaser) is very different, as are the considerations affecting its calculation.

The payment would be a form of recognition that, before the sale, there was an overfunded scheme within the vendor's group from which the vendor might have gained some benefit in the future. Following the sale, the vendor no longer has that opportunity, which has passed to the purchaser instead.

It would be inappropriate for the purchaser to pay to the vendor the whole of this surplus. This would presume that it was open to the scheme's employers to acquire the full present value of the scheme's surplus, which is not the case for a number of reasons:

(a) Only in exceptional cases may an employer receive a refund of surplus assets from its scheme, and even then the scheme rules and legislation will normally require that substantial benefit increases be granted first. Any such refund would, in any event, be subject to a 40 per cent tax charge. These issues are considered in more detail in Chapter 11.

(b) It is more likely that the employer could benefit from the surplus by means of a reduction in its contributions or even a contributions holiday. However, it is by no means certain that the whole of the surplus could be used in this way. For example, if the scheme rules give the trustees a say in the matter, then it is likely that at least some of this surplus would instead have to be used for benefit improvements.

Even if the employer is able to take a contributions holiday in respect of the entire surplus, the benefit of that holiday will only gradually be realised over a period of time. An immediate payment to the vendor in lieu of that contributions holiday, therefore, ought not to be equal to the entire surplus, but should be discounted to take into account the fact that (unlike a contributions holiday) the benefit to the vendor is immediate.

It can be seen from this that agreeing a suitable method for ascertaining the amount of the compensatory payment is likely to prove complex. Often the matter will instead be dealt with between the parties before the sale as part of the purchase price negotiations.

Change of trustees

16.29 Usually, the scheme's trustees will be directors, employees or a subsidiary company of the vendor. If the trustees are to remain with the vendor's group following completion, it will generally be appropriate for them to be replaced as trustees by individuals or by a company within the purchaser's group. The contract may expressly provide for this to be done, and may even require that a deed of removal and appointment of trustees be one of the completion documents.

Considerations may also arise in relation to the issue of member-nominated trustees. This is addressed further in 16.67 below.

TRANSACTIONS INVOLVING A TRANSFER PAYMENT

General

16.30 Where the transaction involves a transfer payment (see 16.19 above), the sale agreement may provide for the company being sold (or, in the case of an asset sale, the purchaser) to participate in the vendor's scheme on a transitional basis for a temporary period after completion. This is not always the case, however, and the following paragraphs, from 16.31 to 16.50 below, assume that there is to be no such transitional period.

The further issues which will become relevant if there is to be a transitional period are considered later in this chapter (see 16.51 onwards).

Methods of calculating transfer payments

Past service reserve

16.31 There are several ways of calculating a bulk transfer payment. Of these, a 'past service reserve' calculation is the one which seeks to produce a sum which is sufficient to provide past service benefits which are equal overall to the benefits that the transferring members could otherwise have expected to receive in respect of their completed membership of the vendor's scheme had there been no sale.

A past service reserve transfer payment is calculated by reference to the length of past pensionable service of the members concerned, but with present pensionable salaries being increased by an actuarially assumed rate of future salary growth. The calculation will also require other assumptions to be made, for instance in relation to the future mortality rates, inflation, rates of withdrawal by members from pensionable service and investment growth.

The figure produced by this calculation will ultimately depend upon the assumptions used. These assumptions should normally therefore be agreed between the respective parties' actuaries before the contract is signed. Two very slightly differing sets of assumptions can produce vastly different results and consequently these negotiations are often hard fought. In reality, the relationships between the assumptions (for instance, the extent by which investment returns are assumed to exceed future salary growth) may have a greater impact on the final calculation than the assumptions themselves.

The purchaser's actuary will normally wish to see a copy of the scheme's most recent actuarial valuation report, so that he can form a view as to whether the assumptions on offer are consistent with the way in which the scheme as a whole is funded. The vendor may refuse to make the valuation report available, but the purchaser may still be able to obtain it through links with members or with trades unions to whom the trustees can be required by law to provide a copy in accordance with the *Occupational Pension Schemes (Disclosure of Information) Regulations 1996 (SI 1996 No 1655)* (see summary at Appendix II).

The valuation report may reveal that the assumptions on offer will produce a smaller transfer payment than would the long-term funding assumptions recommended by the actuary for the purpose of calculating employer's contributions. The purchaser may then argue that the scheme's long-term funding

16.32 *Commercial transactions*

assumptions should be used instead. The vendor's likely response would be that a policy decision had been taken to fund the scheme using more cautious assumptions than were strictly necessary or that different assumptions were appropriate to the group of employees being transferred.

Sensitivity about the scheme's funding assumptions is not the only reason why a vendor may prefer not to make a copy of the valuation report available. Other reasons might be that:

(*a*) the valuation shows that the scheme is in surplus, and this may encourage the purchaser to press for a greater transfer payment; or

(*b*) the valuation shows that the scheme is weakly funded, which in turn may lead the purchaser to ask for an indemnity in respect of any employer's debt that may arise. This aspect is explained further in 16.62 to 16.66 below.

Past service reserve plus share of surplus

16.32 The purchaser may seek a transfer payment that is calculated on a past service reserve basis but which also includes a proportionate share of any surplus funding in the vendor's scheme over and above that.

Although the scheme rules will be relevant, it has been widely accepted since Walton J's decision in *Re Imperial Foods Ltd Pension Scheme [1986] 2 All ER 802* that there is no reason in principle why a purchaser (or the receiving trustees) should expect the transfer payment to include a share of any surplus. The rationale for this view is that, in an ongoing scheme whose rules will require the employers to increase their contributions to make good any underfunding that arises in the future, a surplus in the scheme as at a given time simply reflects the fact that the employers are temporarily ahead with their contributions. The so-called surplus does not represent 'spare' money that should necessarily be available to a receiving scheme.

Transfer payments including a share of a surplus are therefore now comparatively rare. However, they can still occur where, for instance, a very substantial proportion of the vendor's scheme's liabilities is to be transferred in circumstances where the vendor's scheme's rules will make it difficult for the trustees to justify not transferring a share of the surplus, or require a 'share of fund' transfer value to be paid.

Where this does happen, the vendor can be expected to require an increase in the purchase price. The manner in which this should be calculated is complex, but it will be governed by the same considerations as have been mentioned above in the context of 16.28 above.

Cash equivalents

16.33 We saw in Chapter 6 that a member's 'cash equivalent' is the statutory amount which he may be entitled by law to require the trustees to transfer to another scheme. For a group of members, their aggregate cash equivalents will broadly speaking be comparable to the amount which is needed to satisfy the statutory minimum funding requirement in respect of their past service benefits.

In most cases, cash equivalents will produce a lower figure than would a past service reserve. This is primarily because the cash equivalent calculation does not provide for future salary growth.

Where a vendor proposes that the transfer payment be restricted to cash equivalents, this may be because the vendor's scheme is too precariously funded to be able to pay more. If this is so, the purchaser may request a shortfall payment from the vendor representing the difference between the cash equivalents and the higher amount which a past service reserve calculation would have produced (see 16.44 below) or alternatively seek a reduction in the purchase price. If the vendor is not prepared to accede to either of these requests, then there is likely to be an adverse impact on the past service benefits which the purchaser's scheme will be able to offer, unless the purchaser is prepared to make up the shortfall itself. The employment law and industrial relations of this will have to be considered (see Chapter 7), as well as the possibility instead that past service benefits simply be left in the vendor's scheme (rather than transferred).

Sometimes a vendor will offer only cash equivalent transfer payments, even though its scheme can afford to pay more. The scheme rules are likely to be especially relevant in such cases; it may well be that they require the trustees to pay more than the vendor is offering.

Reduced cash equivalents

16.34 In some circumstances, the law may permit the trustees of the vendor's scheme to reduce members' cash equivalent transfer payments, on the basis of the scheme's funding position. The problems which this can raise for the purchaser are essentially the same as those mentioned in 16.33 above, only even more acute. The purchaser should also be particularly concerned about the risk of an employer's debt arising as explained further in 16.62 below.

Other possibilities

16.35 There are, of course, other ways of calculating a transfer payment. For instance, it could be calculated as an agreed percentage of (for example) the amount needed to meet the statutory minimum funding requirement ('MFR') in respect of the transferring members' past service benefits. So, a scheme which, being funded at 104 per cent of the MFR, could afford to pay more than the statutory cash equivalents but was unable to pay a reasonable past service reserve, might pay transfer payments equal to 104 per cent of the MFR in respect of the members concerned.

16.36 Commercial transactions

Timescales, mechanics and calculation adjustments

Timescales and mechanics

16.36 In the absence of a transitional period (see 16.51 onwards), the mechanics of the transfer provisions will tend to revolve around two key dates.

The first of these is the date of completion of the sale, which is for pension purposes will be the date on which the relevant employees' pensionable service in the vendor's scheme will terminate.

The second of these is the date on which the transfer payment becomes payable.

The length of time that is to pass in between the completion date and the payment date will be determined by the sale agreement. In most cases the agreement will provide for certain steps to be taken in between the two dates. In a typical agreement, these might be as follows:

(a) Following the completion date, members are to be invited to join the purchaser's scheme for future service and advised that if they do elect to join they will have a right to transfer their past service benefits to the purchaser's scheme.

(b) The members are to be given a period in which to decide whether to elect for such a transfer. This will normally involve their signing and returning a consent form, and the sale and purchase agreement will often provide for that form to include a discharge from the member to the vendor's scheme's trustees (and possibly the vendor) in respect of any further liability for past service benefits. The information given to members should recommend that they obtain independent financial advice, so as to avoid problems arising under the *Financial Services Act 1986* (see Chapter 10).

(c) Once that period has expired, the parties know which members have elected to transfer. The parties then instruct their actuaries to liaise with a view to calculating the transfer payment in accordance with the method of calculation previously agreed between them. There will usually be a set timescale for this.

(d) Once the calculation of the transfer payment has been agreed, there is a short further period allowed for, at the end of which the payment becomes due. If it has been agreed that the transfer be paid in cash, the transferring trustees may need to realise assets during this period. Alternatively, the parties and their actuaries may agree certain *in specie* transfers of assets.

Timing adjustment

16.37 A past service reserve transfer payment will in these circumstances be calculated as at the date of completion, as that will be the date on which pensionable service terminated and the benefits therefore crystallised.

However, as explained in 16.36 above, the transfer payment will not actually become payable until some time after that. Some provision therefore needs to be included in the agreement specifying how the transfer payment is to be adjusted in respect of the period from completion until the date on which it becomes payable.

An interest calculation can be used, but this may not take proper account of the effects of investment conditions during the period in question. If, for instance, share values were to soar ahead of the agreed interest rate during this period, then the vendor's fund would benefit disproportionately from this, whereas the purchaser's fund would not benefit from it at all. Conversely, were investments instead to fall in value, the effect of an agreed interest rate would be to exacerbate the impact of this upon the vendor's fund, whilst the purchaser's fund would remain insulated from the adverse conditions.

The actuaries may therefore agree a market related 'timing adjustment' in respect of this period. In effect, this means that the past service reserve figure is to be adjusted by a formula representing movements over the period in a notional portfolio consisting of (for instance) 85 per cent equities and 15 per cent gilts. The actuaries will discuss and agree the formula to be used before the sale agreement is signed. The respective schemes' investment strategies can be expected to have some bearing on these discussions.

Interest

16.38 If the transfer payment is not paid until after it has fallen due, a further adjustment will be necessary in respect of the period of late payment.

This may be dealt with simply by continuing to apply the timing adjustment for that further period, but the purchaser may consider that the sale agreement should require a more punitive adjustment as payment by that stage will be overdue. One approach would be to continue to apply the timing adjustment, but to make the sum resulting from it subject to an agreed rate of interest in respect of the period of delay.

Voluntary contributions

16.39 The agreement should also provide for the transfer of assets arising from the payment of money purchase voluntary contributions by those members who elect to transfer their past service benefits. Because of the money purchase nature of these, this will be a simpler provision than those parts of the agreement dealing with the transfer of final salary benefits.

Disputes clause

16.40 There may be circumstances in which, following the sale, the actuaries are unable to agree the calculation of the transfer payment as required by the

16.41 *Commercial transactions*

sale agreement. Alternatively, the sale agreement may require that the past service benefits to be granted by the purchaser's scheme should be equal in overall value to the amount of the transfer payment; this is another area where the actuaries may fail to agree.

Most pensions schedules therefore include a clause providing for disagreements of this nature to be referred to an independent actuary. The clause will normally provide for the independent actuary to act as expert (rather than as arbitrator) as this is generally suitable for disputes of this nature and is less formal than arbitration. The agreement should also make provisions as to who is to bear the expert's costs; for example, whether these are to be borne between the parties equally or, alternatively, as the expert may direct.

Inland Revenue issues

Consent to bulk transfer

16.41 The consent of the Inland Revenue should be sought before making a bulk transfer payment to or from an approved scheme, and the pensions schedule should accordingly make it clear that any obligations in relation to the transfer are subject to this approval being obtained.

The application to the Inland Revenue should be made on form PS 295. In practice, the Inland Revenue is unlikely to object except in the very rare cases where a scheme has such a large surplus that the Inland Revenue requires it to be reduced.

Continued rights

16.42 We saw in Chapter 5 (see 5.6 onwards) that Inland Revenue limits may (subject of the member's precise circumstances) be more generous for a member who joined a scheme before 17 March 1987 or 1 June 1989 than if he had joined on or after those dates. Members who joined before these dates are said to have 'continued rights'.

The Inland Revenue should therefore be asked to confirm that these members of the vendor's scheme may carry on being treated as having 'continued rights' after they join the purchaser's scheme. The *Occupational Pension Schemes (Transitional Provisions) Regulations 1988 (SI 1988 No 1436)* and the *Retirement Benefits Schemes (Continuation of Rights of Members of Approved Schemes) Regulations 1990 (SI 1990 No 2101)* respectively provide for such treatment. It is not strictly necessary to seek the Revenue's approval in all cases but it is generally safest to do so, and should certainly be sought where members already had continued rights in the vendor's scheme arising from a previous transfer in.

Contracting-out

16.43 Separate requirements apply to the transfer of contracted-out benefits. The relevant law is summarised in Chapter 4, starting at 4.75.

Shortfall and excess clauses

Shortfall clause

16.44 As has been mentioned already, the trustees will not be a party to the sale agreement and so will not be bound by its terms. Consequently, except in those cases where the vendor's scheme's rules enable the vendor to direct the amount of the transfer payment, there can be no guarantee that the trustees of that scheme will in fact transfer the amount provided for in the sale agreement. The purchaser will have particular cause for concern if the funding position of the vendor's scheme suggests that its assets may prove insufficient to justify the transfer payment which the parties have negotiated.

The purpose of a shortfall clause, therefore, is to protect the purchaser (and the purchaser's scheme) from the possibility of the trustees transferring less than the amount which the vendor and the purchaser have agreed. The clause will require a payment by the vendor itself (or by a company in its group) to achieve this. The principles surrounding the shortfall payment (including the tax considerations) will be those that have already been considered in the context of 16.27 above.

Excess clause

16.45 An excess clause is essentially the converse of a shortfall clause. Whereas a shortfall clause requires a payment from the vendor, should the trustees of the vendor's scheme pay less than the agreed transfer payment, an excess clause requires a payment from the purchaser should they pay more.

A vendor might insist that, in order to be even-handed, any shortfall clause in the agreement should be accompanied by a mirror-image excess clause. The purchaser, however, may take the view that the vendor's trustees will only exceed the negotiated transfer payment if they are satisfied that their scheme can afford it. Consequently, many excess clauses are expressed so as only to apply to the extent that the trustees have transferred the excess by mistake.

The purchaser's scheme

Type of scheme

16.46 The course of action which ought to create the least disruption to the continuing accrual of members' pension benefits will be a properly funded

16.47 *Commercial transactions*

transfer payment to a final salary scheme of the purchaser, containing similar provisions to those of the vendor's scheme.

Often, however, the purchaser will not have an existing final salary scheme and the number of employees to be transferred may simply not be enough to make the establishment of a final salary scheme specifically for them financially viable. In these circumstances, the purchaser might instead offer membership of a money-purchase scheme or agree to pay contributions to personal pension schemes in relation to the employees concerned.

The vendor will normally require a commitment in the sale agreement that the receiving scheme should be approved (or at least capable or receiving approval), so that the vendor's scheme may properly make the transfer to it. The contracted-out status of the purchaser's scheme should also be addressed, in view of the requirements referred to in 16.43 above.

One related point concerns announcements which the vendor may have made about the purchaser's scheme. When contemplating making announcements to members about an impending sale, vendors will need to bear in mind the case of *Hagen v ICI Chemicals and Polymers Ltd [2001] 64 PBLR, [2001] All ER (D) 273 (Oct)*. This has already been referred to at 7.22 above. In the light of this case, the vendor may want to leave as much detail as possible to be explained by the purchaser, whilst still complying with its duty to provide certain disclosures under *TUPE*. The vendors should ensure that communications are as far as possible recorded in writing and that they take legal advice.

Past service benefits

16.47 If the sale agreement provides for a past service reserve transfer payment to a final salary scheme, the vendor is likely to require some commitment as to what past service benefits the purchaser's scheme will provide. The vendor may prefer that these be determined in the same manner as applies for the calculation of benefits under the vendor's scheme, but this could prove impractical for the purchaser if its own scheme has a different benefit structure.

Instead, the purchaser may (if it is satisfied that the transfer payment will be sufficient) be prepared to agree that the past service benefits will be broadly equivalent (or, if the purchaser agrees to go further than that, at least equal in value) overall to those earned in the vendor's scheme; the vendor, in turn, may consider that this should be tightened so as to apply separately in respect of each member. The agreement may have to make it clear how benefits are to be valued for this purpose.

A more stringent line that a vendor could take would, in effect, be to insist that the whole of the transfer payment is used to provide past service benefits in respect of the employees concerned. This would prevent the purchaser from using any part of the sum to fund a reduction in employers' contributions or to provide benefits for other scheme members. Much will depend upon the trust deeds and funding positions of the respective schemes, but a purchaser may well be reluctant to accept such a suggestion on the ground that it places a more onerous obligation upon it than would previously have applied under the vendor's scheme.

Indeed, the purchaser may be reluctant to give any commitments as to the level of past service benefits at all if it has doubts about the adequacy of the transfer payment being offered.

Where the transfer is to be made to a money-purchase scheme, the question of past service benefits is less controversial. These will normally be whatever the value of each member's portion of the overall transfer payment provides.

Future service benefits

16.48 Purchasers are generally reluctant to commit themselves in the sale agreement to a specific level of benefits in respect of future service. This is partly because to do so would in most cases be a more onerous obligation than the vendor itself had ever assumed, but more particularly because it would fetter the future running of their business.

A purchaser which has decided initially to provide final salary benefits might, therefore, be prepared to commit itself to a particular benefits structure as at the date when the employees join the scheme, but reserve the right to amend or discontinue the scheme at any time after that. In the comparatively rare cases where the purchaser agrees to maintain a particular benefit structure (perhaps because it is receiving a generous transfer payment), this will only normally apply for a limited period.

Transfer agreement

16.49 The nature of the purchaser's scheme and the benefits under it will generally tend to be of greater concern to the transferring trustees than they are to the vendor itself. These trustees may even have adopted a practice of requiring receiving trustees to enter into a transfer agreement with them, dealing specifically with these issues, before they will agree to make a particular transfer payment.

Where this is the case, the vendor may require that a form of transfer agreement is attached to the sale agreement and that the vendor's obligations in relation to any transfer are dependent upon the purchaser's scheme's trustees entering into such an agreement with the vendor's scheme's trustees.

Transfer agreements, and examples of the matters that they will frequently cover, are considered in Chapter 12, 12.42 onwards.

16.50 *Commercial transactions*

Due diligence, warranties and indemnities

16.50 Where the purchaser will not be inheriting the whole of the vendor's scheme, it may not require the same level of warranty protection as described in 16.24 above. This is particularly so in the absence of a transitional period (see 16.30 above), as the purchaser (or, in the case of a share purchase, the company it is buying) will not be participating in the vendor's scheme following completion.

The purchaser should still, however, request a complete copy of the scheme's trust deed and rules and obtain a warranty as to its accuracy. There are two main reasons for needing to see this. The first is to enable the purchaser to satisfy itself that its provisions will not be such as to prevent the agreed pensions schedule from being implemented. If, therefore, the rules show that the power to make bulk transfer payments rests solely with the trustees, then (particularly if the scheme appears to be poorly funded) the purchaser will be forewarned of the importance of obtaining a shortfall clause (see 16.44 above).

The other reason is to enable the purchaser to ascertain the contributions and benefits structure in the vendor's scheme; with this in mind, the purchaser should also seek to obtain copies of members' booklets and should also require a warranty that no changes to the information shown have been proposed or announced. This (together with appropriate membership data) should enable the purchaser's actuary to assess the likely costs to the purchaser of providing the same benefits for future service and suggest what alternative approaches might be available. This information should also reveal any particular expectations the members may have that could prove expensive for the purchaser, such as generous early retirement provisions on redundancy.

The purchaser ought also to request a copy of the latest actuarial valuation report and obtain warranties to the effect that nothing has happened since its effective date which might adversely affect its findings. An understanding of the scheme's funding position will help the purchaser to take a view as to how large a transfer payment it can realistically negotiate. Where there is some indication of underfunding, this will again alert the purchaser to the possible need for a shortfall clause (see 16.44 above) and an indemnity in respect of any employer's debt that may arise (see 16.62 to 16.66 below).

Warranties should also be sought as to the vendor's scheme's tax position (as an approved scheme is not permitted by the Inland Revenue to accept a transfer payment from a scheme that is not approved) and also its contracted-out status (because of the requirements referred to briefly in 16.46 above and set out in chapter 4).

Another area of concern is the equalisation of benefits as between men and women as required by law (see Chapter 9). The purchaser should seek a warranty that these requirements have been met, as a member who is entitled to bring a claim based on a scheme's failure to equalise can also sue the trustees of another scheme to whom the benefits in question have been transferred. If successful, such a claim can prove expensive. It is therefore common for purchasers also to seek an indemnity against this eventuality.

The current state of concern arising from the case of *Beckmann v Dynamco Whicheloe Macfarlane Ltd, Case C-164/00, [2002] 64 PBLR; [2002] All ER (D) 05 (Jun)* (see 16.15 above) may lead to purchasers and vendors negotiating who will bear the commercial risk that a particular scheme benefit will pass following this case. Purchasers may seek indemnities or an adjustment to the purchase price in this connection. They should consider relevant provisions of the vendor's scheme very carefully and ask their actuary to cost these pension rights.

Transitional periods

General

16.51 Transactions involving a transfer payment fall into two main categories, depending upon whether the employees concerned:

(a) cease to be active members of the vendor's scheme from the completion date; or

(b) continue to be active members of the vendor's scheme for a transitional period following the completion date.

The purchaser may wish to have the benefit of a transitional period if it has no suitable scheme in place to receive the transfer payment (or provide future service benefits) and requires a period of time in which to establish one.

In the context of a company sale, this will simply be a case of the company continuing to participate in the scheme for a temporary period after it has been sold out of the vendor's group. In an asset sale, by contrast, it will mean the purchaser (or employer of the transferring employees) being admitted to the vendor's scheme as a participating employer, but only for the agreed transitional period commencing on the completion date.

Previously in this chapter we have considered only those cases where there is no transitional period. Where there is to be a transitional period, further considerations will apply.

Inland Revenue

16.52 Any period of participation in these circumstances by an employer which is not (or has ceased to be) associated with the scheme's principal employer will require the agreement of the Inland Revenue. The sale and purchase agreement should be drawn up in a manner which recognises this. In practice, however, the Revenue can normally be expected to agree to such a period provided it does not exceed 12 months.

16.53 *Commercial transactions*

Role of trustees

16.53 Before agreeing to a period of temporary participation, the vendor should check its scheme rules to see if the trustees have a discretion as to whether or not to permit this. If so, then the vendor will not be in a position to *procure* a transitional period in the sale agreement, and should ensure that the level of commitment required of it under the sale agreement is consistent with those rules.

In most instances, the trustees should be amenable to the agreement of a transitional period of participation, but circumstances may arise where they are not (for instance, if the trustees anticipate that the temporary employer intends to grant artificially high pension increases, to the detriment of the scheme's funding position).

The sale agreement will normally seek to regulate the terms upon which the company or purchaser is to be permitted to participate, as we shall see below. This is another area, therefore, where the rules of the vendors' scheme and the scheme's actuarial assumptions will need to be checked. This can be particularly relevant in the context of contributions, which is considered next.

Employer's contributions

16.54 The parties may either leave the question of contributions during the transitional period to be determined in accordance with the scheme rules, or they can agree a specific rate.

If, for example, the vendor's scheme is overfunded and the participating employers are enjoying a contributions holiday, the vendor is likely to prefer to specify a fixed contribution rate, probably equal to the long-term contribution rate which the actuary would be recommending if the scheme was evenly funded on an ongoing basis. This, of course, is because the purchaser will have made no contribution towards the surplus that has arisen and so the vendor will not wish to see the purchaser derive any benefit from it.

Conversely, the employers may all be paying very high contributions following an unfavourable actuarial valuation report. In these circumstances, the purchaser can be expected to request a lower, specified rate.

Even where a specified rate of contribution is agreed, it may in fact be the vendor's scheme's trustees (rather than the vendor) who have the power to decide contribution rates under the scheme rules. If, therefore, the parties have agreed a fixed rate which tends to favour the purchaser, then the purchaser may also seek an indemnity from the vendor against the possibility of the trustees requiring a higher rate.

Expenses

16.55 Expenses arising during the transitional period may take the form of:

(a) administrative expenses; or

(b) the cost of insuring risk benefits.

They may form part of the contribution rate required to be paid by the purchaser during the transitional period, or be specified in the agreement as a further sum to be paid in addition to those contributions.

Limit on salary increases

16.56 One of the actuarial assumptions by reference to which the vendor's scheme is funded will relate to future salary increases. A transitional period presents some risk to the vendor of the temporarily participating company granting salary increases during that period which significantly exceed this assumption.

Such an increase will inflate the vendor's liabilities for deferred pensions in respect of those members affected by the transaction who elect not to transfer to the purchaser's scheme. It may also increase the amount of the transfer payment, depending on the circumstances (see 16.59 below). This, of course, will be detrimental to the funding of the vendor's scheme.

The vendor may therefore insert a provision requiring the purchaser to procure that pay increases do not rise by more than a certain percentage during the transitional period (often a percentage consistent with the scheme's assumptions). Whether this presents a problem for the purchaser will depend on whether it anticipates granting such increases. If not, then the purchaser may choose to accept the restriction, but with the qualification that the increases may be granted with the consent of the vendor (that consent not to be unreasonably withheld or delayed).

Other obligations of the purchaser during the transitional period

16.57 The sale agreement may also require the purchaser to procure that, during the transitional period, it (or, where appropriate, the participating employer owned by it):

(a) will comply with all the provisions of the vendor's scheme which apply to it as a participating employer;

(b) will not exercise any discretion which it may have in relation to the vendor's scheme without the vendor's consent (usually not to be unreasonably withheld or delayed);

(c) will not by any act or omission prejudice the scheme's exempt approved or contracted-out status;

(d) will not take any steps which might increase the transfer payment; and

(e) will nominate the vendor to act on its behalf in relation to the member-

16.58 *Commercial transactions*

nominated trustee arrangements and its right to be consulted about the scheme's statement of investment principles.

Obligations of the vendor during the transitional period

16.58 Obligations of the vendor under the sale agreement in respect of the transitional period might be as follows:

(a) to keep the scheme in full force and effect;

(b) not to increase benefits in relation to the members concerned; and

(c) not to take any steps which might reduce the transfer payment.

Date as at which past service liabilities are calculated

16.59 The date as at which the past service reserve should be calculated may be either:

(a) the completion date; or

(b) the end of the transitional period.

One of these alternatives may be more consistent with the scheme's trust deed and rules than the other. A number of issues will arise depending upon which of the two dates is to apply:

(i) If the completion date is used, an addition should be made to the calculation of the transfer payment representing the contributions paid by the participating employer in respect of the transferring members, and by the transferring members themselves, during the transitional period (less any part of the employer contributions which relates to the expenses mentioned in 16.55 above).

(ii) If the end of the transitional period is used, then the issue of salary increases during the transitional period (see 16.56 above) becomes particularly relevant, as increases in excess of the assumptions will inflate the calculation of the transfer payment.

(iii) If the end of the transitional period is used, then the timing adjustment (which, in the absence of a transitional period, would operate from the completion date – see 16.37 above) should instead operate from the end of the transitional period.

Admission of new members during the transitional period

16.60 If during the transitional period the purchaser does not have any other scheme in place, it may wish to have new members employed by it (who were not members before completion) admitted to the vendor's scheme during that period. The vendor's views on this are likely to depend on the administrative implications.

It may be that the vendor will draw a distinction between:

(a) applicants who were employed by the company (or within the business) before completion but were at that time serving a 'waiting period' before they could become eligible to join; and

(b) applicants who are recruited as employees by the new owners after completion;

and agree only to admit the first of these two groups.

Due diligence, warranties and indemnities

16.61 The purchaser should obtain the same information, and seek the same protections, as mentioned in 16.50 above.

In addition, however, the fact that there will be a temporary period of participation in the vendor's scheme will necessitate a careful review of the participating employers' obligations under the scheme's trust deed. The issues in relation to employers' contributions have already been mentioned (see 16.54 above) including the possible need for an indemnity from the vendor. A review of the scheme's latest actuarial valuation report may (depending on how recent it is) give some indication as to whether this is likely to be an issue.

The purchaser should also check to see whether the trust deed (or any other document) contains an indemnity by the participating employers in favour of the trustees. If so, more extensive warranties may be necessary to satisfy the purchaser that there is no matter in respect of which it might become liable under that indemnity.

EMPLOYER'S DEBT

General

16.62 We saw in Chapter 12 (see 12.76 onwards) that there are certain circumstances where *section 75* of the *PA 1995* may render an employer liable for a debt to the trustees of an underfunded scheme.

One of these sets of circumstances is especially relevant in the context of this chapter. Under *section 75*, as amended by *regulation 4(3)* of the *Occupational Pension Schemes (Deficiency on Winding Up etc.) Regulations 1996 (SI 1996 No 3128)* (the 'Deficiency Regulations'), an employer will become liable in this way if:

(a) the scheme is one to which *section 75* relates (which in practice covers most approved final salary schemes – see 12.77 above);

(b) the employer ceases to employ persons in a description or category of employment to which the scheme relates whilst at least one other employer continues to do so; and

16.63 *Commercial transactions*

(c) the scheme is at that time underfunded by reference to the statutory minimum funding requirement (the 'MFR'). (See *regulation 3* of the *Deficiency Regulations* and Chapter 11 above for details regarding the MFR).

It can therefore be seen that this will be relevant when a transaction results in a cessation of participation by one or more of the participating employers in an underfunded, approved final salary scheme.

Amount of the debt

16.63 The first stage in calculating the debt is to ascertain the amount by which the scheme as a whole falls short of the MFR. To do this will require an actuarial valuation of the entire scheme.

There are statutory provisions (*section 75(1A)-(1E)* of the *PA 1995* as inserted by *regulation 4* of the *Deficiency Regulations*) which specify how much of this debt will be the responsibility of a given employer. These provisions apply whether the debt has arisen specifically in the context of 16.62 above or any of the other circumstances outlined in 12.80 above.

Where the scheme has more than one participating employer the effect of these provisions is as follows:

(a) If the scheme rules specify how the overall MFR deficit is to be apportioned between the employers for the purpose of calculating the debt, then those rules must be followed (*section 75(1A), PA 1995*).

(b) If (as is more usually the case) the scheme rules are silent on the point, then the amount of the debt due from the employer concerned is:

$$\frac{A}{B} \times C$$

where:

    A   is the amount of the scheme's liabilities which, in the opinion of the actuary (after consultation with the trustees or managers), are attributable to employment with the employer concerned;

    B   is the amount of the scheme's liabilities which, in the opinion of the actuary (after consultation with the trustees or managers), are attributable to employment with any of the employers; and

    C   is the total MFR deficit in the scheme. (See *regulations 3* and *3A* of the *Deficiency Regulations* and Chapter 11 above for details regarding the MFR deficit calculation).

[*Section 75(1A), PA 1995*].

See also 12.80 above regarding when multi-employer schemes are treated as being divided into separate schemes for debt purposes.

The Pensions Bill

16.64 The Pensions Bill contains new provisions regarding debts on employers. It proposes to insert a new *section 75A* in *PA 1995* to provide flexibility in relation to the calculation of a *section 75* debt in circumstances where a participating employer withdraws from a multi-employer scheme. The explanatory notes to the Bill indicate that it is intended for the full buy-out calculation basis to be adopted unless approved arrangements are entered into to ensure that the scheme receives financial support in the future, in which case the scheme's specific funding basis of calculation may be adopted. Further detail on the operation of this new section will be set out in regulations. Clearly the possibility of a *section 75* debt arising, which is calculated on a full buy-out basis, may have a significant impact on the viability of a proposed transaction and the value of a withdrawing company.

Trustees' position

16.65 We have already seen (see 12.82 above) that *section 75* does not as a general rule create any absolute requirement on the trustees to obtain an actuarial valuation or to pursue the debt. Where there is no such obligation, the trustees may decide not to take these steps if, for instance, they are satisfied that the costs of doing so would exceed any amount that the scheme might stand to recover or that no MFR debt will arise.

However, where:

(*a*) (as will be the case here) an event has occurred in relation to one or more (but not all) of the scheme's employers which may give rise to a debt; and

(*b*) any of the circumstances indicating the possibility of an MFR deficit (as specified in *reg 13* of the *Occupational Pension Scheme (Minimum Funding Requirement and Actuarial Valuations) Regulations 1996 (SI 1996 No 1536)* (*the 'MFR Regulations'*)) has occurred;

that regulation *requires* the trustees to obtain an MFR valuation.

Parties' positions

16.66 The purchaser should be concerned about the risk that he may be entering into a transaction which may gives rise to a debt payable by him or by the company he is buying. It would not be wise for the purchaser to assume that, just because the Pensions Bill does not refer to the circumstances in 16.62 it can ignore the possibility of a debt arising.

Even if the purchaser can persuade the vendor to indemnify him against any such debt, there remains the possibility that a considerable period of time might pass before the actuarial calculations are complete and the debt is notified to the purchaser. There is a risk that, by this stage, the vendor may no longer be in a financial position to meet the indemnity. As well as an indemnity, therefore, the

16.66 *Commercial transactions*

purchaser may ask the vendor to procure that the scheme will be valued, and the amount of any debt notified, within a set timescale.

None of this is likely to appeal to the vendor, especially if the scheme's funding is indeed weak. The prospect of an indemnity will be particularly unattractive if the vendor is promising a past service reserve transfer payment backed up by a shortfall clause (see 16.44 above). As for a commitment to procure an MFR valuation within a set timescale, this of course can only serve to increase the likelihood of the indemnity coming into operation. The vendor may require that the purchaser meet the costs of any such valuation, but this, like the surrounding matters, will ultimately be a matter for negotiation.

The possibility of an employer's debt may, therefore, present major issues for the parties, and this highlights the need for early due diligence in relation to the scheme's funding position. It may, however, be possible to lessen the impact of the legislation by structuring the deal, for example, as an asset sale rather than a company sale, as illustrated in the following table:

	Potential size of debt	**Reason**
Company sale, no transitional period	Could be huge.	The purchaser acquires all the company's liabilities. The company may have participated in the vendor's scheme for years and be responsible for a huge proportion of the overall debt. This will relate not only to the company's present employees, but also to pensioners and deferred pensioners formerly employed by it.
Company sale with transitional period	Larger still	As above, except that the extra period of participation will increase any debt still further.
Asset sale, no transitional period	Nil (assuming the vendor of the assets continues to have some employees in the scheme following completion).	No employer will be ceasing to participate in the vendor's scheme.
Asset sale with transitional period	Smaller debt than for corresponding company sale (again, assuming the vendor of the assets continues to have some employees in the scheme following completion).	The purchaser will have participated in the vendor's scheme only for a short time following completion, and so be responsible for a (probably small) proportion of any overall deficit.

MEMBER-NOMINATED TRUSTEES

16.67 We saw in Chapter 3 that certain events (referred to in the legislation as 'relevant events') can cause the trustees of a scheme to re-consider the appropriateness of its arrangements in relation to member-nominated trustees.

A commercial transaction of the sort considered in this chapter will often involve one or more relevant events (although it is worth mentioning here that a bulk transfer is only a relevant event if it is made without the members' consents, and that in the context of these transactions consent is normally obtained). There is further detail on this subject in 3.35 above.

PUBLIC SECTOR TRANSFERS

16.68 Bulk transfers from schemes such as the Principal Civil Service Pension Scheme and other public service pension schemes, of which the Government Actuary's Department is scheme actuary, have separate requirements which must be satisfied if a bulk transfer payment is to be made into a receiving scheme. These situations arise primarily when an outsourcing contract is entered into with a Government body or agency.

In order for the Government Actuary's Department to agree to the transfer of public service scheme benefits, the receiving scheme must satisfy prescribed criteria to their satisfaction. These criteria relate generally to the level of benefits to be provided and the balance of powers in the receiving scheme. The Government Actuary's Department will usually provide a standard pensions schedule setting out their requirements but its provisions can be negotiated to a limited extent, subject to the circumstances of a particular case. Some schemes may be required to make amendments to the scheme rules to satisfy the Government Actuary's Department's criteria. If the necessary criteria are satisfied, the Government Actuary's Department will issue either a 'certificate of broad comparability' or a 'passport'.

The distinction between the passport and the certificate of broad comparability is that the passport attaches to the receiving scheme and is valid for more than one transfer in, only ceasing to be of general application if the Government Actuary's Department's requirements change. A passport is more usually applied for when a new scheme is being established specifically to receive public service transfers. By contrast, a certificate of broad comparability will be required for all schemes without a passport on each occasion on which it is proposed that a transfer be made.

Of course, not all such outsourcing contracts will lead to transfers of benefits. The *Local Government Pension Scheme (Amendment etc.) Regulations 1999* (*SI 1999 No 3438*) provided a new method of addressing pensions on the transfer of employment in the context of local government outsourcing. This method is to admit the new employer to participate in the local government pension scheme. The new employer must enter into an admission agreement

16.68 *Commercial transactions*

with the administering authority, and may also have to acquire an indemnity or bond (*reg 5* of the *Local Government Pension Scheme Regulations 1997 (SI 1997 No 1612)*). The need for an indemnity or bond was previously an absolute requirement, but this changed under the *Local Government Pension Scheme (Amendment) (No 2) Regulations 2003 (SI 2003 No 3004)*. This substituted *regulation 5* with *regulations 5, 5A* and *5B* from 19 December 2003, but with effect from 1 January 2003. The new requirement is that where a new employer will provide services or assets in connection with the function of an existing 'Scheme employer' (the outsourcing Council), as a result of the transfer of the service or assets by means of a contract or other arrangement, that 'Scheme employer' must:

> 'carry out an assessment, taking account of actuarial advice, of the level of risk arising on premature termination of the provision of the service or assets by reason of the insolvency, winding-up or liquidation of the transferee admission body'.

It is only 'where the level of risk identified by the assessment is such as to require it', that the prospective new employer is required to enter into an indemnity or bond. This means that where there are only a handful of employees transferring, for example, there may no longer be a need to go to the expense of providing an indemnity or bond. Where such a document is required, banks usually present their own 'standard' which is then considered by the outsourcing Council's lawyers.

Negotiation of the admission agreement and indemnity or bond is usually a lengthy process and should be started as soon as the overall contract negotiations begin. Prospective new employers are increasingly seeking indemnities from an outsourcing Council as to liabilities – past and future – in the local government pension scheme.

The requirement for a new employer to provide either broadly comparable pension arrangements or admission to the local government pension scheme, is currently only contained in Government guidance, but the Government is in the process of putting this on a statutory basis. *Sections 101* and *102* of the *Local Government Act 2003* provide that local authority transferees will be offered either continued membership of the local government pension scheme or membership of a broadly comparable scheme. However, the provisions are quite short and we will have to wait for appropriate directions to provide the necessary details.

All of the above applies to local authority employees transferring to a new employer as a result of an outsourcing contract. In addition, a Code of Practice has been drawn up in draft, requiring contractors to provide new joiners with membership of the local Government pension scheme, membership of a good quality employer pension scheme – either being a final salary pension scheme or a money purchase pension scheme with matched employee and employer contributions up to six per cent – or a stakeholder pension scheme, under which the employer will match employee contributions up to six per cent. Further details regarding public sector transfers are to be found at 7.22 above.

OTHER TYPES OF SCHEME

Money purchase schemes

16.69 Where the vendor's scheme provides money purchase benefits, the issues are considerably simpler.

In the context of a money purchase occupational scheme, the warranties will focus far less on the sufficiency of the scheme's assets and more on the extent of the liability to contribute (and whether all the contributions due have been paid). There may still, however, be some defined risk benefits, and the purchaser should seek the necessary warranty as to the insurance of these.

If the circumstances give rise to a transfer payment (see 16.19 above), the amount to be transferred will effectively be the sums in the transferring members' money purchase accounts, rather than involving complex valuation methods and assumptions.

If the purchaser is taking over the entire scheme (see 16.20 above), it will also require warranties to satisfy itself that the scheme complies with all relevant legal requirements. However, as illustrated by the table in 1.16 above, money purchase arrangements are less heavily regulated than final salary ones.

If the scheme is a personal pension arrangement, the purchaser will want to see the documentation promising to contribute and information indicating the costs of those contributions. It will also need a warranty that all contributions due have been paid (and that there has been no proposal or announcement to pay higher contributions).

Small self-administered schemes

16.70 Most small self-administered schemes ('SSASs') are money purchase arrangements and so the same principles as mentioned in 16.69 above apply. These are less regulated than other types of scheme in many respects (see 13.34 above), although the purchaser should seek warranties that the investment and borrowing restrictions that apply to such schemes (see Chapter 13) have been observed.

Often the company which the purchaser is buying will be the principal (or only) employer of the SSAS and the vendors will be the scheme members. The vendors (who in these circumstances will probably also be trustees of the SSAS) will wish to retain control over their scheme and so may, as a term of the sale agreement, require that the purchaser executes a deed of amendment transferring (so far as possible) the company's powers under the scheme rules in relation to the SSAS to the trustees. The purchaser may be happy to do this, as long as it is protected from any further liabilities in relation to the SSAS.

16.71 *Commercial transactions*

Unapproved schemes

16.71 The purchaser should seek to obtain as much information as it can about any unapproved schemes that there may be.

As can be seen in the table in 14.12 above, much of the legislation that applies to other schemes does not apply to unapproved arrangements. This will to some extent lessen the level of warranty protection that the purchaser will require, although in assessing the costs of these arrangements it should be borne in mind that the early leaver legislation (see Chapter 6) may apply (even to unfunded arrangements).

The key difference, however, between an unapproved arrangement and any other type of scheme will, of course, be its tax treatment. This is considered in detail in Chapter 14.

CONCLUSION

16.72 This chapter is only an overview, but it should be sufficient to illustrate the complexity and the possible costs implications of pension arrangements in negotiations for the sale or purchase of a company or business. The potential impact of pensions issues for both the vendor and the purchaser should therefore never be underestimated, and the sooner these are addressed the better the chances of the deal progressing to a successful conclusion for both sides.

Chapter 17

Pensions dispute resolution and litigation

INTRODUCTION

17.1 Whilst there has always been scope for disputes to arise over pension schemes, there has been a dramatic growth in this area since the early 1990s. The reasons for this include the increased regulation of pension schemes, the introduction of public bodies to police such schemes, the authority of the Office of the Pensions Ombudsman to adjudicate upon disputes, the introduction of internal dispute resolution procedures and increased public awareness.

The *Maxwell* scandal in the early 1990s, disputes over large surpluses in various privatised industries and, more recently, the *Equitable Life* situation and all the talk of a 'pensions crisis', as a result of the large deficits caused by the stock market slump, have all served to increase public awareness. This increased awareness has translated into an increased number of pensions related complaints. In 2003, the Pension Ombudsman reported an all-time high number of complaints which his office was struggling to keep up with. Similarly, in 2003 OPAS reported a 53% rise in the number of complaints referred to it. As a consequence, the management and resolution of disputes has become an increasingly important factor for trustees in the administration of pension schemes.

The particular relationships of the parties involved in a pension scheme distinguish pensions disputes from normal commercial disputes. This chapter is not intended to be an exhaustive narrative of every type of dispute and procedure. Instead, it is intended to provide an overview of the principal forums for dispute resolution, and, in relation to litigation through the courts, to highlight some of the issues that may arise in pensions cases, including the use of ADR to settle disputes.

NON-COURT FORUMS FOR DISPUTE RESOLUTION

Internal Dispute Resolution Procedure (IDRP)

17.2 *Section 50* of *PA 1995* requires trustees of occupational pension schemes to implement a two stage IDRP to deal with disputes by members and other beneficiaries about matters concerning the scheme. *Section 50*, together

17.3   *Pensions dispute resolution and litigation*

with the *Occupational Pension Schemes (Internal Dispute Resolution Procedures) Regulations 1996 (SI 1996 No 1270)*, set out the detail of who can make a complaint, the information it should contain and how it should be dealt with. This is discussed in more detail in chapter 3.

IDRP should be capable of resolving the majority of the common complaints made by members and beneficiaries against the trustees and managers. It should be noted, however, as stated in paragraph 3.45, that a complaint is exempted from the IDRP if proceedings have already been commenced in a court or other tribunal, or where the Pensions Ombudsman has already commenced an investigation. IDRP is also not the appropriate avenue for pursuing a complaint against an employer, as such complaints fall outside the scope of the procedure.

If the trustees do not implement any 'decision' made under the IDRP which requires implementation, the Pensions Ombudsman would be likely to determine that such failure constitutes 'maladministration' by the trustees, in the event that the member were to complain to him. Also, if the complainant is not satisfied with the 'decision' under the IDRP, the member may refer his complaint to OPAS (see below) and/or the Pensions Ombudsman (the Pensions Ombudsman will ordinarily require a complainant to have made full use of the IDRP before accepting a complaint for investigation – see 3.45 above).

Complaints to Pensions Advisory Service (OPAS)

17.3   OPAS provides free advice and assistance to members of the public who have a complaint about their occupational or personal pension scheme and will seek to resolve a dispute by negotiation and correspondence between the parties. The success of this forum depends to a great extent on the willingness of the parties, as any suggested resolution proposed by OPAS is not directly enforceable. If OPAS cannot resolve the member's complaint, the complaint may then be submitted to the appropriate Ombudsman for resolution. The Pensions Ombudsman encourages individuals complaining to him to have consulted OPAS first. The contact details of OPAS can be found at 2.22 above.

Other forums

Financial Services Authority (FSA) and Financial Ombudsman Service (FOS)

17.4   Where a person has a complaint about the sale and marketing of a pension arrangement, the complaint may be investigated by the FSA (which regulates the industry) or the FOS (which settles disputes between consumers and financial institutions). If the complaint involves a financial product or service, the FOS requires the complaint to be submitted first to the firm involved to be considered under its internal complaints procedure. If the complainant is unhappy with the firm's final response to the complaint, or eight weeks have elapsed from the date the complaint was submitted, without a final response from the firm, the complainant has six months in which to submit the complainant to the FOS. The FOS will first seek to resolve the complaint through an informal process of mediation. If that is unsuccessful, the FOS will conduct a full investigation into the complaint and issue a written determination which is binding on the firm (to a limit of £100,000).

Further information, the relevant forms and contact details can be found on the FOS website: www.financial-ombudsman.org.uk.

The Occupational Pensions Regulatory Authority (Opra)

17.5 Opra regulates the compliance by trustees of occupational pension schemes with *PA 1995* and has a wide range of powers to enforce those regulations. A summary of those powers and Opra's contact details can be found at 2.12 above. Details of the penalties Opra can impose under *PA 1995* are summarised in appendix I.

Employment tribunals

17.6 Disputes concerning an employee's rights under an occupational pension scheme may also be dealt with during the course of employment tribunals. This is discussed in more detail in chapter 7.

Divorce proceedings

17.7 Disputes over pension benefits also arise in the context of divorce proceedings. This is dealt with in more detail in chapter 8 above.

Complaints to Pensions Ombudsman (PO)

17.8 The role of the PO, his jurisdiction and a summary of the applicable procedure is set out in chapter 5 and paragraphs 2.23 to 2.25 of chapter 2. The PO is not permitted to investigate or determine a complaint if proceedings have already been commenced in any court or employment tribunal in connection with matters to which the complaint relates, unless the proceedings began after 30 November 2000 and they have been discontinued without a settlement binding on the complainant. The court has the power to stay court proceedings concerning matters which are the subject of a complaint or dispute before the PO (*sections 146 and 148, PSA 1993*).

Determination

17.9 A determination given by the PO is final and binding on the complainant and any person responsible for the management of the scheme to which the complaint relates (subject to being overturned, on appeal, by the court). The PO has the power to direct any person responsible for the management of the scheme to take, or refrain from taking, such steps as he may specify. Any

17.10 *Pensions dispute resolution and litigation*

determination of the PO is enforceable in a county court as if it were a judgment or order of that court (*section 151, PSA 1993*).

The PO's determination or direction must be in writing and state the grounds upon which it is made. A dissatisfied party may ask for the court's permission to appeal the determination on a point of law. The appeal is heard in the High Court (*section 151(4), PSA 1993*) (see 17.12 below).

Human Rights Act 1998

17.10 The *Human Rights Act 1998* (*HRA 1998*) has been in force since October 2000. *Article 6(1)* of the *European Convention on Human Rights*, which *HRA 1998* incorporates into English law, provides that, in the determination of a person's civil rights and obligations, everyone is entitled to a fair and public hearing within a reasonable time by an independent and impartial tribunal established by law. Following doubts which were raised in connection with the office of the PO in this context, the PO obtained and published an opinion from counsel as to whether *Article 6(1)* applies to investigations by the PO and, if so, whether the PO's practice and procedure satisfy the principles set out in *Article 6(1)*. That opinion is available on the PO's website (www.pensions-ombudsman.org.uk). It concludes that *Article 6(1)* does apply and that the PO's practice and procedure in relation to the holding of oral hearings and otherwise are broadly compatible with *Article 6*. However, particular criticism from legal commentators has been levied at the role and influence of the PO's staff in investigating complaints and producing determinations, and it remains to be seen whether the PO's practice and procedure will be subject to a successful challenge in the High Court under *Article 6(1)*.

COURT PROCEEDINGS

Introduction

17.11 Litigation through the courts has, traditionally, been regarded as costly, time consuming and unpredictable. It is not surprising, therefore, that the Pensions Ombudsman and OPAS are attractive alternative forums in which beneficiaries of pension schemes may pursue their claims. However, court proceedings may be unavoidable in some circumstances, such as where a determination of the Pensions Ombudsman is appealed; where the trustees seek the court's directions on a pensions issue; or where the claimant has no other available forum in which to pursue the claim. Set out below is a summary of the most common types of applications that are made to the court in pensions disputes and a basic explanation of the various procedures under the *Civil Procedure Rules 1998* (*SI 1998 No 3132*) ('*CPR*'), which govern the procedure in the civil courts.

Types of application to court

Appeals from the Pensions Ombudsman (PO)

17.12 Section 151 of *PSA 1993* provides a right of appeal to the High Court on a point of law arising out of a determination given by the PO. Any such appeal will be heard in the Chancery Division of the High Court. The procedure is set out in *Part 52* of the *CPR*, and the *Practice Direction on Appeals*. The party lodging the appeal – the 'appellant' – must file a notice of appeal (known as the 'appellant's notice') at the High Court within 28 days after the date of the PO's determination. A copy must also be served on the PO and the respondent. The appellant's notice should be in a form prescribed by the *CPR* (form N161) and set out the grounds for the appeal, the arguments in support of those grounds, the decision sought from the appeal court and any evidence in support of the appeal. It should be accompanied by a skeleton argument (a summary of a party's submissions) and a bundle of relevant documents.

The other parties to the appeal are referred to as 'respondents', and may include the PO as a respondent. A respondent can ask the appeal court to uphold the PO's determination for reasons different from or additional to those given by the PO, in which case that respondent must file a 'respondent's notice' within 14 days of being served with the appellant's notice. Like the appellant's notice, the respondent's notice should be in a prescribed form (form N162), accompanied by a skeleton argument and bundle of relevant documents.

It is important to note that the time limits referred to above are strict and cannot be varied without the court's permission. This means that once the PO has issued a determination, the parties should take immediate steps to consider whether they wish to appeal and, if so, prepare the relevant documents. Both the appeal notice and the skeleton arguments should be prepared with care because a party will not be able to rely in the appeal on a matter not contained in the appeal notice without the permission of the court. An appeal does not operate as an automatic stay of the determination of the PO unless the court or the PO permits otherwise.

The appeal will be limited to a review of the PO's determination unless the court considers that, in the circumstances, it would be in the interests of justice to hold a rehearing. Oral evidence and evidence which was not before the PO are not allowed to be introduced in the appeal unless the court orders otherwise. The court has power to affirm, set aside or vary any determination made by the PO; refer any claim or issue back to the PO for determination; order a new hearing before the PO, and make orders for the payment of interest on any monies awarded and the parties' costs.

In practice, whilst an employer may have the resources to fund the costs of an appeal, an individual complainant may be reluctant to pursue an appeal given the costs of mounting the appeal and the risk of being ordered to pay the respondent's costs if the appeal is lost. In such circumstances, the potential

17.13 *Pensions dispute resolution and litigation*

appellant may consider applying for a prospective costs order (which is discussed in more detail at 17.35 below) before pursuing an appeal.

In certain appeals the PO may decide that he wishes to participate but, if he does, he will expose himself to a risk that, if he loses, the court may order him to pay the costs of the appeal (*Moore's (Wallisdown) Ltd v Pension Ombudsman [2002] 1 All ER 737*). For this reason, the PO has indicated a reluctance to participate in appeals, except where the issue is of wider public relevance. This approach was reflected in the 2003 case of *Legal & General Assurance Society Ltd v CCA Stationery Ltd [2003] EWHC 2989 (Ch), [2003] ALL ER (D) 233*, in which the court requested the PO's participation in the appeal but the PO declined because of the costs risk. The result was that the appeal hearing went ahead without the participation of the respondents.

The decision of the High Court may be appealed to the Court of Appeal. The court's permission is required and will only be granted if it is considered that the appeal would raise an important point of principle or practice, or there is some other compelling reason to hear it. The Court of Appeal's judgment may, with the court's permission, be appealed to the House of Lords.

It is relevant to note that recent attempts to seek judicial review of the PO's determinations, as an alternative to pursuing an appeal under the procedure explained above, have failed. In those cases, the court referred to the appeal procedure as being the more appropriate means of determining the issues.

Seeking directions from the court

17.13 The court has a wide jurisdiction to provide directions to trustees on matters relating to the administration of a pension scheme (*CPR 64*). Applications to court for such directions usually concern issues arising out of the trustees' exercise of a discretion or a power under the pension scheme's trust deed or rules, or where the meaning of the scheme's trust deed or rules is unclear or ambiguous. For example, the trustees may seek the court's direction because:

(*a*) they are uncertain whether or not a proposed course of action is within their powers;

(*b*) they wish to seek the court's blessing to a proposed course of action which may have a significant impact on the scheme (eg application for a *Beddoe* order – see 17.33 below); or

(*c*) they wish to surrender the exercise of a discretion to the court because they are unable to arrive at a decision for some reason (eg conflict of interest, deadlock).

Such applications are commonly referred to as 'construction' or 'directions' applications. They are not usually of a hostile nature (unless the employer and/or the beneficiaries take exception to what is proposed) and may be distinguished from proceedings in which the trustees' actions are being challenged by a third party, which are usually hostile. Directions applications are usually brought under the simplified *CPR Part 8* procedure (which is discussed in more detail in 17.20 below).

Claims by/against a third party

17.14 These are claims which involve the trustees and third parties ie parties external to the trust. For example, they may include claims involving the trustees' professional advisers over their remuneration or negligence or a claim by trustees against a former trustee for breach of trust. They are usually hostile in nature and are usually brought under the *CPR Part 7* procedure (which is discussed in more detail in 17.21 below).

Rectification

17.15 Where an error is discovered in the drafting of a pension scheme document, such that the document does not reflect accurately the true common intentions of the trustees and the employer, and that error cannot be resolved completely by other means (eg by the proper construction of the document, or by the use of any applicable amendment power which does not offend *section 67, PA 1995*), the trustees may apply to the court to rectify the error. Basically, in order to succeed the trustees would have to provide credible evidence that the error did not reflect accurately the clear and common intentions of the trustees and employer when the wording in the document was drafted. They would have to prove that there is no other effective remedy available, that the mistake is of significant importance such that it justifies the court making an order for rectification and that in all the circumstances it is appropriate to grant rectification (eg there are no legal bars to rectification).

Given the importance of documentary and oral evidence to a rectification application, it is usually made using the *Part 7 procedure* (see 17.21 below), unless there is no dispute on the facts, in which case the *Part 8 procedure* may be more appropriate (see 17.20 below). The trustees and the employer will both be parties to the application and a representative beneficiary (see 17.25 below), or more than one where appropriate, is usually appointed to represent the beneficiaries of the scheme. As a result of the evidential burden on trustees, rectification applications are usually not straightforward, particularly where another party objects to the proposed rectification. They are often made in conjunction with, and as an alternative to, an application for a declaration that the offending document can be properly construed to give effect to the parties' instructions, which, if successful, would mean that the trustees would no longer need to pursue the alternative rectification application.

17.16 *Pensions dispute resolution and litigation*

Outline of procedure

Issues for consideration before commencing court proceedings

17.16 Before embarking on court proceedings, a claimant should consider, in particular, the following important factors:

(a) is the claim being brought within any relevant limitation period prescribed by law? If not, the claim may be time barred.

(b) How will the costs of the proceedings be funded and paid? (Some relevant issues on costs are discussed in 17.29 below.)

(c) Who will be the parties to the proceedings?

(d) What remedy is sought and will it be an effective remedy?

(e) What are the merits of the application?

The answers to these questions will assist a claimant in determining not only whether to commence proceedings in the civil courts, but also the strategy to be adopted in progressing the claim, including whether to pursue alternative dispute resolution methods (Alternative Dispute Resolution ('ADR'), for which see 17.37 below). The decision to commence court proceedings should not be taken lightly, because once commenced, the claimant cannot unilaterally withdraw them without having to pay the other party's costs (unless the other party or the court agrees otherwise).

Beneficiaries and trustees should be aware that the beneficiary may request disclosure by the trustees of certain 'trust documents', which the trustees may be legally obliged to disclose, without the need for litigation. This may assist a beneficiary's investigation into a matter. It is a common law principle that trustees are obliged to disclose 'trust documents' to beneficiaries who have a fixed (as opposed to discretionary) interest in a trust (including a pension scheme) (*O'Rourke v Darbishire [1920] AC 581, [1920] All ER Rep 1*). This obligation has been based on the principle that beneficiaries have the 'proprietary' right to the documents held by the trustees. Trust documents include the trust deed, rules, accounts and all documents relating to the trust, including minutes or trustee meetings. It may also extend to legal advice obtained by the trustees on behalf of scheme, although not usually legal advice obtained in respect of the beneficiary's claim against the trustees or legal advice paid for by the trustees themselves rather than out of trust monies.

This disclosure obligation has not, however, extended to disclosing the trustees' deliberations on and reasons for exercising their discretionary powers under the scheme in a particular way. Therefore, trustees have not had to disclose any document evidencing their reasons and deliberations on that issue, unless there is evidence of improper conduct (*Re Londonderry's Settlement re Peat v Walsh [1964] 3 ALL ER 855; Wilson v. Law Debenture Trust Corporation plc [1995] 2 All ER 337*). If the trustees fail to disclose the disclosable trust documents, they may be ordered by a court to pay the costs of any application that the beneficiary may make to the court to compel such disclosure.

However, this obligation has been affected by two recent decisions.

1. In *Schmidt v Rosewood Trust Ltd [2003] UKPC 26, [2003] 3 ALL ER 76* the court appeared to move away from the 'proprietary right' as the underlying rationale of the obligation and, instead, asserted the court's inherent power to supervise the administration of trusts, and right to order disclosure of any trust documents if it is considered appropriate in all the circumstances. This potentially widens the scope of the disclosure obligation not only in terms of the range of documents that could be disclosable but also the type of beneficiary who may be entitled to disclosure. It remains to be seen how this is further applied in practice by the court.

2. The Pensions Ombudsman indicated in a determination in 2002 (*Allen [L00370]*) that he considered it to be '*good administrative practice*' for pension trustees to give reasons for their decisions and to make minutes of trustee meetings available to beneficiaries with a legitimate interest in the matter, even when exercising discretionary powers. Where he could see no good reason for trustees withholding disclosure of their reasons, he was prepared to determine that the trustees were guilty of maladministration. This approach creates an obvious tension with the approach of the court in the cases referred to in this section. Given the above, trustees who receive a request for documents should consider it carefully, with appropriate advice, before deciding whether to reject it or the extent to which it should be complied with.

(See also a trustee's disclosure obligations pursuant to relevant pensions statutes and regulations at 3.22 above and appendix II.)

Pre-action protocols

17.17 The *CPR* set out steps that the court will expect the parties to undertake before proceedings are commenced. In particular, the court will expect all parties to have complied in substance with the terms of any applicable 'pre-action protocol' in the *CPR*. Whilst there is presently no specific protocol applicable to all types of pension disputes, there is a protocol which applies to professional negligence claims (eg a trustee's claim against his professional advisors for negligence).

Where there is no specific protocol that applies to the dispute in issue, the *Practice Directions on Protocols* (set out in the CPR) set out a pre-action procedure that parties should seek to adhere to with the intention of avoiding litigation in so far as possible. The following procedure is specified, although this may be revised by the parties to suit their particular circumstances provided that the revisions are reasonable.

1. Each party should act reasonably in exchanging information and documents relevant to the claim and generally in trying to avoid the necessity for the start of proceedings.

2. The claimant should write to the defendant setting out its claim. The letter should:

17.17 *Pensions dispute resolution and litigation*

- give sufficient and concise details to enable the recipient to understand and investigate the claim without extensive further information;
- enclose copies of the essential documents which the claimant relies on;
- ask for a prompt acknowledgment of the letter, followed by a full written response within a reasonable stated period (for many claims, a normal reasonable period for a full response may be one month);
- state whether court proceedings will be issued if the full response is not received within the stated period;
- identify and ask for copies of any essential documents not in his or her possession which the claimant wishes to see;
- state (if it is so) that the claimant wishes to enter into mediation or another alternative method of dispute resolution; and
- draw attention to the court's powers to impose sanctions for failure to comply with this practice direction and, if the recipient is unlikely to be represented, enclose a copy of the practice direction.

3. The defendant should acknowledge the claimant's letter in writing within 21 days of receiving it and should state when the defendant will give a full written response. If this is longer than the period stated by the claimant, the defendant should give reasons why a longer period is needed.

4. The defendant's letter should, as appropriate, accept the claim in whole or in part and make proposals for settlement, or state that the claim is not accepted. If the claim is accepted in part only, the response should make clear which part is accepted and which part is not accepted.

5. If the defendant does not accept the claim, or part of it, the response should:

    - give detailed reasons why the claim is not accepted, identifying which of the claimant's contentions are accepted and which are in dispute;
    - enclose copies of the essential documents which the defendant relies upon;
    - enclose copies of documents asked for by the claimant, or explain why they are not enclosed;
    - identify and ask for copies of any further essential documents not in his or her possession which the defendant wishes to see; and
    - state whether the defendant is prepared to enter into mediation or another alternative method of dispute resolution.

6. The claimant should provide requested documents within a reasonably short time or explain in writing why he or she is not doing so.

7. If the claim remains in dispute, the parties should promptly engage in appropriate negotiations with a view to settling the dispute and avoiding litigation.

It should be noted that any documents disclosed by either party in accordance with the above procedure, may not be used for any purpose other than resolving the dispute, unless the other party agrees. Further, if the dispute requires the assistance of an expert, the practice direction suggests that the parties should, wherever possible and to save expense, engage a single agreed expert (eg if an actuary is required to provide a valuation). It should be noted that the court retains a power to refuse an expert's report sought by a party at this stage or refuse that party to claim the costs of an expert report in any subsequent proceedings.

It is important that a party follows this procedure, or any agreed revised procedure, as the court has an express power to apply costs and other sanctions in the event of a party's non-observance.

Whilst the above procedure provides for limited voluntary disclosure of documents, the CPR also provides a mechanism, in certain circumstances, for a potential claimant to apply to the court for an order obliging a potential defendant to anticipated proceedings to disclose documents before those proceedings are commenced (see *CPR 31.16*), although the party making the application will usually have to pay the other party's costs of the application and of complying with any order made.

Procedure in the civil court

17.18 Court procedure in civil cases is governed by the *CPR*, with the exception of appeals, court proceedings are initiated by the issue and service of a Claim Form (which replaces the 'writ' and 'originating summons'). As referred to above, there are two principal procedures under the *CPR* for issuing a claim (as opposed to an appeal) – the Part 7 and Part 8 procedures. They are discussed in more detail below. The Part 7 procedure is the most commonly used procedure in claims involving third parties because such cases involve disputes of fact. The Part 8 procedure is the standard procedure for directions applications by trustees.

Once proceedings have been commenced, the court will allocate the case to one of its three tracks:

(*a*) *Small claims track*: This is for claims worth less than £5,000. It is designed to be an inexpensive and less formal, expedited procedure, in which the strict rules of evidence do not apply. Expert evidence is not allowed without the court's permission and the court allows a party, its lawyer or a lay representative to present its case at the hearing. The court may, if all parties agree, deal with the claim 'on paper' (ie without a hearing).

(*b*) *Fast track*: This is for claims worth between £5,000 and £15,000. It

17.19 *Pensions dispute resolution and litigation*

involves an abbreviated but more formal procedure designed to allow for a trial within a reasonably short timescale, assuming a settlement cannot be reached.

(c) *Multi track*: This is for claims worth over £15,000. It is the most formal procedure of the three tracks, as a result of which cases usually take longer to be determined and are more costly.

Claims issued under the Part 8 procedure are automatically allocated to the multi track, whereas Part 7 claims will be allocated to the appropriate track, according to the value of the claim.

Case management powers

17.19 In all proceedings, the court has wide case management powers. When exercising any power under, or interpreting any rule in, the *CPR*, the court must give effect to what is known as the *'overriding objective'*. The overriding objective stipulates that the court must deal with cases justly (see *CPR Part 1* for a full definition). This includes dealing with the case expeditiously and fairly, and in ways which are proportionate to the amount of money involved; the importance and complexity of the case; and to the financial position of each party. The parties themselves are also required to help the court to further the overriding objective.

The court also has wide powers to penalise parties for their conduct in the proceedings by, for example, disallowing all or any part of their costs, or ordering them to pay another party's costs or, in more serious instances, by striking out their case. As a result, parties should aim to meet time deadlines imposed by the court and conduct themselves appropriately.

Part 8 procedure

17.20 The Part 8 procedure is simpler and is designed to be more efficient than the Part 7 procedure. The Part 8 procedure should be employed where the court's decision is required on a question which is unlikely to involve a substantial dispute of fact or where a practice direction permits or requires its use for that type of proceedings. In pensions cases, a trustee's application for directions (see 17.13 above) is required to be brought under the Part 8 procedure. Whilst third party claims (see 17.14 above) and claims for rectification (see 17.15 above) may also be brought under the Part 8 procedure, such claims will often involve a substantial dispute of fact so the Part 7 procedure is usually more appropriate. The court may, at any time, disapply the Part 8 procedure to any proceedings brought under it. Part 8 claims are automatically allocated to the multi-track.

An outline of the Part 8 procedure is as follows:

(a) Issue and service of claim form

The Part 8 claim form is in a prescribed form and should set out, among other things, the question(s) for determination by the court, the remedy sought and the legal basis for that remedy. Any evidence upon which the claimant wishes to rely at the hearing of the claim should accompany the claim form (set out either in the claim form or in a witness statement, but in both cases verified by a signed statement of truth).

(*b*)   Acknowledgment of service

The defendant must acknowledge service of the claim form within 14 days by filing at court, and serving on all parties, the prescribed form or an appropriately worded letter. In acknowledging service, the defendant should state whether the claim is contested or whether a different remedy is sought. Unlike under the Part 7 procedure, the defendant does not have to serve a defence. If the defendant disputes the court's jurisdiction to hear the claim, an appropriate application should be made within 14 days of acknowledging service. Failure to acknowledge service will result in the defendant not being able to take part in the hearing of the claim without the court's permission.

(*c*)   Evidence

If the defendant wishes to rely on evidence at the hearing, that evidence, in the form of a witness statement with any relevant documents exhibited to it, should be filed and served at the same time as the acknowledgment of service. The claimant then has 14 days in which to serve any evidence in reply, unless an extension of time can be agreed with the defendant(s) or is ordered by the court.

(*d*)   Case management directions

The court may give case management directions when the claim form is issued. It is more usual, however, for the court to give directions after the defendant has acknowledged service or the time limit for acknowledging service has expired. The parties are encouraged to agree, so far as is possible, appropriate case management directions for the court's approval. The court may give such directions without a hearing or by calling a case management conference. Such directions may include the disclosure of documents (see 17.22 below), the exchange of further witness statements (see 17.23 below), the preparation and exchange of expert reports (see 17.24 below), and any other steps that may be necessary for the efficient management of the claim.

(*e*)   Hearing of claim

The hearing of the claim will take place in open court before a judge, unless the court permits it to be held in private. No written evidence may be relied on by a party at the hearing unless it has been served in accordance with the rules or the court gives permission. At the hearing, each party's legal representatives make their oral submissions to the judge. The judge may require or allow a party to give oral evidence at the hearing and may require a witness's attendance for cross examination.

17.20 *Pensions dispute resolution and litigation*

(f) Judgment

After hearing the parties' submissions, the judge will either hand down the judgment at the end of the hearing or may reserve judgment to a future date (in order to allow time for the judge to consider and draft the judgment).

In applications by trustees for directions in the administration of a trust, the court's *Practice Direction to CPR 64* provides additional guidelines, which include the following:

(i) Confidentiality

If the confidentiality of the directions sought is important (such as in a *Beddoe* application – see 17.33 below), the claim form should only give a general description of the remedy sought, with a more detailed explanation set out in the trustee's witness statement.

(ii) Representative parties

The trustees should consider carefully which beneficiaries should be 'representative parties' (see 17.25 below). It may not be necessary for a representative of each class of beneficiary in the pension scheme to be joined as a party to the proceedings because the trustees may be able to present the arguments for or against the application on behalf of some classes of beneficiary (although trustees will need to consider carefully whether it is prudent for them to pursue this course in the circumstances of the application). If the trustees are unable to decide which categories of beneficiaries to join as defendants (for example, where there are many members and categories of interest), the trustees may apply to issue the claim form without naming any defendants (under *CPR 8.2A*). At the same time, they may apply to the court for directions as to which persons to join as parties.

(iii) No defendants required

If the trustees consider that the court may be able to give the directions sought without hearing from any other party, they may apply for permission for the claim form to be issued without naming any defendants (*CPR 8.2A*). However, in the recent case of *Re: Owens Corning Fibreglass (UK) Pensions Plan Ltd (The Times, 8 July 2002)* where a trustee applied for the court's approval of a compromise without informing the beneficiaries, the court indicated that, in most such cases, it would be desirable that potential beneficiaries, or their representatives (eg their union representatives or the pensions committee) be informed about the proposed arrangement and of any related application to the court to allow them to make their views known. The court indicated that, but for overriding considerations specific to that case, as the beneficiaries had not been informed, it would have adjourned the hearing to allow the beneficiaries to be told of the proposed compromise.

(iv) Requirement for a hearing

The court will always consider whether it can deal with the application on paper without the need for a hearing. If the trustees and/or the defendant(s) consider that a hearing is needed, they should state so, with reasons, in their evidence. If the court deals with the application on paper and refuses the application, the parties will be given an opportunity to request a hearing.

(v) Trustees' evidence

The trustees' evidence should disclose fully any matters which are relevant to the application, failing which they may not be protected by the court's order. The court requires such evidence to include a valuation of the trust assets (ie include the latest actuarial valuation); describe the membership profile; if a deficit on winding up is likely, the priority provisions and their likely effect; the significance of the proposed litigation or other course of action for the trust; and why the court's directions are required.

(vi) Consultation with beneficiaries

The trustees' evidence should also describe what, if any, consultation there has been with beneficiaries, and the results of that consultation. As general guidance, unless the members are few in number, the court will not expect any particular steps by way of consultation with beneficiaries (including, where relevant, employers) or their representatives to have been carried out in preparation for the application. If no consultation has taken place, the court may direct that meetings of one or more classes of beneficiaries are held to consider the subject matter of the application, possibly as a preliminary to deciding whether a representative of a particular class ought to be joined as a defendant.

Part 7 procedure

17.21 The Part 7 procedure is used if the Part 8 procedure is inappropriate (eg there is a substantial dispute of fact). The majority of third party claims (see 17.14 above) will therefore be brought under this procedure. The Part 7 procedure usually requires more procedural steps prior to the trial than the Part 8 procedure. An outline of the Part 7 procedure is as follows:

(*a*) Claim form and particulars of claim

The claimant issues and serves a claim form which sets out a basic summary of the claimant's claim. Unlike the Part 8 procedure, the claimant's case is set out in a separate particulars of claim, which contains a detailed description of the claim and the facts on which the claimant relies.

(*b*) Acknowledgment of service

Having been served with the claim form and particulars of claim, the defendant has 14 days to file an acknowledgment of service in the prescribed form, indicating whether it admits the claim, admits part of the claim but contests another part, or contests the entire claim. If the defendant fails to acknowledge service within the prescribed time limit and no extension of time has been agreed, judgment in default may be entered in the claimant's favour.

17.22 *Pensions dispute resolution and litigation*

(c) Defence (and counterclaim if relevant)

If the defendant contests all or part of the claim, unlike under the Part 8 procedure, the defendant must prepare, file and serve a defence within 14 days after being served with the particulars of claim (if no acknowledgment of service has been filed) or 28 days after service of the particulars of claim (if an acknowledgment of service has been filed). If a defence is not filed within the prescribed time limits and no extension of time has been agreed, judgment in default may be entered in the claimant's favour. If the defendant wishes to make a counterclaim against the claimant, this should be served with the defence.

(d) Reply (and defence to counterclaim if relevant)

If the claimant wants to allege facts to answer those alleged in the defence, the claimant may serve a reply. If the defendant has served a counterclaim, the claimant must, at the same time as serving the reply, serve a defence to the counterclaim, failing which judgment in default may be entered in the defendant's favour on the counterclaim.

(e) Case management directions

The court will allocate the case to one of the three court tracks (see 17.18 above) and give case management directions. These typically involve the following (in chronological order):

(i) disclosure and inspection of documents (see 17.22 below);

(ii) exchange of witness statements (see 17.23 below); and

(iii) exchange of expert reports (if necessary), followed by meetings of the experts in order to narrow the issues in dispute (see paragraph 17.24 below).

(f) Trial

The trial of the claim takes place before a judge in open court, at which each party's advocate makes oral submissions, and the witnesses and experts give oral evidence and are cross-examined. At the conclusion of the trial the judge will hand down a written judgment and will make any appropriate costs orders.

Disclosure of documents

17.22 Disclosure in the context of court proceedings is the process by which each party discloses to the other parties to the claim relevant documents within that party's control and in respect of which privilege is not being claimed. The disclosure process aims to ensure that each party has sight of the material that is available to the other parties so that each party can prepare adequately before trial of the proceedings. Disclosure of documents is not always ordered under the Part 8 procedure (see 17.20 above), whereas 'standard disclosure' is usually ordered under the Part 7 procedure (see 17.21 above).

Standard disclosure requires a party to disclose those 'documents' on which it relies, as well as those which adversely affect its own case or another party's case or which support another party's case. The word 'documents' has a wide meaning and includes anything in which information of any description is recorded (eg paper documents, computer files, film, video, photographs). A party must conduct a reasonable search for, and disclose, documents within its control (ie where the party has or had a right to possess it, inspect it or take copies of it.) Disclosure usually takes the form of the parties exchanging a list of documents in a form prescribed in *CPR, Part 31*.

A party is entitled to inspect and take copies of the documents disclosed by another party. However, a party giving disclosure may object to the inspection of certain documents on the grounds that they are legally privileged from inspection (an analysis of the various types of privilege that may be relied upon is outside the scope of the chapter). It should be noted that, as the duty to give disclosure continues to the end of the case, a party should take care when creating new documents in case they also need to be disclosed. A party who gives inadequate disclosure may be compelled by the court to give further disclosure. If a party fails to disclose a document, it may not rely on that document at the trial of the proceedings without the court's permission and, ultimately, if in breach of its obligations, a party may be held to be in contempt of court. (The rules of disclosure are set out in *CPR, Part 31* and should be distinguished from trustees' obligations to disclose information to members under common law and under various pensions statutes and regulations, for which see 3.22 and 17.16 above and appendix II.)

Witness statements and affidavits

17.23 A fact which needs to be proved by the evidence of a witness must, as a general rule, be proved at the trial of the case by the oral evidence of that witness under oath. At any other hearing (ie before the trial) the fact may be proved by the written evidence of the witness (ie in a witness statement or affidavit). A witness statement is a written statement of a witness's evidence. It is signed by the witness and contains a statement that he believes the facts in it are true (a 'statement of truth'). If a witness makes a false statement without an honest belief in its truth, proceedings for contempt of court may be brought. Witness statements have largely replaced affidavits (a written sworn statement), although there may be occasions where an affidavit is still required. There are strict rules governing the form and content of witness statements and affidavits (see *CPR Part 32* and the *Practice Direction on Written Evidence*).

Expert evidence

17.24 Expert evidence is frequently required in pension disputes to assist the court. For example, an expert actuary may be required to give an opinion on the valuation of the assets and liabilities of the pension fund or certain benefits under a pension scheme. The court has wide powers to control the use of expert witnesses in litigation because they are usually expensive and lengthen the

17.25 *Pensions dispute resolution and litigation*

proceedings. Expert evidence is restricted to that which is reasonably required to resolve the proceedings and a party may only call an expert with the permission of the court. In certain circumstances, the court may direct that expert evidence on an issue is to be given by a single expert, jointly instructed by both parties. The expert's overriding duty is to the court and not to the instructing or paying party. An expert will usually give his evidence in the form of a written report, which the parties exchange. Often the court will direct the parties' experts, following the exchange of reports, to meet in order to identify the technical issues in the proceedings and, where possible, reach agreement on those issues. An expert may be called to give oral evidence and be cross examined at the trial of the action. (See *CPR Part 35* and the *Practice Direction – Experts and Assessors* for the rules and guidelines on the use of experts. The Expert Witness Institute and the Academy of Experts have each published their own codes of guidance to experts.

Representation orders

17.25 It is a basic rule under the *CPR* that, where the party making a claim is seeking a remedy to which another person is jointly entitled, every other person who is so jointly entitled to that remedy must be joined as a party to the proceedings, unless the court orders otherwise *(CPR 19.3)*. There is no limit to the number of parties who may be joined to a claim *(CPR 19.1)*. This rule is designed to prevent a multiplicity of proceedings for similar claims and is of particular relevance to litigation involving pension schemes (eg trustees' applications for directions). Whereas the number of trustees of a pension scheme will be small, the number of beneficiaries under the scheme, who may be entitled jointly to a remedy, can be large – often amounting to hundreds, thousands and even tens of thousands. However, for each member or beneficiary of a scheme to be a named party to the litigation in accordance with the basic principle described above would give rise to a procedural and logistical burden which would seriously impair the efficient resolution of the litigation. That said, trustees require certainty that any order made by the court will be binding on all beneficiaries. The practical solution, therefore, is to appoint a party to represent the interests of other similarly interested parties. That party is known as a 'representative party' and may be appointed under two alternative provisions of the *CPR*:

(*a*) If more than one party has the same interest in a claim, the claim may be commenced, or the court may order the claim to be continued, by or against one or more of those parties as representatives of the other parties. Any judgment or order made by the court in the proceedings will bind all the persons represented in the claim (but may only be enforceable by or against a person who is not a party to the proceedings with the consent of the court) (see *CPR 19.6*).

(*b*) In claims concerning the assets of a pension scheme or the meaning of a document, the court may appoint, prior to or after the claim has commenced, a party to represent persons who are (i) unborn, or (ii) cannot be found, or (iii) cannot be easily ascertained. It may also appoint a party to represent a class of persons who have the same interest in a claim and either one or more members of that class fall within (i), (ii) or (iii) above, or if the court considers that the appointment would further the overriding objective of dealing with the claim justly (see 17.19 above) (see *CPR 19.7*). If a representative party has been appointed, the court must give its approval to any compromise of the proceedings, and will only do so where it considers that the compromise is for the benefit of all the represented persons. Any judgment or order made by the court will bind all represented persons unless the court orders otherwise, but can only be enforced by or against a person who is not a party to the claim with the court's consent.

Practical considerations

17.26 Given the frequently large membership of a pension scheme, representation orders provide a practical way for proceedings to be pursued in an efficient and timely manner, and provide certainty for the trustees that the judgment handed down will bind all affected beneficiaries. Where there is more than one distinct category of beneficiaries with a similar interest, it may be necessary to join more than one representative party. As each representative party will require legal representation, the court will usually seek to keep to a minimum the number of representative parties to minimise the costs as much as possible, particularly where the costs are being borne by the pension fund.

Trustees should therefore give proper consideration, at an early stage, as to who should be an appropriate representative party. A proposed representative party should not have a conflict of interest and should have sufficient mental capacity and availability to provide proper instructions to his legal representatives throughout the expected length of the proceedings. If the trustees in Part 8 proceedings are undecided as to who or how many representative parties should be appointed or cannot find a willing volunteer, they may issue the claim form without naming the defendant(s) and seek the court's directions – (see also (iii) in 17.20 above).

It remains arguable whether a person whose interests are represented in proceedings by a representative party may challenge the representation order or challenge a settlement that has been approved by the court on the grounds that it is a breach of that person's right to a fair trial under *Article 6* of the *European Convention on Human Rights*. If a person objects to being represented in an action, a practical solution may be for that person to be joined as a party in his own right (although that person will run the risk that he will have to bear his own legal costs in the event that the court does not permit his costs to be paid from the pension fund). *Article 6* is likely to be of more relevance where a settlement is approved by the court and is binding on a person represented in the proceedings by a representative party, without that person having had a chance to state his own case. To reduce the risk of a successful challenge, trustees should consider giving proper notice of the proceedings to all the persons represented (in so far as they can be ascertained) before the compromise is put to the court for

17.27 *Pensions dispute resolution and litigation*

approval. Such notice should set out the terms of the proposed compromise, a beneficiary's right to object to the compromise and his right to be joined in as a separate party to the proceedings.

This approach was deemed 'desirable' by the court in *Re: Owens Corning Fibreglass (UK) Pensions Plan Ltd [2002] ALL ER 9D) 191*. In that case the court indicated that it would, but for other factors, have adjourned the application to allow the beneficiaries to be informed.

When applying for the court's approval of a settlement, it is common practice for each representative party to obtain a written legal opinion on the merits of the compromise, the purpose of which opinion is to assist the judge in his/her consideration of whether the settlement is for the benefit of all the persons represented.

Trustees representing beneficiaries' interests

17.27 Where proceedings are brought by or against trustees without joining any of the beneficiaries of the pension scheme, any judgment or order made in those proceedings will bind the beneficiaries, unless the court orders otherwise. The court may order otherwise if it considers that the trustees could not or did not in fact represent the interests of those persons in the proceedings (see *CPR 19.7A*). Trustees should therefore consider carefully whether they can and are properly representing the beneficiaries' interests in such proceedings, because if they cannot or are not, it may be necessary to appoint an additional representative party.

Group litigation

17.28 Where there are a number of individual claims by separate persons which all give rise to common or related issues of fact or law (for example, claims by individual members of a pension scheme against the trustees for a breach of trust that has caused each of them loss and which has arisen out of the same facts), the court may order each of the cases to be managed together under a group litigation order. This should be distinguished from a representation order, where each person represented has the same interest in the outcome of a claim. A group litigation order is a useful and efficient mechanism in circumstances where each of the claims are individually small, but collectively large. In principle, it allows for an efficient and cost effective method of determining the claims. (The detailed provisions relating to group litigation orders can be found in *CPR 19.11* and the related *Practice Direction*).

Costs in litigation

17.29 The issue of costs is central to the assessment of whether or not to pursue or defend a claim, what strategy to adopt, in which forum the matter should be pursued, settlement considerations, and whether alternative dispute resolution methods should be explored. It is also an important factor that the court considers when it exercises its case management powers.

General principles

17.30 The court has a broad discretion to award costs (*section 51, Supreme Court Act 1981*). In deciding what costs order (if any) to make, the court will take into account all the circumstances, including the conduct of the parties before and during the litigation, whether a party was only partly successful and any offers of settlement (*CPR 44.3*). The court may penalise a party by denying it costs where it does not approve of that party's conduct or where the party has recovered a lesser amount than a previous offer of settlement which it rejected. Where the court orders a party to pay another party's costs, the amount of those costs will be assessed by the court, unless it can be agreed between the parties. The court may assess those costs summarily at the hearing itself, or conduct a separate detailed assessment of those costs after the hearing. In small claims track cases the court will only award limited costs and will assess those costs at the hearing. In fast track cases the trial costs of the advocate that are awarded are also limited. In multi track cases, there is no prescribed limit on the costs that can be recovered and the amount of those costs will be assessed by the court.

When ordering a party's costs to be assessed, the court will state the basis on which those costs will be assessed. There are two bases:

(*a*) *Standard basis*: This is the usual basis ordered. On this basis the court will only allow costs which are proportionate to the matters in issue and will resolve any doubt which it may have in favour of the paying party.

(*b*) *Indemnity basis*: The court will resolve any doubt it may have in the favour of the receiving party.

The receiving party can expect to recover more of its costs under the indemnity, rather than standard, basis, but on neither basis is the receiving party ever likely to recover 100 per cent of its costs. Indeed, under the standard basis, the receiving party may recover as little as 60 per cent of its costs (or even less). This should be borne in mind at the outset of litigation and when considering offers of settlement.

The general rule followed by the court is that the winner's assessed costs are paid by the loser. In pensions cases involving third parties (see 17.14 above), this rule will usually apply. However, there are special rules that apply to trustees' costs and the costs of applications for directions brought in relation to the administration of a pension scheme. These are discussed below, in 17.31 onwards.

Solicitors are obliged to discuss with clients involved in litigation the possibility of purchasing an 'after-the-event' insurance policy to cover the potential liability to pay costs (his own and/or the other party's) in the event of an unsuccessful outcome. Such policies are yet to make a significant impact in the arena of pensions litigation, but are likely to be of most relevance in the future to claims against or by third parties.

17.31 *Pensions dispute resolution and litigation*

Trustees' costs

17.31 Where a trustee is a party to proceedings in his capacity as trustee, as a general rule he is likely to be entitled to an indemnity out of the trust fund in respect of his legal costs (which may include costs that the trustee is ordered to pay to another party) to the extent that they are not recovered from or paid by another person (*CPR 48.4*) and provided they are properly incurred. In such cases, those costs will be assessed on the indemnity basis. The court may order otherwise if it considers that the trustee has, in all the circumstances, acted improperly (see *section 50A, Practice Direction to CPR 48.4*). By way of example, in the recent case of *Mark Niebhur Todd v Judith Cobb Lady Barton & Others [2002] Ch. (Unreported)*, the Court disallowed a proportion of a trustee's costs which related to an application made by him which the court considered to be unnecessary.

Indemnity and power in trust deed

17.32 A pension scheme's trust deed may contain an indemnity clause which indemnifies the trustees against any costs and liabilities incurred in taking certain action for the benefit of the pension scheme. It may also give the trustees a power to agree to pay from the pension fund the costs of certain other parties to litigation. In the event that the trustees have, and exercise, such a power by agreeing to pay the costs of another party to the litigation (eg in an application to court for directions), it is prudent for the trustees to enter into a formal agreement with that party stipulating what costs may be payable under that agreement and a mechanism for the trustees to control the level of costs incurred. The trustees' prior approval to large items of proposed expenditure (eg expert witness fees, counsel's fees) should also prudently be sought by that party.

In applications to court concerning the administration of a pension scheme, if the trustees have and exercise properly a power to agree to pay the costs of another party to that application, the court will presume, when assessing the amounts of costs payable under that agreement, that (unless the agreement states otherwise) the costs have been reasonably incurred and are reasonable in amount (see *CPR 48.3*). In such a case, a prospective costs order (see 17.35 below) is not required and the trustees are entitled to recover out of the pension fund any costs of another party which they pay pursuant to such agreement (*paragraph 6.2, Practice Direction to CPR 64*).

Beddoe orders

17.33 The proviso to the general rule entitling a trustee to an indemnity out of the trust fund for its costs (see 17.31 above) is that the costs must have been 'properly incurred'. If they are improperly incurred, a trustee may incur personal liability for those costs. To determine what costs are properly incurred, the court will examine all the circumstances of the case including whether the trustee obtained the court's directions before bringing or defending proceedings, acted in the interests of the Scheme or some other interest or conducted himself unreasonably. If trustees propose to commence or defend proceedings against or by a third party, they are able to protect themselves from this risk of personal liability by applying at an early stage for the court's directions on their proposed course of action (this is known as a *'Beddoe'* application, following the Court of Appeal judgment in *Re Beddoe, Downes v Cottam [1893]*). If the court sanctions the proposed action, the trustees can proceed in the comfort that the court regards their action as being proper and reasonable.

A *Beddoe* application is treated as a directions application under *CPR 64* (see 17.13 above). The application must be made in separate proceedings under the Part 8 procedure (see 17.20 above). The trustees should be the claimant and the beneficiaries of the pension scheme the defendants. In the event that a beneficiary is a party to both the main proceedings and the *Beddoe* application and has an interest which conflicts with that of the trustees, the trustees should exercise care not to disclose to that beneficiary privileged information (eg the legal advice of the trustees' lawyer), and that beneficiary may be excluded from all or part of any hearing of that *Beddoe* application.

In a *Beddoe* application, the court is asked to express its view on whether the action proposed by the trustees is proper. To enable the court to express a considered view, the trustees' application should be supported by evidence (in the form of witness statements) giving full disclosure of, among other things, the proposed course of action and the strengths and weaknesses of the trustees' case. This means that the trustees must include in their evidence the advice of an appropriately qualified lawyer on the prospects of success, and other relevant matters to be taken into account, including a costs estimate for the proceedings, any known facts concerning the means of the opposing party to the proceedings, and a draft of any proposed statement of case (see the *Practice Directions* to *CPR 64* for a fuller description of what matters should be included in the evidence and for guidelines on trustee consultation with beneficiaries). If the trustees fail to reveal in full to the court the strengths and weaknesses of their case, they may expose themselves to personal liability, even if the court grants the *Beddoe* order sought.

Depending on the nature of the case, the *Beddoe* application will either be dealt with on paper, without the need for a hearing, or will be referred to a judge in which case a hearing will usually be necessary. If the court allows the trustees to pursue the litigation proposed, it may do so only up to a particular stage in the litigation, thereby requiring the trustees to make a further *Beddoe* application in order to proceed beyond that stage.

However, whilst the above process may afford trustees protection from personal liability for the costs they will incur, the court has become increasingly critical about the tendency of trustees to seek, at considerable cost to the pension scheme, *Beddoe* consent for steps which are clearly in the interests of the pension scheme. This concern is reflected in the court's practice direction which states as follows:

17.34 *Pensions dispute resolution and litigation*

'There are cases in which it is likely to be so clear that the trustees ought to proceed as they wish that the costs of making the application, even on a simplified procedure without a hearing and perhaps without defendants, are not justified in comparison with the size of the fund or the matters at issue.'

[Paragraph 7.2, Practice Direction B to CPR 64]

Trustees should therefore consider carefully, with their legal advisers, the appropriateness of incurring the expense of making a *Beddoe* application. Equally, trustees should have regard to the uncertainties of litigation, even in the most apparently clear cut of cases, and the risk that if *Beddoe* consent is not sought prior to taking a step, the trustees may be held personally liable for their costs (unless they can prove to the satisfaction of the court that they were properly incurred). An assessment of the risk of proceeding without *Beddoe* protection must, therefore, be made by trustees with their legal advisers at the outset. One alternative to incurring the costs of a *Beddoe* application may be for the trustees to seek an indemnity from the employer, particularly if the employer is ultimately liable under the pension scheme's trust deed to make up any shortfall in the assets of the fund.

Beneficiaries' costs

17.34 The indemnity enjoyed by trustees (which is discussed in 17.31 above) is not shared by beneficiaries who are parties to proceedings. However, the court has traditionally sought to divide trust litigation into three categories when considering which party should pay the costs of those proceedings (following the decision in *Re Buckton, Buckton v Buckton [1907] 2 Ch 406*).

1. Proceedings brought by trustees for the court's guidance on the construction of the trust deed or a question arising in the course of the trust's administration. In such cases, the costs of all parties are usually treated as 'necessarily incurred for the benefit of the fund' and ordered to be paid out of the fund on an indemnity basis (such an application is usually brought under *CPR 64*).

2. Applications which are brought by someone other than the trustees, but which raise the types of issues as in 1. above and would have justified an application by the trustees. In this case, the costs are also usually treated as being 'necessarily incurred for the benefit of the fund' and ordered to be paid out of the fund on an indemnity basis (whilst such an application may be made under *CPR 64*, the Practice Direction to *CPR 64* only relates to applications made by trustees, and not other parties).

3. Proceedings in which a beneficiary is making a hostile claim against trustees or another beneficiary. The costs of such proceedings are usually treated in the same way as ordinary litigation and the winner's costs are usually paid by the loser, unless the winner has, in some way, conducted himself inappropriately in connection with the litigation.

These are known as *Buckton* categories 1, 2 and 3 and the court still deems these general guidelines applicable, albeit that it now takes a more robust attitude towards costs (*D'Abo v Paget (No. 2), [2000] WTLR 863*. There is a costs risk to both the trustees and the beneficiaries in the third category of claims, which is a principal reason why trustees generally seek Beddoe consent before pursuing or defending such proceedings, and why beneficiaries prefer to avoid such costs risk and pursue their complaints through the Pensions Ombudsman. It is often difficult, in practice, to assess whether a particular claim is a category 2 or 3 type claim, but given the costs consequences, it is important to reach a conclusion before embarking upon the litigation.

Prospective costs orders

17.35 Whilst the principles in *Buckton* provide a useful guide to what the likely costs order will be at the conclusion of the proceedings, a party may require greater comfort at the outset of the proceedings that its costs will be paid out of the fund no matter what the outcome of the proceedings. For example, a representative beneficiary may not wish to become a party in the proceedings if there is a risk that he or she will incur a personal liability for his/her, and other parties', costs of the proceedings. In applications to the court concerning the administration of a trust (ie under *CPR 64* – see 17.13 above), if the trustees do not have, or decide not to exercise, a power to agree to pay the costs of another party to the application, the trustees or the party concerned may apply to the court for an order that the costs of any party (including the trustees) shall be paid out of the assets of the pension scheme. These are known as 'prospective costs orders' (formerly as 'pre-emptive costs orders') and provide the applicant with the comfort that his costs of the proceedings will be paid, no matter what the outcome of the proceedings.

In Buckton category 1 and 2 cases (see 17.34 above) at the conclusion of the case the court will usually follow the general rule that the parties' costs (including those of any beneficiary) are paid out of the assets of the pension scheme. This makes the grant of a prospective costs order at an earlier stage in the case less problematic. A difficulty arises, however, in Buckton category 3 cases (hostile claims against the trustees). This is because in Buckton category 3 cases, the general rule is that the loser pays the winner's costs. This makes it difficult to make an assessment at any time prior to the full trial as to the likely outcome and therefore the likely costs order the court would make. In the leading case of *MacDonald v Horn [1995] 1 All ER 961* the court overcame this difficulty by deciding that an action by a member of a pension scheme to compel the trustees or others to account to the fund was analogous to what is known as a 'derivative action' by a minority shareholder on behalf of a company. In those circumstances a minority shareholder was entitled to a prospective costs order under the principle in *Wallersteiner v Moir (No 2) [1975] 1 ALL ER 849*. On this basis, the court held that a member of a pension scheme could also be entitled, by analogy, to a prospective costs order in those circumstances. When deciding whether to exercise its discretion to make such an order, the court has in each case a duty, under the *CPR*, to give effect to the overriding objective of dealing with cases justly. This includes ensuring, so far as possible, that the parties are on an equal footing and dealing with the case in a way which is proportionate to the financial position of each party. Such factors are particularly relevant in the pensions context, as the beneficiary who is a party to the case can often be a pensioner with limited financial resources.

Further guidance was given by the court in *Laws v National Grid [1998] PLR 295* where it considered that a prospective costs order should be made where the amount of money in issue is large, the matter in issue affects a large number of persons, the case involves difficult issues of law or fact, and the person applying for the order has substantial support from others in a similar position. In the recent case of *Chessels & ors v BT plc & ors [2002] PLR 141*, the court refused to grant a prospective costs order to a beneficiary to whom it had granted permission to appeal the court's judgment. The court followed the principle that prospective costs orders indemnifying a third party should only be made where the court is satisfied that no other orders can properly be made by the court which is to hear the substantive proceedings. The appeal in this case would, if successful, only benefit a relatively small number of beneficiaries of the scheme, was not for the benefit of the scheme as a whole, and was hostile litigation of the *Buckton* category 3 type in which the court usually awards the winner his costs. The court also reiterated the principle that the fact that the pension scheme had substantial assets, and was in surplus, was not relevant to whether or not it should grant the prospective costs order.

Applications for prospective costs orders can be made at any time during the proceedings but are usually made at the outset, or before a hearing. In the witness statement supporting the application the trustees and the applicant (if different) must give full disclosure of the relevant matters which show that the case is one which falls within the category of cases where a prospective costs order can properly be made. Ordinarily, the court will seek to deal with such an application on paper, without the need for an oral hearing, but if the trustees or any other party think a hearing should be held, they should set out their reasons in the evidence that they file at court. A model form of prospective costs order for straightforward cases is set out in the court's Practice Direction to *CPR 64*. It allows for a party's solicitor to request from the trustees monthly sums on account and for that party's costs to be subject to a detailed assessment by the court on the indemnity basis, unless agreed. It also indemnifies the party against any costs that it is ordered to pay to another party to the proceedings. When granting a prospective costs order the court may set a limit on the costs to be paid (as in *Re AXA Equity & Law Life Assurance Society plc (No 1) [2001] 2 BCLC 447*).

ALTERNATIVE DISPUTE RESOLUTION (ADR)

Introduction

17.36 Alternative Dispute Resolution ('ADR') is the generic phrase used to describe alternative means of resolving a dispute other than by a trial in court.

The use of ADR has developed rapidly over the last twelve years and its importance is actively promoted by the courts. Under the *CPR*, the court is obliged when using its active case management powers to encourage parties to use an ADR procedure if it considers it appropriate and to facilitate the use of such procedure (*CPR 1.4(2)(e)*). In the recent case of *Halsey v Milton Keynes General NHS Trust [2004] EWCA Civ 576, [2004] ALL ER (D) 125*, the Court of Appeal provided some guidelines on the court's approach to ADR (mediation in particular) and to penalising parties who fail to agree to pursue ADR. In summary:

(a) although the court may encourage parties to seek to resolve a dispute through ADR in the strongest terms, it would not order parties to undertake ADR against their will;

(b) as an exception to the general rule that the loser would be ordered to pay the winner's costs, the court may penalise a party, by making an alternative costs order, if that party has acted unreasonably in refusing to agree to ADR;

(c) the burden is on the loser to show why the winner acted unreasonably;

(d) in deciding whether a party had acted unreasonably in refusing to agree to ADR, the court will consider the following, non-exhaustive factors:

- is the nature of the dispute suitable for ADR?. Not every dispute is suitable for ADR, for example, a directions application concerning the construction of the pensions deed may be unsuitable for settlement;

- what are the merits of the case? A party, who reasonably believes that he has a strong case, may reasonably not wish to compromise his position through ADR;

- have any other settlement methods been attempted before? A history of unsuccessful attempts at resolving the dispute may justify a decision not to agree to ADR;

- what are the likely costs of ADR? If the costs of ADR are likely to be disproportionately high, this may justify a party not agreeing to it;

- will ADR cause unreasonable delay? Pursuing ADR will require the commencement or continuation of proceedings to be stayed which may cause unreasonable delay to the resolution of the dispute;

- will ADR have a reasonable prospect of success? The more remote the prospect of ADR resulting in a settlement, the more reasonable a court is likely to regard a refusal by one party to agree to ADR; and

(e) all members of the legal profession should routinely consider with their clients whether their client's disputes are suitable for ADR.

Types of ADR

17.37 There are different forms of ADR, but the principal ones are as follows:

17.38 *Pensions dispute resolution and litigation*

(a) *Mediation.* This is the most common form of ADR. It is a private, without prejudice process of negotiation between the parties, facilitated by an independent qualified mediator. It is non-binding so that a settlement can only be achieved if the parties agree. It is discussed in more detail below.

(b) *Conciliation.* This is a more formal form of mediation, and often involves the use of a formal conciliation service (such as ACAS). The 'conciliator' will often take an active role (ie proffering his views) in the negotiations.

(c) *Expert determination.* This is where the parties agree to refer a (usually) technical issue in dispute for a binding determination by an independent expert. For instance, a pension scheme's trust deed or rules may provide for an actuarial issue to be determined by an independent actuary, or the pensions schedule in a sale and purchase agreement may provide for expert determination in the case of disputes.

(d) *Adjudication.* Like an expert determination, this usually involves the parties agreeing to submit the dispute for determination by a neutral third party (eg a retired judge or experienced lawyer).

(e) *Arbitration.* The process of arbitration takes place in a statutory framework which sets out various rules of conduct. It is common for commercial contracts to contain 'arbitration clauses' which require all disputes to be referred to arbitration. The arbitrator is usually a suitably qualified independent third party who determines the dispute, acting as a judge. The procedure can closely mirror that of court litigation. It is designed to be flexible and less procedural than court litigation. However, it is often regarded as being as time consuming and expensive as court proceedings.

Mediation

17.38 Mediation is the most common form of ADR adopted to settle disputes. Once the parties to a dispute have agreed to mediation, the next step is to appoint a mediator. The Centre for Early Dispute Resolution (CEDR) and ADR Group are two of the most well known bodies that can assist parties in finding and appointing an appropriate mediator and setting up the mediation. They have lists of accredited and suitably experienced mediators. The Association of Pensions Lawyers also maintains a list of mediators with pensions experience (see its website: www.apl.org.uk).

The costs of the mediator(s) (there can be more than one if the parties wish) are usually borne equally by the parties. The costs of a mediation can be substantial as they may include the costs of the mediator, room hire and the costs of the parties' lawyers in preparing for and attending at the mediation. Before the mediation takes place, it is common for each party to exchange brief summaries of their case, if necessary accompanied by supporting documents. The mediation is usually attended by a senior person from each party who has the authority to negotiate and enter into a settlement agreement. The mediation often commences by each party giving an oral summary of its case to the other party in front of the mediator. The mediator may ask questions to clarify a point. Each party then retires to its own private room, and the mediator will visit each party in turn to discuss the structure of a possible settlement and the issues which each party should consider as part of the negotiations. Through this process of 'shuttle diplomacy' the mediator can gauge what possible terms of settlement may be agreeable to the parties and make appropriate suggestions to the parties to facilitate a settlement. As the process is without prejudice and non-binding, a settlement will only be achieved if both parties agree to it.

Practical considerations

17.39 Pension disputes between trustees and third parties are usually hostile, and in such cases, ADR may provide an efficient means of resolving the dispute, thereby avoiding the costs and risk of litigation. Trustees who have the benefit of a *Beddoe* order (see 17.33 above), may wish or need to seek the court's approval of any settlement (although trustees have a power under *section 25* of the *Trustees Act 1925* to enter into a settlement), in which case this should be made clear to the other parties and may affect the choice of ADR method.

Claims against trustees by individual members may also be amenable to ADR, even if those disputes have been referred to the Pensions Ombudsman rather than the court.

Directions applications (see 17.13 above) are not always suitable for resolution by ADR. Some applications, by their nature, are not suitable to ADR (eg where the trustees are requesting the court's approval of a proposed transaction or are surrendering their discretion to the court). Where ADR is possible, there are a number of practical issues which will require consideration, including the following:

(a) Trustees will usually want to avoid negotiating with all the beneficiaries under the pension scheme, not only for logistical reasons but also the difficulty of reaching agreement with all of them. To facilitate negotiations trustees may, therefore, seek the appointment of a representative party with whom they may negotiate. This necessitates the commencement of proceedings prior to ADR being commenced.

(b) Where a settlement is agreed, the trustees may seek the court's approval to that settlement (for example, if a *Beddoe* order has been granted or is sought, or where a representative party has been appointed). In any such application to the court, it is common practice for the trustees and/or the representative party to obtain and present to the court a legal opinion on whether the proposed settlement is in the interests of the members of the pension scheme (see 17.26 above). This means that the court will not examine the proposed settlement on a purely commercial basis, but will also consider to what extent the proposed terms reflect the legal merits of the members' case(s). Further, to produce a reasoned opinion, documents may have to be disclosed and exchanged, if disclosure has not already taken place.

17.39 *Pensions dispute resolution and litigation*

Whilst such factors may provide practical hurdles to be overcome in order for ADR to lead to a successful resolution of the dispute, the advantages of ADR (notably, the potential for a relatively quick, private and less costly settlement of the dispute at an early stage) may justify its use as a means of resolving the dispute. Indeed, parties' solicitors are now expected by the court to consider, in every dispute, the appropriateness of ADR. In all cases, careful consideration should be given as to which form of ADR is most appropriate. If a party is considering rejecting an offer of ADR, it should first consider the guidelines given by the court in *Halsey*. *This may assist in an assessment of whether the rejection is likely to be considered unreasonable, as a refusal to agree to ADR could potentially expose that party to costs sanctions by the court.*

Chapter 18

Insolvency

INTRODUCTION

18.1 There are various types of corporate insolvency regimes ('regimes') under the *Insolvency Act 1986* (as amended) (*'IA 1986'*) supplemented by the *Insolvency Rules 1986* (as amended) (*SI 1986 No 1925*) (*'IR'*) that may affect pension schemes. This Chapter aims to be a general introduction to those regimes, and the relevant persons appointed under them to protect the interests of creditors. This Chapter also details the effect of such regimes on pension schemes.

We have restricted our commentary in this Chapter to the application of the regimes on and in relation to English formed and registered companies. However, it should be noted that entities that are not English formed and registered companies may also be able to become subject to a regime if they have a connection with England and Wales.

CONSEQUENCES OF CORPORATE INSOLVENCY UNDER ENGLISH LAW – THE REGIMES

Company Voluntary Arrangements (CVAs)

18.2 Company Voluntary Arrangements ('CVA's), under *IA 1986, ss 1–7* and *Sch A1* and *IR, Part 1*, are where a company enters into what is effectively a contract with its creditors for either a composition in satisfaction of its debts (an agreement that a debt is to be discharged by payment of a proportion of it), or a scheme of arrangement of its affairs (*IA 1986, s 1*). They are typically initiated by the directors of the company, but can also be initiated by a liquidator or administrator.

CVAs are initiated by the circulation of a proposal which is voted upon by creditors and members of the company. If approved (with or without modifications) the proposal (as modified) becomes the CVA; that is, the contract between the company and its creditors.

There are presently two broad types of CVA available. The original type of CVA is one where a proposal is put together without the benefit of any moratorium against creditor claims/actions. The provisions regulating this type of CVA are

18.3 Insolvency

found in the main body of the *IA 1986, ss 1–7*. The new type of CVA is one that does provide for a moratorium against creditor claims/actions while the proposal is being formulated and put out for approval. It is however, only available to a 'small company' within the meaning of that term in *s 247* of the *Companies Act 1985* ('*CA 1985*') (as amended), provided certain other prescribed criteria are also satisfied. This type of CVA was introduced into the *IA 1986* by the *Insolvency Act 2000* ('*IA 2000*'). The provisions regulating it are to be found in *s 1A* and *Sch A1* of *IA 1986*.

The primary difference between the types of CVAs is that under the original type, the company has no protection from its creditors when formulating the proposal, but under the small company type, it does. That is, there is no bar on creditor action under the original type until and unless (typically) the proposal is approved.

The provisions regulating the content and procedure for approval and implementation of both types of CVA are broadly the same despite the fact that they are separately provided for in the *IA 1986*.

Terms

18.3 The terms of either type of CVA (ie the terms of the 'contract') will depend entirely on what is proposed and accepted (creditors can propose modifications to the proposal put to them) by at least 75 per cent in value of the company's unsecured creditors. (Certain votes will not be taken into account, and/or may render invalid a resolution passed; (*IR, rule 1.19* and *1.54*). For example, a resolution will be invalid if without taking into account the votes of connected creditors, the unconnected unsecured creditors have voted against the proposal. For the definition of 'connected' in this context, please see *s 249* and *s 435* of the *IA 1986*. The terms will also depend on who are entitled to, and do vote on, the proposal, provided that (in general terms) a secured creditor (a creditor who has a valid right of recourse to the assets of the company, as opposed to only a right of action against the company – the latter is an unsecured creditor) or preferential creditor (a creditor whose claim is preferential as defined in *s 386* of the *IA 1986* and *sch 6* of *IA 1986*) cannot be affected by what is proposed without its express consent. This means that the general order of priority of payment of creditors on insolvency will typically not be affected by the CVA. That is, holders of fixed charge security are entitled to the net (less costs of/in connection with the sale) proceeds of sale of the fixed charge asset. Other assets are to be utilised to pay (in the following order) costs; preferential creditors; floating charge holders; and, only then, unsecured creditors. Except for secured creditors (where priority issues will be governed either by law, or if negotiated, by contract – typically, if there is more than one secured creditor, a deed of priority will have been entered into governing not only which creditor has priority to the assets, but also enforcement rights). Creditors in each category will rank *pari passu* (rateably) with each other if there are insufficient funds to pay them all in full.

Members (shareholders) of the company are also required to vote (approval by members is by more than one-half in value of those voting, in person or by proxy, subject only to any express provision in the company's articles) on the proposal (and any proposed modifications). That said, the decision taken by the creditors will prevail, although an aggrieved member can challenge that decision by application to court within 28 days of the last meeting held.

If approved, the CVA binds all persons who:

(*a*)   were entitled to vote on the proposal whether or not they did so; or

(*b*)   would have been entitled to vote on it if they had had notice of the meeting at which the proposal was voted upon.

There is a right (among others) for creditors to challenge a decision taken in the meetings held to approve the proposal by application to court within a 28 day period, the starting date of which period depends on the circumstances. There are two grounds for such a challenge, being:

- the CVA unfairly prejudices the interests of a creditor; and/or
- there has been some material irregularity at or in relation to the meeting at which the proposal was voted upon.

The proposal will nominate a person to be the supervisor of the CVA if it is approved. A licensed insolvency practitioner ('IP') is typically nominated. To be qualified to act as an IP, an individual must be authorised so to act by a specified competent authority or by virtue of his membership to a specified professional body (*s 390* of the *IA 1986* and properly bonded (insured). If an individual purports to act as an IP without being so qualified, he or she commits a criminal offence (*ss 388–389* of the *IA 1986*. Authorisation and membership requires the individual to be generally fit and proper, to meet acceptable levels of education and to have sufficient practical experience in the field. An undischarged bankrupt or a person who has been subject to a disqualification order under the *Company Directors Disqualification Act 1986* is not qualified to act as an IP (*s 390(4)* of the *IA 1986*). That said, since the *IA 2000*, a supervisor can now (subject to certain restrictions) also be any individual who, although not an IP, is a member of a body recognised by the Secretary of State (*s 389A(1)* of the *IA 1986*) and is satisfactorily bonded.

The extent of the supervisor's powers and obligations will be as prescribed in the CVA. In a CVA initiated by the directors of the company, it is typical for the company to continue trading as normal (with its own management), its obligations being simply to make contributions into the CVA from its trading to ultimately satisfy (or part satisfy) creditors' claims. In such a CVA, the supervisor's powers and obligations will typically be limited to monitoring the company's compliance with the CVA terms (defaulting it if the company is in breach), agreeing creditors' claims and making distributions in accordance with the CVA. It is presently rare for a supervisor's powers and obligations to extend to 'running' the company. This means the directors remain in office, although subject to any restriction imposed on them by the CVA. This can lead to some confusion for those dealing with the continuing company.

18.4 Insolvency

Typically, the terms of the CVA will prohibit action being taken against the company in connection with debt and liabilities bound by the CVA. However, action in respect of debt and liabilities outside of the CVA will not be prohibited. This means that if the company is continuing to trade, a creditor incurred by the company after the approval of the CVA will be entitled to take such steps as it deems appropriate against the company for that post CVA debt, including steps to wind up the company.

What effect such steps (and indeed, any actions taken by the company post CVA) will have on the CVA and the funds realised in it will depend on the terms of the CVA. For instance, presentation of a winding-up petition could default the CVA, resulting in it being brought to an end. Typically now, CVAs will provide that funds realised in the CVA are held on trust for the CVA creditors meaning that even if it fails, the funds already realised can be paid to the CVA creditors and do not need to be shared with all of the company's creditors. In such a case of failure however, the CVA creditors are not in principle prevented from also claiming in any liquidation of the company for the full amount of their debts, less the amount received in the CVA. (The inter-relationship between CVAs and liquidation have been the subject of a number of cases and is a difficult area. Presently, the leading case is *NT Gallagher & Son Ltd, Shierson v Thompson, Re [2002] 1 WLR 2380, [2002] 3 All ER 374*. Among other things, it confirms the basic principle that the terms of the CVA are key and should be respected. Also, even if the CVA terms do not expressly refer to a trust being created in respect of CVA funds, wording that in effect implies that to be the intention should be given effect to.)

What happens to the contracts of employees will depend upon the circumstances. It may be that the company seeks to terminate some employment contracts, leaving the employees with claims bound by the CVA. Alternatively, the company may decide that as it is continuing to trade, it wishes to retain its employees. How it does this will depend on circumstances.

The CVA will end when it states it will. A well drawn CVA will contain clear and specific terms about how it will come to an end and in what circumstances, including what happens if the CVA terms are breached.

Liquidation

18.4 This is a regime that can either be initiated by the company voluntarily, or against the company by, among others, its creditors. It provides for the appointment of an IP to the company as a 'liquidator', who takes control of the company's assets, replacing, in effect, the directors, whose powers cease. It represents the beginning of the end for a company and, except in exceptional circumstances, its business, because once the liquidation ends, the company will be automatically dissolved (unless an appeal against dissolution is lodged). It will therefore cease to be a legal entity after the liquidation is completed.

Solvent liquidations

18.5 Solvent liquidations (members' voluntary liquidations ('MVL')) are used where, for example, a company was incorporated for a particular purpose which it has achieved and it is, therefore, no longer required. The aim of a MVL is to realise all remaining assets in the company and to settle all outstanding claims against it (with interest), with a view to realising whatever surplus there is in the company so that it can be distributed to the company's members.

The MVL process is initiated by the company's directors swearing a statutory declaration of solvency (under the threat of criminal liability if they do not do so reasonably) to the effect that they have made a full enquiry into the company's affairs and that having done so, they have formed the view that the company can pay all of its debts and liabilities, including contingent and prospective liabilities, in full within a period not exceeding twelve months. Once they have done this, they then call a meeting of the company's members to pass a special resolution (21 days' notice and a majority of 75 per cent in value of those voting, in person or by proxy) (*s 378* of the *CA 1985*) to put the company into liquidation. The MVL takes effect from the time of the passing of this resolution. If the company is later found, by the liquidator appointed, to be insolvent, he or she has a duty to convert it into a creditors' voluntary liquidation ('CVL'), which is an insolvent liquidation. Unless the company turns out to be insolvent, creditors of companies that go into MVL should be paid in full for their debts.

Insolvent liquidations

18.6 Insolvent liquidations can be either voluntary (CVLs) or compulsory, the latter initiated through the court. These will usually occur where there is no prospect of the company being able to continue trading or of its business surviving in any form, and there is no option but to appoint a liquidator to collect in all the company's assets to distribute them fairly among the company's creditors in the order prescribed in the *IA 1986*.

The general order of priority of payment of creditors on insolvency is that holders of fixed charge security are entitled to the net (less costs of/in connection with the sale) proceeds of sale of the fixed charge asset. Other assets are to be utilised to pay (in the following order) costs; preferential creditors; floating charge holders; and, only then, unsecured creditors, except in regards to secured creditors (where priority issues will be governed either by law, or if negotiated, by contract). Creditors in each category will rank *pari passu* with each other if there are insufficient funds to pay them all in full. The aim of an insolvent liquidation is to ensure a fair distribution to creditors of the company's remaining assets.

Like a MVL, a CVL commences when the members of the company resolve, by extraordinary resolution (75 per cent in value of those voting, in person or by proxy (*s 378* of the *CA 1985,* and *IR, Rule 4.67* contains detailed provisions

18.6 Insolvency

about entitlement to vote.)), to put it into liquidation. The liquidator will be the IP nominated by either the creditors or members.

A compulsory liquidation actually begins on the making of a winding-up order against the company, although after that happening, the liquidation is deemed to have commenced at the time of the presentation of the petition pursuant to which it is wound up (*s 129* of the *IA 1986*).This, among other things, makes vulnerable actions taken by the company between presentation of the petition and the making of an order on that petition (*s 127* of the *IA 1986*). If the company disposes of any of its property in that period, that disposition will be void unless it is authorised or ratified by the court. Even a payment by the company to a creditor during that period could be void on this basis. Generally, such a disposition will only be authorised or ratified if the disposition is likely to benefit all of the company's creditors, or at least not disadvantage them. [*Re Gray's Inn Construction Co. Ltd [1980] 1 WLR 711, [1980] 1 All ER 814.*]

The first liquidator appointed to a company in a compulsory liquidation is typically the 'Official Receiver'. (The Secretary of State appoints a person to the office of Official Receiver and attaches him or her to the High Court of England and Wales, to carry out functions conferred upon him or her by *IA 1986* and by the Secretary of State.) The Official Receiver then has twelve weeks within which to investigate the company's affairs (*s 132* of the *IA 1986*, explains his or her duties) and to call meetings of, amongst others, the creditors of the company for the purpose of their choosing an IP to become the liquidator of the company in his or her place, or to give them notice that he or she will not be doing so, in which case he or she will continue as the liquidator (*s 136* of the *IA 1986*). He or she will typically only call such meetings if there are assets in the company.

The company's business will typically cease on the company going into any form of liquidation. It will only ever continue after liquidation in exceptional circumstances (where it would be beneficial to the winding-up). The liquidator's powers are very wide (*Sch 4* of the *IA 1986*), albeit not all of them can be actioned without the prior sanction of the creditors or the court.

Actions against the company and its property are prohibited without court leave in a compulsory liquidation (*s 130* of the *IA 1986*).This means no actions already commenced against it can be proceeded with, and no new actions can be commenced unless the court gives its leave to that happening. The court will typically only give leave in cases where the normal process of making a claim in the liquidation is not seen as sufficient. The proving process (the process of making a claim in a liquidation is called 'proving' and the claim is called a 'proof' – the rules as to proofs can be found in *IR, Rule 4, Chapter 9*) enables unsecured creditors to make their claim in the liquidation as fully as they wish to (providing such supporting evidence as they deem appropriate), which the liquidator considers in a quasi-judicial capacity. If the liquidator needs more information in order to reach a decision on the claim, he or she can ask for it. If the creditor is ultimately unhappy with the liquidator's decision on their proof (the liquidator can reject all or part of it), the creditor has a right to appeal by making an application to court within 21 days of receiving the liquidator's notice of the rejection. That is, an aggrieved creditor can have 'his or her day' in court if it is needed, but both parties can avoid the cost of litigation where it is not necessary. An unsecured creditor with a simple unsecured claim (eg a simple debt claim) is unlikely to ever get leave to continue or commence proceedings, or indeed, for there to be any benefit to it seeking leave.

There is no such automatic prohibition on proceedings in a voluntary liquidation. That said, the liquidator may apply to court for a stay of any proceedings commenced for the same reasons as outlined earlier in this paragraph 18.6. A liquidator is likely to do so if proceedings for recovery of a simple debt claim are commenced.

The effect of liquidation on employment contracts is not prescribed in the *IA 1986* (as it is in administration and receivership). As a consequence, there is some uncertainty as to what that effect is. It is generally accepted, although there is little firm authority on the point, that in a CVL and MVL, the employees' contracts typically terminate on liquidation, but not because of the liquidation, rather because the company's business has ceased and so their contracts are effectively repudiated. In a compulsory liquidation on the other hand, it is thought that the employees' contracts automatically terminate because of the making of the winding-up order against the company. The reasoning for the distinction between the type of liquidation is not however, clear.

Receivership

18.7 The method typically used by secured creditors to enforce their security is by appointing a receiver or manager over the assets secured in their favour.

In an enforcement context, a receiver is a person who is appointed by a creditor who holds security over a company's assets. The receiver's primary function is to utilise the powers given to him or her to deal with those assets, with the aim of satisfying the debt owed by the debtor to that secured creditor. A receivership appointment is not for the benefit of the company and its creditors as a whole, but rather for the benefit of the secured creditor alone. This means that the receiver owes only limited duties to the company and its creditors. The exact extent of those duties is not clear (there have been a number of cases on this point recently, which have called the extent into question). At the very least, it is presently clear that if the receiver realises any assets, he or she must get the best price reasonably obtainable for those assets in all the circumstances. (See for instance, *Standard Chartered Bank v Walker [1982] 1 WLR 1410, [1982] 3 All ER 938*.)

The receiver will not typically deal at all with the claims of the company's unsecured creditors. He or she would only do so if necessary, such as where the unsecured creditor is a crucial supplier to the company's business, and so to ensure continued supply, the receiver has to agree to pay some or all of the

18.7 Insolvency

unsecured creditor's pre-receivership debt, as well as its new debt. This is what is typically referred to as a 'ransom payment'.

The types of receivership in this context are an administrative receivership and an ordinary receivership, often also referred to as *Law of Property Act 1925* ('*LPA 1925*') receiverships (the *IA 1986* provisions which regulate these appointments are found in *ss 28–49* and *s 72* of the *IA 1986*, (including *ss 72A–72H*), the *LPA 1925* provisions which regulate *LPA 1925* receiverships are found in *ss 99–109* of the *LPA 1925*).

1. Administrative receivers: are those appointed by floating charge holders over all or substantially all of the assets of the company, which typically means that they are appointed over businesses. The *IA 1986* does not contain a right to appoint an administrative receiver. The floating charge must contain that right, otherwise no administrative receiver can be appointed. The appointee must be an IP.

2. Ordinary receivers: are appointed over fixed charge assets – *LPA 1925* receivers being the type of receiver typically appointed by secured creditors where the only asset is land. *LPA 1925* receivers are the only type of receiver appointee that does not need to be an IP. The *LPA 1925* contains a right to appoint a receiver where the security is a mortgage created by deed. Otherwise, a receiver can only be appointed if the security contains a right to appoint. (Most security these days contains a provision that provides that after the security becomes enforceable, the secured creditor can appoint a receiver over the secured assets.)

The ability to appoint an ordinary/*LPA 1925* receiver has not been affected by the recent legislative changes to the *IA 1986* (introduced by the *Enterprise Act 2002*), only the ability to appoint an administrative receiver is affected (*IA 1986 s 72A*). Those changes mean that now unless the floating charge was created before 15 September 2003 or otherwise falls into the list of exceptions (*s 72* of the *IA 1986*), a floating charge holder, who prior to these changes would have had an unrestricted right to appoint an administrative receiver, no longer has that right.

Once a receiver is appointed, it is up to him or her to exercise their powers granted over the secured property as he or she deems appropriate to achieve the purpose for which the appointment has been made (ie to satisfy the debt for the person who appointed him or her). This is because the receiver is not the secured creditor's agent even though the secured creditor appoints him or her. (Under the *IA 1986* and to a limited extent under the *LPA 1925*, and in any event almost always also provided for in the security, the receiver is made the agent of the company over whose assets he or she is appointed. This agency lasts until the company goes into liquidation. So the company is liable in the normal course for the receiver's actions as the receiver's principal. Even after liquidation, the receiver does not become the secured creditor's agent, although his or her exact status after liquidation is not clear. What is clear however, is that the secured creditor does not become liable for the receiver's actions simply because of the liquidation.)

Following appointment, the secured creditor is not involved in the enforcement process (although in practice, the receiver will typically report to the secured creditor along the way). The secured assets are usually managed and sold by the receiver in the company's name. The directors of the company remain in office notwithstanding the appointment, but they cannot exercise any powers over the assets over which the receiver is appointed.

What deductions must be made from any receivership realisations depends upon the nature of those realisations. Secured creditors are entitled to fixed charge realisations without any further deductions following deduction of the costs and expenses of the receivership where it is an *LPA 1925* receivership, or the costs and expenses incurred in connection with those fixed charge assets in an administrative receivership. Floating charge realisations are also available to meet preferential creditor claims, and for floating charges created after 15 September 2003, for payment of the prescribed part. (The prescribed part is a new concept introduced by the *Enterprise Act 2002*. It is a sum (presently up to a maximum of £600,000) of net (after deduction of the costs and preferential creditors) floating charge realisations that must be made available for unsecured creditors save in limited circumstances (mainly, in general terms, where the amount would be small and not cost effective to distribute).

The receiver is given powers to deal with the assets over which he or she is appointed. The powers given and where they can found depend upon the type of appointment. They will often include a power to sell the assets. There are some restrictions to the exercise of that power, prohibiting a sale to the receiver and qualifying the right to sell to associated parties. An *LPA 1925* receiver will not have the power to sell, or indeed any powers other than to receive rent, and possibly insure, issue and accept lease surrenders, unless other powers are given to him or her in the security. The assets do not vest in the receiver, nor do they vest in the secured creditor, but the receiver is able to exercise those powers using the company's name, enabling him or her to pass title to the assets where necessary.

The receivership process does not prevent action being taken against the company by an aggrieved creditor. Indeed, such a creditor could issue a petition to wind-up the company and it could go into liquidation, while still being in receivership. While a liquidation will affect the capacity in which the receiver acts (he or she will no longer act as the company's agent), it will not affect his or her powers over the secured assets.

If the secured assets are all the assets of the company and they are insufficient to pay in full the secured creditor's debt, then there is likely to be nothing left for the unsecured creditors. The unsecured creditors will then be reliant for some recovery on either:

(*a*)   the prescribed part (see above), if applicable; or

(*b*)   successful proceedings within the liquidation, in actions that do not form part of the company's assets.

18.8 *Insolvency*

(There are certain actions that only a liquidator can bring, which if successful will mean the recoveries go into the 'pot' available for unsecured creditors, and do not fall into the assets secured by the secured creditor's security.)

Ultimately, the level of any recovery will depend on the level of costs incurred, and of any unpaid preferential creditors.

Contracts of employment do not automatically terminate when a receiver is appointed. The receiver has 14 days grace after appointment (*s 37* and *44* of the *IA 1986*) to decide whether or not to adopt any contract of employment. If he or she fails to take any steps in connection with any contract of employment within that period, he or she will (on the basis of current case law) be taken to have adopted it (see *Paramount Airways Ltd (No 3), Re [1994] BCC 172*). The liability that the receiver becomes subject to under the adopted contracts of employment depends on the nature of the receivership (see the fourth sub-paragraph of this paragraph). If the receiver decides not to adopt a contract of employment, the contract will be terminated and the employee will be an unsecured creditor of the company (albeit some parts of his claim may be a preferential debt).

ADMINISTRATION

18.8   Administration (see *ss 8–27* of the *IA 1986* for old style administrations and *Sch B1* of the *IA 1986*) was introduced into *IA 1986*, as an alternative process to liquidation, where there is a chance of the company or its business surviving. It was based very loosely on Chapter 11 of the US Bankruptcy Code and is presently the primary formal rescue process available in England. It has recently (since 15 September 2003) been substantially 'revamped' following the *Enterprise Act 2002*. Some of the changes are outlined below.

Administration involves the appointment of an IP to the company (called an administrator), whose purpose is to manage the company (effectively replacing the directors, who remain in office but neither they nor the company can exercise a management power without the administrator's consent) while putting together a proposal for the creditors to vote on which achieves the objectives for which the administrator is appointed. (In both old style and new style administrations, the proposals will be approved if they are approved by a majority in value of those person voting, in person or by proxy, and entitled to vote. Certain votes will not be taken into account, and/or may render invalid a resolution passed (see *IR, Part 2*). For example, a resolution will be invalid if without taking into account the votes of connected creditors, the unconnected unsecured creditors have voted against the proposal. For the definition of 'connected' in this context, please see *s 249* and *s 435* of the *IA 1986*). What that proposal is will depend entirely on the facts and circumstances. In both styles of administration, the proposal should be put to creditors within a short period after the administration is commenced (three months on the old style administrations; *IA 1986, s 23*, and ten weeks in the new style administration, *Sch B1, para 5* of the *IA 1986* – both periods can be extended), the intent being that the administration process should be creditor driven. That is, the ultimate fate of the company should be in the creditors' hands. The administrator may however, before the proposals are put to the creditors, do such things as he or she thinks necessary and appropriate (including sell the company's business) if he or she is of the view that it is in the best interests of the company and its creditors to do so.

Until the recent legislative changes, administration was in effect, an intermediate process in the sense that an administrator had virtually no powers to pay any of the company's creditors within the process. This meant that (unless the court's leave could be obtained to do otherwise, which was becoming increasingly common practice but recently disallowed in a 'typical' administration case) to pay realisations to creditors, administration would have to be exited into another formal insolvency process, such as liquidation. Administrators can now make distributions to secured and preferential creditors within the process, and with court leave, may also be able to make distributions to the company's unsecured creditors, effectively making it possible for administration to be a 'one stop shop'. The general order of priority of payment of creditors in an insolvency applies. See 18.6 and subsequent paragraphs of this paragraph (18.8).

Until the recent legislative changes, there were also four aims the administrator could have been appointed to achieve, being (in summary):

(a) the survival of the company; or

 (i) the entering into by the company of a company voluntary arrangement;

 (ii) the entering into by the company of a scheme of arrangement with its creditors; or

(b) getting a better realisation of the company's assets than would happen if the company is wound up immediately.

Administrations commenced before the 15 September 2003 will have as their purpose(s) one or more of the above points. For administrations commenced on or after 15 September 2003, there is a sliding scale of objectives. The administrator must try and rescue the company as a going concern. There is no definition of 'rescue', making it extremely flexible as to what it might encompass. If the administrator concludes that the company cannot be rescued as a going concern or that the following objective would achieve a better result for all the creditors, his or her next objective is to get a better realisation of the company's assets than would be the case if the company had been immediately wound-up instead of going into administration. Only if he or she concludes that this cannot be done and achieving the following objective will not 'unnecessarily harm' the interests of all creditors, the administrator's third objective is to simply sell the company's assets and distribute the realisations to the secured creditors and the creditors of the company who are preferential under the *IA 1986*.

A key feature of the administration process under both the old style administrations and new style administration is that from initiation (except in one limited

18.8 Insolvency

circumstance for new style administrations, when the moratorium will not commence until later) and until either the application for administration is dismissed or the administration ends, there is a ring-fencing of the company from its creditors' claims and actions (including enforcement by secured creditors). This moratorium even prevents, in certain circumstances, a creditor trying to recover its own property from the company. Such claims can only be pursued with either the leave of the court, or (after the company is in administration) the administrator's consent. Consent/leave will only typically be given when there is some good reason to, such as because the prejudice being suffered by the creditor whose rights have been restricted by the moratorium outweighs the benefit the company/the administration is getting. It is unlikely that a simple unsecured creditor would ever get consent/leave.

There are some limited exceptions to this ring-fencing in the initial period of the moratorium, which include that a secured creditor who can appoint an administrative receiver is still able to appoint one. If the secured creditor does so, administration cannot happen. This gives such floating charge holders some power, although this power has been severely curtailed by the recent restrictions on when such a receiver can be appointed. The intention of the moratorium is to give a company a breathing space and to give it time to enable something to be done.

That said and although the moratorium restricts the ability of secured creditors to enforce their security and gives, once the company goes into administration, the administrator rights (albeit with restriction in the case of fixed charge security) to deal with/dispose of the secured assets, the secured creditors' position in respect of those assets is in very general terms protected, primarily as regards fixed charge security where net proceeds of disposal must be paid to the secured creditor. Their position as a floating charge creditor is less satisfactory. This is because the floating charge realisations are first made available to meet the administration costs, expenses and liabilities and preferential creditors. In addition, for charges created after 15 September 2003, the prescribed part (see 18.7) needs to be considered.

Administrators have very wide powers (principally set out in *Sch 1* of *IA 1986*), which include power to manage the business and sell the company's assets. Administrators take control of the company. They act as agent of the company however, so all actions are in the company's name.

Like administrative receivers, they have 14 days after appointment within which to decide what employment contracts, if any, they want to adopt, with the same consequences (*IA 1986, s 19* for old style administrations, and *para 99* of Schedule B1 for new style administrations).

In addition to those changes other significant changes are that:

- administration is now available as an out of court process (previously, it was only available via an application to court); and
- the time limits of steps within the administration, and the administration

process as a whole, have been shortened/prescribed. For instance, there was no prescribed time within which an old style administration must end. A new style administration will however, end automatically after a year, unless extended. Extensions can happen once with creditor consent but only if the court hasn't already extended it, and after that, consent must be by the court.

NOTIFYING TRUSTEES OF A PENSION SCHEME OF THE APPOINTMENT OF INSOLVENCY PRACTITIONER

18.9 The insolvency practitioner must inform the trustees of a pension scheme that he or she has been appointed within one month of his or her appointment. Failure to do so may be subject to a civil penalty under the *Pensions Act 1995 (PA 1995)*. This is because every employer in relation to a pension scheme is under a duty to notify the pension scheme trustees within one month of the occurrence of an event relating to the employer which will be of material significance to the trustees or their advisors in the exercise of any of their functions under *s 47(9)(a)* of the *PA 1995* and *reg 6(1)(b)* of the *Occupational Pension Schemes (Scheme Administration) Regulations 1996 (SI 1996 No 1715)*. Under *s 10* of the *PA 1995*, Opra can levy a civil penalty if there is failure by an employer to comply with the above information requirements. The maximum penalty is £50,000 for a company and £5,000 for an individual.

In such circumstances, the employer-nominated and member-nominated trustees of the pension scheme may want to resign as trustees of the pension scheme if they are no longer in employment. Those individual trustees that remain may be unwilling to act despite their continuing fiduciary duties to the pension scheme and its members. Under the provisions of *s 39* of the *Trustee Act 1925*, a resignation will be effective where it leaves the pension scheme with at least two persons to act as trustees or a trust corporation. However, the trust deed and rules governing the pension scheme may provide that the pension scheme has a minimum of one trustee. In the case of a corporate trustee the directors may resign their directorships leaving no directors of the corporate trustee in place. The consequences of leaving no directors should be set out in the Memorandum and Articles of Association of the corporate trustee company.

POSSIBLE CLAIMS AGAINST THE PENSION SCHEME BY THE INSOLVENCY PRACTITIONER

18.10 Administrators and liquidators have the power to make applications to the court, for certain transactions that the company has entered into prior to administration or liquidation, to be set aside. In the context of a pension scheme the most obvious vulnerability is under *s 239* of the *IA 1986*, dealing with preferences. A preference is given if a company's actions at a time when it is unable to pay its debts (or as a consequence of which it becomes unable to pay its debts) puts a creditor, amongst others, into a better position in an insolvent liquidation than the creditor would have been if that action had not taken place

18.11 *Insolvency*

and the administrator/liquidator can show that the company was influenced by a desire to put the creditor into such a better position.

This means that, at least in theory, an administrator/liquidator could make a claim in respect of contributions made into the scheme by the employer if he or she can show that the employer was influenced by a desire that the scheme was preferred. For example, the administrator/liquidator may argue that a preference occurred where benefit enhancements occurred or substantial contributions were made into the scheme when the company was in financial difficulties.

INDEPENDENT TRUSTEE REQUIREMENTS

18.11 The insolvency practitioner is under a duty in certain prescribed circumstances to ensure that there is, or that he or she appoints, an independent trustee to the pension scheme where the company of which he or she is an insolvency practitioner participates (*s 22* and *23* of the *PA 1995*,). Further details are contained in Chapter 3. The independent trustee appointment where the only other trustee is the company will remove the company as trustee of the pension scheme. However, even where *s 23* of the *PA 1995*, does not apply where, for example, the company is not sole trustee of the pension scheme, the appointment of an independent trustee may be advisable as conflicts of interest may arise in the negotiation of the pension scheme debt.

Section 25(6) of the *PA 1995*, also requires that reasonable fees of the independent trustee be payable out of the pension scheme's funds regardless of any contrary provisions contained in the trust deed and rules governing the pension scheme. These are paid in priority to all other claims under the pension scheme.

INSOLVENCY OF THE EMPLOYER AND THE WINDING-UP OF A PENSION SCHEME

18.12 When an employer becomes subject to a regime, the following are the typical considerations for the pension scheme trustees:

(*a*) does the pension scheme have to go into wind-up or is it advisable that it does?

(*b*) are there unpaid contributions? If so, how do they rate in the insolvency? Can they be claimed from elsewhere?

(*c*) is there a deficit? How is that deficit calculated and where does it rank in the insolvency?

(*d*) what happens if there is a surplus in the pension scheme?

(*e*) can IP have a claim against the pension scheme arising purely as s consequence of the insolvency?

These considerations are commented on below.

Insolvency 18.12

It is common for occupational pension schemes to include provisions that require the scheme to be wound up (see Chapter 12) in certain circumstances involving the 'insolvency' of the employer or principal employer. In the case of a CVL (see 18.6) the liquidation will be from the date of the passing of the shareholders' resolution. In the case of a compulsory liquidation it will be from the date of the passing of the order for the winding-up of the company (s 247(2) of the *IA 1986*). This date is also relevant as the 'applicable time' for the purposes of the debt calculation under *s 75* of the *PA 1995* (see 18.13).please change to correct ref

Triggering events include:

- the appointment of an insolvency practitioner to the principal employer;
- the principal employer ceasing to trade; and
- the winding-up or liquidation of the principal employer.

Some schemes may simply refer to the company going into 'insolvency'. Unless the context of the pension scheme would infer a meaning otherwise, 'insolvency' can probably be read wide enough to include all of the regimes, particularly given *IA 1986, 247*, but 'liquidation' on the other hand, has a specific and narrower meaning and so would probably only be capable of being read as when the employer goes into formal liquidation (see 18.4 to 18.6). ('Insolvency', in relation to a company, includes the approval of a voluntary arrangement, or the appointment of an administrator or administrative receiver. A company 'goes into liquidation' if it passes a resolution for voluntary winding-up or an order for its winding-up is made by the court at a time when it has not already gone into liquidation by passing such a resolution.)

Where the winding-up of the scheme has not been triggered by the appointment of an insolvency practitioner to the principal employer or the principal employer ceasing to trade it is likely that the appointment of the insolvency practitioner will result in the termination of the contracts of employment of all or most of the employees which may again trigger the winding-up of the scheme. The failure on the part of the principal employer to pay contributions is also a triggering event. However, where the triggering of the winding-up has not occurred even as a result of these events, the trustees may wish to use the power in the scheme rules to wind the scheme up or continue the scheme as a closed scheme for the future.

A trustee claiming a debt under *s 75* of the *PA 1995*, against the employer in a liquidation will be claiming as an unsecured creditor. In the event of the compulsory liquidation of the employer the trustees as unsecured creditors must lodge, with the liquidator, a claim for the deficit debt called 'proof of debt' or 'proof' (unless otherwise ordered by the court) in order for the trustees to seek recovery of the deficit or at least a share in what is available from the liquidation fund.

The trustees of a pension scheme can in certain circumstances enforce any debt or deficit in the pension scheme against the company (see *s 75* of the *PA 1995*).

8.13 *Insolvency*

However, the liquidator, whether appointed by the creditors or the shareholders, can make an application to the court for an order to stay all actions against the company while it remains in voluntary liquidation. In view of the size of most pension scheme deficits, the liquidator is likely to proceed with such an application to prevent the trustees of a pension scheme from taking such action or proceeding with such claims.

Trustees of a pension scheme should be aware that an employer may pass from administration straight into creditors' voluntary liquidation (see 18.6), without passing a resolution. It could be argued in those circumstances that there is no 'applicable time' in which to set the debt calculation under *s 75* of the *PA 1995*(see 18.13).

The trustees governing the pension scheme may not be able to make a debt calculation under *s 75* of the *PA 1995*, unless the trust deed and rules governing the pension scheme make provision for the triggering of the winding-up of the scheme on the appointment of an insolvency practitioner or on the employer ceasing to trade.

Recent decisions indicate that administrators can also exercise the company's powers in relation to the scheme using their general powers (to do all things necessary to manage the affairs of the company) (*Polly Peck International plc (in administration) v Henry [1998] All ER (D) 647*).

There are also a number of cases which suggest that administrative receivers can exercise the company's powers in relation to the pension scheme on the basis that it forms part of the affairs of the company (*Simpson Curtis Pension Trustees Ltd v Readson Limited and others [1994] PLR 289, [1994] OPLR 231*).

DEFICIT OR SURPLUS OF PENSION SCHEME ON INSOLVENCY

Calculation of deficit

8.13 Chapter 12 sets out in detail the effect of a pension scheme being reconstructed or wound up. When the pension scheme has begun winding-up or where a 'relevant insolvency event' has occurred in relation to the employer and if the scheme's assets are less than the value of its liabilities (see Chapter 10) the difference becomes a debt due from the employer to the trustees of the pension scheme. The calculation of the deficit is made under *s 75(3)* of the *PA 1995*, at the applicable time. The applicable time for calculation is:

- any time after the pension scheme has commenced winding-up but before the relevant insolvency event occurs in relation to the employer; and

- when a relevant insolvency event has occurred, immediately before the relevant insolvency event occurs.

In *s 75(4)(a)* of the *PA 1995*, the relevant insolvency event is defined as when a company goes into liquidation within the meaning of *s 247(2)* of *IA 1986*. This includes all types of liquidation including MVLs. Therefore, for the purposes of *s 75* of the *PA 1995*, no debt is triggered when an employer enters into administration, administrative receivership or a CVA. The debt ranks simply as an unsecured claim against the employer.

Where the pension scheme is in wind-up the deficit can be calculated at any time during the winding-up of the pension scheme but before the date of the order for compulsory winding-up or the passing of the resolution to wind-up the company by means of a CVL (18.6)or MVL (18.5). Therefore, the trustees of the pension scheme have a discretion as to the date for the calculation of the deficit (*s 75* of the *PA 1995*) where the pension scheme had commenced winding-up prior to a 'relevant insolvency event' occurring to the employer.

Where a company has gone into compulsory liquidation or into CVL or MVL, the deficit is calculated immediately before the order for compulsory liquidation was passed or immediately before the passing of a resolution by the members to wind-up the company. Therefore, the discretion of the trustees has been removed.

Multi-employer schemes

18.14 Any deficiency under a multi-employer pension scheme is apportioned between the employers in the pension scheme in accordance with any provisions in the pension scheme rules. If the pension scheme rules do not cover the apportionment of the deficiency between employers, the actuary in consultation with the trustees of the pension scheme apportions the deficit between the various employers taking into account the length of adherence and the proportion of the pension scheme's liabilities that each employer has in relation to the pension scheme.

The *Occupational Pension Schemes (Deficiency on Winding-Up etc) Regulations 1996 (SI 1996 No 3128) (as amended)* are silent on whether a debt (*s 75* of the *PA 1995*) recovered from one employer should be applied for the exclusive benefit of that employer's employees or for the benefit of the employees generally. The time for the calculation of the debt in a multi-employer scheme is subject to the provisions of *s 75(3)* of the *PA 1995* (as amended in relation to multi-employer schemes).

If the scheme is being wound up the time for calculation of the debt (*s 75* of the *PA 1995*) is any time after the winding-up commences but before all the participating employers go into liquidation.

If the scheme is not being wound up, the time for calculation of the deficit is immediately before:

- a participating employer ceases to participate at a time other employers continue to participate; or
- a participating employer goes into liquidation.

18.15 *Insolvency*

Funding

18.15 The minimum funding requirement ('MFR') applies to defined benefit schemes only. While the MFR was intended to improve the security of defined benefit scheme members by giving full protection to pensions in payment and providing non-pensioners with a reasonable expectation of receiving their benefits, it is by no means a guarantee that all members will receive their full benefit entitlements. The MFR valuation is an insufficient and inadequate measure of the actual insurance company buy-out costs in relation to members' benefits and therefore provides no guarantee or security to members of their full benefit entitlement.

The actual buy-out costs for pensions in payment are significantly higher than the MFR basis. Therefore, the pension scheme would not have sufficient funds after securing pensions in payment to secure annuities for the remaining members.

Recovery of unpaid contributions to a pension scheme

18.16 Preferential debts rank below contributions and expenses and are paid out of the realisation proceeds prior to any floating charge holder and all unsecured creditors. It is therefore possible that these amounts might be paid in full.

The trustees of the pension scheme can claim the following as preferential debts against the employer:

(a) employee contributions deducted from the employee's earnings but not paid into the scheme in the four months prior to the insolvency of the employer;

(b) unpaid employer contributions to contracted-out defined benefit schemes in the twelve months prior to the insolvency of the employer of no more than three per cent of earnings (or 4.8 per cent if the scheme was non-contributory);

(c) unpaid minimum payment contributions in a money purchase contracted-out scheme in the twelve months prior to the insolvency of the employer of no more than the appropriate secondary Class 1 contributions (including primary Class 1 contributions if the scheme is non-contributory); and

(d) other employer contributions and wages due and unpaid in the four months prior to the insolvency of the employer provided such sums exceed no more than £800 per employee. [*IA 1986, Sch 6* as amended by the *Insolvency Proceedings (Monetary Limits) Order 1986 (SI 1986 No 1996)*].

Where any contributions remain due and unpaid into the scheme and do not fall within the four categories above they will rank as an unsecured debt against the employer.

Recovery from the Secretary of State

18.17 *Sections 123–125* of the *PSA 1993* provide that on application to the Secretary of State in respect of unpaid contributions, payment will be made into the occupational pension scheme in respect of those unpaid contributions. However, the Secretary of State must be satisfied that:

- the employer has become insolvent; and

- at the time the employer became insolvent there remains unpaid relevant contributions that should be paid by the employer to the scheme.

Under *s 123* of the *PSA 1993* an 'insolvent' employer means a situation where:

- a winding-up order or an administration order has been made or a resolution for voluntary winding-up has been passed (see 18.2 to 18.18);

- a receiver or manager has been duly appointed (see 18.7);

- possession is taken, by or on behalf of the holders of any debentures secured by a floating charge, of any property of the company comprised in or subject to the charge; or

- a voluntary arrangement has been proposed (see 18.2 and 18.3).

Relevant contributions are:

- payable by an employer on his or her own account (ie not contributions deducted from the pay of an employee); or

- payable on behalf of an employee provided that the contributions have actually been deducted by the employer from the pay of the employee but not paid over (see *s 124(2)* of the PSA 93).

In respect of contributions due from an employer on his or her own account the amount claimable (see *s 124(3)* and *s 124(3A)* of the *PSA 1993*) is the lower of the following amounts:

- the amount unpaid which had been payable in the twelve months preceding the date of insolvency of the employer;

- the amount certified by an actuary to be necessary to meet the scheme liabilities on dissolution to or in respect of employees of the company (ie the contributions shortfall), in the case of a defined benefit scheme; or

- ten per cent of the total amount of remuneration paid or payable to employees in the twelve months preceding the date of insolvency.

18.18 *Insolvency*

The amount of the claim in respect of unpaid contributions on behalf of an employee (see *s 124–5* of the *PSA 1993*) amounts to those contributions deducted from the pay of the employee during the twelve months preceding the date of insolvency but have not been paid into the scheme.

An application for payment of unpaid contributions must be made by the person 'competent to act' on behalf of the pension scheme (*s 124(1)* of the *PSA 1993*). In practice this will usually be the trustees, but could be the scheme administrator or anyone permitted to act on their behalf, eg a professional adviser may apply for payment. The relevant IP should have copies of all relevant forms for the trustees to complete. Form RP15 is the application form for the claim. The trustees or other 'competent person to act' must complete Part 1 of form RP15 and the relevant IP completes Part 2 of the form. The relevant IP can (if authorised to act for the pension scheme) complete all of form RP15. Form RP16 is the actuarial certificate in respect of defined benefits scheme contributions and will be completed by the actuary. Payment will be made directly to the pension scheme.

The trustees and the relevant IP should together agree the claim amount. The trustees should complete a list of those employees who were also members of the pension scheme and their contribution rates during the twelve month period prior to the appointment of the relevant IP (ie twelve months up to and including the day before the appointment of the relevant IP) so that the relevant IP can calculate the amount of contributions due. A certificate is required from the relevant IP as to the unpaid amounts (unless the Secretary of State waives this requirement).

The right to recover contributions from the employer (including contributions which amount to preferential debts) transfer from the pension scheme to the Secretary of State once payment has been made.

Recovering sufficient sums of unpaid contributions

18.18 In reality the chances of there being a significant sum of unpaid contributions after April 1997 are low as a result of the *PA 1995* requirements. The consequences for late payment of contributions could be that trustees are reported to Opra and fines are imposed.

Compensation can be claimed from the Pensions Compensation Board ('PCB') if the employer is insolvent and the value of the assets of the pension scheme have been reduced and there is reasonable grounds for believing that the reduction is due to an offence which involves dishonesty including an attempt to defraud. In such circumstances:

- the value of the assets immediately before the application is made must be less than 90 per cent of the amount of the liabilities of the pension scheme;
- it must be reasonable in all circumstances that the PCB should assist the members by paying a sum to the trustees.

Application for compensation is made by the trustees of the pension scheme, the administrators, a member or a beneficiary under the pension scheme or a representative of any of the above. The application should be made within twelve months of the later of the insolvency date or when the auditor, actuary or trustees knew or ought to have known that a relevant reduction of value had occurred. This date can be extended by the PCB.

The compensation provisions do not apply to a pension scheme:

- with fewer than two members and no beneficiaries;
- death benefit only schemes where no member has accrued rights;
- where a scheme is not approved by the Inland Revenue; or
- which are public service pension schemes.

The PCB can award an amount equal to the shortfall or such amount as is required to secure 90 per cent of the liabilities of the pension scheme on the settlement date, whichever is the lesser amount.

There is an obligation on the trustees of the pension scheme to take all reasonable steps to recover the lost assets unless to do so would incur disproportionate costs. The PCB can make an interim compensation payment but if it consequently decides that the trustees of the pension scheme were not entitled to such a payment it can recover such amount as they consider appropriate, provided that such recovery would not have the effect of reducing pensions. The PCB can award interim relief if the pension scheme trustees are unable to pay certain prescribed benefits such as retirement pensions, benefits secured by contributions to provide contracted-out benefits under a defined benefit scheme or ill-health pensions.

Surplus of scheme on employer insolvency

18.19 While it is an unlikely event in the light of the current financial circumstances that a surplus is found on the winding-up of a pension scheme, if one becomes available the insolvency practitioner would request the return of the surplus to the employer so that there may be a further distribution to creditors.

Section 76 of the *PA 1995* provides that members must be notified prior of any repayment of surplus being made to an employer. Under *Regulation 7* of the *Occupational Pension Schemes (Payments to Employers) Regulations 1996 (SI 1996 No 2156)* notices must be given to the members of the proposal to return the surplus to the employer. Any member dissatisfied with the proposal to return the surplus to the employer can make representations to the trustees or the employer or ultimately Opra. The surplus in the scheme can be returned to the employer, subject to a 35 per cent tax charge, provided that all the scheme

18.20 *Insolvency*

liabilities have been discharged in full and the trust deed and rules which govern the pension scheme permit the return of surplus and subject to approval by the Inland Revenue.

If the trust deed and rules governing the pension scheme are silent on the return of surplus to the employer or do not permit the return of surplus to the employer, any surplus must be used to augment members' benefits up to the Inland Revenue maximum. In the unlikely event that any surplus remains after augmentation can be returned to the employer.

PENSIONS BILL

18.20 Under the Pensions Bill, as introduced to Parliament in February 2004, it is proposed that there will be a Pensions Regulator (see Chapter 2) whose powers are intended to be more pro-active. The Pensions Regulator will be able to apply for an order under *s 423* of the *IA 1986*, where a debtor has been declared bankrupt or an administration order has been passed. The Pensions Regulator would be acting on behalf of the trustees of the pension scheme or the Pension Protection Fund ('PPF').

The PPF will assume responsibility for eligible schemes where a relevant insolvency event has occurred in relation to the employer (or where the employer is unlikely to be able to continue as a going concern), the scheme is unable to secure its 'protected liabilities' and there is no possibility of a scheme rescue. Defined contribution schemes are not eligible to participate. Relevant insolvency events will include entering administration and passing a resolution for voluntary winding-up without a declaration of solvency. When the PPF assumes responsibility the scheme assets will be transferred to the PPF and the trustees discharged from further responsibility. The Board will then be responsible for paying benefits at the protected liability level.

'Protected liabilities' include 100 per cent of benefits for those already retired or over the scheme's normal pension age, 90 per cent of accrued benefits for other members and 50 per cent pensions for widows and widowers. Up to 25 per cent of the benefit may be taken as a lump sum. Pensions relating to service after 5 April 1997 will be increased at LPI capped at 2.5 per cent and pensions in deferment will be revalued at RPI capped at 5 per cent. The total amount of pension to which any member will be entitled under the PPF is likely to be restricted to £25,000. Further details are expected to be contained in regulations. Also included are all other scheme liabilities (for example fees due to advisers) and winding-up costs.

The Bill also includes proposals which are intended to prevent employers from adjusting their corporate structure in order to avoid pension obligations and to prevent recovery of a debt under *s 75* of the *PA 1995*. This would include transferring assets from an employer which participates in a pension scheme to another associated company such as a service company. The Pensions Regulator (see 2.29) will have powers to impose liability on a person who is associated or connected with the insolvent employer and may order a parent company to provide financial support, while a pension scheme is still in existence.

In addition, the Bill proposes to amend the definition of an insolvency event, so that it will include the conversion of a members' voluntary liquidation (see 18.5) to a creditors' voluntary liquidation (see 18.6).

Appendix I

Penalties under the *Pensions Act 1995* and other legislation

TYPES OF PENALTY

General

The *Pensions Act 1995* carries a number of sanctions for non-compliance, ranging from fines to, in extreme cases, imprisonment. Other Acts and Regulations contain sanctions, but these are usually confined to fines.

Civil penalties

Opra may require a person to pay a penalty in respect of an act or omission in contravention of various requirements of the *1995 Act*. [*PA 1995, s 10*]. The maximum amount of the penalty varies from £5,000 in the case of an individual and £50,000 in any other case to £200 and £1,000 respectively. The time limit for payment is usually 28 days.

Where a penalty is recoverable from a corporate body, and the act or omission was done with the connivance or consent of an officer (or, in some cases, a managing shareholder) of the company, Opra may instead impose a penalty on that person.

Prohibition from acting as a trustee

Opra has the power to prohibit an individual from being a trustee (or director of trustee company). The effect of a prohibition order is that the individual is removed as a trustee. [*PA 1995, s 3*]. Opra also has the power to suspend a trustee [*PA 1995, s 4*]. The effect of the suspension order is to prohibit the trustee from exercising his functions in respect of the scheme(s) in question.

Criminal penalties

Certain transgressions carry criminal sanctions. Penalties for conviction of an offence are:

(*a*)   on summary conviction – a fine not exceeding the statutory maximum; and

Appendix I

(*b*) on conviction on indictment – a fine or imprisonment or both.

Where an offence committed by a corporate body is proved to have been committed with the consent or connivance of an officer or purported officer of the company, that person is guilty of an offence and subject to the same punishment.

Appeals

Opra is required to review its decisions on the application of any person within a certain period, (*PA 1995, s 96(2)*)

Opra may refer any question to the court. In addition, an appeal to court on a point of law is available for any person aggrieved by a review decision or a refusal to undertake a review.

SUMMARY OF PENALTIES

A brief summary of the main transgressions for which penalties may be imposed is set out in the table below. This is not an exhaustive list.

Transgression	*Penalty*	*Can be imposed on*
Failure to give effect to the statutory consultation procedure re member nominated trustees/directors (*sections 17* and *19, PA 1995*)	Civil penalty	Any employer who makes a proposal to opt-out of the member-nominated trustee or member-nominated director requirements
Failure to make arrangements for member-nominated trustees or member-nominated directors or failure to implement arrangements or appropriate rules (*section 21, PA 1995*)	Civil penalty and prohibition order	Any trustee who fails to take all reasonable steps to secure compliance
Failure by trustees or administrators to report to Opra within one month where an insolvency practitioner is acting in relation to an employer of a final salary scheme that there is no trustee (*section 26A, PA 1995*)	Civil penalty	Any trustee who has failed to take all such steps as are reasonable to secure compliance or any person who fails to comply with a duty imposed on him by the section

Appendix I

Transgression	Penalty	Can be imposed on
Acting as an actuary or auditor whilst ineligible to do so by virtue of being a trustee or being connected with or an associate of a trustee (*section 28, PA 1995*)	Criminal offence	Any person so acting
	Prohibition order	Any trustee so acting and any trustee connected with the actuary or auditor so acting
Purporting to act as a trustee whilst disqualified (*section 30, PA 1995*)	Criminal offence	Any person purporting to so act
Accepting or permitting reimbursement for fines or civil penalties imposed under the Act or *PSA 1993* (*section 31, PA 1995*)	Criminal offence	Any trustee who, knowing or having reasonable grounds to believe he has been reimbursed, fails to take all reasonable steps to secure that he is not reimbursed
	Civil penalty and prohibition order	Any trustee who fails to take all reasonable steps to secure that reimbursement is not made.
Failure to give notice (required under *Reg 9, Scheme Administration Regulations 1996* (*SI 1996/1715*)) of trustee meetings where decisions taken by majority (*section 32, PA 1995*)	Civil penalty and prohibition order	Any trustee who fails to take all reasonable steps to secure compliance
Failure to prepare or maintain a statement of investment principles or failure to obtain and consider advice before preparing the statement (*section 35, PA 1995*)	Civil penalty and prohibition order	Any trustee who fails to take all reasonable steps to secure compliance
Failure to obtain and consider proper advice before making an investment (*section 36, PA 1995*)	Civil penalty and prohibition order	Any trustee who fails to take all reasonable steps to secure compliance
Failure to comply with the Act in relation to the payment of surplus to an employer (*section 37, PA 1995*)	Civil penalty and prohibition order	Any trustee who fails to take all reasonable steps to secure compliance

Appendix I

Transgression	Penalty	Can be imposed on
Non-trustee purporting to exercise a power in relation to the payment of surplus to the employer (*section 37, PA 1995*)	Civil penalty	Person purporting to exercise power
Investing in employer-related investments in excess of statutory limit (*section 40, PA 1995*)	Civil penalty and prohibition order	Any trustee who fails to take reasonable steps to secure compliance
	Criminal offence	Any trustee or manager who agreed to make the investment
Placing reliance on the skill and judgement of legal or other specified professional advisers (as to which, see *Reg 2 of the Scheme Administration Regulations 1996* (*SI 1996/1715*)) not appointed by the trustees (*section 47, PA 1995*)	Civil penalty and prohibition order	Any trustee who does so
	Civil penalty	Any manager who does so
Failure to appoint a scheme auditor, scheme actuary or fund manager when required to do so or failure to comply with requirements prescribed regarding the appointment of professional advisers (*section 47, PA 1995*)	Civil penalty and prohibition order	Any trustee who fails to take reasonable steps to secure compliance
	Civil penalty	Any manager who fails to take reasonable steps to secure compliance
Failure without reasonable excuse to obtain audited accounts or an auditor's contribution statement within seven months of end of scheme year (*Occupational Pensions Schemes (Requirement to Obtain Audited Accounts and a Statement from the Auditor) Regulations 1996* (*SI 1996/1975*)).	Prohibition order	Any trustee failing to comply.
	Civil penalty	Any trustee or manager failing without reasonable excuse to take all necessary steps to secure compliance.
Failure to blow the whistle when required to do so (*section 48, PA 1995*) (*Sections (2) and 7–13 have not been brought into force*)	Civil penalty and disqualification from acting as actuary or auditor of specified scheme(s)	Any actuary or auditor

Appendix I

Transgression	Penalty	Can be imposed on
Purporting to act as an auditor or actuary in respect of a scheme while disqualified for failure to blow the whistle (*section 48, PA 1995*) (*Not yet in force*)	Criminal offence	Any person purporting to act
Failure to keep money in a separate account and failure to maintain adequate records relating to trustee meetings and certain transactions as required by regulations (see, in particular, the *Scheme Administration Regulations 1996* (*SI 1996/1715*)) (*section 49, PA 1995*)	Civil penalty and prohibition order	Any trustee who fails to take all reasonable steps to secure compliance
Failure to keep adequate records, as required by regulations (*section 49, PA 1995*)	Civil penalties	Any employer or prescribed person
Deducting contributions from employees' earnings and failing to pay them to the trustees within required time with no reasonable excuse for doing so (*section 49, PA 1995*)	Civil penalty	Employer (unless he is required to pay a penalty under *section 3(7), WRPA* for failures in respect of stakeholder schemes)
Failure to give notice to Opra and the member of the failure of the employer to pay deductions from the employee's earnings to the trustees within the prescribed time (*section 49, PA 1995*).	Civil penalty and prohibition order	Any trustee who fails to take all reasonable steps to secure compliance
	Civil penalty	Any manager who fails to take all reasonable steps to secure compliance
Being knowingly concerned in the fraudulent evasion of the obligation to pay deductions from employee's earnings to the trustees within the prescribed time (*section 49, PA 1995*).	Criminal offence	Any person

Appendix I

Transgression	Penalty	Can be imposed on
Failure to comply with the statutory requirements to keep written records of any determinations or decisions in relation to the winding up of the scheme (*section 49A, PA 1995*)	Civil penalty and prohibition order	Any trustee who fails to take all such steps as are reasonable to secure compliance
	Civil penalty	Any manager who fails to take all such steps as are reasonable to secure compliance
Failure to make and/or implement arrangements for the resolution of disputes (*section 50, PA 1995*)	Civil penalty	Any trustee or manager who fails to take all reasonable steps to secure compliance
Failure to obtain actuarial valuations or certificates when required to do so and failure to make them available to the employer within seven days of their receiving it (*section 57, PA 1995*)	Civil penalty and prohibition order	Any trustee who fails to take all reasonable steps to secure compliance
	Civil penalty	Any manager who fails to take all reasonable steps to secure compliance
Failure to prepare a schedule of contributions in accordance with statutory requirements (*section 58, PA 1995*)	Civil penalty and prohibition order	Any trustee who fails to take all reasonable steps to secure compliance
	Civil penalty	Any manager who fails to take all reasonable steps to secure compliance
Failure to give notice to Opra and to members, or failure to prepare a report, when contributions are not made or the MFR is not met (*sections 59 and 60, PA 1995*)	Civil penalty and prohibition order	Any trustee who fails to take all reasonable steps to secure compliance
	Civil penalty	Any manager who fails to take all reasonable steps to secure compliance
Failure to apply the assets of the scheme in the statutory order on a winding-up or allowing a person other than the trustees or managers to apply those assets (*section 73, PA 1995*)	Civil penalty and prohibition order	Any trustee who fails to take all reasonable steps to secure compliance
	Civil penalty	Any manager who fails to take all reasonable steps to secure compliance

Appendix I

Transgression	Penalty	Can be imposed on
Exercising a power to distribute excess assets on a winding-up to an employer without having complied with the statutory requirements (*sections 76 and 77, PA 1995*)	Civil penalty and prohibition order	Any trustee who fails to take all reasonable steps to secure compliance
	Civil penalty	Any person other than the trustees who purports to exercise the power (under *section 76, PA 1995* only).
Failure to obtain recoverable funds where this would not entail disproportionate cost whilst making an application to the Compensation Board (*section 81, PA 1995*)	Prohibition order	Any trustee who fails to take all reasonable steps to secure compliance
Failure to prepare a schedule of payments for a money purchase scheme (*section 87, PA 1995*)	Civil penalty and prohibition order	Any trustee who fails to take all reasonable steps to secure compliance
	Civil penalty	Any manager who fails to take all reasonable steps to secure compliance
Failure to make payments to a money purchase scheme in accordance with the schedule of payments (*section 88, PA 1995*)	Civil penalty	Employer
Failure to notify Opra and members within the required time where payments have not been made in accordance with the schedule of payments (*section 88, PA 1995*)	Civil penalty and prohibition order	Any trustee who fails to take all reasonable steps to secure compliance
	Civil penalty	Any manager who fails to take all reasonable steps to secure compliance
Failure to provide information and documents to Opra, delaying or obstructing an Opra Inspector (*section 101, PA 1995*) or neglects or refuses to produce a document to the Compensation Board (*section 111, PA 1995*)	Criminal offence (punishable by fine only)	Any person

Appendix I

Transgression	Penalty	Can be imposed on
Knowingly or recklessly providing Opra or the Compensation Board with information that is false or misleading in a material particular that Opra (*section 101, PA 1995*) or the Compensation Board (*s 111*) may require.	Criminal offence	Any person
Intentionally altering, suppressing, concealing or destroying documents that Opra may require (*section 101, PA 1995*) or the Compensation Board (*s 111*) may require.	Criminal offence	Any person
Failure to provide certain information to the Registrar (*Register of Occupational and Personal Pension Schemes Regulations 1997* (*SI 1997/371*))	Civil penalty	Any person who fails to comply without reasonable excuse
Disclosing any restricted information obtained by Opra without authorisation (*section 104, PA 1995*)	Criminal offence	Opra or any person who receives the information directly or indirectly from them
Failure to provide a statement of guaranteed cash equivalent when required to do so or failure to comply with a transfer notice given by an eligible member (*section 153, PA 1995/section 93A, 99* and *101 PSA 1993*) (Includes statements/transfers in respect of pension credit benefits.)	Civil penalty	Any trustee or manager who fails to take all reasonable steps to secure compliance
Failure to disclose documentation and information when required to do so (Regulations made under *section 41, PA 1995*)	Civil penalty and prohibition order	Any trustee who has failed to take all reasonable steps to secure compliance
	Civil Penalty	Any manager who has failed to take all reasonable steps to secure compliance

Appendix I

Transgression	Penalty	Can be imposed on
Failure to obtain actuarial certification or failure to comply with consent requirements before modifying the scheme to the detriment of member's accrued rights (Regulations made under *section 67, PA (1995)*)	Civil penalty	Any person who fails to comply
Failure to issue appropriate notice within one month following determination to defer winding-up of scheme or as to when liabilities are to be determined (*Winding-up Regulations 1996 (SI 1996/3126)* made under *section 38, PA 1995*)	Civil penalty	Any person who fails to comply
Failure to make a report regarding a scheme's winding-up where required to do so (*section 72A, PA 1995*) (part of this section came into force partially from 1 March 2002 for the purpose of making regulations and rules and partially from 1 April 2002. However, the remainder of the section is still not in force.)	Civil penalty and prohibition order	Any trustee who has failed to take all reasonable steps to secure compliance
	Civil penalty	Any manager who has failed to take all reasonable steps to secure compliance
Failure to comply with a direction given by Opra to facilitate winding-up (*section 72C PA 1995*).	Civil penalty and prohibition order	Any trustee who fails, without reasonable excuse, to take all reasonable steps to secure compliance with the direction
	Civil penalty	Any manager or other person to whom a direction is given who fails, without reasonable excuse, to take all reasonable steps to secure compliance

Appendix I

Transgression	Penalty	Can be imposed on
Failure to secure that the requirements for a registered stakeholders scheme are fulfilled at the time the application for registration is made (*section 2, WRPA 1999*)	Civil penalty and prohibition order	Any trustee who made the application
	Civil penalty	Any prescribed person who made the application
Failure to secure that the conditions for registration of a stakeholders scheme are fulfilled while the scheme is registered (*section 2, WRPA 1999*)	Prohibition order and civil penalty	Any trustee who fails to take all reasonable steps to secure compliance
	Civil penalty	Any other prescribed person who fails to take all reasonable steps to secure compliance
Knowingly or recklessly providing Opra with information which is false or misleading in a material particular (*section 2, WRPA 1999*)	Criminal offence	Any person applying for registration of a pension scheme under the *Act*
Failure to comply with duty to facilitate access to stakeholders pension scheme (*section 3, WRPA 1999*)	Civil penalty	Employer
Failure to discharge liability in respect of a pension credit within the implementation period (*section 33, WRPA 1999*)	Civil penalty (*see Reg 5 SI 2000/1053*)	Any trustee or manager who has failed to take all reasonable steps to ensure that liability in respect of the credit is discharged before the end of the implementation period.
Failure to notify Opra of a failure to discharge liability for a pension credit within the implementation period (*section 33, WRPA 1999*)	Civil penalty (*see Reg 5 SI 2000/1053*)	Any trustee or manager who has failed to take all reasonable steps to ensure the obligation is performed.
Failure to notify Opra of the failure to comply with the transfer notice in respect of a pension credit benefit (*section 33, WRPA 1999*)	Civil penalty	Any trustee or manager who has failed to take all reasonable steps to ensure that the obligation is performed
Failure to provide a statement of entitlement to members when applied for by a member (*section 93A, PSA 1993*)	Civil penalty	Any trustee or manager who has failed to take such steps as are reasonable to secure compliance

Appendix I

Transgression	Penalty	Can be imposed on
Failure to carry out what a member of the scheme requires within six months of the necessary date as regards the exercise of the option conferred by *section 95, PSA 1993* (*section 99, PSA 1993*)	Civil penalty	Any trustee or manager who has failed to take all such steps as are reasonable to ensure it was so done
Failure on application of an eligible member of a salary related occupational pension scheme, to provide him with a written statement of the amount of cash equivalent of his pension credit benefit under the scheme (*section 101H, PSA 1993*)	Civil penalty	Any trustee or manager who has failed to take all such steps as are reasonable to secure that the obligation was performed
Failure to notify Opra of the failure to comply with transfer notice before the end of the period for compliance (*section 101J, PSA 1993*)	Civil penalty	Any trustee or manager who has failed to take all steps as are reasonable to ensure that the notice was complied with before the end of the period for compliance
Failure to prepare/maintain a record for direct payment arrangements regarding contributions to personal pension schemes or to send a copy of the record to the trustees or managers (*section 111A, PSA 1993*)	Civil penalty	Employer (unless he is required to pay a penalty under *section 3(7), WRPA 1999* for failures in respect of stakeholder pensions)
Failure to notify Opra and/or the employee where contributions shown on the record of the direct payment arrangements had not been paid before the due date or failure to provide information to employee at specified intervals (*section 111A, PSA 1993*)	Prohibition order	Any trustee who has failed to take all reasonable steps to secure compliance

Appendix I

Transgression	Penalty	Can be imposed on
Failure to pay the contribution payable under direct payment arrangements to the trustee/managers of the scheme on or before its due date (*section 111A, PSA 1993*)	Civil penalty	Employer
Failure to provide information regarding transfer of accrued rights without consent (*Reg 27B, Occupational Pension Schemes (Preservation of Benefit) Regulations 1991 (SI 1991/167)*)	Civil penalty	Any person who fails without reasonable excuse to comply
Failure to provide information to member on termination of pensionable service (*Reg 27B, Occupational Pension Schemes (Preservation of Benefit) Regulations 1991 (SI 1991/167)*)	Civil penalty	Any person who fails without reasonable excuse to comply
Failure to provide information to members within two months of the appointment of an independent trustee (*Reg 7, SI 1997/252*)	Civil penalty	Any person who fails without reasonable excuse to comply
Failure to pay the Occupational and Personal Pension Schemes Levy (*Reg 13, Levy Regulations 1997 (SI 1997/666)*)	Civil penalty	Any person who fails without reasonable cause to comply
Failure to provide specified information regarding pension sharing (*Reg 9, Pensions on Divorce etc. (Provision of Information) Regulations 2000 (SI 2000/1048)*)	Civil penalty	Any trustee or manager who fails without reasonable excuse to comply
False statements on application for approval or in order to secure tax relief (*sections 605A, 619, 653 and 658, ICTA 1988*)	Civil penalty	Any person making such statements either fraudulently or negligently (*section 605A, ICTA 1988*) or knowingly (otherwise)

Appendix I

Transgression	Penalty	Can be imposed on
Failure to provide information to the Revenue when required to do so, or failure to keep books, documents and other records as required (*sections 605* and *651A, ICTA 1988*)	Civil penalty	Any person failing to comply
Carrying on a Regulated Activity while unauthorised, or outside the exempt regime (*section 23, FSMA 2000*)	Criminal offence	Any person acting in the course of business
Communicating an invitation or inducement to engage in investment activity (*section 25, FSMA 2000*)	Criminal offence	Any person acting in the course of business
An unfit and improper individual carrying out functions in relation to a Regulated Activity for an Authorised Person (*section 56, FSMA 2000*)	Prohibition order	Any person who is deemed to be unfit and improper by the FSA
Failure to comply with a statement of principle issued by the FSA (*section 66, FSMA 2000*)	Civil penalty or statement of misconduct	Any approved person issued with a statement of principle
Knowing concern in a contravention, by a relevant authorised person, of a requirement imposed on that authorised person by, or under, the *FSMA 2000* (*section 66, FSMA 2000*)	Civil penalty or statement of misconduct	Any approved person
Engaging in, or by act or omission encouraging or requiring another to engage in, market abuse (*section 123, FSMA 2000*)	Civil penalty or statement indicating engagement in market abuse	Any person or persons privy to unpublished price sensitive information

Appendix I

Transgression	Penalty	Can be imposed on
Failure to notify the FSA of a step which would result in the acquiring of control over, additional kind of control or an increase in the relevant kind of control over, a UK authorised person (*section 118, FSMA 2000*)	Criminal offence (punishable by fine only) (see *section 191, FSMA 2000*)	Any person under a duty to notify
Failure to notify the FSA of a step which would result in ceasing to have control over, or reducing relevant control over, a UK authorised person (*section 190, FSMA 2000*)	Criminal offence (punishable by fine only) (see *section 191, FSMA 2000*)	Any person under a duty to notify
Failure to abide by a notice of objection issued by the FSA (*section 191, FSMA 2000*)	Criminal offence	Any person subject to a notice of objection
Contravention of a requirement relating to authorised persons under the *FSMA 2000* (*section 205* and *206, FSMA 2000*)	Civil Penalty or statement of contravention issued by the FSA	Any authorised person
Communicating an invitation or inducement to participate in an unauthorised collective investment scheme (*section 241, FSMA 2000*)	Civil action by a private person	Any authorised person
Disclosure or use of confidential information by, or obtained from, a primary recipient without the relevant consent (*section 352, FSMA 2000*)	Criminal offence	Any person who is in possession of confidential information
On application to the FSA or the Secretary of State there is a reasonable likelihood, possibility or actual case of a relevant requirement under the act being contravened (*section 380, FSMA 2000*)	Injunction	Any person

Appendix I

Transgression	Penalty	Can be imposed on
Accruing profit or causing loss as a result of a contravention or knowing involvment in a contravention of a relevant requirement (*section 382, FSMA 2000*)	Restitution order	Any person
Making a statement, promise or forecast which is known to be misleading, false or deceptive in a material particular (*section 397, FSMA 2000*)	Criminal offence	Any person
Dishonestly concealing any material facts whether in connection with a statement, promise or forecast made by the offender or otherwise (*section 397, FSMA 2000*)	Criminal offence	Any person
Recklessly making (dishonestly or otherwise) a statement, promise or forecast which is misleading, false or deceptive in a material particular (*section 397, FSMA 2000*)	Criminal offence	Any person
Knowingly or recklessly giving the FSA information which is false or misleading in a material particular in purported compliance with any requirement imposed by or under the Act (*section 398, FSMA 2000*)	Criminal offence (punishable by fine only)	Any person

Human Rights Act implications of Opra's powers

As a public Authority, it is unlawful for Opra to act in a way that is incompatible with rights under the European Convention on Human Rights.

The Convention article of primary relevance for Opra is Article 6(1), which lays down certain requirements in relation to the determination of a person's civil rights and obligations and in relation to criminal charges. Extra requirements are laid down in relation to criminal procedures in Articles 6(2) and 6(3). How might these apply to Opra's activities?

Appendix I

Prohibition orders

There is some debate over whether the imposition of a prohibition order would be subject to the requirements of Article 6(1). It would be more likely to be the case where a professional trustee is the subject of the prohibition order.

Fines

The imposition of fines under *section 10* of *PA 1995* certainly involves the determination of a person's civil rights and obligations and, it has been suggested, could be regarded in the nature of a criminal penalty. If the fines are to be regarded as criminal penalties, then the absence of the availability of legal aid is of concern as this is required under Article 6 for the purposes of criminal proceedings.

In addition, there is currently no right to a public hearing in relation to the imposition of a penalty under *section 10*. The ECHR case law suggests that it is sufficient that the opportunity is given to the person in question. However, it may be difficult for Opra to deny a hearing if a person requests it.

Finally, there are some question marks over whether Opra are sufficiently impartial to comply with Article 6(1), particularly if the fines imposed can be categorised as criminal penalties. There may be an argument that, although different members of Opra investigate to those who adjudicate, Opra may unconsciously favour the arguments of their own staff. Any problems that arise in this regard can be overcome, provided that there is an adequate appeals procedure. In the case of Opra, all decisions are subject to review (*section 96(2), PA 1995*) and can then be appealed on a point of law only (*section 97, PA 1995*). This latter point may cause difficulties as an appeal is only permitted on a point of law. If the appeal court cannot make a finding of fact, it will need to have the option of remitting the matter back to Opra and this will only be possible if there are sufficient adjudicators to hear it, leaving aside those who took the original decision and those who reviewed it.

Appendix II

Summary of the Application of the Occupational Pension Schemes (Disclosure of Information) Regulations 1996 (*SI 1996 No 1655*) (The 'Disclosure Regulations') to Approved Schemes, and other Requirements to Disclose Information

To be disclosed	Disclosure to	Form of disclosure	When
CONSTITUTION OF THE SCHEME (Regulation 3, Disclosure Regulations) *(all schemes)*			
The contents of: • The trust deed or other document constituting the scheme; • The rules (if not in above document); • Any documents amending, supplementing or superseding any of the above; • A document setting out the names and addresses of participating employers, if not in the above documents. Reference to (or text of) relevant provisions of Acts or Statutory Instruments set out or referred to in the above documents. English translation if necessary.	• Members, prospective members and their spouses; • Beneficiaries; • Recognised trade unions. *Only information relevant to an individual need be disclosed to him/her or to his/her trade union.*	• Copy for inspection, free of charge at a place which is reasonable; or • Personal copy at a reasonable charge (ie cost of copying, postage & packaging) or, if publicly available, notice of where a copy may be obtained from.	On request, within two months of the request being made.

Appendix II

To be disclosed	Disclosure to	Form of disclosure	When
BASIC INFORMATION ABOUT THE SCHEME (Regulation 4 and Schedule 1, Disclosure Regulations) (*all schemes*)			
Membership Categories of people who are eligible to be members and whether they are admitted: • only on their own application; or • automatically unless they request not to be admitted; or • subject to the consent of their employer. The conditions of eligibility for membership. The period of notice (if any) which a member must give to terminate his pensionable service. Whether and on what conditions (if any), a member may re-enter pensionable service before normal pension age. **Contributions** How employers' contributions are determined. How members' ordinary contributions are determined. What arrangements are made for members to pay additional voluntary contributions.	• Members, prospective members and their spouses • Beneficiaries; • Recognised trade unions. *Only information relevant to an individual need be disclosed to him/her or to his/her trade union.*	No specified form but must include a written statement that further information is available, giving address to which enquiries should be sent.	As of course, to every prospective member or, if not practicable to do so, within two months of his becoming a member. To the extent that any information has not been given to a person who was a member or pensioner on 5 April 1997, it must be given to that person by 5 April 1998 (or, in the case of a deferred member, within two months of him becoming a pensioner, if later). Otherwise, on request, (unless the same information was provided in the 12 months prior to the request being made), as soon as practicable and in any event, within two months of the date of receipt of request.

(cont'd)

Appendix II

To be disclosed	Disclosure to	Form of disclosure	When
(cont'd) **Scheme details** Whether the scheme is a tax-approved scheme and, if not, whether an application for tax-approval has been made. Which of the relevant employments are, and which are not, contracted-out. The short title of the enactment (if any) which provides for: • the setting up of the scheme; and • the determination of the rate or amount of the benefits. **Benefits** Normal pension age under the scheme (except simplified defined contribution schemes). What benefits are payable and how they are calculated (including how pensionable earnings are defined and the rate at which benefits accrue and including, in a contracted out money purchase or hybrid scheme, that the amount of assets allocated for the provision of protected rights benefits are increased, how they are increased and why that method is used). The conditions on which benefits are paid. *(cont'd)*			*(cont'd)* Details of material changes must be drawn to attention of members and beneficiaries (but not excluded persons) before the change if practicable, but in any event, within three months after the change.

Appendix II

To be disclosed	Disclosure to	Form of disclosure	When
(cont'd) Whether and, if so, when and on what conditions, survivors' benefits are payable. Which benefits, if any, are payable only at some person's discretion.			
Whether there is a power under the scheme to increase pensions after they have become payable, and, if so, who may exercise it, and to what extent it is discretionary.			
Where the scheme is a hybrid scheme for contracting-out purposes, the circumstances in which the nature of a member's accrued rights may alter and a statement that the trustees will notify the member if his rights are affected.			
Administration What arrangements are made, and in what circumstances, for estimates or statements of a guaranteed cash equivalent, for the refund of contributions and the preservation or transfer of the accrued rights of early leavers.			
Whether, and the circumstances in which, the trustees will accept cash equivalents and provide transfer credits and whether this is discretionary.			
If applicable, a statement to the effect that the trustees have directed that any cash equivalent shall not take into account discretionary benefits.			
A statement summarising the way in which transfer values are calculated.			
A statement that an annual report is available on request (except public sector schemes).			
(cont'd)			

Appendix II

To be disclosed	Disclosure to	Form of disclosure	When
(cont'd) Whether information about the scheme has been given to the Registrar of Occupational and Personal Pension Schemes			
Unless the scheme is exempt, what procedures it has for the internal resolution of disputes, including the address and job title of the person to be contacted.			
A statement that the Occupational Pensions Advisory Service is available to assist in connection with queries and unresolved disputes and the address at which it may be contacted.			
A statement that the Pensions Ombudsman may investigate and determine any complaint or dispute of fact or law in relation to an occupational pensions scheme and the address at which he may be contacted.			
A statement that the Occupational Pensions Regulatory Authority is able to intervene in the running of schemes where trustees, employers or other professional advisers have failed in their duties, and in certain other circumstances, and the address at which it may be contacted.			
The address to which enquiries about the scheme generally or about an individual's entitlement to benefit should be sent.			

Appendix II

To be disclosed	Disclosure to	Form of disclosure	When
INFORMATION TO BE MADE AVAILABLE TO INDIVIDUALS (Regulation 5 and Schedule 2, Disclosure Regulations) *(all schemes)*			
Pensions *(all schemes)* The amount of benefit which is payable and if a benefit is payable periodically: • the conditions (if any) subject to which payment will be continued; and • the provisions (if any) under which the amount payable may be altered. The rights and options (if any) available on the death of a member or beneficiary, and the procedures for exercising them.	Any person to whom a benefit has become, or is about to become, payable.	Information plus written statement that further information is available, giving address to which enquiries should be sent.	As of course, before or within one month (two months where the person is retiring before normal pension age) after date on which benefit becomes payable.
If the amount of benefit is to be altered (other than under a provision already notified to the person concerned): • the amount of benefit which is payable to the person; and • the rights and options (if any) available on the person's death and the procedures for exercising them.	Any person in receipt of a benefit.	Information plus written statement that further information is available, giving address to which enquiries should be sent.	As of course, before or within one month after the later of the date of the decision to make the alteration and the effective date of the alteration.
Active members, deferred members and pension credit members: All schemes except money purchase schemes • in the case of an active member: – the amounts of the member's and his survivors' benefits which would be payable (ignoring future salary increases) from normal pension age or death if his pensionable service were to terminate either (at the trustees discretion) within one month of the date on which the information is given or on his normal pension age; and *(cont'd)*	Any member.	Information plus written statement that further information is available, giving the address to which enquiries should be sent.	On request (unless within 12 months of information being given following a similar request), as soon as practicable, and in any event within two months of the request.

633

Appendix II

To be disclosed	Disclosure to	Form of disclosure	When
(cont'd) – the amount of any death in service benefits which would be payable if he died within one month of the date on which the information is given, with details of how those benefits are calculated (except simplified deferred contributions schemes). • In the case of a deferred member, the date pensionable service ceased and the amounts of his own and his survivors' benefits payable from normal pension age or death. • In either case the information must include: – date on which member's pensionable service commenced; – the accrual rate or formula for calculating the member's own benefits and any survivors' benefits; – the amount of the member's pensionable remuneration on the relevant date (ie for an active member the date when the information is given or a date within a month thereof and for a deferred member, the date pensionable service ceased); and – details of how any deduction from benefits is calculated. • In the case of a pension credit member, the amounts of his own benefits and of any survivors' benefits payable from normal pension age or death. The information in respect of a pension credit member must include: – the method or formula for calculating the member's own benefits and any survivors' benefits; and – details of how any deduction from benefits is calculated. *(cont'd)*			

Appendix II

To be disclosed	Disclosure to	Form of disclosure	When
(cont'd) **All members: Money purchase schemes.** In the case of a scheme which provides money purchase benefits (excluding stakeholder schemes): • the amount of contributions (before the making of any deductions) credited to the member during the preceding scheme year and, where the scheme is contracted-out, the contributions attributable to: – the minimum payments required to be made in respect of the member by his employer during the preceding year; – any rebate payments made by the DWP; – the age-related payments (if any) made by the DWP; and – the date of birth used in determining the appropriate age-related percentage and name and address of whom to contact should the date of birth be incorrect. • in the case of a simplified defined contribution scheme, the amount or fraction of contributions applied to insure death benefits; *(cont'd)*	Each member who is eligible for money purchase benefits (except excluded persons).	Information plus written statement that further information is available, giving address to which enquiries should be sent.	As of course, within 12 months of the end of each scheme year.

635

Appendix II

To be disclosed	Disclosure to	Form of disclosure	When

(cont'd)
● the value of:
  – the member's protected rights as at a specified date;
  – the member's accrued rights (other than protected rights) at the same or another specified date; and
  – the cash equivalent of the member's rights, if different.
● in the case of a pension credit member:
  – his safeguarded rights under the scheme as at a specified date; and
  – his accrued rights other than his safeguarded rights under the scheme at the same or another specified date; and
  – his cash equivalent if different.
● an illustration of the amount of the pension which would be likely to accrue to a member, or be capable of being secured by him at retirement in respect of his money purchase benefits that may arise under the scheme.			

Hybrid schemes Where a hybrid scheme is contracted-out and under the rules of the scheme an earner's service is contracted-out, employment will cease to qualify him for benefits under one part of the scheme but begin to qualify him for benefits under another part of the scheme. ● the date he begins to qualify for different benefits; and ● the basis on which his rights accrued after that date will be contracted-out. *(cont'd)*	Each member who ceases to qualify under one part of the scheme and begins to qualify for benefits under the other part of the scheme.	Information plus written statement that further information is available, giving address to which enquiries should be sent.	Within two months after the date on which his service begins to qualify him for different benefits.

Appendix II

To be disclosed	Disclosure to	Form of disclosure	When
(cont'd) **Money purchase schemes** Where a scheme is, or has been a money-purchase scheme or provides money purchase benefits, the options available to the member within the scheme rules.	Each member and pension credit member who is eligible for money purchase benefits.	Information plus written statement that further information is available, giving address to which enquiries should be sent.	As of course, at least six months prior to normal pension age or date of retirement (or within seven days if less than six months until retirement).
Money purchase schemes ceasing to contract out Where a scheme ceases to be a contracted-out money purchase scheme:	Each member who has ceased to be contracted-out.	Information plus written statement that further information is available, giving address to which enquiries should be sent.	In respect of the notification that the scheme has ceased to be contracted-out, as soon as practicable but in any event within one month of the scheme ceasing to contract out
notice that, and the date on which, the scheme ceased to be such a scheme; the options available in respect of protected rights; and			In respect of the other information, as soon as practicable and in any event within four months of the scheme ceasing to contract out.

(cont'd)

Appendix II

To be disclosed	Disclosure to	Form of disclosure	When

(cont'd)
• if the scheme is not able to meet its liabilities in full, an account of the amount by which accrued rights safeguarded rights and protected rights have been reduced, and of the action taken by the scheme, or which is open to the member to take, to restore their value.
In the case of a pension credit member:
• the value of the pension credit member's safeguarded rights under the scheme as at a specified date; and
• the value of the pension credit member's accrued rights (other than his safeguarded rights) under the scheme at the same or another specified date; and
• his cash equivalent if different.
In the case of a member other than a pension credit member:
• the amount of contributions (before any deductions) credited to the member during the immediately preceding scheme year including contributions attributable to:
    – the minimum payments required to be made in respect of the member by his employer during the preceding year;
    – any rebate payments made by the DWP;
    – the age-related payments (if any) made by the DWP; and
    – the date of birth used in determining the appropriate age-related percentage and the name of whom to contact and their address should the date of birth be incorrect;
(cont'd)			

Appendix II

To be disclosed	Disclosure to	Form of disclosure	When
(cont'd) in the case of a simplified defined contribution scheme, the amount or fraction of contributions applied to insure death benefits • the value of: – the member's protected rights as at a specified date; – the member's accrued rights (excluding protected rights) as at the same or another specified date; – the cash equivalent of the member's rights, if different.			
Contingent beneficiaries (*all schemes*) Where a member or beneficiary has died: • the rights and options (if any) available to the contingent beneficiary, and the procedures for exercising them; and • the provisions under which any contingent pension may or will be increased, and the extent to which such increases are discretionary or a statement that there are no such provisions.	Any contingent beneficiary who is at least 18 and whose address is known to the trustees. Personal representative of the deceased or any person entitled to act on behalf of the contingent beneficiary.	Information plus written statement that further information is available, giving address to which enquiries should be sent. Information plus written statement that further information is available, giving address to which enquiries should be sent.	As of course, as soon as practicable and in any event within two months of trustees receiving notification of the death. On request (unless within three years of information being given to same person in same capacity), as soon as practicable and in any event within two months of request being made.
Transfers (*all schemes*) Whether the member or prospective member is entitled to acquire transfer credits in exchange for a cash equivalent or other transfer payment provided by another scheme, and if so, a statement of those transfer credits. *(cont'd)*	Any member or prospective member.	Information plus written statement that further information is available, giving address to which enquiries should be sent.	On request (unless within twelve months of information being given following a similar request) within two months of request.

Appendix II

To be disclosed	Disclosure to	Form of disclosure	When
(cont'd) **Winding-up (all schemes)** Where, after 5 April 1997, trustees have commenced winding-up the scheme or a section of a multi-employer scheme which is to be treated as a separate scheme: • notification of the winding-up and the reasons for it; • notification of whether death benefits will continue to be payable; • if the independent trustee requirements apply, notification that at least one of the trustees is required to be an independent person; • what action is being taken to establish the scheme's liabilities and to recover any assets; when it is anticipated final details will be known; and (where the trustees have sufficient information) an indication of the extent to which, the actuarial value of accrued rights are likely to be reduced. *(cont'd)*	All members, all persons entitled to a pension credit and beneficiaries (except excluded persons) (but only active members in relation to the second point).	Information plus written statement that further information is available, giving address to which enquiries should be sent.	As of course, as soon as practicable and in any event within one month of the winding up trigger. In addition, in the case of the final point, at least once in every successive 12 month period until the completion of the winding up.

640

Appendix II

To be disclosed	Disclosure to	Form of disclosure	When
(cont'd) Where, before 6 April 1997, trustees have commenced winding up the scheme or a section of a multi-employer scheme which is to be treated as a separate scheme: • what action is being taken to establish the scheme's liabilities and to recover any assets; • when it is anticipated final details will be known; and • (when the trustees have sufficient information) an indication of the extent to which the actuarial value of accrued rights is likely to be reduced.	All members and beneficiaries (except excluded persons).	Information plus written statement that further information is available giving address to which enquiries should be sent.	At least once in every successive 12 month period beginning with the date of commencement of the winding up and ending with the date of completion of the winding up.
Where trustees are engaged in winding-up the scheme or a section of a multi-employer scheme which is to be treated as a separate scheme: • the amount of benefit which is payable to the person; • if a benefit is payable periodically: – the provisions (if any) under which the amount payable may be altered; – the conditions (if any) subject to which payment will be continued; • (except in the case of money purchase schemes) if the member is not entitled to payment of benefits an estimate of amount of the member's own benefits and of his survivors' benefits which are expected to be payable from normal pension age or death; • notification of: – whether, and if so by how much, the benefits are reduced because of insufficient scheme resources; – who has or will become liable to pay benefits after scheme is wound up.	Every beneficiary and every member who is entitled to payment of benefits (except excluded persons).	Information plus written statement that further information is available, giving address to which enquiries should be sent.	As soon as practicable and in any event within three months the trustees having discharged their liabilities.

(cont'd)

Appendix II

To be disclosed	Disclosure to	Form of disclosure	When
(cont'd) Where a report has been made by the trustees or managers of the scheme to Opra under *section 72A of PA 1995* a copy of the report must contain the following: • name of scheme; • date on which winding up commenced; • scheme registration number; • statement as to the nature of the benefits provided by the scheme; • statement as to whether an independent trustee has been appointed; • name and address of scheme actuary (if relevant); • name and address of any third party administrator; • estimate of when winding up will be completed; • statement as to what steps have been taken in the winding up, what steps remain and when each step is estimated to be completed • a statement as to whether any particular difficulties are hindering the winding up.)	Any member or beneficiary who requests a copy.	Written report.	Within two months of the request.
Stakeholder Pensions Where stakeholder scheme is removed from the register of such schemes: • notification of that fact and of the fact that it is required to commence winding-up under the rules.	Every member (except excluded persons).	Information plus written statement that further information is available giving address to which enquiries should be sent.	Within two weeks of being notified of the removal from the register.

Appendix II

To be disclosed	Disclosure to	Form of disclosure	When
AVAILABILITY AND CONTENT OF ANNUAL REPORT (Regulation 6, Disclosure Regulations) *(all schemes except certain public sector schemes (Reg. 6(2))*			
A document which contains: • the audited accounts and the auditor's statement required under *s 41 of PA 1995* for the scheme year to which the document relates; • the latest actuarial statement given under *s 41 of PA 1995*; • the latest annual certificate obtained in accordance with Minimum Funding Requirement Regulations; • the names of the persons, including the directors of any sole trustee company, who were trustees during the relevant year; • the provisions of the scheme (or articles of association in the case of a sole trustee company) in relation to appointing and removing trustees (or directors of the sole trustee company); • the names of the professional advisers and others who have acted for the trustees during the year, with an indication of any change since the previous year; • the address to which enquiries about the scheme generally or about an individual's entitlement to benefit should be sent; • the number of active, deferred and pensioner members and beneficiaries as at any one date during the scheme year;	• Members and prospective members and their spouses; • Beneficiaries; • Recognised trade unions.	• Personal copy of latest report/information free of charge (on first request) plus written statement that further information is available, giving address to which enquiries should be sent; • Copies of reports/information for previous five years available: – for inspection (free of charge) at a place that is reasonable; or – personal copy (at a reasonable charge) plus written statement that further information is available, giving address to which enquiries should be sent.	To be available within seven months of end of each scheme year which ends after 6th April 1997 and to be provided within two months of request.

(cont'd)

Appendix II

To be disclosed	Disclosure to	Form of disclosure	When

(cont'd)
● except in a money purchase scheme, the percentage increases made during the year to pensions in payment and deferred pensions and a statement of the extent to which they are discretionary (if variable for different individuals, state the maximum, minimum and average);
 	
● (except in the case of insured money purchase scheme)a statement, where applicable, explaining:
  – why any cash equivalents paid during the year were not calculated and verified in accordance with legislative requirements;
  – why cash equivalents paid during the year were less than the amount for which legislation provides and when full values were or will be available; and
  – whether, and if so how, discretionary benefits are included in the calculation of transfer values;
 	
● a statement as to whether the accounts have been prepared and audited in accordance with s 41 of PA 1995 (unless exempt), and if not, the reasons why not, and a statement as to how the situation has been or is likely to be resolved;
 	
● details of who has managed the investments during the year and the extent of any delegation by the trustees;
 	
● confirmation of whether the trustees have produced a statement of investment principles in accordance with s 35 of PA 1995 (unless exempt), advising that a copy is available on request;
 	
(cont'd)			

Appendix II

To be disclosed	Disclosure to	Form of disclosure	When

(cont'd)
• a statement as to the trustees' policy on the custody of the scheme's assets (except in relation to a wholly insured scheme);
• unless exempt from the requirement to produce a statement of investment principles, an investment report containing:
  – a statement by the trustees, or fund manager, providing details of any investments which were not made in accordance with the statement of investment principles, giving the reasons why and explaining what action, if any, has been or will be taken to resolve the position;
  – a review of the investment performance during the year and a period of between three and five years ending with the year, including an assessment of the nature, disposition, marketability, security and valuation of the scheme's assets;
• a copy of any statement made on the resignation or removal of the auditor or actuary;
• where the scheme has employer-related investments a statement:
  – as to a percentage of the scheme's resources so invested;
  – if that percentage exceeds 5 per cent, as to the percentage of the scheme's resources which are not subject to the statutory restrictions; and
  – if the statutory restriction on employer-related investments is exceeded, the steps taken (or to be taken) to secure compliance, and when those steps will be taken.
(cont'd)			

645

Appendix II

To be disclosed	Disclosure to	Form of disclosure	When
(cont'd) **NB** *Reference to reports/information in relation to a scheme year ending before 6 April 1997 are deemed to include references to copies of documents made available under reg 9 of the Occupational Pension Schemes (Disclosure of Information) Regulations 1986.*			
AVAILABILITY OF ACTUARIAL VALUATION, SCHEDULE OF CONTRIBUTIONS, PAYMENT SCHEDULE AND STATEMENT OF INVESTMENT PRINCIPLES (Regulation 7, Disclosure Regulations) *Public service schemes are exempt.*			
Latest actuarial valuation required under: • s 41(1) and (2)(c) of PA 1995; • s 57(1)(a) of PA 1995, if appropriate. Schedule of contributions or payment schedule required under s 58 or s 87 of PA 1995, if appropriate. Latest statement of principles governing decisions about investment required under s 35 of PA 1995.	• Members, prospective members and their spouses; • Beneficiaries; • Recognised trade unions.	• Copy for inspection, free of charge at a place which is reasonable; • Personal copy at reasonable charge. Document must be accompanied by a written statement that further information is available, giving address to which enquiries should be sent.	On request, within two months of the request being made.

Appendix II

To be disclosed	Disclosure to	Form of disclosure	When
LIMITED DISCLOSURE IN RELATION TO UNAPPROVED SCHEMES (Regulation 8, Disclosure Regulations) (*All schemes other than public sector schemes*)			
• What benefits are payable under the scheme and how they are calculated (including how pensionable earnings are defined and the rate at which benefits accrue). • What arrangements are made and in what circumstances for estimates of cash equivalents, statements of entitlement to guaranteed cash equivalents, refunds to contributions and preservation or transfer of accrued rights in relation to early leavers. • Whether information about the scheme has been given to the Registrar of Occupational and Personal Pension Schemes. • What procedures the scheme has for the internal resolution of disputes and the address and job title of the person to be contacted in order to have recourse to these. • A statement that the Occupational Pensions Advisory Service is available at any time to assist members and beneficiaries of the scheme in connection with pension queries and the resolution of disputes and the address at which OPAS may be contacted.	• Members. • Prospective members. • Recognised trade unions.	Written statement that further information is available, giving address to which enquiries should be sent.	As of course to every prospective member and, where not practical, to a person within two months of his becoming a member.
(cont'd)			

647

Appendix II

To be disclosed	Disclosure to	Form of disclosure	When
(cont'd) • A statement that the Pensions Ombudsman may investigate and determine any complaint of fact or law in relation to an occupational pension scheme and the address at which he may be contacted. • A statement that the Regulatory Authority is able to intervene in the running of schemes where trustees, employers or professional advisers have failed in their duties and the address at which it may be contacted. • The address to which enquiries about the scheme generally or about an individual's entitlement to benefit should be sent. • A statement as to which of the benefits are and which are not funded and, where benefits are funded, the manner in which they are secured. • A statement that the provisions of *PA 1995* are not applicable to the scheme (subject to certain exceptions).			
INFORMATION TO BE FURNISHED TO EARLY LEAVERS (Regulation 27A, the Occupational Pension Schemes (Preservation of Benefit) Regulations 1991) *(all schemes)*			
Any information relating to the rights and options available to a member whose pensionable service terminates before he attains normal pension age.	Any member or prospective member.	To be furnished in writing.	As soon as practicable and, in any event, within two months of the request being made (unless within 12 months of information being given following a similar request). *(cont'd)*

648

Appendix II

To be disclosed	Disclosure to	Form of disclosure	When
(cont'd)	Any deferred member.	To be furnished in writing.	As of course as soon as practicable and, in any event, within two months of notification of termination of pensionable service.
Information whether a refund of contributions is, or would be, available in any circumstances together with an estimate of the amount of the refund and an explanation of the method of calculation.	Any person who has paid contributions to the scheme (which have not already been refunded).	To be furnished in writing.	As soon as practicable and, in any event, within two months after request (unless he has already been told that there will be no refund or the request is within 12 months of information being given following a similar request).
TRANSFER OF MEMBER'S ACCRUED RIGHTS WITHOUT CONSENT (Regulation 12(4B), the Occupational Pension Schemes (Preservation of Benefit) Regulations 1991) *(all schemes)*			
Information about the proposed transfer and details of the value of the rights to be transferred including rights in respect of death in service benefits and survivors' benefits.	Those members being transferred.	In writing.	Not less than one month before the proposed transfer is due to take place.
CASH EQUIVALENTS AND TRANSFER VALUES (Regulation 11, the Occupational Pension Schemes (Transfer Values) Regulations 1996) *(all schemes)*			
The 'Schedule 1' Information i.e: Whether a cash equivalent is available or would be available if pensionable service were to terminate and, if so: • an estimate of the amount and date used for basis of calculation; *(cont'd)*	Active members of any scheme. Deferred members of a money purchase scheme.	To be provided by the trustees in writing.	As soon as practicable and, in any event, within three months of the member's request (such request not being one made less than 12 months since the last occasion when the information was provided).

Appendix II

To be disclosed	Disclosure to	Form of disclosure	When
(cont'd) • the accrued rights to which it relates; • whether any part of the estimated part of the cash equivalent is attributable to additional benefits awarded at the discretion of the trustees or which will be awarded if their established custom continues unaltered; • if appropriate, a Regulation 8(2) statement indicating that calculation of the estimated cash equivalent does not take account of discretionary benefits and a statement that the trustees must get the actuary's written report (which must be available to the member) before including such liabilities. • Notification of any reduction of the member's cash equivalent including: the reasons for and the amount of the reduction; an estimate of the date (if any) by which an unreduced cash equivalent will be available; a statement of the member's right to obtain further estimates; a statement explaining that the member has a further three months from the date on which the member was informed of the reduction to make an application to take the cash equivalent as reduced. A copy of the actuary's written report (where the trustees of a scheme have directed that discretionary benefits will not be included in the calculation of cash equivalents) *(cont'd)*	Any active or deferred member of any scheme.	A copy of the written report to be sent to the member.	Within one month of that member's request.

650

Appendix II

To be disclosed	Disclosure to	Form of disclosure	When

(cont'd)
The statement of entitlement to a guaranteed cash equivalent shall be accompanied by:
• 'Schedule 1 Information' in relation to any cash equivalent of or transfer value in relation to the member's money purchase benefits (if any) under the scheme calculated by reference to the guarantee date;
• A statement as to:
  – where the trustees have given a direction indicating that the cash equivalent does not take account of discretionary benefits, indication that the trustees have been obliged to obtain the actuary's written report (of which the member can request a copy) before excluding such benefits from the calculation of the cash equivalent;
  – whether, for what reasons and by what amount the member's cash equivalent has been reduced as well as the paragraph of reg 8 which has been relied upon, together with an estimate of the date by which it will be possible to make available a guaranteed cash equivalent which is not so reduced;
  – the terms and effect of reg 6(3) (no right to make an application for a guaranteed statement of entitlement within 12 months of the last application);
  – an explanation of the member's right to take the guaranteed cash equivalent and the need for that member to submit a written application to do so within three months beginning on the guarantee date;
  – an explanation that in exceptional circumstances the guaranteed cash equivalent may be reduced and that member will be so informed if that is the case.
(cont'd)
	An active or deferred member whose membership has terminated at least one year before normal retirement age.	Statement/Report in writing.	Within a period of ten working days after the 'guarantee date' (which must be within a period of three months beginning with the date of the member's application).

651

Appendix II

To be disclosed	Disclosure to	Form of disclosure	When

(cont'd)
• Notification of any member's reduction or increase in guaranteed cash equivalent under Regulation 9 including:
  – the reasons for and the amount of the reduction/increase;
  – an estimate of the date (if any) by which an unreduced guaranteed cash equivalent will be available;
  – indication of the paragraph of Regulation 9 which has been relied upon;
  – a statement explaining that the member has a further three months from the date on which the member was informed of the reduction / increase to make a written application to take the guaranteed cash equivalent as reduced/increased.
	Relevant member	In writing	Within ten days of reduction/increase

WINDING-UP (Regulation 11, The Occupational Pension Schemes (Winding-Up) Regulations 1996 (all schemes)			
Details of any determination made: • to defer winding up the scheme; • as to the time when the priorities into which the liability in respect of any person falls under s 73(3) of PA 1995 is fixed; or • as to the time when the amounts or descriptions of liabilities of the scheme are to be determined for the purposes of any rule of the scheme setting out the scheme's winding-up priorities.	The members of the scheme; Any other person whose entitlement to payment of a pension or any other benefit under the scheme has arisen.	In writing.	Within one month of the date that the determination is made.

Appendix II

To be disclosed	Disclosure to	Form of disclosure	When
MODIFICATION on winding-up (Section 71A, PA 1995 and Regulation 8 of the Occupational Pension Schemes (Winding up Notices and Reports etc) Regulations 2002)			

Where the trustees or managers make an application to Opra to modify the scheme in accordance with *section 71A of PA 1995*, a notice setting out:
(a) the modification requested;
(b) the effects, if any, which the modification would or might have:
    (i) on benefits under the scheme that are in payment at the time of the application, and
    (ii) on benefits under it which are or may be payable at a later time.
(c) the reason for requesting the modification;
(d) whether any previous application has been made to the court or to Opra for an order to make the modification requested by the application or any similar modification, (only to be included in notice to insolvency practitioner);
(e) whether the modification would reduce the value of the assets, if any, which might otherwise be distributed to that employer on the winding up;
(f) the date of the notice;
(g) a statement that the recipient may make representations to Opra about the modification requested by the application during the period of one month beginning with the date specified in (f).
	Members
	 The insolvency practitioner (if the modification would reduce the value of the assets which might otherwise be distributed to the employer on the winding up).
		In writing	Before the trustees or manager make the application to Opra.

653

Appendix II

To be disclosed	Disclosure to	Form of disclosure	When
DIVORCE (Regulation 4, The Pensions on Divorce etc (Provision of Information) Regulations 2000) *(all schemes)*			

• The full name of the pension arrangement and address to which any order or provision should be sent.
• In the case of an occupational pension scheme whether the scheme is winding up and, if so, the date of commencement of the winding up and the name and address of the trustees who are dealing with the winding up.
• In the case of an occupational pension scheme whether a cash equivalent of the member's rights would be reduced if calculated on the date the trustees received notification that a pension sharing order or provision may be made.
• Whether the person responsible for the pension arrangement is aware of the member's rights being subject to any of the following and, if so, to specify which
  – an order under *s 23 of the Matrimonial Causes Act 1973* (so far as it includes provision made by virtue of *ss 25B or 25C* of that Act)
  – an order under *s 12A(2) or (3) of the Family Law (Scotland) Act 1985* which relates to benefits or future benefits to which the member is entitled under the pension arrangement
  – an order under *Art 25 of the Matrimonial Causes (Northern Ireland) Order 1978* so far as it includes provision made by virtue of *Art 27B or 27C* of that order.
  – A forfeiture order.
  – A bankruptcy order.
 	
(cont'd)
	To the member;
	The Court.
			Within 21 days of the date when the trustees received notification that a Pension Sharing Order or provision may be made or if later a date set by the court.

Appendix II

To be disclosed	Disclosure to	Form of disclosure	When
(cont'd) – An order of sequestration on a member's estate or the making of an appointment on his estate of a judicial factor under *s 41 of the Solicitors (Scotland) Act 1980*. • Whether the member's rights under the pension arrangement include any rights which are not shareable. • If not provided previously, whether the trustees require any charges to be paid and, if so, whether prior to the commencement of the implementation period those are required to be paid in full, or the proportion which is required. • Whether the trustees may levy additional charges and, if so, the scale which is likely to be charged. • Whether the member is a trustee of the pension arrangement. • Whether the trustees may request information about the member's state of health if a pension sharing order or provision were made. • Whether the trustees require information in addition to that specified in *reg 5* of the *Pensions on Divorce etc (Provision of Information) Regulations 2000* in order to implement the pension sharing order or provision.			

Appendix II

To be disclosed	Disclosure to	Form of disclosure	When
Regulation 2: Basic Information about Pensions and Divorce			
• A valuation of pension rights or benefits accrued under the member's pension arrangement not available to the spouse of the member. • A statement that on the member's request or pursuant to a court order a valuation of pension rights or benefits will be provided to the member or the Court. • A statement summarising the way in which the valuation is calculated. • The pension benefits which are included in the valuation. • Whether the trustees offer membership to a person entitled to a pension credit and, if so, the types of benefit available. • Whether the trustees intend to discharge their liability for a pension credit other than by offering membership. • A schedule of charges which will apply. • Any other information relevant to any power relating to matters specified in s 23(1)(a) of the *Welfare Reform and Pensions Act 1999* and which is not specified in Schs 1 or 2 to the *Occupational Pension Schemes (Disclosure of Information) Regulations 1996* or Schs 1 or 2 of the *Personal Pension Scheme (Disclosure of Information) Regulations 1987* (available to the Court only). At the same time as providing the information set out above, the trustees may supply informaiton specified in reg 4 of the *Pensions on Divorce etc Regulations 2000*	• Member. • Member's spouse. • Court.		On request within three months beginning with the date the trustees receive the request or order for the provision of information; or within six weeks if the member has notified the trustees on the date of the request or order that the information is needed in connection with proceedings commenced under any of the provisions referred to in s 23(1)(a) of the *Welfare Reform and Pensions Act 1999*; or within such shorter period as the Court may specify; or if the request does not include a request for a valuation or if the member's spouse requests the information under reg 2(3) of *The Pensions on Divorce etc Regulations 2000*, within one month of the date of receipt of the request or Court order.

Appendix II

To be disclosed	Disclosure to	Form of disclosure	When
Regulation 6, Provision of Information after the death of the person entitled to the pension credit			
Where the person entitled to the pension credit dies before the trustees have discharged their liability, the trustees must notify relevant persons: – how the trustees intend to discharge their liability; – whether the trustees intend to recover charges and, if so, a schedule of those charges; – a list of any further information required in order to discharge the order.	Any person whom the trustees consider should be notified.	In writing.	Within 21 days of receipt of the notification of death.
Regulation 7, Provision of Information after receiving a pension sharing order			
On receipt of a pension sharing order or a provision: – a notice of charges; – a list of information relating to the transferor or the transferee or (where reg 6 (1) of the *Pensions on Divorce etc Regulations 2000* applies); – a person other than the person entitled to the pension credit, which has been requested already, which the trustees need or which remains outstanding; – a notice of implementation; or – a statement of why the trustees are unable to implement the pension sharing order or agreement.	The transferor or transferee or where *reg 6(1)* of the *Pensions on Divorce etc Regulations 2000* applies to the person other than the person entitled to the pension credit (referred to in *reg 6* of the *Implementation and Discharge of Liability Regulations*).	In writing.	Within 21 days of receipt of the pension sharing order or provision or, in the case of a notice of implementation, the later of the days specified in *section 34(1)(a)* and *(b)* of the *Welfare Reform and Pensions Act 1999*.

Appendix II

To be disclosed	Disclosure to	Form of disclosure	When
Regulation 8, Provision of Information after Implementation of an Order			
Notice of discharge of liability including: *(where the transferor's pension is not in payment)* – the value of the transferor's accrued rights on a cash equivalent basis; – the value of the pension debit; – the amount deducted by way of charges; – the value of the transferor's rights after the deductions of the pension debit and charges; – the transfer day; **OR** *(where the transferors pension is in payment)* – the value of the transferor's benefits on a cash equivalent basis; – the value of the pension debit; – the amount of the pension which was in payment before the pension credit liability was discharged; – the amount of pension payable following the deduction of the pension debit; – the transfer day; – the amount of any unpaid charges; – how those charges will be recovered; **OR** (in the case of a transferee whose pension is not in payment and who will become a member) – the value of the pension credit: – the amount deducted by way of charges; – the value of the pension credit after deduction of charges; *(cont'd)*	Transferor or transferee or the person entitled to the pension credit by virtue of reg 6 of the *Implementation and Discharge of Liability Regulations*.		Within 21 days of the date of discharge of the pension credit.

658

Appendix II

To be disclosed	Disclosure to	Form of disclosure	When
(cont'd) – the transfer day; – any periodical charges to be made including when and how those charges will be recovered; – information concerning membership of the pension arrangement which is relevant to the transferee; **OR** (in the case of the transferee who is transferring his pension credit rights out of the pension arrangement from which those rights were derived): – the value of the pension credit; – the amount of any charges deducted; – the value of the pension credit after the deduction; – the transfer day; – details of the pension arrangement including its name, address, reference number, telephone number and where available the business facsimile number and electronic mail address to which the pension credit has been transferred: **OR** (in the case of a transferee who has reached normal benefit age on the transfer day and whose pension credit liability has been discharged) – the amount of pension credit benefit to be paid to the transferee; – the date when the pension credit benefit is to be paid to the transferee; – the transfer date; *(cont'd)*			

Appendix II

To be disclosed	Disclosure to	Form of disclosure	When
(cont'd) – details of any unpaid charges and how those charges will be recovered; **OR** (in the case of a person entitled to the pension credit by virtue of reg 16 of the Implementation and Discharge of Liability Regulations): – the value of the pension credit rights; – any amount deducted by way of charges; – the value of the pension credit after deduction of charges; – the transfer day; – details of any unpaid charges, including how and when those charges will be recovered.			
PROVISION OF INFORMATION AFTER RECEIPT OF AN EAR MARKING ORDER *(all schemes)*			
● If a member's pension is not in payment, a list of circumstances in respect of any changes which the member or spouse must notify to the trustees. ● (except in Scotland) if the order is made in respect of a member whose pension is in payment the notice will include: – the value of the pension rights or benefit of the member; – the amount of the member's pension after implementation of the order. – the first date when a pension pursuant to the order is to be made. – a list of the circumstances which the member and spouse must notify to the trustees. *(cont'd)*	● Member. ● Spouse.	In writing.	Within 21 days of receipt of the order.

Appendix II

To be disclosed	Disclosure to	Form of disclosure	When
(cont'd) – (to member only) the amount of the member's pension currently in payment and the amount of the member's pension after the order has been implemented. (*NB These two items are also listed in the items to be notified to member and spouse*). ● In any event: – the amount of any charges not yet paid by the member or spouse in respect of the provision of information and how those charges will be recovered including the date when payment is required in whole or in part, the sums payable by the member and spouse respectively and whether the sum will be deducted from payments of pension to the member or from payments for the spouse.			
Regulation 3, Information about Pensions and Divorce: valuation of pension benefits			
Information set out in reg 11 and Sch 1 to the Occupational Pension Schemes (Transfer Values) Regulations 1996.	● Any member.	In writing.	Within ten working days after the 'valuation date' elected by the trustees and upon the request of the member as Petitioner or Respondent in proceedings for divorce, nullity of marriage or judicial separation, or upon request by the court.

Index

Absence from work 1.21
Accounts
  audited 2.8
  contents 2.8
  form 2.8
  requirement to obtain audited 2.8
  statement of 2.8
Accrued rights
  employer's duties 7.12
  statutory protection 12.18–31
  trustees' duties 7.12
Actuarial valuations
  see also Actuary
  discontinuance basis 11.11
  final salary schemes 11.8
  money purchase schemes 11.9
  ongoing
    basic requirements 11.10
    discontinuance basis 11.11
    past service reserve basis 11.12
  past service reserve basis 11.12
  reference scheme valuation 4.7
  types 11.7
    final salary schemes 11.8
    money purchase schemes 11.9
Actuary
  appointment 2.4
  approval 2.4
  divorce and valuation of benefits 8.4
  experience 2.4
  penalties 2.5
  qualifications 2.4
  reference scheme valuation 4.7
  requirements 2.4
  role 2.3
  trustees
    appointment 2.4
    ineligibility 2.7
    resignation 2.4
  whistleblower, as 2.5
Additional voluntary contributions
  deferring benefits 1.32
  income drawdown 1.32
  Pensions Bill 2004, proposals 12.92

Address
  Inland Revenue, Savings, Pensions, Share Schemes (IR SPSS) 2.10
  National Insurance Services to Pensions Industry 2.24
  National Association of Pension Funds 2.33
  Pensions Advisory Service (OPAS) 2.25
  Pensions Compensation Board (PCB) 2.22
  Pensions Management Institute (PMI) 2.32
  Pensions Ombudsman 2.28
  Registrar of Occupational and Personal Pension Schemes 2.12
Administration 18.8
Administration expenses
  taxation of exempt approved occupational pension schemes 5.39
Adoption leave 9.34
ADR *see* Alternative dispute resolution
Advertisements
  investment 10.27
Age
  see also Retirement ages
  discrimination 7.32, 9.16, 9.29
  equalisation 1.6
  hazardous occupations, retirement age 5.5
  membership of occupational schemes 1.24
  sportsmen, retirement age 5.5
  State pensions 1.6
Agency workers 9.33
Agents
  fund manager's liability for breach of trust by 10.45
  selection and supervision 10.30
Alternative dispute resolution (ADR)
  basic principles 17.36

Index

Alternative dispute resolution (ADR) – *contd*
practical considerations 17.39
  directions applications 17.39
  trustees' position 17.39
types
  adjudication 17.37
  arbitration 17.37
  conciliation 17.37
  expert determination 17.37
  mediation 17.37, 17.38

Amendment of scheme rules
amendment 12.17
basic meaning 12.2, 12.8
closing scheme to future entrants 12.29
conversion to money purchase 12.31
court order 12.9
different benefits for future entrants 12.30
entitlements and accrued rights, statutory protection
  accrued rights defined 12.20
  basic provisions 12.18
  certification requirements 12.21
  consent requirements 12.22, 12.24, 12.25
  entitlement 12.20
  member defined 12.19
  practical issues 12.23
future entrants
  closing scheme to 12.29
  different benefits for 12.30
future service benefits 12.27, 12.28
future service benefits, reduction 12.27, 12.28
methods 12.8, 12.25
modification orders 12.10
money purchase, conversion to 12.31
past service benefits, reduction 12.26
power in scheme rules
  effect of winding-up 12.14
  exercise 12.13
  need 12.12
  restrictions 12.16
  retrospective amendments 12.15
trustees' statutory powers 12.11

Annuities
clustering 15.16
death benefits 15.14
deferred annuities in small self-administered schemes *see under* Small self-administered schemes
lump sum 15.13
purchase 12.61, 12.69

Anti-franking
GMPs and 4.64

Appropriate personal pension schemes (APPS)
appropriate scheme certificate 15.40
forms of 15.40
minimum contributions 15.41
protected rights *see* Protected rights
providers 15.40
SERPS, contracting-out 15.40
supervision by NICO 15.40

Associated persons
definition 3.6
independent trustees 3.6
trustees 2.7, 3.6

Audit and Pension Scheme Service 2.10

Audited accounts
requirement to obtain 2.8

Auditors
appointments 2.8
associated persons 2.8
connected persons 2.8
requirement to appoint 2.8
requirements 2.8
role 2.8
trustees and 2.8
whistleblower, as 2.8

Badges of trade *see under* Trading

Bankruptcy
bankruptcy restriction orders 1.56
conduct 1.56
contributions, excessive 1.56
discharge 1.56
Enterprise Act 2002 1.56
estate 1.51
excessive contributions 1.56
extension of period of 1.56

Index

Bankruptcy – *contd*
forfeiture clause 1.51
income payments agreements 1.56
Income Payments Order 1.53, 1.56
official receiver 1.56
pensions in payment 1.53
protective trusts 1.51
trustee in bankruptcy 1.53, 1.54, 1.56
trustees and 3.2
unapproved schemes 1.54
vesting of estate 1.54
Welfare Reform and Pensions Act, effect 1.52, 1.55

Beddoes orders 17.33, 17.34

Benefits *see also* Death benefits
basic issues 9.9
charge 1.49
equal treatment
  actuarial factors 9.13
  additional voluntary contributions 9.14
  bridging pensions 9.12
  derived rights 9.10
  transfer 9.11
final salary schemes *see under* Final salary schemes
Inland Revenue requirements 1.32
lien 1.49
money purchase schemes *see under* Money purchase schemes
personal pension schemes *see under* Personal pension schemes
rules detailing 1.18
set-off 1.49
taxation
  exempt approved occupational pension schemes *see* Taxation of exempt approved occupational pension schemes
  funded unapproved schemes 14.3, 14.4
  personal pension schemes 15.31
  unfunded unapproved schemes 14.3, 14.4

Borrowing
small self-administered schemes 13.13

Bought-out benefits 6.28

Bribes
fund manager's duty not to accept 10.42

Bulk transfers
after commencement of winding-up 12.48, 12.85
background 12.32
basic meaning 12.3
before commencement of winding-up
  amount to be transferred 12.50
  background 12.48
  power to make 12.49
benefits protection 12.35
comparison of balance of powers 12.37
contracted-out schemes 12.41
examples 12.3
funding disparity 12.36
indemnity 12.47
Inland Revenue approval 12.40
long term future of schemes 12.38
members' consents 12.33
overview 12.90
past service benefits 12.46
power to make
  after commencement of winding-up, before 6 April 1997 12.86
  after commencement of winding-up, after 5 April 1997 12.86
  before commencement of winding-up 12.49
receiving scheme, amendments 12.46
transfer agreement 12.42
  indemnity 12.47
  past service benefits 12.46
  receiving scheme, amendments 12.46
  transfer amounts 12.44
  transferring scheme, amendments 12.43

Index

Bulk transfers – *contd*
  transfer amount 12.44
  after commencement of
    winding-up, after
    6 April 1997 12.89
  after commencement of
    winding-up, before
    6 April 1997 12.88
  trustees, issues for 12.34
  benefits protection 12.35
  comparison of balance of
    powers 12.37
  funding disparity 12.36
  long term future of
    schemes 12.38
  winding-up, other ways of
    securing benefits 12.39
Business purchase 7.22
Business reorganisation *see also* Transfers of undertakings
  Acquired Rights Directive 7.22
  business purchase 7.22
  purchase of a company with
    its own name 7.21
  purchase of subsidiary
    participating in parent's
    scheme 7.23

Cadbury Committee 10.46
Capital gains tax
  changes to regime 14.18
  FURBS and 14.18
  tapering relief 14.18
Cash equivalent
  acquisition of right to 6.44
  calculation
    final salary benefits, basic
      transfer value 6.48
    money purchase benefits,
      basic transfer value 6.49
  customary discretionary
    benefits taken into
    account 6.50
  disclosure requirements 6.60
  exercising right
    benefits to be provided by
      receiving arrangement 6.54
    making relevant application 6.52
    splitting a cash equivalent 6.53

Cash equivalent – *contd*
  guaranteed statement of
    entitlement 6.45
  hybrid schemes 6.61
  losing the right to 6.47
  partial cash equivalents 6.46
  reduction of 6.51
  summary of procedure 6.63
  transitional arrangements 6.62
  trustee's duties after exercise
    of right
    compliance with member's
      request 6.55
    consequences of delay 6.58
    discharges of trustees 6.59
    extensions of time limits 6.57
    variations of time limits 6.57
Cash equivalent transfer value basis (CETV) 8.4
Charge
  benefits 1.49
Civil penalties Appendix I
Closed schemes
  member-nominated
    trustees/directors 3.25
COEG *see* National Insurance Services to Pensions Industry
COMBS *see* Contracted-out mixed benefit schemes (COMBS)
  commencement after 5 April
    1997 Winding-up
    scheme 12.74
Commercial transactions
  assets *see* share/asset sale
    below
  basic issues 16.1, 16.72
  due diligence 16.6
  employer's debt *see*
    Employer's debt
  final salary schemes 16.1
  funding 16.4
  indemnities 16.5
  money purchase schemes 16.69
  public sector transfers 16.68
  purchaser takes over whole
    scheme
    change of trustees 16.29
    due diligence 16.23
    funding 16.26–28

Index

Commercial transactions – *contd*
  purchaser takes over whole scheme – *contd*
    indemnities   16.25
    overfunded scheme   16.28
    protection of purchaser   16.22–25
    underfunded scheme   16.27
    warranties   16.24
  sale agreement
    adjustment of share price   16.10
    consistency with scheme rules   16.11
    documents   16.7–13
    indemnities   16.10
    parties   16.7
    pensions schedule   16.9
    warranties   16.8
  share/asset sale
    actuary's letter   16.13, 16.14–17
    deed of substitution   16.17
    disclosure letter   16.12
    distinction between shares and assets   16.14–17
    employer's debt   16.16
    employment aspects   16.15
    sale agreement *see* sale agreement above
  small self-administered schemes   16.70
  transfer payments *see* Transfer payments
  types of scheme involved   16.2
  unapproved schemes   16.71
  warranties   16.5, 16.8, 16.24

Commercial transactions member-nominated trustees   16.67

Commission
  trust busting   6.56

Commutation of pension
  conditions for   4.14
  occupational pension schemes   1.47
  trivial   4.14

Company
  as trustee   2.2

Compensation
  lump sum   7.26
  part-time workers   7.26
  taxation   7.26

Conflict of interest
  fund managers   10.41

Connected persons
  definition   3.6
  independent trustees   3.6
  trustees   2.7, 3.6

Constructive trustees   3.9

Consultation
  member nominated trustees/directors   3.31

Contracted-out mixed benefit schemes (COMBS)
  cessation   4.33
  election   4.32
  governing legislation   4.31
  transitional provisions   4.34

Contracted-out money purchase scheme (COMPS)   4.3
  benefits payable on death   4.26, 4.27
  minimum payments   4.22
  suspension and forfeiture   4.28

Contracting-out
  basic aims   4.1
  divorce rights   4.67
  final salary schemes *see under* Final salary schemes
  history   4.2
  legislative changes, proposed   4.74
  minimum payments   4.20, 4.21
  money purchase schemes *see under* Money purchase schemes
  National Insurance and   4.1
  public sector   16.68
  rights on divorce   4.67
  SERPS   4.3, 4.68
  simplification   1.3, 4.66
  stake-holder schemes   4.68
  supervision of formerly contracted-out schemes   4.65
  transfers between schemes
    basic aims   4.35
    contracted-out final salary to contracted-in final salary   4.36
    contracted-out final salary to contracted-out final salary   4.37

Index

Contracting-out – *contd*
   transfers between schemes – *contd*
     contracted-out final salary
       to contracted-out
         money purchase   4.38
     contracted-out final salary
       to contracted-out
         personal pension   4.38
     contracted-out money
       purchase to another
       contracted-out money
       purchase   4.40
     contracted-out money
       purchase to another
       contracted-out
         personal pension   4.40
     contracted-out money
       purchase to
       contracted-in money
       purchase   4.39
     contracted-out money
       purchase to
       contracted-in personal
       pension   4.39
     contracted-out money
       purchase to
       contracted-out final
       salary   4.41
     summary   4.42
   triennial re-certification   4.17

Contracting-out certificate
   COEG and   4.4
   compliance   4.4
   election for issue, variation or
      surrender   4.4, 4.43
     compliance   4.4, 4.43
     issue   4.4
     making election   4.47–49
     notice of explanation   4.46
     notice of intention   4.44, 4.45
     procedures   4.4
     requirement   4.4
     responsibility   4.4
     supporting documents   4.49
     surrender   4.51
     timing of election   4.48
   employer
     contracting-out number
       (ECON)   4.4
     ECON   4.4
   final salary schemes and   4.4

Contracting-out certificate – *contd*
   holding company certificates   4.52
   issue   4.4
   National Insurance Services
     to Pensions Industry and   4.4
   NICO and   4.4
   periodic return system   4.53
   requirement   4.4
   responsibility   4.4
   surrender   4.51
   variation
     election *see* election for
       issue, variation or
       surrender
     major variations   4.50
     minor variations   4.50
     notice of explanation   4.46
     notice of intention   4.44, 4.45
     procedures   4.4

Contribution record
   National Insurance   1.7

Contributions to occupational pension schemes *see also*
   Additional voluntary
     contributions
   bankruptcy   1.56
   employer's contributions
     basic contributions   1.25
     final salary schemes   1.26
     Inland Revenue
       requirements   1.28
     money purchase schemes   1.27
   excessive benefits   1.32
   excessive contributions   1.56
   final salary schemes
     employer's   1.26
     notice of failure to pay   1.26
     offences   1.26
     records   1.26
     schedule of payments   1.26
     whistle-blowing offences   1.26
   free standing additional
     voluntary contributions   1.31
   Inland Revenue
     requirements 1.27   1.32
   late payments, report to Opra   1.26, 2.2
   life assurance   15.29
   members' contributions   1.29
     excessive benefits   1.32

Index

Contributions to occupational pension schemes – *contd*
members' contributions – *contd*
  free standing additional voluntary contributions   1.31
  Inland Revenue restrictions   1.32
  ordinary contributions   1.30
  refunds   5.36
  tax advantages   5.28
  voluntary contributions   1.31
money purchase schemes
  basic contributions   1.27
  notice of failure to pay   1.27
  offences   1.27
  schedule of payments   1.27
  whistle-blowing offences   1.27
notice of failure to pay
  final salary schemes   1.26
  money purchase schemes   1.27
offences
  final salary schemes   1.26
  money purchase schemes   1.27
ordinary contributions   1.30
part-time employers   5.28, 5.30, 7.26, 9.5
records, final salary schemes   1.26
refunds   5.36
schedule of payments
  final salary schemes   1.26
  money purchase schemes   1.27
tax advantages   5.28
voluntary contributions   1.31
whistle-blowing offences   1.26, 1.27

Corporate trustees   3.3, 3.4

Costs   17.12, 17.31, 17.32
basic principles   17.29, 17.30
Beddoe orders   17.33
beneficiaries' costs   17.34
indemnity in trust deed   17.30
Pensions Ombudsman   17.12
power in trust deed   17.30
prospective costs orders   17.35
shared costs orders   11.31
trustees'   17.31, 17.33

Creditors
arrangement   3.2
trustees   3.2

Credits *see* Pension credits

Criminal penalties   Appendix I
non-payment of contributions to money purchase schemes   1.27
stakeholder pensions   2.15
whistle-blowing offences   1.26, 1.27

Custodianship
agreements   10.38
appointment   10.38
fund managers   10.38
global custody agreements   10.38
liability   10.38
sub-custodians   10.38

Customs and Excise

Data protection legislation
compliance   3.54–56
data processors   3.59
manual data   3.55
registration of pension fund trustees   3.57
transitional relief   3.56

Death benefits
April 2006 regime   5.50
equal treatment   9.6
final salary schemes   1.39, 1.40
funded unapproved schemes   14.22
lump sum   1.39, 1.43, 15.13
maternity   9.39
money purchase schemes   1.42
personal pension schemes
  annuities   15.14
  lump sum   1.39, 1.43, 15.13
  spouse's/dependant's pension   1.40, 1.43
statement of wishes   1.39
taxation
  death in service after normal retirement date   5.23
  dependants' benefits   5.21
  early leaver   5.22
  lump sum payable on death in service before normal retirement date   5.20
  spouse's benefits   5.21
  termination of employment   7.20
unfunded unapproved schemes
  insurance   14.27–32
  taxation   14.26

Deed of substitution   16.17

Index

Deferred pay
  pensions as   7.12
Deficits
  insolvency, on   8.13
  winding-up scheme   12.65, 12.73
Defined benefit schemes *see under* Final salary schemes
Defined contribution schemes *see under* Money purchase schemes
Delegation
  fund managers   10.40, 10.41
  investment   10.30, 10.47
  trustees   3.19, 10.47
Department of Work and Pensions   2.35
  Simplicity, Security and Choice: Working and Saving for Retirement   1.3
Dependant
  death benefits   1.40, 1.43
  taxation   5.21
  final salary schemes   1.40
  money purchase schemes   1.43
  surrender of benefits in favour of   1.48
Detriment
  right not to suffer   7.35
Directors
  emoluments   5.4
  member nominated *see* Member-nominated trustees/directors
Disability discrimination
  adoption absence   7.29
  basic definition   1.23
  bringing a claim   7.28
  compliance with legislation   7.28
  employment terms   7.28
  European Community law   7.28
  justification defence   1.23, 7.28
  less favourable treatment   1.23, 7.28
  maternity absence   7.29
  membership of occupational pension schemes and   1.23
  number of employees   7.28
  parental absence   7.29
  paternity absence   7.29
Disclosure of information *see* Information

Disclosure letter
  in commercial transactions   16.12
Discretionary benefits
  preservation   6.22
Discrimination
  see also Disability discrimination; Equal treatment; Sex discrimination
  age   7.32, 9.16, 9.29
  basic equality   7.25
  belief   7.31
  European Community law   7.28, 7.30, 9.16, 9.29
  fixed-term (temporary) workers   1.24, 7.27
  marital status   7.30
  part-time workers   7.26
  religious   7.31
  same sex partners   7.30
  transsexuals   7.25, 7.33
Dismissal *see also* Employment protection; Termination of contracted-out employment; Termination of employment
Disposal of assets
  taxation of exempt approved occupational pension schemes   5.31
Dispute resolution
  see also Alternative dispute resolution (ADR); Litigation
  background   17.1
  court proceedings   17.11
    application   17.12
    civil court   17.18
    directions   17.13
    pre action protocols   17.17
    procedure, outline of   17.16
    rectification of error   17.15
  employment tribunals   17.6
  Financial Ombudsman Service (FOS)   17.4
  Financial Services Authority (FSA)   17.4
  human rights and   17.10
  internal dispute resolution procedure (IDRP)   17.2

Dispute resolution – *contd*
Occupational Pensions
  Regulatory Authority
  (OPRA) 17.5
Pensions Advisory Service
  (OPAS) 17.3
Pensions Ombudsman (PO) 17.8–9
time limits 17.4

Dividends
tax credits, abolition 11.19
taxation of exempt approved
  occupational pension
  schemes 5.27

**Divorce, impact on pension
  rights** *see also* Pension
  sharing
actuaries' role 8.4
basic issues 8.1
cash equivalent transfer value
  basis (CETV) 8.4, 8.23
charges 8.25
charges, recommended scale 8.26
charging for earmarking
  orders 8.7
clean break 8.2
contracting-out rights 4.67
court orders, ambit 8.6
credit benefits 8.18
  charges 8.25, 8.26
  charges, recommended
    scale 8.26
  disclosure of information 8.24
  indexation 8.19
  information disclosure 8.24
  MNT legislation and 8.20
  safeguarded rights 8.27
  section 67 protection 8.21
  valuation 8.23
  winding-up treatment 8.22
disclosure and earmarking
  orders 8.8
disclosure of information 8.24
division of assets 8.2
earmarking orders 8.3
  charging for 8.7
  disclosure and 8.8
  pension sharing and 8.30
  taxation and 8.31
  transfers of 8.5
exempt approved schemes 8.1
external transfer option 8.14

Divorce, impact on pension rights –
  contd
family law court jurisdiction 8.1
Family Proceedings Rules 8.28
funded schemes and 8.14
future 8.32
information disclosure 8.24
inheritance tax liability 8.3
internal transfer option 8.14
jurisdiction of courts 8.1
Law Commission report 8.1
orders available 8.3
Pension Law Review
  Committee report 8.1
pension sharing *see* sharing of
  pension below
powers of court 8.3
pre-1995 law 8.1, 8.2
property, treatment of 8.2
safeguarded rights 8.27
scheme documentation,
  post-10 May 2000 8.29
shareable rights 8.9
statutory provisions 8.9, 8.14
taxation and 8.31
transfer options, pros and
  cons 8.17
statutory provisions 8.3, 8.9, 8.14
taxation 8.31
transfers of earmarked
  benefits 8.5
types of order 8.3
valuation of benefits 8.4, 8.23

Documentation
approval 1.18
definitive 1.18
disclosure 3.22
employee share ownership
  plans 5.3

Due diligence
commercial transactions 16.6, 16.23
transfer payments 16.50, 16.61

Early leavers
basic treatment 6.1
benefits payable, final salary
  schemes 1.36
death benefits 5.22
ill-health and 9.24
incapacity 5.16

Index

Early leavers – *contd*
    legislation, relationship to
        scheme rules   6.8
    money purchase schemes and   1.43
    occupational pension schemes   1.10
    other than on grounds of
        incapacity   5.17
    preservation legislation,
        enforcement   6.9
    schemes affected   6.7
    taxation of exempt approved
        occupational pension
        schemes   5.15
    transfer of undertakings   16.15
Early retirement *see* **Early leavers**
Earmarking orders *see under* **Divorce, impact on pension rights**
Earnings-related pension component   1.9, 1.11
EC law *see* **European Community law**
Employee
    definition by Inland Revenue   1.21
    part-time *see* **Part-time employees**
    rights *see* **Employee's rights**
    stable relationships   7.26
    trustee as   2.2
Employee share schemes   5.3–5.4
Employee's rights
    contract of employment   7.2
    pension scheme
        documentation   7.3
    exclusion in deed and rules   7.19
    pension scheme
        documentation   7.2
    redundancy   7.15
    unfair dismissal   7.16
    wrongful dismissal   7.17
Employers
    definition   12.82
    lien   7.24
    National Insurance Services
        to Pensions Industry and   2.24
    as trustees   2.2
Employer's debt
    basic legislation   12.78, 16.62
    commercial transactions   16.16, 16.62–65

Employer's debt – *contd*
    compromise   12.84
    deficiency, parties position   16.66
    deficiency payments
        amount of debt   16.63
        basic circumstances   16.62
        trustees' position   16.65
    employer defined   12.82
    impact   12.84
    minimum funding
        requirement   12.84
    Pensions Bill 2004   16.64
    recoverability of   12.84
    relevant insolvency events   12.80
    schemes affected   12.79
    valuation of assets and
        liabilities   12.83
    when debt arises   12.81
Employer's duties
    accrued rights   7.12
    basic obligations   7.4
    death in service benefits   7.20
    equal treatment ensurement   9.19
    fiduciary duties   7.5
    good faith   7.6, 7.7, 7.10
        contracting out of duty   7.8
        to whom duty owed   7.9
    Icarus   7.5
    Imperial case   7.6, 7.7
        contracting out of duty   7.8
        limits to duty of care   7.7
        post *Imperial*   7.7
        to whom duty owed   7.8
    Mettoy   7.5
    reconstruction and   12.6
    reduction in benefits in
        ongoing scheme   7.10, 7.11
    termination of benefits   7.10, 7.11
Employment protection
    Acquired Rights Directive   7.22
    basic pension issues and   7.1, 7.36
    business reorganisation *see* **Business reorganisation**
    contract of employment
        eligibility to join pension
        scheme   7.2
        rights   7.1, 7.2
        senior executives   7.2
        wording of   7.2
        written statement of terms
        and conditions   7.2

Index

Employment protection – *contd*	
detriment, right not to suffer	7.35
employee, financial circumstances	7.7
exclusion in deed and rules	7.19
express pension promise	7.18
Group Personal Pension (GPP)	7.18
lien	7.24
no requirement to run a pension scheme	7.1
redundancy	7.15
time off	
for performance of duties	7.34
for training	7.34
traditional approach	7.1
transfer of undertakings	7.22
trustees	
acting in best interests of beneficiaries	2.2, 7.13
appointment	3.11
basic duties	7.13
basic rights	3.10
disclosure of options	7.14
employee leaving service	7.14
liaison with employer	7.14
removal	3.11
retirement	3.11
unfair dismissal	7.16, 7.35
burden of proof	7.16
compensation	7.16
death in service benefits	7.20
definition	7.16
pension rights and	7.16
tribunals guidance	7.16
wrongful dismissal	7.17
compensation	7.17
damages	7.17
death in service benefits	7.20
Employment tribunals	
guidance	7.16
Enterprise Act 2002	1.56
Entry onto premises	
Occupational Pensions Regulatory Authority (Opra) and	2.17
Equal treatment	
see also Maternity	
access	
basic principles	9.2

Equal treatment – *contd*	
access – *contd*	
part-time employees *see* part-time employees *below*	
actuarial issues	9.27
basic equality	1.22, 7.25, 9.1
benefits	
actuarial factors	9.13
additional voluntary contributions	9.14
basic requirements	9.9
bridging pensions	9.12
death in service	9.6
derived rights	9.10
money purchase benefits	9.15
retirement ages *see* retirement ages *below*	
transfers	9.11
case law summary	9.40
contracted-out schemes	9.29
death in service benefits	9.6
development of law	9.1
EC law effect	9.1
eligibility	
basic principles	9.2
part-time employees *see* part-time employees *below*	
employers duty to ensure	9.19
employment law considerations	9.22
equal treatment	9.1, 9.16
fixed-term workers	9.5, 9.8
guaranteed minimum pensions (GMPs)	9.29
ill-health early retirement	9.24
Inland Revenue requirements	9.28
legislation summary	9.40
life expectancy and	9.1
lower earnings limit	9.6
new employees	9.23
part-time employees	
claims	9.5
exclusion from membership	9.3, 9.4
membership conditions	9.6
Part-time Workers Regulations	9.7
Pensions Bill 2004	9.1
reference scheme test	9.29

Index

Equal treatment – *contd*
  retirement ages
    contractual retirement age   9.14
    state retirement age   9.16
    under pension scheme   9.17
  same sex partners   7.30, 9.30
  scheme amendments   9.21
  sex equality   7.25
  single sex schemes   9.25
  statutory provisions   9.1
  summary of legislation and case law   9.40
  transfers   9.26
  transsexuals   7.25, 733
  trustees' role   9.19

European Community law
  age discrimination   9.16, 9.29
  direct effect   9.1
  disability discrimination   7.28
  discrimination   7.28, 7.30–7.32, 9.16, 9.29
  equal treatment   9.1, 9.16
  fixed-term employees   7.27
  part-time employees   7.26, 9.7
  redundancy   9.11, 16.15
  retirement age   9.16
  same sex partners   7.30–7.32
  temporary workers   9.33
  transfer of undertakings   7.22, 9.8

Excessive contributions   1.32
  bankruptcy   1.55

Exclusion clauses
  breach of trust   3.50
  trust deeds   3.50
  trustees   3.50

Expenses
  trustees   3.13

Fees
  stakeholder pensions, registration of   2.15
  trustees   3.13

Fiduciary duties
  employers' duties   7.5
  fund manager's
    basic duty   10.39
    bribes, not to accept   10.42
    conflict of interest   10.41
    not to delegate   10.40
    taking advantage of position   10.43

Fiduciary duties – *contd*
  fund manager's – *contd*
    ultra vires   10.44

Final salary schemes
  actuarial valuations   11.8
  benefits   1.14
    early retirement   1.36
    incapacity   1.36
    late retirement   1.37
    leaving service other than on retirement   1.41
    lump sum death benefits   1.39
    normal retirement age   1.35
    spouse's/dependant's pension   1.40
    tax free lump sum on retirement   1.39
    voluntary and involuntary retirement, distinction   1.36
  contracting-out   4.1
    post-6 April 1997 service   4.5
    pre-6 April 1997 service   4.5
    qualitative test   4.2
    quantitative test   4.2
  contributions to occupational pension schemes
    employer's   1.26
    notice of failure to pay   1.26
    offences   1.26
    records   1.26
    schedule of payments   1.26
    whistle-blowing offences   1.26
  hybrid schemes   1.16
  occupational pension scheme, types of benefit   1.13–1.16
  offences   1.26
  qualitative test   4.2
  quantitative test   4.2

Finance Bill 2004   1.3, 1.34, 13.1, 14.38

Financial futures, dealings in
  taxation of exempt approved occupational pension schemes   5.31

Financial Services Authority
  pensions and divorce   8.17
  objectives   10.25

Financial Services Ombudsman
  time limits   17.4

Index

Fixed-term workers
  comparators 9.7, 9.8
  continuity of employment 9.8
  discrimination 1.24, 7.27
  equal treatment 9.5, 9.8
  European Community law 7.27
  less favourable treatment 9.8
  occupational pensions 7.27
  pro rata benefits 1.24
  remuneration 7.27
Forfeiture of benefits 1.50, 1.51
Free standing additional voluntary contributions (FSAVC) 1.31, 1.32, 9.14
  contracting-out 4.3
Frozen schemes
  modifications 11.30
Fund income
  see also Funding
  certificates of deposit 5.31
  financial futures 5.31
  investment income 5.31
  options trading 5.31
  overfunding 5.32
  stock lending fees 5.31
  taxation of exempt approved occupational pension schemes
    certificates of deposit 5.31
    financial futures 5.31
    investment income 5.31
    options trading 5.31
    overfunding 5.32
    stock lending fees 5.31
  trading 5.33
  underwriting commission 5.31
Fund managers
  agents, liability for breach of trust 10.45
  appointment requirement 2.9
  breach of trust by agents, liability 10.45
  bribes, duty not to accept 10.42
  custodianship 10.38
  delegation of investment power 2.9, 10.40, 10.47
  duties arising from appointment 10.32–38
    custodianship 10.38
    investment discretion 10.33
    liability 10.34

Fund managers – *contd*
  duties arising from appointment – *contd*
    uninvested cash 10.35
    valuation and reports 10.37
    voting 10.36
  fiduciary duties 10.39
    conflict of interest 10.41
    not to accept bribes 10.42
    not to delegate 10.40
    taking advantage of position 10.43
    ultra vires 10.44
  investment discretion 10.33
  liability 10.47
    breach of trust by agents 10.45
    duties arising from investment 10.32–38
    protection 10.47
  regulated activities 2.10
  supervision 10.27, 10.31
  taking advantage of position 10.43
  trustees' selection and supervision 10.28
    agents 10.30
    post-1995 10.30
    pre-1995 10.29
    statutory power 10.30
  voting rights 10.36, 10.46
Funded unapproved schemes
  April 2006 regime 5.54
  capital gains tax 14.18
  company law implications 14.37
  contributions 14.3
  employers (NI) contributions, treatment of 14.36
  establishment 14.11
  final salary 14.34
  Financial Services and Markets Act 14.35
  income tax 14.4, 14.17
  inheritance tax 14.19
  investment 14.35
  National Insurance contributions 14.36
  taxation
    basic approach 14.13
    capital gains 14.18
    death benefits 14.22
    employee's position 14.16
    employer's position 14.15

Index

Funded unapproved schemes – *contd*
  taxation – *contd*
    gains   14.17
    grossing-up   14.16
    income tax   14.4, 14.17
    inheritance tax   14.19
    money and assets, going into scheme   14.14–16
    money and assets, coming out of scheme   14.21, 14.22
    reporting requirements   14.20
    retirement benefits   14.21
    simplification   14.39

Funding
  see also Fund income
  actuarial valuations *see* Actuarial valuations
  basic requirements   11.1
  minimum requirement *see* Minimum funding requirement
  practice   11.6
  pre-1995 Act requirements   11.2
  contracting-out requirements   11.4
  disclosure   11.5
  Inland Revenue requirements   11.3

FURBS *see* Funded unapproved schemes

Gender reassignment   7.33, 9.30
Gender Recognition Bill   7.25, 9.32
GMPs *see* Guaranteed minimum pensions
Good faith, employer's duty of   7.6, 7.7, 7.10, 7.35
  contracting out of duty   7.8
  to whom duty owed   7.9
Goode Committee Report
  basic recommendations   1.2
  minimum funding requirement   11.13
Green Paper 2002   3.40, 5.1, 7.1
Group Personal Pension (GPP)   7.18
Guaranteed minimum pensions (GMPs)
  anti-franking   4.64
  calculation   4.12
  conditions   4.11

Guaranteed minimum pensions (GMPs) – *contd*
  contracting-out and   4.2
  the future   4.15
  pre-6 April 1997 service   4.5
  equal treatment and   9.29
  equalisation   4.16, 9.29
  reference scheme test   9.29
  spouses   4.13
  trivial commutation   4.14

Hazardous occupations, retirement age of people with   5.5
History of pension provision   1.2
HM Treasury/Inland Revenue. *Simplifying the Taxation of Pensions*   1.3
Human rights
  European Convention on Human Rights   7.33
  implications of penalties   Appendix I
  transsexuals   7.25, 7.33
Hybrid schemes
  benefits and   1.16
  cash equivalent   6.61
  provision for   6.61

Incapacity
  basic definition   1.36
  benefits payable on final salary schemes   1.36
  permanent   1.36
Income drawdown
  additional voluntary contributions   1.32
  lump sum   15.13
Income payment agreements   1.56
Income Payments Orders   1.53, 1.56
Income tax
  funded unapproved schemes   14.4, 14.17
  unfunded unapproved schemes   14.4
Indemnities
  basic meaning   16.5
  commercial transactions   16.5, 16.10, 16.25
  distinguished from warranties   16.5
  employer's debt   16.25
  enforcement   16.5

Index

Indemnities – *contd*
  sale agreements   16.10
  transfer payments   16.50, 16.61
  trust deed and   3.51

Independent trustees
  non-statutory appointments   3.6
  statutory appointments
    appointment   3.6
    associated person   3.6
    connected person   3.6
    discretionary powers   3.6
    independent person   3.6
    information to members   3.6
    insolvency information and   3.6
    multi-employer schemes and   3.6
    reasonable fees   3.6

Information
  disclosure requirement
    summary   Appendix II
    trustees   3.22
    winding up   12.53
  internal dispute resolution, requirement   3.40
  occupational pension schemes, information disclosure requirements, summary   Appendix II
  Occupational Pensions Regulatory Authority (Opra), information, disclosure and obtaining   2.17
  Pensions Compensation Board (PCB), obtaining information   2.22
  personal pension schemes, disclosure of information   15.50
  reasons   3.22
  Registrar of Occupational and Personal Pension Schemes, provision to   2.12
  Small self-administered schemes (SSASs), information sources   13.1
  trustees' duties, disclosure to members   3.22

Information Commissioner   2.34

Inheritance tax
  divorce and   8.3
  funded unapproved schemes   14.19
  lump sum death benefits and   1.38

Inland Revenue
  see also IR Savings, Pensions, Share Schemes Office (IR SPSS); Taxation of exempt approved occupational pension schemes; Taxation of personal pension schemes; Unapproved arrangements
  business streams   2.10
  Green Paper 2002   1.3, 3.40, 5.1, 7.1
  Savings, Pensions, Share Schemes   2.10
    office address   2.10
    organisation   2.10
  Simplifying the Taxation of Pensions   1.3
  trust busting   6.56

Insolvency   18.1
  administration   18.8
  Company Voluntary Arrangements (CVAs)   18.2
  deficit, and   8.13
  employer's debt   12.80
  independent trustee requirements   18.11
  information   3.6
  insolvency events   12.80
  liquidation   18.4
  Pensions Bill 2004, proposals   12.93, 18.20
  practitioner   18.9, 18.10
  receivership   18.7
  surplus, and   8.13
  trustees, appointment of   3.6
  winding-up of pension scheme   18.12

Institutional Shareholders Committee   10.49

Internal dispute resolution
  arrangements   3.40
  basic information   3.40
  complainant   3.41
  deceased member and   3.41
  details set out   3.40
  exempted disagreements   3.47
  first stage
    giving decision   3.44

Index

Internal dispute resolution – *contd*
  first stage – *contd*
    making application   3.43
    nominated person   3.42
    giving decision
      first stage   3.44
      second stage   3.46
  Green Paper 2002   3.40
  making application
    first stage   3.43
    second stage   3.45
  minor and   3.41
  nominated person, first stage   3.42
  Pensions Bill 2004   3.48
  procedure   3.40
  prospective member and   3.41
  second stage
    giving decision   3.46
    making application   3.45
  trustees   3.40

Investment
  advertisements   10.27
  advisers *see* Fund managers
  badges of trade *see under* Trading
  income tax exemption   10.3
  Institutional Shareholders Committee   10.49
  meaning   10.2
  personal pension schemes
    generally   15.51
    SIPPs, member directed investments   15.52
  Pensions Bill 2004   10.23
  power
    basic derivation   10.14
    sources   10.14
    statutory power   10.15
    under trust instrument   10.13, 10.16
  self-invested personal pension scheme (SIPP) *see under* Self-appointed personal pension scheme
  small self-administered schemes *see under* Small self-administered schemes
  stakeholder schemes,
    generally   15.41

Investment – *contd*
  stakeholder schemes schemes,
    SIPPs, member directed investments   15.52
  statement of principles   10.49
  trading *see* Trading
  trustees' duties   3.16, 10.16
    acting in best interests of beneficiaries   10.18
    appropriateness of investment   3.16
    delegation   3.16
    diversification   3.16, 10.19, 10.20
    duty of care   3.14
    employer-related investment, restrictions   10.24
    ethical considerations   10.21
    income production   10.1
    investment powers   2.9, 3.16
    moral considerations   10.21
    principles   10.19, 10.23
    prudent man test   10.19
    review investments   10.22
    standard required   10.19
    statutory obligations   10.23, 10.24
    suitability of investment   10.19
  voluntary code of practice, proposals (Myners Report)   10.48
    activism   10.48
    appropriate benchmarks   10.48
    clear objectives   10.48
    effective decision making   10.48
    expert advice   10.48
    explicit mandates   10.48
    focus on asset allocation   10.48
    performance measurement   10.48
    regular reporting   10.48
    transparency   10.48

Investment business
  activities that constitute   10.26
  basic requirements   10.25
  Financial Services and Markets Act   10.25–27
  trustees' position   10.27
    authorisation   10.27
    common investment funds   10.27
    supervision of fund managers   10.27

Index

Investment income
  taxation of exempt approved occupational pension schemes   5.27
Investment Management Agreement (IMA)   2.9
Investment managers *see* Fund managers
IR Savings, Pensions, Share Schemes Office (IR SPSS)
  disclosure to Opra   2.17
  organisations incorporated   2.10
  responsibilities   2.10
  role   2.10
  stakeholder pensions, approval   1.57

Late retirement
  benefits payable on final salary schemes   1.37
  short service benefits, alternatives to   6.27
  taxation of exempt approved occupational pension schemes   5.28
Lien
  benefits   1.49
  employer's   1.49, 7.24
Life interests, forfeiture clauses and   1.51
Life assurance
  contributions   15.29
Life offices
  taxation of exempt approved occupational pension schemes   5.40
Limited price indexation (LPI)   1.45, 6.39
Liquidation   18.4
  insolvent, when   18.6
  solvent, when   18.5
  trustees   3.2
Litigation
  see also Dispute resolution
  basic issues   17.11
  costs
    basic principles   17.29, 17.30
    Beddoe orders   17.33
    indemnity in trust deed   17.30
    power in trust deed   17.30
    prospective costs orders   17.35

Litigation – *contd*
  costs – *contd*
    trustees'   17.31, 17.33
  procedure
    affidavits   17.23
    case management powers   17.19
    Civil Procedure Rules (CPR)   17.15
    disclosure of documents   17.22
    expert evidence   17.24
    fast track   17.15
    group litigation   17.28
    multi-track   17.15
    Part 7 procedure   17.21
    Part 8 procedure   17.20
    pre-action   17.16
    representation orders   17.25, 17.26
    small claims track   17.15
    witness statements   17.23
  types
    claims by/against third party   17.14
    Pension Ombudsman appeals   17.12
    seeking directions   17.13
Loans
  by small self-administered schemes
    permitted   13.21
    to associated employers   13.22
    to employers   13.22
Local government schemes   1.1
Long service benefit
  definition   6.15
Lump sums
  annuities   15.13
  compensation   7.26
  income drawdown   15.13
  Pensions Update   5.11
  personal pensions   15.13
  retirement benefits   5.11
  taxation of exempt approved occupational pension schemes   5.35
  trust busting   6.56

Maladministration   2.27, 3.22
Marital status, discrimination and   7.30

Index

Maternity
- accrued rights   9.34
- additional maternity leave   9.34
- basic equality requirements   9.34
- continuous employment   9.34
- contractual remuneration   9.36
- death benefits   9.39
- final salary schemes   9.37
- money purchase schemes   9.38
- paid maternity leave   5.4, 9.34
- maternity allowance   9.34
- minimum period   9.34
- notifications   9.34
- ordinary maternity leave   9.34
- right to   9.34
- Parental Leave Directive   9.34
- pay   9.34, 9.35
- Pensions Updates   5.4
- statutory provisions   9.34
- 'Maxwell scandal'   1.2

Meetings
- trustees
  - conduct   3.24
  - decisions   3.24
  - quorum   3.24
  - records of meetings   3.21, 3.24
  - requirements   3.24

Member-nominated trustees/ directors
- alternative arrangements
  - approval   3.28, 3.36, 3.38
  - approval period   3.30
  - changes   3.38
  - consultation procedure   3.31
  - objection procedure   3.32
  - procedure   3.30
- appointment   3.8, 3.25
- appropriate rules   3.28
  - cessation of approval   3.36
  - prescribed   3.28
- approval   2.2, 3.28, 3.30, 3.36, 3.38
- arrangements   3.27
  - duty to secure   3.25
- cessation of approval of appropriate rules   3.36
- changes to arrangements   3.38
- Child Support Act and draft Regulations   3.25
- closed schemes   3.25
- consultation procedure   3.31

Member-nominated trustees/directors – *contd*
- duty to secure arrangements for selection   3.25
- exceptions to member nomination requirements   3.25
- functions   3.27
- Green Paper   3.25
- legislation   3.25
- minimum number   3.27
- Myners Report   2.2
- objection procedure   3.32
- opt-out   3.25, 3.30
  - *see also* alternative arrangements above
- pensioner members   3.27
- Pensions Bill 2004   3.39
- Pickering Report   3.25
- prescribed appropriate rules   3.29
- proposals
  - alternative arrangements   3.30
  - ballot procedure   3.33
  - consultation procedure   3.31
  - objection procedure   3.32
  - timescales   3.33, 3.35
  - schemes established after 6 April 1997   3.35
  - schemes established before 6 April 1997   3.33
- qualifying members   3.27
- regulations   2.2, 3.25
- removal   3.27
- review of arrangements   3.25
- selection   3.25
- special cases   3.37
- term of office   3.27
- vacancies   3.27
- winding-up scheme   3.25

Membership of occupational schemes
- disability discrimination   1.23
- equal access   1.22
- Inland Revenue requirements   1.21
- non-compulsory membership   1.20

MFR *see* Minimum funding requirement

Minimum funding requirement   1.26
- annual certification   11.27
- basic requirements   11.14
- components   11.14

Index

Minimum funding requirement – *contd*
consequences of
    non-compliance   11.32
employer's debt   12.84
guidance   11.14
initial reforms   11.33
need for solvency standard   11.13
non-compliance   11.32
reforms   11.33
replacement proposals   11.33, 11.34
requirements   11.14
schedule of contributions
    certification by actuary   11.21
    content   11.20
    contracting out   11.22
    extension of schedule period   11.25
    record keeping   11.24
    revision of schedule   11.23
    supervision by OPRA   11.26
    time limits   11.20
scheme modifications
    frozen schemes   11.30
    multi-employer schemes   11.29
    paid-up schemes   11.30
    shared cost schemes   11.31
serious underprovision   11.28
test   11.14, 11.19
trustees' role   11.14
underfunding suspected   11.18
valuations   11.15
    assets   11.19
    basis   11.19
    contracted-out schemes   11.19
    debts in multi-employer schemes   11.18
    exceptional circumstances   11.18
    first MFR valuation   11.16
    gilts   11.19
    liabilities   11.19
    new serious underfunding suspected   11.18
    subsequent valuations   11.17
    test   11.19

Minimum solvency requirement
proposal   11.13

Minors
internal dispute resolution   3.41

Mixed benefit schemes *see* Contracted-out mixed benefit schemes (COMBS)

MNDs *see* Member-nominated trustees/directors

MNTs *see* Member-nominated trustees/directors

Model Rules   15.4

Modification orders   12.10
conditions   12.10
notice   12.10
Opra   2.14

Modifications
frozen schemes   11.30
paid-up schemes   11.30
shared cost schemes   11.31

Money purchase schemes
annuities   1.42
benefits   1.15, 9.14
    annuities   1.42
    death benefits   1.43
    determination   1.42
    leaving service, benefits on   1.44
    pension   1.42
    spouse's/dependants' provision   1.43
commercial transactions   16.69
contracting-out   4.1, 4.3
    minimum payments *see* Protected rights
    requirements   4.19
contributions to occupational pension schemes
    basic contributions   1.27
    notice of failure to pay   1.27
    offences   1.27
    whistle-blowing offences   1.27
costs   1.15
death benefits   1.43
funding   1.15
individual account, notional   1.15
notice of failure to pay   1.27
offences   1.27
pension   1.42
spouse's/dependants' provision   1.43

Multi-employer schemes
independent trustees and   3.6

Myners Report   2.2, 10.48

Index

National Association of
  Pension Funds (NAPF)   2.33
National Health Service
  scheme   1.1
National Insurance
  contribution   1.7
  unapproved arrangements   14.36
National Insurance Services to
  Pensions Industry
  (NISPI)   2.11
  address   2.24
  employers and   2.24
  functions   2.11, 2.24
  responsibilities   2.24
Normal pension age
  definition   6.14
  determination   6.23
Normal retirement age   9.28
Normal retirement date   5.5

Obstruction
  Opra   2.17
Occupational Pension schemes
  absence from work   1.21
  advantages   1.11
  age for membership   1.24
  basic definition   1.11
  basic meaning   1.11
  benefits
    final salary schemes *see
      under* Final salary
      schemes
    Inland Revenue
      requirements   1.33
    money purchase schemes
      see under Money
      purchase schemes
    when payable   1.34
  benefits, inalienability
    basic right   1.46
    exceptions, bankruptcy   1.51–56
    exceptions, charge   1.49
    exceptions, commutation of
      pension   1.47
    exceptions, forfeiture   1.50
    exceptions, lien   1.49
    exceptions, set-off   1.49
    exceptions, surrender in
      favour of spouse
      and/or dependant   1.48
  centralised schemes   1.19

Occupational Pension schemes – *contd*
  commutation of pension   1.47
  contributions *see*
    Contributions to
    occupational pension
    schemes
  establishment   1.12, 1.18
  exceptions, surrender in
    favour of spouse and/or
    dependant   1.48
  exempt approved schemes
    advantages   1.11
    bankruptcy   1.51
    basic description   1.11
    contributions   5.1
    discretion to approve   5.1
    final remuneration   5.4
    mandatory approval   5.1
    maximum benefits   5.1
    normal retirement date   5.5
    remuneration   5.2, 5.3, 5.4
    requirements   5.1
    taxation   5.39
  fixed-term workers   7.27
  forfeiture   1.50
  increasing pensions in
    payment   1.45
  information disclosure
    requirements,
    summary   Appendix II
  Inland Revenue requirements,
    employer's contributions   1.28
  legislation governing   1.17
  lien   1.49
  members' contributions basic
    contribution   1.29
  money purchase schemes *see
    under* Money purchase
    schemes
  ordinary contributions   1.30
  procedure for becoming a
    member   1.24
  set-off   1.49
  stakeholder pensions *see*
    Stakeholder pension
    schemes
  statutory provisions   1.11
  structures   1.11
  types of benefit   1.13
    final salary schemes   1.14
    hybrid schemes   1.16

Index

Occupational Pension schemes – *contd*
  types of benefit – *contd*
    money purchase schemes   1.15
    unfunded   1.11
    voluntary contributions   1.31
Occupational Pensions Board (OPB)
  dissolution   2.11
  functions   2.11
  New Kind of Regulator   2.11
  OPRA and   2.11
  Pickering Report   2.11
Occupational Pensions Regulatory Authority (Opra)
  cost of   2.17
  determinations   2.16
  disclosure of information   2.17
  establishment   2.13
  information obtaining   2.17
  'New Kind of Regulator'   2.11
  non-cooperation with   2.17
  obstruction   2.17
  powers
    applications to court   2.14
    appointment of additional trustees   2.14
    circulation of statements   2.14
    directions to trustees   2.14
    disqualification   2.14
    modification orders   2.14, 12.10
    penalties imposition   2.14, Appendix I
    prohibition   2.14
    suspension   2.14
    winding-up of schemes   2.14
  reporting to   2.2
  'traffic light' framework   2.5, 2.6
  restricted information, disclosure   2.17
  stakeholder pensions   2.15
Offences *see* Criminal offences
Official Receiver   1.56
Ombudsman *see* Financial Services Ombudsman, Pensions Ombudsman
OPAS *see* Occupational Pensions Advisory Service (OPAS); Pensions Advisory Service

OPB *see* Occupational Pensions Board (OPB)
Open Market Option   15.12
Opra *see* Occupational Pensions Regulatory Authority (Opra)
Options, trading in
  taxation of exempt approved occupational pension schemes   5.31
Overseas arrangement
  transfer of accrued rights   6.25

Paid-up schemes
  modifications   11.30
Partnership Shares   5.3–5.4
Part-time employees
  back-dated rights   5.6, 5.28, 9.7
  compensation   7.26
  contributions   5.28, 5.30, 7.26, 9.5
  discrimination   7.26, 9.5
  European Community law   7.26, 9.7
  sex discrimination   9.5
  taxation   5.26, 5.28, 5.30, 7.26, 9.5
  transfer payment   7.26
Paternity leave   9.34
Penalties
  appeals   Appendix I
  civil and criminal   Appendix I
  fines   Appendix I
  human rights implications   Appendix I
  OPRA role   Appendix I
  prohibition from acting as trustee   Appendix I
Pension
  definition   1.1
  framework of law   1.1
  history   1.2
  pay as you go   1.1
  Pension credits   8.18
  charges   8.25, 8.26
  charges, recommended scale   8.26
  disclosure of information   8.24
  indexation   8.19
  information disclosure   8.24
  limited price indexation   1.45
  MNT legislation and   8.20
  pension sharing   8.18–8.27
  safeguarded rights   8.27
  section 67 protection   8.21

Index

Pension – *contd*
  valuation 8.23
  winding-up treatment 8.22
  Pension liberation schemes 6.56
Pension Protection Fund (PPF) 1.3, 2.1, 2.23, 2.30, 7.3, 12.95
Pension sharing
  basic concept 8.9
  credits 8.10, 8.12, 8.18
  charges 8.25, 8.26
  charges, recommended scale 8.26
  disclosure of information 8.24
  indexation 8.19
  information disclosure 8.24
  MNT legislation and Pensions Bill 2004 8.20
  Pensions Bill 2004 8.32
  safeguarded rights 8.27
  section 67 protection 8.21
  valuation 8.23
  winding-up treatment 8.22
  death of ex-spouse prior to discharge of liability 8.15
  debits 8.10, 8.11
  earmarking and 8.30
  external transfer option 8.14, 8.17
  funded schemes and 8.14
  future 8.32
  implementation period 8.13
  internal transfer option 8.14, 8.17
  limited price indexation 1.45
  shareable rights 8.9
  small self-administered schemes 8.16
Pensionable service
  definition 6.12
Pensioneer trustees 3.5
Pensions Advisory Service (OPAS)
  address 2.25
  Ombudsman, assistance with complaint 2.25
  role 2.25
Pensions Bill 2004 1.3, 1.31, 1.45, 2.1, 2.29
  additional voluntary contributions 12.92
  employer's debt 16.64
  equal treatment 9.1

Pensions Bill 2004 – *contd*
  insolvency 18.20
  definition 12.93
  internal dispute resolution 3.48
  member-nominated trustee 3.39
  minimum funding requirement 11.34
  pension credits 8.32
  Pension Protection Fund 12.95
  scheme modifications 12.96
  scheme specific funding requirement 12.94
  stakeholder schemes 15.59
  statement of investment principles 10.23
  surplus, repayment of 11.51
  trustee, role of 3.1, 3.23
Pensions Compensation Board (PCB)
  address 2.22
  amount of payments 2.20
  assistance availability 2.20
  determinations 2.19
  establishment 2.19
  funding 2.21
  future 2.23
  interim payments 2.20
  making a claim 2.20
  obtaining information 2.22
  period for making claim 2.20
Pensions Consultation Committee 7.11
Pensions Green Paper 2002 3.40, 5.1, 7.1
Pensions Management Institute (PMI) 2.32
Pensions Ombudsman
  address 2.28
  appointment 2.26
  compensation 2.28
  costs 17.12
  determinations 2.28
  fairness 2.28
  growth of use 2.26
  investigation of complaint 2.28
  jurisdiction summary 2.27
  maladministration 2.27
  natural justice 2.28
  powers to demand papers 2.28
  respondents 2.28
  role 2.26

Pensions Ombudsman – *contd*
  time limits for referral 2.27
Pensions Registry
  winding-up notification 12.76
Pensions Regulator 2.1, 2.31, 2.33
Pensions scheme
  basic meaning 1.1
  equal treatment *see* Equal treatment
  funding *see* Funding
  occupational *see* Occupational pension schemes
  personal *see* Personal pension schemes
  private arrangements 1.1
  reconstruction *see* Reconstruction
  small-self-administered *see* Small self-administered
  stakeholder *see* Stakeholder pension pension schemes
  state *see* State
  unapproved *see* Unapproved arrangements
  winding-up *see* Winding-up
Pensions Update
  employee share ownership plans, participation in 5.3–5.4
  lump sums 15.13
  maternity leave 5.4
  normal retirement age 9.28
  Partnership Shares 5.3
  part-time employees 5.26, 5.28, 5.30, 7.26, 9.5
  personal pensions 15.13, 15.49
  retirement benefits, tax free lump sum 5.11
  restrictive undertakings, participation in 5.3–5.4
  Share Incentive Plans 5.1
  tax position 5.26
  transfer payments 15.29
Personal pension schemes
  approval, requirement 15.1
  availability 15.1
  basic concept 15.1
  benefits
    annuity, payable after death of member 15.14
    annuity payable to a member 15.12

Personal pension schemes – *contd*
  benefits – *contd*
    basic provisions 15.10
    cash accumulation scheme 15.10
    clustering 15.16
    lump sum, payable on death of member 15.15
    lump sum, tax free payable to member 15.13
    pension date 15.11
    retirement date 15.11
  concurrent membership with occupational pension scheme 15.7
  contributions
    application 15.29–31
    basic provisions 15.25
    earnings threshold, higher than 15.28
    earnings threshold, up to 15.27
    employer option 15.25
    incapacity insurance, post 6 April 2001 15.30
    incapacity insurance, pre 6 April 2001 15.31
    ineligible, repayment 15.32
    life assurance purchase 15.29
    maximum 15.26
    minimum 15.25
    net relevant earnings 15.28
    paid in error 15.32
  details 15.1
  disclosure of information 15.50
  income withdrawal
    background 15.17
    by member 15.18
    death of member on or after pension date, where annuity purchases 15.19
    death of member before pension date 15.21
    death of member where income drawdown had started 15.20
    no provision for survivor's family 15.23
    provision for survivor's family 15.22
  Inland Revenue approval
    administrator 15.3

Index

Personal pension schemes – *contd*
Inland Revenue approval – *contd*
  application, personal
    pension scheme   15.4
  application, stakeholder
    schemes   15.5
  Model Rules   15.4
  providers   15.2
investment *see under*
  Investment
lump sum   15.13
membership
  concurrent with
    occupational pension
    scheme   15.7
  conditions   15.6
  miscellaneous requirements   15.9
  relevant earnings   15.8
net relevant earnings   15.28
Open Market Option   15.12
pension date   15.11
reasons for introduction   15.1
retirement annuity contract
  (RAC)   15.1
retirement date   15.11
self-invested *see* Self-invested
  personal pension scheme
  (SIPP)
Stamp Duty   15.54
taxation *see* Taxation of
  personal pension
  schemes
transfer payments   15.49
transfer values
  nil certificates   15.48
  right to a cash equivalent   15.46
  transfers from personal
    pension scheme   15.49
  transfers to personal
    pension scheme   15.47

Personal insolvency *see*
  Bankruptcy

Pickering Report
consolidation of legislation   2.11
member-nominated trustees   3.25
'New Kind of Regulator'   2.11
Pensions Green Paper 2002   1.3, 3.40, 5.1, 7.1
reference scheme test   9.29

Preservation
see also Cash equivalent;
  Early leavers;
  Revaluation; Short
  service benefit; Transfer
  values
basic provisions   6.1
date of payment of preserved
  benefits   6.23
death in service benefits not
  preserved   6.21
defined terms
  2 years' qualifying service   6.11
  linked qualifying service   6.13
  long service benefit   6.15
  normal pension age   6.14
  pensionable service   6.12
  short service benefit   6.16
discretionary benefits   6.22
Inland Revenue limits   6.29
legislation enforcement   6.9
requirements   6.2

Private pensions schemes *see
also* Personal pension
schemes, funding

Professional bodies
Departmenet for Work and
  Pensions   2.35
National Association of
  Pension Funds (NAPF)   2.33
Pensions Management
  Institute (PMI)   2.32

Prohibition order   Appendix I

Protected rights
occupational pension schemes
  age-related rebates   4.23
  benefits payable on death
    after retirement   4.26
  benefits payable on death
    before retirement   4.27
  forfeiture   4.28
  giving effect to   4.25–30
  identification   4.21
  incentive payments   4.24
  lump sum and   4.29, 4.30
  member's pension   4.25
  suspension   4.28
  trivial commutation   4.29
  valuation   4.21
personal pension schemes
  benefits   15.42

Protected rights – *contd*
  personal pension schemes – *contd*
    death of member and
      spouse's pension   15.43
    premium   15.45
    transfer   15.44
Protective trusts   1.51
PSO *see* Pension Schemes
  Office (PSO)
Public sector transfers   16.68
Purchase of company *see also*
  Commercial transactions;
  Transfer payments

Reasons
  disclosure of   3.22
  maladministration   3.22
  trustees   3.22
Receivership   18.7
Reconstruction
  basic definition   12.1
  bulk transfers *see* Bulk
    transfers
  definition   12.1
  employers' duties   12.6
  examples of scheme
    amendments   12.2, 12.8
    see also Amendment of
      scheme rules
  Pensions Bill 2004, proposals 12.96
  powers to carry out   12.5
  trustees' duties   12.7
  winding-up *see* Winding-up
    scheme
Reduction of surplus *see*
  Surplus, reduction
Redundancy
  entitlements   7.15
  European Community law   9.11,
                              16.15
  transfer of undertakings   16.15
Reference scheme test
  actuarial certification   4.7
  certificate   4.7
  equal treatment   9.29
  guaranteed minimum pension   9.29
  more than one benefit
    structure, schemes with   4.8
  more than one employer,
    schemes with   4.9

Reference scheme test – *contd*
  post-6 April   1997 4.5
    test   4.7
  Pickering Report   9.29
  provisions   4.6
  qualifying earnings   4.10
  scheme   4.6
  spouses   4.6, 4.7, 4.10
  stringency   4.10
  test   4.7
**Registrar of Occupational and
  Personal Pension Schemes**
  address   2.12
  establishment   2.12
  functions   2.12
  provision of information to   2.12
Registration
  stakeholder pensions, fees for 2.15
'Relevant contributions'   7.22
Remuneration
  basic aims   5.2
  employee share ownership
    plans   5.3
  final   5.4
  fixed-term workers   7.27
  maternity leave   5.4
  maternity pay   9.34, 9.35
  trustees   3.13
Retirement
  age discrimination   9.15, 9.16
  benefits, tax free lump sum   5.11
  change in nature of
    employment   5.15
  definition   1.36
  equalisation   9.16, 9.17
  meaning of   5.15
  normal date of   5.5
  retirement annuity contract
    (RAC)   15.1
Revaluation
  application of requirements   6.32
  basic aims   6.31
  basic entitlement   6.3
  benefits other than GMPs   6.4
  determination of applicable
    method   6.33
    average salary method   6.34
    final salary method *see*
      final salary method
      below
    flat rate method   6.35

Index

Revaluation – *contd*
  determination of applicable method – *contd*
    money purchase method   6.36, 6.38
    final salary method
      appropriate revaluation percentage, application   6.42
      appropriate relevant percentage, calculation   6.41
      basic method   6.39
      revaluation percentage   6.40
    GMPs   6.5
    see also Guaranteed minimum pensions

Same sex partners, discrimination and   7.30, 9.30
S2P *see* State second pension
Sale of Company *see* Commercial transactions; Transfer payments
Same sex partners
  civil partnerships   9.31
  equal treatment   9.30
  Gender Recognition Bill   9.32
Schedule of contributions
  actuary certification   1.26, 11.21
  content   11.20
  contracting out   11.22
  extension of period   11.25
  final salary schemes   1.26
  rate of contributions   1.26
  requirement   1.26
  revision   11.20, 11.23
  summary of requirements   11.21
  supervision by Opra   11.26
  time limits   11.20
Schedule of payments
  exemptions   1.27
  failure to maintain   1.27
  money purchase schemes   1.27
  rates of payment   1.27
  requirement   1.27
Scheme specific funding requirement   12.94
Self-invested personal pension scheme (SIPP)
  application for approval   15.4
  basic concept   15.1

Self-invested personal pension scheme (SIPP) – *contd*
  investments
    member directed   15.52
    requirements   15.53
SERPS
  annual rate   1.9
  contracting-out   1.9, 15.40–45
    APPS   15.40
    minimum contributions   15.41
    see also Protected rights
  earnings limit   1.9
  entitlement   1.9
  protected rights, *see also* Protected rights
  state pension and   1.4
  surplus earnings   1.9
Set-off
  benefits   1.49
Sex discrimination
  justification   9.29
  part-time workers   9.5
  same sex partners   9.30
  sex equality   7.25
  transsexuals   7.25, 7.33
Sex equality *see* Equal treatment
Shared costs scheme
  modifications   11.31
Shares
  Share Incentive Plans   5.3–5.4
  small self-administered schemes, investment   13.23
Sharing pensions *see* Divorce, impact on pension rights of
Short service benefit
  alternatives
    basic permission   6.24
    bought-out benefits   6.28
    early retirement   6.26
    late retirement   6.27
    money purchase benefits   6.29
    transfer payments   6.25
  calculation
    basic method   6.18
    same basis as long service benefit   6.19
    uniform accrual   6.20
  qualifying for   6.17
Simplification   5.41, 14.38
  contracting out   1.2, 4.66

Index

Simplification – *contd*
  funded unapproved schemes 14.39
  Simplifying the Taxation of Pensions. HM Treasury/Inland Revenue consultation paper 1.3, 7.1
  tax treatment, of 5.41
  unfunded unapproved schemes 14.40

Small self-administered schemes (SSASs)
  basic structure 13.1
  borrowing by 13.13
    amount 13.13
    pensioner trustee and 13.13
  commercial transactions 16.70
  deferred annuities
    actuary's certificate 13.9
    basic principles 13.8
    borrowing 13.10
    drawdown 13.12
    investment in property 13.11
    loans 13.10
    share purchases 13.10
  definition 13.3
  divorce and sharing of pensions 8.16
  documentation, incorporation of provisions 13.5
  funding
    basic principles 13.6
    deferred annuities *see* deferred annuities above
    spreading of special contributions 13.7
  future 13.36
  Green Paper 2002 13.36
  information sources 13.1
  Inland revenue, withdrawal of approval 13.31
  investment by 13.36
    co-ownership requirements 13.15
    co-signatory requirements 13.15
    Financial Services and Markets Act 13.14
    pensioner trustee and 13.15
    prohibited investments *see* prohibited investments below

Small self-administered schemes (SSASs) – *contd*
  investment by – *contd*
    real property *see* real property, investment in below
    self-investment 13.24
    shares 13.23
  loans
    permitted 13.21
    to associated employers 13.22
    to employers 13.22
  pensioneer trustee 13.4
    appointment 13.4
    basic definition 13.4
    borrowing and 13.13
    'connected' defined 13.4
    death 13.4
    investment requirements 13.15
    as member of scheme 13.4
    notification of appointment 13.4
    prohibitions 13.4
    requirement 3.5, 13.2, 13.4
    resignation 13.4
    termination of appointment 13.4
  Pensions Act 1995 13.34
  prohibited investments
    personal chattels 13.16
    residential property 13.17
    substantial shareholdings 13.18
    transactions between approved and non-approved schemes 13.19
    transactions with members or connected persons 13.20
  real property, investment in
    leasing 13.27
    permitted investments 13.26
    prohibitions 13.25
  regulatory framework
    background 13.2
    definition of SSAS 13.3
    incorporation in documentation 13.5
    pensioneer trustee 13.4, 13.13, 13.15
  tax avoidance
    basic concerns 13.28
    bona fides 13.30
    transactions 13.29

Index

Small self-administered schemes (SSASs) – *contd*
- trading — 13.32
- transfers — 13.35
- trustee — 13.4
- VAT — 13.33
- withdrawal of IR approval — 13.31

Social security
- legislation — 1.2

Sportsmen, retirement age — 5.5

Spouse
- death benefits — 1.40, 1.43
- taxation — 5.21
- final salary scheme, benefits — 1.40
- money purchase scheme, benefits — 1.43
- surrender of benefits in favour of spouse — 1.48

SSAS *see* Small self-administered schemes

Stakeholder pension schemes — 15.1
- background — 1.57
- charging — 1.58
- concurrent membership with occupational scheme — 15.7
- criminal offences — 2.15
- duty on employers — 1.58
- employees not entitled to access — 15.7
- employer's contribution — 15.28
- Inland Revenue approval, application — 15.5
- investment *see under* Investment
- legal structure — 1.58
- minimum contributions — 1.58
- Occupational Pensions Regulatory Authority — 2.15
- Open Market Option — 15.12
- Pensions Bill 2004 — 15.59
- registration, fees for — 2.15
- regulation — 1.58
- trustees — 2.15

Stamp Duty — 15.54
- In specie transfers — 15.55

Stamp Duty Land Tax (SDLT) — 15.56
- In specie transfers — 15.57

State earnings-related pension scheme *see* SERPS

State Pension Credit — 1.5

State pensions
- age — 1.6
- application for — 1.8
- basic — 1.1, 1.5
- categories — 1.4
- contracting-out *see* Contracting-out
- National Insurance contribution — 1.7
- SERPS *see* SERPS

State second pension (S2P) — 4.69
- benefits — 4.70
- contracting-out of — 4.73
- incapacity benefit and — 1.10
- low earnings threshold (LET) — 1.10
- lower earnings limit (LEL) — 1.10
- non-earners — 4.71
- qualifying earnings factor (QEF) — 1.10
- SERPS replacement — 1.10
- severe disablement allowance and — 1.10
- upper earnings threshold (UET) — 1.10

Statement of investment principles — 10.23

Stock lending fees
- taxation of exempt approved occupational pension schemes — 5.31

Subsidiary participating in parent's scheme, purchase of — 7.23

Surplus
- consequences of overfunding — 11.42
- definition — 11.35
- insolvency, on — 8.13
- issue of — 11.36
- ongoing schemes
  - ownership — 11.37
  - reduction — 11.47
- overfunding, consequences — 11.42
- ownership, ongoing schemes — 11.37
- Pensions Bill 2004 — 11.51
- payment to employer — 11.43
- reduction
  - basic requirements — 11.39
  - consequences of overfunding — 11.42
  - ongoing schemes — 11.47
  - overfunding, consequences — 11.42

Index

Surplus – *contd*	
reduction – *contd*	
payment to employer	11.43
sanctions for non-compliance	11.44
Schedule22 variations	11.41
schemes to which legislation applies	11.40
trust law requirements	11.45–47
under PA1995	11.47–51
winding-up schemes	11.48
sanctions for non-compliance	11.44
Schedule 22 variations	11.41
trust law requirements	
exercise of trustees' powers	11.46
powers under trust instrument	11.45
trustees	12.53
winding-up schemes	11.38, 11.48
Surrender of benefits	
spouse/dependant, in favour of	1.48
Suspension order	
Occupational Pensions Regulatory Authority (Opra)	2.14
Taxation	
April 2006 regime	
annual allowance	5.45
benefits	5.48, 5.49, 5.50
funded unapproved retirement schemes	5.54
investment	5.52
lifetime allowance	5.43, 5.44
pension age	5.47
pension sharing	5.51
registered schemes	5.42
tax-free lump sum	5.46
tax relief on contributions	5.53
unfunded unapproved retirement schemes	5.54
compensation	7.26
divorce and	8.31
exempt approved occupational pension schemes *see* Taxation of exempt approved occupational pension schemes	
part-time employees	5.26, 5.28, 5.30, 7.26, 9.5

Taxation – *contd*	
personal pension schemes *see* Taxation of personal pension schemes	
Simplifying the Taxation of Pensions. HM Treasury/Inland Revenue consultation paper	1.3, 5.40
trust busting	6.56
Taxation of exempt approved occupational pension schemes	
administration expenses	5.39
advantages	5.1
employees' contributions	5.28
employers' contributions	5.26
fund income *see under* fund income below	
pension sharing	5.27, 5.29
approval	5.1
basic aims	5.1
benefits paid out	
lump sums	5.35, 5.37
pension benefits	5.34
refunds of contributions	5.36
transfer payments	5.38
death benefits	
death in service after normal retirement date	5.23
dependants' benefits	5.21
early leavers	5.22
lump sums payable on death in service before normal retirement date	5.20
spouses benefits	5.21
early retirement	
basic rules	5.15
incapacity	5.16
leaving service benefits	5.18
other than on grounds of incapacity	5.17
pension debit	5.17
fund income	
basic exemptions	5.31
certificates of deposit, profits on gains	5.31
disposal of assets	5.31
financial futures dealings	5.31
investment income	5.31
overfunding	5.32
stock lending fees	5.31

691

Index

Taxation of exempt approved occupational pension schemes – *contd*
fund income – *contd*
  trading 5.33
  trading by
    exempt-approved
      schemes 5.31
  underwriting commissions 5.31
late retirement 5.19
life offices 5.40
mandatory approval 5.1
maximum benefits 5.1
  basic provision 5.11
  pension at normal
    retirement date
  maximum total benefits 5.7
  pension sharing easement 5.8
  post-17 March 1997
    member 5.10
  pre-17 March 1997
    member 5.9
  pension sharing easement 5.12
  post-1 June 1989 member 5.14
  post-17 March but
    pre-31 May 1989
    member 5.13
  pre-17 March 1987
    member 5.12
  regimes 5.6
normal retirement date 5.5
pension sharing 5.1, 5.27, 5.29
remuneration 5.2, 5.3
  basic year payment 5.4
  earnings cap 5.3
  final 5.4
  fluctuating emoluments 5.4
  permitted maximum 5.3
  three year averaging 5.4
requirements 5.1
retained benefits 5.24
retirement after normal
  retirement date 5.19

Taxation of personal pension schemes
benefits 15.39
employer's contributions,
  relief for 15.37
fund 15.38
member's contributions
  basic provisions 15.33

Taxation of personal pension schemes – *contd*
member's contributions – *contd*
  carrying back contributions 15.36
  carrying forward tax reliefs
    post 6 April 2001 15.35
    pre 6 April 2001 15.34
  employer's contribution 15.33
  higher rate 15.33

Temporary workers *see also*
  Fixed-term workers
agency workers 9.33
European Community 9.33

Termination of contracted-out employment
cessation of employment 4.55
generally 4.54
non-cessation of employment 4.56
revaluation
  GMPs 4.61
  post-1967 contracted-out
    salary related rights 4.62
  protected rights 4.63
securing contracted-out rights
  basic aims 4.57
  reinstatement into SERPS 4.58
  retention of liability 4.59
  transfer to another
    arrangement 4.60

Termination of employment
contracting-out *see*
  Termination of
  contracted-out
  employment
employer's duties
  basic duties 7.10
  deliberate discontinuance
    of scheme 7.11
  good faith 7.10
  issue of new contracts 7.11
  exclusion in deed and rules 7.19
  lump sum death in service
    benefits 7.20
  redundancy 7.15
  trustees' role 7.13, 7.14
  unfair dismissal 7.16
  wrongful dismissal 7.17

Trading
badges of trade
  application of 10.11
  circumstances of realisation 10.9

Index

Trading – *contd*
  badges of trade – *contd*
    frequency or number of
      similar transactions   10.7
    length of period of
      ownership   10.6
    motive   10.10
    powers under trust
      instrument   10.13
    presumption against
      trading   10.12
    subject matter of realisation   10.5
    supplementary work with
      property realised   10.8
  classification for taxation   5.33
  investment or   10.3
  tax exemptions   10.3
  taxation
    classification for   5.33
    of income of exempt
      approved schemes   5.31

Transsexuals   7.25, 9.32

Transfer payments
  see also Commercial
    transactions
  alternative structures   16.21
  basic considerations   16.18
  basic issues   16.30
  calculation
    agreed percentage of MFR   16.35
    cash equivalents   16.33
    other possibilities   16.35
    past service reserve   16.31
    past service reserve plus
      share of surplus   16.32
    reduced cash equivalents   16.34
    timing adjustment   16.37
  circumstances
    involving transfer   16.19
    not involving transfer   16.20
    other approaches   16.21
  contracting out   16.43
  disputes clause   16.40
  due diligence   16.50, 16.61
  excess clause   16.45
  improper transfers   15.49
  indemnities   16.50, 16.61
  Inland Revenue issues
    consent to bulk transfer   16.41
    continued rights   16.42
    interest   16.38

Transfer payments – *contd*
  mechanics   16.36
  part-time employees   7.26
  personal pensions   15.49
  purchaser's scheme
    future service benefits   16.48
    past service benefits   16.47
    transfer agreement   16.49
    type of scheme   16.46
  shortfall clause   16.44
  structures, alternative   16.21
  timescales   16.36
  timing adjustment   16.37
  transitional periods
    admission of new members   16.60
    categories   16.51
    date for calculation of past
      service liabilities   16.59
    due diligence   16.61
    employer's contributions   16.54
    expenses   16.55
    indemnities   16.61
    Inland Revenue   16.52
    obligations of purchaser   16.57
    obligations of vendor   16.58
    salary increase limits   16.56
    trustees' role   16.53
    warranties   16.61
  trust busting   6.56, 6.57
  voluntary contributions   16.39
  warranties   16.50, 16.61

Transfer of undertakings
  early retirement   16.15
  employment protection   7.22, 16.15
  European Community law   7.22, 16.15
  public sector   16.68
  redundancy   16.15

Transfer values
  basic protection   6.1, 6.43
  cash equivalent *see* Cash
    equivalent
  personal pension schemes *see*
    under Personal pension
    schemes
  statutory entitlements   6.6

Transsexuals   7.33, 9.30

Trust
  as basis for occupational
    pension schemes   1.18
  busting   6.56, 6.57

Index

Trust – *contd*
    corporations   3.4
    protective   1.51

Trustees
    access to documents   3.22
    accrued rights   7.12
    acting in accordance with trust deeds and rules   3.15
    actuary
        appointment   2.4
        resignation   2.4
    agents, selection and supervision   10.30
    appointment   3.11
    associated persons   2.7, 3.6
    auditors and   2.7
    bankruptcy and   1.53, 1.54, 1.56, 3.2
    basic duties   7.13
    Beddoes orders   17.33, 17.34
    breach of trust   3.50
    bulk transfers and   12.36
    collection of contributions   3.20
    company as   2.2
    connected persons   2.7
    constructive trustees   3.9
    corporate trustees   3.3
    costs   17.31, 17.30
        Beddoes orders   17.33
        beneficiaries' costs   17.34
    creditors' arrangement   3.2
    Data protection legislation *see* Data protection legislation
    delegation   3.19
    delegation of investment discretions   3.16
    detriment, right not to suffer   7.35
    disclosure   3.22
    disqualifications   3.2
    distribution of a surplus   3.60
    duties
        acting in accordance with trust deeds and rules   3.15
        collection of contributions   3.20
        delegation   3.19
        delegation of investment discretions   3.16
        distribution of a surplus   3.60
        financial benefits   3.12

Trustees – *contd*
    duties – *contd*
        impartiality between different classes of beneficiaries   3.17
        information, disclosure to members   3.22
        investment decisions and   3.16, 3.60
        not to profit from position   3.13
        Pensions Bill 2004   10.51
        prudence   3.14
        receipts, payments and records, keeping   3.21
        reconstruction   12.7
        statutory duty of care   3.14
        to employer   3.60
    employers as   2.2
    employment protection
        appointment   3.11
        basic rights   3.10
        removal   3.11
        retirement   3.11
    equal treatment role   9.19
    exemption clauses   3.50
    expenses   3.13
    fees   3.13
    financial benefits   3.12
    impartiality between different classes of beneficiaries   3.17
    independent trustees *see* Independent trustees
    individual trustees   3.3
    ineligibility   2.7
    information, disclosure to members   3.22
    internal dispute resolution *see* Internal dispute resolution
    investment *see under* Investment
    liability   3.49
    liability, protection from *see* protection from liability below
    liability, protection from *see under* protection from liability
    maladministration   3.22
    meetings
        conduct   3.24

Index

Trustees – *contd*
meetings – *contd*
  decisions 3.24
  notice of 3.24
  quorum 3.24
  record 3.24
member-nominated trustees
  see Member-nominated trustees/directors
minimum funding requirement 11.14
Myners Report 2.2, 3.14
not to profit from position 3.13
Opra
  powers to appoint 2.14, 3.11
  powers to direct 2.14
  powers to disqualify 3.2, 3.11
  powers to prohibit 3.1, 3.11
  powers to suspend 3.1
penalties 2.2, 3.1
pensioner trustees 3.4
Pensions Bill 2004 3.23
professional 3.50
professional advice, seeking of 3.18
prohibition Appendix I, 3.1
protection from liability
  basic liability 3.49
  court's discretion 3.52
  exclusion clauses 3.50
  exoneration clauses 10.47
  indemnity clauses 3.51
  insurance 3.53
  investment decisions 10.47
prudence 3.13
public trustees 3.4
reasonable fees 3.13
reasons 3.22
receipts, payments and records, keeping 3.21
removal 3.11
remuneration 3.13
representation orders and 17.26, 17.27
requirements 2.2
retirement 3.11
role 2.2, 3.1
scheme rules amendment, statutory powers 12.11
share ownership and voting rights 10.46

Trustees – *contd*
small self-administered schemes (SSASs) 13.4
stakeholder pensions 2.15
statutory duty of care 3.14
surplus 12.72
suspension 3.1
trust corporations 3.4
types
  constructive trustees 3.9
  corporate trustees 3.3
  independent trustees *see* Independent trustees
  individual trustees 3.3
  pensioner trustees 3.4
  public trustees 3.4
  trust corporations 3.4
unfair dismissal, right not to suffer 7.35

Unapproved arrangements
basis use 14.1
company law implications 14.37
death benefits, insuring
  beneficiary's tax liability 14.30
  employee's tax position 14.29
  employer's tax position 14.28
  premium payment 14.27
  proceeds paid to employer, tax liability 14.31
  proceeds paid to trustees, tax liability 14.32
  employer (NI) contributions, treatment of 14.36
establishment
  formal board resolution 14.9
  funded arrangements 14.11
  reporting to Inland Revenue 14.9
  unfunded arrangements 14.10
Financial Services and Markets Act 14.35
funded *see* Funded unapproved schemes
investment 14.35
National Insurance contributions 14.36
offshore arrangements 14.33
schemes, basis use 14.1
types
  basic types 14.2

695

Index

Unapproved arrangements – *contd*
  types – *contd*
    commercial considerations   14.5
    final salary or money
      purchase   14.8
    funded or unfunded   14.3–6
    group or individual
      arrangement   14.7
    security   14.6
    taxation considerations   14.4
  unfunded *see* Unfunded
    unapproved schemes
Unfair dismissal   7.16
  as trustee   7.35
Unfunded unapproved schemes
  application of legislation   14.12
  April 2006 tax regime   5.54
  benefits   14.3
  commercial considerations   14.5
  establishment   14.10
  income tax   14.4
  legislation, application of   14.12
  security   14.6
  taxation
    death benefits   14.26
    income tax   14.4
    payment of benefits   14.23
    retirement benefits   14.24, 14.25
    simplification   14.40
United States
  pension fund voting rights   10.46
Updates *see* Pensions Updates
UURBS *see* Unfunded
  unapproved schemes

Valuations
  actuarial *see* Actuarial
    valuations
  minimum funding   11.15
VAT
  small self administered
    schemes   13.32
Vesting   1.2, 1.54
Voting
  duty to exercise rights   10.46
  fund managers   10.36, 10.46
  trustees   10.46
  United States   10.46

Warrant
  Opra   2.17
Warranties
  breach   16.5
  commercial transactions   16.5, 16.8, 16.24, 16.50
  enforcement   16.5
  indemnity distinct from   16.5
  protection of purchaser   16.24
  sale agreements   16.7, 16.8, 16.50, 16.61
  transfer payments   16.51
Whistleblowing
  actuary   2.5
  auditors as   2.8
Wilful default   10.47
Winding-up scheme
  additional voluntary
    contributions   12.92
  annuities purchase,
    commencement after
    5 April 1997   12.69
  basic meaning   12.4
  beneficiaries, missing or
    unknown   12.77
  circumstances   12.4
  commencement after 5 April 1997
    annuities purchase   12.69
    basic provisions   12.66
    deficits   12.73
    priorities   12.67, 12.68
    surplus, payment to
      employers   12.72
    surplus, power to increase
      benefits   12.71
    transfers out   12.70
    trustees' discharge of
      liability   12.74
  commencement before
    6 April 1997
    deficits   12.65
    expenses   12.60
    purchase of annuities   12.61
    surplus, power to increase
      benefits   12.63
    surplus, payment to
      employers   12.64
    transfers out   12.62
  deferral by trustees
    disclosure requirements   12.57

696

Winding-up scheme – *contd*
  deferral by trustees – *contd*
    power under scheme rules 12.54
    priorities 12.56
    statutory power 12.55
  disclosure requirements
    during 12.53, 12.75
  divorce and 8.22
  employer's debt *see*
    Employer's debt
  IR SPSS notification 12.76
  insolvency 18.12
    definition 12.93
  missing beneficiaries 12.77
  notification of regulatory
    bodies 12.76
  Pension Protection Fund 12.95
  Pensions Registry,
    notification 12.76
  process
    overview 12.58

Winding-up scheme – *contd*
  process – *contd*
    see also commencement
      after 5 April 1997
      above; commencement
      before 6 April 1997
      above
  scheme specific funding
    requirement 12.94
  statutory protection 1.2
  surplus
    payment to employers 12.72, 12.64
    power to increase benefits 12.63, 12.71
  triggering
    court application 12.52
    events 12.51
    new legislation 12.53
    Opra application 12.52
    unknown beneficiaries 12.77
Wrongful dismissal 7.17